Advances in Machine Learning and Mathematical Modeling for Optimization Problems

Advances in Machine Learning and Mathematical Modeling for Optimization Problems

Editors

Francois Rivest
Abdellah Chehri

MDPI • Basel • Beijing • Wuhan • Barcelona • Belgrade • Manchester • Tokyo • Cluj • Tianjin

Editors
Francois Rivest
Royal Military College of Canada
Canada

Abdellah Chehri
Royal Military College of Canada
Canada

Editorial Office
MDPI
St. Alban-Anlage 66
4052 Basel, Switzerland

This is a reprint of articles from the Special Issue published online in the open access journal *Mathematics* (ISSN 2227-7390) (available at: https://www.mdpi.com/si/mathematics/Mach_Lear_Math_Mod_Optim_Probl).

For citation purposes, cite each article independently as indicated on the article page online and as indicated below:

LastName, A.A.; LastName, B.B.; LastName, C.C. Article Title. *Journal Name* **Year**, *Volume Number*, Page Range.

ISBN 978-3-0365-7740-1 (Hbk)
ISBN 978-3-0365-7741-8 (PDF)

© 2023 by the authors. Articles in this book are Open Access and distributed under the Creative Commons Attribution (CC BY) license, which allows users to download, copy and build upon published articles, as long as the author and publisher are properly credited, which ensures maximum dissemination and a wider impact of our publications.

The book as a whole is distributed by MDPI under the terms and conditions of the Creative Commons license CC BY-NC-ND.

Contents

About the Editors . . . . **vii**

Abdellah Chehri and Francois Rivest
Editorial for the Special Issue "Advances in Machine Learning and Mathematical Modeling for Optimization Problems"
Reprinted from: *Mathematics* **2023**, *11*, 1890, doi:10.3390/math11081890 . . . . **1**

Ramy A. Othman, Saad M. Darwish and Ibrahim A. Abd El-Moghith
A Multi-Objective Crowding Optimization Solution for Efficient Sensing as a Service in Virtualized Wireless Sensor Networks
Reprinted from: *Mathematics* **2023**, *11*, 1128, doi:10.3390/math11051128 . . . . **7**

Suad Abdeen, Mohd Shareduwan Mohd Kasihmuddin, Nur Ezlin Zamri, Gaeithry Manoharam, Mohd. Asyraf Mansor and Nada Alshehri
S-Type Random k Satisfiability Logic in Discrete Hopfield Neural Network Using Probability Distribution: Performance Optimization and Analysis
Reprinted from: *Mathematics* **2023**, *11*, 984, doi:10.3390/math11040984 . . . . **31**

Dong Wei, Renjun Wang, Changqing Xia, Tianhao Xia, Xi Jin and Chi Xu
Edge Computing Offloading Method Based on Deep Reinforcement Learning for Gas Pipeline Leak Detection
Reprinted from: *Mathematics* **2022**, *10*, 4812, doi:10.3390/math10244812 . . . . **77**

Connor Little, Salimur Choudhury, Ting Hu and Kai Salomaa
Comparison of Genetic Operators for the Multiobjective Pickup and Delivery Problem
Reprinted from: *Mathematics* **2022**, *10*, 4308, doi:10.3390/math10224308 . . . . **97**

Wadi Khalid Anuar, Lai Soon Lee, Hsin-Vonn Seow and Stefan Pickl
A Multi-Depot Dynamic Vehicle Routing Problem with Stochastic Road Capacity: An MDP Model and Dynamic Policy for Post-Decision State Rollout Algorithm in Reinforcement Learning
Reprinted from: *Mathematics* **2022**, *10*, 2699, doi:10.3390/math10152699 . . . . **119**

Muhammad Saeed, Muhammad Ahsan, Muhammad Haris Saeed, Atiqe Ur Rahman, Asad Mehmood, Mazin Abed Mohammed, et al.
An Optimized Decision Support Model for COVID-19 Diagnostics Based on Complex Fuzzy Hypersoft Mapping
Reprinted from: *Mathematics* **2022**, *10*, 2472, doi:10.3390/math10142472 . . . . **189**

Chun-Yao Lee, Meng-Syun Wen, Guang-Lin Zhuo and Truong-An Le
Application of ANN in Induction-Motor Fault-Detection System Established with MRA and CFFS
Reprinted from: *Mathematics* **2022**, *10*, 2250, doi:10.3390/math10132250 . . . . **209**

Sung-Jin Lee, Jun-Seok Yun, Eung Joo Lee and Seok Bong Yoo
HIFA-LPR: High-Frequency Augmented License Plate Recognition in Low-Quality Legacy Conditions via Gradual End-to-End Learning
Reprinted from: *Mathematics* **2022**, *10*, 1569, doi:10.3390/math10091569 . . . . **227**

Dawan Chumpungam, Panitarn Sarnmeta and Suthep Suantai
An Accelerated Convex Optimization Algorithm with Line Search and Applications in Machine Learning
Reprinted from: *Mathematics* **2022**, *10*, 1491, doi:10.3390/math10091491 . . . . **251**

About the Editors

Francois Rivest

Francois Rivest, Ph.D., has been an associate professor in the Department of Mathematics and Computer Science at the Royal Military College of Canada (RMC) since 2010 and a member of the Center for Neuroscience Studies at Queen's University since 2011. Dr. Rivest received his M.Sc. degree in Machine Learning from McGill University (Dean's Honours List) and his Ph.D. degree in computational neuroscience from the University of Montreal. His current research focuses on understanding how animals learn so quickly, in particular timing, in order to develop better representation construction algorithms for real-time machine learning. His research interests include the brain's dopaminergic system, animal interval timing, machine reinforcement learning, and automatic construction of representations.

Abdellah Chehri

Abdellah Chehri, Ph.D., is an associate professor in the Department of Mathematics and Computer Science at the Royal Military College of Canada (RMC). Dr. Chehri received his master's degrees in Digital Communications and Signal Processing from the University Nice-Sophia Antipolis-Eurecom (France) and his Ph.D. degree in Electrical Engineering, with applied research in Information Communication and Telecommunications, from the University Laval (Quebec City). Dr. Chehri has received many prestigious awards, including the Dean's Scholarship Award, Postdoctoral Studies (University Ottawa), Scholarship Fund to Support Success (Laval University), Japan Society for the Promotion of Science, MITACS, and NSERC Postdoctoral Fellowship. He has been listed among the top 2% cited scientists reported by Stanford University since 2020. His research interests include big data, data analytics, AI/ML, IoT (Internet of Things) for the real-time response and control of autonomous intelligent systems, intelligent biometric monitoring systems, ML/federated learning in wireless systems, and unmanned aerial vehicle communications.

Editorial

Editorial for the Special Issue "Advances in Machine Learning and Mathematical Modeling for Optimization Problems"

Abdellah Chehri * and Francois Rivest

Mathematics and Computer Science, Royal Military College of Canada, Kingston, ON K7K 7B4, Canada; francois.rivest@rmc.ca
* Correspondence: chehri@rmc.ca

Citation: Chehri, A.; Rivest, F. Editorial for the Special Issue "Advances in Machine Learning and Mathematical Modeling for Optimization Problems". *Mathematics* 2023, 11, 1890. https://doi.org/10.3390/math11081890

Received: 10 April 2023
Accepted: 12 April 2023
Published: 17 April 2023

Copyright: © 2023 by the authors. Licensee MDPI, Basel, Switzerland. This article is an open access article distributed under the terms and conditions of the Creative Commons Attribution (CC BY) license (https://creativecommons.org/licenses/by/4.0/).

Machine learning and deep learning have made tremendous progress over the last decade and have become the de facto standard across a wide range of image, video, text, and sound processing domains, from object recognition to image generation. Recently, deep learning and deep reinforcement learning have begun to develop end-to-end training to solve more complex operation research and combinatorial optimization problems, such as covering problems, vehicle routing problems, traveling salesman problems, scheduling problems, and other complex problems requiring general simulations. These methods also sometimes include classic search and optimization algorithms for machine learning, such as Monte Carlo Tree Search in AlphaGO.

Starting from the above considerations, this Special Issue aims to report the latest advances and trends concerning advanced machine learning and mathematical modeling for optimization problems. This Special Issue intends to provide a universally recognized international forum to present recent advances in mathematical modeling for optimization problems. We welcomed both theoretical contributions as well as papers describing interesting applications. Papers invited for this Special Issue considered aspects of this problem, including:

- Machine learning for optimization problems;
- Statistical learning;
- End-to-end machine learning;
- Graph neural networks;
- Combining classic optimization algorithms and machine learning;
- Mathematical models of problems for machine learning;
- Optimization method for machine learning;
- Evolutionary computation and optimization problems;
- Applications such as scheduling problems, smart cities, etc.

After reviewing submissions, we accepted a total of nine papers for publication.

The Internet of Things (IoT) encompasses many applications and service domains, from smart cities, autonomous vehicles, surveillance, and medical devices, to crop control. Most experts regard virtualization in wireless sensor networks (WSNs) as the most revolutionary technological technique in these areas. Due to node failure or communication latency and the regular identification of nodes in WSNs, virtualization in WSNs presents additional hurdles.

In the contribution by Othman et al. [1], "A Multi-Objective Crowding Optimization Solution for Efficient Sensing as a Service in Virtualized Wireless Sensor Networks", the authors present a novel architecture for heterogeneous virtual networks on the Internet of Things. They propose to embed the architecture in WSN settings to improve fault tolerance and communication latency in service-oriented networking. Moreover, the authors utilize the Evolutionary Multi-Objective Crowding Algorithm (EMOCA) to maximize fault tolerance and minimize communication delay for virtual network embedding in WSN environments for service-oriented applications focusing on heterogeneous virtual networks in the IoT. Unlike the current wireless virtualization approach, which uses the Non-dominated Sorting Genetic Algorithm-II (NSGA-II), EMOCA uses both domination and diversity criteria in the evolving population for optimization problems. The analysis of the results demonstrates that the proposed framework successfully optimizes fault tolerance and communication delay for virtualization in WSNs.

Scholars have recently introduced various non-systematic satisfiability studies on Discrete Hopfield Neural Networks to address the lack of interpretation. Although a flexible structure was established to help generate a wide range of spatial solutions that converge on global minima, the fundamental issue is that the existing logic completely ignores the distribution and features of the probability dataset, as well as the literal status distribution.

In the study by Abdeen et al. [2], "S-Type Random k Satisfiability Logic in Discrete Hopfield Neural Network Using Probability Distribution: Performance Optimization and Analysis", the authors consider a new type of non-systematic logic known as S-type Random k Satisfiability, which employs a novel layer of a Discrete Hopfield Neural Network and plays a significant role in identifying the predominant attribute likelihood of a binomial distribution dataset. Establishing the logical structure and assigning negative literals based on two specified statistical parameters is the objective of the probability logic phase. Abdeen et al. examined the performance of the proposed logic structure by comparing a proposed metric to current state-of-the-art logical rules. As a result, they discovered that the models have a high value in two parameters that efficiently introduce a logical structure in the probability logic phase. In addition, the study observed that implementing a Discrete Hopfield Neural Network reduced the cost function. The authors employed a novel statistical method of synaptic weight assessment to investigate the influence of the two proposed parameters on the logic structure. Overall, they revealed that regulating the two proposed parameters positively impacts synaptic weight management and the generation of global minimum solutions.

Traditional leak detection methods for gas pipelines necessitate task offloading decisions in the cloud, which has poor real-time performance. Edge computing provides a solution by allowing decisions to be made directly at the edge server, improving real-time performance; however, energy is the new bottleneck. In "Edge Computing Offloading Method Based on Deep Reinforcement Learning for Gas Pipeline Leak Detection", Wei et al. [3] concentrate on the real-time detection of gas transmission pipeline leaks. As a result, the authors propose a novel detection algorithm that combines the benefits of both the heuristic algorithm and the advantage actor-critic (AAC) algorithm.

The proposed detection algorithm seeks to optimize and ensure real-time pipeline mapping analysis tasks and maximize the survival time of portable gas leak detectors. Because the computing power of portable detection devices is limited due to their battery power, the main problem posed in this study is how to account for node energy overhead while ensuring system performance requirements.

Wei et al. establish the optimization model by introducing the concept of edge computing and using the mapping relationship between resource occupation and energy consumption as a starting point to optimize the total system cost (TSC). This is constituted of the transmission energy consumption of the node, the local computing energy consumption, and the residual electricity weight.

To reduce TSC, the algorithm employs the AAC network to make task scheduling decisions and determine whether tasks should be offloaded. Furthermore, it uses heuristic strategies and the Cauchy–Buniakowsky–Schwarz inequality to allocate communication resources.

Their experiments show that their proposed algorithm can meet the detector's real-time requirements while consuming less energy. Compared to the Deep Q Network (DQN) algorithm, their proposed algorithm saves approximately 56% of the system energy. It saves 21%, 38%, 30%, 31%, and 44% of energy consumption compared to the artificial gorilla troops Optimizer (GTO), the black widow optimization algorithm (BWOA), the exploration-enhanced grey wolf optimizer (EEGWO), the African vulture optimization algorithm (AVOA), and the driving training-based optimization (DTBO). Moreover, it saves 50% and 30% compared to entirely local computing and fully offloading algorithms, respectively. Meanwhile, this algorithm's task completion rate is 96.3%, the best real-time performance among these algorithms.

The pickup and delivery problems are pertinent problems in our interconnected world. Efficiently moving goods and people can decrease costs, emissions, and time. In the contribution by Little et al. [4], "Comparison of Genetic Operators for the Multi-Objective Pickup and Delivery Problem", the authors develop a genetic algorithm to solve the multi-objective capacitated pickup-and-delivery problem by adapting standard benchmarks.

They aim to reduce the total distance traveled and the number of vehicles employed. Based on NSGA-II, the authors investigate the effects of inter-route and intra-route mutations on the final solution. Little et al. introduce six inter-route operations and sixteen intra-route operations. Then, they calculate the hypervolume to compare their impact directly. In addition, the authors present two unique crossover operators tailored to this problem.

Their methodology identified optimal results in 23% of the instances in the first benchmark. In most other models, it generated a Pareto front within 1 vehicle and 20% of the best-known distance. Users can select the routes that best suit their requirements due to the presence of multiple solutions.

In a disaster, the road network is often compromised in capacity and usability conditions. This is a challenge for humanitarian operations delivering critical medical supplies. In the contribution by Anuar et al. [5], "A Multi-Depot Dynamic Vehicle Routing Problem with Stochastic Road Capacity: An MDP Model and Dynamic Policy for Post-Decision State Rollout Algorithm in Reinforcement Learning", the authors optimize vehicle routing for a Multi-Depot Dynamic Vehicle-Routing Problem with Stochastic Road Capacity (MD-DVRPSRC) using the Markov Decision Processes (MDP) model. They use the Post-Decision State Rollout Algorithm (PDS-RA) as a look-ahead approach in an Approximate Dynamic Programming (ADP) solution method. The authors execute a PDS-RA for all assigned vehicles to effectively solve the problem. The agent then decides at the end.

For the PDS-RA, Anuar et al. propose five types of constructive base heuristics. Firstly, they propose the Teach Base Insertion Heuristic (TBIH-1) to investigate the partial random construction approach for non-obvious decisions. The paper presents TBIH-2 and TBIH-3 as extensions to the TBIH-1 to demonstrate how experts could execute the Sequential Insertion Heuristic (I1) and Clarke and Wright (CW) in a dynamic setting, respectively. Additionally, the authors propose TBIH-4 and TBIH-5 (TBIH-1 with the addition of Dynamic Look-ahead SIH (DLASIH) and Dynamic Look-ahead CW (DLACW)). The goal is to improve the on-the-fly constructed decision rule (dynamic policy on the fly) in look-ahead simulations.

COVID-19 has shaken the world economy and affected millions of people in a brief period. COVID-19 has countless overlapping symptoms with other upper respiratory conditions, making it challenging for diagnosticians to diagnose correctly. Several mathematical models have been presented for their diagnosis and treatment. In "An Optimized Decision Support Model for COVID-19 Diagnostics Based on Complex Fuzzy Hypersoft Mapping", Saeed et al. [6] propose a mathematical framework based on a novel agile fuzzy-like arrangement, the complex fuzzy hypersoft (CFHS) set, a combination of the complex fuzzy (CF) and the hypersoft sets (an extension of the soft set).

First, the authors develop the CFHS elementary theory, which considers the amplitude term (A-term) and phase term (P-term) of complex numbers simultaneously to address uncertainty, ambivalence, and mediocrity of data. This new fuzzy-like hybrid theory is versatile in two parts.

First, it provides access to a wide range of membership function values by broadening them to the unit circle on an Argand plane and incorporating an additional term, the P-term, to account for the periodic nature of the data. Second, it divides the distinct attributes into corresponding sub-valued sets for easier comprehension. The CFHS set and CFHS mapping, with its inverse mapping (INM), can manage such issues. They validate their proposed framework by connecting COVID-19 symptoms to medications. This work also includes a generalized CFHS mapping [6], which can assist a specialist in extracting the patient's health record and predicting how long it will take to overcome the infection.

With the fourth industrial revolution developing, the way factories operate will no longer be the same. Factory automation can save labor and avoid equipment failures with online fault-detection systems. In recent years, various signal-processing methods have received much attention in the problem of fault-detection systems. In the article by Lee et al. [7], "Application of ANN in Induction-Motor Fault-Detection System Established with MRA and CFFS", the authors propose a fault-detection system for faulty induction motors (bearing faults, inter-turn shorts, and broken rotor bars) based on a multiresolution analysis (MRA), correlation and fitness values-based feature selection (CFFS), and artificial neural network (ANN).

For induction–motor–current signature analysis, Lee et al. compare two feature-extraction methods: the MRA and the Hilbert Huang transform (HHT). This work compares feature-selection methods to reduce the number of features while maintaining the best detection system accuracy to reduce operating costs. In addition, the proposed detection system is tested with additive white Gaussian noise, and the best signal-processing and feature-selection methods are chosen to create the best detection system. According to their results, features extracted from MRA outperform HHT using CFFS and ANN. The authors also confirm that the CFFS significantly reduces operation costs (95% of the features) while maintaining 93% accuracy using ANN in their proposed detection system.

Detection and recognition of scene text, such as automatic license plate recognition, is a technology with various applications. Although numerous studies have been conducted to increase detection performance, accuracy decreases when low-resolution and low-quality legacy license plate images are input into a recognition module.

In "HIFA-LPR: High-Frequency Augmented License Plate Recognition in Low-Quality Legacy Conditions via Gradual End-to-End Learning", Lee, S.-J. et al. [8] propose a model for high-frequency augmented license plate recognition. They integrate and collaboratively train the super-resolution and the license plate recognition modules using a proposed gradual end-to-end learning-based optimization. To train their model optimally, the authors propose a holistic feature extraction method that effectively precludes the generation of grid patterns from the super-resolved image during training.

Moreover, to exploit high-frequency information that affects license plate recognition performance, the authors propose a high-frequency augmentation-based license plate recognition module. In addition, they present a three-step, gradual, and end-to-end learning process based on weight immobilization. Their three-step methodological approach optimizes each module for robust performance in recognition. The experimental outcomes demonstrate that their model outperforms extant methods in low-quality legacy conditions for the UFPR and Greek vehicle datasets.

In machine learning, the convex minimization problem in the sum of two convex functions is fundamental. Many authors have analyzed this problem due to its applications in various fields, such as data science, computer science, statistics, engineering, physics, and medical science. These applications include signal processing, compressed sensing, medical image reconstruction, digital image processing, and data prediction and classification. In the contribution by Chumpungam et al. [9], "An Accelerated Convex Optimization Algorithm with Line Search and Applications in Machine Learning", the authors introduce a new line search technique and use it to build a novel accelerated forward–backward algorithm for solving convex minimization problems in the sum of two convex functions, one of which is smooth in a real Hilbert space.

The authors demonstrate a weak convergence to a solution of the proposed algorithm in the absence of the Lipschitz assumption on the gradient of the objective function. Furthermore, they evaluate its performance by applying the proposed algorithm to classification problems on various data sets and comparing it to other line search algorithms. The authors' experiments show that their proposed algorithm outperforms other line search algorithms.

The articles presented in this Special Issue provide insights into fields related to "Advances in Machine Learning and Mathematical Modeling for Optimization Problems", including models, performance evaluation and improvements, and application developments. We wish that readers can benefit from the insights of these papers and contribute to these rapidly growing areas. We also hope that this Special Issue sheds light on major developments in the area of machine learning and mathematical modeling for optimization problems and attracts the attention of the scientific community to pursue further investigations leading to the rapid implementation of these techniques.

Acknowledgments: We would like to express our appreciation to all the authors for their informative contributions and to the reviewers.

Conflicts of Interest: The authors declare no conflict of interest.

References

1. Othman, R.A.; Darwish, S.M.; Abd El-Moghith, I.A. A Multi-Objective Crowding Optimization Solution for Efficient Sensing as a Service in Virtualized Wireless Sensor Networks. *Mathematics* **2023**, *11*, 1128. [CrossRef]
2. Abdeen, S.; Kasihmuddin, M.S.M.; Zamri, N.E.; Manoharam, G.; Mansor, M.A.; Alshehri, N. S-Type Random k Satisfiability Logic in Discrete Hopfield Neural Network Using Probability Distribution: Performance Optimization and Analysis. *Mathematics* **2023**, *11*, 984. [CrossRef]
3. Wei, D.; Wang, R.; Xia, C.; Xia, T.; Jin, X.; Xu, C. Edge Computing Offloading Method Based on Deep Reinforcement Learning for Gas Pipeline Leak Detection. *Mathematics* **2022**, *10*, 4812. [CrossRef]
4. Little, C.; Choudhury, S.; Hu, T.; Salomaa, K. Comparison of Genetic Operators for the Multiobjective Pickup and Delivery Problem. *Mathematics* **2022**, *10*, 4308. [CrossRef]
5. Anuar, W.K.; Lee, L.S.; Seow, H.-V.; Pickl, S. A Multi-Depot Dynamic Vehicle Routing Problem with Stochastic Road Capacity: An MDP Model and Dynamic Policy for Post-Decision State Rollout Algorithm in Reinforcement Learning. *Mathematics* **2022**, *10*, 2699. [CrossRef]
6. Saeed, M.; Ahsan, M.; Saeed, M.H.; Rahman, A.U.; Mehmood, A.; Mohammed, M.A.; Jaber, M.M.; Damaševičius, R. An Optimized Decision Support Model for COVID-19 Diagnostics Based on Complex Fuzzy Hypersoft Mapping. *Mathematics* **2022**, *10*, 2472. [CrossRef]
7. Lee, C.-Y.; Wen, M.-S.; Zhuo, G.-L.; Le, T.-A. Application of ANN in Induction-Motor Fault-Detection System Established with MRA and CFFS. *Mathematics* **2022**, *10*, 2250. [CrossRef]
8. Lee, S.-J.; Yun, J.-S.; Lee, E.J.; Yoo, S.B. HIFA-LPR: High-Frequency Augmented License Plate Recognition in Low-Quality Legacy Conditions via Gradual End-to-End Learning. *Mathematics* **2022**, *10*, 1569. [CrossRef]
9. Chumpungam, D.; Sarnmeta, P.; Suantai, S. An Accelerated Convex Optimization Algorithm with Line Search and Applications in Machine Learning. *Mathematics* **2022**, *10*, 1491. [CrossRef]

Disclaimer/Publisher's Note: The statements, opinions and data contained in all publications are solely those of the individual author(s) and contributor(s) and not of MDPI and/or the editor(s). MDPI and/or the editor(s) disclaim responsibility for any injury to people or property resulting from any ideas, methods, instructions or products referred to in the content.

Article

A Multi-Objective Crowding Optimization Solution for Efficient Sensing as a Service in Virtualized Wireless Sensor Networks

Ramy A. Othman [1], Saad M. Darwish [2,*] and Ibrahim A. Abd El-Moghith [3]

1 World Trans Group, Alexandria 5423002, Egypt
2 Department of Information Technology, Institute of Graduate Studies and Research, Alexandria University, Alexandria 21544, Egypt
3 Almotaheda Company for Construction & Paving Roads, Alexandria 5432078, Egypt
* Correspondence: saad.darwish@alexu.edu.eg

Abstract: The Internet of Things (IoT) encompasses a wide range of applications and service domains, from smart cities, autonomous vehicles, surveillance, medical devices, to crop control. Virtualization in wireless sensor networks (WSNs) is widely regarded as the most revolutionary technological technique used in these areas. Due to node failure or communication latency and the regular identification of nodes in WSNs, virtualization in WSNs presents additional hurdles. Previous research on virtual WSNs has focused on issues such as resource maximization, node failure, and link-failure-based survivability, but has neglected to account for the impact of communication latency. Communication connection latency in WSNs has an effect on various virtual networks providing IoT services. There is a lack of research in this field at the present time. In this study, we utilize the Evolutionary Multi-Objective Crowding Algorithm (EMOCA) to maximize fault tolerance and minimize communication delay for virtual network embedding in WSN environments for service-oriented applications focusing on heterogeneous virtual networks in the IoT. Unlike the current wireless virtualization approach, which uses the Non-dominated Sorting Genetic Algorithm-II (NSGA-II), EMOCA uses both domination and diversity criteria in the evolving population for optimization problems. The analysis of the results demonstrates that the proposed framework successfully optimizes fault tolerance and communication delay for virtualization in WSNs.

Keywords: fault tolerance; virtualization; internet-of-things; multi-objective optimization; evolutionary crowding algorithm

MSC: 37M05; 37-04

1. Introduction

To accommodate the ever-expanding range of services offered by the IoT, network virtualization has been heralded as a crucial future-proofing mechanism for the Internet [1]. Through virtualization, a computer's hardware may be abstracted into a set of logical units that can then be shared across several users and, in some cases, competing software programmers. Multiple applications will be able to cohabit on the same virtualized WSNs, making this a potential strategy that can enable efficient use of WSN implementations [2]. The virtualization of networks has been proposed as a component of future inter-network communication models that might make it simple to integrate new functions into the Internet without requiring fundamental changes to the underlying architecture. The evolution of Internet structures would be hastened by this [3].

As a whole, the network virtualization environment is made up of individual network nodes and the connections between them. A virtual topology is created when virtual nodes are linked together via virtual connections to overcome the limitations of a single

connection, such as low bandwidth. The same physical hardware can host many virtual networks, each of which may have drastically different features. Resource-virtualization technologies also make things more abstract, which gives network operators a lot of freedom in how they run and change the network [4].

Sensing as a service (SaaS), which may be carried out in conjunction with network as a service (NaaS), is one of several fascinating application areas where the concept of WSN virtualization can be put to use. WSN virtualization enhances IoT security, resource usage, and administration, and decreases energy consumption [5]. Figure 1 shows how WSN visualization can be performed by making it easier for different kinds of networks to work together on the same physical infrastructure. The current four-tiered virtualization architecture for WSN networks is designed to cut down on unnecessary duplication of sensor networks across various IoT use cases [6–8].

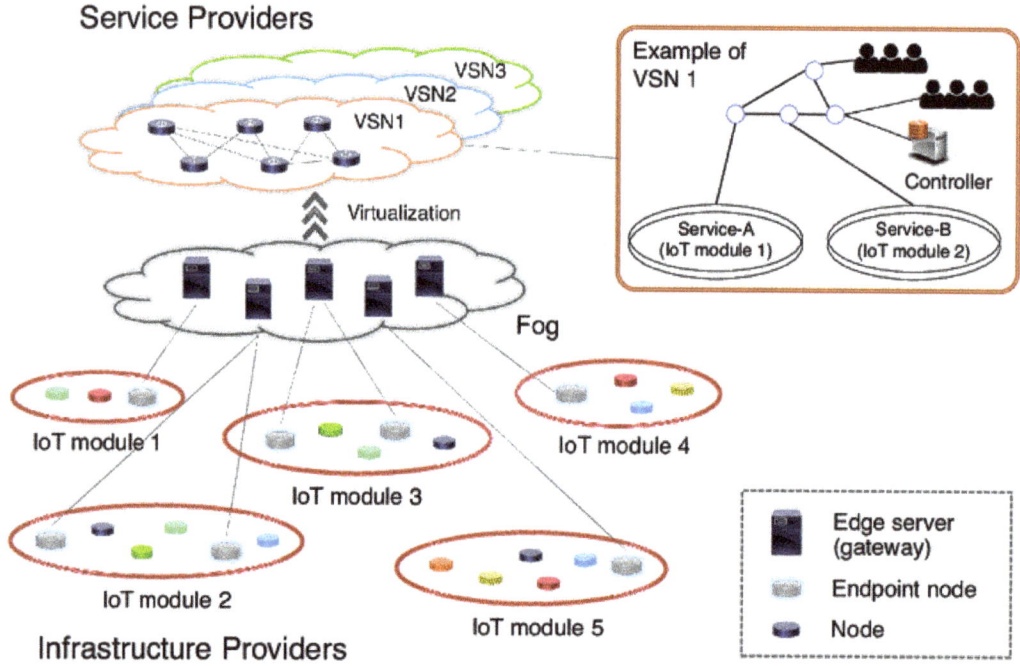

Figure 1. Architecture for virtualized wireless sensor networks.

The current virtualized wireless sensor networks architectures have not taken into account the possibility of a communication breakdown on a virtual network as a result of a breakdown in communications on real-world WSN networks. All nodes in a WSN are susceptible to failures such as node failures, communication failures, or internal component malfunctions of the sensors (such as a transceiver, CPU, battery, etc.) due to the wide variety of risk or hazard situations in which WSNs are deployed. Additionally to sensor attributes (low cost, compact size, high quality, etc.) [9], WSN technology has a number of challenges, but fault tolerance is by far the most significant of these. Due to the severity of these problems, it is even more important to include procedures and ways to remedy these flaws and reinforce their operation in order to boost fault tolerance [10].

In many scientific and technical contexts, it is important to simultaneously maximize many objectives while weighing the tradeoffs between them. Recent years have seen extensive studies devoted to the development of effective algorithms for resolving such multi-objective optimization (MOO) challenges. To solve MOO issues, these algorithms employ a population of candidate solutions, investigating a number of non-dominated solutions simultaneously. This is in contrast to the single-solution-at-a-time approach taken by conventional methods. In this process, the authors in [11] used a probabilistic approach to the formulation of a novel evolutionary multi-objective crowding algorithm (EMOCA). A middle ground between the issues of dominance and variety in the expanding population appears to be provided by their method.

In this context, this paper presents a novel architecture for heterogeneous virtual networks in the IoT that may be embedded into WSN settings to improve fault tolerance and decrease communication latency in service-oriented networking. Since fault tolerance and communication latency are often two conflicting objectives in WSN settings, the problem can be formulated as a reactive optimization of fault tolerance and communication delay, which in our case is carried out by adapting an evolutionary multi-objective crowding algorithm (EMOCA). EMOCA's novel method lies in its use of a non-domination ranking scheme and a probabilistic technique to decide whether an individual's offspring will be considered during the replacement-selection phase. EMOCA incorporates diversity preservation as an integral part of the algorithm. Compared with the well-known non-dominated sorting genetic algorithm NSGA-II, EMOCA discovers a diverse set of non-dominated solutions with near-uniform spacing [11]. Simulations are used to find out how well EMOCA performs at optimizing fault tolerance for virtualization in WSNs.

The remaining sections of the paper are as follows: the literature on virtual network embedding's fault tolerance is discussed in Section 2. Section 3 lays forth the specifics of the multi-objective optimization problem's mathematical formulation and EMOCA's application toward resolving it. The simulation environment, metrics, and performance comparisons are discussed in Section 4, and a summary is provided in Section 5.

2. Related Works

This section will provide an overview of some of the studies that have been carried out on fault tolerance in virtual network embedding (VNE). We surveyed the literature and classified past research into three broad classes: that focusing on link failure, that focusing on node failure, and that focusing on multi-objective optimization for network survival. We will next move on to a discussion of virtualization as a contributing area in WSNs. Many approaches have been suggested to strengthen VNE's dependability against the failure of the substrate resources, and many researchers have attempted to address the VNE problem using these mechanisms [12].

There are two main types of solutions to VNE survivability issues that have been identified in the literature: (a) proactive solutions that involve reserving resources in advance of a potential failure, and (b) reactive solutions that respond to a failure by immediately initiating a restoring mechanism [13]. In this case, each link's backup-storage quota has been depleted to be used for protection and restoration. Survivability techniques based on connection restoration and protection are useful from a commercial standpoint, but they have certain limitations. In many instances, the reactive method might cause data loss. The survivability measurement also does not account for the fault-tolerance capabilities of connections or communication latency [13].

Reactive solutions utilize a path-selection algorithm to determine backup pathways for each underlying connection before any VNE request is received. An existing embedding technique is then used to create the virtual node and link it to the subsequent request. With increased data loads, failure can cause a significant loss of data, and the backup mechanism may not be able to restore the VNE [14]. In [15], the authors presented the link-based backup strategy as a preventative measure against link failure. A portion of each core link's backup bandwidth is reserved in advance of any incoming VN request during the setup process. In this case, the backup bandwidth is scheduled ahead of time, before a problem occurs, which is preferable. Further, the VN embedding process requires fewer computational resources. With the shared pre-allocation method, backup bandwidth is held regardless of the VN requests, meaning it might not be used if even a small number of VN requests come at once.

To choose the most suitable virtual link for failure recovery, a hybrid technique was presented in [16]. In contrast to the reactive approach, which seeks to reallocate any capacity negatively impacted by a large request, the preventative approach embeds virtual links into numerous core channels to promote resistance to attacks and efficiency in resource use. This method depends on the WSN's remaining hardware resources, which may not be enough to fix the virtual network on a very busy network. An approach for identifying the alternate link among the impacted virtual network (VN) resources is introduced in [17]. While a dynamic recovery method is useful in general, it is especially useful when physical failures cause additional downtime and resources are limited. This approach demands a full VN reset, which takes a long time and makes the service inaccessible.

The authors in [18] presented a two-step methodology for restoring the whole VN of the failed attachment node. First, a graph is built to request VN with a virtual link backup contract, and then the improved VN is requested on the core set by employing both the redundant and K-redundant schemes. While this strategy may help optimize the allocation of certain resources, it may not be able to do so for all of them. It is recommended to set aside a spare node and link for every vital node in the network. A second two-step strategy for restoring VN is presented in [19]. The VN is augmented using virtual nodes (V_{Nodes}) and virtual links (V_{Links}) in the first stage, and sensor networks are then given access to this improved VN in the second stage. In the worst event, each V_{Node} needs to have a backup set aside. The research in [20] offered an enhanced VN based on a failover method to minimize backup resources. Despite being resource-efficient, this method is unworkable because V_{Nodes} frequently migrate.

Contrary to these approaches, in [21], the authors presented a joint optimization approach to assign both primary and backup resources. Although heuristic-based mapping quickly tackles single-node failure, the complexity and inconvenience of considering backup resources and the possibility of node and connection failure are inherent in this embedding technology. A method for improving long-term viability with minimal operating expenses was discussed in [22], which takes advantage of the spatial distribution of VNE's physical resources. A heuristic-based method was used for the smaller network, while an integer linear programming model was used for the larger one. It has been hypothesized that this is a multi-commodity network-flow issue. Since smaller networks often have faster physical connectivity, location data have less of an effect. If the structure of the virtual networks is altered, undesirable topology-based survival characteristics will emerge as a direct result. Even though there are more and more factors that take survival into account, the use of single-objective optimization approaches has stopped progress toward the best values for network parameters [23–26].

To improve fault tolerance in WSN virtualization, the popular MOO approach of non-dominated sorting based on a genetic algorithm (NSGA-II) is developed in [4]. Through a process of chromosomal sorting, NSGA-II is modified to address the optimization issue. The technique of sorting prioritizes chromosomes depending on competing criteria. Concerning solution dispersion and convergence to the genuine Pareto optimal, NSGA-II performs better than other Pareto-optimal approaches. However, there are drawbacks to the framework because of restrictions on the dissemination of consistency in some issues. Moreover, crowded comparisons can restrict the convergence. Virtualization proposals for WSNs tend to focus on improving resource (sensor) usage via the use of application-centric multitasking and the abstraction of sensors according to their use (i.e., virtual sensors).

The research in [27] investigated the challenge of finding the optimal lifetime and number of relay nodes for a network operating in three-dimensional environments. To achieve a better compromise between two goals, a new method is suggested. The technique combines a decomposition-based multi-objective evolutionary algorithm with a targeted local search to improve its component parts. In [28], the controller placement problem, which is a multi-objective optimization problem, is stated for selecting the optimal location for Software Defined Network (SDN) controllers to improve WSN performance. Considerations such as cost, time, and dependability are among the constraints that are applied here.

In addition, a novel adaptive population-based cuckoo optimization (APB-CO) is used to position controllers optimally.

The work in [29] discussed WSN resource allocation for combined time-slot assignment, channel allocation, and power control. This study analyses resource dependency to design a two-stage resource-allocation optimization technique for a non-convex issue with diverse research aims and computing complexity. First, a graph-coloring technique for time-slot assignment is created for conflict-free sensor information interchange. Based on the first stage of this technique, combined power control and channel allocation are examined and articulated as a multi-objective optimization problem to solve the tradeoff between energy efficiency and network capacity maximization under link interference and load-balancing constraints. In their work, multi-objective hybrid-particle swarm optimization yields Pareto-optimal solutions.

In [30], the time function of the goal function perception matrix is presented, taking into account the features of low-power and real-time performance of sensor nodes in WSN. In order to limit the perceptual nodes' inherent bias, a constraint on the number of targets they can detect is suggested; a weighted factor on the utility function is employed to ensure users are treated fairly; and finally, an optimization model of multi-objective resource allocation is established. To effectively allocate resources, a new technique is presented that builds on top of a modified version of simulated annealing (SA), bringing together the speedy optimization capabilities of SA with the robust search capabilities of logistic chaos.

The authors in [31] presented a multi-objective protocol (MOP) that maximizes network lifespan and residual energy using a mixed-integer linear-programming (MILP) optimization technique. Within the boundaries of the nodes that make up a given target, sets of MILP are solved locally. Therefore, within the same coverage nodes, energy is conserved. This research takes into account the goals of optimizing network residual energy and neighbor node connections. In order to determine which nodes to deactivate, each round's local MILP solution is used to identify the nodes that have the lowest connection to their neighbors and are thus the most heavily used throughout the routing process.

For 5G systems that support the Internet of Things, the research in [32] developed a new method of clustering based on optimization via network slicing. By using network slicing and cluster construction, multi-objective improved seagull optimization-based clustering with network slicing (MOISGO-CNS) aims to improve 5G systems' energy efficiency and load distribution. Both ISGO-based clustering and IGSO using bidirectional long short-term memory (BiLSTM) form the backbone of the MOISGO-CNS method. Two-hop connectivity ratio, residual energy, and link quality are the three metrics used to build a fitness function in the IGSO-based clustering method. In addition, the ISGO algorithm is developed as part of the network-slicing process in order to pick hyperparameters for optimum slicing classification performance. See [33,34] for an updated review of multi-objective optimization in wireless sensor networks. Recent studies that have looked at the crucial research of node and network-level virtualization in WSNs for the IoT [35,36] and applications show this to be the case [6,8,37–39].

In general, the problem with employing evolutionary algorithms for improving fault tolerance in WSN virtualization is that they cannot determine whether or not a solution is optimum; they can only determine whether or not it is "better" than other solutions that they already know about. It is also tricky to provide accurate weights to the objective functions, run the algorithm numerous times, and end up with various Pareto-optimal solutions; and Pareto-front concaves are notoriously difficult to analyze. A key challenge in the development of effective algorithms is the incorporation of diversity mechanisms into evolutionary algorithms for multi-objective optimization problems. This is the case for problems with an exponentially large number of possible non-dominated goal vectors. An acceptable approximation of the Pareto front is what we are aiming to obtain.

We look at how this can be carried out using the diversity mechanism of crowding dominance and highlight where this idea is demonstrably beneficial to handle internal failure perspectives in virtualization in WSNs. We use EMOCA as an MOO technique to maximize fault tolerance and minimize communication delay. The performance of EMOCA is compared with that of the well-known non-dominated sorting genetic algorithm NSGA-II. According to [11], EMOCA performs better than the other algorithm in eight of the nine test problems when it comes to convergence and diversity. It always finds a wide range of solutions that are not dominant.

3. The Proposed Framework

Here we cover the topic of virtualization's fault tolerance in WSNs. We evaluate a network structure with four layers. There is the "physical" layer, which is made up of the real sensor nodes, and then there is the "virtualization" layer, which creates additional "virtual" sensors that can perform additional jobs and services beyond what the "physical" layer can. In the third layer, known as the "access layer", different WSNs are developed based on the fault-tolerant incorporation of mission-oriented sensors. There is an access agent for every embedded network. The applications layer is where the IoT's smart applications, such as humidity, fire monitoring, temperature, etc., are represented to the end users who really benefit from them. In order to implement the suggestion, the access layer is modified.

Every node in a traditional sensor network cooperates to deploy sensors at the same level [24]. When many sensor networks operate together and share the same physical location, they form the Virtual Sensor Network (VSN). The same domain hosts a variety of physically distinct sensor networks. As part of a larger wireless sensor network, it is established by the sensor nodes that are most relevant to a certain activity or use case at that moment [20]. But in a virtual sensor network, the nodes work together to complete a specified task at a precise moment. To create a virtual sensor network, logical connections must be made between cooperating sensor nodes. Depending on the phenomenon being monitored or the function being served, nodes may be organized into distinct virtual sensor networks. The capability for network construction, utilization, adaptation, and maintenance of a subset of sensors working on a given job should all be provided by the virtual sensor network protocol. The proposed framework's flowchart is shown in Figure 2, and the mathematical terminology used to describe its key processes is included in Table 1.

Say we have a sensor network with nodes dispersed over the network region N_A. Assume mesh topology, meaning all nodes are connected. This network supports virtual networks. Assume a link-route breakdown causes s^v and d^v's link connection to fail. The wireless sensor network connects source physical sensor s^p and destination physical sensor d^p nodes. Investigate all possible paths between s^p and d^p to discover a fault-tolerant alternative. To find these routes, you must know the expected number of intermediary nodes. By calculating the average distance to the nearest-neighboring node, we may count the paths. Obtaining the sensor's probability density function (pdf) is all that is required to compute the nearest-neighbor sensor's distance; pdf is the probability of a neighbor sensor within r and $(r + \Delta r)$, where r is the transmission radius and Δr is the incremental distance. The physical wireless sensor network is considered to have a uniform sensor distribution λ such that [4].

$$\int_{N_A} \lambda \, dN_A = 1 \Rightarrow \lambda = \frac{1}{N_A} \tag{1}$$

For any two sensors separated by a distance between r and $(r + \Delta r)$, the probability $P^c_{r|(r+\Delta r)}$ of the closest-neighbor sensor is equal to the product of the probabilities that one of the sensors is present at the distance $P^s_{r|(r+\Delta r)}$ and that none of the other sensors are closer $P^0_{<r}$. Assume that the N_n sensor nodes in the network can only send data at a distance of 0.5 rad to the destination d^p. In this case, $P^c_{r|(r+\Delta r)}$ can be computed as:

$$P^c_{r|(r+\Delta r)} = P^0_{<r} \cdot P^s_{r|(r+\Delta r)} \tag{2}$$

$$P^c_{r|(r+\Delta r)} = [1 - P^s_{<r}] \cdot \left[P^s_{r|(r+\Delta r)} \right] \quad (3)$$

$$P^c_{r|(r+\Delta r)} = \left[1 - \sum_{j=1}^{N_n} \binom{N_n}{j} \left(\frac{\lambda \pi r^2}{2}\right)^j \left(1 - \frac{\lambda \pi r^2}{2}\right)^{N_n - j} \right] \cdot \left[\sum_{j=1}^{N_n} \binom{N_n}{j} \int_r^{r+\Delta r} \left(\frac{2\lambda \pi r \cdot dr}{2}\right)^j dr \cdot \int_r^{r+\Delta r} \left(1 - \frac{2\lambda \pi r \cdot dr}{2}\right)^{N_n - j} dr \right] \quad (4)$$

$$P^c_{r|(r+\Delta r)} = (1 - \lambda \pi r^2)^{N_n} \left[1 - \left(1 - \lambda \pi \left(rdr + dr^2\right)\right)^{N_n} \right] \quad (5)$$

$$P^c_{r|(r+\Delta r)} = (1 - \lambda \pi r^2)^{N_n} \left[1 - \left\{ 1 - \binom{N_n}{1} \cdot \left(\lambda \pi (rdr + dr^2)\right) + \binom{N_n}{2} \cdot \left(\lambda \pi (rdr + dr^2)\right)^2 \ldots \right\} \right] \quad (6)$$

$$P^c_{r|(r+\Delta r)} = (1 - \lambda \pi r^2)^{N_n} \left[N_n \lambda \pi r dr + N_n \lambda \pi dr^2 - \binom{N_n}{2} \cdot \left(\lambda \pi (rdr + dr^2)\right)^2 \ldots \right] \quad (7)$$

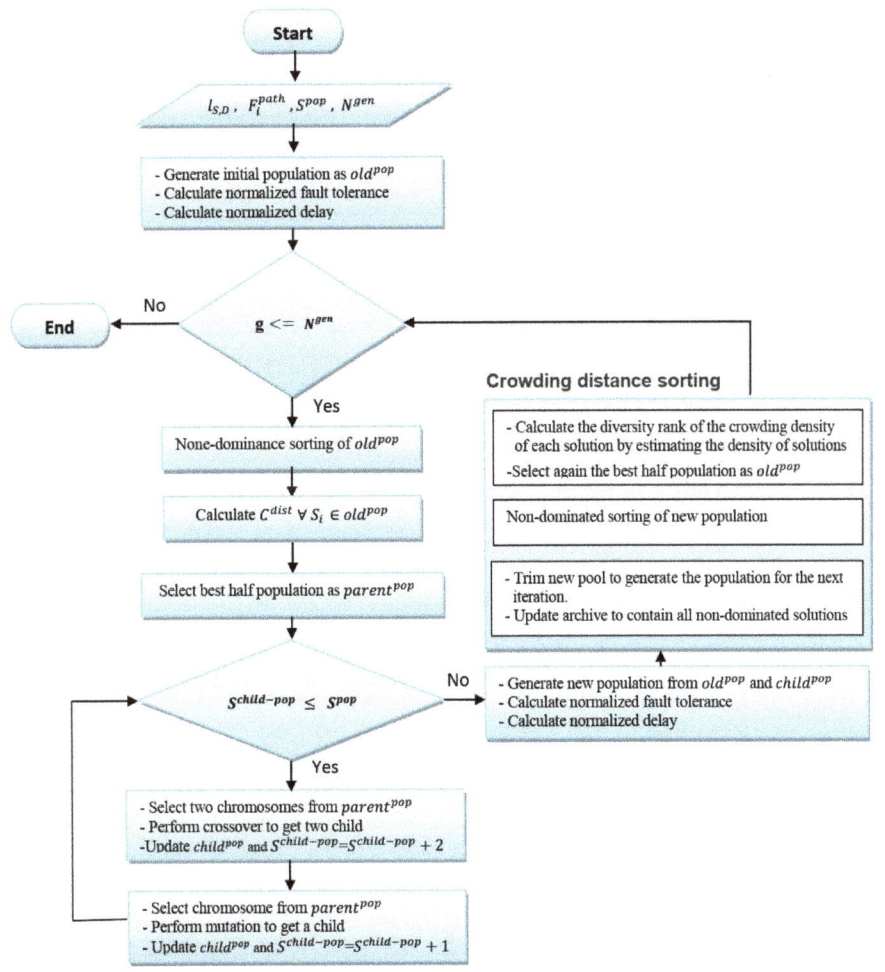

Figure 2. Flowchart of the proposed framework.

Table 1. Mathematical Nomenclature.

Notation	Description
s^v	Virtual source sensor of a link failure
d^v	Virtual destination sensor of a link failure
s^p	Source physical sensor
d^p	Destination physical sensor
N^p	Total number of paths between s^p and d^p
N_n	Number of sensors in the network
N_A	Network area
N_{in}	Number of intermediate nodes between s^v and d^v
$E(r)$	Expected closest-neighbor distance
r	Distance of nearest-neighbor sensor
Δr	A small incremental distance in r
λ	Density of sensors in the network
$P^c_{r\|(r+\Delta r)}$	Probability of closest sensor between r and $r + \Delta r$
$P^s_{r\|(r+\Delta r)}$	Probability of some sensor between r and $r + \Delta r$
$P^0_{<r}$	Probability of no sensor at less than r distance
S_i or S_{ij}	The ith sensor or the jth virtualization of ith sensor
$f_{r(r)}$	Probability density function (pdf) of closest-neighbor distance
R	Transmission range of sensors
D	Distance between s^p and d^p
$(N_{in} - 2)_{ck}$	Number of paths with k intermediates
FT^p_i	Fault tolerance of ith path
FT^l_i	Fault tolerance of ith link
CD^p_i	Communication delay of ith path
CD^l_i	Communication delay of ith link
CH_i	The ith chromosome
N_{re}	Number of retransmissions for a success
$e_{i,j}$	Packet error rate of a link between nodes i and j
$d^l_{i,j}$	Degree estimation of a link between nodes i and j
d^e_i	Degree of ith node
a	Decision variable
$d_{i,j}$	Distance between nodes i and j
S_p	Propagation speed
S_t	Transmission speed
S_{pkt}	Size of packet
S^{pop}	Size of chromosome population
N^{gen}	Number of generations during solution optimization
$l_{S,D}$	Link between s^p and d^p
F^{path}_i	Fault tolerance of ith path
D^s_i	Dominance set of ith solution
S_i	The ith solution of the population
np	The number of solutions that dominate p
F_j	The jth front
$S^{child-pop}$	Size of child population
R_i	Rank of ith solution

In order to calculate the probability density function of the nearest-neighbor distance $f_r(r)$, we can use the limit in Equation (7) as:

$$f_r(r) = \lim_{dr \to 0} \frac{P^c_{r|(r+\Delta r)}}{dr} = N_n \lambda \pi r (1 - \lambda \pi r^2)^{N_n} \qquad (8)$$

Considering R as transmission range of sensors, the expected closest-neighbor distance (r) can be expressed as

$$E(r) = \int_0^R r f_r(r) dr = \int_0^R N_n \lambda \pi r^2 \left(1 - \lambda \pi r^2\right)^{N_n} dr \qquad (9)$$

$$E(r) = \left[\frac{-r(1-\lambda\pi r^2)}{\lambda\pi(N_n+1)}\right]_0^R + \int_0^R \frac{(1-\lambda\pi r^2)^{N_n+1}}{\lambda\pi(N_n+1)} dr \qquad (10)$$

$$E(r) = \left[\frac{1}{\lambda\pi(N_n+1)}\sum_i^{N_n+1}\binom{N_n+1}{i}\frac{(-\lambda\pi r^2)^i r}{i+1}\right]_0^R \qquad (11)$$

$$E(r) = \frac{\sqrt{N_A}}{\lambda\pi^{\frac{3}{2(N_n+1)}}}\sum_i^{N_n+1}\frac{(-1)^i}{i+1} \qquad (12)$$

It can be shown that there are exactly $(N_{in}-2)_{ck}$ pathways from s^p to d^p with exactly k intermediary nodes, where

$$k = \left\{1,2,3,\ldots\left(\left\lfloor\frac{D}{E(r)}\right\rfloor - 1\right)\right\} \qquad (13)$$

$$N_{in} = \left(\left\lfloor\frac{D}{E(r)}\right\rfloor - 1\right) \qquad (14)$$

D represents distance between s^p and d^p. The equation for the total number of routes, N^p, from s^p to d^p is as follows:

$$N^p = (N_{in}-2)_{C_1} + (N_{in}-2)_{C_2} + \cdots + (N_{in}-2)_{C_{(N_{in}-2)}} \qquad (15)$$

$$N^p = \left\{(N_{in}-2)_{C_0} + (N_{in}-2)_{C_1} + \cdots + (N_{in}-2)_{C_{(N_{in}-2)}}\right\} - 1 \qquad (16)$$

$$N^p = 2^{N_{in}} - 1 \qquad (17)$$

If we want to maximize fault tolerance (FT), we can write it as:

$$\text{Maximize } FT = \max_{i=1,2,\ldots,N^p}\left(FT_i^p\right) \qquad (18)$$

$$FT_i^p = \frac{1}{\left(\left\lfloor\frac{D}{E(r)}\right\rfloor - 1\right)}\sum_{i=s^p, j=1}^{i=(\lfloor\frac{D}{E(r)}\rfloor-1), j=d^p} FT_{i,j}^l \qquad (19)$$

FT_i^p is the fault tolerance of the ith path from source s^p to destination d^p, and $FT_{i,j}^l$ is the fault tolerance of a link between an adjacent pair of nodes. The ordered set of nodes of ith path is represented by S_i^{op}

$$S_i^{op} = \left\{s^p, 1, 2, \ldots, \left(\left\lfloor\frac{D}{E(r)}\right\rfloor - 2\right), \left(\left\lfloor\frac{D}{E(r)}\right\rfloor - 1\right), d^p\right\} \qquad (20)$$

Similar to how the maximize FT function is written, the communication-delay (CD) minimization function is given by:

$$\text{Minimize } CD = \min_{i=1,2,\ldots,N^p}\left(CD_i^p\right) \qquad (21)$$

$$CD_i^p = \frac{1}{\left(\left\lfloor\frac{D}{E(r)}\right\rfloor - 1\right)}\sum_{i=s^p, j=1}^{i=(\lfloor\frac{D}{E(r)}\rfloor-1), j=d^p}\left(\frac{CD_{i,j}^l}{CD_{max}^l}\right) \qquad (22)$$

15

CD_i^p represents delay of ith path from s^p to d^p, $CD_{i,j}^l$ is the delay of a link between an adjacent pair of nodes, and $i,j \in S_i^{op}$. The maximum link delay among all the links is represented by CD_{max}^l. The optimization issue outlined above has the following restrictions:

$$0 < FT_i^p \leq 1,\ 0 < FT_i^l \leq 1,\ 0 < CD_i^p \leq 1,\ 0 < \frac{CD_{i,j}^l}{CD_{max}^l} \leq 1 \qquad (23)$$

The problem can be formulated as a reactive optimization of fault tolerance and communication delay, which is accomplished in our case by adapting an evolutionary multi-objective crowding algorithm (EMOCA). The number of objectives being optimized for is the primary dividing line between single- and multi-objective streamlining. When there are several competing goals, there is no best way to solve the situation at hand. There are a few possible good solutions. Pareto-optimal solutions are those that maximize utility with the fewest costs. As far as all goals go, the Pareto front does not provide a single solution that is optimal. Accordingly, all Pareto-front solutions are valuable without any problem-specific knowledge regarding the relative importance of different goals. Finding numerous such solutions that represent tradeoffs between goals is the primary aim of multi-objective optimization [40,41].

The primary objectives of multi-objective evolutionary algorithms (MOEAs) include: (1) settling on a Pareto-optimal solution set; and (2) acquiring a wide variety of options that are evenly spaced. When solutions are distributed unevenly, the Pareto front becomes crowded in certain areas. The EMOCA solution prioritizes variety throughout the algorithm to solve this problem [11]. Evolutionary operators such as crossover and mutation, in addition to chromosomal sorting through the non-dominance concept and diversity, are used to alter the solutions in EMOCA. After multiple cycles, the EMOCA eventually arrives at a collection of tradeoffs known as the Pareto front. Unlike an aggregate optimization strategy that only offers one solution, this set of alternatives gives the system designer many to choose from. The main structure of EMOCA is illustrated in Algorithm 1. Now we will discuss each of EMOCA's distinct steps [11].

Algorithm 1: EMOCA main structure

1. Initialize.
2. For the number of iterations determined by computational bounds, do:
    2.1. Generate Mating Population.
    2.2. Generate offspring by crossover followed by mutation.
    2.3. Create a new pool consisting of parents and some offspring.
    2.4. Trim new pool to generate the population for the next iteration.
    2.5. Update archive to contain all non-dominated solutions

---

Mating Population Generation: As a means of increasing the number of viable mates, EMOCA uses a system of binary tournament selection. An individual's fitness level is equal to their non-dominance rank plus their diversity rank. Individuals' non-dominance ranks are determined using the non-dominated sorting algorithm presented in [42–44]. Each individual within the population is compared to the others to determine dominance. This gives initial non-dominated front solutions. The first front's solutions are temporarily discarded, and then the preceding method is repeated until no non-dominated fronts remain. Solutions from the same non-dominated front are ranked equally.

For diversity rank, NSGA-II crowding's distance metric determines each solution's crowding density. To determine the density of solutions around a specific solution in a front, we calculate the average distance of two solutions along each goal (two solutions on either side of the solution x_i). Front boundary solutions have an infinite crowding distance. For all other solutions within a front, the following Algorithm 2 is used to assign the crowding distance [36]. Greater crowding distance in a solution suggests more variety (diversity). Based on their crowding distance, the solutions in the population are rated and ordered.

Algorithm 2: Crowding distance measure

1. For each solution x_i of front F, initialize crowding distance $d(x_i)$ to be 0;
2. For each objective function f_m do:
   2.1 Sort the solutions in F along objective f_m;
   $d(x_i) = d(x_i) + f_m(\text{the individual that precedes xi in the sorted sequence})$
   $\qquad\qquad\qquad - f_m(\text{the individual that follows xi in the sorted sequence})$

New Pool Generation: After comparing each child to one of its randomly selected parents, taking dominance and crowding density into account, a new pool consisting of all the parents and some of the offspring is formed. Possible outcomes include the following three scenarios:

- Case 1: The child gets introduced to the new pool if it is dominant over the parent.
- Case 2: The probability of acceptance of the children is calculated using the crowding distance measure if the parent is dominant over the offspring. The probability P that a child will be included in the new pool if it has a larger crowding distance than its parent is:

$$P = 1 - exp((\delta(parent) - \delta(offspring)) \tag{24}$$

δ denotes the crowding distance of a solution. A more diverse child with a larger crowding distance than its parent has a greater chance of survival. More diverse solutions are rewarded by being given a chance to thrive in subsequent generations.

- Case 3: In cases where the parent and offspring are not dominant over one another, the offspring will be included in the new pool if its crowding distance is greater than that of the parent.

Trimming New Pool: Both non-domination rank and diversity rank are used to sort the new pool. Thus, the diversity rank is used to compare alternatives that have the same non-domination rating. The new population will be made up of the initial items of the sorted list of fronts $F_1, F_2, \ldots, F_n$ where elements of $F_i + 1$ are dominated only by elements in $F_1, F_2, \ldots, F_i$. All generations of non-dominated solutions are saved in EMOCA's archive.

For the most part, EMOCA relies on an individual's diversity score to determine whether or not their offspring will be allowed to join the new population. While EMOCA does not tolerate offspring who are dominant like their parents, it does allow some low-quality offspring to remain in the population, provided they have sufficient variety. The result is a more well-rounded and interesting population. Although NSGA-II allows all viable offspring to go on into the next generation, EMOCA only allows a small percentage to do so. Therefore, whereas NSGA-II executes non-dominated sorting on a population of size 2N, where N is the population size, EMOCA executes non-dominated sorting on a population size between N and $2N$. With this, EMOCA's computational complexity decreases [11].

3.1. Chromosome Representation

In EMOCA's solution space for an optimization problem, a chromosome CH_i is an ordered collection of intermediate nodes S_i^{op} that begins with source s^p and ends with d^p. Genes in the chromosomal model are represented by each node in the set.

$$CH_i = \left\{ s^p, 1, 2, \ldots, \left(\left[\frac{D}{E(r)}\right] - 2\right), (|D/E(r)| - 1), d^p \right\}^{FT,CD} \tag{25}$$

$$FT_{i,j}^l = \left(1 - \sum_{t=0}^{N_{re}} (e_{i,j})^t (1 - e_{i,j})\right) + d_{i,j}^l \tag{26}$$

Given a connection with packet error rate $e_{i,j}$ and degree estimate of the link $d_{i,j}^l$, we may calculate the number of retransmissions, N_{re}, that will be necessary for a successful transmission. In this case, a path's cumulative fault tolerance is calculated by adding the fault tolerances of its individual connections. With the help of packet-error-rate-based link-quality estimation and neighbor-density-based degree estimation, we are able to calculate a link's fault tolerance $FT_{i,j}^l$. The degree estimation can be derived from Equation (27) where d_i^e and d_j^e are the degrees of nodes i and j, respectively, and α is a decision variable varying between 0 and 1.

$$d_{i,j}^l = \begin{cases} 1, & d_i^e = d_j^e = N_n - 1 \\ 1 - \alpha^{d_i^e}, & d_i^e = d_j^e < N_n - 1 \\ 1 - \alpha^{\frac{(d_i^e - d_j^e)^2}{d_i^e + d_j^e}}, & |d_i^e - d_j^e| > 0 \end{cases} \quad (27)$$

When calculating the communication delay $CD_{i,j}^l$, we factor in interference for the connection, which is based on the link quality, as well as propagation and transmission delay where $d_{i,j}$ is the distance between the pair of nodes i and j, S_p represents propagation speed, S_{pkt} is the packet size, and s_t represents transmission speed.

$$CD_{i,j}^l = \left(1 - \sum_{t=0}^{N_{re}} (e_{i,j})^t (1 - e_{i,j})\right) + \frac{d_{i,j}}{S_p} + \frac{S_{pkt}}{s_t} \quad (28)$$

3.2. Crossover and Mutation

The crossover procedure involves randomly swapping a collection of nodes between two chromosomes from the population (all paths between s^p and d^p). The exchange is limited to nodes that are reachable both downstream and upward. Larger group sizes are desirable in the earlier stages (lower generations) of a solution. Generation number and chromosomal pair size determine crossover group size. Due to the recurrence of intermediate nodes, chromosomes after crossover operations (also called offspring in optimization theory) are repaired. Intermediate nodes in the parent chromosome but not in the offspring are considered during repair. If two randomly chosen nodes on the chromosome can be reached (present as neighbors) from their respective descendant nodes, then the mutation process will swap their positions.

3.3. Non-Dominance and Crowding-Distance-Based Sorting for Chromosomes

Using non-dominance, chromosomes are sorted. Multiple competing goals are used to arrange chromosomes. Consider population chromosomes CH_i and CH_j. According to Pareto optimum, a chromosome CH_i dominates CH_j if at least one of its fitness values is higher than CH_j's and the other fitness values are equal. Multi-objective optimization in communication networks favors Pareto-optimal prioritizing [40,41]. For two goals, it is:

$$CH_i > CH_j = \begin{cases} CH_i(FT) > CH_j(FT), \wedge CH_i(CD) \not< CH_j(CD) \\ CH_i(CD) > CH_j(CD), \wedge CH_i(FT) \not< CH_j(FT) \end{cases} \quad (29)$$

The population's chromosomes are sorted by fitness using the non-dominance notion. Non-dominant chromosomes rank first in the population. Only one chromosome in a population ranks second. Population-wise, chromosomes dominated by two others rank third. Each chromosome's crowding distance is computed after ranking. The next generation is chosen via a tournament method.

Algorithm 3 lays out the whole process that was followed to obtain an optimal solution, for which a population (paths between pairs of sources and destinations) of size S^{pop} is formed by randomly scattering the decision variable throughout some allowed range (low, high). Non-dominance-based sorting old^{pop} is used to order the population. To determine the objective-1 normalized fault tolerance and the objective-2 normalized delay for each $S_i \in old^{pop}$, the best half of the population is selected, and for each S_i the crowing distance C^{dist} is computed from all points excluding boundary points. Using the tournament-selection approach, the best half of the population is chosen based on the rank of ith solution R_i and crowding distance C^{dist}. By introducing mutations and performing crossovers, a superior solution may be generated from a preselected parent population. The optimal half of the population is once again chosen from the whole population. These procedures are iterated until the stop criterion is met (the maximum number of generations is reached) in order to produce optimal chromosomes. The time complexity of EMOCA is $O(2 \times S^{pop} \times N^{gen})$, where S^{pop} is size of the old population and N^{gen} represents the number of generations. The number of generations, and hence the amount of time it takes to run, is indirectly determined by the size of the network. As a result, the time needed for each generation might change based on the system's hardware.

In summary, convergence is emphasized by the concept of non-domination rank. During the period of tournament selection and population reduction, variety is preserved by the use of diversity rank. It is also possible to apply the crowding distance to the parameter space [11]. In contrast, we measure crowding in the target space to determine the optimal solution. When compared to NSGA-II and other multi-objective evolutionary algorithms (MOEAs) such as multi-objective ant-colony optimization (MOACO) and multi-objective particle-swarm optimization (MOPSO), EMOCA's most distinguishing features include:

- When selecting whether or not to include a new generation into the population, EMOCA takes into account each individual's diversity score. In contrast to MOEAs, which eliminate offspring who take after a single parent, EMOCA lets some low-quality offspring to persist in the population so long as they contribute to genetic variety. In a nutshell, this contributes to a more diverse population.
- While NSGA-II allows all viable offspring to go on into the next generation, EMOCA allows just a small percentage to do so. Thus, whereas NSGA-II can only carry out non-dominated sorting on a population of size $2N$, EMOCA can perform non-dominated sorting on populations with sizes ranging from N to $2N$. The computational burden placed on EMOCA is therefore decreased.
- In EMOCA, both non-domination and diversity are equally weighted by a single measure (the total rank) used for mate selection. This tremendously aids efforts to diversify and improve the quality of the available mating pool. But MOEAs and NSGA-II employ non-domination rank as the major criterion for selecting the mating pool. As a result, the resulting mate pool could not be as diverse as it otherwise would be.

The next section details the simulations run to assess the framework's efficacy, paying special attention to the parameters of the test beds, the metrics used, and the analysis of the resulting data. Two goals were set to accomplish simulations based on case studies. To begin, the number of generations has an influence on fault-tolerant optimization's efficacy, which is then used to determine how well it performs. Second, network density is a key indicator of fault-tolerant optimization's effectiveness.

Algorithm 3: EMOCA for solving the optimization problem

Input: S^{pop}, N^{gen}, $l_{S,D}$, F_i^{path}
Starting with generate initial population size S^{pop}. Then saving one copy of population as "old^{pop}".
For each $S_i \in old^{pop}$
        Calculate objective-1 normalized fault-tolerance using Equation (19)
        Calculate objective-2 normalized delay using Equation (22)
End for
  g = 1;
While (g $\leq N^{gen}$)
    Non-dominated sorting (old^{pop})
    For each $S_i \in old^{pop}$
        Calculate D_i^s
    End for
    j = 1,
    For each $S_i \in old^{pop}$
        If ($D_i^s = \phi$)
          $F_j = F_j \cup S_i$, $R_i = 1$
        End if
    End for
    j = 2,
    For each $S_i \in old^{pop}$
    If ($D_i^s \neq \phi$ && $R_i == j - 1$)
        $F_j = F_j \cup S_i$, $R_i = 1$, $j = j + 1$
    End if
End for
Crowding_distance (old^{pop})
    Assume C^{dist} from boundary point (group of solution) to ∞ for any solution.
    For each $S_i \in old^{pop}$
        Calculate C^{dist} from all point excluding boundary points
    End for
Select the best half population as $parent^{pop}$ considering R_i & C^{dist} using tournament selection approach.
    $child^{pop} = \phi$
    $S^{child-pop} = 0$
While ($S^{child-pop} \leq S^{pop}$)
    Randomly select two chromosomes from the parent population.
    Perform crossover to produce two child chromosomes.
    Update $child^{pop}$ and $S^{child-pop} = S^{child-pop} + 2$
    Randomly choose a chromosome from parent population.
    Mutate chromosome to produce a child chromosome
    Update $child^{pop}$ and $S^{child-pop} = S^{child-pop} + 1$
End while
    Generate new population of size ($2 \times S^{pop}$) by $old^{pop} \cup child^{pop}$
    Calculate normalize fault-tolerance using Equation (19).
    Calculate normalized delay using Equation (22).
    Non-dominated sorting ($Nold^{pop} \cup child^{pop}$)
    Crowing_distance ($old^{pop} \cup child^{pop}$)
    Select again the best half population as old^{pop} using rank and C^{dist}
End while
Output: optimized chromosomes

4. Experimental Results

In order to evaluate the proposed framework in virtual networks, the NS2 network simulator employs C++ to develop the simulation's primary classes. The major classes of the simulation include 'NetworkNode', 'VirtualNode', 'RandomProvider', 'PathSearch', and 'MainApp'. All the characteristics of a node in a network, such as position, list of neighbors, link delay with neighbors, and fault tolerance of associated links, are implemented in 'NetworkNode'. At 'VirtualNode', tasks are processed using an interface-based architecture. Different sets of network nodes are generated at random by the 'RandomProvider' for each simulation run. PathSearch is a tool for optimizing virtual network generation with respect to delay and fault tolerance. The simulation is run on a machine with a 64-bit UBUNTU operating system (Linux), 16 GB of RAM, and an Intel Core i7-11700K processor running at 3.6 GHz. Three sets of randomly formed networks of 100, 500, 1000, 1500, and 2000 nodes are constructed using the Poisson distribution method. For each of four distinct networks, the EMOCA algorithm is run for 500, 1000, 1500, and 2000 generations in an effort to maximize fault tolerance and minimize communication latency. The most recent generation's chromosomes in the results table stand in for the most recent set of optimized values.

Parameter and setting values utilized in the simulations are listed in Table 2. Sensors are deployed in a range of 100 to 1000, according to a specific deployment pattern, with a maximum transmission radius of 30 m, uniformly and randomly distributed across the circle with area $N_A = 1500$ m^2. The initial energy level J of each sensor is the same. The power consumed while transmitting, receiving, and in the idle state are 175 mJ, 175 mJ, and 0.015 mJ, respectively. The power consumed for sensing is equal to 1.75 µJ. For focusing on coverage measurement, a sensing range of 10 m and a transmission range of 30 m are considered during the simulation. Transmission delays due to propagation have been deemed insignificant for the simulation region chosen. Each experiment was repeated 30 times using the specified simulation settings and variables, and the arithmetic mean was used to optimize the data record with a 95% degree of confidence.

Table 2. Basic parameter setting for simulation.

Parameter	Value
Simulation area	1500 m^2
Simulation time	600 s
Number of nodes	100 – 1000
Bandwidth	40 Kbps
Transmission range	15 m to 30 m
Receiving range	15 m
Initial node energy	30 J
Packet type	UDP
Channel type	Wireless
Antenna model	Omni
MAC protocol	IEEE 802.11
Query period	3 s
Hello timeout	1 s

4.1. Comparative Results

In Figures 3–6, we see how EMOCA, NSGA-II, and multi-objective versions of both optimization algorithms, which include particle-swarm optimization (PSO) and ant-colony optimization (ACO), perform while optimizing a network with 100 nodes across 500–2000 generations. Herein, the comparative algorithms were employed as black-box versions with their default parameters (open-source code from GitHub). It is evident that EMOCA outperforms other comparative algorithms in terms of optimization performance, with regards to both fault tolerance and communication latency. The finding demonstrates that virtualized WSNs based on EMOCA can successfully deal with failure. More specifically, the optimal values for fault tolerance and communication latency are 0.67 and 0.02, respectively. This is because packet-error rate is a reliable predictor of fault tolerance. For the multi-objective version of ACO, the optimal value of fault tolerance is approximately 0.57 and the optimal value of communication delay is approximately 0.038. However, for the multi-objective version of PSO, the optimal values of fault tolerance and communication delay are 0.31 and 0.11, respectively.

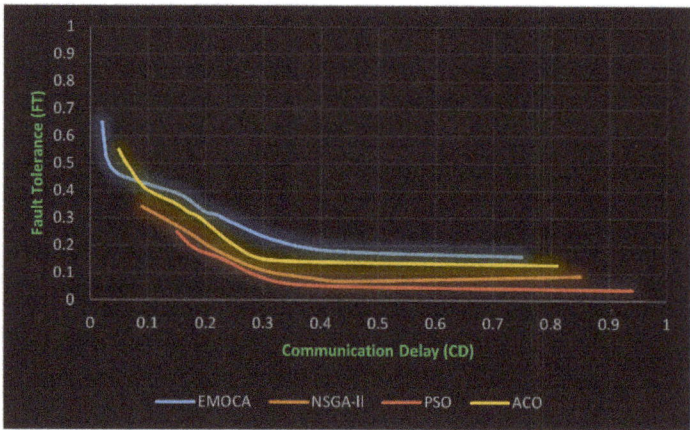

Figure 3. Optimized chromosome with 100 nodes after 500 generations.

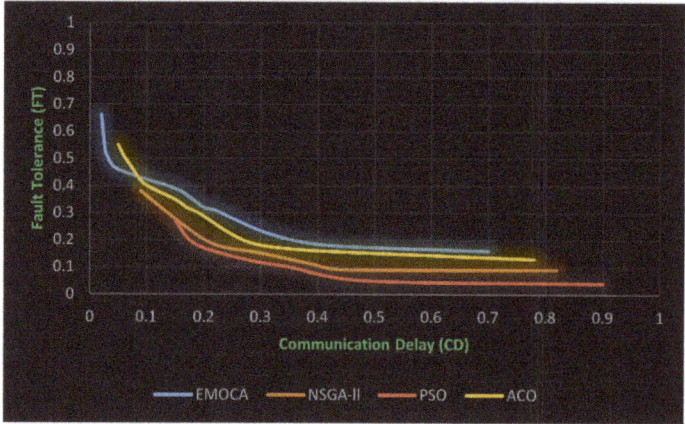

Figure 4. Optimized chromosome with 100 nodes after 1000 generations.

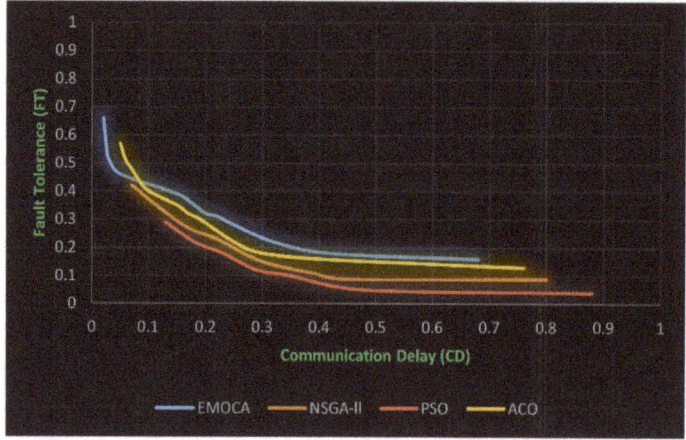

Figure 5. Optimized chromosome with 100 nodes after 1500 generations.

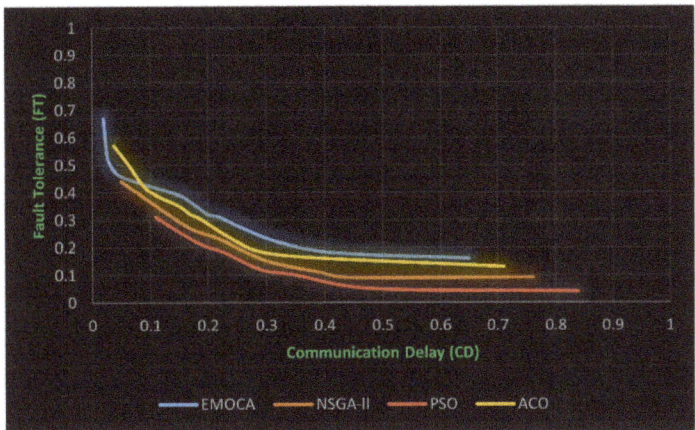

Figure 6. Optimized chromosome with 100 nodes after 2000 generations.

The optimal value of fault tolerance for NSGA-II is around 0.44, whereas the optimal value of delay is approximately 0.05. This is because a fault-tolerant estimate is reliant on the degree of connection. In a wireless environment, the estimate is inappropriate. Having a large number of chromosomes also increases latency and decreases fault tolerance. In addition, because of the reduced size of the network (100 nodes), the effect of a larger number of generations on the final, optimized chromosome is far less dramatic. It is difficult to tell what makes one set of results distinct from the next. This is because there are fewer possible paths to create in more compact networks.

The network is scaled up to 500 nodes in order to amplify the optimization performance gap between generations. Figures 7–10 display a comparison of optimization performance with increasing network size. The results show that when both goals are included, EMOCA achieves greater optimization performance than NSGA-II and multi-objective versions of both ACO and PSO. Specifically, the fault tolerance value of the latest optimized chromosome is about 0.92, while the communication latency value is around 0.015. This is because more paths are available in more extensive networks, allowing for the selection of connections of higher quality, with higher fault tolerance and reduced communication latency. There is a tradeoff between fault tolerance and communication latency, with the optimal value for each ranging around 0.82, 0.06 for ACO; 0.72, 0.08 for NSGA-II; and 0.59, 0.1 for PSO, respectively. The pace at which the system converges on an optimal solution has slowed, and the number of optimized chromosomes has decreased. Additionally, the bigger network (500 nodes) mitigates the negative effects of increasing the number of generations on the optimized chromosome.

The convergence rate toward the ideal solution is boosted by increasing the network size to 1000 nodes. Figures 11–14 display a comparison of the optimization convergence rates. As expected, the results show that EMOCA has a higher optimization convergence rate compared to NSGA-II, ACO, and PSO for both goals. Comparatively, the optimum chromosomal value for communication latency is about 0.010, whereas the fault-tolerance value is around 0.98. This is because, as the size of the network grows, more and more paths become suitable for use, allowing for more discriminatory tolerance in the paths that are ultimately chosen. The optimal fault tolerance for ACO chromosomes is around 0.82, whereas the optimum communication delay is about 0.06. The optimal fault tolerance for NSGA-II chromosomes is around 0.78, whereas the optimum communication delay is about 0.07. The optimal fault tolerance for PSO chromosomes is around 0.59, whereas the optimum communication delay is about 0.1. In addition, when the size of the network is ramped up, the proportion of optimized chromosomes grows. In both cases, you will find that the chromosomes are packed closely together. We can also observe that the Pareto front obtained by EMOCA covers a wider region of the objective space compared to the Pareto fronts obtained by the other algorithms.

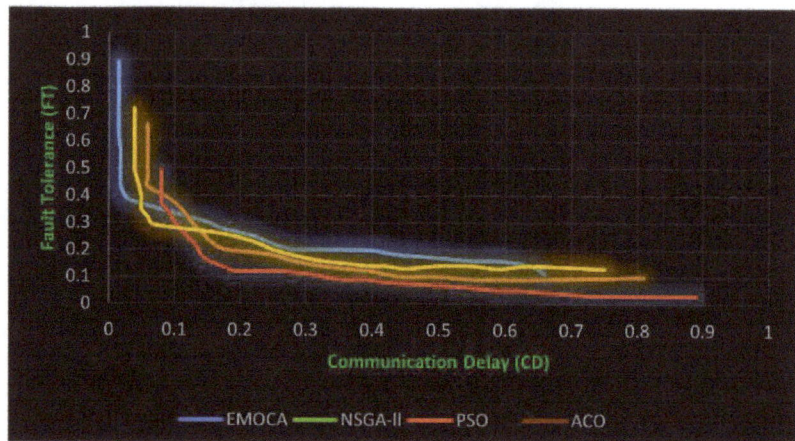

Figure 7. Optimized chromosome with 500 nodes after 500 generations.

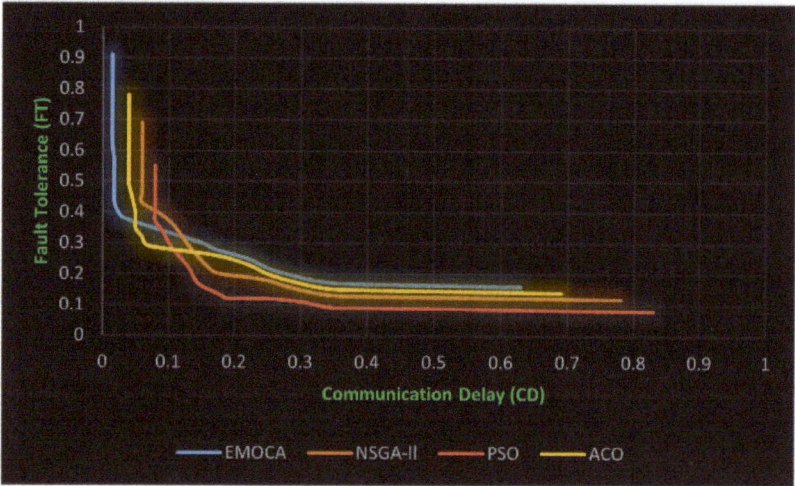

Figure 8. Optimized chromosome with 500 nodes after 1000 generations.

4.2. Summary of Results

We can also observe that the Pareto front obtained by EMOCA covers a wider region of the objective space compared to the Pareto fronts obtained by the other algorithms. EMOCA yields much smaller values for the crowding distance of a solution compared to competing techniques. EMOCA finds a wide variety of non-dominated solutions spaced out almost uniformly. These characteristics enable EMOCA algorithms to search for solutions in a much larger space with less complexity, and the results show that the EMOCA approach was capable of providing more accurate solutions at a lower computational complexity than the existing compared methods.

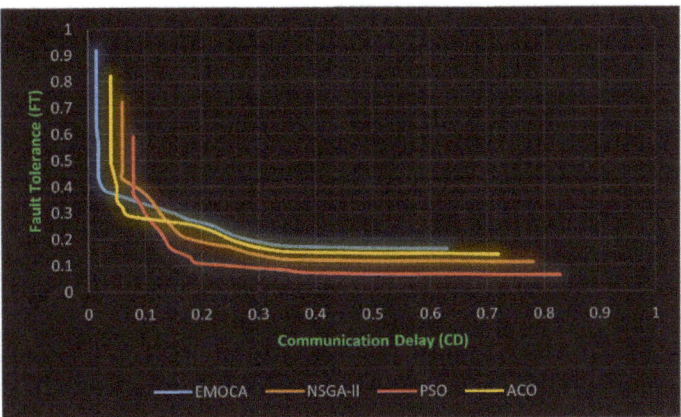

Figure 9. Optimized chromosome with 500 nodes after 1500 generations.

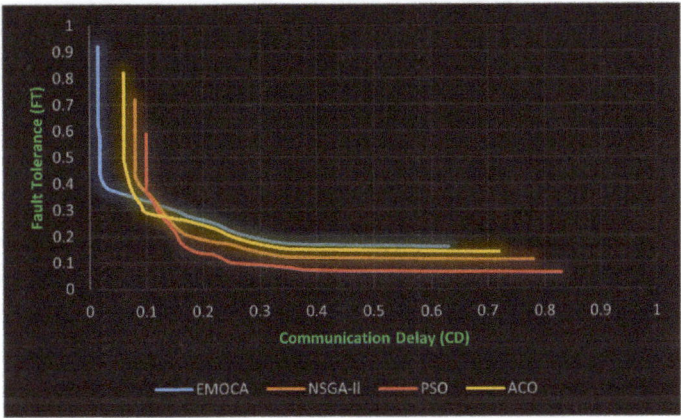

Figure 10. Optimized chromosome with 500 nodes after 2000 generations.

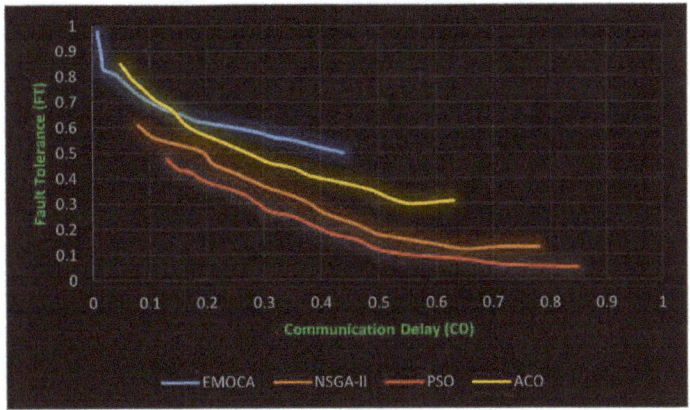

Figure 11. Optimized chromosome with 1000 nodes after 500 generations.

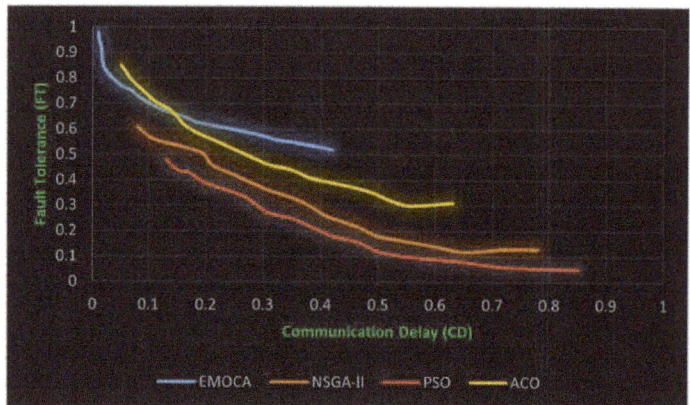

Figure 12. Optimized chromosome with 1000 nodes after 1000 generations.

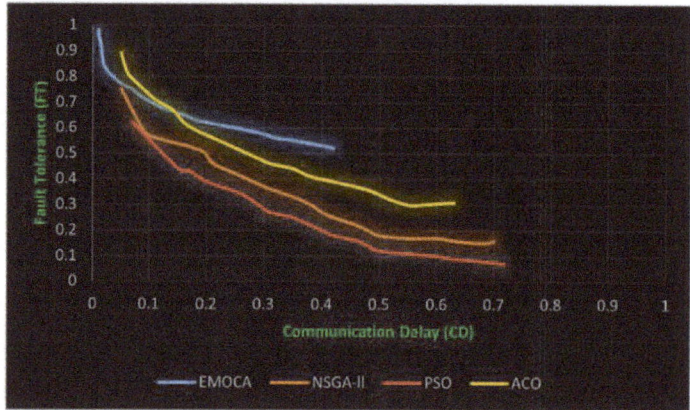

Figure 13. Optimized chromosome with 1000 nodes after 1500 generations.

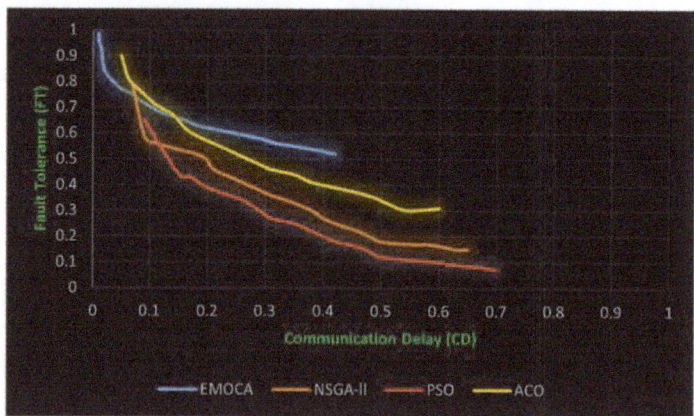

Figure 14. Optimized chromosome with 1000 nodes after 2000 generations.

Algorithms built on the NSGA-II framework outperform their PSO-based counterparts. Here are several explanations that might be at play. Because of NSGA-II's crossover and mutation processes, chromosomes may be shifted across huge distances in the solution space. Additionally, in NSGA-II, there is no correlation between individual chromosomes and the present local or global best results. Such capabilities allow NSGA-II based VNE algorithms to explore solutions in a considerably broader area than is possible with the PSO method alone. On the other hand, only the "best" particle shares its knowledge in PSO-based VNE algorithms. In contrast to PSO-based algorithms, those based on ACO vary in the calculation rank of the nodes, which affects the sequence in which virtual node consolidation and pheromone computing occur. As a result, EMOCA algorithms are a viable option for multi-objective optimization since they may provide more workable solutions.

5. Conclusions and Future Work

Both diversity and convergence are crucial for VNE optimization techniques. A system designer who is interested in analyzing several tradeoff alternatives in order to make an informed decision would not benefit from a Pareto set with few solutions concentrated in a certain location of the Pareto front. In this study, we demonstrate how we optimized two conflicting objectives—fault tolerance and communication latency in virtualized WSNs—by concentrating on heterogeneous network requirements for IoT applications through utilizing an EMOCA framework that uses a stochastic replacement-selection technique that includes both non-domination and diversity. In order to address the issues of fault tolerance and communication latency in virtualized WSNs, a mathematical formulation of a multi-objective optimization problem is presented. Using NSGA-II as a benchmark, we found that EMOCA's optimization framework was superior to the current standard. Simulation results demonstrate that EMOCA outperforms superior optimization techniques produced with fewer generations. Moreover, the time to achieve the optimization outcomes is reduced compared to the best current methods. This proves the effectiveness of the suggested framework in terms of convergence and diversity, since a diverse range of non-dominated solutions is constantly discovered. The successful performance of EMOCA in optimization challenges across a broad range of sectors, such as routing and battery life in virtualized WSNs, will be considered in future research work. This is in addition to expanding the current work to include many other objective functions besides fault tolerance and communication delay.

Author Contributions: Conceptualization, S.M.D.; methodology, S.M.D. and R.A.O.; software, R.A.O.; validation, S.M.D and I.A.A.E.-M.; formal analysis, S.M.D. and I.A.A.E.-M.; investigation, S.M.D.; resources, R.A.O.; data curation, R.A.O. and I.A.A.E.-M.; writing—original draft preparation, S.M.D., I.A.A.E.-M. and R.A.O.; writing—review and editing, S.M.D.; visualization, R.A.O. and I.A.A.E.-M.; supervision, S.M.D.; project administration, R.A.O. and I.A.A.E.-M.; funding acquisition, R.A.O. All authors have read and agreed to the published version of the manuscript.

Funding: This research received no external funding.

Institutional Review Board Statement: The study did not require ethical approval.

Informed Consent Statement: Not applicable.

Data Availability Statement: The study did not report any data.

Conflicts of Interest: The authors declare no conflict of interest.

References

1. Mahapatra, S.; Singh, B.; Kumar, V. A survey on secure transmission in internet of things: Taxonomy, recent techniques, research requirements, and challenges. *Arab. J. Sci. Eng.* **2020**, *45*, 6211–6240. [CrossRef]
2. Borsatti, D.; Davoli, G.; Cerroni, W.; Raffaelli, C. Enabling Industrial IoT as a Service with Multi-Access Edge Computing. *IEEE Commun. Mag.* **2021**, *59*, 21–27. [CrossRef]
3. Rawat, D.B. Fusion of Software Defined Networking, Edge Computing, and Blockchain Technology for Wireless Network Virtualization. *IEEE Commun. Mag.* **2019**, *57*, 50–55. [CrossRef]
4. Kaiwartya, O.; Abdullah, A.H.; Cao, Y.; Lloret, J.; Kumar, S.; Shah, R.R.; Prasad, M.; Prakash, S. Virtualization in Wireless Sensor Networks: Fault Tolerant Embedding for Internet of Things. *IEEE Internet Things J.* **2017**, *5*, 571–580. [CrossRef]

5. Wu, H.; Zhou, F.; Chen, Y.; Zhang, R. On virtual network embedding: Paths and cycles. *IEEE Trans. Netw. Serv. Manag.* **2020**, *17*, 1487–1500. [CrossRef]
6. Li, Y.; Zhang, Z.; Xia, S.; Chen, H.-H. A Load-Balanced Re-Embedding Scheme for Wireless Network Virtualization. *IEEE Trans. Veh. Technol.* **2021**, *70*, 3761–3772. [CrossRef]
7. Murakami, M.; Kominami, D.; Leibnitz, K.; Murata, M. Drawing inspiration from human brain networks: Construction of interconnected virtual networks. *Sensors* **2018**, *18*, 1133. [CrossRef]
8. Sivakumar, S.; Vivekanandan, P. Efficient fault-tolerant routing in IoT wireless sensor networks based on path graph flow modeling with Marchenko–Pastur distribution (EFT-PMD). *Wirel. Netw.* **2020**, *26*, 4543–4555. [CrossRef]
9. Mahmud, M.; Kaiser, M.S.; Rahman, M.M.; Shabut, A.; Al-Mamun, S.; Hussain, A. A Brain-Inspired Trust Management Model to Assure Security in a Cloud Based IoT Framework for Neuroscience Applications. *Cogn. Comput.* **2018**, *10*, 864–873. [CrossRef]
10. Zhang, Z.; Mehmood, A.; Shu, L.; Huo, Z.; Zhang, Y.; Mukherjee, M. A survey on fault diagnosis in wireless sensor networks. *IEEE Access* **2018**, *6*, 11349–11364. [CrossRef]
11. Rajagopalan, R.; Mohan, C.; Mehrotra, K.; Varshney, P. *An Evolutionary Multi-Objective Crowding Algorithm: (EMOCA)*; Technical Report; EECS Department, Syracuse University: Syracuse, NY, USA, 2005.
12. Bao, N.-H.; Sahoo, S.; Kuang, M.; Zhang, Z.-Z. Adaptive path splitting based survivable virtual network embedding in elastic optical networks. *Opt. Fiber Technol.* **2019**, *54*, 102084. [CrossRef]
13. Cao, H.; Wu, S.; Hu, Y.; Liu, Y.; Yang, L. A survey of embedding algorithm for virtual network embedding. *China Commun.* **2019**, *16*, 1–33. [CrossRef]
14. Cao, H.; Hu, H.; Qu, Z.; Yang, L. Heuristic solutions of virtual network embedding: A survey. *China Commun.* **2018**, *15*, 186–219. [CrossRef]
15. Awoyemi, B.S.; Alfa, A.S.; Maharaj, B.T. Network Restoration in Wireless Sensor Networks for Next-Generation Applications. *IEEE Sens. J.* **2019**, *19*, 8352–8363. [CrossRef]
16. Liu, Y.; Han, P.; Hou, J.; Zheng, J. Resource-Efficiently Survivable IoT Services Provisioning via Virtual Network Embedding in Fiber-Wireless Access Network. *IEEE Access* **2019**, *7*, 65007–65018. [CrossRef]
17. Lu, B.; Huang, T.; Sun, X.-C.; Chen, J.-Y.; Liu, Y.-J. Dynamic recovery for survivable virtual network embedding. *J. China Univ. Posts Telecommun.* **2014**, *21*, 77–84. [CrossRef]
18. Shahriar, N.; Chowdhury, S.R.; Ahmed, R.; Khan, A.; Fathi, S.; Boutaba, R.; Mitra, J.; Liu, L. Virtual Network Survivability Through Joint Spare Capacity Allocation and Embedding. *IEEE J. Sel. Areas Commun.* **2018**, *36*, 502–518. [CrossRef]
19. Cao, H.; Wu, S.; Aujla, G.S.; Wang, Q.; Yang, L.; Zhu, H. Dynamic Embedding and Quality of Service-Driven Adjustment for Cloud Networks. *IEEE Trans. Ind. Inform.* **2019**, *16*, 1406–1416. [CrossRef]
20. He, F.; Oki, E. Backup Allocation Model with Probabilistic Protection for Virtual Networks against Multiple Facility Node Failures. *IEEE Trans. Netw. Serv. Manag.* **2021**, *18*, 2943–2959. [CrossRef]
21. Su, Y.; Meng, X.; Kang, Q.; Han, X. Survivable Virtual Network Link Protection Method Based on Network Coding and Protection Circuit. *IEEE Access* **2018**, *6*, 67477–67493. [CrossRef]
22. Shahriar, N.; Ahmed, R.; Chowdhury, S.R.; Khan, A.; Boutaba, R.; Mitra, J. Generalized Recovery From Node Failure in Virtual Network Embedding. *IEEE Trans. Netw. Serv. Manag.* **2017**, *14*, 261–274. [CrossRef]
23. Song, A.; Chen, W.-N.; Gu, T.; Yuan, H.; Kwong, S.; Zhang, J. Distributed Virtual Network Embedding System With Historical Archives and Set-Based Particle Swarm Optimization. *IEEE Trans. Syst. Man Cybern. Syst.* **2019**, *51*, 927–942. [CrossRef]
24. Kaur, T.; Kumar, D. Particle Swarm Optimization-Based Unequal and Fault Tolerant Clustering Protocol for Wireless Sensor Networks. *IEEE Sens. J.* **2018**, *18*, 4614–4622. [CrossRef]
25. Shahriar, N.; Ahmed, R.; Chowdhury, S.R.; Alam Khan, M.; Boutaba, R.; Mitra, J.; Zeng, F. Virtual Network Embedding With Guaranteed Connectivity Under Multiple Substrate Link Failures. *IEEE Trans. Commun.* **2019**, *68*, 1025–1043. [CrossRef]
26. Azeem, N.; Tarrad, I.; Hady, A.; Youssef, M.; El-kader, S. Shared sensor networks fundamentals, challenges, opportunities, virtualization techniques, comparative analysis, novel architecture and taxonomy. *J. Sens. Actuator Netw.* **2019**, *8*, 29. [CrossRef]
27. Tam, N.T.; Hung, T.H.; Binh, H.T.T.; Vinh, L.T. A decomposition-based multi-objective optimization approach for balancing the energy consumption of wireless sensor networks. *Appl. Soft Comput.* **2021**, *107*, 107365. [CrossRef]
28. Qaffas, A.; Kamal, S.; Sayeed, F.; Dutta, P.; Joshi, S.; Alhassan, I. Adaptive population-based multi-objective optimization in SDN controllers for cost optimization. *Phys. Commun.* **2023**, *25*, 102006. [CrossRef]
29. Hao, X.; Yao, N.; Wang, L.; Wang, J. Joint resource allocation algorithm based on multi-objective optimization for wireless sensor networks. *Appl. Soft Comput.* **2020**, *94*, 106470. [CrossRef]
30. Tang, M.; Xin, Y.; Qiao, Y. Multi-objective resource allocation algorithm for wireless sensor network based on improved simulated annealing. *AdHoc Sens. Wirel. Netw.* **2020**, *47*, 157–173.
31. Tounsi, M.; Mahlous, A. A Multi-objective model for optimizing network lifetime in wireless sensor network. *Int. J. Comput. Sci. Inf. Secur.* **2016**, *14*, 562–596.
32. Sheena, B.; Snehalatha, N. Multi-objective metaheuristic optimization-based clustering with network slicing technique for Internet of Things-enabled wireless sensor networks in 5G systems. *Trans. Emerg. Telecommun. Technol.* **2022**, *2022*, e4626. [CrossRef]
33. Singh, O.; Rishiwal, V.; Chaudhry, R.; Yadav, M. Multi-objective optimization in WSN: Opportunities and challenges. *Wirel. Pers. Commun.* **2021**, *21*, 127–152. [CrossRef]

34. Fei, Z.; Li, B.; Yang, S.; Xing, C.; Chen, H.; Hanzo, L. A survey of multi-objective optimization in wireless sensor networks: Metrics, algorithms, and open problems. *IEEE Commun. Surv. Tutor.* **2016**, *19*, 550–586. [CrossRef]
35. Zahoor, S.; Mir, R.N. Resource management in pervasive Internet of Things: A survey. *J. King Saud Univ. Comput. Inf. Sci.* **2018**, *33*, 921–935. [CrossRef]
36. Yaqoob, A.; Ashraf, M.; Ferooz, F.; Butt, A.; Khan, Y. WSN Operating Systems for Internet of Things (IoT): A Survey. In Proceedings of the IEEE International Conference on Intelligent Computing, Lahore, Pakistan, 1–2 November 2019; pp. 1–7.
37. Luo, H.; Wu, K.; Ruby, R.; Liang, Y.; Guo, Z.; Ni, L.M. Software-Defined Architectures and Technologies for Underwater Wireless Sensor Networks: A Survey. *IEEE Commun. Surv. Tutor.* **2018**, *20*, 2855–2888. [CrossRef]
38. Qiu, T.; Zhao, Z.; Zhang, T.; Chen, C. Underwater Internet of Things in Smart Ocean: System Architecture and Open Issues. *IEEE Trans. Ind. Inform.* **2019**, *16*, 4297–4307. [CrossRef]
39. Zhang, X.; Cao, Y.; Peng, L.; Ahmad, N.; Xu, L. Towards Efficient Battery Swapping Service Operation Under Battery Heterogeneity. *IEEE Trans. Veh. Technol.* **2020**, *69*, 6107–6118. [CrossRef]
40. Hasan, M.; Al-Rizzo, H. Optimization of sensor deployment for industrial internet of things using a multi-swarm algorithm. *IEEE Internet Things J.* **2019**, *6*, 10344–10362. [CrossRef]
41. Rajagopalan, R. Multi-Objective Optimization Algorithms for Sensor Network Design. In Proceedings of the IEEE 11th Annual Conference on Wireless and Microwave Technology (WAMICON), Melbourne, FL, USA, 12–13 April 2010; pp. 1–4.
42. Maier, H.; Razavi, S.; Kapelan, Z.; Matott, L.; Kasprzyk, J.; Tolson, B. Introductory overview: Optimization using evolutionary algorithms and other metaheuristics. *Environ. Model. Softw.* **2018**, *114*, 195–213. [CrossRef]
43. Gustavo, H.; Fernando, G.; Rodrigo, T.; Flávio, V. Multi-attribute decision making applied to financial portfolio optimization problem. *Expert Syst. Appl.* **2020**, *158*, 113527.
44. Biswas, A.; Pal, T. A comparison between metaheuristics for solving a capacitated fixed charge transportation problem with multiple objectives. *Expert Syst. Appl.* **2020**, *170*, 114491. [CrossRef]

Disclaimer/Publisher's Note: The statements, opinions and data contained in all publications are solely those of the individual author(s) and contributor(s) and not of MDPI and/or the editor(s). MDPI and/or the editor(s) disclaim responsibility for any injury to people or property resulting from any ideas, methods, instructions or products referred to in the content.

Article

S-Type Random k Satisfiability Logic in Discrete Hopfield Neural Network Using Probability Distribution: Performance Optimization and Analysis

Suad Abdeen [1,2], Mohd Shareduwan Mohd Kasihmuddin [1,*], Nur Ezlin Zamri [3], Gaeithry Manoharam [1], Mohd. Asyraf Mansor [3] and Nada Alshehri [2]

1. School of Mathematical Sciences, Universiti Sains Malaysia, Penang 11800 USM, Malaysia
2. College of Sciences, King Saud University, Riyadh 11451 KSU, Saudi Arabia
3. School of Distance Education, Universiti Sains Malaysia, Penang 11800 USM, Malaysia
* Correspondence: shareduwan@usm.my; Tel.: +60-46534769

Abstract: Recently, a variety of non-systematic satisfiability studies on Discrete Hopfield Neural Networks have been introduced to overcome a lack of interpretation. Although a flexible structure was established to assist in the generation of a wide range of spatial solutions that converge on global minima, the fundamental problem is that the existing logic completely ignores the probability dataset's distribution and features, as well as the literal status distribution. Thus, this study considers a new type of non-systematic logic termed S-type Random k Satisfiability, which employs a creative layer of a Discrete Hopfield Neural Network, and which plays a significant role in the identification of the prevailing attribute likelihood of a binomial distribution dataset. The goal of the probability logic phase is to establish the logical structure and assign negative literals based on two given statistical parameters. The performance of the proposed logic structure was investigated using the comparison of a proposed metric to current state-of-the-art logical rules; consequently, was found that the models have a high value in two parameters that efficiently introduce a logical structure in the probability logic phase. Additionally, by implementing a Discrete Hopfield Neural Network, it has been observed that the cost function experiences a reduction. A new form of synaptic weight assessment via statistical methods was applied to investigate the effect of the two proposed parameters in the logic structure. Overall, the investigation demonstrated that controlling the two proposed parameters has a good effect on synaptic weight management and the generation of global minima solutions.

Keywords: discrete hopfield neural network; non-systematic satisfiability; probability distribution; binomial distribution; statistical learning; optimization problems; travelling salesman problem; evolutionary computation

MSC: 37M22; 37M05

Citation: Abdeen, S.; Kasihmuddin, M.S.M.; Zamri, N.E.; Manoharam, G.; Mansor, M.A.; Alshehri, N. S-Type Random k Satisfiability Logic in Discrete Hopfield Neural Network Using Probability Distribution: Performance Optimization and Analysis. *Mathematics* **2023**, *11*, 984. https://doi.org/10.3390/math11040984

Academic Editors: Francois Rivest and Abdellah Chehri

Received: 14 December 2022
Revised: 17 January 2023
Accepted: 20 January 2023
Published: 15 February 2023

Copyright: © 2023 by the authors. Licensee MDPI, Basel, Switzerland. This article is an open access article distributed under the terms and conditions of the Creative Commons Attribution (CC BY) license (https:// creativecommons.org/licenses/by/ 4.0/).

1. Introduction

A Discrete Hopfield Neural Network (DHNN) is a significant type of Artificial Neural Network (ANN) that employs a learning model based on association features formulated by Hopfield and Tank [1]. ANNs have long been used as a mathematical method with which to solve a range of issues [2–8]. DHNN is a recurrent ANN with feedforward connections that comprise interconnected neurons in which every neuron output is fed back into every neuron input. Neurons are stored in either a binary or bipolar form in the input and output neurons of the DHNN structure [9]. Further, to approximate optimization solutions for problems, the structures of DHNN have been extensively modified. This network has many interesting behaviors. Fault tolerance is also a feature of the Content Addressable Memory (CAM) technique, which has an infinite capacity for pattern storage and is useful for its converging iterative process [10]. Numerous applications have made use of DHNNs, including optimization problems [1], clinical diagnosis [11–13], the electric power sector [14], the investment sector [15], location detectors [16], and others. Despite the importance of using the intelligent decision systems of the DHNN to solve optimization problems, it is necessary to implement the symbolic rule to guarantee that the DHNN always converges to the ideal solution, because recent studies failed to conduct a thorough analysis of a DHNN based on neural connections. This issue was solved by Wan Abdullah [17], who suggested a logical rule for ANNs by associating each neuron's connection with a true or plausible interpretation.

The Wan Abdullah approach is a novel approach, and it is interesting to note that the synaptic weight is determined by matching the logic cost function and the Lyapunov energy function. This approach led to better performance than traditional teaching techniques such as Hebbian learning with respect to obtaining the synaptic weight during the training phase. A more specific logical rule has been developed since the logical rule was first introduced in the original DHNN. Sathasivam [18] decided to expand the work of Wan Abdullah and proposed Horn Satisfiability (HORNSAT) as a new Satisfiability (SAT) concept. This study introduced the Sathasivam method of relaxation to improve the finalized state of neurons. This proposal demonstrates the strong capabilities of the HORNSAT in terms of reaching the absolute minimum amount of energy. The outcome demonstrates that logical rules can be included in DHNNs. Nevertheless, because DHNNs relax too quickly and offer fewer possibilities for neurons to interchange information, more local minimum solutions result, which makes it difficult to understand how different logical rules affect DHNNs. This motivated the emergence of a new era of research with different perspectives, beginning with Kasihmuddin et al. [9], who introduced systematic k Satisfiability (kSAT) for k = 2, 2 Satisfiability (2SAT). With each clause containing two literals and all clauses joined by a disjunction, the implementation of 2SAT in a DHNN was reported to achieve a high global minima ratio while keeping computational time to a minimum. Subsequently, Mansor et al. [19] continued the research by proposing a high degree of order of kSAT for k = 3, namely, 3 Satisfiability (3SAT), in a DHNN. With each clause containing three literals and all clauses joined by a disjunction, the proposed 3SAT in a DHNN increases the storage capacity of a network because each neuron's number of local minimum solutions tends to be low. Despite the success of the implementation of systematic logic in DHNNs, this approach lacks control with respect to distributing the number of negative literals as well as regarding a variety of clauses. Furthermore, as the number of such neurons increases, the efficiency of the training phase in the DHNN decreases. During the testing phase of DHNNs, there is less neuronal variation. Sathasivam et al. [20] clarified that the rigidity of the logical structure contributes to overfitting solutions in DHNNs. When the number of neurons is large, the restricted number of literals per clause results in suboptimal synaptic weight values, thereby decreasing the likelihood of locating diverse global minima solutions. The necessity of variance in the recovered solutions ensures that the search space is well-explored. Further stated by [21], DHNNs are still vulnerable to various challenges, including a lack of generality as a result of non-flexible logical rules and a strict logic structure, despite the fact that the accuracy of research acquired from the real-world dataset has been satisfactory.

Due to the need for a different logical clause set that contributes to the degree of connection between the logical formulae, Sathasivam et al. [20] proposed a non-systematic SAT called Random k Satisfiability (RANkSAT) by using first-order and second-order logic 2SAT in conjunction, where k = 1, 2; Random 2 Satisfiability (RAN2SAT); and all clauses are connected by disjunction. RAN2SAT introduces a flexible logic structure that contributes to the generation of more logical inconsistency, which expands the diversity of synaptic weights. The proposed RAN2SAT in a DHNN achieved about 90% of the global minima ratio with fewer neurons. Due to the necessity of increasing the storage capacity of RAN2SAT and dealing with the absence of interpretation in a typical systematic satisfiability logic and limited $k \leq 2$, Karim et al. [22] were inspired to resolve this problem and thus proposed a flexible logic structure that increases storage capacity by incorporating third-order clauses into the formulation. Random 3 Satisfiability (RAN3SAT) suggests three logical ($k = 1, 3$; $k = 2, 3$; and $k = 1, 2, 3$) literal structures per clause, and for all clauses to be joined by a disjunction. This increases the capacity of the DHNN to recover neuronal states based on different logical orders, which can lead to a variety of convergent interpretations of global minimum solutions. Both RANkSAT types experience difficulty regarding the selection system in terms of the composition represented by the first, second, and third logical formulations, which is still poorly defined. Thus, the combination of correct interpretations is restricted to the number of k-order clauses with a predefined term assigned in the logical formula.

Another fascinating study on non-systematic logic with a different perspective was introduced by Alway et al. [23]; this solution increases the representation of 2SAT compared to 3SAT clauses in non-systematic SAT logic through an assigned 2SAT ratio (r^*) in DHNN in order to decrease the duplication of final neuron state patterns. The proposed Major 2 Satisfiability (MAJ2SAT) in the DHNN successfully provides more neuronal variation. Zamri et al. [24] introduced Weighted Random k Satisfiability (rSAT) as a non-systematic method with a proposed logical structure that ideally produces the proper rSAT logical structure using a Genetic Algorithm (GA) by taking into account the desired proportion of negative literals (r). Another method introduced by Sidik et al. [25] consisted of altering the rSAT logic phase by adding a binary Artificial Bee Colony algorithm to guarantee that negative literals are distributed properly. The proposed rSAT in a DHNN with a weighted ratio of negative literals leads to a significant global minima ratio. Nonetheless, despite this significant advancement in controlling the logical structure of selecting clauses and using a metaheuristic approach to distribute the number of negative literals, these techniques fail to account for the representation of the probability distribution of the dataset in the selection system.

Unique, flexible logical systems were formed by combining systematic and non-systematic approaches with a unique perspective. This approach leads to a great potential for solution diversity as it randomly generates a number of clauses. Guo et al. [26] proposed Y-Type Random 2 Satisfiability (YRAN2SAT), in which a number is randomly assigned to the first-order and second-order clauses, while further final states can be retrieved by YRAN2SAT in a DHNN with the minimum global energy. With high order logic, Gao et al. [27] proposed a G-Type Random k Satisfiability (GRAN3SAT) system, in which a set of clauses of first, second, and third orders is randomly generated. In a DHNN, GRAN3SAT can exhibit a larger storage capacity and is capable of investigating complex dimensional issues. Despite this success, its system of selection still has a flaw: there is no clear system with which to control a distribution over the desired number of negative literals based on the probability distribution of a dataset.

The Probabilistic Satisfiability problem (PSAT) involves assigning probabilities to a set of propositional formulations and deciding whether this assignment is consistent. The pioneering work was introduced by George Boole [28] as another perspective. He proposed the PSAT to determine if he could discover a probability measure for truth assignments that satisfy all assessments. The PSAT framework was developed to demonstrate these details as logical sentences with linked probabilities to infer the likelihood of a query sentence. The PSAT was initially suggested by George Boole and, subsequently, was refined by Nilsson [29]. This intelligent perspective was followed by different studies [30–33], which all aimed to integrate the probability tools into satisfiability without considering their implementation in a DHNN. The present study addresses this gap by introducing a probability distribution to the prevailing attribute in the data set, which is represented in a DHNN through desire logic.

There are no studies in this area regarding the way in which the probability distribution for literals with SAT may be represented in a DHNN. Thus, the findings addressing this issue can be used to guarantee the most effective search for satisfying interpretations. Therefore, this study introduces S-type Random k Satisfiability ($\delta kSAT$), where $k = 1, 2$

($\delta 2SAT$) and with the probability distribution of the prevailing attribute in the simulation dataset. It aims to address the problem regarding RANkSAT, where k randomizes structural issues by utilizing two statistical features, the probability distribution and the sample size formula, to obtain an estimator for the binomial distribution dataset. In addition to helping to assign the negative literal that was mapped to the prevailing attribute in a dataset with a non-systematic logical RAN2SAT, the main feature of RAN2SAT is its structural flexibility, which takes advantage of another logical rule, 2SAT, whereas the non-systematic logical rule provides a more diversified solution [34,35]. Furthermore, the probability distribution is used to control the composition's probability of appearing in first- and second-order logic to avoid a poorly explained or lack of interpretation in non-systematic SAT by providing suitable logical combinations depending on the dataset's distribution. Moreover, the logic system uses the binomial distribution's sample size to determine the appropriate number of negative literals based on the predetermined proportion appearing in the dataset. Then, the clauses are distributed in each order depending on the probability distribution governing appearance. This approach will help us determine the appropriate weight of a negative literal number in logic systems based on the distributed clauses in order to create suitable solutions [24]. Notably, researchers tend to neglect negative literals because they are indirectly mapped errors in a logical structure [36]; however, in this study, negative literals represent the prevailing attribute in a binomial distribution that has only two characteristics.

Our proposed logical rule will provide flexibility with respect to controlling the overall structure of $\delta 2SAT$ in terms of the dataset's characteristics by combining both the effects of statistical parameters and non-systematic features to identify suitable neuronal variation and diversity in the proposed logic. The main aims of this study are as follows:

(a) To formulate a novel logical rule called S-Type Random k Satisfiability, where k = 1, 2 and statistical tools are integrated to structure first- and second-order logic in order to select the most suitable number of negative literals.

(b) To propose a probability logic phase to determine the probability of the appearance of the number of the first- and second-order literals and the distribution of the desired number of negative literals on every clause by considering the selected dataset.

(c) To implement the proposed S-Type Random 2 Satisfiability as a symbolic structure in the Discrete Hopfield Neural Network by reducing the logical inconsistency of the corresponding zero-cost function's logical rule, as well as determine the synaptic weight of the DHNN that achieves the cost function equivalent to the satisfied $\delta 2SAT$.

(d) To compare the effectiveness of $\delta 2SAT$ with respect to producing the appropriate logical structure during the probability logic phase before training in the Discrete Hopfield Neural Network by using three proposal metrics in accordance with the existing benchmark works.

(e) To examine the capability of the proposed $\delta 2SAT$ under the current logical rules with respect to the training and testing phase, demonstrate synaptic weight management, and ascertain the quality of neuronal states' efficiency in the DHNN via well-known performance metrics.

(f) To investigate the proposed $\delta 2SAT$ system's structural behavior during the training phase and thereby demonstrate the flexibility of this logical structure by using a novel form of analysis—synaptic weight analysis—via the mean of the synaptic weights.

The framework of this paper is as follows: The motivation for this study is described in detail in Section 2. An overview of $\delta 2SAT$'s structure is given in Section 3. The integration of $\delta 2SAT$ into a DHNN is described in Section 4. Section 5 explains the experimental setup and performance assessment metrics incorporated into the simulation. In Section 6, the effectiveness of the proposal logic in a DHNN is discussed and analyzed, with comparisons made to several existing logical structures with regard to various parameters and phases. The conclusions and future work are presented in Section 7 at the end of the article.

2. Motivation

2.1. Issue with the Identified Probability Distribution

With reference to the structural issue regarding existing systematic and non-systematic satisfiability, that is, the systematic logic kSAT [19,37], the relevant approaches in this respect implement random selection for the literal states from within clauses, where the clauses are selected uniformly, without regard to the individual probability or chance of appearing in the required population dataset. Whereas the non-systematic logic RANkSAT [20,22] structure is defined randomly, wherein the clauses are selected uniformly. Moreover, the chance of obtaining both negative and positive literals is uniformly distributed [38], with both outcome having an equally likely chance of appearing. This implies that the population follows a uniform distribution and is thus considered a limited option. In this study, we address this research gap by giving the clauses and negative literals inside clauses the priority of a population dataset's probability distribution, and when the dataset has two characteristics, i.e., negative and positive literals, we assign the negative literal for the prevailing attribute that is withdrawn from a binomial distribution.

2.2. Initialization for the Number of Clauses and Number of Neuron

The investigation into controlling the general structure of SAT is still ongoing. Cai and Lei's [39] work proposed a Partial Maximum Satisfiability (PMAXSAT) clausal weighting mechanism, with a positive integer as its weight. This method demonstrated the power of weight in terms of controlling the distribution of a logical structure based on the desired result. Conversely, Always et al. [23] suggested a non-systematic logical rule, MAJ2SAT, which seeks to create bias in the selection of 2SAT over 3SAT via the r^* ratio. The MAJ2SAT system successfully provides more neuronal variations that increase the composition of the 2SAT with the same number of neurons. Despite the benefit of extracting information from real datasets that exhibit the behaviors of 2SAT and 3SAT, the persistent issue is the system of selection, which limits the value of r in the set of limited pre-defined intervals and is chosen randomly without considering a dataset's probability distribution. Therefore, we propose the non-systematic logical rule $\delta 2SAT$, which incorporates a probability logic phase to calculate the probability of first- and second-order clauses appearing from the dataset by determining the required number of literal and clauses.

2.3. Initialization for the Number of Negative Literals

The structure of SAT should be subjected to a systematic analysis to avoid the poor description of a dataset. Dubois and Prade [40] examined the role of logic in dealing with uncertainty in an ANN. The work concluded that it was crucial to use the generalization method to determine how many negative literals should be distributed for technical convenience. Zamri et al. [24] introduced rSAT with the (logic phase) as a new phase to produce a non-systematic logical structure based on the ratio of negative literals. The ratio is generated in the logic phase by employing GA to increase the logic phase's effectiveness. Nevertheless, the findings showed that the proposed model performed well, indicating that having a dynamic distribution of negative literals will benefit the generation of global minimum solutions with different states of the final neurons. One of the limitations of the weighting scheme is the method of choosing the number of negative literals, where the value of r is in the set of limited pre-defined intervals and is subject to the issue of random system selection without considering the probability distribution of literals.

Alway and Zamri's studies motivated the current study, in which we propose the non-systematic logical rule $\delta 2SAT$, which incorporates a probability logic phase to calculate the appearance-related probability distribution in the first-order and second-order clauses from the real dataset by predetermining the required number of neurons or number of clauses via harnessing the behavior of 2SAT so as to explore a wider solution space and extract information from datasets, as well as assign the number of negative literals required for logic by using the sample size formula with a predefined, prevailing attribute proportion from the dataset that will be exposed in the logic.

2.4. Synaptic Weight Performance Using Statistical Analysis

The research on satisfiability in DHNNs suffers from a lack of statistical analysis, especially in terms of synaptic weight, which is considered the backbone for the global minimum solution achieved during testing phases. We determine synaptic weight by contrasting the cost function with Lyapunov energy. The previous studies on systematic and non-systematic approaches were limited in terms of assessing the performance accuracy of the logic in different phases, as mentioned in [9,21,22]. The synaptic weight was analyzed at several points in this study since they were not completely comprehensible in [20,26], wherein the authors describe the dimensions of the synaptic weight values. In addition, [27] measured the accuracy of the error in the synaptic weight by evaluating the differences between the synaptic weight obtained by Wan's method and the synaptic weight achieved in the training phase. The gap was addressed in this study by using new statistical tests to capture the impact of changing the synaptic weight during training phases due to the absence of statistical tools in the synaptic weight analysis.

3. S-Type Random 2 Satisfiability Logic

S-Type Random 2 Satisfiability ($\delta 2SAT$) is a new category of non-systematic-clause SAT in which the probability distribution is used to assign prevailing attributes in the dataset via two methods: First, depending on the dataset requirements, we assigned the probability of the appearance of first- and second-order logic. Second, we used the sample size from a binomial population [41] to ascertain the appropriate number of negation literals inside each clause based on its assigned probability since the probability of a negative literal appearing follows a binomial distribution. The novelty of the mentioned methods is that they determine the suitable weight of negative literal numbers (ξ) in logic depending on the probability clauses distributed, which will lead to greater structural diversity. In addition, the negative literal number is not fixed, and by increasing or decreasing the probability of obtaining a literal number in the logic system, there is greater flexibility in the dataset.

Our approach can be introduced as a form of non-systematic logic comprising n literals per T clauses. It is a general form of RANkSAT logic, where $k = 1,2$ is expressed in the k Conjunctive Normal Form (kCNF). The components of the S-Type Random 2 Satisfiability Logic problem are as follows:

(a) A set of h variables, $\tau_1, \tau_2, \tau_3, \ldots \tau_h$, where $\tau_i \in \{-1, 1\}$ for all items in our logic system;

(b) A set of h non-redundant literals r_i, where r_i is the positive (r_i) or a negative ($\neg r_i$) nature of a literal;

(c) A set of λ distinguishable clauses, $T_1, T_2, T_3, \ldots T_\lambda$, where every clause is composed of h literals joined by $\wedge$ logical (AND) Booleans, which is distributed as follows:

   i. A set of x first-order clauses: $T_1^{(1)}, T_2^{(1)}, T_3^{(1)}, \ldots T_x^{(1)}$, $x \in \mathbb{N}$.

   ii. A set of y second-order clauses: $T_1^{(2)}, T_2^{(2)}, T_3^{(2)}, \ldots T_y^{(2)}$, where $T_y^{(2)} = (r_i \vee r_j)$, $y \in \mathbb{N}$.

The general formulation of S-Type Random 2 Satisfiability is given as follows:

$$\Theta_{\delta 2SAT} = \bigwedge_i^x T^{(1)} \bigwedge_j^y T^{(2)} \quad \text{for } k = 1,2 \tag{1}$$

$$T_i^k = \begin{cases} (r_i), & k = 1 \\ (r_i \vee r_j), & k = 2 \end{cases} \tag{2}$$

where $\Theta_{\delta 2SAT}$ in Equation (1) is $\delta 2SAT$ for $k = 1, 2$. The difference between $\delta 2SAT$ and RAN2SAT lies in the selection system for the number of clauses and the number of negative literals in $\delta 2SAT$. This system is established under the condition that the number of clauses corresponds to:

$$\begin{cases} x_m = p(x) \cdot \lambda_m \\ y_m = p(y) \cdot \lambda_m \end{cases} \tag{3}$$

where λ_m denotes the total number of literals λ_1 or total number of clauses λ_2; y_m and x_m denote the number of literals in the first- and second-order clauses or the number of clauses when $m = 1, 2$, respectively; $y_m, x_m \geq 0$ represent clauses T_i^k for different values of k; and $p(x_m)$ and $p(y_m)$ denote the probability of first- and second-order logic appearing, which is calculated by the Laplace formula [42] to find the probability A_{y_m} from population Ω expressed as follows:

$$p(y_m) = \frac{|A_{y_m}|}{|\Omega|} \quad (4)$$

$|A_{y_m}|$ represents a number of elements that contain a prevailing attribute from the total number of a dataset $|\Omega|$ in this study. We will denote the probability of second-order $p(y_m)$ by Y, which is considered as the first parameter in $\delta 2SAT$.

The number of negated literals that exist in each T_i^k will be determined by ξ, where $\xi \in \mathbb{N}$ is the negative literal number used to obtain ρ in the dataset [41] and is calculated as follows:

$$\xi = \frac{\lambda_m \rho_0 (1-\rho_0)}{(\lambda_m - 1)(d^2/z^2) + \rho_0 (1-\rho_0)} \quad (5)$$

where:

ρ: The pre-defined negative literal proportion required in the logic system (Second parameter in Logic).

ρ_0: the negative literal proportion in the population (which is available before the survey; if no estimate of ρ_0 is available prior to the survey, a worst-case value of $\rho_0 = 0.5$ can be used to determine the sample size).

d: the margin of error (or the maximum error) of the negative literal proportion, which is calculated as follows:

$$d = Z_\alpha \sqrt{\frac{\rho(1-\rho)}{\lambda}} \quad (6)$$

Z: the upper $\alpha/2$ point of the normal distribution when $\alpha = 0.01$, where Significance Level = P (type I error) = α.

The distribution of the number of negated literals in each order logic clause T_i^k is dependent on the value β_k, where:

$$\begin{cases} \beta_1 = (\xi \times p(x)) \\ \beta_2 = (\xi \times p(y)) \end{cases} \quad (7)$$

In (7), β_1 and β_2 denote first- and second-order logic, respectively, and $\sum \beta_k$ is the total number of negated literals existing in $\delta 2SAT$ logic, where:

$$\sum \beta_i - \xi = 0 \quad (8)$$

The structure of $\Theta_{\delta 2SAT}$ is believed to provide more variations and greater diversity of the final neuron states and to be able to find more global solutions in other solution spaces via two effective parameters: Y and ρ. The implementation of S-type Random k Satisfiability logic in this study is outlined in Figure 1.

Probability Logic Phase in $\delta 2SAT$

The probability logic phase was developed to assess the features of a prevailing attribute in the dataset via probability distribution, which are then reflected in the logic system by the two parameters Y and ρ; this differs from the logic phase in *r*SAT [24], where the phase is established to allocate the correct ratio of the negative literals and the position in the *r*SAT logic via metaheuristics. The main purpose for the probability logic phase is to extract the required information from the dataset, and then generate the correct structure of RAN2SAT logic depending on the dataset features assigned by the two probability Equations (3) and (5). Subsequently, once the desired logic has been attained, the probability logic phase is complete. This section will introduce some logic generated from the dataset using the two parameters Y and ρ; the restriction in the probability logic phase is as follows:

$$p(y_m) + p(x_m) = 1, \ p(y_m) > p(x_m), \ p(x_m) \neq 0 \tag{9}$$

whose probability function can be defined as follows (Nilsson 1986) [29]:

$$\begin{cases} p(\lambda) = 1 \\ r_i \wedge r_j \equiv 0, \text{ its mutually exclusives, then} \\ p(r_i \wedge r_j) = p(r_i) + p(r_j) \end{cases} \tag{10}$$

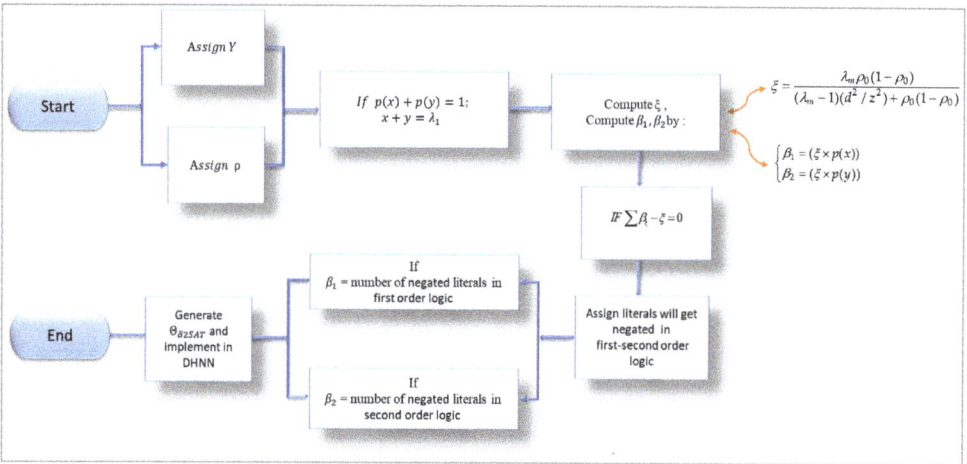

Figure 1. Block diagram of the proposed S-type Random 2 Satisfiability logic $\Theta_{\delta 2SAT}$.

According to the applied method for the determination of probability, there are two types of $\delta 2SAT$: First, there is the type of probability logic phase that determines the probability of the appearance of the number of first-order logic and second-order logic literals λ_1 and the distribution of the desired number of negative literals in each clause depending on the selected dataset. Second, there is the type of probability logic phase that determines the probability of the appearance of the number of first-order logic and second-order logic clauses λ_2 and the distribution of the desired number of negative literals in each clause depending on the selected dataset. Table 1 introduces some possible examples of two cases of the logic of $\delta 2SAT$ that can be used to generate the dataset using Equations (4), (5) and (7) when $\rho = 0.7$.

Table 1. Possible structures of $\delta 2SAT$ when $\rho = 0.7$.

λ_m	ξ	Y	Possible $\delta 2SAT$
$\lambda_1 = 10$	6	0.6	Case 1: $\neg r_1 \wedge r_2 \wedge \neg r_3 \wedge r_4 \wedge (r_5 \vee \neg r_6) \wedge (r_7 \vee \neg r_8) \wedge (\neg r_9 \vee \neg r_{10})$
	6	0.8	Case 2: $\neg r_1 \wedge \neg r_2 \wedge (r_3 \wedge \neg r_4) \wedge (r_5 \vee \neg r_6) \wedge (r_7 \vee \neg r_8) \wedge (r_9 \vee \neg r_{10})$
$\lambda_2 = 5$	4	0.6	Case 3: $\neg r_1 \wedge r_2 \wedge (r_3 \wedge \neg r_4) \wedge (r_5 \vee \neg r_6) \wedge (r_7 \vee \neg r_8)$
	5	0.8	Case 4: $\neg r_1 \wedge (r_2 \vee \neg r_3) \wedge (r_4 \vee \neg r_5) \wedge (r_6 \vee \neg r_7) \wedge (r_8 \vee \neg r_9)$

We observe that applying the same probability to more clauses λ_2 results in a reduced number of first-order logic items than applying it to a greater number of neurons λ_1; notably, the number of unique logic combinations that a probability logic phase can create by using a specific value of the two parameters Y and ρ is $\binom{x}{1} \times \binom{y}{1}$. Algorithm 1 presents the pseudocode for the steps taken to generate the $\Theta_{\delta 2SAT}$, which starts with the determination of the value of the two parameters Y and ρ; then, by applying the constraint of the logic in Equation (9), the probability logic phases operate under the following conditions: (a) $\rho \neq 0.5$, because we need to expose the prevailing attribute. (b) The z is a random number generated to ensure the negative values will be distributed in the logic phase randomly. (c) The loop will run w times to ensure that the logic system will be correctly generated. (d) The probability logic phase ends when Equation (8) is satisfied, at which point the DHNN training phase begins.

The limitation that we observed in $\delta 2SAT$'s logic structure is the position of negative literals; these are selected randomly depending on z random numbers, and this randomization clearly effects results in an inconsistent interpretation. In addition, there are no redundant literals. Also, due to the high probability of 2SAT, the Exhaustive Search (ES) algorithm is unable to find the best number of instances of first-order logic for a small number of clauses that satisfies Equation (9). The utilization of $\Theta_{\delta 2SAT}$ in a DHNN is presented as $DHNN - \delta 2SAT$. In the next section, we clarify how $\Theta_{\delta 2SAT}$ functions as a representational command to control the neurons of the DHNN mappings.

Algorithm 1: Pseudocode for generating the probability of logic phases

Input: $\lambda_m, \rho, p(y_m)$, Set of r_i
Output: The best $\Theta_{\delta 2SAT}$
Begin
  Generate $\Theta_{\delta 2SAT}$
  Initialized λ_m;
  Initialized Proportion ρ;
  Initialized Second-order clauses $p(y_m)$;
  Calculate The number of first- and second-order clauses
  While
  $(\beta_1 \leq y \& \beta_2) \leq x \& (\beta_1 + \beta_2) = \zeta \& p(y_m) + p(x_m) = 1 \& p(y_m) > p(x_m) \& y_m + x_m = \lambda_m \& y_m/2 = 0, x_m \neq 0)$
  Do
    Calculate y_m, x_m by Equation (3);
    Calculate ζ by Equation (5);
    Calculate $\beta_1 \& \beta_2$ by Equation (7);
  End while
  distributed negative literal in logic
  While $(w \leq 1000)$ do
  While $(b = \beta_1 \& \rho \neq 0.5 \& b^* = \beta_2)$do
  for $(u = 0 \text{ to } x_m)$ do
  Generate random number z;
  Generate proportion to be initial negative literal $\rho*$;
  IF $(\rho* \geq z)$ THEN
  $\neg r_i$;
  $(b = b + 1)$;
  ELSE
  r_i;
  End IF
  End for
  for $(u = 0 \text{ to } y_m)$ do
  Generate random number z;
  Generate proportion to be initial negative literal $\rho*$;
  IF $(\rho* \geq z)$ THEN
  -B;
  $(b^* = b^* + 1)$;
    Else
    B;
    End IF
    End for
    End While
  End While
End

Note: $b, b*$ is a counter.

4. $\Theta_{\delta 2SAT}$ in Discrete Hopfield Neural Network

A DHNN is a type of free, self-feedback information comprising N interconnected neurons with no hidden layers. The neurons are updated one at a time; Ref. [23] asserts that the possibility of neuronal oscillations is eliminated by asynchronous updating. This network has parallel computing, quick convergence, and is also effective in terms of its CAM capacity, which has encouraged researchers to use DHNNs as mediums for solving challenging optimization problems. A general description of the state of activated neurons in a DHNN is provided below:

$$S_i = \begin{cases} 1, & \sum_{j}^{N} W_{ij} S_j \geq \varepsilon \\ -1, & \text{otherwise} \end{cases} \quad (11)$$

where the synaptic weight from unit i to unit j is W_{ij}. The synaptic weight of a DHNN is always symmetrical, whereby $W_{ij} = W_{ji}$, and has no self-looping, $W_{ii} = W_{jj} = 0$. S_i represents the state of neuron j; ε is a predetermined threshold value, and in this study, $\varepsilon = 0$ to guarantee a uniform decrease in DHNN energy [18]; and h is the number of logic variables. The $\delta 2SAT$ is implemented in a DHNN according to the following equation ($DHNN - \delta 2SAT$), due to the requirement for a symbolic rule that can control the network's output and decrease logical inconsistency by minimizing the network's cost function. To derive the cost function $E_{\Theta_{\delta 2SAT}}$ of $\Theta_{\delta 2SAT}$, the following formula can be used:

$$E_{\Theta_{\delta 2SAT}} = \sum_{i=1}^{x} \left(\prod_{i=1}^{1} \Psi_{ij} \right) + \sum_{i=1}^{y} \left(\prod_{i=1}^{2} \Psi_{ij} \right) \quad (12)$$

where x_2 and y_2 are the number of clauses. The inconsistency of $\Theta_{\delta 2SAT}$, denoted as Ψ_{ij}, is specified in Equation (13), as literals are possible in $\Theta_{\delta 2SAT}$:

$$\Psi_{ij} = \begin{cases} \frac{(1-S_r)}{2}, & \text{if } \neg r \\ \frac{(1+S_r)}{2}, & \text{if } r \end{cases} \quad (13)$$

where r denotes the random literals assigned in $\Theta_{\delta 2SAT}$. If $\frac{(1+S_r)}{2} = 0$, which leads to $E_{\Theta_{\delta 2SAT}} = 0$; this indicates that all clauses in $\Theta_{\delta 2SAT}$ are satisfied with the value of the mean task for the logic program during the training phase (i.e., a consistent interpretation is found). A consistent interpretation will help the logic program to derive the correct synaptic weight of $\Theta_{\delta 2SAT}$ clauses, and the Wan Abdullah (WA) method [17] can be used to directly compare the cost function and Lyapunov energy function of the DHNN to determine the values of W_{ij}. However, it is noted that the DHNN's synaptic weight can be effectively trained using a traditional approach such as Hebbian learning [1]; nevertheless, Ref. [43] demonstrated that the (WA) method, when compared to Hebbian learning, can achieve the optimal synaptic weight with minimal neuron oscillation. Synaptic weight is a building block (matrix) of CAM. Therefore, a specific output-squashing mechanism will be applied to every neuron in $DHNN - \delta 2SAT$ via the Hyperbolic Tangent Activation Function (HTAF) to retrieve the correct logic pattern of the CAM; according to Karim et al. [22], the equation is expressed as follows:

$$\tanh(h_i) = \frac{e^{h_i} - e^{-h_i}}{e^{h_i} + e^{-h_i}} \quad (14)$$

A DHNN's testing phase allows for the asynchronous updating of the neuronal state based on the following equation:

$$h_i = \sum_{j=1, j \neq i}^{N} W_{ij}^{(2)} S_j + W_j^{(1)} \quad (15)$$

h_i represents the network's local field, where $W_{ij}^{(2)}$ is the second-order synaptic weight and $W_j^{(1)}$ is the first-order synaptic weight. By applying the HTAF to the h_i values, the final state of the neurons is retrieved, and the neuron states $S_i(t)$ are updated by:

$$S_i(t) = \begin{cases} 1, & \text{if } \tanh(h_i) \geq 0 \\ -1, & \text{otherwise} \end{cases} \tag{16}$$

The information that results in $E_{\Theta_{\delta 2SAT}} = 0$ must be present in the neuron's final state [44], which corresponds to $H_{\Theta_{\delta 2SAT}}$, the Lyapunov energy function [18]:

$$H_{\Theta_{\delta 2SAT}} = -\frac{1}{2} \sum_{i=1, i \neq j}^{n} \sum_{j=1, j \neq i}^{n} W_{ij}^{(2)} S_i S_j - \sum_{i=1}^{n} W_i^{(1)} S_i \tag{17}$$

The convergence of the energy will indicate when the degree of convergence has reached a stable state according to [22]. This is supported by Sathasivam [18], who states that if a DHNN is stable and oscillation-free, the Lyapunov energy will reach its lowest value (the equilibrium state). Hence, [45] a DHNN will always converge to the global minimum energy. One can see the convergence of the final neuron state based on the following Equation:

$$\left| H_{\Theta_{\delta 2SAT}} - H_{\Theta_{\delta 2SAT}}^{\min} \right| \leq Tol \tag{18}$$

where $H_{\Theta_{\delta 2SAT}}^{\min}$, the final neuron state, produces the anticipated global minimum energy and is calculated as follows:

$$H_{\Theta_{\delta 2SAT}}^{\min} = -\left(\frac{x_2}{2} + \frac{y_2}{4}\right) \tag{19}$$

where x_2 and y_2 denote the number of first- and second-order clauses, respectively. Algorithm 2 is an example of the $DHNN - \delta 2SAT$ given in pseudocode, which explains the processes of the training phase and testing phase of $DHNN - \delta 2SAT$. Conventionally, the logic program employs a 2^n search space to find consistent interpretations by ES in the training phase.

Figure 2 illustrates the schematic diagram of $DHNN - \delta 2SAT$. Different orders of $k = 1, 2$ are shown in two different blocks. In the orange block, there are two inputs and an output (I/O) line, which are green and yellow, representing the two types of logic distributed by clauses and neuron, respectively. Inside the orange box, the second-order clauses are depicted, and every line represents the connection of the neuron state via weights. On the right side, the dashed blue line denotes the first-order clause that is present in this phase as well, with two (I/O) lines: green and yellow. On the inside, the line represents the connection of the neuron state via weights. The satisfied clauses from the two boxes will result in $E_{\Theta_{\delta 2SAT}} = 0$; the figure only represents the satisfied clauses of $\Theta_{\delta 2SAT}$.

Algorithm 2: Pseudocode of $DHNN - \delta 2SAT$

Begin
    Probability logic phase
    Initialized $\Theta_{\delta 2SAT}$;
    Training phase
    do
    According to Equation (12), minimize cost function;
    Use WA method to calculate Synaptic weight and store it in CAM;
    According to Equation (19), calculate global minimum energy $H_{\Theta_{\delta 2SAT}}^{\min}$;
    End
    Testing phase
    Initialize Random neuron state;
    do
    According to Equation (14), calculate the HTAF;
    According to Equation (15), calculate the local field;
    According to Equation (16), update neuron state;
    End
    According to Equation (17), calculate the final neuron energy;
    By using Equation (18), confirm global or local minimum energy;
    Recognize global or local minimum solutions;
        Global minima solutions
    Else
        Local minima solutions
End

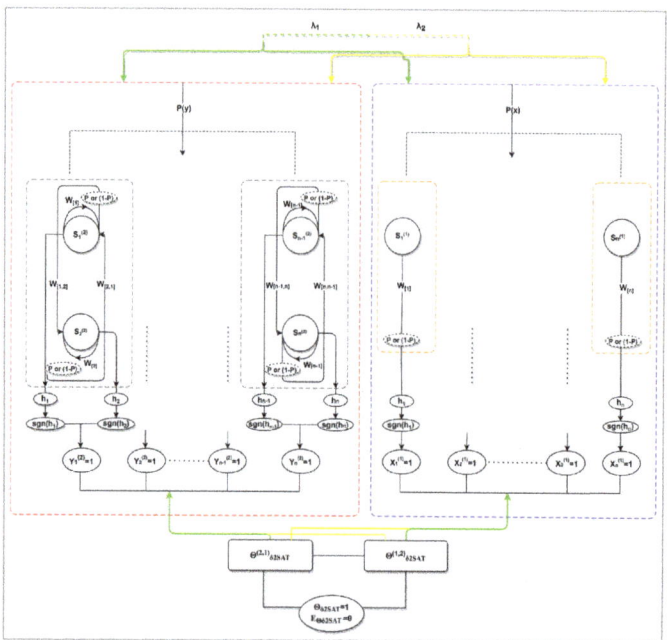

Figure 2. Schematic diagram of $DHNN - \delta 2SAT$ for both types of logic; the total of literal is n for first-second-order logic.

5. Experimental Procedure for Testing DHNN -δ2SAT

In this section, we explain the proposed logic output and evaluate it using several evaluation metrics at all phases to guarantee the effectiveness of adding statistical parameters in RAN2SAT, which aimed to produce $\Theta_{\delta 2SAT}$ logic. Furthermore, the simulation platform, the assignment of parameters, and the metrics for performance are all explained. All models were used with the ES algorithm, where the algorithm utilizes trial and error to achieve a cost function that is minimized ($E_{\Theta_{\delta 2SAT}} = 0$) [23].

5.1. Simulation Platform

All simulations were carried out using an open-source software, visual basic C++ (Version 2022), and a 64-bit Windows 10 operating system. To avoid biases in the interpretation of the results, the simulations were run on a single personal computer equipped with an Intel Core i5 processor. The open-source software **R** studio was used to perform the statistical analysis. Eight different simulations—depending on the statistical parameters (probability and proportion)—were conducted, including those involving different numbers of clauses and neurons. In addition, different numbers of logic combinations (η) were tested in this study.

Each simulation's specifics are as follows:

(a) Various range of parameter Y. This section assesses and examines the effects of the various probabilities that can be obtained from the dataset applied to $\delta 2SAT$. The performance metrics at each phase and the effect of parameter alterations on $\Theta_{\delta 2SAT}$ were determined.

(b) Various proportions of negative literals, ρ. In this section, we evaluate the impact of different proportions of negative literals on $\Theta_{\delta 2SAT}$, evaluating the performance metrics at each phase and determining the effects of parameter alterations on the proposed logic.

(c) A variety of logic structure analyses. In this section, we compare $\Theta_{\delta 2SAT}$ with a number of well-known logical rules in terms of the diversity-satisfying clauses of the logical rule.

(d) Synaptic weight mean analysis for $\Theta_{\delta 2SAT}$ models' simulation includes boxplot and whiskers and a probability function curve.

5.2. The Parameter Setting in Probability Logic Phase

The proposed model incorporates a probability logic phase. As we previously mentioned, there are two types of $\Theta_{\delta 2SAT}$ depending on the probability that is applied to the number of neurons or the number of clauses. Numerous types of simulations are conducted to examine the impacts of different probabilities and several types of expected negative literal proportions on the dataset, in which the probability logic phase is dependent upon the dataset. The different probability logic phase will be denoted as $\delta_\gamma 2SAT\rho$, where $\gamma = 1, 2$ (1 refers to the probability with respect to the number of neurons and 2 refers to the probability of the number of clauses), and ρ refers to the negative literal proportion; the overall model can be denoted as $\delta_1 2SAT_{0.9}$. Another type of logic is possible if the range of the probability parameter Y with respect to the number of neurons or clauses stated in the simulation step generates only one type of neuron or clause state, and this will yield a systematic 2SAT during initialization, which is not covered in this study; alternatively, the first-order logic clauses will correspond to more than second-order logic. When this occurs, the proposed system's structural benefit cannot be seen because only one specific type of solution can be found in the final neuron state. In order to prevent these two types of logic, it is proposed that $Y > 0.5$, wherein more features of second-order as opposed to first-order logic are implemented in the DHNN. In parallel, to determine the range proportion, we proposed $\rho > 0.5$ to determine the correct number of negative literals that represent the prevailing attribute in the dataset, and we also considered $\rho_0 = 0.5$ since there is no available information prior to the survey; the symbols of the stages are presented in Table 2.

Table 2. Parameter list for probability logic phases.

Parameter	Parameter Values
Predefined proportion range (ρ)	[0.6, 0.9]
Negative literal proportion (ρ_0)	0.5
Probability second-order logic range (Y)	[0.6, 0.9]
The upper $\alpha/2$ point of the normal distribution (Z)	2.576
Significance Level (α)	0.01
Number of learning stages in probability logic phases (ω)	1000

5.3. Parameter Setup of $DHNN - \delta_\gamma 2SAT\rho$

All simulations were run with 100 logical combinations ($\eta = 100$). This method aids the DHNN model's analysis and the approximate evaluation of the efficacy of the proposed logic in a DHNN with various distributions of the two parameters Y and ρ. The number of total literals in the logic system is represented by the number of neurons (λ_1) in the DHNN. We chose a specific number of neurons: $5 < \lambda_1 < 50$. For the DHNN, we apply a relaxation procedure in accordance with [18]. We select $R = 3$ in this context because a further reduction in the potential neuron oscillation has been observed, and a value of R greater than 4 will yield the same outcome as [27]. Table 3 summarizes the establishment of all the parameters necessary for $DHNN - \delta_\gamma 2SAT\rho$. In addition, it is notable that each $\delta_\gamma 2SAT\rho$ has a neuron combination that is equivalent to the other DHNN logic systems, which eliminates the issue of a small sample size.

Table 3. List of parameters for $DHNN - \delta 2SAT$.

Parameter	Parameter Values
Number of Learning stages (v)	100 [9]
Number of Combinations (η)	100 [9]
Number of Trials (φ)	100 [44]
Number of Neurons (λ_1)	$5 < \lambda_1 < 50$
Tolerance value (Tol)	0.001 [18]
Method of determining synaptic weight	Wan Abdullah (WA) [17]
Rate of relaxation (R)	3 [18]
Time of threshold CPU	24 h [20]
Learning iteration (ϕ)	$\phi \leq v$ [26]
Initialization of neuron states	Random [27]
Training Algorithm	Exhaustive Search
Threshold constraint of DHNN (θ)	0 [9]
Activation function	HTAF [22]
Order of clauses	First- and second-order logic

5.4. Performance Metrics

The objective of each phase includes the evaluation of the performance of the proposed model. Therefore, this study will utilize several performance metrics to assess the efficacy of each simulation in the different phases with respect to the $DHNN - \delta_\gamma 2SAT\rho$ model to verify the effectiveness of the proposed logic system in terms of the probability logic, learning, and testing analysis phases.

5.4.1. Assessment Logic Structure

The probability logic phase is the phase in which the correct logic sequence is generated and that controls the number of clauses and negative literals by solving Equations (3), (5) and (7). We attempt to evaluate the features of the output logic by comparing it with other models to guarantee well-produced logic in terms of clauses and negative numbers, which will the acquirement of the minimum cost function given in Equation (12). To determine the appropriate synaptic weight based on the main objective of this phase, we express three features: (a) the number of negative literals affected by parameter ρ, (b) the weights of the second-order logic clauses affected by parameter Y, and (c) the full-negativity second-order logic clauses affected by the two parameters Y and ρ. The goal is to compare these features to determine whether the probability logic phase will be successful in achieving the desired logic system by changing this parameter and demonstrating its excellence with respect to expressing the logic features. The parameter ρ controls the proportion of negative literals; hence, in this section, we test the effectiveness of this parameter based on several different aspects, which are provided below.

The proportion of negativity: in the probability logic phase, the optimal value of negative literals in the logic system will be assigned ξ, which is a constant ratio that is dependent on λ_1, and the probability of negative literals in the logic system will be computed using the following equation:

Probability Of total Negativity (PON):

$$\text{PON} = \frac{1}{\eta} \sum_{i=1}^{\eta} \frac{\xi}{\lambda_1} \qquad (20)$$

Equation (20) is derived from a Laplace formula [42]; we need to test whether the change in ρ will affect the probability of a negative literal structure occurring in the two types of logic compared to other forms of logic that introduce random proportions of negative literals in the logic structure. When compared to other types of logic, this matrix's scale, if corresponding to the necessary proportion, gives us the correct negative literal probability in the logic structure. While analyzing the deviation of the negative literal in terms of the whole logic system, we introduce a second measure to determine the state of the negative literals in the whole logic system, as shown below:

Negativity Absolute Error (NAE):

$$\text{NAE} = \frac{1}{\eta} \sum_{i=1}^{\eta} \frac{|\lambda_1 - \xi|}{\xi} \qquad (21)$$

The proposed NAE scale measures the amount of error that is not negative if it fits the desired proportion in Equation (5). The optimal NAE is zero, which is equivalent to the required number of negative literals.

The probability of the full negativity of second-order logic: Full negativity second-order $(\neg r_i \vee \neg r_j)$ logic helps us to represent a greater number of the attributes in the final solution. The main objective of the $\delta 2SAT$ is to control the number of negative literals and second-order logical items in the logic structure. We need to expose the features of second-order logic as mentioned previously to fully enjoy the benefits of 2SAT in terms of our proposed logic system. Therefore, the next measure is presented as follows:

Full-Negativity Absolute Error second clauses (FNAE):

$$\text{FNAE} = \frac{1}{\eta} \sum_{i=1}^{\eta} \frac{|\xi_{2SAT} - \lambda_{2SAT}|}{\lambda_{2SAT}} \qquad (22)$$

where ξ_{2SAT} is the number of full negativity second-order clauses and λ_{2SAT} is the number of second-order clauses in a specific string of logic. The accuracy of the logic will be measured by the FNAE scale in terms of generating the full-negative second-order clauses, which are expressed as $(\neg r_i \vee \neg r_j)$, from the rest of the second-order clauses, that is, $(\neg r_i \vee r_j)$, $(r_i \vee \neg r_j)$, and $(r_i \vee r_j)$. Similarly, using this scale, we will address the effectiveness degree of the two factor parameters Y and ρ with respect to their significance in terms of altering the second-order clauses. We can determine if the required logic can represent the prevailing attributes by the properties of this measure. The optimal best of FNAE scale is zero, which is equivalent to the required number fully negative second-order clauses.

To address the effect of a parameter Y in the second-order weight, we propose the weighted error measure, which gives the accuracy of the changing of the effect of Y in both proposed logic types when compared to other logic systems, as follows:

Weight Full-Negativity Absolute Error (WFNAE):

$$\text{WFNAE} = \frac{1}{\eta} \sum_{i=1}^{\eta} \frac{\left(\left| \zeta_{2SAT} - \overline{\lambda}_{2SAT} \right| \right) \times w(y_m)}{\sum_{i=1}^{\eta} \lambda_{2SAT}} \quad (23)$$

where $\overline{\lambda}_{2SAT}$ is the mean number of second-order clauses, and $w(y_m)$ is the weight of second-order clauses, which equals Y because the Laplace formula determines an equally likely probability for all the elements. Using this measure, we can determine the effect of Y on the amount of deviation of the full negative clauses from the mean. We can calculate the real weight for this deviation by multiplying it with the weighted $w(y_m)$. A large scale signifies a high degree of representation in terms of the weight of the negative strings, which greatly improves our understanding of the weight of dominating attribute in logic. By comparing the scale to the other reasoning and assigning weight to that prioritized (completely negative sentences), the deviance is biased towards. Table 4 lists the symbols that we require during this phase.

Table 4. List of parameters used in $DHNN - \delta2SAT$ experimental setup.

Parameter	Parameter Name
$F_{desierd}$	Maximum fitness
F_i	Current fitness
W_E	Expected Synaptic weight obtained by the Wan method.
W_A	Actual synaptic weight
λ_1	Total number of neurons
ζ	The Total of negative literals in logic system
$p(y_m)$	The probability of obtaining second-order clauses
ζ_{2SAT}	The number full-negativity second-order clauses
λ_{2SAT}	The number of second-order clauses
$\overline{\lambda}_{2SAT}$	The mean number of second-order clauses
$H_{\Theta_{\delta2SAT}}$	Minimum energy value
$H_{\Theta_{\delta2SAT}}^{min}$	Final energy
R_G	Ratio of global minimum solutions
$G_{\Theta_{\delta2SAT}}$	Number of global minimum solutions
S_i	Neuron state
S_i^{max}	Benchmark neuron state
$Sokal$	Sokal and Michener Index
R_{tv}	The Ratio of cumulative neuronal variation

5.4.2. Assessment during the Training Phase

In the training phase, we achieved satisfying assignments of the clauses, which generated the optimal synaptic weights in terms of $\Theta_{\delta,2SAT\rho}$ by minimizing Equation (12). The Root-Mean-Square Error (RMSE) has been used as a basic statistical metric for measuring the quality of a model's prediction in many fields [24], and it is utilized to identify the quality of the training phase, wherein the value of RMSE training (RMSEtrain) signifies the root square of the error between the neurons' desired fitness value $F_{desierd}$ generated and their current fitness F_i [22]. The RMSEtrain formula is:

$$\text{RMSE}_{train} = \sqrt{\frac{1}{v} \sum_{i=1}^{\eta \times v} (F_i - F_{desierd})^2} \quad (24)$$

The optimal value of the RMSE in the DHNN model is achieved when it is zero, which means the WA method derived the correct synaptic weight. Furthermore, a good model is achieved when the measure is between 0–60. Whereas the Root-Mean-Square Error in synaptic weight (RMSEweight) used will be assessed based on the following formula

$$\text{RMSE}_{weight} = \sqrt{\frac{1}{v \times \eta} \sum_{i=1}^{\eta \times v} (W_E - W_A)^2} \quad (25)$$

where W_E denotes the Expected synaptic weight obtained by the WA method, and W_A is the actual synaptic weight obtained in the testing phases; this measure gives us a complete understanding of the error produced by the WA method, wherein the best result is 0, which corresponds to Equation (12).

5.4.3. Assessment for Testing Phase

In the event that the suggested network satisfies the requirement in Equation (18), the proposed $DHNN - \delta 2SAT$ will act in conformance with the embedded logical rule during the testing phase. The final neuron state will enter a state of minimum energy, which corresponds to the cost function of the proposed $DHNN - \delta 2SAT$ logical rule. Therefore, based on the synaptic weight generated in the training phase, we evaluate the quality of the retrieved final neuron states (global), namely, the minima solutions. Thus, we apply the next measure as follows: Global minima ratio (R_G)—the goal of the global minima ratio is to assess the retrieval efficiency of the $DHNN - \delta 2SAT$. The formula of the R_G is:

$$R_G = \frac{1}{\eta \times \varphi} \sum_{i=1}^{\lambda_1} G_{\Theta_{\delta 2SAT}} \tag{26}$$

where $G_{\Theta_{\delta 2SAT}}$ is the number of global minimum solutions that satisfy condition (18) after being distributed in Equation (19), φ is the number of trials in the training phase, and η is the logical combination for each run. This metric was frequently used in articles such as [21,38] to assess the proposed $DHNN - \delta 2SAT$'s convergence property.

The second measure in the testing phase is the Root-Mean-Square Error energy (RMSEenergy) [22], which is used to evaluate the minimization of energy achieved by $DHNN - \delta 2SAT$. The energy profile can be determined using RMSE$_{energy}$:

$$\text{RMSE}_{energy} = \sqrt{\frac{1}{v \times \varphi} \sum_{i=1}^{\eta \times v} \left(H_{\Theta_{\delta 2SAT}} - H_{\Theta_{\delta 2SAT}}^{\min} \right)^2} \tag{27}$$

We use RMSEenergy to analyze the converge of $\delta 2SAT$ to determine the actual energy difference between the absolute minimum energy $H_{\Theta_{\delta 2SAT}}^{\min}$ and the final minimum energy $H_{\Theta_{\delta 2SAT}}$.

5.4.4. Similarity Index

The similarity index [38] and cumulative neuronal variation [24] can be used to evaluate SAT performance using a DHNN. The similarity index values will be compared with benchmark neuron states $S_i^{\max}$ to determine the quality of each optimal final neuron state that achieved global lowest energy, as indicated in the following formula:

$$S_i^{\max} = \begin{cases} 1, & r_i \\ -1, & \neg r_i \end{cases} \tag{28}$$

where 1 denotes a positive literal of r_i, and -1 denotes a negative literal of $\neg r_i$ in each clause. It should be noted that the benchmark neuron states are the DHNN model's ideal neuron states that satisfy the conditions in Equation (18). The retrieved final neuron states are compared to the benchmark neuron states indicated in Table 5 to provide a comprehensive comparison of the benchmark neuron states and final neuron states.

Table 5. Variables' similarity index specifications.

Variable	$S_i^{\max}$	S_i
e	−1	−1
f	1	1
g	−1	1
h	1	−1

The overall comparison of the benchmark and final neuron states is conducted as follows [9]:

$$C_{S_i,S_i^{\max}} = \{(S_i, S_i^{\max})|i = 1, 2, \ldots, n\} \tag{29}$$

According to Case 1 in $\Theta_{\delta 2SAT}$ given in the examples in Table 1, the final neuron states are generalizable, as follows: $S_i^{\max} = (-1, 1, -1, 1, 1, -1, 1, -1, -1, -1)$.

In this study, we selected a well-known measure with which to determine the similarity index for diverse perspectives, namely, that developed by Sokal and Michener (Sokal) [46], which will be employed to evaluate the viability of the recovered final neuron states. It should be noted that Sokal measures the similarity of negative cases of S_i with S_i^{max} over a range of (0, 1). The formulation is as follows:

$$Sokal(S_i, S_i^{max}) = \frac{f+e}{f+e+h+g} \tag{30}$$

The Ratio of Cumulative Neuronal variation (R_{tv}) is used because the testing phase uses the DHNN's ability to directly memorize the final neuron states ratio without the need to create a new state. This is expressed as follows:

$$\begin{cases} R_{tv} = \frac{1}{\varphi \times \eta \times v} \sum_{i=1}^{\varphi} \sum_{i=1}^{\eta v} E_i, \\ E_i = \begin{cases} 1, & S_i \neq S_i^{max} \\ 0, & S_i = S_i^{max} \end{cases} \end{cases} \tag{31}$$

where E_i denotes the points scores used to assess the difference between newly recovered final neuron states and the benchmark neuron states. The symbol that we require for this Testing and Training phase is shown in Table 4.

5.5. Comparison of Method and Baseline Models

Since this study focuses on investigating $\delta_\gamma 2SAT\rho$ performance with respect to its logical behavior, we need to investigate the $\delta_\gamma 2SAT\rho$'s performance in terms of Y and ρ with regard to constructing a good logical structure in the probability logic phase. Therefore, we compare $\delta_\gamma 2SAT\rho$ with the existing logic systems in DHNNs based on the logic structures, testing phases, and the quality of the solution to examine two behaviors relating to logic:

(a) The effects of controlling a number of clauses on the second-order weight and non-systematic logic structure.
(b) The capability of $\delta 2SAT$ to control the negative literals and accurately reflect the behavior of the dataset.

In order to examine the logic in a DHNN after its implementation, we also compare its final neuron state's quality to that of RAN2SAT. We also evaluate the variation introduced by the testing phase, global minima solutions, and variation of neurons. The most recent logic systems with a 2SAT structure were selected for this reason, and one of their features was the decision to compare the logic systems' structures. Each clause contains two literals and all clauses are joined by a disjunction.

(a) 2SAT [37]: This is a systematic logical rule that was implemented into a DHNN, with each clause containing two literals. It is a special type of logic of general Boolean satisfiability. Each phrase in the 2SAT model can withstand no more than one suboptimal neuron update, leaving it more akin to a two-dimensional decision-making system. When included into logic mining, this logic system has demonstrated good applicability in task classification. Neuron counts varied from $5 < \lambda_1 < 50$.
(b) MAJ2SAT [23]: The initial focus of the effort was on developing the current non-systematic SAT logic structure. MAJ2SAT suggests structural modifications when considering unbalanced clauses. The unbalanced feature result from different compositions of 2SAT and 3SAT. As a result, MAJ2SAT prefers a greater number of 2SAT clauses. Moreover, to avoid any bases, we limited the number of neurons ranging from $5 < \lambda_1 < 50$.
(c) RAN2SAT [20]: This system is a second-order and first-order clause logical rule that was implemented in a DHNN as an initial form of non-systematic logic. The $\delta_\gamma 2SAT\rho$ has no structural differences compared to RAN2SAT but consists of a logic probability phase. Due to the connection of the first-order clause, RAN2SAT is reported to provide a greater variety in terms of synaptic weight. Although each literal state was chosen at random, the number of clauses in each order can be determined in advance. Specifically, the number of neurons ranged from $3 < \lambda_1 < 50$.
(d) RAN3SAT [22]: This work expanded on the previous work by [20], incorporating higher-order logic of 3SAT clauses in a non-systematic SAT structure, which improved the lack of interpretability of the current non-systematic SAT by storing more neurons per clause. Although the number of clauses for each sequence was selected at random, each literal state was defined. In this case, again, we restricted the number of neurons; the range was $6 < \lambda_1 < 50$.

(e) YRAN2SAT [26]: This system is known as the Y-Type Random 2-Satisfiability logical rule. YRAN2SAT's novelty is introduced by randomly generating first- and second-order clauses. It is a combination of systematic and non-systematic logic. YRAN2SAT can explore the search area with a high potential for solution diversity by adding the features of both clauses. YRAN2SAT introduces remarkable logical flexibility, while the number of all clauses is predefined by the user and the literal states are defined at random. The range of the number of neurons is $1 < \lambda_1 < 50$.

(f) rSAT [24]: This is a new, non-systematic satisfiability logic class, known as Weighted Random k Satisfiability for k = 1, 2, which includes a weighted ratio of negative literals and adds a new logic phase to produce a non-systematic logical structure based on the number of negative literals specified. More diverse final neuron states were obtained by integrating rSAT into a DHNN. The proposed model showed outstanding promise as an advanced logic-mining model that can be used further in the forecasting and prediction of real-world problems. In this study, we select (r = 0.5) because it has been discovered that it performs well in the logic phase of the rSAT [24]. The range of the number of neurons was $5 < \lambda_1 < 50$.

5.6. Benchmark Dataset

In this study, the proposed model generated bipolar interpretations randomly from a simulated dataset. More specifically, the logical illustration that was used in the simulations will serve as the foundation for the structure of the simulated data. The simulated dataset is commonly used in the modeling and evaluation of the efficacy of SAT logic programming, as demonstrated in the work of [18,22,27].

5.7. Statistical Test

This section provides a brief definition of the statistical measures that will be used in this study for two purposes (description and testing):

(a) The measure of central tendency is defined as "the statistical measure that designates a single value as being indicative of a whole distribution" [47]. Therefore, we selected two measures: (a) The average, which is known as the arithmetic mean (or, simply, "Mean"). It is calculated by adding all of the values in the dataset and dividing them by the number of observations. One of the most significant measures is the central tendency measure. The mean has the disadvantage of being sensitive to extreme values/outliers, especially when the sample size is small. As a result, it is ineffective as a measure of central tendency for a skewed distribution [48]. Its formula is expressed as follows:

$$\overline{X} = \frac{\sum_{i=1}^{n} x_i}{n*} \tag{32}$$

where $\overline{X}$ denotes the mean, x_i represents the set of data, and $n*$ denotes the sample size of the data.
(b) The median is the value that, when all observations are arranged in ascending/descending order, occupies the central position. It divides the frequency distribution into two halves, is not biased by outliers, and is determined by the following formula [49]:

$$\widetilde{X} = \begin{cases} \frac{x_{\frac{n*}{2}} + x_{\frac{n*}{2}+1}}{2}, & \text{if } n* \text{ even} \\ x_{\frac{n*+1}{2}}, & \text{if } n* \text{ odd} \end{cases} \tag{33}$$

where $\widetilde{X}$ denotes the median, and $n*$ denotes the sample size of the data.

(b) The measure of dispersion: Variability measures inform us about the distribution of the data and allow us to compare the dispersion of two or more sets of data. We can determine whether the data are stretched or compressed using dispersion metrics, namely, the Standard Deviation (SD), which evaluates variability by considering the distance between each score and the distribution's mean as a reference point. It is a variance square root and gives an indication of the standard deviation or average separation from the mean. It is presented as follows:

$$\sigma x \; (SD) = \frac{\sum_{i=1}^{n}(X_i - \overline{X})^2}{n*-1} \tag{34}$$

(c) The boxplot and whiskers (measure of position): The boxplot (Tukey1977) [50] is a well-known tool for displaying significant distributional features of a dataset. The classical box-plot displays the quartiles $\mathbb{Q}_1, \mathbb{Q}_2, \mathbb{Q}_3$, and whiskers, where the median is equal $\mathbb{Q}_2$, which is used to estimate the 25th ($\mathbb{Q}_1$) and 75th ($\mathbb{Q}_3$) quantiles, thus providing an estimate of the interquartile range $IQR = \mathbb{Q}_3 - \mathbb{Q}_1$. The range of the majority of the data (the whisker's length) ends at those values just inside the whisker's "limits" (referred to as "fences" and defined by $LF = \mathbb{Q}_1 - 1.5 \times (IQR)$ and $UF = \mathbb{Q}_3 - 1.5 \times (IQR)$, lower ($LF$) and upper ($UF$) respectively. Observations outside the whiskers (the outliers), observations beyond the fences [51], plotted individually, are defined as the data points outside the boundaries. When comparing different datasets, the boxplot is particularly helpful. Instead of using a Table of Values, we can quickly compare all reported statistics across numerous datasets. The simple, effective design of the boxplot aids the comparison of summary statistics (location, spread, and range of the data in the sample or batch).

(d) The Laplace Principle of Probability states that in a space of elementary events Ω, where each element has the same chance of appearing, the probability of a compound event, A, is equal to the ratio of outcomes that are favorable to the occurrence of all other outcomes. This is demonstrated by the formula in Equation (4):

(e) The probability density function curve is a schematic illustration of the probability of random variable density function that is given by:

$$f(x) = \int_{-\infty}^{\infty} f_x(x).dx \tag{35}$$

where $f(x)$ denotes the probability density function for random variables; the shape provides a visualization of the distribution of continuous random variables and provides the probability that a continuous random variable's value will fall within a specific interval.

(f) The Wilcoxon signed-rank test: The Wilcoxon signed-rank test was introduced for the first time by Frank Wilcoxon in 1945 [52]. It is a one-sample location problem-based nonparametric test that is used to test the null hypothesis wherein the median of a distribution equals some value ($H_0 : \bar{X} = 0$) for data that are skewed or otherwise (i.e., do not follow a normal distribution). It can be used instead of a one-sample t-test or paired t-test, or for ordered categorical data with a normal distribution. If (p-value $\leq \alpha$), the null hypothesis is rejected; this is strong evidence that the null hypothesis is invalid, i.e., the result of the median is significant. The Formula for the Wilcoxon Rank Sum Test (W) for x_i independent random variable is:

$$W = \frac{W_s^* - \frac{\pi(\pi+1)}{4}}{\sqrt{\frac{\pi(\pi+1)(2\pi+1)}{24}}} \tag{36}$$

where π = number of pairs whose difference is not 0. W_s^* = smallest of the absolute values of the sums of x_i. The symbols of these statistics are listed in Table 6. The details of the implementation of $\Theta_{\delta 2SAT}$ into DHNN is presented in Figure 3, which contains the probability logic, the learning and testing phases, and the evaluation metric in each phase.

Table 6. Parameters List for $DHNN - \delta 2SAT$.

Parameter	Parameter Name
$\bar{X}$	The arithmetic mean
$\tilde{X}$	The median
σx	Standard deviation
$\mathbb{Q}_1$	First quartile
$\mathbb{Q}_2$	Second quartile
$\mathbb{Q}_3$	Third quartile
IQR	Interquartile range
LF	Lower fences
UF	Upper fences
$f(x)$	Probability density function for random variables
W_s^*	Smallest of absolute values of the sum of x_i in Wilcoxon test
W	Wilcoxon test value (sum of smallest and largest absolute values of the sum x_i)

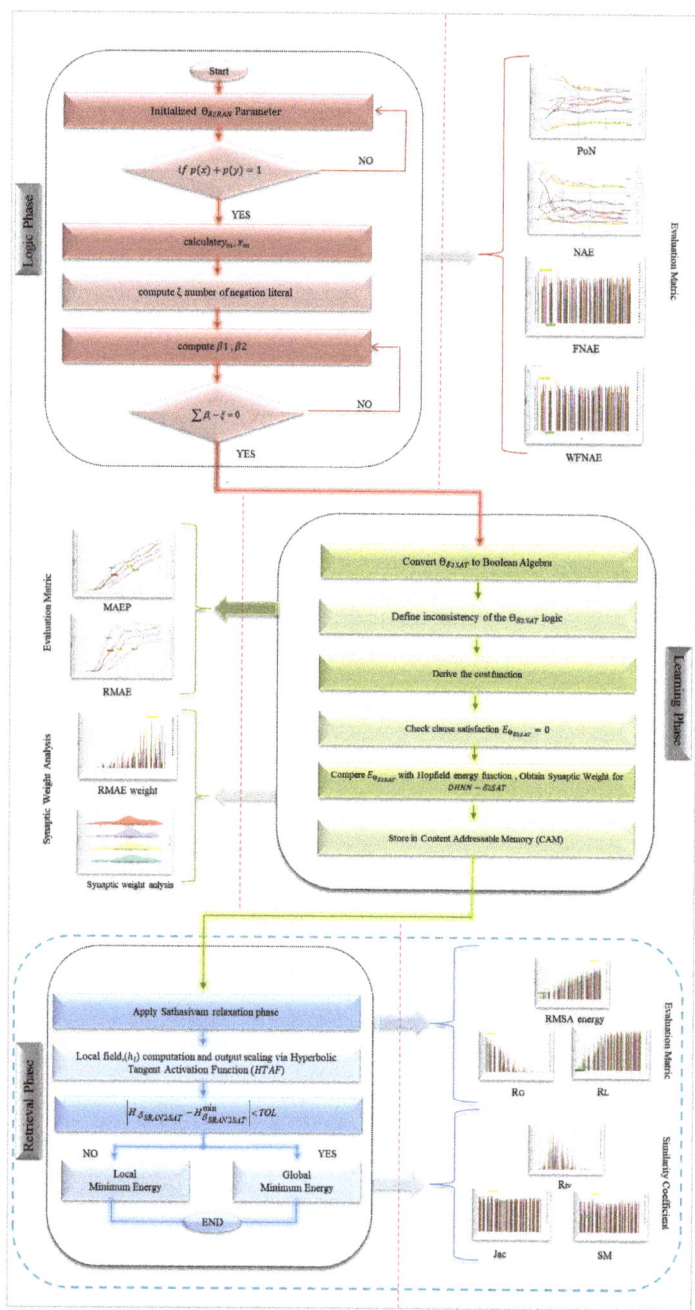

Figure 3. Flowchart of $DHNN - \delta 2SAT$ and Experimental evaluation.

6. Results and Discussion

In this section, we describe the suggested logical output and evaluate it using a variety of evaluation metrics throughout all three phases to ensure that the addition of statistical tools to the RAN2SAT structure and the produced $\delta_\gamma 2SAT\rho$ logic was effective. Furthermore, the simulation platform, assigned parameters, and the metrics' performance are discussed in this section. It is important to note that we have not considered any optimization during the probability logic phase, as in Zamri et al.'s [24] work; the training phase, as proposed in [21,38]; or the testing phase, as proposed in [9,53].

6.1. Logic Structure Capability

The probability phases give us different models in terms of negative literals and second-order logic with respect to the two parameters Y and ρ. Since both parameters fall within the [0,1] interval, we can generate an endless (infinite) number of 2SAT models using both parameters. For the majority of the representations of 2SAT, we chose to use Y ($p(y_m)$) more frequently than $p(x_m)$ so that the results would be in the range (0.6–0.9). In this study, we chose values of ρ greater than 0.5 in the range (0.6–0.9) of the probability logic phases to obtain a greater representation of the negative numbers in order to study the predominating attributes in the dataset, as we previously mentioned.

We selected the most significant differences from the two intervals and designated them as models, which are illustrated in Table 7, in order to examine the efficacy of the two parameters with different numbers of λ_m, where $5 < \lambda_1 < 50$ so at improve the benefits compared with other recently developed produced logic systems. Subsequently, we will test two $\delta_\gamma 2SAT\rho$ types with different numbers of λ_m, Y, and ρ; these values are selected considering the significant change in probability and negative literals. Notably, values of $\rho = 1$ will be disregarded because we do not need all literals to be negative because the structure will not represent the Binomial distribution dataset. Moreover, the $DHNN - \delta 2SAT$ will give one satisfied interpretation of a first-order clause [54]; on the other hand, $Y = 1$ will give us second-order logic. It is important to emphasize that we do not consider a systematic $\delta 2SAT$ logical system in this study. Table 7 shows the names of two $\delta_\gamma 2SAT\rho$ types for different possible models depending on the two parameters Y and ρ, as well as other logic symbols.

Table 7. The logical symbols in the experiment.

Y	ρ	$\delta_1 2SAT\rho$	$\delta_2 2SAT\rho$
0.6	0.6	A1	Q1
	0.7	A2	Q2
	0.8	A3	Q3
	0.9	A4	Q4
0.7	0.6	A5	Q5
	0.7	A6	Q6
	0.8	A7	Q7
	0.9	A8	Q8
0.8	0.6	A9	Q9
	0.7	A10	Q10
	0.8	A11	Q11
	0.9	A12	Q12
0.9	0.6	A13	Q13
	0.7	A14	Q14
	0.8	A15	Q15
	0.9	A16	Q16

The negativity representation: The PON measure in the different logic models has been tested by Equation (20). The PON represents the probability of the appearance of a negative literal in the entire logic system in all combinations with different λ_1. It is necessary to control the negative literals in order to determine the prevailing attributes in the dataset, as negative literals will ensure more negativity in the final neurons; then, we can ensure that the attribute will appear in the solution space by helping the DHNN find the optimal solution [24].

The Figure 4, a line representation, shows different layers of logic in different proportions for both types of $\delta_\gamma 2SAT\rho$. At the same time, for other groups, $\rho = 0.5$ for rSAT logic, and ρ = random for other logic systems (YRAN2SAT, MAJ2SAT, RAN3SAT, 2SAT, and RAN2SAT). The reason why this is in the minimum levels of the proposed logic for the $\delta_\gamma 2SAT\rho$ is because, as was already noted, the probability of receiving a negative literal for the SAT is incredibly low. The highest two layers were recorded as $\rho = 0.9$ and $\rho = 0.8$ in both types of $\delta_\gamma 2SAT\rho$, respectively. By applying Equation (5), we obtain the best number of negative literals for all λ_1, which is similar to the third layer for the other two groups, where $\rho = 0.6$ and $\rho = 0.7$ were the lowest probabilities in both types of $\delta_\gamma 2SAT\rho$, which, by the change in the proportional parameter ρ, indicates the success in terms of producing the desired number of negative literals in the logic system, representing the predominate attributes in our dataset. Additionally, there was a direct correlation between the number of neurons in each class of the desired proportion and the proportions where a high PON recorded low probability when the number corresponded to λ_1. When the number is less than 17 and after 31 for λ_1, the PON becomes approximately stable. This is because the d in Equation (6) in the sample size equation always selects the optimal sample that reflects the number of negative literals, even if the number of neurons is low. Table 8 provides detailed information on the PON in each proportion group for the two types of logic. Note that group ($\rho = 0.9$) recorded the maximum PON and highest mean value of the PON with low σ in both types of $\delta_\gamma 2SAT_{0.9}$; the small σ indicates a different number of neurons λ_1, and this provides the nearest value of the PON means, and that result is highly similar within each group for all models and increases in accordance with the Y increasing in the models for both types, namely, $\delta_1 2SAT\rho$ and $\delta_2 2SAT\rho$. the small σ indicate, with different number of neuron λ_1, it provides the nearest value of PON mean's, and that result is highly similar within each group for all models and increases in accordance with the Y increasing in models for both types, namely, $\delta_1 2SAT\rho$, $\delta_2 2SAT\rho$. However, we can also note that the PON mean of the other logic systems is closest, indicating that the minimal PON value was recorded in YRANSAT with a minimum mean of 0.4966 and a low SD(σ) = (0.015), which indicates that it was also the lowest for different numbers of neurons, but we can also notice that the PON mean of other logic systems is closest, showing low values for different numbers of neurons that were less than or equal to 0.5. The PON results prove the flexibility of $\delta_\gamma 2SAT\rho$'s structure in terms of controlling the literals' states.

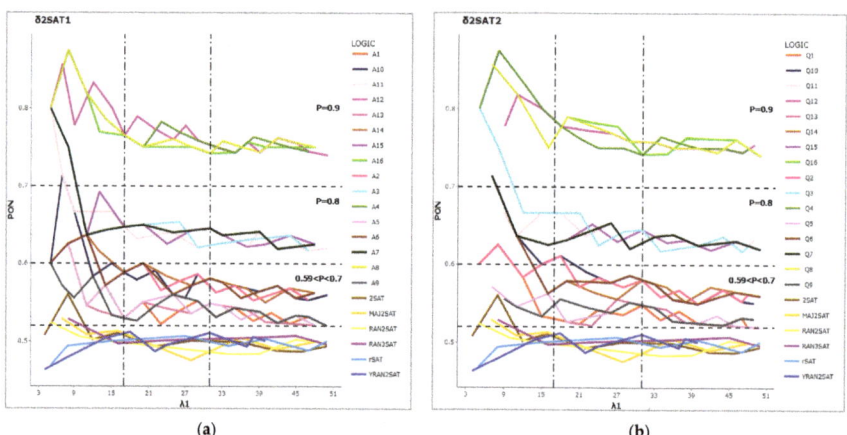

Figure 4. PON line representation for models in both types of logic (a) $\delta_1 2SAT\rho$, (b) $\delta_2 2SAT\rho$, and recently developed logic systems.

The accuracy of the models is evaluated by the NAE measure in Equation (21) in terms of the amount of error that is non-negative or the quantity of the negative literal status for the entire logic system in each proportion group for both types of $\delta_\gamma 2SAT\rho$ models. According to Figure 5, in the line representation, note that the effect of the proportional changes in the logic restructure guarantees that the best RAN2SAT is required, or effective of the prevailing attribute in the dataset where different proportions give us different layers. The details of Figure 5 can be found in Table 9, which shows the minimum values of the NAE that were recorded in a group $\rho = 0.9$ where A4 in $\delta_2 2SAT_{0.9}$ was recorded as the lowest error by (0.1429). It should be observed that the median value (0.3090) was the lowest possible value, indicating that the A4 for all n neurons of λ_1 always had a lesser error in the middle sections. Additionally, it should be noted that all models in the same group, A16, A12, and A8, have very similar median values (0.333, 0.31, and 0.320), which is because, as shown in the PON, this group has the highest probability for the representation of a negative literal, which is accomplished by the proportion $\rho = 0.9$. Similarly, in $\delta_2 2SAT_{0.9}$, Q4 recorded the lowest error as 0.1429, but the least median was recorded by Q16 (0.13125), which means the minimum error lies in the middle values with respect to the number of neurons λ_1. Moreover, it can be noted from Figure 5 that for a small number of neurons λ_1, Q4 has fewer NAE values than Q8, Q12, and Q16. However, the reverse is true for the middle values of Q16 compared to Q12, Q8, and Q4, as mentioned before regarding the effect of Y in λ_1. However, in Table 9 the value of the median has very small differences from the model in group $\rho = 0.9$. As discussed in terms of the PON, this indicates the successfulness of the proportion of representation in the logic system. The highest NAE value was observed to be for rSAT with a high median, where $r = 0.5$ with the nearest value of NAE for the other logic systems (YRAN2SAT, MAJ2SAT, RAN3SAT, 2SAT, and RAN2SAT); as previously mentioned, there was a lack of representation of the negative literals in the logic system, as they recorded the least degree of the probability of the appearance of negative literals.

Table 8. PNO results for models with both types of logic, $\delta_1 2SAT\rho$ and $\delta_2 2SAT\rho$, and recently developed logic systems' details determined by Wilcoxon test for median divided by ρ value.

ρ	Model	Mean	SD	Min	Max	Model	Mean	SD	Min	Max
0.6	A1	0.5483	0.0294	0.5217	0.6250	Q1	0.5454	0.0318	0.5200	0.625
	A5	0.5503	0.0290	0.5208	0.6250	Q5	0.5392	0.0165	0.5200	0.5714
	A9	0.5460	0.0211	0.5200	0.6000	Q9	0.5392	0.0115	0.5227	0.5556
	A13	0.5368	0.0100	0.5208	0.5500	Q13	0.5319	0.0134	0.5200	0.5556
0.7	A2	0.5827	0.0253	0.5526	0.6364	Q2	0.5779	0.0215	0.5500	0.625
	A6	0.5812	0.0246	0.5556	0.6364	Q6	0.5850	0.0466	0.5500	0.7143
	A10	0.5858	0.0405	0.5532	0.7143	Q10	0.5863	0.0353	0.5500	0.6667
	A14	0.5829	0.0242	0.5500	0.6364	Q14	0.5668	0.0097	0.5526	0.5806
0.8	A3	0.6565	0.0524	0.6170	0.8000	Q3	0.6558	0.051	0.6170	0.8000
	A7	0.6558	0.0501	0.6190	0.8000	Q7	0.6384	0.0257	0.6200	0.7143
	A11	0.6481	0.0441	0.6170	0.8000	Q11	0.6410	0.0172	0.6170	0.6667
	A15	0.6481	0.0441	0.6170	0.8000	Q11	0.6410	0.0172	0.6170	0.6667
0.9	A4	==0.7753==	0.0362	0.7429	==0.8750==	Q4	0.7716	0.0378	0.7400	==0.8750==
	A8	0.7709	0.0360	0.7419	==0.8750==	Q8	0.7704	0.0349	0.7400	0.8571
	A12	0.7730	0.0315	0.7400	0.8571	Q12	==0.7678==	0.0217	0.7447	0.8182
	A16	0.7578	0.0206	0.7419	0.8182	Q16	0.7623	0.0183	0.7400	0.7895
random	2SAT	0.5041	0.0211	0.4870	0.5600					
	MAJ2SAT	0.5021	0.0159	0.4750	0.5286					
	RAN2SAT	0.4982	0.0131	0.4829	0.5240					
	RAN3SAT	0.5056	0.0121	0.4962	0.5288					
	YRAN2SAT	==0.4966==	0.0152	==0.4625==	0.5117					
0.5	rSAT	0.4900	0.0100	0.4700	0.5100					

Note: The yellow highlights indicate the highest number in the column and the green indicates the smallest number in the column.

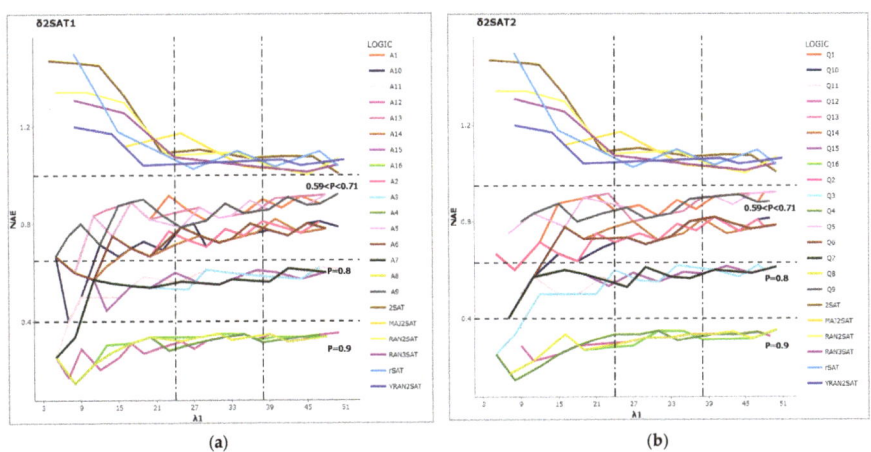

Figure 5. NAE line representation for models in both types of logic (**a**) $\delta_1 2SAT\rho$, (**b**) $\delta_2 2SAT\rho$, and recently developed logic systems.

Table 9. Maximum and minimum NAE results for models with both types of logic $\delta_1 2SAT\rho$, $\delta_2 2SAT\rho$, and recently developed logic systems with details determined by Wilcoxon test for median divided by ρ value.

ρ	Model	Min	Max	Median	W	Model	Min	Max	Median	W
0.6	A1	0.6	0.9167	0.8571	120	Q1	0.6	0.9231	0.875	120
	A5	0.6	0.92	0.8333	120	Q5	0.75	0.9231	0.8634	78
	A9	0.6667	0.9231	0.85	190	Q9	0.8	0.913	0.8571	91
	A13	0.8182	0.92	0.8536	78	Q13	0.8	0.9231	0.9	45
0.7	A2	0.5714	0.8095	0.7417	105	Q2	0.6	0.8182	0.75	136
	A6	0.5714	0.8	0.75	120	Q6	0.4	0.8182	0.753	78
	A10	0.4	0.8077	0.75	190	Q10	0.5	0.8182	0.7333	91
	A14	0.5714	0.8182	0.7361	78	Q14	0.7222	0.8095	0.76923	45
0.8	A3	0.25	0.6207	0.5635	105	Q3	0.25	0.6207	0.5635	136
	A7	0.25	0.6154	0.56	120	Q7	0.4	0.6129	0.5848	78
	A11	0.25	0.6207	0.5833	190	Q11	0.5	0.6207	0.5714	91
	A15	0.4444	0.6087	0.5714	78	Q15	0.5333	0.6154	0.5862	45
0.9	A4	0.1429	0.3462	0.309	105	Q4	0.1429	0.3514	0.3274	136
	A8	0.1428	0.3478	0.32	120	Q8	0.1667	0.3514	0.3191	78
	A12	0.1667	0.3514	0.3125	190	Q12	0.2222	0.3429	0.3182	91
	A16	0.2222	0.3478	0.3333	78	Q16	0.2667	0.3514	0.3125	45
random	2SAT	1.005	1.47	1.097	55					
	MAJ2SAT	1.018	1.171	1.076	10					
	RAN2SAT	0.999	1.34	1.086	36					
	RAN3SAT	1.012	1.309	1.058	21					
	YRAN2SAT	1.039	1.2	1.062	28					
0.5	rSAT	1.03	1.501	1.1	36					

Note: The results highlighted in yellow indicate the highest number in the column and the green indicates the smallest number in the column, (p-value < 0.00), for all models in terms of Wilcoxon test, which means that H_0 should be rejected.

The probability of full negativity of second-order logic: We examined the ability of several models incorporating the two types of $\delta_\gamma 2SAT\rho$ to produce full-negativity second-order clauses with greater accuracy compared to other recently developed logic systems by manipulating two parameters, Y and ρ, using the FNAE measure for the second-order clause in Equation (22). Obtaining full negativity second-order logic guarantees that the prevailing attribute in the desired logic structure is represented. Figure 6, a columnar representation, shows the result of the FNAE measure, the higher accuracy achieved by A8 and A4 in $\delta_1 2SAT\rho$, and Q4 in $\delta_2 2SAT\rho$ that obtained a value of (0) for FNAE. This is due to the effect of the two parameters in this model, for which the proportion of negative number is $\rho = 0.9$, with a lower probability than other models in second-order logic where $Y = 0.6, 0.7$, which means that all second-order clauses are satisfied by negative numbers because of the small representation of second-order clauses. Based on the same figure, the low accuracy obtained by A1 and Q1, which obtain the maximum number in terms of the FNAE logic (0.8930, 0.8650), is the reason for the low representation of the negative proportion in the logic system. Thus, if we need greater representation of the prevailing attributes in the desired logic structure, we should choose the A8 and A16 from $\delta_1 2SAT_{0.9}$ and Q4 from $\delta_2 2SAT_{0.9}$. Model A4 recorded higher accuracy using the lowest value of the FNAE median (0.3995), which means the minimum error lies is in the middle values for all neuron quantities λ_1. We also note the proportion of negative literals is $\rho = 0.9$, which means there are more second-order negative clauses in the models in $\delta_1 2SAT\rho$ recorded in model Q12, where the lowest FNAE median was (0.4147). The accurate results regarding the FNAE measure are listed in Table 10. It is evident that the ratios of the negative literals are $\rho = 0.9$ and $Y = 0.9$, indicating that the model has a higher fraction of negative, second-order representations. Comparing these results to those of other state-of-the-art logic systems, all of them provide low accuracy due to a higher median value, which indicates that the mean lacks the ability to accurately represent the full-negative second-order values in this model. RAN2SAT performs the best among the logic systems. The latest logic systems give higher errors because the fluctuation in predetermine for assigning second-order logic and low represent for negative literal that indicate the $\delta_1 2SAT\rho$ and $\delta_2 2SAT\rho$ is flexible more than the recent logic systems in controlling of two parameters.

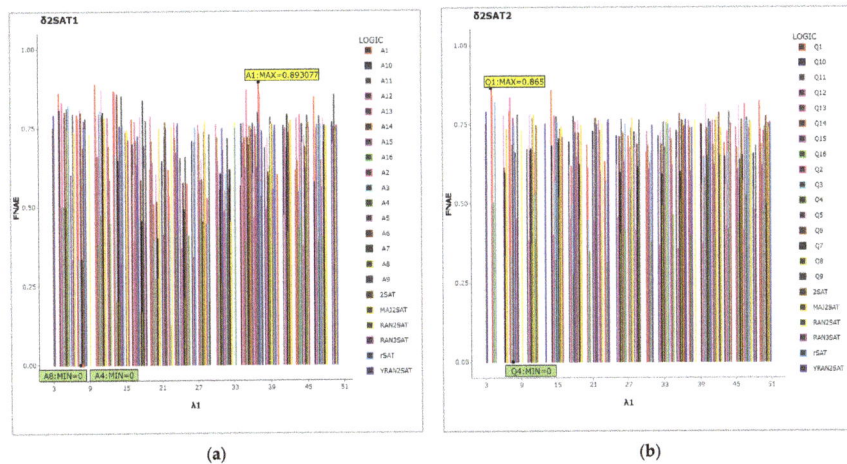

(a) (b)

Figure 6. FNAE column representation for models in both types of logic (a) $\delta_1 2SAT\rho$, (b) $\delta_2 2SAT\rho$, and recently developed logic systems.

Table 10. Maximum and minimum FNAE results for models in both types of logic $\delta_1 2SAT\rho$, $\delta_2 2SAT\rho$, and recently developed logic systems with details determined by Wilcoxon test for median.

Model	Min	Max	Median	W	Model	Min	Max	Median	W
A1	0.5650	0.8931	0.6186	120	Q1	0.6322	0.8650	0.7472	120
A2	0.5071	0.8683	0.7688	105	Q2	0.5722	0.8400	0.6993	136
A3	0.3333	0.8025	0.4825	105	Q3	0.3333	0.7633	0.5678	136
A4	0.0000	0.5525	0.3996	91	Q4	0.0000	0.7594	0.4527	120
A5	0.5756	0.8700	0.7186	120	Q5	0.6576	0.8141	0.7322	78
A6	0.5129	0.8560	0.6860	120	Q6	0.5763	0.7856	0.7000	78
A7	0.3333	0.7975	0.5950	120	Q7	0.4962	0.7043	0.6179	78
A8	0.0000	0.7488	0.4440	105	Q8	0.3333	0.7378	0.5017	78
A9	0.6570	0.8515	0.7775	190	Q9	0.6818	0.7880	0.7660	91
A10	0.5753	0.8050	0.6925	190	Q10	0.6475	0.7489	0.6938	91
A11	0.4712	0.7231	0.6047	190	Q11	0.5418	0.6840	0.6225	91
A12	0.3217	0.7510	0.4488	190	Q12	0.3538	0.4773	0.4148	91
A13	0.7068	0.7860	0.7651	78	Q13	0.7254	0.7615	0.7386	45
A14	0.6445	0.7594	0.7125	78	Q14	0.6745	0.7383	0.7018	45
A15	0.5445	0.6700	0.6245	78	Q15	0.6009	0.6467	0.6196	45
A16	0.3780	0.5044	0.4204	78	Q16	0.3965	0.4742	0.4177	45
2SAT	0.6850	0.7682	0.7502	55					
MAJ2SAT	0.7350	0.7800	0.7505	36					
RAN2SAT	0.7300	0.7658	0.7441	36					
RAN3SAT	0.7100	0.7700	0.7530	21					
YRAN2SAT	0.7225	0.7900	0.7514	45					
rSAT	0.7400	0.8200	0.7500	78					

Note: The results highlighted in yellow indicate the highest number in the column and the green indicates the smallest number in the column, (p-value < 0.00) for all models in terms of Wilcoxon test, it means reject H_0.

A high result in the WFNAE measure in Equation (23) indicates that full-negative second-order logic is more greatly represented. By using this scale, the weight of the sentences in the logic has been evaluated, and the Y parameter may be used to determine whether the model is desirable because the highest probability gives the highest weight. The maximum probability, as shown in Figure 7, is the highest weight represented and is obtained by A16, Q16 in $\delta_1 2SAT_{0.9}$, and $\delta_2 2SAT_{0.9}$, respectively, and 0 for YRANSAT, because it also produces first-order logic. In Table 11, note the highest significant median value was achieved by the A16 and Q16 models (0.4477 and 0.4691, respectively), and the lowest significant median value was achieved by the YRANSAT (0) WFNAE value. This would ensure that the prevailing attribute has the highest representation in our logic compared to other state-of-the-art logic systems, in addition to its ability to minimize and maximize changes in Y. In conclusion, it is evident that the two parameters, Y and ρ, have a direct impact on the probability distribution dataset in the $\delta_\gamma 2SAT\rho$ logic structure.

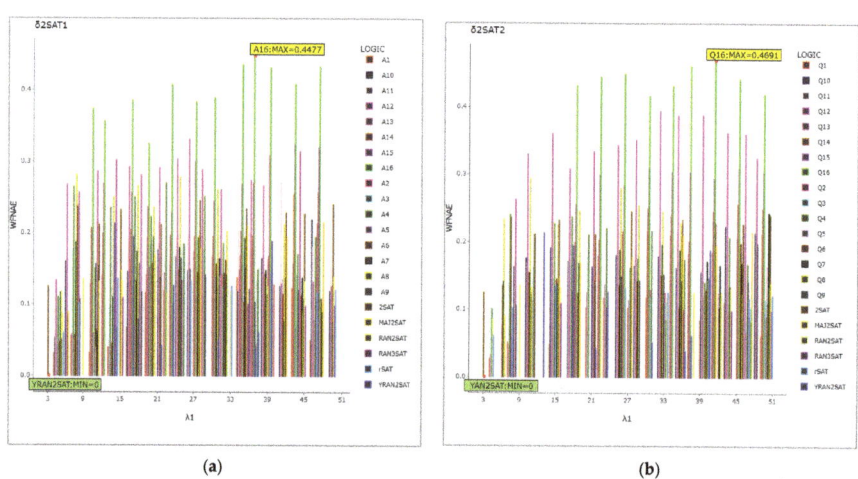

Figure 7. WFNA column representation for models in both types of logic (a) $\delta_1 2SAT\rho$, (b) $\delta_2 2SAT\rho$ and recently developed logic systems.

Table 11. Maximum and minimum WFNAE results for models in both types of logic $\delta_1 2SAT\rho$, $\delta_2 2SAT\rho$ and recently developed logic systems with details determined by Wilcoxon test for median.

Model	Median	Min	Max	W	Model	Median	Min	Max	W
A1	0.1162	0.0308	0.1373	120	Q1	0.0889	0.0270	0.1181	120
A2	0.0721	0.0374	0.1501	105	Q2	0.1058	0.0320	0.1369	136
A3	0.1506	0.0559	0.1849	105	Q3	0.1293	0.0832	0.1789	136
A4	0.1896	0.1100	0.2695	105	Q4	0.1904	0.0818	0.2400	136
A5	0.1024	0.0390	0.1486	120	Q5	0.1258	0.0782	0.1653	78
A6	0.1140	0.0448	0.1616	120	Q6	0.1353	0.1017	0.1977	78
A7	0.1409	0.0608	0.1943	120	Q7	0.1702	0.1380	0.2432	78
A8	0.2014	0.0910	0.2800	120	Q8	0.2304	0.1233	0.2931	78
A9	0.1141	0.0507	0.1646	190	Q9	0.1412	0.1056	0.1980	91
A10	0.1563	0.0520	0.2184	190	Q10	0.1760	0.1552	0.2233	91
A11	0.1906	0.1333	0.2708	190	Q11	0.2157	0.1685	0.2851	91
A12	0.2732	0.1262	0.3305	190	Q12	0.3517	0.2628	0.3945	91
A13	0.1630	0.1284	0.2131	78	Q13	0.2058	0.1744	0.2158	45
A14	0.1973	0.1673	0.2571	78	Q14	0.2386	0.1992	0.2563	45
A15	0.2676	0.2040	0.3245	78	Q15	0.3029	0.2544	0.3086	45
A16	0.3977	0.3244	0.4477	78	Q16	0.4414	0.4158	0.4691	45
2SAT	0.2300	0.1250	0.2447	55					
MAJ2SAT	0.1734	0.0883	0.2141	36					
RAN2SAT	0.1287	0.0850	0.1393	36					
RAN3SAT	0.0987	0.0575	0.1088	21					
YRAN2SAT	0.0610	0.0000	0.2131	36					
rSAT	0.1200	0.0600	0.1500	36					

Note: The results highlighted in yellow indicate the highest number in the column and the green indicates the smallest number in the column, (p-value < 0.00) for all models in terms of Wilcoxon test, it means reject H_0.

6.2. Training Phase Capability

This phase's objective is to evaluate the efficiency of various $\delta_\gamma 2SAT\rho$ structures produced in the probability logic phase, which were trained in a DHNN and minimize the logical inconsistencies using Equation (12), to obtain the correct synaptic weight. In this phase, ES obtained consistent interpretations for $\Theta_{\delta_\gamma 2SAT}$ and derived the correct synaptic weight for the logic system. If the model arrived at an inconsistent interpretation ($E_{\Theta_{\delta 2SAT}} = 0$), the $DHNN - \delta 2SAT$ model will reset the whole search space and generate a new one until $\phi = v$. The error of the maximum fitness of logic, which is represented by the total clause from the achieved fitness, is calculated by employing RMSEtrain and RMSEweight to quantify the error in the training phase via Equations (24) and (25), respectively. Figures 8 and 9 show different RMSEtrain, and RMSEweight results for both types of $\delta_\gamma 2SAT\rho$, when ($v = 100$); for both types of $\delta_\gamma 2SAT\rho$, RMSEtrain was described to undergo an exponential increase (logistic growth) with a rate of growth equal to $|F_i - F_{desired}|$ and a linear positive increase in RMSEweight. According to [26], the error value in the training phase starts off low when the learning set is small because it is more difficult to fit the larger learning set. In this instance, as λ_1 rises, more iterations are required for the DHNN to locate SAT structures with satisfying interpretations, and the training phase metrics obtain 0 value when λ_1 is small. When the value of Y is high, there is always low error because the structure of second-order logic helps ES by becoming satisfied ($F_i = F_{desired}$) to a greater extent than first-order logic and because the probability of finding a consistent interpretation for each $\delta_\gamma 2SAT\rho$ clause follows a binomial distribution, which measures the effect of flexible structure by changing in two parameters Y and ρ in terms of the RMSEtrain and RMSEweight results [24]. As shown in Figures 8 and 9, high probability of obtaining second-order Y makes it easier to locate optimal interpretations [22], which means the WA method will derive the correct synaptic weight. On the other hand, when Y decreases, it signifies that the probability of the first-order clauses being satisfied is very low for 2SAT. Due to its limited number of interpretations, the non-systematic logical rule with first-order clauses reduces the cost function of the logic.

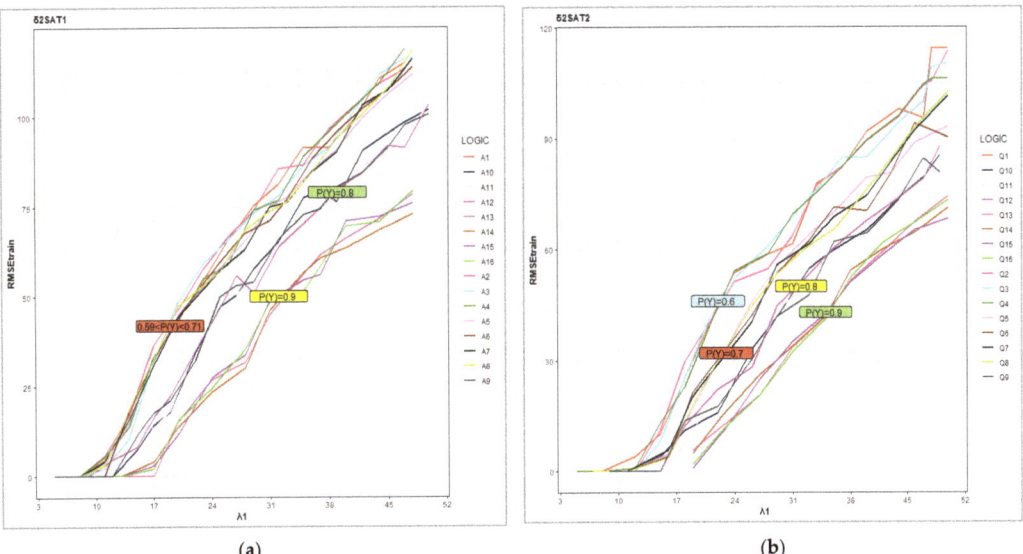

Figure 8. RMSEtrain line representation for models in both types of logic (**a**) $\delta_1 2SAT\rho$, (**b**) $\delta_2 2SAT\rho$.

Table 12 records the values in Figure 8; in the line representation, it is noted for $\delta_1 2SAT\rho$ large RMSEtrain reported for A4 (118.895) that follows group $Y = 0.6$, have the smallest number for 2SAT at the same time, the result of the RMSEtrain median gives us the more significant result reported by group $Y = 0.7$, whereas A8(68.5274) has a large RMSEtrain value without any effect by outlier for all λ_1; thus, when Y decreases, the ES could not find a consistent interpretation for first-order logic. The low RMSEtrain median go for group $Y = 0.9$ were A14 (38.16665), which also indicates a large number of 2SAT that make it simpler for ES to achieve consistent interpretation. For $\delta_2 2SAT\rho$ a large error was reported for the $Y = 0.6$ group in Q1(114.342) because of a small number of 2SAT.

For the median result, we note that Q3(64.7599) reported a high RMSEtrain in the same group, and group $Y = 0.9$ reported a lower value with respect to Q16 (41.0488), which indicates it has the same behavior for $\delta_1 2SAT\rho$; it is worth noting here that large Y and ρ have large fitness errors. It is clear in Q(4,8,12,16) that when $\rho = 0.9$ in both measures, that means it is difficult for ES to become satisfied for negative literals, because the extreme value for negative literal makes it difficult to achieve optimal fitness, as mentioned in [24]. Due to the limited room for searching, it is challenging for ES to be applied to large Y in small λ_1. Finally, the mechanism of ES in the training phase of DHNN is only effective when λ_1 is small and effected by a high number of neurons because of the non-randomized operator [24]. The training phase can be improved further by embedding a learning algorithm in a DHNN and using global and local search operators [26]. This approach may aid in the search for optimal $\Theta_{\delta_\gamma 2SAT\rho}$ interpretations and ensures that logical inconsistencies are minimized.

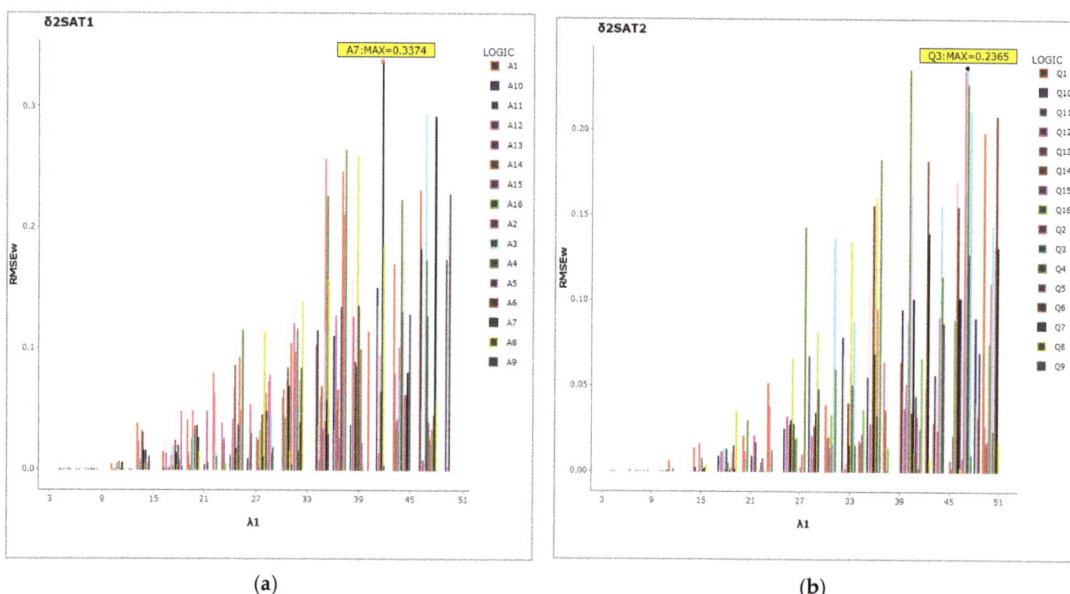

Figure 9. RMSEweight column representation for models in both types of logic (a) $\delta_1 2SAT\rho$, (b) $\delta_2 2SAT\rho$.

From Figure 9, column representation, the RMSEweight for two types $\delta_\gamma 2SAT\rho$ models help to better understand the fitness of the neuron state. Based on the results, the value of 0 was obtained in different quantities of λ_1 in the interval [5,18] in different models in both types of $\delta_\gamma 2SAT\rho$; then, the values started to fluctuate at large λ_1—the maximum RMSEweight values were reported for A7 and Q3, where the values of the negative literals were large ($\rho = 0.9$) and where λ_1 was large. In Table 13, which corresponds Figure 9, it is reported that the maximum RMSEweight values in terms of the median are A1(0.0791) and Q10(0.0548), wherein the ρ is small. In addition, a small result was reported for A16 (0.0075) and Q14(0.0048), where the negative numbers are large, which is clearly the result of the RMSEweight being affected by the fitness clauses that were measured by RMSEtrain, because the ES is could not find the interpretation for a clause with a high value of λ_1 then the DHNN could not derive the correct synaptic weight by WA methods when the result was more than zero. The fluctuation in the result is because the DHNN is selected the random number for weight if $E_{\Theta_{\delta 2SAT}} \neq 0$ after the number of iterations ϕ reaches the maximum. In conclusion, it is evident that two parameters, Y and ρ, have a direct impact on the probability distribution dataset during the testing phases.

Table 12. Maximum and minimum RMSEtrain results for models in both type of logic $\delta_1 2SAT\rho$, $\delta_2 2SAT\rho$ details by Wilcoxon test for median.

Y	Model	Min	Max	Median	W	Model	Min	Max	Median	W
0.6	A1	0	114.965	65.6734	78	Q1	0.0000	114.342	61.3433	91
	A2	0	113.345	62.2179	78	Q2	0.0000	113.745	59.2203	91
	A3	0	116.34	62.4112	78	Q3	0.0000	110.381	64.7599	91
	A4	0	118.895	56.8860	78	Q4	0.0000	106.132	64.1423	105
0.7	A5	0	111.853	65.3299	91	Q5	0.0000	93.0699	59.5461	55
	A6	0	113.982	67.6314	78	Q6	0.0000	93.8776	57.8688	55
	A7	0	116.327	63.0476	91	Q7	0.0000	101.459	58.5859	55
	A8	0	118.617	68.5274	91	Q8	0.0000	102.528	57.0719	55
0.8	A9	0	100.822	53.1695	120	Q9	0.0000	84.5754	41.8091	55
	A10	0	101.922	50.3786	120	Q10	0.0000	85.4868	41.6653	66
	A11	0	103.015	50.6162	120	Q11	0.0000	82.3286	43.8634	55
	A12	0	103.388	51.0294	136	Q12	0.0000	87.8521	44.6654	55
0.9	A13	0	78.5366	38.3444	45	Q13	5.8309	74.3707	41.7971	45
	A14	0	72.9383	38.16665	55	Q14	5.0000	71.2881	41.6413	45
	A15	0	76.0526	41.35185	55	Q15	1.0000	68.2202	42.4853	45
	A16	0	79.4921	41.86575	55	Q16	2.0000	73.2871	41.0488	45

Note: The results highlighted in yellow indicate the highest number in the column and the green indicates the smallest number in the column, (p-value < 0.00) for all models in terms of Wilcoxon test, it means reject H_0.

Table 13. Maximum and minimum RMSEweight results for models in both types of logic $\delta_1 2SAT\rho$, $\delta_2 2SAT\rho$ and details by Wilcoxon test for median.

Y	Model	Min	Max	Median	W	Model	Min	Max	Median	W
0.6	A1	0	0.2458	0.0791	91	Q1	0.0000	0.1978	0.0295	55
	A2	0	0.2567	0.0485	91	Q2	0.0000	0.2340	0.0241	55
	A3	0	0.2943	0.0321	78	Q3	0.0000	0.2365	0.0145	91
	A4	0	0.2642	0.0242	78	Q4	0.0000	0.2350	0.0193	105
0.7	A5	0	0.1134	0.0364	136	Q5	0.0000	0.1700	0.0093	55
	A6	0	0.0887	0.0397	78	Q6	0.0000	0.2077	0.0304	91
	A7	0	0.3374	0.0261	91	Q7	0.0000	0.1389	0.0319	91
	A8	0	0.2591	0.0138	78	Q8	0.0000	0.1598	0.0134	55
0.8	A9	0	0.2277	0.0175	91	Q9	0.0000	0.1268	0.0321	55
	A10	0	0.1821	0.0110	120	Q10	0.0000	0.1012	0.0548	55
	A11	0	0.2023	0.0228	120	Q11	0.0000	0.1079	0.0396	55
	A12	0	0.1265	0.0135	120	Q12	0.0000	0.0368	0.0207	66
0.9	A13	0	0.0790	0.0389	45	Q13	0.0004	0.0639	0.0178	45
	A14	0	0.0990	0.0250	55	Q14	0.0016	0.0358	0.0048	45
	A15	0	0.0423	0.0213	55	Q15	0.0005	0.0246	0.0171	45
	A16	0	0.0427	0.0075	55	Q16	0.0005	0.0885	0.0329	45

Note: The results highlighted in yellow indicate the highest number in the column and the green indicates the smallest number in the column, (p-value < 0.00) for all models in terms of Wilcoxon test, it means reject H_0.

6.3. Testing Phase Capability

Optimal testing phase is achieved when $E_{\Theta_{\delta 2SAT}} = 0$ retrieved optimal synaptic weight, after $DHNN - \delta 2SAT$ completing checking clause satisfaction and generating optimal synaptic weight through the WA method. The final state of the neuron will converge towards the global minimum energy. It is important to evaluate testing phase because DHNN frequently produces similar final neuron states as opposed to novel final neuron states [55]. Therefore, we compare the $\delta_\gamma 2SAT\rho$ logic with the recent logic systems by global minima ratio matric. If the model is unable to reach a global solution, this indicates that it is trapped in a local solution, which makes it impossible to determine whether the proposed $DHNN - \delta 2SAT$ is satisfied or not.

Figure 10, column representation, shows the global minima ratio results, calculated by Equation (26) for two types $\delta_\gamma 2SAT\rho$ and state-of-the-art logic systems, without considering any optimizer, to assess the actual testing phase capability for of $DHNN - \delta 2SAT$. Where the optimal result for global minima ratio R_G is 1, we can note in Figure 10 that all are capable of retrieving the optimal synaptic weight values in small λ_1 and then it decreases linearity with large λ_1, because the ES is unable to manage synaptic weight in the training phase and will be susceptible to retrieving non-optimal neuron states and ensnared in local minima. A model's ability to achieve maximum global minima ratio demonstrates that the suggested SAT is effectively integrated into DHNN. Maximum global minima ratio reported for YRAN2SAT, rSAT, and (A1, A11, Q11) models in $\delta_\gamma 2SAT\rho$. The reason for YRAN2SAT recorded the high global minima ratio for small λ_1 [26] because the flexibility in the structure offers an accurate result. Table 14 gives the Figure 10 numerical result, from the R_G median results without effect from the outliers, note both type $\delta_\gamma 2SAT\rho$ achieve near result to other latest logic systems. High median goes for MAJ2SAT because the structure of logic that (2SAT,3SAT) [23], also the fare literals state represent in rSAT [24] make it achieved highly R_G. Based on Table 14, from R_G median, there is a high effect for two parameters Y and ρ in $\delta_\gamma 2SAT\rho$, small λ_1 in the DHNN for small Y and ρ can retrieval the right synaptic weight such as (A1,Q1), but from median, the high Y and ρ achieved more global minimum than other such as A(13,14,15), Q(9,10,13,14). It can say the proposed models showcased the efficiency of $\delta_\gamma 2SAT\rho$ to control DHNN as a symbolic structure that causes network convergence. Since the local field in Equation (15) drives the neuron's final state in accordance with the behavior of the second and first-order clause, it exhibits the same behavior as the non-systematic RAN2SAT structure presented by [20].

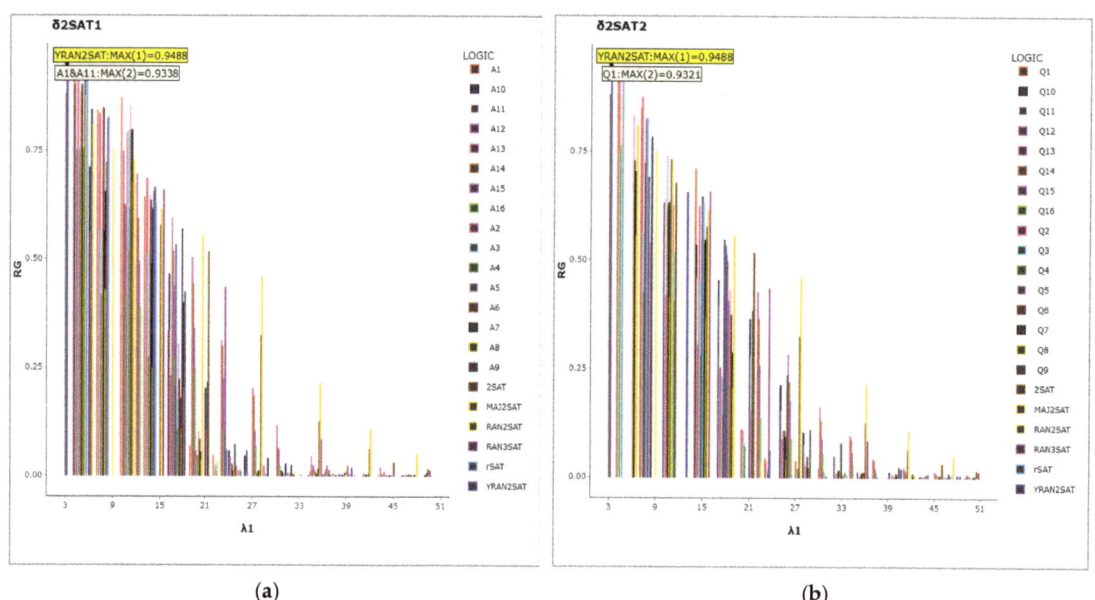

Figure 10. Column representation for models in both types of logic (**a**) $\delta_1 2SAT\rho$, (**b**) $\delta_2 2SAT\rho$ and recently developed logic systems.

Table 14. Maximum R_G results for models in both type of logic $\delta_1 2SAT\rho$, $\delta_2 2SAT\rho$ and RAN2SAT details by Wilcoxon test for median.

Model	Median	Max	W	Model	Median	Max	W
A1	0.0200	**0.9338**	66	Q1	0.0197	**0.9321**	105
A2	0.0133	0.9125	105	Q2	0.0152	0.9191	136
A3	0.0194	0.7945	91	Q3	0.0097	0.7479	136
A4	0.0077	0.7468	91	Q4	0.0099	0.7603	105
A5	0.0061	0.8855	91	Q5	0.0185	0.8322	78
A6	0.0096	0.9008	120	Q6	0.0299	0.7276	78
A7	0.0092	0.7970	120	Q7	0.0170	0.7025	78
A8	0.0058	0.7551	105	Q8	0.0162	0.5546	78
A9	0.0563	0.9093	190	Q9	**0.1084**	0.7822	91
A10	0.0437	0.9009	153	Q10	0.1014	0.6888	91
A11	0.0200	**0.9338**	66	Q11	0.0740	0.6787	91
A12	0.0204	0.7479	171	Q12	0.0240	0.5382	91
A13	**0.1576**	0.7467	78	Q13	0.0945	0.5113	45
A14	0.1226	0.6243	78	Q14	0.0864	0.4968	45
A15	0.0815	0.6197	78	Q15	0.0560	0.4055	45
A16	0.0434	0.4152	78	Q16	0.0261	0.2097	45
2SAT	0.4190	0.8789	55				
MAJ2SAT	**0.5050**	0.8076	36				
RAN2SAT	0.0172	0.8756	36				
RAN3SAT	0.2580	0.8213	21				
YRAN2SAT	0.0178	**0.9488**	21				
rSAT	0.0000	0.9200	28				

Note: The Yellow highlighted to indicate the highest number in the column, (p-value < 0.00) for all models in terms of Wilcoxon test, it means reject H_0.

The purpose of finding the RMSEenergy in Equation (27) is to calculate the difference between the final energy and the absolute minimum energy, as stated in condition Equation (18). indicates whether or not the solutions produced by $DHNN - \delta 2SAT$ are optimal, it must assess the flexibility of $\delta_\gamma 2SAT\rho$ by determining the value of RMSEenergy. Based on Figure 11 column representation, was reported to small λ_1 achieve less RMAEenergy value for all models, which indicates a successful convergence towards the optimal final neuron state, after which the final energy difference fluctuates as the number of λ_1 increased. This phenomenon occurs as a result of the decreased probability of receiving cost function $E_{\Theta_{\delta 2SAT}} = 0$, as clear in RMSEtrain which leads to higher energy, and $DHNN - \delta 2SAT$'s ineffective learning strategy. As the number of λ_1 increases, some synaptic weights become suboptimal, resulting in final neuron states stuck in local minimum energy. Additionally, Sathasivam [18] claims that during the DHNN testing phase, suboptimal neuron updates are what caused the local minimum energy to exist. Suboptimal neuron updates in this situation will result in more incomplete sentences, which raises the energy gap. When the logical formulation containing 2SAT was incorporated into $DHNN - \delta 2SAT$ we said the $\delta_\gamma 2SAT\rho$ behaved like the traditional non-systematic logical rule RAN2SAT. As shown in Figure 11 it can be observed that the adverse impact of negative literal with high number of λ_1 in logic where A4 Q12 recorded the highest value of RMSEenergy and A1 Q1 when number of λ_1 small is the opposite, from Table 15 gives from the Figure 11 the median of RMSEenergy gives us the accurate result where the small median go for A13, Q9 with low value parameter ρ and A8, A16 with high value parameter ρ give high RMSEenergy error. This demonstrates that when most neuron states are negative, tend to converge towards local minimum energy. In conclusion, it is evident that two parameters, Y and ρ, have a direct impact on the probability distribution dataset during the testing phases.

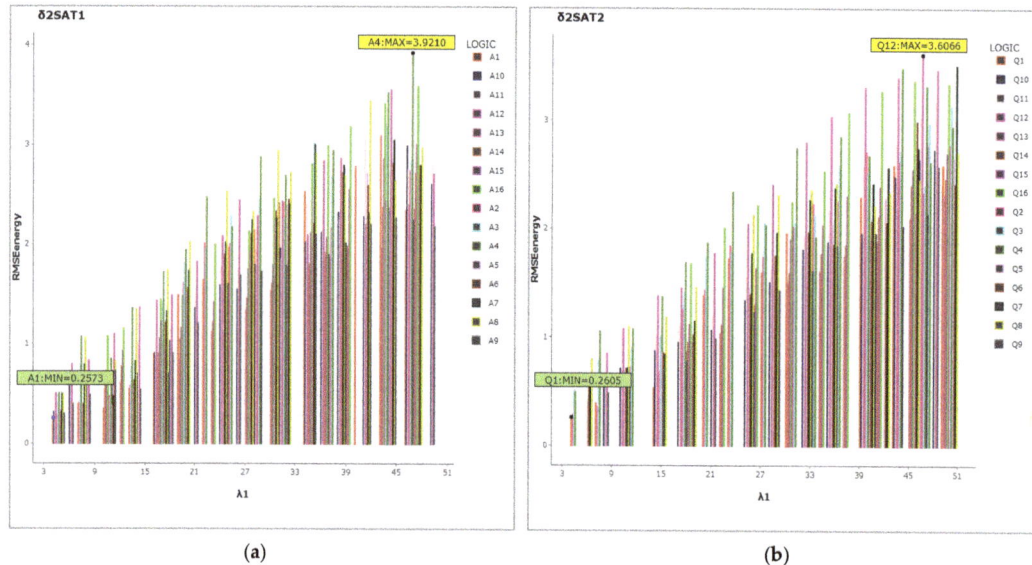

Figure 11. RMSEenergy column representation for models in both types of logic (a) $\delta_1 2SAT\rho$, (b) $\delta_2 2SAT\rho$.

Table 15. Maximum and minimum RMSEenergy results for models in both type of logic $\delta_1 2SAT\rho$, $\delta_2 2SAT\rho$ details by Wilcoxon test for median.

Model	Median	Min	Max	W	Model	Median	Min	Max	W
A1	1.8703	0.2573	3.0905	120	Q1	1.9596	0.2606	2.7905	120
A2	1.9854	0.2958	2.7368	105	Q2	1.9339	0.2844	2.7724	120
A3	2.1074	0.4555	3.1800	105	Q3	2.0517	0.5021	3.1297	136
A4	2.3208	0.5032	3.9210	105	Q4	2.1874	0.4896	3.4820	136
A5	1.9285	0.3384	2.7783	120	Q5	1.7077	0.4096	2.6531	78
A6	2.1017	0.3150	2.8161	120	Q6	1.8026	0.5526	2.9892	78
A7	2.2435	0.4680	3.0432	120	Q7	2.1137	0.5819	3.5014	78
A8	2.5302	0.4949	3.4379	120	Q8	2.2589	0.7982	2.7102	78
A9	1.6867	0.3012	2.2621	190	Q9	1.4306	0.4812	2.5811	91
A10	1.5883	0.3148	2.9905	190	Q10	1.5079	0.6127	2.7328	91
A11	1.7648	0.5055	3.0828	190	Q11	1.6259	0.6307	3.1733	91
A12	2.0895	0.5021	3.5483	190	Q12	2.4068	0.8465	3.6066	91
A13	1.4357	0.5445	2.3507	78	Q13	1.6090	0.8600	2.3148	45
A14	1.5348	0.7222	2.7120	78	Q14	1.7685	0.9484	2.4639	45
A15	1.7717	0.7171	3.0085	78	Q15	2.0352	1.1185	2.6995	45
A16	2.2963	1.0788	3.5845	78	Q16	2.5315	1.6824	3.3637	45

Note: The results highlighted in yellow indicate the highest number in the column and the green indicates the smallest number in the column, (p-value < 0.00) for all models in terms of Wilcoxon test, it means reject H_0.

6.4. Similarity Index Analysis

For final neurons' quality states only compare both type of $\delta_\gamma 2SAT\rho$ with RAN2SAT because $\delta_\gamma 2SAT\rho$ consider the enhancement and developing for RAN2SAT, also, they have the same structure behavior, we tested the variation introduced by the testing phase for $\delta_\gamma 2SAT\rho$ models and final neurons' quality state compared with RAN2SAT, where the degree of state redundancy for the DHNN model training phases is indicated by the similarity index of the final neuron state. A standard has been introduced indexing metrics, which is Sokal index, and consider the effective metric known as the ratio of total neurons variation R_{tv}.

Firstly, consider the lower Sokal in Equation (30) in the similarity index matrices indicates that the final neuron states obtained are highly distinct to the benchmark states. According to Figure 12, a column representation to both types of $\delta_\gamma 2SAT\rho$ reported low values, which imply higher more variety solution than other recorded by A16, Q16m but Q1, A5 recorded high value, due to parameter ρ. Table 16 translates Figure 12, which clarifies numerically, where the A16, Q16 reported low median value. Where all logic has the $\rho = 0.9$ and $Y = 0.9$ record low value, it indicates that there is more negative neuron and less first-order logic provides the final neuron state and the benchmark state distinction as shown in blue numbers in Table 16, Q, A (4,8,12,16). In other words, the low negativity and greater representation for first-order logic give us a high Sokal, as shown in Q, A (1,5,9,13) with a red number.

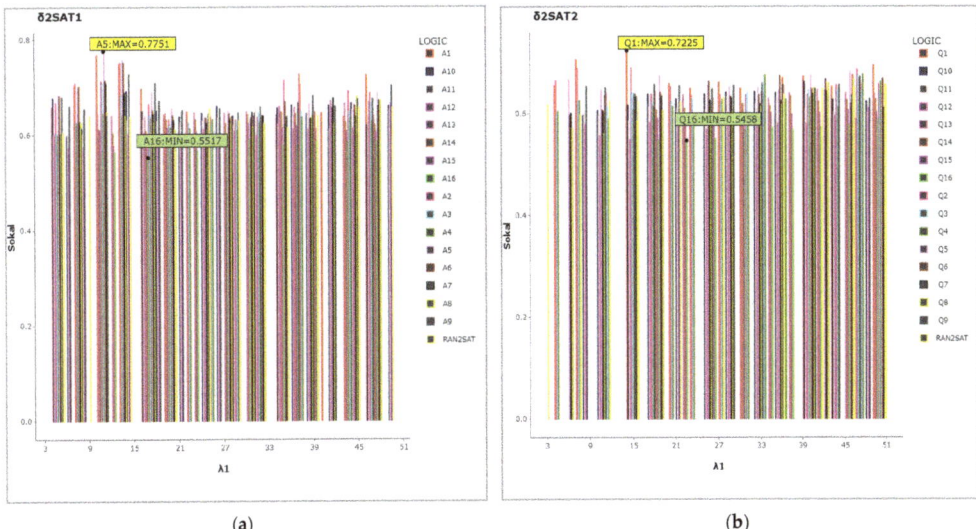

(a)   (b)

Figure 12. Sokal column representation for models in both types of logic (a) $\delta_1 2SAT\rho$, (b) $\delta_2 2SAT\rho$ and RAN2SAT.

Secondly, the effective parameter known as the ratio total variation of neurons R_{tv} In Equation (31). From the Figure 13 its clearly a column representation to both types giving us different number of variation solution for different number of λ_1 because of the effect of two parameter Y and ρ in the training phase. The highly oscillation recorded for $\delta_1 2SAT\rho$ in $14 < \lambda_1 < 20$ and $14 < \lambda_1 < 26$ for $\delta_1 2SAT\rho$ models and the highest oscillation value is recorded for A16 in $17 < \lambda_1 < 20$. For $\delta_2 2SAT\rho$. The highly oscillation recorded in $14 < \lambda_1 < 26$ for $\delta_1 2SAT\rho$ models and the highest oscillation value is traced for Q15 in $13 < \lambda_1 < 23$. At the same time both type of $\delta_\gamma 2SAT\rho$ models affected by a number of neurons, they start the ups and downs in different λ_1 according to the effect of two parameter Y and ρ. The total oscillation for some of models is rich to zero when $\lambda_1 < 5$, $\lambda_1 > 39$ such as A (1,3,4,5,8,10,12) and so low for others models $\delta_1 2SAT\rho$, also Q1,Q4 when $\lambda_1 < 5$, $\lambda_1 > 35$ for $\delta_2 2SAT\rho$, we can be said there are no significant variations for high than 37, also we can note here the effect of Y, it can't achieve the global solution for low Y because the ES will disturb the $\delta_\gamma 2SAT\rho$ model in order to reach the optimal training phase (known as learn inconsistent interpretation), from Figure 10, global solutions acquired by $\delta_\gamma 2SAT\rho$ models grow as λ_1 decrease as introduce previously. Table 17 for numerical result for Figure 13 note the effect of increase ρ where the logic has $\rho > 0.7$ recorded the highest high number of R_{tv}, where the highest variation go for A16 (0.2149) and Q15 (0.2084), and also can see the $\delta_2 2SAT\rho$ record high R_{tv} than $\delta_1 2SAT\rho$ in general, the reason her the $\delta_2 2SAT\rho$ give less number of first-order logic than $\delta_1 2SAT\rho$ for the same Y that was mention previously in Table 1, then the ES will deal with fewer numbers for first-order logic where it difficult to reach the optimal training phase. Moreover, Figure 13 presents the reason for the decrease when

λ_1 increases the hard achieved global solution. It was observed that the RAN2SAT behave similarly to the $\delta_\gamma 2SAT\rho$, with a high R_{tv} recorded of (0.1764) at the same time as its increase in the interval $13 < \lambda_1 < 42$ and then decrease with a high λ_1. The impact of the global minimum solution R_{tv} is related to the number of neurons. As λ_1 rises, the probability of the number of global solutions reduces. We can conclude from the above results that R_{tv} is related to the occurrence of other neuron states that lead to global minimum solutions in other domain adaptations [22].

Table 16. Maximum and minimum Sokal results for models in both types of logic $\delta_1 2SAT\rho$, $\delta_2 2SAT\rho$ and RAN2SAT details by Wilcoxon test for median.

Model	Median	Min	Max	W	Model	Median	Min	Max	W
A1	0.6483	0.6367	0.7667	120	Q1	0.6601	0.6350	0.7225	120
A2	0.6771	0.6212	0.7512	105	Q2	0.6527	0.6337	0.6887	136
A3	0.6335	0.6020	0.7074	105	Q3	0.6341	0.5993	0.6747	136
A4	0.6286	0.5988	0.6447	105	Q4	0.6189	0.5884	0.6757	136
A5	0.6632	0.6360	0.7751	120	Q5	0.6509	0.6324	0.6810	78
A6	0.6556	0.6329	0.7509	120	Q6	0.6385	0.5965	0.6730	78
A7	0.6369	0.6000	0.7074	120	Q7	0.6271	0.5997	0.6423	78
A8	0.6232	0.6024	0.6790	120	Q8	0.6095	0.5593	0.6662	78
A9	0.6594	0.6374	0.7266	190	Q9	0.6536	0.6284	0.6709	91
A10	0.6493	0.5974	0.6915	190	Q10	0.6276	0.5960	0.6614	91
A11	0.6288	0.5987	0.6547	190	Q11	0.6051	0.5850	0.6322	91
A12	0.6027	0.5702	0.6702	190	Q12	0.5790	0.5468	0.6096	91
A13	0.6453	0.6377	0.6651	78	Q13	0.6385	0.6167	0.6459	45
A14	0.6277	0.6031	0.6475	78	Q14	0.6228	0.6058	0.6335	45
A15	0.6080	0.5770	0.6227	78	Q15	0.5977	0.5836	0.6060	45
A16	0.5783	0.5517	0.5890	78	Q16	0.5665	0.5458	0.5863	45
RAN2SAT	0.6379	0.6007	0.6564	55					

Note: The results highlighted in yellow indicate the highest number in the column and the green indicates the smallest number in the column, (p-value < 0.00) for all models in terms of Wilcoxon test, it means reject H_0.

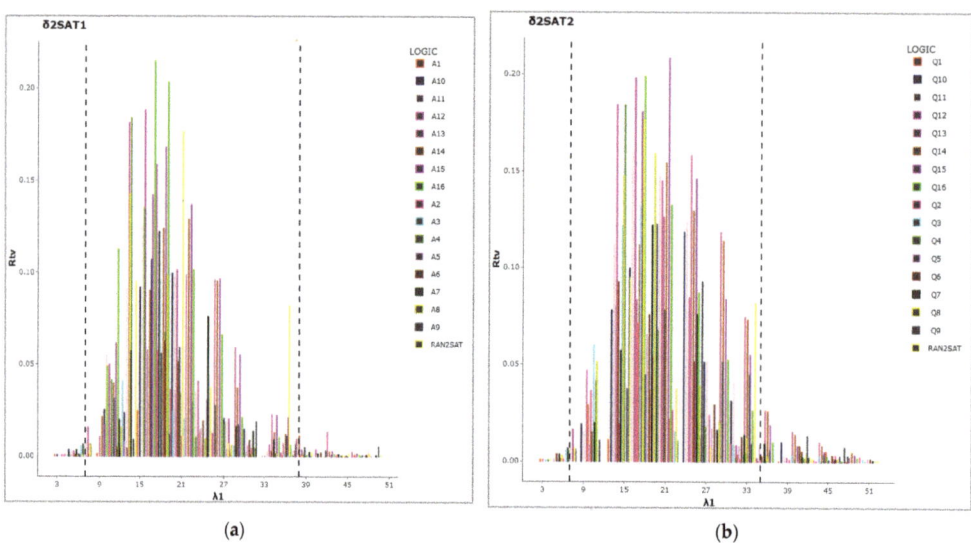

Figure 13. Column representation for models in both types of logic (**a**) $\delta_1 2SAT\rho$, (**b**) $\delta_2 2SAT\rho$ and RAN2SAT.

Table 17. Maximum and minimum R_{tv} results for models in both types of logic $\delta_1 2SAT\rho$, $\delta_2 2SAT\rho$ and RAN2SAT.

Model	Min	Max	Model	Min	Max
A1	0.0000	0.0246	Q1	0.0000	0.0364
A2	0.0003	0.0573	Q2	0.0002	0.0712
A3	0.0000	0.0962	Q3	0.0001	0.1327
A4	0.0000	0.1469	Q4	0.0000	0.1840
A5	0.0000	0.0347	Q5	0.0003	0.0804
A6	0.0004	0.0624	Q6	0.0013	0.0926
A7	0.0001	0.1031	Q7	0.0006	0.1219
A8	0.0000	0.1423	Q8	0.0002	0.1587
A9	0.0005	0.059	Q9	0.0028	0.0929
A10	0.0000	0.1067	Q10	0.0007	0.1225
A11	0.0002	0.1413	Q11	0.0003	0.1596
A12	0.0000	0.188	Q12	0.0002	0.1979
A13	0.0027	0.0984	Q13	0.002	0.1581
A14	0.0009	0.1288	Q14	0.0047	0.1542
A15	0.0015	0.1678	Q15	0.0033	0.2084
A16	0.0008	0.2149	Q16	0.0018	0.1987
RAN2SAT	0.0004	0.1764			

Note: The results highlighted in yellow indicate the highest number in the column and the green indicates the smallest number in the column.

6.5. Synaptic Weight Analysis

The mean is important because it signifies the location of the dataset's centre value, it contains information from each observation in a dataset. When a dataset is skewed or contains outliers, the mean may be untrue. We are utilizing various statistical tests to aid us comprehend the behaviors of synaptic weight to deduce information about the performance of logic in the training phases for further inquiry in synaptic weight distribution. The descriptive statistic of mean synaptic weight is a novel perspective in synaptic weight analysis, and we consider the mean of full logic to obtain a meaningful result in this analysis of our study by using the following formula:

$$\text{Mean of } \delta 2SAT = \sum_{i=1}^{\eta \times v} \left(\frac{\sum_{i=1}^{\eta} W_{ri} + \sum_{j=1}^{\eta} W_{rj} + \sum_{j=1}^{\eta} W_{rjrj+1}}{\lambda_1} \right) \quad (37)$$

where $W_{ri} = \pm 0.5$ synaptic weight for first-order logic, $W_{rj} = \pm 0.25$ synaptic weight for second-order logic literals, $W_{rjrj+1} = \pm 0.25$ synaptic weight for second-order logic clauses. An example of the formula is shown as follows:

$$\begin{cases} \delta 2SAT = \neg a \wedge b \wedge (\neg e \vee \neg f) \wedge (\neg k \vee l) \\ \text{Mean of } \delta 2SAT = \frac{-.5 + .5 + (-.25 - .25 - .25) + (-.25 + .25 + .25)}{6} = 0.0833 \end{cases} \quad (38)$$

The center value located in a dataset is carries a piece of information from every observation in a dataset; accordingly the mean will give the information of the center value for all synaptic weight in logic, where they affect together in cos function on training phases, in this study the mean for 100 combinations been calculated in training phase as sampling size for each logic in both type of $\delta_\gamma 2SAT\rho$, so we have 100 individual results for the means that have the same characteristic in two parameters Y and ρ. It is worth noting that all means' values were tested first using appropriate tests that yielded significant p-values to ensure a correct outcome. The logic value signifies that features will be statistically defined by the curve of probability density function $f(x)$, representing points and (boxplot and whiskers), denoted as (Raincloud Plot), and we want to achieve the following by using these figures:

(a) The probability density function $f(x)$ the curve will give an accurate result data behaviors (symmetric or skewness) so that we can determine if there is an outlier or if all value is distributed normality in the $\delta_1 2SAT\rho$ and $\delta_2 2SAT\rho$ logic (a normal bell curve indicating there is no outlier, and this logic has a high probability of achieving satisfaction in terms of Y and ρ).

(b) The representing points the spread of mean values, while the boxplot and whiskers explain the amount of spread around the median, along with the details of an outlier from the median value given by whiskers sides.

This investigation will look at the impact of mean value analysis in evaluating the $DHNN - \delta 2SAT$ during the training phase. We consider the highest λ_1 in each logic systems combination to calculate the mean, so we have λ_1 between 48,50 to obtain more accurate results. In the training phase, the synaptic mean value was determined using the ES effect to uncover inconsistent interpretations that offer us a basic understanding about the behavior of logic and achieving satisfied. There are 4 figures for both types of $\delta_\gamma 2SAT\rho$, each figure includes a probability density function curve, the representing point, and (boxplot and whiskers), its classification depending on the Y values in both types of $\delta_\gamma 2SAT\rho$, where they have the same structure because it is the key affected parameter in the mean values discussed as follows: For both $\delta_1 2SAT\rho$ and $\delta_2 2SAT\rho$:

(a) When $Y = 0.6$ noted the following from Figure 14:

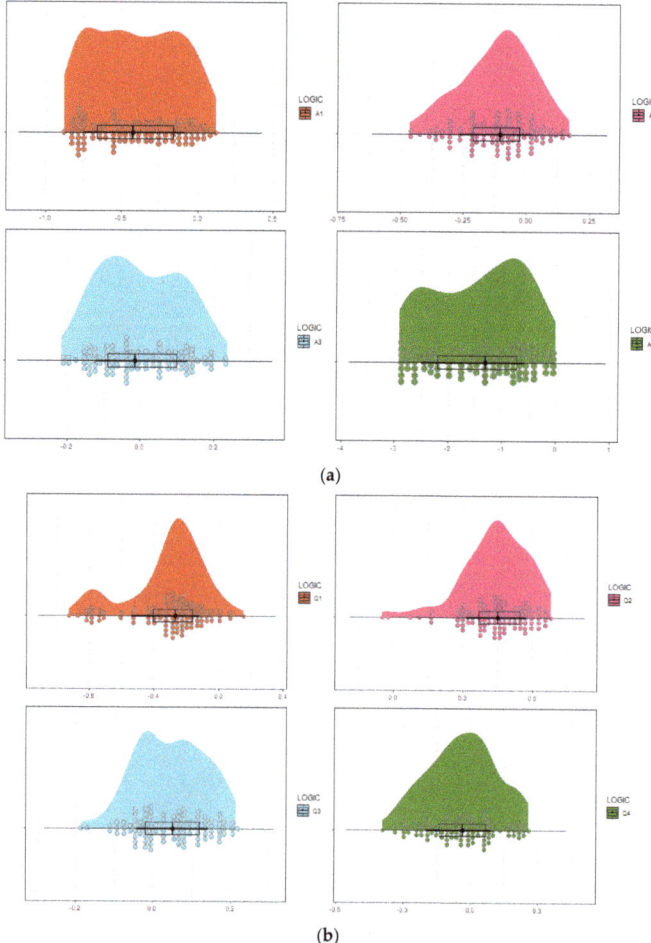

Figure 14. The Raincloud Plot analysis for (a) $\delta_1 2SAT\rho$, (b) $\delta_2 2SAT\rho$ synaptic weight means when $Y = 0.6$.

$\delta_1 2SAT\rho$ probability function curve shows thin-tailed on two sides, so it is fairly to be a symmetric ship, which indicates that outliers are infrequent (an observation is considered an outlier if it differs numerically from the rest of the data), and the values for the mean tend to be normal for A (1,2,3,4), whereas the probability function curve Q3,4 are similar in behavior for $\delta_1 2SAT\rho$. It is fairly to a symmetric ship, so it has thin tailed on two sides and rare outliers, but Q1,2 shows different results because it tends to be non-symmetric by the heavier tail on the left which means that there are a lot of outliers. This result will be supported by the boxplot and whiskers. When we look at interquartile ranges, IQR (the lengths of the boxes), the longer it is, the more dispersed the data are, and the shorter it is, the less dispersed the data are. It can be observed that the $\delta_1 2SAT\rho$ is highly dispersed from the median compared to $\delta_2 2SAT\rho$ since the IQR range is higher in A (1,2,3,4) than Q (1,2,3,4). In addition, in terms of outlier, when checking a box plot, an outlier is defined as a data point that lies outside the box plot's whiskers, the $\delta_1 2SAT\rho$ and $\delta_2 2SAT\rho$ have the approximate behavior of a huge outlier, but it can be noted that the $\delta_1 2SAT\rho$ has more outlier than $\delta_2 2SAT\rho$ because ES could not achieve inconsistent interpretation in the training phase due to the $\delta_2 2SAT\rho$ models structure that leads to a random value for synaptic weight. Finally, the boxplot clearly shows that the distribution is nonsymmetric for $\delta_1 2SAT\rho$ and $\delta_2 2SAT\rho$, as previously explained (the distribution is symmetric when the median is in the center of the box and the whiskers are nearly the same on both sides of the box), in both logic systems. The reasons for these results are:

In terms of Y parameter, the number of first-order logic that has a $p(x_m) = 0.4$ in logic value that pulls the logic curve to the sides because the suboptimal synaptic weight for first-order logic is clearly in the distribution tail and box-whiskers plot also $\delta_2 2SAT\rho$ has more 2SAT than $\delta_1 2SAT\rho$ for the same Y parameter, and that reflects in the spread of value in the boxplot, which is high in $\delta_1 2SAT\rho$. This indicates a high variation between the mean values ES failed to find a consistent interpretation. In terms of ρ parameter, from the boxplot also, we can observe that the effect of ρ gives more negative synaptic weight, but we should also consider the value of W_{BB} that was positive in clauses $(\neg r_i \lor r_j)$, $(r_i \lor \neg r_j)$ and $(r_i \lor r_j)$ that affected 2SAT clauses mean values, because it is noted in $\delta_2 2SAT\rho$ there is no effect for ρ, as mentioned previously, it has more 2SAT clauses than $\delta_1 2SAT\rho$ for the same Y. Therefore, the ES tend to obtain consistent interpretation that is reflected in the mean values of whole synaptic weight logic. Conversely, for $\delta_1 2SAT\rho$ the effect of ρ is clearer in the mean values, with most points of the values located on the negative side.

(b) When $Y = 0.7$ noted the following from Figure 15 as follows:

The probability function curve for $\delta_1 2SAT\rho$ exhibits the same behavior for $Y = 0.6$, indicating that it is a symmetric ship with normal mean values. It has a thin tailed on two sides, so outliers are infrequent. For $\delta_2 2SAT\rho$ it is a little different, all Q (5,6,7,8) is symmetric. Then, the mean values tend to be normal and have a light tail, except for Q6, as we see in the curve, it is a fat tail, therefore there are a lot of outliers on both sides. The boxplot and whiskers tell the same story for $Y = 0.6$. When we look at the box side, we can see that the $\delta_1 2SAT\rho$ is highly dispersed from the median compared than the $\delta_2 2SAT\rho$ because the value of IQR is higher in A (4,5,6,7) than the Q (4,5,6,7). Moreover, in terms of an outlier, we can observe that the $\delta_1 2SAT\rho$ and $\delta_2 2SAT\rho$ both have the approximate behavior of a huge outlier, but the $\delta_1 2SAT\rho$ is more outlier than $\delta_2 2SAT\rho$ except for Q6. Most logic has an outlier and, at the same time, is a short box (which implies that high-frequency data tends to be more fat-tailed). Finally, from the boxplot, the non-symmetric shape in both for $\delta_1 2SAT\rho$ and $\delta_2 2SAT\rho$ can be seen clearly. The reasons for these results are justified as follows:

In terms of Y parameter, the number of second-order logic clauses that have a $p(x_m) = 0.3$ is considered a bit high, especially in high λ_1 which generates $E_{\Theta_{\delta 2SAT}} \neq 0$ that pulls the logic curve to the two sides because the suboptimal synaptic weight is clearly in the tail of probability curve distribution and boxplot-whiskers. For $\delta_2 2SAT\rho$, it has more 2SAT clauses than $\delta_1 2SAT\rho$, for the same Y parameter. This reflects in the spread of value in the boxplot at its highest more than in $\delta_1 2SAT\rho$. Therefore, it shows a high variation between mean values because ES failed to find consistent interpretations. In terms of ρ parameter, boxplot in $\delta_1 2SAT\rho$ and $\delta_2 2SAT\rho$ are reflected in a negative synaptic weight value. Both models have the parameter of $Y = 0.6$, the spread of data affected by ρ in 2SAT clauses and it affects the value of the mean which tends to be positive, as we mentioned previously. Finally, as seen in the Q6, the reasons for right fat-tailed the number of high second-order logic sentences that generate suboptimal synaptic weight, resulting in positive mean values.

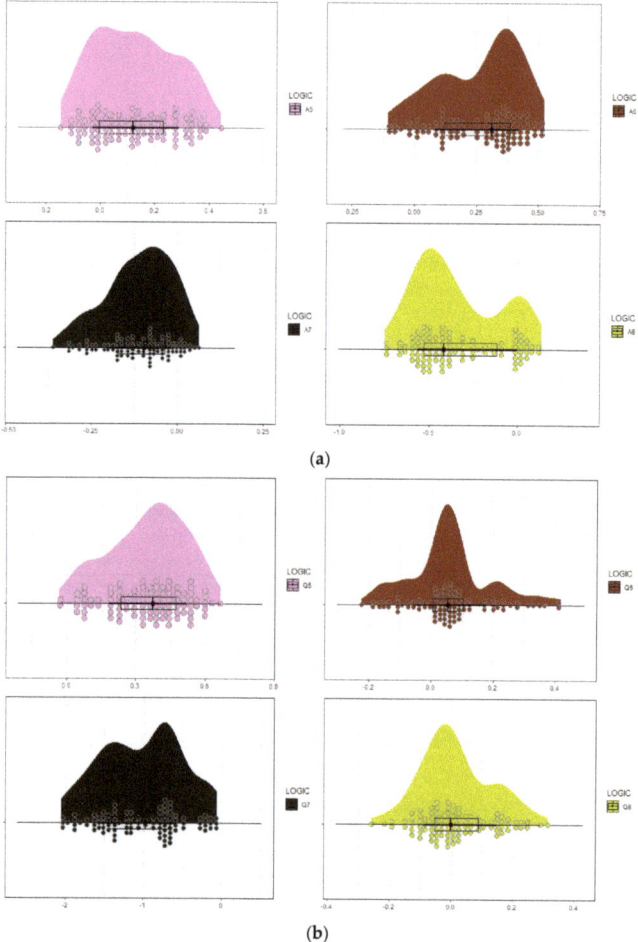

Figure 15. The Raincloud Plot analysis for (**a**) $\delta_1 2SAT\rho$, (**b**) $\delta_2 2SAT\rho$ synaptic weight means when $Y = 0.7$.

(c) When $Y = 0.8$ is observed from Figure 16 as follows:

Where the 2SAT clauses are the common clauses, for $\delta_1 2SAT\rho$ the curve shows semi normal ship in A (9.11,12) with a semi skewed in A10, the light tail on the two sides with less outlier is in all $\delta_1 2SAT\rho$. On the other side, $\delta_2 2SAT\rho$ gives near result where Q (10,12) is fairly to be symmetric ship, the mean values tend to be normal, it has a thin-tailed in two sides, Q (9.11) tend to be non-symmetric, the light tail in the two sides with less outlier is on all $\delta_2 2SAT\rho$. The boxplot and whiskers for $\delta_1 2SAT\rho$ and $\delta_2 2SAT\rho$, is highly sparse from the median comparison because the IQR range is higher in A (9,10,11,12) than Q (9,11,12), and shorter in Q10. In the terms outlier, from a box plot whiskers, the $\delta_1 2SAT\rho$ and $\delta_2 2SAT\rho$ have approximate behavior of huge outliers on both sides, but we can note the Q11 is more outlier on the left than others and Q9 is more outlier on the right. Finally, based on the boxplot, it clarifies both logic systems have non symmetric curves. The reasons for these results are justified as follows:

In terms of Y parameter, the number of first-order logic clauses that have a small appearance probability that makes the range values of mean is high in the two previous Figures 14 and 15. It is clear here in these figures the $\delta_1 2SAT\rho$, $\delta_2 2SAT\rho$ obtaining (0.5) synaptic weight is small, so most of the means value range is small that led to less spread curve line, on the other side, the high representation of 2SAT clauses makes the length of the box highest because the volatile in the mean values of 2SAT clauses it gives a different result depending on negative literal, where $(\neg r_i \vee r_j)$, $(r_i \vee \neg r_j)$ and $(r_i \vee r_j)$ have the mean values different from $(\neg r_i \vee \neg r_j)$ the effect also by ES algorithm searching and that effect in cost function in Equation (12), that pull the logic curve and boxplot-whiskers into sides, that reflects in the spread of values in boxplot its highest than in $Y = 0.6, 0.7$. In terms of ρ parameter, its high effect here, in boxplot in $\delta_1 2SAT\rho$ and $\delta_2 2SAT\rho$ is clearly in the range of values, most of it full in the negative side, more clearly in Q, A(11,12) because the mean values of full negative second-order logic clauses it is highest here as we clarify in FNAE matric. It is also noted for Q (9,10), A10 is in the positive side because the ρ is small therefore, the mean will be positive and ES algorithm searching tend to find inconsistent interpretation. This indicates the effect of the parameter ρ but A9 still has first-order logic, which makes the data spread in two sides with light tail. However, in Q10 and Q12, the tail because the extreme mean values that come from full negative clauses and first-order logic clauses.

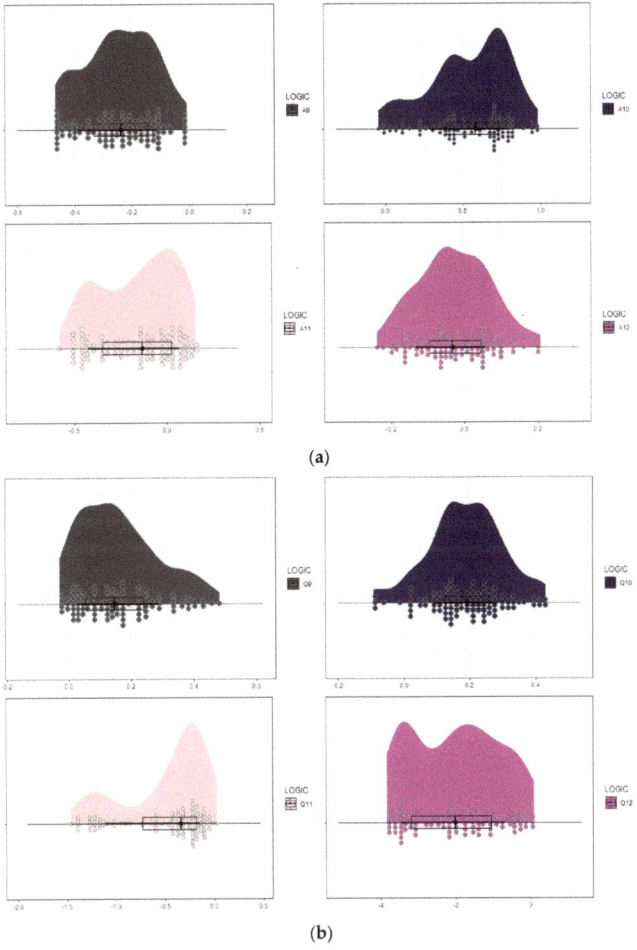

Figure 16. The Raincloud Plot analysis for (**a**) $\delta_1 2SAT\rho$, (**b**) $\delta_2 2SAT\rho$ synaptic weight means when.

(d)　　When $Y = 0.9$ is observed from Figure 17 as follows:

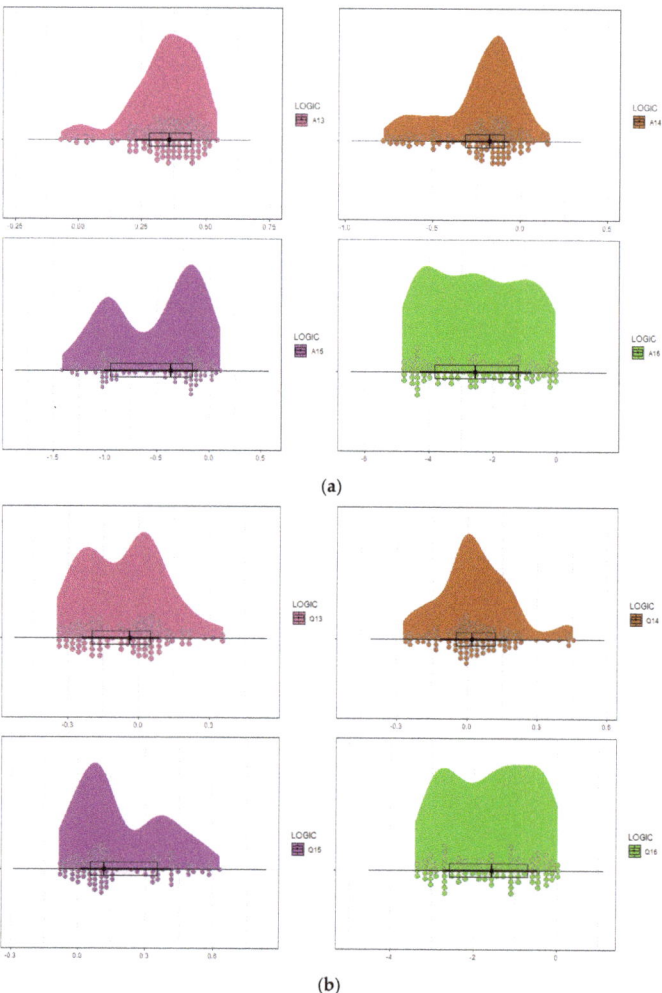

Figure 17. The Raincloud Plot analysis for (**a**) $\delta_1 2SAT\rho$, (**b**) $\delta_2 2SAT\rho$ synaptic weight means when $Y = 0.9$.

The $\delta_1 2SAT\rho$ probability function curve indicates that it is reasonable to be a symmetric shape in A(15,16), but A14 tends to be non-symmetric, with a thin tail in two sides, implying that outliers are infrequent. Whereas A13 is left–right skewed and heavy-tailed, which implies that there a lot of outliers on the left, but in $\delta_2 2SAT\rho$, Q (13,14,16) is symmetrical. While Q15 tends to be non-symmetric, they have a thin tailed on two sides, implying that outliers are infrequent. Moreover, Q14 is heavily tailed which indicates there is a lot of outliers, but Q13, 16 have light tails and outliers are infrequent. When we look at interquartile ranges, we can observe that $\delta_1 2SAT\rho$, A (15,16) is considerably distributed from the median compared to A (13,14) because the IQR range is similarly high in $\delta_2 2SAT\rho$. Meanwhile, Q (13,15,16) is highly dispersed from the median compared to Q (14) because the IQR range is highest in terms of an outlier. When reviewing box whiskers, the $\delta_1 2SAT\rho$ and $\delta_2 2SAT\rho$ have the approximate behavior of a huge outlier however, we can note that Q, A (13,14,) is more outlier than Q, A (15,16). Finally, from the boxplot, it is clearly the non-symmetric for $\delta_1 2SAT\rho$ and $\delta_2 2SAT\rho$ as we previously mentioned. The reasons for these results are justified as follows:

In terms of Y parameter, the number of second-order logic clauses that have the smallest appearance, so the mean values are high, is clear in the $\delta_1 2SAT\rho$, $\delta_2 2SAT\rho$ figures. Moreover, the majority of 2SAT clauses representing, make the spread in all length box highest in $\delta_1 2SAT\rho$, $\delta_2 2SAT\rho$

because of the volatility in the mean of 2SAT clauses, as mentioned previously. This effect in the logic curve and pulling the logic curve into the two sides also for boxplot-whiskers, which reflect in the dispersion of value in boxplot is more than $Y = 0.6, 0.7$. In terms of the ρ parameter, it has a high effect as well, in the boxplot in $\delta_1 2SAT\rho$ and $\delta_2 2SAT\rho$, it is clearly in the range of value, most of it fails in the negative side also more clearly in Q, A (15,16) because the mean of full negative second-order logic clauses is highest here. As we explain in the FNAE metric, for other logic A, Q (14, 13) still has more first-order logic, which causes the mean spread in two directions and a heavy tail in Q14 and A13 due to the extrema value that occurs due to the full negative clauses and second-order logic clauses.

From this result, we can note the significance of the synaptic weight analysis; it gives a summary of the search space area for a specific algorithm in training phases, and it is clarified by the mean synaptic weight results, which give the center of search space (optimal) and the wide by the range of spread (suboptimal) from the previous result the mean synaptic weight gives a general perspective for the mechanism of ES algorithm in this search space. Thus, we can observe the behavior of working in this limited space, as well as the behaviors of obtaining a solution using optimal and suboptimal synaptic weights. The ES has a unique search space that is heavily influenced by the number of neurons and the structure of logic.

6.6. The Limitation of the DHNN-δ2SAT

One of the limitations of $DHNN - \delta 2SAT$ in this study is that the proposed hybrid network DHNN only considers propositional logic programming. The DHNN is unable to embed other variant of logic, such as predicate logic, fuzzy logic, or probabilistic logic due to the nature of Hopfield Neural Network proposed by Pinkas [56] that are limited to symmetric connectionist network, as well as the DHNN's low storage capacity and the cost function proposed by Wan Abdullah (1992), which only considers bipolar neurons. Conversely, this study takes a number of neurons limits is less than 52 because of ES. Consequently, as we improve, will replace ES by metaheuristics such as Artificial Bee Colony Algorithm [57] and Election Algorithm [58]. Despite DHNN flexibility, $\delta 2SAT$'s the quality of solutions offered needed to be improved. We can increase the iterations numbers required in our simulations by increasing the number of learning. The proposed model may yield more variation neurons, less errors, and a global minimum solution with more iterations.

6.7. Summary

In this section, we provide a brief summary of the beneficial properties of the logical structure of the proposed model; moreover, we provide a simple summary of the most important accomplishments of the proposed logic system, clarifying the findings given in the Results and Discussion section with respect to the following points:

(a) Probability logic phases were applied to introduce various models to address dataset-related requirements. Notably, one of the most significant advantages of $\delta kSAT$ is that it can generate multifarious models by controlling parameters that are revealed from the dataset features in the logic system. It is a flexible logic system, but this is not discussed in this study. The parameters can be used to generate models of logic that can be systematic when $p(x_m) = 0$, transforming to 2SAT and when $p(y_m) = 0$, it becomes first-order logic or it can be high-order non-systematic when $k = 3$, and it can be SRAN3SAT for order $k = 1, 2, 3$ or $k = 2, 3$ or $k = 1, 3$ by adding a new parameter $p(z_m)$. In this case, regarding the probability of third clauses, we consider the probability concept $p(z_m) + p(y_m) + p(x_m) = 1$, when $p(y_m) = 0$ and $p(x_m) = 0$, it becomes 3SAT. The main differences between $\delta kSAT$ and other logic systems such as YRAN2SAT, RAN3SAT, and RAN2SAT, as well as other systematic logic systems such as 2SAT and 3SAT, are the factors of probability, wherein the dataset will choose the best structure by controlling the probability parameter; in addition, the terms of negative literals determined from the dataset and distributed in clauses depend on the probability parameter, whose two main features render the $\delta kSAT$ unique.

(b) The testing and the training phases were examined. By applying Equations (24) and (25) in the testing phase, the results show that the proposed model obtained optimal synaptic weight after checking the clauses' satisfaction. It also generated optimal synaptic weight through the WA method for the small number of neurons and high parameter values. Equations (26) and (27) in the training phase showed that the efficiency of the probability logic phase produced various logical structures in the DHNN compared to the current systems.

(c) A novel analysis of the synaptic weight for $DHNN - \delta 2SAT$ was introduced, which was termed the descriptive statistic of mean synaptic weight. Previously, there have been various statistical tests used to study the behaviors of synaptic weight to deduce information about the performance of a proposed logic system in the training phases. Whereas, in this study, the descriptive statistical method analyzed the synaptic weight distribution by obtaining the mean of the synaptic weight in the testing phase.

(d) Notably, in the Results and Discussion section, the sample size in Equation (5) gives us the best number of negative literals for the desired logic needed to obtain satisfaction. Of particular significance are the models $\delta_1 2SAT\rho$ and $\delta_2 2SAT\rho$, which have a high proportion ($\rho = 0.9$) and high probability ($Y = 0.9$) introduced by probability logic phases, have the best structure as clarified by the measures used in the study (PON, NAE, and FNAE), and tended to be the best models in the training and testing phases, which are also shown by the similarity index measures. This result is the opposite of that obtained by Zamri et al. [24], which concluded a value of $r = 0.5$ for negative literal works efficiently in the logic phase and yielded a better structure than (r = 0.1, 0.9). The reason behind these contrary findings is that the proportion is dependent on the d value in Equation (6), which gives a margin of error dependent on the Z value; additionally, there is the probability of second-order logic Y drawn from the dataset, which affected the $\delta_\gamma 2SAT\rho$ models—all these factors rendered it the best in terms of logic structure.

(e) In this study, the probability distribution from the contributed data set successfully generated an efficient, new logical structure for a DHNN. The discussion section considered the introduction of the comparative analysis of the $\delta 2SAT$ with other existing SATs, for which the proposed model was superior in several aspects, as shown in Table 18.

Table 18. A summary of comparative analysis between $\delta 2SAT$ and other SATs.

Contribution	$\delta 2SAT$	rSAT	MAJ2SAT	2SAT	RAN3SAT	RAN2SAT	YRAN2SAT
Organized phase	✓	✓					
System for selecting clauses	✓		✓				
System for selecting negative literals	✓	✓					
Systematic structure	✓			✓			✓
Non-Systematic structure	✓	✓	✓		✓	✓	✓

7. Conclusions and Future Work

It is critical to create a non-systematic logical framework in a DHNN, employing parameters conducive to building a flexible final neuronal state. This study introduced a new probability logic phase that assigns the probability of the first- and second-order clauses and the desired negative literals appearing in each sentence, which helped to address the requirements of datasets. Statistical tools govern the creation of $\Theta_{\delta 2SAT}$ during the probability logic phase. The novel logic probability phase of the proposed $\delta 2SAT$ model provides a new enhancement with which to shape the logic structure according to the dataset, for which it was found that these models have high values in two parameters ($Y = 0.9, \rho = 0.9$) of two $\delta_\gamma 2SAT\rho$ types, which introduced efficient logic structures in the probability logic phase. The new logic was embedded in the $DHNN - \delta 2SAT$ by reducing the logical inconsistency of the corresponding zero-cost function's logical rule. The achieved cost function that corresponds to satisfaction was used to calculate the synaptic weight of the DHNN's effectiveness with a $\delta 2SAT$ logical structure, which was examined using three proposal metrics in comparison with state-of-the-art methods, such as 2SAT, MAJ2SAT, RAN2SAT, RAN3SAT, YRAN2SAT, and rSAT. The final neuron state was assessed based on various initial neuron states, statical method parameters, and various metric performances, such as learning errors, synaptic weight errors, energy profiles, testing errors, and similarity metrics, which were compared with existing benchmark works. To further demonstrate the efficiency and robustness of the proposed $\Theta_{\delta 2SAT}$, it was validated using four different second-order probability distributions with four different proportions of extensive simulations. Further, a new prospective logical investigation was introduced in this study, which consisted of the analysis of the mean of synaptic weight for $DHNN - \delta 2SAT$ to evaluate the existence of a flexible logical structure. The findings demonstrated that the proposed $\delta 2SAT$ was successful in achieving a flexible logical structure with a prevailing attribute dataset compared to other state-of-the-art SAT. For future work: (1) A metaheuristic analysis of the probability logic phase would aid the selection of the negative literals' positions in a logic system. (2) A metaheuristic analysis of the training phases would aid the satisfaction of Equation (12). (3) A metaheuristic analysis of the testing phases would aid the generation of a vast range of space solutions. (4) Synaptic weight analysis can be applied in the training phases to address the effects of the energy function and global solutions on the synaptic weight. Moreover, we can add the measure of variability to address the deviation in the results. Notably, the robust architecture of ANNs integrated with our proposed logic would serve as a good foundation for real-life applications such as Natural Disaster prediction. In this context, each neuron would represent the attributes from the data, such as rainfall trends, river levels, and drainage and ground conditions. These attributes will be embedded into the logic-mining approach proposed by [45], which will lead to the formation of induced logic, which, in turn, has predictive and classificatory abilities. In other developments, the proposed logic system would be indispensable in finding the optimal route in the Travelling Salesman Problem.

Author Contributions: Conceptualization, methodology, software, writing—original draft preparation, S.A.; formal analysis, validation, N.E.Z.; supervision and funding acquisition, M.S.M.K.; writing—review and editing, G.M.; visualization, N.A.; project administration, M.A.M. All authors have read and agreed to the published version of the manuscript.

Funding: This research was supported by Ministry of Higher Education Malaysia for Transdisciplinary Research Grant Scheme (TRGS) with Project Code: TRGS/1/2022/USM/02/3/3.

Data Availability Statement: Not applicable.

Acknowledgments: The authors would like to express special thanks to all researchers in the Artificial Intelligence Research Development Group (AIRDG) for their continued support.

Conflicts of Interest: The authors declare no conflict of interest.

Abbreviations

Notation	Explanation
AI	Artificial Intelligence
DHNN	Discrete Hopfield Neural Network
ANN	Artificial Neural Network
CAM	Content addressable memory
SAT	Satisfiability
HORNSAT	Horn Satisfiability
2SAT	2 Satisfiability
3SAT	3 Satisfiability
RAN2SAT	Random 2 Satisfiability
RAN3SAT	Random 3 Satisfiability
MAJ2SAT	Major 2 Satisfiability
YRAN2SAT	Y-Type Random 2 Satisfiability
GRAN3SAT	G-Type Random k Satisfiability
PSAT	Probabilistic Satisfiability Problem
rSAT	Weighted Random k Satisfiability
PMAXSAT	partial maximum satisfiability
GA	Genetic Algorithm
ES	Exhaustive Search
HTAF	Hyperbolic Tangent Activation Function
WA	Wan Abdullah method
CNF	Conjunctive Normal Form
RMSE	Root-Mean-Square Error
PON	Probability of total negative
NAE	Negativity Absolut Error
FNAE	Full negativity Absolut Error second clauses
WFNAE	Weight Full negativity Absolut Error
ρ_0	pre-defined proportion range
ρ	negative literal proportion
α	Significance Level
Z	the upper $\alpha/2$ point of the normal distribution
w	Number of learning in probability logic phases

Symbol	Description
τ_i	literal
$T_x^{(1)}$	First-order clause
$T_y^{(2)}$	Second order clause
Y	Probability second-order logic range
λ_1	Number of literals/neurons
λ_2	Total clauses
x	Number of the second-order clauses
y	Number of the first-order logic clauses
$\Theta_{\delta 2SAT}$	General formula of $\delta 2SAT$
W_{ij}	Synaptic weight between i and j
W_{ii}	Synaptic weight of neuron i
$F_{desierd}$	Maximum fitness
F_i	Current fitness
W_E	Expected Synaptic weight that obtained by Wan method
W_A	Actual synaptic weight
ζ	The Total of negative literal in logic
$p(y_m)$	The probability of obtaining second-order clauses
ζ_{2SAT}	The number full negativity second-order clauses
λ_{2SAT}	The number of second-order
$\overline{\lambda}_{2SAT}$	The mean number of second-order clauses
$H_{\Theta_{\delta 2SAT}}$	Minimum energy value
$H_{\Theta_{\delta 2SAT}}^{min}$	Final energy
R_G	Ratio of global minimum solutions
$G_{\Theta_{\delta 2SAT}}$	Number of global minimum solutions
S_i	Neuron state
S_i^{max}	Benchmark neuron state
Sokal	Sokal and Michener Index
R_{tv}	The Ratio of cumulative neuronal variation
h_i	local field
$b, b*$	Counter
v	Number of Learning
η	Number of neuron combination
φ	Number of Trials
Tol	Tolerance value
R	Relaxation rate
ϕ	Learning iteration
θ	Threshold constraint of DHNN
$E_{\Theta_{\delta 2SAT}}$	The cost function of the DHNN-YRAN2SAT
$\overline{X}$	The arithmetic mean
$\widetilde{X}$	The median
σx	Standard deviation
$\mathbb{Q}_1$	First quartile
$\mathbb{Q}_2$	Second quartile
$\mathbb{Q}_3$	Third quartile
IQR	Interquartile range
LF	Lower fences
UF	Upper fences
$f(x)$	Probability density function for random variables
W_s^*	Smallest of absolute values of the sum of x_i in Wilcoxon test
W	Wilcoxon test value (sum of smallest and biggest of absolute values of the sum x_i)

References

1. Hopfield, J.J.; Tank, D.W. "Neural" computation of decisions in optimization problems. *Biol. Cybern.* **1985**, *52*, 141–152. [CrossRef]
2. Basheer, I.A.; Hajmeer, M. Artificial neural networks: Fundamentals, computing, design, and application. *J. Microbiol. Methods* **2000**, *43*, 3–31. [CrossRef] [PubMed]
3. Egrioglu, E.; Baş, E.; Chen, M.-Y. Recurrent Dendritic Neuron Model Artificial Neural Network for Time Series Forecasting. *Inf. Sci.* **2022**, *607*, 572–584. [CrossRef]

4. Gonzalez-Fernandez, I.; Iglesias-Otero, M.; Esteki, M.; Moldes, O.; Mejuto, J.; Simal-Gandara, J. A critical review on the use of artificial neural networks in olive oil production, characterization and authentication. *Crit. Rev. Food Sci. Nutr.* **2019**, *59*, 1913–1926. [CrossRef]
5. Juan, N.P.; Valdecantos, V.N. Review of the application of Artificial Neural Networks in ocean engineering. *Ocean Eng.* **2022**, *259*, 111947. [CrossRef]
6. Liao, Z.; Wang, B.; Xia, X.; Hannam, P.M. Environmental emergency decision support system based on Artificial Neural Network. *Saf. Sci.* **2012**, *50*, 150–163. [CrossRef]
7. Shafiq, A.; Çolak, A.B.; Sindhu, T.N.; Lone, S.A.; Alsubie, A.; Jarad, F. Comparative Study of Artificial Neural Network versus Parametric Method in COVID-19 data Analysis. *Results Phys.* **2022**, *38*, 105613. [CrossRef]
8. Tran, L.; Bonti, A.; Chi, L.; Abdelrazek, M.; Chen, Y.-P.P. Advanced calibration of mortality prediction on cardiovascular disease using feature-based artificial neural network. *Expert Syst. Appl.* **2022**, *203*, 117393. [CrossRef]
9. Mohd Kasihmuddin, M.S.; Mansor, M.; Md Basir, M.F.; Sathasivam, S. Discrete mutation Hopfield neural network in propositional satisfiability. *Mathematics* **2019**, *7*, 1133. [CrossRef]
10. Gosti, G.; Folli, V.; Leonetti, M.; Ruocco, G. Beyond the maximum storage capacity limit in Hopfield recurrent neural networks. *Entropy* **2019**, *21*, 726. [CrossRef] [PubMed]
11. Hemanth, D.J.; Anitha, J.; Son, L.H.; Mittal, M. Diabetic retinopathy diagnosis from retinal images using modified hopfield neural network. *J. Med. Syst.* **2018**, *42*, 1–6. [CrossRef]
12. Channa, A.; Ifrim, R.-C.; Popescu, D.; Popescu, N. A-WEAR bracelet for detection of hand tremor and bradykinesia in Parkinson's patients. *Sensors* **2021**, *21*, 981. [CrossRef] [PubMed]
13. Channa, A.; Popescu, N.; Ciobanu, V. Wearable solutions for patients with Parkinson's disease and neurocognitive disorder: A systematic review. *Sensors* **2020**, *20*, 2713. [CrossRef] [PubMed]
14. Veerasamy, V.; Wahab, N.I.A.; Ramachandran, R.; Madasamy, B.; Mansoor, M.; Othman, M.L.; Hizam, H. A novel rk4-hopfield neural network for power flow analysis of power system. *Appl. Soft Comput.* **2020**, *93*, 106346. [CrossRef]
15. Chen, H.; Lian, Q. Poverty/investment slow distribution effect analysis based on Hopfield neural network. *Future Gener. Comput. Syst.* **2021**, *122*, 63–68. [CrossRef]
16. Dang, X.; Tang, X.; Hao, Z.; Ren, J. Discrete Hopfield neural network based indoor Wi-Fi localization using CSI. *EURASIP J. Wirel. Commun. Netw.* **2020**, *2020*, 1–16. [CrossRef]
17. Abdullah, W.A.T.W. Logic programming on a neural network. *Int. J. Intell. Syst.* **1992**, *7*, 513–519. [CrossRef]
18. Sathasivam, S. Upgrading logic programming in Hopfield network. *Sains Malays.* **2010**, *39*, 115–118.
19. Mansor, M.; Kasihmuddin, M.; Sathasivam, S. Artificial Immune System Paradigm in the Hopfield Network for 3-Satisfiability Problem. *Pertanika J. Sci. Technol.* **2017**, *25*, 1173–1188.
20. Sathasivam, S.; Mansor, M.A.; Ismail, A.I.M.; Jamaludin, S.Z.M.; Kasihmuddin, M.S.M.; Mamat, M. Novel Random k Satisfiability for k ≤ 2 in Hopfield Neural Network. *Sains Malays.* **2020**, *49*, 2847–2857. [CrossRef]
21. Bazuhair, M.M.; Jamaludin, S.Z.M.; Zamri, N.E.; Kasihmuddin, M.S.M.; Mansor, M.; Alway, A.; Karim, S.A. Novel Hopfield Neural Network Model with Election Algorithm for Random 3 Satisfiability. *Processes* **2021**, *9*, 1292. [CrossRef]
22. Karim, S.A.; Zamri, N.E.; Alway, A.; Kasihmuddin, M.S.M.; Ismail, A.I.M.; Mansor, M.A.; Hassan, N.F.A. Random satisfiability: A higher-order logical approach in discrete Hopfield Neural Network. *IEEE Access* **2021**, *9*, 50831–50845. [CrossRef]
23. Alway, A.; Zamri, N.E.; Karim, S.A.; Mansor, M.A.; Mohd Kasihmuddin, M.S.; Mohammed Bazuhair, M. Major 2 satisfiability logic in discrete Hopfield neural network. *Int. J. Comput. Math.* **2022**, *99*, 924–948. [CrossRef]
24. Zamri, N.E.; Azhar, S.A.; Mansor, M.A.; Alway, A.; Kasihmuddin, M.S.M. Weighted Random k Satisfiability for k = 1, 2 (r2SAT) in Discrete Hopfield Neural Network. *Appl. Soft Comput.* **2022**, *126*, 109312. [CrossRef]
25. Muhammad Sidik, S.S.; Zamri, N.E.; Mohd Kasihmuddin, M.S.; Wahab, H.A.; Guo, Y.; Mansor, M.A. Non-Systematic Weighted Satisfiability in Discrete Hopfield Neural Network Using Binary Artificial Bee Colony Optimization. *Mathematics* **2022**, *10*, 1129. [CrossRef]
26. Guo, Y.; Kasihmuddin, M.S.M.; Gao, Y.; Mansor, M.A.; Wahab, H.A.; Zamri, N.E.; Chen, J. YRAN2SAT: A novel flexible random satisfiability logical rule in discrete hopfield neural network. *Adv. Eng. Softw.* **2022**, *171*, 103169. [CrossRef]
27. Gao, Y.; Guo, Y.; Romli, N.A.; Kasihmuddin, M.S.M.; Chen, W.; Mansor, M.A.; Chen, J. GRAN3SAT: Creating Flexible Higher-Order Logic Satisfiability in the Discrete Hopfield Neural Network. *Mathematics* **2022**, *10*, 1899. [CrossRef]
28. Boole, G. The Laws of Thought (1854). *Walt. Mabe.* **1911**, *2*, 450–461.
29. Nilsson, N.J. Probabilistic logic. *Artif. Intell.* **1986**, *28*, 71–87. [CrossRef]
30. Andersen, K.A.; Pretolani, D. Easy cases of probabilistic satisfiability. *Ann. Math. Artif. Intell.* **2001**, *33*, 69–91. [CrossRef]
31. Caleiro, C.; Casal, F.; Mordido, A. Generalized probabilistic satisfiability. *Electron. Notes Theor. Comput. Sci.* **2017**, *332*, 39–56. [CrossRef]
32. Semenov, A.; Pavlenko, A.; Chivilikhin, D.; Kochemazov, S. On Probabilistic Generalization of Backdoors in Boolean Satisfiability. In Proceedings of the Thirty-Sixth AAAI Conference on Artificial Intelligence (AAAI-22), Virtual, 22 February–1 March 2022.
33. Fu, H.; Liu, J.; Wu, G.; Xu, Y.; Sutcliffe, G. Improving probability selection based weights for satisfiability problems. *Knowl.-Based Syst.* **2022**, *245*, 108572. [CrossRef]
34. Wang, Y.; Xu, D. Properties of the satisfiability threshold of the strictly d-regular random (3, 2s)-SAT problem. *Front. Comput. Sci.* **2020**, *14*, 1–14. [CrossRef]

35. Schawe, H.; Bleim, R.; Hartmann, A.K. Phase transitions of the typical algorithmic complexity of the random satisfiability problem studied with linear programming. *PLoS ONE* **2019**, *14*, e0215309. [CrossRef] [PubMed]
36. Saribatur, Z.G.; Eiter, T. Omission-based abstraction for answer set programs. *Theory Pract. Log. Program.* **2021**, *21*, 145–195. [CrossRef]
37. Kasihmuddin, M.S.M.; Mansor, M.A.; Sathasivam, S. Hybrid Genetic Algorithm in the Hopfield Network for Logic Satisfiability Problem. *Pertanika J. Sci. Technol.* **2017**, *25*, 139–152.
38. Sathasivam, S.; Mansor, M.A.; Kasihmuddin, M.S.M.; Abubakar, H. Election Algorithm for Random k Satisfiability in the Hopfield Neural Network. *Processes* **2020**, *8*, 568. [CrossRef]
39. Cai, S.; Lei, Z. Old techniques in new ways: Clause weighting, unit propagation and hybridization for maximum satisfiability. *Artif. Intell.* **2020**, *287*, 103354. [CrossRef]
40. Dubois, D.; Godo, L.; Prade, H. Weighted logics for artificial intelligence—An introductory discussion. *Int. J. Approx. Reason.* **2014**, *55*, 1819–1829. [CrossRef]
41. Thompson, S.K. Sample size for estimating multinomial proportions. *Am. Stat.* **1987**, *41*, 42–46.
42. Sheynin, O.B.P.S. Laplace's Work on Probability. *Arch. Hist. Exact Sci.* **1976**, *16*, 137–187. [CrossRef]
43. Sathasivam, S.; Wan Abdullah, W.A.T. Logic mining in neural network: Reverse analysis method. *Computing* **2011**, *91*, 119–133. [CrossRef]
44. Kasihmuddin, M.S.M.; Jamaludin, S.Z.M.; Mansor, M.A.; Wahab, H.A.; Ghadzi, S.M.S. Supervised Learning Perspective in Logic Mining. *Mathematics* **2022**, *10*, 915. [CrossRef]
45. Bruck, J.; Goodman, J.W. A generalized convergence theorem for neural networks. *IEEE Trans. Inf. Theory* **1988**, *34*, 1089–1092. [CrossRef]
46. Sokal, R.R. A statistical methods for evaluating systematic relationships. *Univ. Kans. Sci. Bull.* **1958**, *38*, 1409–1438.
47. Gravetter, F.J.; Wallnau, L.B.; Forzano, L.-A.B.; Witnauer, J.E. *Essentials of Statistics for the Behavioral Sciences*; Cengage Learning: Boston, MA, USA, 2020.
48. Manikandan, S. Measures of central tendency: The mean. *J. Pharmacol. Pharmacother.* **2011**, *2*, 140. [PubMed]
49. Manikandan, S. Measures of central tendency: Median and mode. *J. Pharmacol. Pharmacother.* **2011**, *2*, 214.
50. Tukey, J.W. Exploratory data analysis. In *Addison-Wesley Series in Behavioral Science: Quantitative Methods*; Addison-Wesley: Reading, MA, USA, 1977; Volume 2.
51. Hoaglin, D.C.; Iglewicz, B.; Tukey, J.W. Performance of some resistant rules for outlier labeling. *J. Am. Stat. Assoc.* **1986**, *81*, 991–999. [CrossRef]
52. Wilcoxon, F. Individual Comparisons by Ranking Methods. *Biom. Bull.* **1945**, *1*, 80–83. [CrossRef]
53. Zamri, N.E.; Azhar, S.A.; Sidik, S.S.M.; Mansor, M.A.; Kasihmuddin, M.S.M.; Pakruddin, S.P.A.; Pauzi, N.A.; Nawi, S.N.M. Multi-discrete genetic algorithm in hopfield neural network with weighted random k satisfiability. *Neural Comput. Appl.* **2022**, *34*, 19283–19311. [CrossRef]
54. Darmann, A.; Döcker, J. On simplified NP-complete variants of monotone 3-sat. *Discret. Appl. Math.* **2021**, *292*, 45–58. [CrossRef]
55. Ong, P.; Zainuddin, Z. Optimizing wavelet neural networks using modified cuckoo search for multi-step ahead chaotic time series prediction. *Appl. Soft Comput.* **2019**, *80*, 374–386. [CrossRef]
56. Pinkas, G. Symmetric neural networks and propositional logic satisfiability. *Neural Comput.* **1991**, *3*, 282–291. [CrossRef] [PubMed]
57. Karaboga, D.; Basturk, B. Artificial Bee Colony (ABC) Optimization Algorithm for Solving Constrained Optimization Problems. *Found. Fuzzy Log. Soft Comput.* **2007**, *4529*, 789–798.
58. Emami, H.; Derakhshan, F. Election algorithm: A new socio-politically inspired strategy. *AI Commun.* **2015**, *28*, 591–603. [CrossRef]

Disclaimer/Publisher's Note: The statements, opinions and data contained in all publications are solely those of the individual author(s) and contributor(s) and not of MDPI and/or the editor(s). MDPI and/or the editor(s) disclaim responsibility for any injury to people or property resulting from any ideas, methods, instructions or products referred to in the content.

Article

Edge Computing Offloading Method Based on Deep Reinforcement Learning for Gas Pipeline Leak Detection

Dong Wei [1], Renjun Wang [1,2,3,4], Changqing Xia [1,2,3,4,*], Tianhao Xia [2,3,4], Xi Jin [2,3,4] and Chi Xu [2,3,4]

1. School of Information Science and Engineering, Shenyang University of Technology, Shenyang 110870, China
2. State Key Laboratory of Robotics, Shenyang Institute of Automation, Chinese Academy of Sciences, Shenyang 110016, China
3. Key Laboratory of Networked Control Systems, Chinese Academy of Sciences, Shenyang 110016, China
4. Institutes for Robotics and Intelligent Manufacturing, Chinese Academy of Sciences, Shenyang 110169, China
* Correspondence: xiachangqing@sia.cn

Abstract: Traditional gas pipeline leak detection methods require task offload decisions in the cloud, which has low real time performance. The emergence of edge computing provides a solution by enabling offload decisions directly at the edge server, improving real-time performance; however, energy is the new bottleneck. Therefore, focusing on the gas transmission pipeline leakage detection scenario in real time, a novel detection algorithm that combines the benefits of both the heuristic algorithm and the advantage actor critic (AAC) algorithm is proposed in this paper. It aims at optimization with the goal of real-time guarantee of pipeline mapping analysis tasks and maximizing the survival time of portable gas leak detectors. Since the computing power of portable detection devices is limited, as they are powered by batteries, the main problem to be solved in this study is how to take into account the node energy overhead while guaranteeing the system performance requirements. By introducing the idea of edge computing and taking the mapping relationship between resource occupation and energy consumption as the starting point, the optimization model is established, with the goal to optimize the total system cost (TSC). This is composed of the node's transmission energy consumption, local computing energy consumption, and residual electricity weight. In order to minimize TSC, the algorithm uses the AAC network to make task scheduling decisions and judge whether tasks need to be offloaded, and uses heuristic strategies and the Cauchy–Buniakowsky–Schwarz inequality to determine the allocation of communication resources. The experiments show that the proposed algorithm in this paper can meet the real-time requirements of the detector, and achieve lower energy consumption. The proposed algorithm saves approximately 56% of the system energy compared to the Deep Q Network (DQN) algorithm. Compared with the artificial gorilla troops Optimizer (GTO), the black widow optimization algorithm (BWOA), the exploration-enhanced grey wolf optimizer (EEGWO), the African vultures optimization algorithm (AVOA), and the driving training-based optimization (DTBO), it saves 21%, 38%, 30%, 31%, and 44% of energy consumption, respectively. Compared to the fully local computing and fully offloading algorithms, it saves 50% and 30%, respectively. Meanwhile, the task completion rate of this algorithm reaches 96.3%, which is the best real-time performance among these algorithms.

Keywords: edge computing; deep reinforcement learning; heuristic algorithm; task offloading; resource allocation

MSC: 68W99

1. Introduction

With the advent of 5G, high-performance computing and other technologies in industry have developed in the direction of high real-time engagement and low energy consumption, and many delay-sensitive and computationally intensive applications and services have emerged. Although cloud computing can provide sufficient computing resources, a large amount of traffic generated in the process of task delivery to the cloud will likely lead to network congestion, unpredictably high delay, and massive transmission energy consumption, and a distributed computing method is needed to solve these problems. Edge computing makes this feasible. To move computing to the edge of the network solves the problem of high latency of cloud services and makes up for the lack of computing resources of end devices to a certain extent.

Although edge computing provides a feasible solution for such scenarios, it entails the problem of using limited resources to realize high real-time performance and low energy consumption. Much research has been performed in this field, with good results. The main concern is to balance low latency and low energy consumption, which can effectively solve the offloading problem when the attributes of the task set to be processed are known. However, such solutions have the common limitation of low robustness, which will lead to a chain reaction when unexpected tasks enter the system, sharply degrading system performance. This is more likely to occur when tasks arrive in real time. Sun et al. [1] proposed a task offloading algorithm based on a hierarchical heuristic strategy, aiming to minimize the task delay and energy consumption, but it assumes the task set to be scheduled is known, without taking into account sudden tasks. Similarly, Li et al. proposed a task offloading algorithm based on deep reinforcement learning, which is based on a known task set, to schedule tasks [2].

Taking the leak detection of a natural gas transmission pipeline as an example, once a leak occurs, there is a great danger. Detectors need to work in the leak area. The faster they locate the leak point, the less the security risk; hence this scenario demands high reliability in real time. Many portable gas leak detectors depend on the collection of infrared or other spectral images for image analysis [3]. Because the detector must constantly change its position during operation, it needs to feedback results immediately so that it will not miss the leak point. However, due to the size of the detector, its computing and battery capacity have certain limitations. It is difficult to complete some complex recognition tasks on time, which greatly affects detection efficiency and accuracy. Figure 1 shows the workflow of the solution. By introducing edge computing, complex image processing tasks generated by the detection equipment can be uploaded to the cloud and processed quickly, which can enable the accurate and quick location of the leak point.

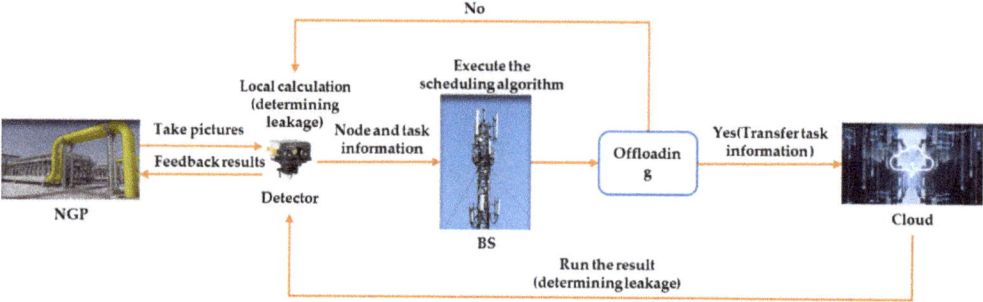

Figure 1. Workflow of edge computing in natural gas pipeline detection.

This paper proposes a natural gas leak detection algorithm that combines edge computing task offloading with portable natural gas leak detection technology—a real-time multi-leak detection algorithm based on the improved advantage actor-critic (AAC) method—to improve the detection efficiency and endurance of instruments. We consider a three-tier edge computing architecture with cloud-side and end-to-end collaboration, where the portable gas leak detector is at the end of the system and has some computing power itself. To improve the efficiency and range of the detector, the image analysis task must be offloaded, so as to determine where to process the task and allocate resources to it. The current system state is determined, and this is input to the constructed AAC network to determine the processing position of tasks in the system. The results obtained from the network are optimized using the proposed heuristic algorithm. At the same time, the allocation strategy of communication resources is determined, and tasks are scheduled and executed according to the offloading results. By analyzing the problem, improving the detection efficiency and range of the existing detection instruments can address the objectives in the edge computing task offloading problem, that is, to improve the real-time performance and minimize the energy consumption of the edge computing system as much as possible. This paper makes the following contributions:

1. The system real-time requirements and energy consumption limits are modeled in a unified manner. Tasks arrive and are unloaded in real time in order to be close to the real situation to the maximum extent, which enables the proposed algorithm in this study to achieve good practical relevance.
2. A real-time multi-leak detection algorithm based on the improved AAC is proposed to solve the problem in that traditional reinforcement learning methods are difficult to converge and traditional heuristics cannot fully consider various influencing factors. The proposed algorithm in this paper allows the AAC algorithm to complement the traditional heuristics, and the AAC algorithm can fully take into account the impact of various environmental factors on the unloading results while also taking into account the long-term payoff of the system. However, the AAC algorithm is a reinforcement learning algorithm whose convergence effect is not stable enough, so this paper supplements the AAC algorithm with a heuristic algorithm to correct the obtained results in order to ensure that the proposed algorithm can at least achieve the performance of the heuristic algorithm. Moreover, through detailed mathematical analysis, the condition that the proposed heuristic algorithm obtains the minimum value of total system cost (TSC) is proved to hold.
3. We compare the performance of the proposed algorithm with that of the deep Q network (DQN), the artificial gorilla troops optimizer (GTO), the black widow optimization algorithm (BWOA), the exploration-enhanced grey wolf optimizer (EEGWO), the African vultures optimization algorithm (AVOA), and the driving training-based optimization (DTBO), and two other baseline algorithms. Experiments show that the proposed algorithm reduces the energy consumption by 56% compared to DQN. Compared with GTO, BWOA, EEGWO, AVOA and DTBO algorithms, the energy consumption is reduced by 21%, 38%, 30%, 31% and 44%, respectively. The energy consumption is reduced by 50% compared to the fully local computing algorithm, and by 30% compared to the fully offloading algorithm. Meanwhile, the task completion rate of this algorithm reaches 96.3%, which is the best real-time performance among these algorithms. In addition, the proposed algorithm in this paper has a faster convergence speed than the DQN algorithm.

The remainder of this paper is organized as follows. Section 2 describes related work. Section 3 presents the proposed system model and describes the problem. Section 4 details the main steps of the proposed algorithm. Section 5 compares the performance of the proposed algorithm with baseline algorithms such as DQN and GTO through experiments. Section 6 concludes the paper.

2. Related Work

Many studies have been conducted on the task offloading problem of edge computing, which is NP-hard, and all solutions thus far have been approximate. However, different optimization techniques can be used such that the approximate solution converges to the optimal solution. These solutions start either with machine learning or traditional means such as greedy heuristics, integer optimization, branch delimitation, game theory, or convex optimization. The two most important factors in edge computing are latency and energy consumption.

2.1. Traditional Task Offloading Methods

Kan et al. proposed a heuristic algorithm for offloading tasks to MEC servers considering radio and computational resources with the goal of minimizing the average task latency, which was shown by experiments to achieve excellent results under different latency requirements [4]. Due to the relative lack of infrastructure, they introduced drones to assist in edge computing, and proposed a USS algorithm [5] that can satisfy the task processing latency constraint in the multiuser case. Wang, Shen, and Zhao introduced a dynamic penalty function in a study of edge computing in the smart grid domain, and proposed an improved algorithm for solving Lagrange multipliers [6], which overcomes the shortcomings of traditional grid systems that cannot provide deterministic services, and can effectively improve the overall system revenue and reduce the average delay of user tasks. Li et al. considered event-triggered decision systems, whose goal is to optimize the average system revenue to satisfy the average delay constraint for different priority services [7]. Ref. [8] presented designs of online computing task scheduling methods for multi-server edge computing scenarios [8]. Sun et al. [9] considered an ultra-dense network environment that supports edge computing. Constantly moving users dynamically generate computational tasks in the network, which need to be offloaded to the base station for computation. In order to minimize the average delay given a limited energy budget, users need to make mobility management decisions about base station association and switching based on their service requirements without knowing future information.

System energy consumption has long been a concern among edge computing researchers, as an important component of system cost, and especially in mobile edge computing, where energy consumption directly affects system endurance and reliability. Michael proposed a hybrid method based on particle swarm optimization and the gray wolf optimizer [10] to optimize the energy consumption of MEC task offloading. Ding and Zhang [11] proposed a game theory-based computational offloading strategy for massive IoT devices, which improves data transfer and reduces task energy consumption using the beneficial task offloading theory.

Delay and energy consumption factors are usually considered together, and are important factors affecting the user experience. Researchers can decide whether to optimize delay or energy consumption based on specific requirements. Some studies have considered the minimum energy consumption while satisfying the latency constraint using heuristic algorithms [12,13]. Others have proposed a more flexible optimization objective, synthesizing both into a cost objective, where the weights of delay and energy consumption in the cost formulation can be changed according to the case [14,15]. Ref. [16] considered two different cases of adjustable and non-adjustable CPU frequency of APs. A linear relaxation based approach and an exhaustive search based approach are proposed to obtain the offloading decision for these two cases, respectively. The method aims to minimize the total task ground execution delay and the energy consumption of the mobile device (MD) [16]. In order to trade-off the two metrics of energy consumption and computational latency, a Liapunov-based algorithm was proposed in Ref. [17] for computing task offloading decisions in mobile edge computing systems. The algorithm greatly reduces the energy consumption of the device while satisfying the latency constraint [17]. Ref. [18] investigated the computational offloading and scheduling problem, which seeks to minimize the cost per mobile device, where the cost is defined as a linear combination of task completion time and energy consumption. In addition, the literature considers inter-device communication and competition for computational resources. The problem is also defined formally using a game model, and a decentralized algorithm is designed to achieve a pure policy Nash equilibrium [18]. Tang et al. modeled the multi-user computational offloading problem in an uncertain wireless environment as a non-cooperative game based on PT, and then proposed a distributed computational offloading algorithm to obtain a Nash equilibrium, which minimizes the user overhead [19]. Yi et al. considered that tasks are randomly generated by mobile users and proposed a mechanism based on queuing model. This is used to maximize social welfare and achieve the equilibrium of the noncooperative game among mobile users [20].

Task offloading algorithms based on the above studies are based on ideal mathematical models, and cannot consider all the factors that affect the optimization objective, which limits their task offloading performance. To solve this problem, a new class of offloading methods has been proposed, using deep learning techniques, with good results.

2.2. Machine Learning Task Offloading Methods

To cope with the variability of edge computing application environments, Wang and Jia et al. proposed a meta-reinforcement learning-based approach to solve the computational offloading problem [21], which enables fast adaptation to dynamic scenarios without updating too many parameters. A joint task offloading and bandwidth allocation problem was considered for multiuser computational offloading, with the goal of minimizing the overall delay in completing user tasks, using a DQN approach to find the optimal solution [22].

Wang Jin et al. [23] found that studies using DRL for task offloading rarely focus on the dependencies between tasks, and proposed a DRL offloading method that can address dependent tasks. The general dependency of tasks was modeled as a directed acyclic graph (DAG), and an S2S neural network captured the features of the DAG and output the offloading strategy. The method can use delay, energy consumption, or tradeoffs of both as optimization objectives.

In Ref. [24], the authors are the first to attempt to consider end-device energy consumption in a deep learning-based modeling of MEC partial offloading schemes [24]. They propose a novel partial offloading scheme EEDOS based on a fine-grained partial offloading framework, in which the cost function comprehensively considers important parameters such as residual energy of end-devices and energy consumption of previous application components. Dai and Niu [25] used unmanned aerial vehicles (UAVs) to assist edge servers for task offloading, minimizing the energy consumption of all mobile end devices by jointly optimizing UAV trajectories, task association, and the resource allocation of computation and transmission. They reduced the problem complexity by decomposing the joint optimization problem into the subproblems of UAV trajectory planning, task association scheduling, and resource allocation of computation and transmission. A proposed hybrid heuristic and learning-based scheduling strategy (H2LS) algorithm incorporated long short-term memory neural networks, fuzzy c-means, deep deterministic policy gradients, and convex optimization techniques.

As with traditional optimization techniques, most of the research on the application of deep learning in offloading edge computing tasks focuses on the integrated consideration of delay and energy consumption. To focus on only one of these aspects can bring the results closer to the optimal solution, at the price of a narrow range of practical applications. Yang and Lee proposed a deep supervised learning-based dynamic computing task offloading approach (DSLO) for mobile edge computing networks [26], minimizing the delay and energy consumption by jointly optimizing the offloading decision and bandwidth allocation problem. Cao et al. proposed a multi-intelligent deep reinforcement learning (MADRL) scheme [27] to solve the multichannel access and task offloading problems in edge computing-enabled Industry 4.0, which allows edge devices to collaborate and significantly reduce computational latency and mobile device energy consumption relative to traditional methods. Huang et al. [28] considered a mobile edge computing system, in which each user has multiple tasks transferred to the edge server over a wireless network. They proposed a deep reinforcement learning based approach to solve the problem of joint task offloading and resource allocation. In Refs. [29,30], the authors proposed to use deep reinforcement learning methods to solve the task offloading problem in mobile edge computing, and made some progress, obtaining better latency and energy consumption than when using deep learning [29,30].

Although the above deep learning-based solutions have achieved good results, they have limitations if we only consider how to optimize the latency and energy consumption of task processing. In the problem addressed in this paper, each image analysis task is generated in real time, and the optimization goal of low latency can cause some tasks to have low processing latency, at the cost of some subsequent tasks that exceed their deadlines; hence, they cannot guarantee overall high real-time performance. We propose an AAC and heuristic policy-based task offloading algorithm that simultaneously considers overall task execution in real time and low energy consumption, and use it to optimize the performance of a portable gas leak detector. The algorithm reduces the energy consumption of the detector as much as possible by jointly optimizing the task offloading location and resource allocation problems while ensuring completion within the deadline.

3. System Model and Problem Description

3.1. System Model

The edge computing system (ECS) consists of a cluster of cloud servers, a wireless communication base station with small edge servers, and K portable gas leak detectors, $\gamma = \{U_1, U_2, U_3, \ldots \ldots, U_k\}$; each detector U_i can generate in time order a series of independent image recognition tasks, each task of all detectors is generated in real time and cannot be split, and the set of tasks can be denoted by $\Gamma_i = \{T_{i,1}, T_{i,2}, T_{i,3}, \ldots \ldots T_{i,N}\}$; each task has six attributes, and any task i can be denoted as $T_i = \{j, s_i, d_i, D_i, cy_i, \omega_i\}$, where j is the serial number of the detector, s_i is the release time of task i (in seconds), d_i is the relative deadline of the task, D_i is the size of the data carried by the task (in Mb), cy_i is the CPU processing cycle required by the task, and ω_i is its priority. An example of the system model is shown in Figure 2. The cloud server has sufficient resources for the detectors, so there is no need to consider the waiting and preemption of tasks in the cloud, and only one task can be processed at a time on a detector. The task offloading algorithm is deployed on the edge server in the communication base station, and the information changes of each node are transmitted to the edge server in real time. In this model, the tasks to be offloaded are generated by the detector in real time, and each task is indivisible. Considering that the offloading decision requires knowledge of the global information of the system, while the system that transmits the main task parameters is not a complete model and the base station is very close to the detector and there is no conflict in the transmission process, the offloading algorithm generates comparable and almost negligible communication energy consumption and delay whether it is executed on the detector or on the base station equipped with the edge computing server [1]. The edge server has more arithmetic power and faster execution, so the communication base station is left in charge of the communication function and makes the offloading decision, based on which the detector offloads the computational task to the cloud or processes it locally. If offloaded to the cloud, the cloud server will return the results after processing, and the energy consumption of the detector during the offloading process includes that for transmission and local processing.

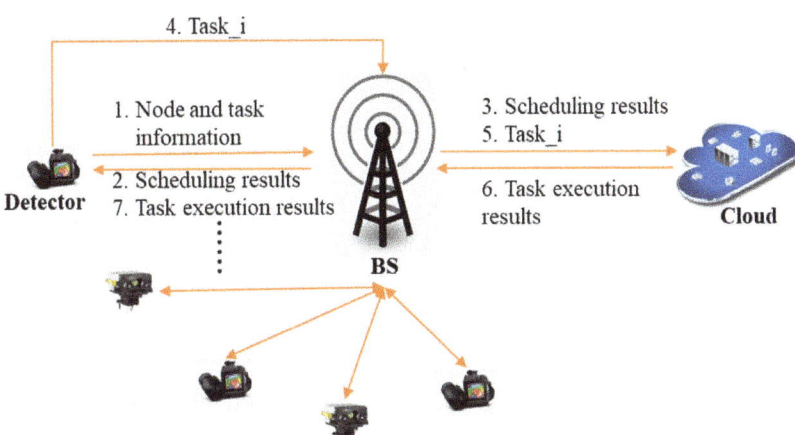

Figure 2. System model.

3.2. Description of problem

Since each task in the system can be chosen to be executed either locally or in the cloud, an offloading decision variable is introduced to indicate the execution location of a task,

$$\pi_i^C = \begin{cases} 0 & \text{Task executed locally,} \\ 1 & \text{Task executed in the cloud} \end{cases} \quad (1)$$

The transmission power of all edge devices (detectors) is P. The data transmission rate assigned for any task i is r_i, the average CPU frequency of the cloud server is F^C, and the CPU frequency of the edge device is f_i^L. Therefore, the time to locally execute task T_i of edge device U is

$$t_i^L = \frac{cy_i}{f_i^L} \quad (2)$$

The local execution energy consumption of a task is

$$e_i^L = a * \left(f_i^L\right)^2 * cy_i \quad (3)$$

If a task is unloaded, its unloaded transfer time is

$$t_i^{LC} = \frac{D_i}{P} \quad (4)$$

The cloud processing time of a task is

$$t_i^C = \frac{cy_i}{F^c} \quad (5)$$

The offloading transmission energy consumption of a task is

$$e_i^T = \frac{P_i * D_i}{r_i} \quad (6)$$

where a is the chip-related energy consumption coefficient of edge device U [31].

The mathematical model described in this paper must optimize the objectives of the real-time system and the total energy consumption of edge devices for synergistic optimization while considering load balancing. To achieve the joint optimization of the above objectives, the model optimization objective is transformed to the total system cost TSC,

$$TSC = \min_{r_i, \pi_i^L} \sum_{1}^{M} \left(1 - \pi_i^C\right) * a * \left(f_i^L\right)^2 * cy_i + \pi_i^C * \frac{\overline{E}}{E_i} * \frac{P_i * D_i}{r_i} \quad (7a)$$

$$\pi_i^C = \{0, 1\} \quad (7b)$$

$$0 \leq f_i^L \leq F_i^L \quad (7c)$$

$$0 \leq E_i \leq 1 \quad (7d)$$

$$0 \leq \sum_{i=1}^{M} r_i \leq R \quad (7e)$$

where E_i is the remaining power percentage of edge device i, and $\overline{E}$ is the average power percentage of all devices that are idle and must perform offload tasks.

Equation (7a) is the weighted sum of the local execution energy consumption and offload transmission energy consumption for task i, and $\frac{\overline{E}}{E_i}$ is the distance between the remaining power of each device and the average power. A larger $\frac{\overline{E}}{E_i}$ indicates that the remaining power of the device is farther from the average power. To reduce the energy consumption of the device, it has the opportunity to share more communication resources (faster data transmission rate) when the system performs bandwidth resource allocation [1]

Constraints 7b, 7c, 7d, and 7e refer to the offloading decision variables, range of CPU frequency variation per device, range of power percentage variation per edge device, and range of data transfer rate variation per device, respectively.

The variables involved in the model are shown in Table 1.

Table 1. Model variables.

Symbol	Definition
s_i	Task i release time
d_i	Task i relative deadline
D_i	Amount of data carried by task i
w_i	Task i priority
π_i^C	Offload decision variables
t_i^L	Task i local execution time
t_i^{LC}	Task i offload transfer time
t_i^C	Task i cloud execution time
e_i^L	Task i local execution energy consumption
e_i^T	Task i offload transfer energy consumption
r_i	Task i assigned data transfer rate
E_i	Percentage of power remaining in detector
$\overline{E}$	Average power percentage of detectors idle and performing offload tasks
TSC	Total system cost

4. Task Offloading Algorithm

The proposed task offloading algorithm has two parts. The AAC algorithm gives the scheduling location of the task. The initial offloading decision is obtained by the heuristic algorithm, based on which the AAC network is updated. The heuristic algorithm can be solved quickly for the NP-hard problem, but the suboptimal solution found by this method has room for improvement. Reinforcement learning is used to optimize the obtained unloading strategy. The algorithms are described below.

4.1. Heuristic Algorithm

The heuristic algorithm considered in this paper takes Equation (7a) as the optimization objective. Since the optimization for the TSC is an NP-hard problem, the deep reinforcement learning algorithm is used to first determine whether the new arrival task is to be offloaded, and the Cauchy–Buniakowsky–Schwarz inequality is used to derive the transmission rate allocation, and thus the processing time for each task. If the processing time exceeds the task deadline, the processing position of the task is redetermined according to the priority of the task, and the transfer rate allocation is calculated. Iterations continue until an approximate optimal solution is found.

The Cauchy–Buniakowsky–Schwarz inequality is often applied to quickly solve n-dimensional inequalities [32] and its application to solve the system communication resource allocation can simplify computations and reduce the execution time of the offloading algorithm. When using this inequality, we must first ensure that the left-hand side of the inequality can be split into two non-negative expressions multiplied together.

Theorem 1. *If the inequality* $R * \sum_{1}^{M} \frac{\pi_i^C * \frac{\overline{E}}{E_i} * P_i * D_i}{r_i} \geq \left(\sum_{i}^{M} \sqrt{\pi_i^C * \frac{\overline{E}}{E_i} * P_i * D_i} \right)^2$ *satisfies both* $R > 0$ *and* $\sum_{1}^{M} \frac{\pi_i^C * \frac{\overline{E}}{E_i} * P_i * D_i}{r_i} \geq 0$, *the equality sign holds when and only when*

$$r_i^* = \frac{R * \sqrt{\pi_i^C * \frac{\overline{E}}{E_i} * P_i * D_i}}{\sum_{i=1}^{M} \sqrt{\pi_i^C * \frac{\overline{E}}{E_i} * P_i * D_i}} \tag{8}$$

Additionally, when $r_i = r_i^*$, *TSC obtains the minimum value.*

Proof of Theorem 1. It is known that R is the total transmission rate of the system, which is always positive, and each term in $\sum_{1}^{M} \frac{\pi_i^C * \frac{\overline{E}}{E_i} * P_i * D_i}{r_i}$ is greater than or equal to zero, which satisfies the condition of use of the Cauchy–Buniakowsky–Schwarz inequality. Then the following inequalities are solved by combining the constraints, and the specific solved process is stated in Equation (9) for the optimization objective expression (7a) and its constraint (7e):

$$R * \sum_{1}^{M} \frac{\pi_i^C * \frac{\overline{E}}{E_i} * P_i * D_i}{r_i} \geq \sum_{i}^{M} r_i * \sum_{1}^{M} \frac{\pi_i^C * \frac{\overline{E}}{E_i} * P_i * D_i}{r_i} \geq \left(\sum_{i}^{M} \sqrt{\pi_i^C * \frac{\overline{E}}{E_i} * P_i * D_i} \right)^2. \tag{9}$$

According to the Cauchy–Buniakowsky–Schwarz inequality, if there exists some r_i not equal to 0, the equality sign holds when and only when there exists a real number X such that for every $i = 1, 2, \ldots, n$, there is $r_i * X + \frac{\pi_i^C * \frac{\overline{E}}{E_i} * P_i * D_i}{r_i} = 0$, i.e.,

$$r_i^* = \frac{R * \sqrt{\pi_i^C * \frac{\overline{E}}{E_i} * P_i * D_i}}{\sum_{i=1}^{M} \sqrt{\pi_i^C * \frac{\overline{E}}{E_i} * P_i * D_i}} \tag{10}$$

and when $r_i = r_i^*$, TSC obtains the minimum value, and the theorem is proved. □

In the task scheduling process of the real-time edge system in this paper, not only should we consider making the energy consumption of the edge devices as low as possible, but the tasks should meet the deadline requirements to the maximum extent to improve the real-time performance of the whole system. In traditional scheduling methods, often only the remaining execution time or deadline of a task is used to reflect that the urgency of task execution evaluation criteria is too singular. We propose a dynamic priority evaluation method that integrates the initial priority, remaining execution time, deadline, and idle time of a task. The dynamic task priority Ω_i is composed of the preemption cost δ_i of the task and the execution urgency φ_i,

$$\Omega_i = \delta_i * \varphi_i \tag{11}$$

where

$$\delta_i = \frac{\omega_i}{t_i^{LC} + t_i^C} \quad (12)$$

Tasks have different levels of importance. Equation (12) integrates the initial priority of tasks and deadlines, which can ensure that important tasks can be completed on the basis of as many tasks as possible that are close to the deadline and can also be executed, which protects the tasks being executed to some extent. The task execution urgency is

$$\varphi_i = q^{\frac{t_i^{LC}+t_i^C}{d_i-t}} \quad (13)$$

where t is the current moment and $q \in (1, \infty)$. The execution urgency of the task decreases as the task is executed, which in turn gives a somewhat greater chance of execution for newly arrived tasks.

4.2. Deep Reinforcement Learning Algorithms

To perform further optimization based on the task unloading decision obtained from the heuristic strategy, a deep reinforcement learning model, AAC, is considered to perform the unloading decision for the newly arrived task. The network structure of the model is shown in Figure 3.

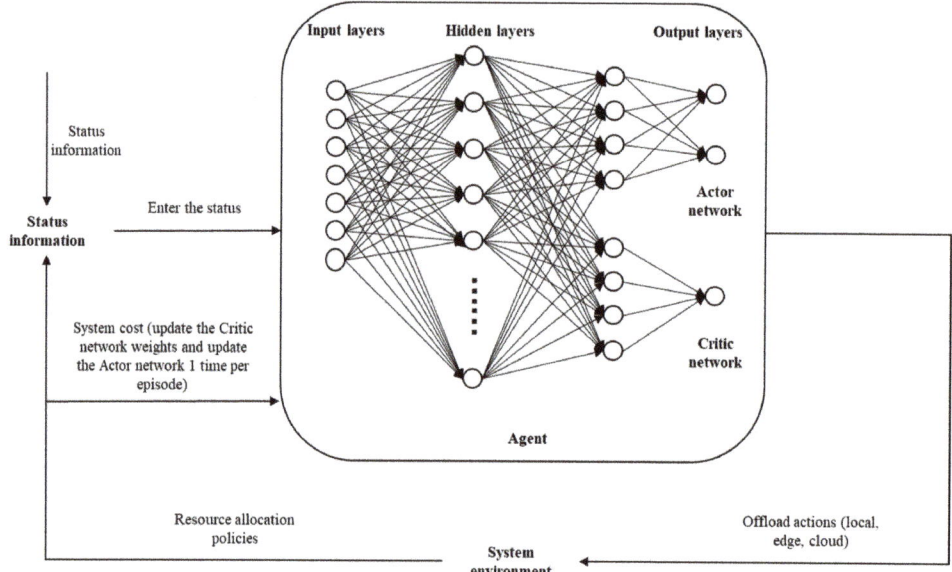

Figure 3. Advantage actor-critic network structure.

From Figure 3 above, we can see that the AAC network is composed of two subnetworks, actor and critic, where the first two layers of the two sub-networks are shared, in order to reduce the complexity of the model and speed up the network convergence. Meanwhile, the hidden layers of both sub-networks consist of 256 × 128 neurons, which is the best combination chosen after several attempts in the experiments. Through keeping the other conditions of the experiment constant, only the number of neurons in the network was allowed to increase evenly between 64 × 64 and 256 × 256. We found that too few neurons make the training unstable and difficult to converge, while too many neurons lead to overfitting. Optimal model performance is only achieved when the number of neurons is varied to near 256 × 128.

The offloading decision is a prerequisite for resource allocation. We discuss the three elements of the reinforcement learning-based offloading decision method: environment, action, and reward.

1. Environment state S

The superiority of the state will have a great impact on the final training effect of the model. In this model, the environment state includes the state of the task and the external environment. The model is updated only when a new task arrives, and these arrive in chronological order, so the task's own state includes the properties of the new task, and the external environment state has the remaining power E_i of each node in the system at this time, the average remaining power $\overline{E}$, the CPU speed f_i^L of the node generating the task, the average CPU speed F^C of the cloud, and the number of tasks to be transmitted in the system.

2. Action a

In the reinforcement learning model, the action is the decision made by the agent, and there are only two actions in this scheduling model: transmission and non-transmission.

3. Reward function

The output of the reinforcement learning model is the probability $p_\theta(a|S)$ of selecting different actions in a certain state. To measure the goodness of an action, the system cost TSC is used as the reward.

The AAC algorithm first defines an initial actor π to interact with the environment, as shown in Figure 4. The collected information is used to train the critic network to estimate the value function V, which is the sum of the rewards received by the system after performing an action until the end of the interaction. The actor network is updated and iterated until both networks converge. The actor network parameters are updated as follows:

$$\widetilde{\nabla R_\theta} \approx \frac{1}{N} \sum_{n=1}^{N} \sum_{t=1}^{T_n} (LSC_t^n + V^\pi(S_{t+1}^n) - V^\pi(S_t^n)) \nabla log p_\theta(a_t^n | S_t^n) \tag{14}$$

$$\theta = \theta - \eta * \widetilde{\nabla R_\theta} \tag{15}$$

where $\widetilde{\nabla R_\theta}$ is the gradient of the mean of the reward sum of multiple trajectories, and θ is the parameter of the actor network. Since the optimization goal is to reduce energy consumption while satisfying the real-time performance of the task, which is the opposite of the goal of maximizing the reward of reinforcement learning, gradient descent is used to update the network.

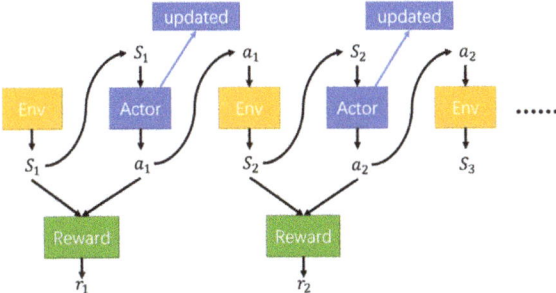

Figure 4. Trajectory of interaction between actor π and environment.

4.3. Algorithm Process

We combine the heuristic algorithm and deep reinforcement learning algorithm, using the AAC network for offloading decisions, and a heuristic algorithm for resource allocation, as shown in Algorithm 1.

Algorithm 1: Offloading algorithm for edge computing tasks based on deep reinforcement learning.

Input: Number of training rounds M, set of tasks G_{M*L} used for training, number of edge devices N, CPU frequency f_i^L, energy consumption factor α, transmission power P_i, CPU frequency F^C of cloud server, total data transmission rate R available to system, learning rate of actor and critic networks

Output: Trained Advantage Actor-critic model, total energy consumption of system, and task completion rate

1. Initialize model and related parameters;
2. Let actor π interact with environment
3. **for** i = 1 to M **do**
4.   Storing j-th task in i-th subtask set in training set in a list;
5.   Updating status of environment and storing it in the list;
6.   Input environmental state parameters to actor network, and record action a selected by network with probability p;
7.   Determining value of offloading decision variable π_i^C based on recorded actions;
8.   **while** flag = True
9.   Passing value of π_i^C into Equation (7a) and using Equations (8) and (9) to derive allocation of data transfer rate r;
10.   Substitute r back into Equation (7a) to find value of TSC at this point, and use Equations (4) and (5) to calculate expected transmission time t_i^{LC} and execution time t_i^C for task;
11.   **if** $d_i < t_i^{LC} + t_i^C$
12.   Calculating priority of all tasks being transmitted and pending transmission and forcing selection of lowest priority task to be executed locally;
13.   **end if**
14.   **if** All tasks that are subject to offload meet deadlines
15.   flag = False
16.   **end if**
17.   Storing track data;
18. **end for**
19. Training critic network using stored trajectory data and storing output V of critic network each time;
20. Training actor network once more with data stored in steps 6, 18, and 20;
21. **end for**
22. **return** Trained Advantage Actor-critic model, total energy consumption of system, along with task completion rate;

The core part of Algorithm 1 uses a heuristic algorithm and the AAC network, which is a deep reinforcement learning network model. In the edge computing scenario considered in this paper, task offloading, and resource allocation is an NP-hard problem. At the same time, the uncertainty of task arrival poses a great challenge for task offloading. Facing this multi-objective optimization problem, traditional optimization techniques (e.g., linear programming) have difficulty in obtaining better results [33]. In addition, deep reinforcement learning has two advantages in facing the above problem: (1) compared with many one-time optimization methods, deep reinforcement learning can adjust the strategy with the change of environment; (2) its learning process does not need to know the relevant a priori knowledge about the law of network state change over time [34, 35]. In fact, the heuristic algorithm is the basis on which the present model can operate efficiently, and the main purpose of the AAC is to further optimize the optimization results derived from the heuristic algorithm. The heuristic algorithm performs the optimization search by introducing the Cauchy–Buniakowsky–Schwarz inequality, which can reduce the number of iterations and greatly accelerate the solution efficiency by using the conclusion of Theorem 1.

The AAC model is improved from the actor-critic model. In the actor-critic model, both Q-network (Network to evaluate good and bad actions) and V-network (Network to evaluate good and bad status) need to be estimated, which is not only time-consuming, but also has greater uncertainty. In the AAC model, the expectation of the V-network is directly used to estimate the Q-network, that is, the critic network is allowed to learn the Advantage value directly instead of the Q value. In this way, the assessment of behavior is not only based on how good the behavior is, but also on how much the behavior can be improved. The benefit of the advantage function is that it reduces the variation in the values of the policy network, and stabilizes the model, giving the AAC model superior convergence.

5. Experimental Results and Analysis

Simulation experiments are used to demonstrate the performance of the proposed algorithm. All parameters are chosen according to real scenarios. As shown in Table 2, the number of portable detection devices is set to 10, their computational power is 0.2 GCycles/s, and that of the cloud is 10 GCycles/s. The transmission power (w) of the portable devices is a random number in (0.1,0.2), with a total system transmission rate of 800 Mb/s. The amount of data for each task is (10,40) Mb, and the required computation period is (0.01,0.3) GCycles. The arrival time of the task conforms to a uniform distribution [36].

Table 2. Simulation parameters.

Parameter	Value
Number of items of testing equipment K	10
Local computing capability f_i^L	0.2 GCycles/s
Cloud server computing capability F^C	10 GCycles/s
Transmitted power P_i	(0.1,0.2) w
Total system transmission rate R	800 Mb/s
Computation cycles required per task cy_i	(0.01,0.3) GCycles

To demonstrate the performance of the improved AAC-based multi-leakage real-time detection algorithm, the algorithm and the DQN algorithm are trained simultaneously in the same environment. The proposed algorithm is also compared with two benchmark algorithms, that is, task fully local computation and full offloading. Meanwhile, in order to better represent the performance of the proposed algorithm in this paper, we also compare it with a series of excellent heuristics, such as GTO [37], BWOA [38], EEGWO [39], AVOA [40] and DTBO [41].

The variations in the total cost TSC per iteration based on the improved AAC multi-leakage real-time detection algorithm and the DQN algorithm in this experimental setting are shown in Figure 5. From Figure 5, it can be seen that the proposed algorithm in this paper has nearly stabilized and the model reached convergence at 50 rounds of training, while the DQN algorithm only shows a significant trough when the training reaches 700 rounds. Although both use a 256 × 128 network structure, the AAC algorithm allows for more stable training and faster convergence due to the presence of the critic network. The figure also shows that the total cost per round of the proposed algorithm is lower than that of the DQN algorithm, so it is better in terms of overall performance. In Figure 6, the vertical coordinate indicates the total system energy consumption. The energy consumption variation curve of the improved AAC-based multi-leakage real-time detection algorithm is approximately 56% lower than that of the DQN algorithm after convergence. The AAC algorithm is improved on the basis of the DQN algorithm, which overcomes the problem of unstable training of the DQN algorithm. Moreover, the AAC algorithm in this paper is not used alone, it works as a further enhancement after the heuristic algorithm gets the suboptimal solution of the model. Therefore, this algorithm can obtain a large improvement relative to the DQN algorithm.

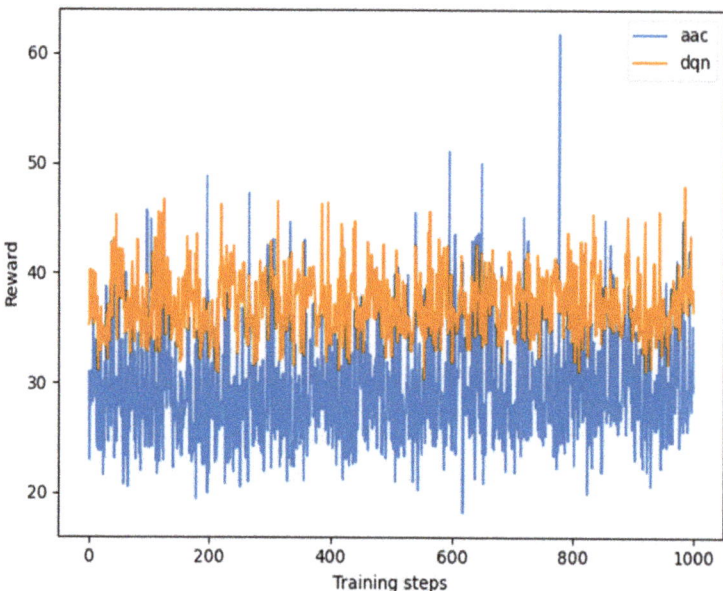

Figure 5. TSC based on improved AAC multi-leakage real-time detection algorithm and DQN algorithm.

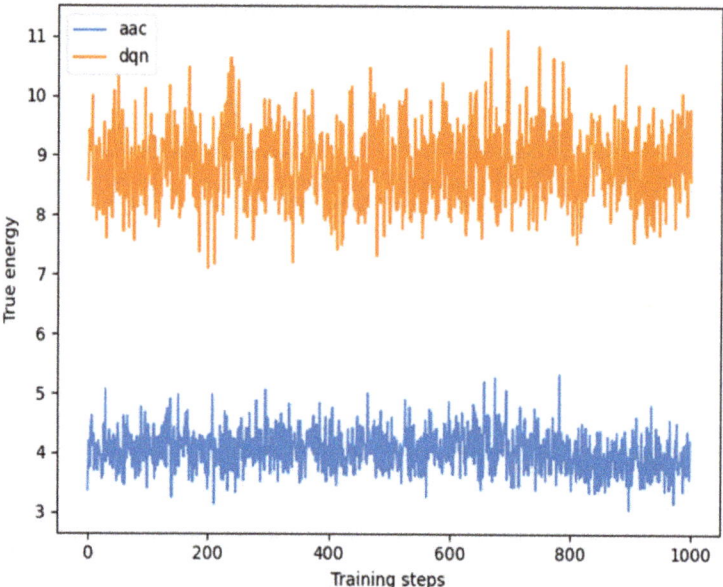

Figure 6. Total system energy consumption based on improved AAC multi-leakage real-time detection algorithm and DQN algorithm.

Figures 7 and 8 compare the line graphs of the energy consumption of the improved AAC-based multi-leakage real-time detection algorithm to the fully local computation algorithm and the fully offloading algorithm. Since these two algorithms are not machine learning algorithms, there is no training process, so it is not necessary to compare the algorithm convergence here. They show that the system using the improved AAC-based multi-leakage real-time detection algorithm has better total energy consumption than the two baseline algorithms, thus saving approximately 50% of the energy consumption compared to the fully local calculation, and saving approximately 30% of the energy consumption compared to the fully unloaded algorithm. To make the experiments more realistic, the test tasks have different amounts of data and complexity; thus, having them all executed locally or in the cloud would result in higher energy consumption due to the underutilization of system resources. At the same time, if we combine Figures 5–7 together for comparison, we can see that the system energy consumption of the DQN algorithm is around 9, which would be slightly higher than the 6.5 energy consumption for local computation and 5.3 energy consumption for full offloading. This is due to the fact that in the scenario considered in this paper, the task to be offloaded is so random that the performance of the DQN algorithm is no longer sufficient for this scenario, and incorrect predictions can waste a lot of energy.

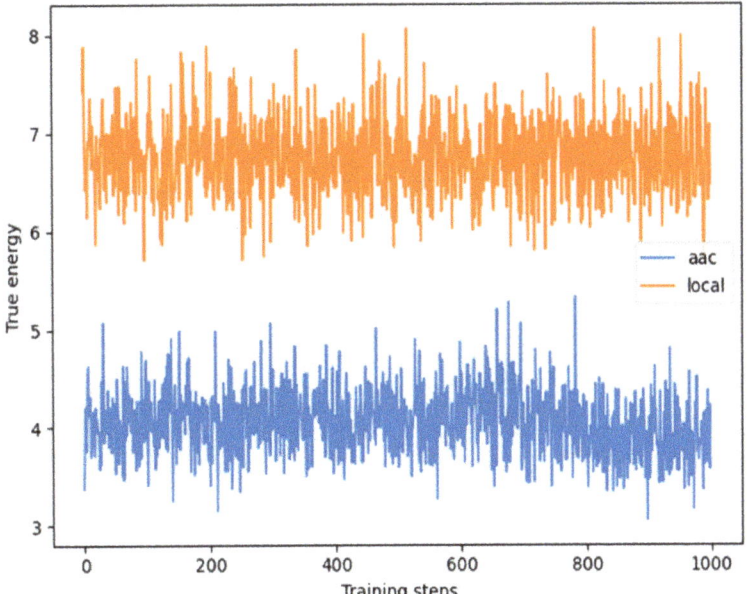

Figure 7. Total system energy consumption based on improved AAC multi-leakage real-time detection algorithm with fully locally calculated system.

Figure 9 shows the comparison of the total system energy consumption between the proposed algorithm and some current excellent heuristics. With a simple calculation, we can conclude that the proposed algorithm saves 21%, 38%, 30%, 31% and 44% of energy consumption compared to the GTO, BWOA, EEGWO, AVOA and DTBO algorithms, respectively. If combined with Figures 6–8, it can be seen that all these heuristics used for comparison in the experiments perform well. Nevertheless, the proposed algorithm outperforms them. Thus, we can say with more certainty that due to the addition of deep reinforcement learning, the performance of the traditional heuristic algorithm can be brought to a higher level.

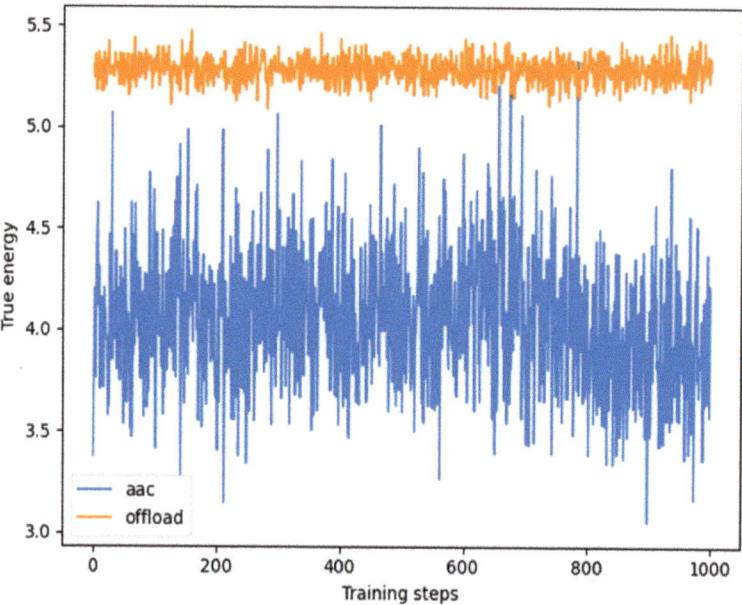

Figure 8. Total system energy consumption based on improved AAC multi-leakage real-time detection algorithm with fully offloaded system.

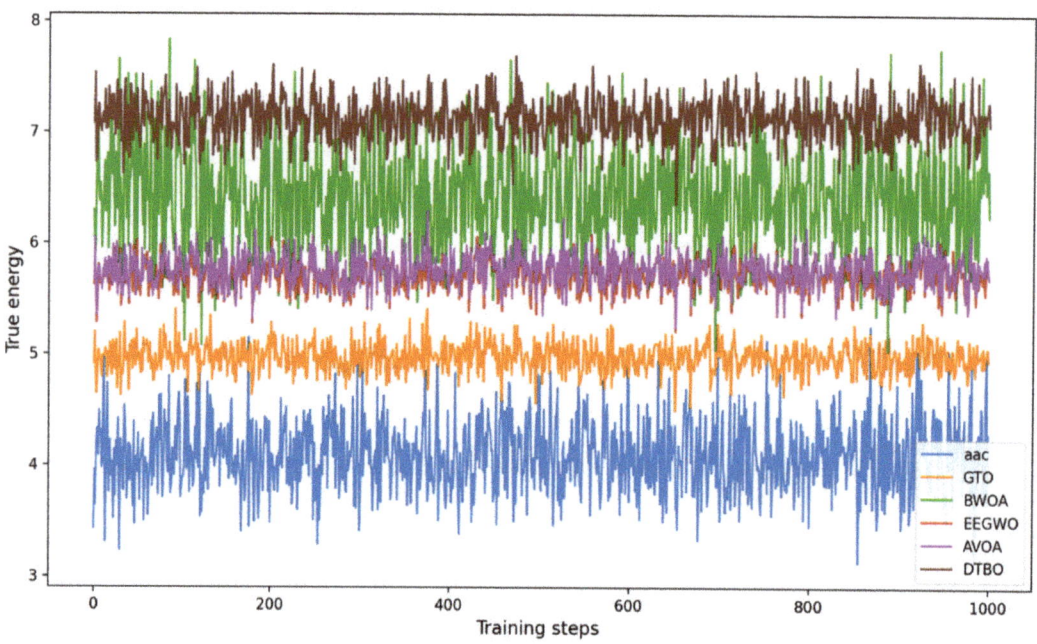

Figure 9. Total system energy consumption based on improved AAC multi-leakage real-time detection algorithm with some excellent current heuristics algorithms.

In this experiment we also obtained another metric to evaluate the performance of the algorithms, namely the task completion rate. Based on the output of the code, we can obtain the task completion rate of 96.4% for the proposed algorithm and 93.2% for the DQN algorithm; the corresponding values were 92.8%, 90.3%, 89.4%, 94.3% and 91.1% for the GTO, BWOA, EEGWO, AVOA and DTBO algorithms, respectively. The task completion rates for the fully local computing and fully offloading algorithms were 86.7% and 93.4%, respectively. According to the experimental results, the use of the proposed algorithm in this paper allows the highest execution success rate of the tasks, indicating that this algorithm has the best real-time performance and can ensure that as many tasks as possible are completed before the deadline. The task completion rate of the fully local computing algorithm is the lowest, which is mainly due to the high complexity of the task and the limited computing power of the nodes.

From the experiments designed in this paper, we can know that this algorithm design idea is reasonable and effective. It is based on the principle of using heuristic algorithm for initial optimization at first, and then further optimization using deep reinforcement learning. It can bring about more efficient task offloading for edge computing, which not only ensures the real-time performance of the algorithm, but also further reduces the system energy consumption compared to the current better optimization-seeking algorithms such as GTO.

6. Conclusions and Future Work

We studied an edge computing task offloading and resource allocation problem in a natural gas pipeline leak detection scenario, with the optimization goal of minimizing energy consumption while ensuring high real-time performance of the system. Due to the unpredictability of computational tasks, deep reinforcement learning was used to solve this problem. Using the AAC algorithm framework, the final offloading strategy was obtained by fully considering minimizing the overall system cost and continuously optimizing the task offloading strategy, followed by optimizing the allocation of communication resources through a heuristic algorithm based on the Cauchy–Buniakowsky–Schwarz inequality. Simulation results show that this algorithm has a faster convergence speed compared to the DQN algorithm, while the energy consumption is reduced by 56%. Although heuristics such as GTO, BWOA, EEGWO, AVOA and DTBO have better performance than the DQN algorithm, the proposed algorithm still saves 21%, 38%, 30%, 31% and 44% of energy consumption compared to them, respectively. The energy consumption is reduced by 50% compared to the fully local computation, and by 30% compared to the fully offloaded algorithm. This algorithm also has the highest task completion rate with the highest real-time performance. Furthermore, this paper proves a sufficient condition for the heuristic algorithm to achieve a suboptimal solution using the Cauchy–Buniakowsky–Schwarz inequality. From the performance of the DQN algorithm in the experiments, due to the strong real-time nature of the scenario in this paper and the strong uncertainty of the system environment, the model convergence speed of the reinforcement learning algorithm alone is slow, and at the same time, incorrect offloading predictions also tend to lead to higher energy consumption. Finally, the proposed algorithm in this paper is also not optimal for certain application scenarios. This algorithm uses a complex deep reinforcement learning model in order to meet the performance requirements of task arrival scenarios in real time. In contrast, for deterministic scenarios where the set of tasks to be offloaded is known and no prediction of future tasks is required, simpler heuristics, such as linear programming algorithms, etc. can achieve the same or even better performance, and the latter is clearly the better choice.

In this paper, the communication environment of the system is simplified while modeling, and the interference factor of the channel is not considered. The allocation of network resources in the edge computing system is also idealized and will be studied in detail in the next work in conjunction with SDN technology. In future work, we will also further consider the mutual cooperation among edge nodes, in order to maximize the utilization of system idle resources and further reduce the system's energy consumption. In order to further improve this model, we will also allocate computation and storage resources in edge and cloud servers in a more granular way.

Author Contributions: Conceptualization, D.W., R.W. and C.X. (Changqing Xia); Formal analysis, R.W. and C.X. (Changqing Xia); Funding acquisition, C.X. (Changqing Xia); Methodology, R.W.; Project administration, C.X. (Changqing Xia), X.J. and C.X. (Chi Xu); Resources, D.W. and C.X. (Changqing Xia); Software, R.W. and T.X.; Supervision, D.W.; Validation, R.W.; Writing—original draft, R.W.; Writing—review and editing, C.X. (Changqing Xia). All authors have read and agreed to the published version of the manuscript.

Funding: This work was partially supported by National Key Research and Development Program of China (2022YFB3304004), the National Natural Science Foundation of China (61903356, 61972389, 62133014, 62022088, 62173322 and U1908212), the National Natural Science Foundation of Liaoning province (2022JH6/100100013), and the Youth Innovation Promotion Association CAS (2020207, 2019202, Y2021062).

Data Availability Statement: Not applicable.

Conflicts of Interest: The authors declare no conflict of interest.

References

1. Sun, C.; Li, H.; Li, X.; Wen, J.; Xiong, Q.; Wang, X.; Leung, V.C.M. Task Offloading for End-Edge-Cloud Orchestrated Computing in Mobile Networks. In Proceedings of the 2020 IEEE Wireless Communications and Networking Conference (WCNC), Seoul, Republic of Korea, 25–28 May 2020; pp. 1–6. [CrossRef]
2. Li, J.; Gao, H.; Lv, T.; Lu, Y. Deep reinforcement learning based computation offloading and resource allocation for MEC. In Proceedings of the 2018 IEEE Wireless Communications and Networking Conference (WCNC), Barcelona, Spain, 15–18 April 2018; pp. 1558–2612. [CrossRef]
3. Zhang, X.; Jin, W.; Li, L.; Wang, X.; Qin, C. Research progress on passive infrared imaging detection technology and system performance evaluation of natural gas leakage. *Infrared Laser Eng.* **2019**, *48* (Suppl. S2), 47–59. [CrossRef]
4. Kan, T.; Chiang, Y.; Wei, H. Task offloading and resource allocation in mobile-edge computing system. In Proceedings of the 2018 27th Wireless and Optical Communication Conference (WOCC), Hualien, Taiwan, 30 April–1 May 2018; pp. 1–4. [CrossRef]
5. Tan, T.; Zhao, M.; Zhu, Y.; Zeng, Z. Joint Offloading and Resource Allocation of UAV-assisted Mobile Edge Computing with Delay Constraints. In Proceedings of the 2021 IEEE 41st International Conference on Distributed Computing Systems Workshops (ICDCSW), Washington, DC, USA, 7–10 July 2021; pp. 21–26. [CrossRef]
6. Wang, Q.; Shen, J.; Zhao, Y.; Li, G.; Zhao, J.; Zhang, Y.; Guo, Y. Offloading and Delay Optimization Strategies for Power Services in Smart Grid for 5G Edge Computing. In Proceedings of the 2022 IEEE 6th Information Technology and Mechatronics Engineering Conference (ITOEC), Chongqing, China, 4–6 March 2022; pp. 1423–1427. [CrossRef]
7. Li, Q. An Actor-Critic Reinforcement Learning Method for Computation Offloading with Delay Constraints in Mobile Edge Computing. *arXiv* **2019**, arXiv:1901.10646. [CrossRef]
8. Han, Z.; Tan, H.; Li, X.; Jiang, S.; Li, Y.; Lau, F.C.M. OnDisc: Online Latency-Sensitive Job Dispatching and Scheduling in Heterogeneous Edge-Clouds. *IEEE/ACM Trans. Netw.* **2019**, *27*, 2472–2485. [CrossRef]
9. Sun, Y.; Zhou, S.; Xu, J. EMM: Energy-Aware Mobility Management for Mobile Edge Computing in Ultra Dense Networks. *IEEE J. Sel. Areas Commun.* **2017**, *35*, 2637–2646. [CrossRef]
10. Mahenge, M.P.J.; Li, C. Energy-efficient task offloading strategy in mobile edge computing for resourceintensive mobile applications. *Digit. Commun. Netw.* **2022**, *8*, 19–37. [CrossRef]
11. Ding, X.; Zhang, W. Computing Unloading Strategy of Massive Internet of Things Devices Based on Game Theory in Mobile Edge Computing. *Math. Probl. Eng.* **2021**, *2021*, 1–12. [CrossRef]
12. Guo, H.; Liu, J. Collaborative Computation Offloading for Multiaccess Edge Computing Over Fiber–Wireless Networks. *IEEE Trans. Veh. Technol.* **2018**, *67*, 4514–4526. [CrossRef]
13. Gu, B.; Zhou, Z.; Mumtaz, S.; Frascolla, V.; Kashif Bashir, A. Context-Aware Task Offloading for Multi-Access Edge Computing: Matching with Externalities. In Proceedings of the 2018 IEEE Global Communications Conference (GLOBECOM), Abu Dhabi, United Arab Emirates, 9–13 December 2018; pp. 1–6. [CrossRef]
14. Ni, W.; Tian, H.; Lyu, X.; Fan, S. Service-dependent task offloading for multiuser mobile edge computing system. *Electron. Lett.* **2019**, *55*, 839–841. [CrossRef]
15. Luo, J.; Deng, X.; Zhang, H.; Qi, H. QoE-Driven Computation Offloading for Edge Computing. *J. Syst. Archit.* **2019**, *97*, 34–39. [CrossRef]
16. Dinh, T.Q.; Tang, J.; La, Q.; Quek, T.Q.S. Offloading in Mobile Edge Computing: Task Allocation and Computational Frequency Scaling. *IEEE Trans. Commun.* **2017**, *65*, 3571–3584. [CrossRef]

17. Wu, H.; Sun, Y.; Wolter, K. Energy-Efficient Decision Making for Mobile Cloud Offloading. *IEEE Trans. Cloud Comput.* **2020**, *8*, 570–584. [CrossRef]
18. Jošilo, S.; Dán, G. Computation Offloading Scheduling for Periodic Tasks in Mobile Edge Computing. *IEEE/ACM Trans. Netw.* **2020**, *28*, 667–680. [CrossRef]
19. Tang, L.; He, S. Multi-User Computation Offloading in Mobile Edge Computing: A Behavioral Perspective. *IEEE Netw.* **2018**, *32*, 48–53. [CrossRef]
20. Yi, C.; Cai, J.; Su, Z. A Multi-User Mobile Computation Offloading and Transmission Scheduling Mechanism for Delay-Sensitive Applications. *IEEE Trans. Mob. Comput.* **2020**, *19*, 29–43. [CrossRef]
21. Wang, J.; Hu, J.; Min, G.; Zomaya, A.Y.; Georgalas, N. Fast Adaptive Task Offloading in Edge Computing Based on Meta Reinforcement Learning. *IEEE Trans. Parallel Distrib. Syst.* **2021**, *32*, 242–253. [CrossRef]
22. Huang, L.; Feng, X.; Zhang, C.; Qian, L.; Wu, Y. Deep reinforcement learning-based joint task offloading and bandwidth allocation for multi-user mobile edge computing. *Digit. Commun. Netw.* **2019**, *5*, 10–17. [CrossRef]
23. Wang, J.; Hu, J.; Min, G.; Zhan, W.; Ni, Q.; Georgalas, N. Computation Offloading in Multi-Access Edge Computing Using a Deep Sequential Model Based on Reinforcement Learning. *IEEE Commun. Mag.* **2019**, *57*, 64–69. [CrossRef]
24. Ali, Z.; Jiao, L.; Baker, T.; Abbas, G.; Abbas, Z.H.; Khaf, S. A Deep Learning Approach for Energy Efficient Computational Offloading in Mobile Edge Computing. *IEEE Access* **2019**, *7*, 149623–149633. [CrossRef]
25. Dai, B.; Niu, J.; Ren, T.; Hu, Z.; Atiquzzaman, M. Towards Energy-Efficient Scheduling of UAV and Base Station Hybrid Enabled Mobile Edge Computing. *IEEE Trans. Veh. Technol.* **2022**, *71*, 915–930. [CrossRef]
26. Yang, S.; Lee, G.; Huang, L. Deep Learning-Based Dynamic Computation Task Offloading for Mobile Edge Computing Networks. *Sensors* **2022**, *22*, 4088. [CrossRef]
27. Cao, Z.; Zhou, P.; Li, R.; Huang, S.; Wu, D. Multiagent Deep Reinforcement Learning for Joint Multichannel Access and Task Offloading of Mobile-Edge Computing in Industry 4.0. *IEEE Internet Things J.* **2020**, *7*, 6201–6213. [CrossRef]
28. Huang, L.; Feng, X.; Qian, L.; Wu, Y. Deep Reinforcement Learning-Based Task Offloading and Resource Allocation for Mobile Edge Computing. In Proceedings of the MLICOM 2018: Machine Learning and Intelligent Communications, Hangzhou, China, 6–8 July 2018; Springer: Cham, Switzerland, 2018; pp. 33–42. [CrossRef]
29. Huang, L.; Bi, S.; Zhang, Y.J.A. Deep Reinforcement Learning for Online Computation Offloading in Wireless Powered Mobile-Edge Computing Networks. *IEEE Trans. Mob. Comput.* **2020**, *19*, 2581–2593. [CrossRef]
30. Chen, X.; Zhang, H.; Wu, C.; Mao, S.; Ji, Y.; Bennis, M. Optimized Computation Offloading Performance in Virtual Edge Computing Systems Via Deep Reinforcement Learning. *IEEE Internet Things J.* **2019**, *6*, 4005–4018. [CrossRef]
31. Liu, Y.; Lee, M.; Zheng, Y. Adaptive multi-resource allocation for cloudlet-based mobile cloud computing system. *IEEE Trans. Mob. Comput.* **2015**, *15*, 2398–2410. [CrossRef]
32. Tan, L.; Zhang, X.; Zhou, Y.; Che, X.; Hu, M.; Chen, X.; Wu, D. AdaFed: Optimizing Participation-Aware Federated Learning With Adaptive Aggregation Weights. *IEEE Trans. Netw. Sci. Eng.* **2022**, *9*, 2708–2720. [CrossRef]
33. Wen, G.; Ge, S.; Chen, C.L.; Tu, F.; Wang, S. Adaptive Tracking Control of Surface Vessel Using Optimized Backstepping Technique. *IEEE Trans. Cybern.* **2019**, *49*, 3420–3431. [CrossRef]
34. Yang, Y.; Gao, W.; Modares, H.; Xu, C. Robust Actor–Critic Learning for Continuous-Time Nonlinear Systems With Unmodeled Dynamics. *IEEE Trans. Fuzzy Syst.* **2022**, *30*, 2101–2112. [CrossRef]
35. Vu, V.; Pham, T.; Dao, P. Disturbance observer-based adaptive reinforcement learning for perturbed uncertain surface vessels. *ISA Trans.* **2022**, *130*, 277–292. [CrossRef]
36. Cao, Y.; Jiang, T.; Wang, C. Optimal radio resource allocation for mobile task offloading in cellular networks. *IEEE Netw.* **2014**, *28*, 68–73. [CrossRef]
37. Abdollahzadeh, B.; Gharehchopogh, F.; Mirjalili, S. Artificial gorilla troops optimizer: A new nature-inspired metaheuristic algorithm for global optimization problems. *International J. Intell. Syst.* **2021**, *36*, 5887–5958. [CrossRef]
38. Hayyolalam, V.; Kazem, A. Black Widow Optimization Algorithm: A novel meta-heuristic approach for solving engineering optimization problems. *Eng. Appl. Artif. Intell.* **2020**, *87*, 103249. [CrossRef]
39. Long, W.; Jiao, J.; Liang, X.; Tang, M. An exploration-enhanced grey wolf optimizer to solve high-dimensional numerical optimization. *Eng. Appl. Artif. Intell.* **2018**, *63*, 63–80. [CrossRef]
40. Abdollahzadeh, B.; Gharehchopogh, F.; Mirjalili, S. African vultures optimization algorithm: A new nature-inspired metaheuristic algorithm for global optimization problems. *Comput. Ind. Eng.* **2021**, *158*, 107408. [CrossRef]
41. Dehghani, M.; Trojovská, E.; Trojovský, P. A new human-based metaheuristic algorithm for solving optimization problems on the base of simulation of driving training process. *Sci. Rep.* **2022**, *12*, 9924. [CrossRef]

Article

Comparison of Genetic Operators for the Multiobjective Pickup and Delivery Problem

Connor Little *, Salimur Choudhury, Ting Hu and Kai Salomaa

School of Computing, Queen's University, Kingston, ON K7L 3N6, Canada
* Correspondence: connor.little@queensu.ca

Abstract: The pickup and delivery problem is a pertinent problem in our interconnected world. Being able to move goods and people efficiently can lead to decreases in costs, emissions, and time. In this work, we create a genetic algorithm to solve the multiobjective capacitated pickup and delivery problem, adapting commonly used benchmarks. The objective is to minimize total distance travelled and the number of vehicles utilized. Based on NSGA-II, we explore how different inter-route and intraroute mutations affect the final solution. We introduce 6 inter-route operations and 16 intraroute operations and calculate the hypervolume measured to directly compare their impact. We also introduce two different crossover operators that are specialized for this problem. Our methodology was able to find optimal results in 23% of the instances in the first benchmark and in most other instances, it was able to generate a Pareto front within at most one vehicle and +20% of the best-known distance. With multiple solutions, it allows users to choose the routes that best suit their needs.

Keywords: optimization; vehicle routing; genetic algorithm; local search; pickup and delivery

MSC: 90C59

Citation: Little, C.; Choudhury, S.;
Hu, T.; Salomaa, K. Comparison of
Genetic Operators for the
Multiobjective Pickup and Delivery
Problem. *Mathematics* **2022**, *10*, 4308.
https://doi.org/10.3390/
math10224308

Academic Editors: Abdellah Chehri
and Francois Rivest

Received: 27 September 2022
Accepted: 10 November 2022
Published: 17 November 2022

Publisher's Note: MDPI stays neutral
with regard to jurisdictional claims in
published maps and institutional affiliations.

Copyright: © 2022 by the authors.
Licensee MDPI, Basel, Switzerland.
This article is an open access article
distributed under the terms and
conditions of the Creative Commons
Attribution (CC BY) license (https://
creativecommons.org/licenses/by/
4.0/).

1. Introduction

The pickup and delivery problem is a problem that has gained significant popularity since its inception. Much of its interest is due to strong applications in industry across several important problems such as supply chain routing, distribution, ride hailing, food delivery, etc. [1]. In recent years, in part due to the emergence of COVID-19, these problems have been brought to the forefront of the public consciousness. It has been harder to fulfill the demands of a global population. Supply chains have been hit particularly hard leading to a sharp decrease in the number of goods that have been shipped [2]. The need for robust and efficient solutions is more important than ever.

The pickup and delivery problem is a variation on vehicle routing [3]. Specifically, this paper addresses the multiobjective capacitated pickup and delivery problem (PDP) with time windows. Vehicle routing, in turn, is a generalization of the travelling salesman problem. Vehicle routing expands upon its predecessors by allowing multiple routes and multiple vehicles while still maintaining the goal of minimizing the total distance or time travelled. The pickup and delivery problem further expands on vehicle routing by adding precedence to pairs of nodes, pickup nodes and delivery nodes [3]. Each pickup node must be visited prior to the corresponding delivery node. The added precedence constrains the problem in unique ways such that many algorithms developed for regular vehicle routing must be altered. The added constraints of capacity and time windows further restrict operations on the solution.

The pickup delivery problem also has some additional constraints which are important to this version of the problem. All vehicles start and end at the same location called a depot. The fleet is assumed to have all the vehicles be the same and travel at uniform speeds to simplify the problem. It is assumed that no node is visited twice as the pickup and delivery only needs to be completed once. If a vehicle must travel through a node to arrive at another node, this is simply ignored.

As pickup delivery with time windows is NP-hard [1], there have been many attempts to develop heuristics. One class of heuristics which have had success in solving the multiobjective PDP is genetic algorithms. With the introduction of NSGA-II (Non-dominated Sorting Genetic Algorithm II) [4], evolutionary algorithms have a strong framework for modelling this kind of problem. Standard techniques to approach multiobjective problems include assigning weights to different objective values or solving them one at a time. The latter essentially turns the problem into a sequential single-objective problem. NSGA-II introduces nondominated sorting which allows solutions to be ranked according to numerous objectives without specifying precedence or weights, by sorting solutions into dominating fronts. Further, a crowding distance allows the comparison between within each front while still avoiding the previous issues. This allows better solutions to propagate without placing bias or preference to any one solution.

The large majority of current research into the pickup and delivery problem is single objective. This is insufficient in practice in many cases. Real-world scenarios are dynamic with many factors such as profit, vehicle count, or greenhouse emissions being factors in determining routes. Even the visual nature of the routes can determine whether a solution will be utilized in practice [5]. The research that does explore multiobjective pickup and delivery often reduces it down into a weighted single-objective problem, adding bias and eliminating diverse solutions [6]. This area of research has also grown with the recent popularity in green vehicle routing. Green vehicle routing often attempts to minimize environmental impacts alongside reducing costs and distance, making it a prime candidate for multiobjective techniques.

To improve upon NSGA-II, mutation and crossover operators can be specified. There are many different mutation and crossover operators that can be utilized for travelling salesman problems and their variants [7].

This paper introduces several local search operators to quantify and compare them. There are two main classifications of operators that are covered: inter-route operations and intraroute operations. As multiple inter-route operations need to be included in order to cover the search space, an ablation study is utilized to explore each operator's effectiveness. Intraroute operations are compared directly.

The paper is structured as follows. Section 2 reviews the current state of works in the field of multiobjective pickup and delivery. Section 3 formally introduces the problem and supply a linear programming model for the problem. Section 4 introduces the genetic algorithm and explains its properties. Section 5 shows results and finally, Section 6 concludes with a discussion of the results and future directions.

2. Background and Related Work

The pickup and delivery problem is a well-researched problem within the literature. There are numerous different variations and distinctions, each presenting different challenges. A full taxonomy was constructed by Berbeglia et al. [8].

Being a combinatorial optimization problem, much of the research is looking into heuristics to speed up computation time. Multiobjective capacitated pickup and delivery with time windows (MOCPDPTW) is an extension of the vehicle routing problem. The highly constrained nature of the problem makes designing heuristics a unique challenge. One important paper for multiobjective problems is "A fast and elitist multiobjective genetic algorithm: NSGA-II" by Deb et al. [4]. This paper proposed an efficient framework for multiobjective evolutionary algorithms. Based on nondominated sorting, fronts were assembled. Fronts are collections of solutions based on how many other solutions are dominated. This allowed direct comparisons of groups of solutions.

Evolutionary algorithms such as genetic algorithms and memetic algorithms are common approaches to solve the multiobjective pickup and delivery problem. Bravo, Rojas, and Parada [9] focused on green vehicle routing, specifically on reducing pollution.

They introduced an MO-PRP (multiobjective pollution routing problem) model which considered customers serviced, distance travelled, and fuel consumption. This could involve introducing additional variables to capture each objective. Chami et al. [10] offered a hybrid algorithm that combined genetic algorithms with a local search to optimize distance and cost. They did not cover time windows in their formulation. Fatemi-Anaraki et al. [11] also offered a hybrid genetic algorithm which first clustered the nodes before creating an initial population using one genetic algorithm. After the population had been generated, NSGA-II was run to find the final solutions. Fatemi-Anaraki et al. [11] aimed to minimize greenhouse emissions and cost of travel. Their formulation also did not contain time windows. Garcia-Najera and Gutierrez-Andrade [12] attempted to solve the multiobjective capacitated pickup and delivery problem with time windows by designing their own evolutionary algorithm based on solution domination. Gong et al. [13] used a bee-inspired algorithm to solve the MOCPDPTW. Their framework combined NSGA-II with the bee-evolutionary-guided algorithm to minimize fuel consumption, waiting time, and distance. Again, their model abstained from considering time windows. Li, Sahoo, and Chiang [14] designed their evolutionary algorithm based on R2 indicators. Velasco et al. [15] formulated their problem assuming the vehicles would be helicopters with no need for time windows. They designed a genetic algorithm based on NSGA-II as well and improved upon it with local search operators. Wang and Chen [16] explored genetic algorithms with numerous different mutations in order to minimize vehicles and minimize travel distance. Finally, Zhu et al. [17] introduced a memetic algorithm with locality-sensitive-hashing local-search operators. They did not include time windows in their analysis.

There has been much exploration outside of the field of evolutionary computing as well. Grandinetti [18] solved the problem by an ϵ-constraint method. This involved iteratively solving constrained single objective functions to approximate the Pareto front. Ren et al. [19] designed a variable neighbourhood search algorithm. Their methodology generated the solutions, perturbed them with nonoptimal search operators, before improving them again in hopes of leaving local optima. Wang et al. [6] compared two different frameworks for MOCPDPTW: multiobjective local search (MOLS) and multiobjective memetic algorithms (MOMA). Zou, Li, and Li [20] used particle swarm optimization hybridized with a variable neighbourhood search.

The majority of the work done in the domain of vehicle routing and pickup and delivery has been conducted on single objective functions. This is slowly changing as the demand and the types of problems encountered change. The number of multiobjective papers has been increasing in recent years. Previous surveys mention very few instances of MO-PDP [21] but in the last 5 years, there has been papers by Chami et al. [10], Li et al. [14], Gong et al. [13], and Bravo et al. [9], amongst others. The consequence of single-objective work taking the majority of the attention is that many ideas have not been applied in this domain. Carrabs, Cordeau, and Laporte [22] worked on the single-objective version of the problem and introduced novel local search operators based on combining pickups and deliveries into single entities. In recent years, the exploration of multiobjective problems has become more prevalent. The increase in attention is driven in part by green vehicle routing. Green vehicle routing aims to not only reduce the distance and the number of vehicles but also to reduce the emissions the routes will produce.

One drawback of all of these papers is that most abstain from describing their methodology in full. The mutation and crossover operators are overlooked or implemented far more simply than they need to be. The work by Bravo et al. [9] did not mention which operators were chosen, making replication and derivation of their work difficult. Others, such as the work by Chami et al. [10], only tested one operator: the swap operator. This operator, while a classic genetic algorithm operator, does not take into account the structure of the problem. Our work aims to further help the creation and study of genetic algorithms by giving other researchers a jumping-off point when creating their algorithms. We aim to compare and contrast how different operators affect the final solutions so that a more intelligent algorithm design can be implemented.

3. Problem Definition

The capacitated pickup and delivery with time windows problem is built on a complete directed graph $G = \{N, A\}$. N is the set of nodes and is further broken down into $N = \{0\} \cup P \cup D$, where 0 is the depot, $P = \{1, 2, \ldots, n\}$ is the set of all pickups and $D = \{n+1, n+2, \ldots, 2n\}$ is the set of all deliveries. n is the number of requests. Pickup and delivery locations always come in pairs. Explicitly, for any pickup i, the corresponding delivery is $n + i$ with n being the number of pickup and delivery pairs. The depot defines the starting and ending location for all vehicles.

For each pickup or delivery node, there is additional information supplied. Given a node $i \in N$, there exists q_i, d_i, ETW_i, and LTW_i. q_i designates the demand at node i. For pickups, this represents the space needed in the vehicle to pick an item up and is positive, while for deliveries it is negative to represent the removal of an item from the vehicle. d_i is the service time at each node. This represents the amount of time it takes to perform a pickup or delivery. Finally, $[ETW_i, LTW_i]$ are the early time window and late time window, respectively. This represents the time when a vehicle can visit and the service can be performed. Should a vehicle arrive prior to ETW_i, it has to wait, and should a vehicle arrive after LTW_i, the route is invalid.

We are also given a set K of vehicles. Each vehicle must keep track of how much it is carrying and how long it has been travelling. Let Q_i, k be the total capacity of a vehicle at a given node. As a vehicle traverses through the graph, the latter is updated to add q_i. For nodes a vehicle does not visit, this value is irrelevant. Let B_i, k be the time at which a vehicle has arrived at a given node. For each visited node, this should add the travel time and the service time of the node. Again, should a vehicle not visit a node, this value is irrelevant.

A is the set of all edges between the nodes $A = \{(i, j) | i, j \in N, i \neq j\}$. Each element (i, j) in A has an associated cost $C_{i,j}$. This typically represents distance or time to travel.

In addition to G, we also receive the max capacity of each vehicle Q. As this version of the problem has a homogeneous fleet, it is a constant. The max route time is implicitly supplied by the latest time that the depot may be visited. Again, we are assuming a homogeneous fleet, so all vehicles travel at the same speed and have the same capacity.

Let x_i, j, k be a decision variable to determine if a vehicle k travels from node i to node j. This is a multiobjective problem so there are two objective functions to minimize.

$$\min \sum_{i \in N, k \in K} x_{i,0,k}$$

Objective 1 aims to minimize the total number of vehicles used.

$$\min \sum_{i,j \in N, i \neq j} c_{i,j} * x_{i,j,k}$$

Objective 2 minimizes the total travel time that a vehicle takes. This does not take into account waiting time to not incentive idling.

With these objectives, the following constraints are added to construct a linear programming model:

$$\sum_{k \in K} \sum_{j \in N} x_{i,j,k} = 1 \ \forall i \in N \tag{1}$$

$$\sum_{j \in N} x_{i,j,k} - \sum_{j \in N} x_{n+i,j,k} = 0 \ \forall i \in P, k \in K \tag{2}$$

$$\sum_{j \in N} x_{0,j,k} = 0 \ \forall k \in K \tag{3}$$

$$\sum_{j \in N} x_{j,i,k} - \sum_{j \in N} x_{i,j,k} = 0 \ \forall i \in N, k \in K \tag{4}$$

$$\sum_{j \in N} x_{j,0,k} = 0 \ \forall k \in K \tag{5}$$

$$x_{i,j,k} * (Q_{i,k} + q_j) <= Q_{j,k} \ \forall i \in N, j \in N, k \in K \tag{6}$$

$$max[0, q_i] <= Q_{i,k} <= min[Q, Q + q_i] \ \forall i \in N, k \in K \tag{7}$$

$$x_{i,j,k} * (B_{i,k} + c_{i,j} + d_j) <= B_{j,k} \ \forall i \in N, j \in N, k \in K \tag{8}$$

$$b_{i,k} + c_{i,n+i} + q_{n+i} <= b_{n+i,k} \ \forall i \in P, k \in K \tag{9}$$

$$ETW_i <= B_{i,k} <= LTW_i \ \forall i \in N, k \in K \tag{10}$$

$$x_{i,j,k} \in [0,1] \tag{11}$$

Constraint 1 enforces that each node is visited once and only once across all vehicles. As the pickup delivery problem with time windows assumes a complete graph, it is assumed that any intermediate stops are irrelevant. Constraint 2 is to enforce that pickup and delivery pairs are in the same route. If a vehicle picks up a product, it must also be the one to deliver it. Constraints 3, 4, and 5 ensure that a subroute is consistent and both starts and ends at the depot. In other words, the vehicle must start and stop at the depot, while also making a cycle. Constraints 6, 7, and 8 guarantee that the routes always arrive within the allowed time window. Equations (9) and (10) guarantee that a vehicle always has a sufficient capacity for the route it is assigned to. Lastly, Constraint 11 enforces that the decision variable be a Boolean variable.

The above is a 3-index model of the pickup and delivery problem with time windows, constructed by [23]. With mixed-integer programming, the objectives are solved hierarchically. First, the minimum number of vehicles are found by solving the model with only one objective. The number of vehicles is then set constant by adding an equality constraint, and the model is rerun with the second objective function to find the minimum distance.

4. Genetic Algorithm

The motivation behind constructing a genetic algorithm heuristic is the size of the problem. MOCPDPTW is NP-hard [1], as it extends the vehicle routing problem (VRP) which is provably NP-hard. This makes finding solutions increasingly difficult as the size of the problem increases. Using Gurobi, the three-index model was unable to find solutions to 50 request instances within the time limit of an hour. The two-index model [24] was able to find solutions but they were worse than using simple construction heuristics such as the cheapest insertion method. Heuristics are required as they trade speed for solution quality. For unexplained notations and for those unfamiliar with evolutionary computing, the reader is referred to a review by Katoch et al. [25] or the introduction by Mitchell [26]. A survey on genetic algorithms with respect to capacitated vehicle routing is provided by Karakatič and Podgorelec [21].

4.1. Solution Representation

For this problem, we encoded a solution (chromosome in genetic algorithms) as an array of arrays. Each array in the outer array represented the route a vehicle would take. Each route was a permutation of nodes sampled from N. An example route can be seen in Figure 1. For each pickup, the corresponding delivery, x + n, appears after. Each route is implicitly known to start and end at the depot, so those nodes are added during the evaluation step.

| 3 | 4 | 2 | (4 + n) | (3 + n) | (2 + n) | 1 | 5 | (1 + n) | (5 + n) |

Figure 1. Example route with 5 pickups and 5 deliveries; n = 5.

4.2. Initial Population

The populations were initialized using the insertion heuristics as construction heuristics. First, we predicted an upper bound on the number of vehicles that were available to cap the number of routes generated. Each route was seeded with a random request. This ensured that each individual would be different. Afterwards, a cheapest parallel insertion heuristic was used. This algorithm is explained in Algorithm 1. Given a solution, each request is inserted into each possible location and the cost is calculated. The solution with the cheapest cost is kept and the process is repeated with the next request. This inserts the request which minimizes the total route time. Once each request has been inserted, a 2-opt algorithm is run on each route to improve the initial solutions.

Algorithm 1 Parallel Insertion

Input: Insertion heuristic H, insertion operator I, local search operator O, number of routes K
Output: A feasible solution

1: *routes* ← List of K empty lists
2: Let *requests* be a set of pickup and delivery pairs
3: Initialize each route in *routes* with a randomly chosen *request* from *requests*
4: Remove each inserted *request* from *requests*
5: **while** Not all *requests* are inserted **do**
6:    *newSolution* ← None
7:    *bestRequest* ← None
8:    **for** each *idx*, *route* in *routes* **do** ▷ At the end newSolution contains the best request inserted in the best location
9:       Choose *request* with H
10:      Insert *request* into *newRoute* with I
11:      Improve *newRoute* with O
12:      **if** *newRoute* is feasible **then**
13:         **if** *newSolution* is None **then** ▷ If this is the first valid insertion
14:            *newSolution* ← *routes*
15:            *newSolution*[*idx*] ← *newRoute*
16:            *bestRequest* ← *request*
17:         **else**
18:            *tempSolution* ← *routes*
19:            *tempSolution*[*idx*] ← *newRoute*
20:            **if** *tempSolution* is better than *newSolution* **then**
21:               *newSolution* ←*tempSolution*
22:               *bestRequest* ← *reqest*
23:            **end if**
24:         **end if**
25:      **end if**
26:    **end for**
27:    **if** *newSolution* is None **then** ▷ The request cannot be inserted anywhere
28:      *bestRequest* ← random request from *requests*
29:      Append *routes* with new route containing *bestRequest*
30:    **else**
31:      *routes* = *newSolution*
32:    **end if**
33:    Remove *bestRequest* from *requests*
34: **end while**
35: **return** *routes*

4.3. Evaluation

Our genetic algorithm utilized NSGA-II to enable multiple objectives. The first objective was to minimize the total distance over all routes. This did not include waiting time or service time. Service time was constant across all nodes, so adding it did not change the solutions relative to each other. The waiting time was the time during which a vehicle was simply sitting idle. This could occur if a vehicle arrived prior to the earliest time window.

The second objective was to minimize the number of vehicles needed. This evaluation step was different from the linear programming version as nondominated sorting was used instead of hierarchical methods.

4.4. Selection

Selection followed the standard given by NSGA-II [4]. For parent selection, a binary tournament was employed with replacement. Parents were chosen iteratively until the number of parents was equal to two times the population. This allowed for the number of offspring to be equal to the population. The offspring were then generated by performing a crossover and a mutation operation before being added into the population. Selecting the next generation was done by sorting the combined offspring and prior population into fronts by which nodes they dominated/were dominated by. They were then sorted within each front by the crowding distance. The individuals were then chosen based hierarchically on their front, followed by their crowding distance until the new population was the same size as the old population. This framework is the same as the $(\mu + \lambda)$ framework [26].

4.5. Crossover

Due to the highly constrained nature of the problem, a specialized crossover function was used. The crossover function began by initializing an empty solution. Iteratively, a route was selected from each parent until no route was left in either parent. If that route contained only pickup and delivery pairs which had not been seen prior, the route was appended to the solution as is. If a route had a node which had already been included, that pickup delivery pair was removed, and the rest of the route was kept intact. The shortened route was then added to the solution. At the end, the routes added got smaller due to nodes being removed. As a final optimization step, all routes with 2 or fewer pickup and delivery nodes were removed from the solution, and the pickup and delivery pairs were extracted. These requests were then reinserted into the solution in a parallel fashion. The final solution was then returned. The intuition for allowing partial routes was that it did not separate requests that were often paired together. This crossover function was called route crossover with ejection. For an example of how this works, see Figure 2.

First Parent	2, 2+n, 3, 3+n	1, 1+n	5, 5+n, 4, 4+n	
Second Parent	2, 1, 2+n, 4, 4+n 1+n,	3, 3+n, 5, 5+n		
Offspring 1st Iteration, route 1 is taken	2, 2+n, 3, 3+n			
Offspring 2nd Iteration, route 2 is taken	2, 2+n, 3, 3+n	5, 5+n		
Offspring 3rd Iteration, route 3 is taken	2, 2+n, 3, 3+n	5, 5+n	4, 4+n	
Offspring Final Iteration, route 1 is taken	2, 2+n, 3, 3+n	5, 5+n	4, 4+n	1, 1+n

Figure 2. Example of crossover without ejection. The final offspring would then have all "small" routes removed and reinserted.

A second crossover operator was tested. Developed by Wang et al. [6] and Alvarenga and Mateus [27]. Wang et al. [6] and Alvarenga and Mateus [27] chose routes iteratively but only accepted routes that could be added in their entirety. Those that could not had all nodes set aside to be reinserted into the surviving routes.

In our trials it was found that the first crossover operator produced slightly better results, so in the results, we opted to use that one. A crossover rate of 1/5 was used. The crossover algorithm is described in Algorithm 2.

Algorithm 2 Crossover Operation

    Input: Parent A, parent B   **Output:** A single offspring C

1: $offspring \leftarrow []$
2: **while** A and B are not empty **do**
3:     Select a random subroute from A
4:     **for** each elem in subroute **do**
5:         **if** elem in $offspring$ **then**
6:             Remove elem from subroute
7:         **end if**
8:     **end for**
9:     Append subroute to $offspring$
10:     Select a random subroute from B
11:     **for** each elem in subroute **do**
12:         **if** elem in $offspring$ **then**
13:             Remove elem from subroute
14:         **end if**
15:     **end for**
16:     Append subroute to $offspring$
17:     **for** each subroute in $offspring$ **do**
18:         **if** size of subroute <=2 **then**
19:             Reinsert all element into routes in $offspring$
20:         **end if**
21:     **end for**
22: **end while**
23: Return $offspring$

4.6. Mutation

Mutation was divided into two stages. The first step was to perform an inter-route operation. This moved nodes between each subroute. The second step was to perform intraroute optimizations. After a route was chosen, it searched an operational neighbourhood for an improved solution. The motivation behind exploring different mutation operators stemmed from the lack of diversity within the literature. Of those that employ intra-route operations, swap mutations are by far the most common mutation. Chami et al. [10], Gong et al. [13], Garcia-Najera and Gutierrez-Andrade [12], and Zhu et al [17] all used a variation of this operator.

4.6.1. Inter-Route Operations

There were six inter-route mutations applied.

- Mutation 1: single-pair relocation
    - Removes a single pickup and delivery pair from a random route and attempts to insert it into another route.
- Mutation 2: double-pair relocation
    - Randomly selects 2 routes and attempts to swap a pickup and delivery pair between them.
- Mutation 3: customer relocation
    - Randomly picks a route and attempts to add a random pickup and delivery pair.
- Mutation 4: best-customer relocation
    - Randomly picks a route and attempts to add the pickup and delivery pair according to a heuristic

- Mutation 5: route ejection
    - Selects a route and unassign all pickup and delivery pairs. Afterwards, it attempts to insert all of them.
- Mutation 6: route divide
    - Selects a route and creates 2 new routes out of the pickup and delivery pairs.

These 6 mutations were given an equal probability of occurring. Each of these mutations required an insertion operator. To make the most general insertion operators, we followed the algorithms as described in Algorithms 1 and 3. These inter-route operations were inspired by the works of Wang and Chen [16] and Yanik, Bozkaya, and Dekervenoael [28].

Algorithm 3 Sequential Insertion

Input: Insertion heuristic H, insertion operator I, local search operator O
Output: A feasible solution

1: *routes* ← []
2: Let *requests* be a set of pickup and delivery pairs
3: **while** True **do**
4:     *newRoute* ← []
5:     **while** Not all *requests* are inserted **do**
6:         *tempRoute* ← *newRoute*
7:         Choose *request* with H
8:         Insert *request* into *newRoute* with I
9:         Improve *newRoute* with O
10:        **if** *newRoute* is feasible **then**
11:            Remove *request* from *requests*
12:        **else**
13:            Append *tempRoute* to *routes*
14:            break
15:        **end if**
16:    **end while**
17:    **if** *requests* is empty **then**
18:        return *routes*
19:    **end if**
20: **end while**

For the sequential insertion, a heuristic, an insertion operator, and a local search operator were supplied. Starting with an empty solution, routes were built iteratively by choosing a request based on the insertion heuristic and the insertion operator. Once the optimal request had been inserted, the resulting route was improved by the local search operator until it could not be improved anymore. If at any point a new pickup and delivery pair could not be inserted, the route was added to the solution as is and a new route was started with the previously uninserted pair. These processes were repeated until all requests were inserted.

The parallel insertion heuristic worked very similarly. Given a starting number of vehicles k, k routes were initialized with a randomly chosen request. The optimal request across all routes were chosen via the insertion heuristic and operator. Only one route was improved at each iteration. From there, the route was improved with the local search operator and inserted into the solution. If a request could not be inserted into any route, a new route was appended much like the sequential variation.

4.6.2. Insertion Operators

Another consideration in the design was which insertion operators to use. As mentioned previously one can insert in both parallel and sequential fashions. There are also several heuristics to improve which requests get inserted and where to insert. Common methods include the cheapest insertion, which inserts the request that minimizes the total distance, the furthest insertion, which maximizes the total distance, and the random insertion, which places a random request.

We found that choosing requests via the cheapest insertion method was the most useful method. Moreover, our trials found that the number of vehicles had little effect on the final result. As such, choosing a number of initial routes for the parallel insertion operator was not impactful. In the end, we chose to use the parallel construction heuristic for our initial populations. While both produced similar results, the parallel construction was able to create more varied populations and therefore had more diversity throughout.

4.6.3. Intraroute Operations

In addition to insertion operators, the routes are often further optimized with local search operators. Multiple local search operators are tested and explained in Table 1 below. Some were standard genetic algorithm operators such as the swap mutation while others were more problem-specific such as the blocked 2-opt operator. A blocked operation involves grouping the pickup and delivery pairs into single entities. The idea is to keep pickup and delivery pairs together. Sequentially going down a list, the nodes are added into a bin starting with a pickup and until the corresponding delivery node is reached. After the first bin has been filled, the route is restarted at the next pickup node and the process repeats until all pickup and delivery pairs are considered. All nodes between a pickup and delivery pair are included in the group and as such this results in multiple copies of some nodes. The original decoding by [22] was LIFO (last in, first out) and assumed that there would never be any overlap. To address this, only the first copy of a node was kept when converting back into a normal route. This can be further seen in Table 2. Operations were then performed on these groups instead of individual elements. The reasoning for this was to preserve precedence. If pickup and delivery pairs moved together, it was impossible for the precedence to be violated.

4.7. Datasets

When choosing a dataset, there is often many factors to consider. For nonstandard PDP, there is no consensus on a benchmark dataset, with most papers generating their own [1]. While this does allow data to be curated for any problem, there is the issue on how representative of real-world scenarios the synthesized data will be.

One dataset we elected to use comes from Sulzbach Sartori and Buriol [29]. This dataset is an open-source dataset based on geographical data from capital cities. It supplies several instances of varying node counts and incorporates real-world travel time to ensure that it is representative of actual data. We used 25 instances with 100 nodes. The input instances were labelled with the city they were based on, the number of nodes, and the instance number. In this case bar-n100-2 would be the second instance in Barcelona with 100 nodes.

In addition, we also used the well-known Li Lim [30] dataset. This is a commonly used benchmark dataset for the pickup and delivery problem. It uses Euclidean distances between points and hierarchically solves for the number of vehicles and then distance. Li Lim [30] distinguished their instances based on how the nodes were arranged. Lr instances were randomly distributed, lc instances were clustered, and lrc instances were partially distributed randomly.

Table 1. Descriptions of each local search operator.

Mutation	Description
Swap	Selects 2 nodes in a route and attempts to switch them.
Displacement	Selects a subroute of a fixed size within a route and translates it.
Insertion	Special case of displacement mutation with size 1.
Gaussian displacement	Selects a subroute of a randomly chosen size within a route and translates it.
K-Opt	Removes k edges and attempt to reconnect them.
Blocked K-Opt	Combines nodes into request blocks, removes k edges and attempts to reconnect them.
End request swap	Swaps the delivery of one request with the pickup of another later on.
Request Swap	Swaps a pickup and delivery with another pickup and delivery node within the same route.
Boundaries	Half of the time, performs a request swap and half of the time, performs an end request stop.

Table 2. Example of a route that has been blocked.

3, 4, 2, 4 + n, 3 + n	4, 2, 4 + n	2, 4 + n, 3 + n, 2 + n	1, 5, 1 + n	5, 1 + n, 5 + n

Both datasets can be trivially adapted into multiobjective instances. Moreover, both datasets come with the best-known solution which was treated as the optimal solution with respect to the lower bound and for calculating optimality. Optimality gaps were calculated through the equation

$$1 - (\text{Found solution}/\text{best known solution})$$

5. Results

All instances were run for a max time of 30 min or a max epoch of 300 on an i7-9750H CPU with 16 GB of RAM. A population of 50 was utilized. A time limit of 1800 s was applied, should the algorithm fail to terminate within that time. The total results for each instance can be found in Appendix A.

The max epochs of 300 was chosen arbitrarily such that the time limit was the more important factor. This allowed the algorithms to compare highly complex operations against very efficient operators without heavily biasing the results towards search techniques with larger neighbourhoods. Measuring epochs instead of time limits biases the algorithm towards complex and costly operations. Very rarely did instances hit the epoch limit as opposed to the time limit. In this instance, convergence meant that all genomes within the population had the same fitness value, essentially reducing the diversity to 0. Convergence is important as if the population is still very diverse, it means that the local optimum has not been reached yet, while if the diversity is 0, then no more learning can be done. Test runs were run in 10 min intervals on the first five instances of the Li Lim dataset in order to empirically choose these values. The 2-opt operator was chosen for these runs. These runs held all other parameters constant. For a time limit of 10, the algorithm did not converge at all, still having around 16 fronts on average. In four out of five cases the 20 min test run converged, while when given 30 min, all test cases converged. As the time got longer the solutions got better. A final time limit of 30 min was chosen to allow a greater chance at convergence, especially given more complex operators. On the final run, with a 30 min time limit, the algorithm converged about 25% of the time.

The population size was chosen in much the same fashion. Using a grid search technique, population sizes of 25, 50, and 100 were tested. A time limit of 30 min was allotted. On the five test instances, a populations size of 50 was found to perform the best. A population size of 25 had the population converge very early on, preventing further learning from taking place. With a population size of 50, there was still some diversity within the population. A population size of 100 was far too large for the problem. Within 30 min, none of the five test cases had converged and the four instances had upwards of 60 fronts. Of the resulting best solutions, all five came from the test case where the population size was 50. With 25 and 50, the optimal solution was found twice.

The results from the Li Lim dataset can be seen in Table A1. This table lists the instance name, the best solution and our found solution. The solutions are in the form of number of vehicles, distance travelled. Our algorithm was able to find the optimal (best known) result in 13 out of 56 instances. In the rest of the trials, we were able to find results within one vehicle and within 10% in most cases for the distance. The worst result we achieved was on the instance lr205 in which our three-vehicle solution was only 27% within optimality in regard to distance. Our five-vehicle solution was within 13%, however. Four of our results were 20% or higher, while in forty-three instances our result was within 10% of optimality. Omitting the lr 200 instances, the average distance optimality gap was 4% as seen in Table 3. When nodes were randomly distributed, our algorithm performed the worst. The proposed algorithm performed the best when the nodes were clustered, in which 9 out of 17 were optimal. In three cases, our algorithm was able to reduce the total distance to below that of the best-known solution. Often, the genetic algorithm would converge to a local optimum and would then cease learning. The addition of the 4-opt mutation was able to help remove solutions from this pool on occasion.

Table 3. Summary on Li-Lim benchmark.

Instance	Distance Optimality Gap	Vehicle Optimality Gap
lc 100 instances	−0.0462	0.0416
lc 200 instances	0.02983	0.0
lr 100 instances	0.0402	0.0790
lr 200 instances	0.1364	0.2424
lrc 100 instances	0.0441	0.0658
lrc 200 instances	0.04779	0.1562

The results from the Sulzbach Sartori and Buriol's [29] dataset can be seen in Table A2, and summarized in Table 4. This dataset was more complex than the previous one, with our algorithm not always converging within a 30 min time limit. As such, our algorithm was not able to solve to optimality in any of the instances. Despite this, we were able to solve the problem in every case and produce solutions within one vehicle and an average of 2.97% of the optimal distance on average. Distancewise the worst solution was bar-n100-6 with an optimality gap of 11.81%. It was one of two total solutions with a gap larger than 10%. It is not surprising that we did not find that many optimal solutions within the specified time limit. Our algorithm had a lot of overhead dedicated to finding many feasible solutions as opposed to finding one optimal solution. Maintaining multiple unique genomes allow a greater diversity and more options for choosing a final solution.

Table 4. Summary on Sulzbach Sartori and Buriol's benchmark.

Instance	Distance Optimality Gap	Vehicle Optimality Gap
bar instances	0.0550	0.0694
ber instances	0.0292	0.1360
nyc instances	0.0388	0.2666
poa instances	0.0019	0.1170

A secondary study was conducted to determine which inter-route and intraroute operators would be most effective.

To choose which intraroute operations to utilize, a comparison was generated. For each operator five trials were run on five different instances. Each trial was run using identical parameters. Each run had a population of 50 and was run for 200 epochs. Initial populations were generated with a parallel construction and then solved to be 2-opt optimal. The crossover rate was 0.2 and the starting number of vehicles was chosen to be slightly higher than the known best solution, typically higher than four.

For each run, the total number of fronts and the number of unique solutions were measured to quantify the diversity of the population, as seen in Table 5. Table 6 measures the solution quality. The points at the Pareto front and the hypervolume were measured to compare the quality of the solutions. For each operator the z score of the hypervolume was also recorded. This allowed a direct measurement of how much better each operator was in comparison. Table 7 aggregates all of the trials.

Table 5. Local search operators effects on diversity of bar-n100-1 [29].

Local Search Operator	Final # of Fronts	Number of Unique Solutions
No-op	1	1
Swap mutation	3	19
Blocked swap mutation	2	6
Insertion mutation	3	6
Blocked insertion	1	3
Displacement mutation	3	13
Blocked displacement mutation	3	10
Gaussian displacement mutation	1	6
Blocked Gaussian displacement mutation	1	5
2-Opt	1	5
Blocked 2-opt	1	3
3-Opt	8	12
Blocked 3-opt	7	27
4-Opt	1	8
Blocked 4-opt	1	5
Boundary operators	2	15

Each operator with the exception of the 4-opt operator was run in a dynamic programming fashion, fully exhausting the neighbourhood to ensure the best move was made. For the 4-opt and blocked 4-opt operators, this was infeasible due to the size of the search space, so a Monte Carlo framework was used. One hundred random neighbourhood moves were tested and the best one was used for this iteration of local search.

Table 6. Local search operators effects on solution quality of bar-n100-1 [29].

Local Search Operator	(Vehicle Count, Distance) in Front 0	Hypervolume	z Score
No-op	(7, 774)	126	−1.40152
Swap mutation	(6, 779), (7, 776)	245	0.59139
Blocked swap mutation	(6, 797), (7, 762)	241	0.5244
Insertion mutation	(6, 754)	292	1.37851
Blocked insertion mutation	(6, 797), (7, 766)	237	0.45742
Displacement mutation	(6, 779), (7, 764)	257	0.79236
Blocked displacement mutation	(7, 783)	117	−1.55225
Gaussian displacement mutation	(6, 837), (7, 815)	148	−1.03308
Blocked Gaussian displacement mutation	(6, 782), (7, 771)	247	0.62489
2-Opt	(6, 768)	264	0.90959
Blocked 2-opt	(6, 776), (7, 778)	248	0.64164
3-Opt	(7, 798)	102	−1.80345
Blocked 3-opt	(6, 794), (7, 769)	237	0.45742
4-Opt	(6, 790), (7, 787)	223	0.22296
Blocked 4-opt	(7, 770)	130	−1.33453
Boundaries operators	(6, 786), (7, 773), (8, 771)	241	0.5244

Reference Point 8, 900.

The results indicated that the 2-opt operator was the best move by a decently large margin. The 3-opt operator move was too slow to test exhaustively and so failed to converge like the other trials. The 4-opt operator had the largest variance of any operator. On some runs it found the best solution and on some it found the worst. The standard array of mutation operators performed adequately but were not able to compare to more specialized operators.

As for diversity, out of those that converged, the 4-opt operator had the best diversity within each front, with an average of eight unique individuals per front. Insertion mutation had the worst diversity averaging only 1.8 fronts and 5.6 individuals.

To address both diversity and solution quality, a combination of 4-opt and 2-opt was used in the final model.

To assess the effectiveness of each intraroute operator an ablation study was conducted. There were seven different scenarios run over five different instances. All runs held all parameters constant aside from the inter-route operations. They were run for 200 epochs with a population of 50. The initial population was created with parallel insertion and the 2-opt operator, with the intraroute operation also using the 2-opt operator. The 2-opt operator is a standard local search operator for variants on the travelling salesman problem. It involves selecting two edges and swapping them, effectively generating two new routes.

In each scenario, a single inter-route operation was removed to assess its effect on the final solution. Results are in Tables 8–10. Figure 3 shows the average hypervolume value over time and Figure 4 shows how minimum distance is affected. The hypervolume is a special measurement that calculates the area of the solution space and a reference point that is larger in magnitude than any given point in all dimensions. This area allows a direct comparison of the solutions generated. It was first introduced by Ziztler and Theile [31] in 1999. The main benefit of this measure is that it makes no assumptions on any knowledge about the Pareto front, which the other measures require.

Table 7. Local search operators summary statistics.

Local Search Operator	Mean Z Score	Mean # of Fronts	Mean # of Unique Solutions
No-op	−0.51334	2.4	6.4
Swap mutation	−0.043814	2.6	13.2
Blocked swap mutation	0.97958	3.4	12.6
Insertion mutation	0.33991	1.8	5.8
Blocked insertion mutation	0.32763	1.6	8.2
Displacement mutation	0.3491	2.2	8.2
Blocked displacement mutation	−0.31909	2.8	12.6
Gaussian displacement mutation	−0.179226	1.8	8.4
Blocked Gaussian displacement mutation	−0.16168	2.4	10.8
2-Opt	0.87708	2	8
Blocked 2-opt	0.118585	3.6	11
3-Opt	−1.22385	6.6	21.4
Blocked 3-opt	0.17869	4.8	16.6
4-Opt	0.16474	1.6	12.8
Blocked 4-opt	−0.80439	3	14.6
Boundaries operators	0.044518	3.8	18.6

The experiment tested how much each pickup and delivery operation affected the end result. For each operator, the genetic algorithm was run with all other parameters fixed. The only difference was the inclusion of each operator. Each run was executed with a population of 40, over 300 epochs. All other parameters were held constant.

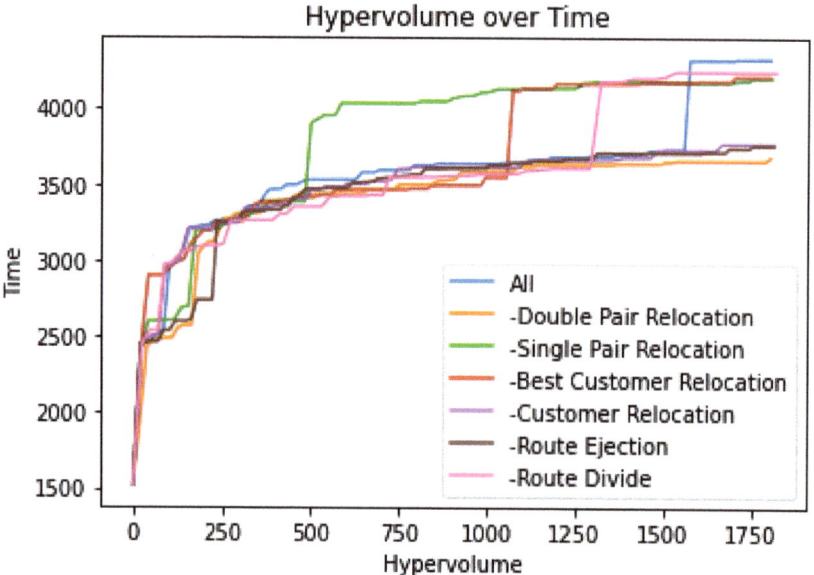

Figure 3. Hypervolume after removing each inter-route operator.

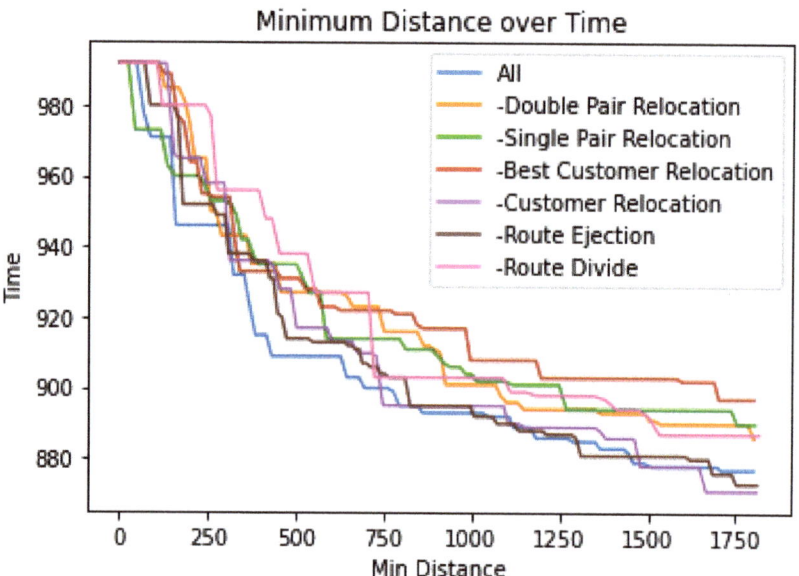

Figure 4. Minimum distance after removing each inter-route operator.

Table 8. Inter-route operation effects on diversity of bar-n100-5 [29].

Inter-Route Operator	Final # of Fronts	Number of Unique Solutions
All	1.8	5
Double-pair relocation	1	4
Single-pair relocation	3	28
Best-customer relocation	3	13
Customer relocation	1	8
Route ejection	1	5
Route divide	2	9

Table 9. Inter-route operation effects on solution quality of bar-n100-5 [29].

Inter-Route Operator	(Vehicle Count, Distance) in Front 0	Hypervolume
All	(6, 780), (7, 772)	248
Double-pair relocation	(6, 785), (7, 782)	233
Single-pair relocation	(6, 784), (7, 761)	255
Best-customer relocation	(6, 805), (7, 776)	219
Customer relocation	(6, 806), (7, 777)	217
Route ejection	(7, 746)	154
Route divide	(6, 788), (7, 770)	242

Reference Point 8, 900.

Table 10. Inter-route operation effects on solution quality of bar-n100-5 [29] Part 2.

Inter-Route Operator	Mean Z Score	Mean # of Fronts
All	1	1
Double-pair relocation	3	19
Single-pair relocation	2	6
Best-customer relocation	3	6
Customer relocation	1	3
Route ejection	3	13
Route divide	3	10

Reference Point 8, 900.

6. Discussion and Conclusions

In this work we formulated a genetic algorithm based on NSGA-II for solving the multiobjective capacitated pickup and delivery problem with time windows. We built two generic metaheuristics which allowed solution construction and insertion and explored six different inter-route operations and sixteen different intraroute operations. We found that adding intraroute operations in addition to inter-route operations greatly improved solution quality, with 2-opt being the best operator we trialed.

Of the inter-route operations, all of the tested operators benefited the end result. The variety of each operator enabled a good diversity within the population. The intraroute operators had more interesting results. Standard genetic algorithm operators such as mutation tended to perform poorly. Operators that took structure into account such as k-opt performed much better. Blocking the results did not have as much success despite taking more of the problem into consideration.

Our work does contain some limitations. Without proper benchmarks within the literature, it is difficult to compare results directly. Additionally, future work would involve exploring different ways to maintain diversity, as our algorithm was occasionally stuck in local optima. There are many ways that this could be implemented, either by speciation, island models, or geographical encodings.

Author Contributions: Conceptualization, C.L., K.S., T.H. and S.C.; methodology, C.L.; software, C.L.; validation, C.L.; investigation, C.L.; data curation, C.L.; writing—original draft preparation, C.L.; writing—review and editing, K.S., T.H. and S.C.; visualization, C.L.; supervision, K.S., T.H. and S.C.; project administration, C.L. and S.C. All authors have read and agreed to the published version of the manuscript.

Funding: This research is funded by Vector Scholarship in Artificial Intelligence and NSERC CGS-M 2021 scholarships of Connor Little, as well as NSERC discovery grant received by Dr. Salimur Choudhury (RGPIN-2018-1507).

Institutional Review Board Statement: Not applicable.

Informed Consent Statement: Not applicable.

Data Availability Statement: Li Lim dataset [30]: https://www.sintef.no/projectweb/top/pdptw/li-lim-benchmark/ (accessed on 25 September 2022).

Conflicts of Interest: The authors declare no conflict of interest.

Abbreviations

The following abbreviations are used in this manuscript:

PDP   Pickup and delivery problem
MOCPDPTW   Multiobjective capacitated pickup and delivery problem with time windows

Appendix A

Below are Tables A1 and A2 and displaying the found and best solutions for each instance in the Li Lim [30] and Sulzbach Sartori and Buriol [29] datasets, respectively.

Table A1. Results on Li-Lim's benchmark.

Instance	Best Solution	Found Solution
lc101	(10, 828.94)	(10, 828.94)
lc102	(10, 828.94)	(10, 828.94)
lc103	(9, 1035.35)	(10, 829.56) *
lc104	(9, 860.01)	(10, 818.60) *
lc105	(10, 828.94)	(10, 828.94)
lc106	(10, 828.94)	(10, 828.94)
lc107	(10, 828.94)	(10, 828.94)
lc108	(10, 826.44)	(10, 828.94)
lc109	(9, 1000.60)	(10, 828.94) *
lc201	(3, 591.56)	(3, 591.56)
lc202	(3, 591.56)	(3, 591.56)
lc203	(3, 591.17)	(3, 648.05), (4, 637.87)
lc204	(3, 590.60)	(3, 674.84)
lc205	(3, 588.88)	(3, 588.88)
lc206	(3, 588.49)	(3, 597.31)
lc207	(3, 588.29)	(3, 588.29)
lc208	(3, 588.23)	(3, 589.44)

Table A1. *Cont.*

Instance	Best Solution	Found Solution
lr101	(19, 1650.80)	(20, 1700)
lr102	(17, 1487.57)	(17, 1519.98)
lr103	(13, 1292.68)	(13, 1337.34), (14, 1333.39)
lr104	(9, 1013.39)	(10, 1067.19)
lr105	(14, 1377.11)	(15, 1486.85)
lr106	(12, 1252.62)	(12, 1287.67), (13, 1271.09)
lr107	(10, 1111.31)	(10, 1111.31)
lr108	(9, 968.97)	(9, 970.74)
lr109	(11, 1208.96)	(12, 1251.53)
lr110	(10, 1159.35)	(12, 1226.60)
lr111	(10, 1108.90)	(12, 1203.15)
lr112	(9, 1003.77)	(11, 1075.88)
lr201	(4, 1253.23)	(4, 1311.34), (5, 1291.02), (6, 1289.23)
lr202	(3, 1197.67)	(4, 1287.83)
lr203	(3, 949.40)	(3, 1042.40)
lr204	(2, 849.05)	(3, 1053.58)
lr205	(3, 1054.02)	(3, 1342.12), (4, 1211.80), (5, 1191.29)
lr206	(3, 931.63)	(3, 970.70)
lr207	(2, 903.06)	(3, 1120.39), (4, 1116.43)
lr208	(2, 734.85)	(3, 891.17)
lr209	(3, 930.59)	(4, 1030.60)
lr210	(3, 964.22)	(3, 1188.75), (4, 1179.80)
lr211	(2, 911.52)	(3, 1097.17), (4, 1007.62)
lrc101	(14, 1708.80)	(14, 1708.80)
lrc102	(12, 1558.07)	(13, 1608.49)
lrc103	(11, 1258.74)	(11, 1275.32)
lrc104	(10, 1128.40)	(10, 1128.40)
lrc105	(13, 1637.62)	(14, 1734.76)
lrc106	(11, 1424.73)	(13, 1531.88)
lrc107	(11, 1230.14)	(12, 1399.75)
lrc108	(10, 1147.43)	(11, 1188.12)
lrc201	(4, 1406.94)	(5, 1494.95)
lrc202	(3, 1374.27)	(4, 1440.29)
lrc203	(3, 1089.07)	(4, 1153.20)
lrc204	(3, 818.66)	(3, 914.81), (4, 887.48)
lrc205	(4, 1302.20)	(4, 1310.28)
lrc206	(3, 1159.03)	(3, 1159.03)
lrc207	(3, 1062.05)	(3, 1066.68)
lrc208	(3, 852.76)	(4, 953.59)

Results in which distance was improved are indicated wtih an *.

Table A2. Results on Sulzbach Sartori and Buriol's benchmark.

Instance	Best Solution	Found Solution
bar-n100-1	(6, 733)	(6, 776), (7, 766)
bar-n100-2	(5, 554)	(5, 608), (6, 579)
bar-n100-3	(6, 746)	(6, 803), (7, 777)
bar-n100-4	(12, 1154)	(13, 1217), (14, 1193)
bar-n100-5	(6, 838)	(6, 909), (7, 877)
bar-n100-6	(3, 788)	(4, 933), (5, 894), (6, 890), (7, 881)

Table A2. *Cont.*

Instance	Best Solution	Found Solution
ber-n100-1	(12, 1857)	(14, 1848) *
ber-n100-2	(6, 1491)	(7, 1569)
ber-n100-3	(3, 713)	(4, 745), (5, 702), (6, 695) *
ber-n100-4	(3, 494)	(3, 555)
ber-n100-5	(5, 944)	(5, 966)
ber-n100-6	(14, 2147)	(16, 2108) *
ber-n100-7	(7, 1935)	(8, 2043), (9, 2039)
nyc-n100-1	(6, 634)	(6, 731), (7, 665)
nyc-n100-2	(4, 567)	(4, 603), (5, 587), (6, 583)
nyc-n100-3	(3, 492)	(4, 477)
nyc-n100-4	(2, 535)	(3, 589)
nyc-n100-5	(2, 671)	(3, 702)
poa-n100-1	(12, 1589)	(14, 1637)
poa-n100-2	(15, 1539)	(16, 1645), (17, 1640)
poa-n100-3	(10, 1301)	(11, 1329), (12, 1311)
poa-n100-4	(7, 1668)	(9, 1586) *
poa-n100-5	(6, 624)	(6, 630), (7, 626)
poa-n100-6	(3, 562)	(3, 601), (4, 574), (5, 572)
poa-n100-7	(5, 779)	(6, 743), (7, 731)

Results in which distance was improved are indicated with an *.

References

1. Koç, Ç.; Laporte, G.; Tükenmez, İ. A review of vehicle routing with simultaneous pickup and delivery. *Comput. Oper. Res.* **2020**, *122*, 104987. [CrossRef]
2. Xu, Z.; Elomri, A.; Kerbache, L.; El Omri, A. Impacts of COVID-19 on Global Supply Chains: Facts and Perspectives. *IEEE Eng. Manag. Rev.* **2020**, *48*, 153–166. [CrossRef]
3. Parragh, S.N.; Doerner, K.F.; Hartl, R.F. A survey on pickup and delivery problems: Part II: Transportation between pickup and delivery locations. *J. Betriebswirtschaft* **2008**, *58*, 81–117. [CrossRef]
4. Deb, K.; Agrawal, S.; Pratap, A.; Meyarivan, T. A fast and elitist multiobjective genetic algorithm: NSGA-II. *IEEE Trans. Evol. Comput.* **2002**, *6*, 182–197. [CrossRef]
5. Tomasz, M. Visual Attractiveness of the Routes in the Vehicle Routing Problem. Mater's Thesis, University Wien, Wien, Austria, 2018.
6. Wang, J.; Zhou, Y.; Wang, Y.; Zhang, J.; Chen, C.L.; Zheng, Z. Multiobjective Vehicle Routing Problems with Simultaneous Delivery and Pickup and Time Windows: Formulation, Instances, and Algorithms. *IEEE Trans. Cybern.* **2016**, *46*, 582–594. [CrossRef]
7. Abdoun, O.; Abouchabaka, J.; Tajani, C. Analyzing the Performance of Mutation Operators to Solve the Travelling Salesman Problem. *arXiv* **2012**, arXiv:1203.3099.
8. Berbeglia, G.; Cordeau, J.F.; Gribkovskaia, I.; Laporte, G. Static pickup and delivery problems: A classification scheme and survey. *Top* **2007**, *15*, 1–31. [CrossRef]
9. Bravo, M.; Rojas, L.P.; Parada, V. An evolutionary algorithm for the multi-objective pick-up and delivery pollution-routing problem. *Int. Trans. Oper. Res.* **2019**, *26*, 302–317. [CrossRef]
10. Chami, Z.A.; Manier, H.; Manier, M.A.; Fitouri, C. *A Hybrid Genetic Algorithm to Solve a Multi-Objective Pickup and Delivery Problem*; Elsevier B.V.: Amsterdam, The Netherlands, 2017; Volume 50, pp. 14656–14661. [CrossRef]
11. Fatemi-Anaraki, S.; Mokhtarzadeh, M.; Rabbani, M.; Abdolhamidi, D. A hybrid of K-means and genetic algorithm to solve a bi-objective green delivery and pick-up problem. *J. Ind. Prod. Eng.* **2021**, *39*, 146–157. [CrossRef]
12. Garcia-Najera, A.; Gutierrez-Andrade, M.A. An evolutionary approach to the multi-objective pickup and delivery problem with time windows. In Proceedings of the 2013 IEEE Congress on Evolutionary Computation, Cancun, Mexico, 20–23 June 2013; pp. 997–1004. [CrossRef]
13. Gong, G.; Deng, Q.; Gong, X.; Zhang, L.; Wang, H.; Xie, H. A Bee Evolutionary Algorithm for Multiobjective Vehicle Routing Problem with Simultaneous Pickup and Delivery. *Math. Probl. Eng.* **2018**, *2018*, 2571380. [CrossRef]
14. Naik, N.; Jenkins, P.; Savage, N.; Yang, L.; Naik, K.; Song, J.; Boongoen, T.; Iam-On, N. Fuzzy hashing aided enhanced YARA rules for malware triaging. In Proceedings of the 2020 IEEE Symposium Series on Computational Intelligence (SSCI), Canberra, Australia, 1–4 December 2020.
15. Velasco, N.; Dejax, P.; Guéret, C.; Prins, C. A non-dominated sorting genetic algorithm for a bi-objective pick-up and delivery problem. *Eng. Optim.* **2012**, *44*, 305–325. [CrossRef]
16. Wang, H.F.; Chen, Y.Y. A genetic algorithm for the simultaneous delivery and pickup problems with time window. *Comput. Ind. Eng.* **2012**, *62*, 84–95. [CrossRef]

17. Zhu, Z.; Xiao, J.; He, S.; Ji, Z.; Sun, Y. A multi-objective memetic algorithm based on locality-sensitive hashing for one-to-many-to-one dynamic pickup-and-delivery problem. *Inf. Sci.* **2016**, *329*, 73–89. [CrossRef]
18. Grandinetti, L.; Guerriero, F.; Pezzella, F.; Pisacane, O. The Multi-objective Multi-vehicle Pickup and Delivery Problem with Time Windows. *Procedia—Soc. Behav. Sci.* **2014**, *111*, 203–212. [CrossRef]
19. Ren, X.; Huang, H.; Feng, S.; Liang, G. An improved variable neighborhood search for bi-objective mixed-energy fleet vehicle routing problem. *J. Clean. Prod.* **2020**, *275*, 124155. [CrossRef]
20. Zou, S.; Li, J.; Li, X. A hybrid particle swarm optimization algorithm for multi-objective pickup and delivery problem with time windows. *J. Comput.* **2013**, *8*, 2583–2589. [CrossRef]
21. Karakatič, S.; Podgorelec, V. A survey of genetic algorithms for solving multi depot vehicle routing problem. *Appl. Soft Comput. J.* **2015**, *27*, 519–532. [CrossRef]
22. Carrabs, F.; Cordeau, J.F.; Laporte, G. Variable Neighbourhood Search for the Pickup and Delivery Travelling Salesman Problem with LIFO Loading. *INFORMS J. Comput.* **2007**, *19*, 618–632. [CrossRef]
23. Cordeau, J.F.O. A Branch-and-Cut Algorithm for the Dial-a-Ride Problem. *Oper. Res.* **2003**, *54*, 573–586. [CrossRef]
24. Furtado, M.G.S.; Munari, P.; Morabito, R. Pickup and delivery problem with time windows: A new compact two-index formulation. *Oper. Res. Lett.* **2017**, *45*, 334–341. [CrossRef]
25. Katoch, S.; Chauhan, S.S.; Kumar, V. A review on genetic algorithm: Past, present, and future. *Multimed. Tools Appl.* **2021**, *80*, 8091–8126. [CrossRef] [PubMed]
26. Mitchell, M. *An Introduction to Genetic Algorithms*; MIT Press: Cambridge, MA, USA, 1998.
27. Alvarenga, G.B.; Mateus, G.R. A Two-Phase Genetic and Set Partitioning Approach for the Vehicle Routing Problem with Time Windows. In Proceedings of the Fourth International Conference on Hybrid Intelligent Systems (HIS'04), Kitakyushu, Japan, 5–8 December 2004.
28. Yanik, S.; Bozkaya, B.; Dekervenoael, R. A new VRPPD model and a hybrid heuristic solution approach for e-tailing. *Eur. J. Oper. Res.* **2014**, *236*, 879–890. [CrossRef]
29. Sartori, C.S.; Buriol, L. Instances for the Pickup and Delivery Problem with Time Windows based on open data. In *Mendeley Data*; 2020. [CrossRef]
30. Li, H.; Lim, A. A Metaheuristic for the Pickup and Delivery Problem with Time Windows. *Int. J. Artif. Intell. Tools* **2001**, *12*, 173–186. [CrossRef]
31. Zitzler, E.; Thiele, L. Multiobjective Evolutionary Algorithms: A Comparative Case Study and the Strength Pareto Approach. *IEEE Trans. Evol. Comput.* **1999**, *3*, 257–271. [CrossRef]

 *mathematics*

Article

A Multi-Depot Dynamic Vehicle Routing Problem with Stochastic Road Capacity: An MDP Model and Dynamic Policy for Post-Decision State Rollout Algorithm in Reinforcement Learning

Wadi Khalid Anuar [1,2], Lai Soon Lee [2,3,*], Hsin-Vonn Seow [4] and Stefan Pickl [5]

1. Department of Logistics and Transportation, School of Technology Management and Logistics, Universiti Utara Malaysia, Sintok 06010, Kedah, Malaysia; wadikhalidanuar@gmail.com
2. Laboratory of Computational Statistics and Operations Research, Institute for Mathematical Research, Universiti Putra Malaysia, Serdang 43400, Selangor, Malaysia
3. Department of Mathematics and Statistics, Faculty of Science, Universiti Putra Malaysia, Serdang 43400, Selangor, Malaysia
4. Faculty of Arts and Social Sciences, Nottingham University Business School, University of Nottingham Malaysia Campus, Semenyih 43500, Selangor, Malaysia; hsin-vonn.seow@nottingham.edu.my
5. Fakultät für Informatik, Universität der Bundeswehr München, 85577 Neubiberg, Germany; stefan.pickl@unibw.de
* Correspondence: lls@upm.edu.my

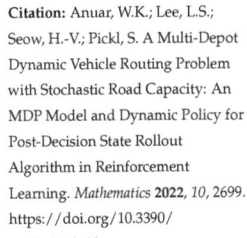

Citation: Anuar, W.K.; Lee, L.S.; Seow, H.-V.; Pickl, S. A Multi-Depot Dynamic Vehicle Routing Problem with Stochastic Road Capacity: An MDP Model and Dynamic Policy for Post-Decision State Rollout Algorithm in Reinforcement Learning. *Mathematics* 2022, *10*, 2699. https://doi.org/10.3390/math10152699

Academic Editors: Francois Rivest and Abdellah Chehri

Received: 2 June 2022
Accepted: 26 July 2022
Published: 30 July 2022

Publisher's Note: MDPI stays neutral with regard to jurisdictional claims in published maps and institutional affiliations.

Copyright: © 2022 by the authors. Licensee MDPI, Basel, Switzerland. This article is an open access article distributed under the terms and conditions of the Creative Commons Attribution (CC BY) license (https://creativecommons.org/licenses/by/4.0/).

Abstract: In the event of a disaster, the road network is often compromised in terms of its capacity and usability conditions. This is a challenge for humanitarian operations in the context of delivering critical medical supplies. To optimise vehicle routing for such a problem, a Multi-Depot Dynamic Vehicle-Routing Problem with Stochastic Road Capacity (MDDVRPSRC) is formulated as a Markov Decision Processes (MDP) model. An Approximate Dynamic Programming (ADP) solution method is adopted where the Post-Decision State Rollout Algorithm (PDS-RA) is applied as the lookahead approach. To perform the rollout effectively for the problem, the PDS-RA is executed for all vehicles assigned for the problem. Then, at the end, a decision is made by the agent. Five types of constructive base heuristics are proposed for the PDS-RA. First, the Teach Base Insertion Heuristic (TBIH-1) is proposed to study the partial random construction approach for the non-obvious decision. The heuristic is extended by proposing TBIH-2 and TBIH-3 to show how Sequential Insertion Heuristic (SIH) (I1) as well as Clarke and Wright (CW) could be executed, respectively, in a dynamic setting as a modification to the TBIH-1. Additionally, another two heuristics: TBIH-4 and TBIH-5 (TBIH-1 with the addition of Dynamic Lookahead SIH (DLASIH) and Dynamic Lookahead CW (DLACW) respectively) are proposed to improve the on-the-go constructed decision rule (dynamic policy on the go) in the lookahead simulations. The results obtained are compared with the matheuristic approach from previous work based on PDS-RA.

Keywords: reinforcement learning; Markov decision processes; approximate dynamic programming; rollout algorithm; constructive base heuristic; vehicle routing problem

MSC: 90C40; 90B15; 90C59

1. Introduction

Recent events have shown that the occurrence of a disaster continues to claim many lives despite the growing number of relief organisations to support and help the victims throughout the world. In the case of the 2015 Nepal earthquake, for example, nearly 9000 lives were lost, and 23,000 people were injured [1]. In the event, critical medical supplies and health personnel were far from lacking, given aid rushed into Nepal as soon as the news went out. The relief supplies received worldwide were so large in volume that the Kathmandu airport was overwhelmed with the sudden increase in air traffic [2]. However, these life-changing resources could not be distributed accordingly and in a timely manner given the lack of coordination between the local and international relief aid providers. This led to inefficiencies in executing relief operations [1,2]. The fact that Nepal is a landlocked country without any sea access also exacerbated the logistical challenges further, as seen from the bottleneck problem in Kathmandu airport [3]. The hilly topography of Nepal is prone to landslides [1,2,4], while continuous aftershocks damaged the road infrastructure, such as the Pasang Lhamu and Araniko highways [5], which compromised the road network to the disaster zone [4,6]. Additionally, the sudden onset of the disaster meant that there was limited availability of vehicles and little preparation for emergency logistics operations [4]. The viability of the long-term humanitarian operations with the available vehicles, with regards to safety and logistics and asset management, were also in question since the road network was compromised [4]. This hindered efficient relief operations in terms of transport and delivery [4,7].

Meanwhile, urgent local medical supplies were rapidly diminishing as both field and local hospitals were overrun by victims seeking immediate treatment [2,8]. If the relief aid and supplies that were laying dormant at the Tribhuvan Airport could have been channelled through effectively, it would certainly have helped alleviate the problem of the urgent need for medical supplies and treatment.

In terms of disaster management preparedness, this case study serves to highlight the critical role of transportation in the event of a disaster. Transportation service is a crucial element when it comes to humanitarian logistics operation, in particular the in-country transportation for delivery of relief supplies [4]. From the 2015 Nepal earthquake event, some observations have been made with regards to ensuring efficient delivery of goods through vehicle routing. The study in [4] pointed out that the geographical topology and mountainous landscapes of Nepal as well as the second earthquake tremors and weather conditions during the event heavily impacted the delivery speed, especially involving the last mile of the delivery. In the disaster event, the road condition and capacity were compromised by major accidents, causing traffic density and loss of cargo [4]. Furthermore, there was an overwhelming demand for the limited number of trucks in terms of capacity and availability due to critical delay and backlogs. This increased the price of transport vehicle procurement to as high as 40%. Additionally, the lack of a decision support system (DSS) to monitor and track transport vehicles, coupled with untrained drivers, also led to a serious shortage of reliable transportation. Landslides, in particular, limited the routing to certain areas. In addition, the risk of accidents due to a unfamiliar route was significant and not helped by landslides which are sensitive to weather conditions. As such, intelligent routing and communication access is pivotal for this particular vehicle routing problem.

The proposed Multi-Depot Dynamic Vehicle-Routing Problem with Stochastic Road Capacity (MDDVRPSRC) model addresses such delivery problems in the setting of relief humanitarian operations by incorporating the aforementioned challenges. The problem of a bottleneck could be solved if "mini" airports were erected at strategic locations (multi-depot). The problem of limited transport vehicles in terms of availability and capacity could be addressed at some length through transport vehicles performing split deliveries which is known to be a cheaper alternative by almost 50% [9]. Furthermore, these vehicles could also perform multi-trip deliveries. Communication among Logistics Service Providers (LSPs) and their local contacts helps in updating the road network conditions which may hint towards dynamic problem modelling, with information updates at regular intervals. The uncertainty which is the pivotal aspect of efficient delivery operations should be addressed in terms of dynamic and stochastic settings of road capacity and conditions within the road network [4,7].

The Markov Decision Processes (MDP) modelling framework offers a natural way to address these dynamic and stochastic aspects of the problem. However, incorporating these aspects leads to an exponential growth of state, action and outcome spaces which is needed when solving such a real and complex problem. To deal with the curse of dimensionality [10], the Approximate Dynamic Programming (ADP) approach is commonly applied to solve the problem from the Machine Learning (ML) (Reinforcement Learning, RL) perspective. To address the large outcome space, the Post-Decision State (PDS) is applied as an extended version of the basic MDP modelling framework [11].

The ADP approach is usually applied to approximate the value of the next state s_{k+1} or the value of the action a_k when solving the Bellman equation [12]. In ADP, the lookahead approach is suitable when dealing with the large action and outcome space that constitutes part of the curse of dimensionality. In this paper, the known Post-Decision State Rollout Algorithm (PDS-RA) [13] is applied as part of the lookahead approach in the ADP.

A base heuristic in the PDS-RA is taken as the guiding policy for the decision rule applied as the state transitions within the lookahead horizon. In modelling the VRP through the MDP framework, the decision rule is generally the assignment of vehicles when the state transitions. In the rollout, the transition occurs in the lookahead horizon beginning from the potential next state s_{k+1} to the lookahead end state s_K. In other words, the base decision rule is a route computed for all vehicles to navigate within the future lookahead horizon. In the case of MDDVRPSRC, however, assigning vehicles based on a computed route, which is computed once, becomes problematic. This is due to the stochastic road capacity which may render the computed route unusable in the next lookahead update. One way to navigate around this is to have the route build dynamically on the go by a simple constructive heuristic known as a base heuristic.

From the decision rule or route obtained through this approach at each iteration, only the first assignments of the constructed route are applied while the rest are ignored. This method is feasible and practical due to the less expansive computation performed by the simple constructive heuristic. Here, the Teach Base Insertion heuristic (TBIH-1) is proposed to balance the random exploration and to guide the exploitation by dictating obvious assignments. Extending from this, the authors apply two known constructive heuristics: Sequential Insertion Heuristic SIH(I1) and Clarke and Wright (CW), in a dynamic setting and embed them into the TBIH-1(as proposed TBIH-2 and TBIH-3). To the best of our knowledge, no paper has shown how these constructive heuristics can be executed, as proposed, in a PDS-RA setting. We further derived from these two heuristics: TBIH-4 and TBIH-5 that seek, within their algorithm, promising vehicle assignments by looking up to two steps ahead. To deal further with the large action space, most research provides some mechanism to segregate or cluster vehicles with a specific set of customers to serve. Due to the stochastic road capacity, such mechanism is difficult to adopt. Thus, further approximation is made when computing the optimal action $a_k^\star$ with regards to executing the PDS-RA. Through this proposed method, each PDS-RA is executed for each vehicle for every potential assignment that can be given to that vehicle.

The contributions made in this paper are as follows: first, the novel MDDVRPSRC is proposed in a disaster event setting based on the modelling framework of MDP. Next, TBIH-1 heuristic is proposed in this work along with four extended variants, namely TBIH-2, TBIH-3, TBIH-4, and TBIH-5. By doing so, it is shown how SIH(I1) and CW can be applied in the dynamic setting of route-based MDP for PDS-RA [14]. The authors also show how these two can be extended by looking up to two steps ahead. Finally, it is also shown and validated how the near optimal decision can be approximated further by disintegrating the collective assignment decisions to an individual near optimal decision. To the best of our knowledge, both the MDDVRPSRC MDP model and the five base heuristics applied in the PDS-RA algorithm are novel and have not yet been proposed.

This work is the extension of research published by [15], where the damage determination of the roads within the road network is referred from. Furthermore, the Poisson stochastic distribution of a stochastic road capacity is also referred from. In this paper, the dynamic and stochastic MDDVRPSRC MDP model is presented to complement the earlier research in [15] that modelled the Deterministic Multi-Depot VRP with Road Capacity (D-MDVRPRC) as well as the two-stage Stochastic Integer Liner Programming (SILP) model of a Multi-Depot VRP with Stochastic Road Capacity (MDVRPSRC-2S). To solve the MDP Model presented in this paper via the PDS-RA algorithm, the five base heuristics are proposed as an alternative to the "cluster first, route second" approach that cannot be applied. Meanwhile, to benchmark these heuristics, the matheuristic rollout presented in [15] is applied where tractable.

This paper is organised as follows: Section 2 describes the literature review focusing on the proposed model and base heuristics. Section 3 describes the problem of MDDVRPSRC where some elements of the models have been referenced from the authors' previous work. The known PDS-RA approach is briefly described in Section 4 as well as how the optimal decision is approximated through the proposed mechanism. Additionally, variants of the proposed base heuristics are presented here. Section 5 presents the computational results. while Section 6 synthesises the findings. Finally, Section 7 concludes the paper.

2. Literature Review

An extensive synthesis of the literature on works adapting VRP for humanitarian operations can be found in [16,17]. In [17], numerous papers within the last decade (as of 2020) have been reviewed in terms of the application of VRPs for three selected humanitarian operations. Various modelling aspects, such as dynamic and stochastic problem, multi-disaster phase, multi-objectives, multi-trips, multi-depots, split delivery and more, which are relevant to the model proposed in this work, are elaborated. Furthermore, the solution approaches applied are also discussed in detail, especially the challenges when dealing with stochastic and dynamic VRPs. Ref. [15] extends the findings by discussing some papers applying VRP outside the field of humanitarian operation settings but are still relevant to the model that was proposed. Meanwhile, the RL adaptation in solving Supply Chain Management (SCM) is discussed in [18]. Additionally, the adoption of RL in VRP and TSP is discussed in [19].

2.1. Stochastic Vehicle Routing Problem for Humanitarian Operations

The survey in [20] discussed the recent dynamic VRP for various applications from 2015 to 2021. From the analysis of their work, it could be observed that the research focusing on dynamic problems usually also address stochastic problems. The opposite, however, may not necessarily be true. As such, some discussion on research works regarding stochastic VRP for humanitarian operations is warranted to complement those discussed in [17]. For example, the recent work of [21] addressed the Inventory Routing Problem (IRP) with an uncertain traffic network. Here the distribution of essential multi-commodities in the chaotic post-disaster phase among relief shelters and distribution centers is modelled through the network flow model. The uncertain traffic network is due to the magnitude of the earthquake's attributes, such as the earthquake's magnitude and the time of its occurrence. Such attributes also affect the vehicle speeds when making split deliveries. Apart from the optimized routing decision, the efficiency of the commodities distribution is further improved through the optimized inventory decision. Both are computed via the simulation optimization technique where the Sample Averaging Approximation (SAA) method is applied.

On the other hand, Ref. [22] presented a two-stage Location Routing Problem (LRP) of distributing first aid relief materials post-earthquake disaster where the complex demand uncertainty is addressed. Here the mixture of uncertain demand from the perspective of randomness (probabilistic theory) and fuzziness (possibility theory) due to the merging of subjective and objective data forms the hybrid demand uncertainties. A scenario-based stochastic demand over a specified interval per scenario is considered for stochastic probabilistic programming due to the strong relationship between events/scenarios such as post-earthquakes and aftershocks and the demands' uncertainty. As such, the demand parameter is considered a fuzzy random variable. In the two-stage robust programming model, the decision for locating a warehouse among existing warehouses is first determined, while the routing and distribution decision is computed in the second stage. The objective is to minimize the cost of warehouse location and the penalty induced by unsatisfied demand. Here the equivalent crisp model is represented by the Basic Possibilistic Chance Constraint Programming (BPCCP) model and later modified as the two-stage robust programming model to overcome the drawback of BPCCP. A small-scale instance problem based on the actual case study of Hamadan province of Iran, a location prone to earthquakes, is applied to verify the model proposed. The solution obtained using CPLEX indicates that the demand satisfaction level is significantly higher than in conventional scenario-based stochastic programming.

Meanwhile, the work proposed in [23] focused on the redistribution of food to charitable agencies, such as homeless shelters and soup kitchens, by picking up the resource (food) from donors such as grocery stores and restaurants. Here the objective is to assure fairness in distributing the donated foods while also considering the waste implicitly through the constraints introduced. The demand from charitable agencies and the resource (donation) are stochastic in this problem. Additionally, equity is the rate between allocated amounts to respective agencies over the total demands. Some assumptions are made, such as unlimited vehicle capacities and that all donors must be visited before distribution is performed. A decomposition strategy in the form of a heuristic is applied to solve the problem where the recipients and donors are clustered first. Then the route is computed for respective clusters, and resources are allocated for each recipient.

Another multi-objective problem is addressed in [24] to deliver both non-perishable and perishable items to demand points considering uncertainty, such as the location and number of relief centers that should be established at the demand points as well as the delivery means of the relief item post-disasters. A Mixed-Integer Non-Linear programming (MINLP) model is formulated to minimise the total distance travelled, the maximum travelled distance between relief centers and demand points, and the total cost associated with acquiring the relief items and vehicles utilized as well as the inventory cost. This model is solved by GAMS software for small-scale instances. Meanwhile, the larger instances are solved by a Grasshopper Optimization Algorithm (GOA) metaheuristic.

Ref. [25] addressed another multi-objective problem involving the COVID-19 pandemic. In this problem, multi-period collection and delivery of multi-products in a single open and close loop Supply Chain (SC) is modelled through the formulation of transportation problems and the Pick and Delivery VRP (PDVRP). Here the open and close supply chain system involving reusable and non-reusable products is transferred from hybrid depots that produce and recycle the products through a forward and reverse flow. The transfer collection centers located in the affected COVID-19 areas acted as the intermediary between the depots and the hospitals. Heterogeneous vehicles traverse the forward and reverse flow via PDVRP from the transfer collection centers to the hospitals when delivering products through split delivery while receiving the old product for reproduction. Various uncertain parameters are defined involving vehicle cost, production cost, the demand from the hospitals, and the returned products when computing for multiple decision variables focusing on the number and routing of the vehicles, production and return of products, shipping, and inventory of products. Finally, a robust optimization approach is applied where the Tchebycheff method is adopted to solve the complex problem.

A complex problem of relief distribution within the humanitarian logistics network and victim evacuation is addressed by [26]. This problem is based on the Facility Location Problem (FLP) and VRP, where the uncertain demand, transportation time, miscellaneous cost, injured victims, and facility capacity are considered. Moreover, the formulated problem involves stakeholders, such as the suppliers of relief materials (e.g., charitable organizations), the distribution centers, the emergency centers that distribute the aids, distribution units where the evacuated victims are located, and hospitals to which they are sent to for further treatment. Thus, the decisions are based on locating and distributing relief materials and allocating evacuated victims assigned to respective routed vehicles. Multi-objectives are also addressed where the total humanitarian logistics cost, the total time of relief operations, and the variation between the lower and upper bound of the transportation cost of the distribution centers are minimized. The uncertainties in the form of inconsistencies and unclear and inaccurate information are captured through the neutrosophic fuzzy set. These uncertainties are prioritized and dealt with, respectively, through the neutrosophic set and the robust optimisation, where the latter deals with the uncertainties associated with worst-case planning involving victims, facility capacity, and relief supply.

The work by [27] similarly addressed the LRP through the Conditional Value at Risk with Regret (CVaR-R) bi-objective mixed nonlinear programming model in dealing with relief distribution post-disaster. In this problem, the optimal decisions include selecting distribution centers to be made operational among all existing distribution centers, the number of vehicles that should be assigned, the assignment of vehicles to respective demand points, and the allocation of relief aids delivered to each of these demand points. The concept of regret when making these decisions due to inaccurate expectations of demands allows for a novel chance constraint programming approach introduced through the CVaR-R measure. The regret value for each objective to: (1) minimise the total waiting time of demand points and (2) minimise the total system cost is measured by defining possible demand scenarios with respective probability. For each demand scenario, the difference between the ideal objective values (from the deterministic model) and the objective values computed given the demands in each scenario is determined, from which the worst-case scenarios are identified and applied to compute the CVaR-R. To solve the problem model, the Nash Bargaining Solution (NBS) approach is applied with the help of a hybrid Genetic Algorithm (GA) when solving the single LRP version of the problem (via the GA) as well as determining the Pareto frontier (via the Non-Dominated Sorting GA Algorithm II (NSGA-II)) used to compute the NBS.

Finally, Ref. [28] also addressed the risk decision factor regarding the relief distribution with uncertain travel time. This problem is formulated based on the multi-level network via a mixed integer programming model to minimise the total arrival time of vehicles delivering relief materials to only selected demand points instead of satisfying demand for all demand points. Furthermore, the near-optimal delivery route computed ensures that a particular service level is reached throughout the operation by formulating the associated constraints. By introducing the risk-averse approach, the objective function is adapted by incorporating the standard deviation term representing the risk of the decision regarding uncertain time travel. Meanwhile, the non-additional term is the expected total arrival that needs to be minimized. Both are weighted to balance the importance of risk to the decision maker when computing for the near-optimal decision. Here, the Variable Neighbourhood Search (VNS) is employed to solve the problem based on the data obtained from the Haiti earthquake case study in 2010.

2.2. Markov Decision Processes Model for Humanitarian Operations

In this paper, the current trends of VRP in the scope of MDP modelling are discussed. It could be derived from [17] that MDP modelling for VRPs in the setting of humanitarian operations is scarce. This is supported by the finding that only [29] addressed the problem in humanitarian operations. Ref. [29] looked at multiple humanitarian operations, such as delivery and search and rescue, by incorporating the Relief Assessment Team (RAT) and the Emergency Relief Team (ERT), using the Decision-Making Agent (DMA) to coordinate the former two. The problem is modelled as an MDP with multiple random parameters, such as the demand and stability of the transport link. Here, the RAT is tasked to assess affected areas and dynamically report the demand situation for each zone. ERT, on the other hand, is tasked to serve the zones assigned by the DMA. Meanwhile, decisions are composed by assigning various combinations of aid organisations to a specified affected zone, as well as routing decisions for both the ERT and RAT. Finally, Q-learning is applied to solve the problem involving a maximum of 7 RAT and 10 ERT.

Other than papers reviewed by [17], there are works such as [30] which plan evacuation routing for the last minute disaster preparedness phase. In this problem, residents are evacuated prior to disaster occurrence via buses that pick up stochastic resident evacuees at bus stops. The problem is modelled as a single trip operation with a homogeneous fleet of vehicles within a finite horizon. Here, the action or decision is the assignment of the next pick-up point for each of the vehicles and the number of evacuees taken, suggesting a split delivery operation. The small instance of the problem is solved exactly using structured value iteration. Meanwhile, dynamic re-routing is applied for a large-scale problem through a reduced network flow MIP and Robust MIP (RMIP) model. Beyond these aforementioned works, related works on modelling a VRP through the framework of the MDP for humanitarian operations are sparse.

Instead, the MDP application is used to address humanitarian operations that revolve around the coverage problem, the allocation problem, the path planning, and the scheduling problem. Ref. [31] computed the evacuation routes during a disaster by modelling the problem as an MDP model. However, the work cannot be regarded as a VRP as the target application is not specified in terms that would constitute a VRP, such as the vehicles' availability or their capacity. Similarly, Ref. [32] used the MDP model to address the problem of clearing the debris from blocked edges or roads in an optimal assignment with uncertain clearance resources. In the post-disaster event, the optimal decision was computed considering the delivery of aid or service for demand nodes. Then we have [33] who addressed the problem of congestion in terms of hospital facilities as well as limited ambulances to rescue patients in the aftermath of a disaster. Considering the stochastic treatment time and transportation availability, the decision for such planning was to allocate ambulances to affected patients and to choose which medical facility the ambulance should be headed for. Two types of vehicles are considered: a dedicated ambulance for a location and another ambulance with flexibility in terms of the location. The latter might suggest split delivery. However, neither capacity nor comprehensive routing were considered in this problem. Dynamic patient treatment times were updated, and the problem was solved based on proposed heuristics that applied a myopic approach with policy improvement.

2.3. Markov Decision Processes Model for Industrial Problems and the Application of Approximate Dynamic Programming

Apart from the application for humanitarian operations, the MDP modelling framework has also been adopted for industrial problems since 2000. Interestingly, most of the early works are dedicated to solve the single VRP with stochastic demand such as in [34–37]. The study in [38] is among the first to look into the theoretical aspect of the pick-up and delivery of a single vehicle-routing problem with stochastic request using MDP modelling. The focus on the multi-vehicle problem is seen later in [39–41] for a VRP with stochastic demands. On the other hand, Ref. [42] deviated from stochastic demands by addressing the problem with stochastic customers or stochastic requests. In this type of application, various different and diverse solution strategies were adopted. This contrasted with the problem with stochastic demands which mainly applied the lookahead approach such as the PDS-RA.

Meanwhile, in [14,43] the route-based MDP was introduced as opposed to the conventional formulation of an MDP addressing a VRP while incorporating a dynamic route plan at every decision epoch. This framework was applied in [44] to solve the problem of maximising the number of services within the same period for stochastic service requests using the Value Function Approximation (VFA). The problem was to decide which new stochastic request should be accepted and which should be postponed to the next operation period. Apart from the fixed working time, multi-periods would be considered as multi-trip operations. VFA was applied as one of the ADP solution approaches allowing for online computation while dealing with the decision and outcome spaces. Through the VFA, the state space was segregated based on common features. The resulting MDP model led to a huge number of decision points which was dealt with by introducing a classification of multi-period operations. The application of VFA as shown here is commonly known to ignore some details of the state due to the aggregation mechanism within. The same authors in [45] alleviated this problem by proposing a hybrid of two ADP approaches: the VFA and the Rollout Algorithm (RA) to address the stochastic request for a single vehicle-routing problem. The authors later addressed the same problem in [46] with a different hybrid mechanism of VFA and RA by having the second part of the simulation horizon driven by a base policy dictated by the VFA. This method was effective in increasing the solution quality while reducing the computation time. A single vehicle-routing problem was also addressed by [47] with regards to taxi routing when searching for a passenger. In this MDP model, the transition probability is derived from the taxi–passenger matching probability on a link. Here, an enhanced value iteration was applied to solve the problem by reformulating Bellman's Equation into a series of matrix operations.

2.4. Approximate Dynamic Programming in Machine Learning

As can be seen from the example mentioned above, aside for [47], ADP is commonly adopted as a solution approach for problems formulated in MDP. The ADP emerged as a means to solve real and practical MDP problem models. This is due to the complexity of the MDP model that increases exponentially due to the explosion of state, outcome, and action spaces [48,49]. Such problem renders the exact solution to be prohibitive as shown in [50,51]. Afterwards, Ref. [52] coined the term ADP which is otherwise known as RL or neuro–dynamic programming. The interest in ADP sparked around the mid–1990s when it was extensively written on by [53,54]; although the ideas and concepts could be found dating back to the 1950s. For instance, Ref. [55] described the concept of approximating the value of a position in a chess game which is based on the state of the board. He likened the concept to an experienced player evaluating a move roughly but not based on all possible scenarios. Later, Ref. [12], when introducing dynamic programming, hinted at the idea with the mention of value space and approximation. Then [56] not only applied the idea of [55] in evaluating a position move, but also showcased the practical use of the lookahead approach while approximating the value of a move in the game of checkers. At the same time, he considered the possibility of remembering all the positions and moves, much like the concept of a dynamic lookup table. The work was further improved in [57] with regards to a tree search lookahead with an improved alpha–beta pruning scheme based on the memorisation of a board position, known as the book-learning procedure. The basic ideas from the aforementioned works were explored further resulting in pivotal works of [58–60] which formed what is known as the modern era of ADP [53]. Following that, Refs. [61–63] in his experiments with the game Backgammon afterwards demonstrated the practical application of ADP to solve real and complex problems.

2.5. Rollout Algorithm and Post-Decision State Rollout Algorithm in Approximate Dynamic Programming

The authors take advantage of the well-known operations of the VRP from the humanitarian operations' perspective and propose that the model based on MDP is adopted for MDDVRPSRC with a known variant of RA (PDS-RA) being applied to solve the problem online. The intuition for the lookahead approach as elaborated above can be identified back to the work of [55] who thought of evaluating a move by thinking ahead in a lookahead manner. The RA is based on the same principle but is refined by means of the quality of the lookahead which depends on the base policy applied. Furthermore, the horizon of the lookahead plays an important role as was mentioned by [64,65]. Another crucial aspect of the rollout is the Monte Carlo sampling that would enable the multiple lookaheads to account for the stochastic parameter for the simulated episode. Finally, the number of simulations performed would also contribute to a better mean approximation of the state or PDS value. The RA is proposed by [48] belonging to the class type of policy iteration in reinforcement learning. Note that [34] was among the first to develop a specified RA in solving sequencing problems. This work was extended in [35] for a single VRP. In [49], the performance of the rollout policy is compared to the optimistic approximate policy iteration for the single VRP. The former showed a better performance. Cyclic heuristic is applied as the base policy for the RA in [66] to solve the problem of of a VRP with stochastic demand (VRPSD) as well as the problem of the Travelling Salesmen Problem (TSP) with stochastic travel time. The former was also addressed by [36] who presented the two–stage stochastic programming solution approach and compared it to the online approach using RA. The outcome space was addressed exactly for all these problems up to this point. However, Ref. [37] managed to tackle this challenging computation approach by applying Monte Carlo sampling instead in a single- and two-stage RA. The computation was shown to have shrunk by 65% when compared with [35].

In [39], the multi-vehicle VRPSD is finally addressed. The challenges that come with the multi-vehicle problem is addressed through clustering to dedicate a set of different customers to each vehicle. An offline a priori route is computed for respective vehicles, and RA is only applied if a route failure occurred. Although RA was not applied from the get-go, this work highlighted the potential of a clustering mechanism when dealing with a multi-vehicle VRP. This was seen in [40] who made the clustering mechanism dynamic at every decision point as the status of stochastic demands were being updated. The problem was then solved by proposed variants of RA making use of the extension of the MDP framework, pre-decision state (PRE) ,and post-decision state (PDS) , advocated by [67]. Here, the base policy applied was the fixed route heuristic. This heuristic was relaxed forming a known restocking fixed route heuristic in [41], from which policies were iterated and obtained through a local search. These policies were evaluated with the help of the optimal value computed by dynamic programming to help with pruning the search space in the search for a more effective rollout base policy. This base policy was then applied in the RA to obtain a more optimal policy for the problem. The same concept was applied in [68] for the same problem, apart from the duration limit for a single vehicle, where a hybrid of backward and forward recursive dynamic programming was applied instead. In the work of [42], the authors applied RA with the cheapest insertion heuristic as the base policy for the problem of single VRP with stochastic requests. The solution was compared with the solution obtained from a greedy heuristic and VFA, respectively. Meanwhile, Ref. [69] proposed a framework for applying RA for the dynamic and stochastic VRP as an ADP solution approach. In [45], PDS–RA was applied with the VFA method driving the decision rule for the lookahead.

2.6. Rollout Algorithm as Matheuristic

An RA with which the base heuristic is driven by the policy of applying a mathematical programming method could be regarded as a matheuristic method. Among those who applied such a technique are [15,70–73]. In the work of [70], the authors addressed the scheduling problem with RA, where the decision rule was obtained using the quadratic programming approach. In [71], the Mixed Integer Linear Programming (MILP) was applied to obtain the decision rule for the RA in solving the problem of inventory routing with a single vehicle. Such approaches were also seen in [72,73] for solving the inventory routing problem. In other works, Ref. [15] proposed a matheuristic RA method to solve the multi-vehicle routing problem for humanitarian delivery operations by reducing the two-stage stochastic programming model to two reduced models that was dependent on the vehicle's mode of operation: replenishment or serving an emergency shelter.

2.7. Knowledge Gap and Research Contribution

By referring to Section 2.2, it is very clear that a humanitarian VRP, which is being addressed through machine learning, is still lacking. Meanwhile, from the industrial problem's perspective, the literature available shows that solving the VRP problem via reinforcement learning and RA are largely limited to stochastic demands, customers, or request problems. No such approach applied has addressed the problem with stochastic road capacity. The authors intend to fill this gap.

Furthermore, addressing the VRP through MDP formulation and the RA solution method is often limited to those of a single-vehicle problem as seen in the work [35–37,41,42,45,49,66,68]. This is evident even in the published works of the last five years. Those who solve multi-vehicle problems such as the work [39–41] often resort to a clustering or decomposition method of the vehicles to a set of different customers. Such a method, with the exception of a dynamic decomposition method, could not be performed when addressing MDDVRPSRC as the road capacity; thus the route is uncertain. Furthermore, it is not clear how a dynamic clustering or decomposition method could address the problem with stochastic road capacity while also accounting for the split delivery and multi-trip operations. To the best of the authors' knowledge, there is no literature that has proposed the method of building the decision rule on the go, guided by the constructive heuristic as the policy while performing the rollout. Similarly, no known variants of such heuristics have been introduced to allow for decision ruling on the go. Here the authors intend to fill the research gaps by proposing the application of proposed heuristics (TBIH-1–TBIH-5) within the PDS-RA adopted from [13]. In terms of the modelling approach, to the best of the authors' knowledge, no literature addresses the MDDVRPSRC, whether in the form of a mathematical programming model or in the MDP formulation, especially in humanitarian operations settings. Most literature for MDP formulation in VRPs addressed multi-trip operations only for on-route failure occasions. For example, the work such as [74] addressed the split operation also when triggered by the event of route failure due to stochastic demands. Literature such as [44,45] which addressed the multi-period operations, however, do not include the possibility of split delivery operations. Furthermore, most of these models only described operations involving a single vehicle. We differ from existing literature by intentionally allowing multi-trip operation as well as split delivery to address the limitation of delivery trucks during a disaster event rather than a result of route failure. Addressing multi-vehicles leads to the explosion of action space and is often very difficult to solve without resorting to a clustering approach. The authors therefore present here how with a moderate number of destination nodes in various simulated road network, the MDDVRPSRC could be solved without utilising a clustering or dynamic clustering method.

3. MDDVRPSRC MDP Model

3.1. Problem Statement

The problem of MDDVRPSRC focuses on the delivery problem, one of the crucial humanitarian operations during a disaster and post-disaster event. Here, the road network is represented as an undirected incomplete graph $G = (H, E)$ in graph theory. H is the set of nodes in graph G such that $H = \{D\} \cup \{S\} \cup \{N\}$ where $D, S,$ and N are the set of depots, emergency shelters, and connecting nodes respectively. The connecting nodes represent the junction connecting the edges $(i, j) \in E$, representing the roads such that $E = \{(i,j) : i,j \in N \cup S \cup D, i \neq j\}$. Note that emergency shelters whose demands are satisfied can act as connecting nodes for vehicles to travel through.

In MDDVRPSRC, the medical supplies are to be delivered to temporary erected emergency shelters, $s \in S$, with different demands, w_s, by a homogeneous fleet of vehicles, $m \in M$, with capacity, q_m. The delivery of medical supplies is conducted via split delivery to account for the limited number of vehicles during the sudden onset of a disaster. Vehicles are allowed to perform multi-trip deliveries throughout the humanitarian operations to satisfy all the demands. The vehicle capacity, q_m, can be replenished to a full capacity, Q, as soon as they return to the depot, $d \in D$. All vehicles must be dispatched throughout the operation until the total demand is satisfied as there is no guarantee that any assigned vehicles might reach their designated emergency shelter. More on this point, a vehicle is considered stranded when it is unable to travel to the next node on the way to the depot for the consecutive decision points of ST once the total demand is satisfied. Unless such an event occurs, all vehicles must return to the depot. However, they are not constrained as to which depot they should return to, advocating the flexibility needed for the humanitarian operations.

All throughout the operation, the road capacity, $r_{i,j}$, is uncertain. The mean road capacity for each road, (i, j), as well as the capacity distribution deteriorates as the operation time progresses for all damaged roads [15]. The deteriorating road capacity mean is due to the damages inflicted by the subsequent post-disaster events, such as tremors of an earthquake. This is simulated as the outward radial circles originating from the epicentre of the earthquake [15]. For more information of road capacity distribution, road damage determination, and simulation of earthquake tremors, refer to the work of [15].

3.2. Agent Solving MDDVRPSRC in Reinforcement Learning

In reinforcement learning, an agent learns to make decisions based on given information of the system. The information is given in the form of the state representation of the system as well as the transition of the state when making a constrained action or decision. An agent learns to make optimal decisions based on the series of interactions it has made from making decisions and in return obtained rewards. An MDP model formulates how an agent sees the system through: (i) the state representation, (ii) how the system transitions, (iii) the constrained actions or decisions it is allow to make as well, and (iv) the reward it received from making a decision. In this work, the agent perceived the problem as a MDDVRPSRC and will make a near optimal decision at every decision point. This agent then becomes a part of the DSS for delivering critical medical supplies during a disaster.

The agent learns of the aforementioned delivery operations of the MDDVRPSRC through a series of discrete states it observes at each decision point, k, beginning with the initial state, s_0, until the end state, s_K, representing the end of delivery operations. The Pre-Decision State (PRE), s_k, represents the state of the operations at decision point, k, prior to decision, a_k, computed by the agent. The state observed by the agent after decision, a_k, is made and denoted as the Post-Decision State (PDS), $s_k^{a_k}$. These states (PRE and PDS) are described through the state variables l, t, q, w, e, and r, respectively:

- l: current location of all vehicles;
- t: the next arrival time to next destination of all vehicles;
- q: the capacity status of all vehicles;
- w: the demand status for all nodes;
- e: the occupancy status of road (i, j) in relation to vehicle m;
- r: the road capacity of all roads or edges.

In the MDDVRPSRC MDP formulation, an agent computes a decision, a_k, to send a fleet of vehicles to a destination node based on the state that it observed, s_k. Once the decision a_k is executed, the PRE transitions to PDS, $s_k^{a_k}$, deterministically and waits for the next decision point, $k+1$, which is triggered at T_{k+1} by the arrival of one or more vehicles $m \in M'_{k+1}$ simultaneously at the emergency shelter $s \in S$ or connecting node $n \in N$ or depot $d \in D$.

Once the decision point $k+1$ is triggered, the random road capacities $\hat{r}_{i,j}$ are observed for all roads $(i, j) \in E$ through the dynamic update from the locals at the arrival destinations. At this point, the PDS transitions to PRE, s_{k+1}, stochastically and the PRE state variables e_k and r_k are updated. This new random information is now known to the agent (via the updates of e_k and r_k) who then uses it to compute the next decision, a_{k+1}, for all vehicles. Once the decision a_{k+1} is computed, the PRE transitions to PDS, $s_{k+1}^{a_{k+1}}$. At the same time, demand $w_h, \forall h \in S$ is served or the vehicle's capacity is replenished or neither (when a vehicle arrives at connecting node $h \in H \cap \{S + D\}$) depending on where the vehicles arrived. Hence, the variables of PDS representing the next destination, l^{a_k}, arrival time to next destination t^{a_k}, capacity, q^{a_k}, status edges travelled, e^{a_k} and demand status, w^{a_k} are updated accordingly. The MDDVRPSRC formulation that follows is developed by referring to [75] and the work of [13]. All parameters, state variables. and decision variables are listed in Tables 1 and 2.

Table 1. MDDVRPSRC: Parameters.

Parameters	
N	connecting node set
D	depot set
S	shelter set
H	$N \cup S \cup D$
E	set of edges $E = \{(i,j) : i,j \in N \cup S \cup D, i \neq j\}$
M	set of vehicles
K	end decision point
s_k	state at decision point k prior to decision a_k being made, PRE
$s_k^{a_k}$	state at decision point k after decision a_k is made, PDS
s_K	termination PRE state
k	decision point such that $k \in \mathbb{N} \cap \{0, K\}$
M_k'	set of vehicles that arrived at their assigned destination at decision point k where $M_k' \subset M$
T_k	time at decision point k such that $T_k \in \mathbb{R}$
t_{wait}	waiting time for vehicle arrived at a node but is assigned to remain stationary at current node such that $t_{\text{wait}} \in [0, \inf)$
$A(s_k)$	decision set of all possible decisions at decision point k given s_k
$A^\pi(s_k)$	MDP decision rule at decision point k following policy π given s_k
$\varrho^\pi(s_k)$	on-the-go constructed lookahead decision rule at decision point k following policy π given s_k
$\eta^\pi(s_k)$	decision rule computed through construction heuristic or CPLEX determined by policy π at decision point k given s_k in the lookahead horizon
O_m'	set of all potential destination for vehicle m at i for all $(i,j) \in E$ where $O_m' \subset H$
O_m	reduced decision space set for a single vehicle m in rollout given that $O_m \subset O_m'$
Q	maximum capacity of vehicles after replenishment at depot
$c_{i,j}$	cost incurred if edge (i,j) is travelled such that $c_{i,j} \in \mathbb{R}$
$t_{i,j}$	time travelled of edge (i,j) such that $t_{i,j} \in \mathbb{R}$
$W(k)$	random information at decision point k
$r_{i,j}$	deterministic road capacity $r_{i,j} \in \mathbb{Z}^\star$, where $\mathbb{Z}^\star = \mathbb{Z}^+ \cup \{0\}$ observed at decision point k
$\hat{r}_{i,j}$	stochastic road capacity $\hat{r}_{i,j} \in \mathbb{Z}^\star$
$p_{i,j}$	damage unit sustained by road (i,j) [15], such that $p_{i,j} \in \mathbb{N}$
Z	a large negative arrival time for vehicles resting at depot when all demand is served
$G2$	a larger constant acting as reward or penalty
ST	a limit on how many times a vehicle is allowed to be stationary (stranded) consecutively in terms of decision points
$F(m,i)$	function that adds consecutive decision points for all stranded vehicle m at i when all demand is served and all other vehicle is at depot consecutively starting from decision point k_{strand_0} to current decision point k_{strand_k} such that $F : (m,i) \rightarrow \{k_n \vert k_{n-1} - k_n = 1\}_{n=k_{\text{strand}_0}}^{k_{\text{strand}_k}} : \forall k_{\text{strand}_k} \leq ST \quad m \in M, \quad i \in H, \quad r_{i,j} = 0 \quad \forall (i,j) \in E$
λ	discount factor in Bellman Equation [12]
π	policy $\pi \in \Pi \subset \mathbb{N}$ that affect the decision rule $\varrho^\pi(s_k) : s_k \rightarrow a_k$
$R_k(s_k, a_k)$	reward for the agent for making decision a_k at decision point k when observing(given) the state s_k
$R_{k,m}(s_k, a_k)$	individual reward of vehicle m at decision point k

Table 2. MDDVRPSRC: State and Decision Variables.

PRE and PDS Variables	
l_k,	vector of next destination $\forall m \in M$ at decision point k, such that $l_k \in H^{\|M\|} = [l_0, l_1, \ldots, l_{\|M-1\|}]$
l^{a_k},	vector of next destination $\forall m \in M$ at decision point k, such that $l^{a_k} \in H^{\|M\|} = [l_0^{a_k}, l_1^{a_k}, \ldots, l_{\|M-1\|}^{a_k}]$
t_k,	vector of arrival time $\forall m \in M$ to assigned destination at decision point k, such that $t_k \in \mathbb{R}^{\|M\|} = [t_0, t_1, \ldots, t_{\|M-1\|}]$
t^{a_k}	vector of arrival time $\forall m \in M$ to assigned destination at decision point k, such that $t^{a_k} \in \mathbb{R}^{\|M\|} = [t_0^{a_k}, t_1^{a_k}, \ldots, t_{\|M-1\|}^{a_k}]$
q_k,	vector of vehicle capacity $\forall m \in M$ at decision point k, such that $q_k \in \mathbb{R}^{\|M\|} = [q_0, q_1, \ldots, q_{\|M-1\|}]$
q^{a_k},	vector of vehicle capacity $\forall m \in M$ at decision point k, such that $q^{a_k} \in \mathbb{R}^{\|M\|} = [q_0^{a_k}, q_1^{a_k}, \ldots, q_{\|M-1\|}^{a_k}]$
w_k,	vector of demand for all node $i \in H$ at decision point k, such that $w_k \in \mathbb{R}^{\|M\|} = [w_0, w_1, \ldots, w_{\|H-1\|}]$
w^{a_k},	vector of demand for all node $i \in H$ at decision point k, such that $w^{a_k} \in \mathbb{R}^{\|M\|} = [w_0^{a_k}, w_1^{a_k}, \ldots, w_{\|H-1\|}^{a_k}]$
r_k,	vector of road capacity for all edges $(i,j) \in E$ at decision point k, such that $r_k \in \mathbb{R}^{\|E\|} = [r_{i,j}]_{\forall (i,j) \in E}$
r^{a_k},	vector of road capacity for all edges $(i,j) \in E$ at decision point k, such that $r^{a_k} \in \mathbb{R}^{\|E\|} = [r_{i,j}]_{\forall (i,j) \in E}$
e_k,	vector of road occupancy of each vehicle for all $(i,j,m) \in \{(i,j,m) : \forall m \in M, \forall (i,j) \in E\}$ at decision point k, such that $e_k \in \{0,1\}^{\|\{(i,j,m): \forall m \in M, \forall (i,j) \in E\}\|} = [e_{i,j,m}]_{\forall (i,j,m) \in \{(i,j,m): \forall m \in M, \forall (i,j) \in E\}}$ 1 if edge (i,j) travelled by specific vehicle m, 0 otherwise
e^{a_k},	vector of road occupancy of each vehicle for all $(i,j,m) \in \{(i,j,m) : \forall m \in M, \forall (i,j) \in E\}$ at decision point k, such that $e^{a_k} \in \{0,1\}^{\|\{(i,j,m): \forall m \in M, \forall (i,j) \in E\}\|} = [e_{i,j,m}^{a_k}]_{\forall (i,j,m) \in \{(i,j,m): \forall m \in M, \forall (i,j) \in E\}}$ 1 if edge (i,j) travelled by specific vehicle m, 0 otherwise
Decision Variable	
a_k	vector of next assigned destination for vehicles, such that $a_k \in H^{\|M\|} = [a_1, a_2, \ldots, a_{\|M\|}] \in A(s_k)$

3.3. MDDVRPSRC Formulation

The pre-decision state (PRE) s_k is a multi dimensional vector consisting of other vectors representing each state variable, respectively. Within this vector are the state variables defined in Table 2:

$$s_k = [l_k, t_k, q_k, w_k, r_k, e_k]. \tag{1}$$

The PDS representation shares the same features as the PRE differs only by annotation and that its variables are updated after decision a_k is made:

$$s_k^{a_k} = [l^{a_k}, t^{a_k}, q^{a_k}, w^{a_k}, r^{a_k}, e^{a_k}]. \tag{2}$$

Once the decision point is triggered, based on the minimum current values within the arrival time vector t^{a_k}, at:

$$T_k = \min_{m \in M, t_m^{a_k} \geq 0} t^{a_k}, \tag{3}$$

the respective decision/assignment is computed for all vehicles including those that arrived as shown in Equation (4) below:

$$M'_k = \underset{m \in M, t_m^{a_k} \geq 0}{\arg\min} \; t^{a_k}. \tag{4}$$

Here, the vehicle that is still en route to its destination during the decision point k is denoted by $\{m \in M \setminus M'_k\}$.

In the MDDVRPSRC, the decision a_k is a $|M|$ dimensional vector in a decision space (a set) $A(s_k)$ given the state s_k. The decision involves assigning the next destination for all vehicles at every decision point k,

$$a_k = a \in H^{|M|} = [a_0, a_1, \ldots, a_{|M-1|}] \in A(s_k). \tag{5}$$

However, the decision space $A(s_k)$ for MDDVRPSRC is too large to obtain a good solution within reasonable computation efforts. Therefore, for every decision point k, the decision by the agent is computed as proposed in [15] where the reduced decision set for a single vehicle O_m is as defined for the rollout in Table 1:

$$\begin{aligned}
A(S_k) = \{a_k \in H^{|M|} : \\
a_m = j, \forall \{m \in M'_k : i = l_m, j \neq i, r_{i,j} > 0, w_j \neq 0, q_m \neq 0, j \in O_m : O_m \subset S\} \\
a_m = j, \forall \{m \in M'_k : i = l_m, j \neq i, r_{i,j} > 0, \sum_{h \in H} w_h \neq 0, q_m = 0, j \in O_m : O_m \subset D\} \\
a_m = j, \forall \{m \in M'_k : i = l_m, j \neq i, r_{i,j} > 0, \sum_{h \in H} w_h = 0, i \notin D, j \in O_m : O_m \subset D\} \\
a_m = i, \forall \{m \in M'_k : i = l_m, j, d \neq i, r_{i,d} > 0, r_{i,j} = 0, \sum_{h \in H} w_h \neq 0, q_m \neq 0, \\
\quad j, d \in O'_m, d \in D\} \\
a_m = i, \forall \{m \in M'_k : i = l_m, j, s \neq i, r_{i,j} > 0, r_{i,s} = 0, \sum_{h \in H} w_h \neq 0, q_m \neq 0, \\
\quad j, s \in O'_m, s \in S\} \\
a_m = i, \forall \{m \in M'_k : i = l_m, \sum_{h \in H} w_h = 0, i \in D\} \\
a_m = i, \forall \{m \in M'_k : i = l_m, j \neq i, r_{i,j} = 0 \;\; \forall (i,j) \in E\} \\
a_m = j, \forall \{m \in M'_k : i = l_m, j \neq i, r_{i,j} > 0, \sum_{h \in H} w_h \neq 0, q_m \neq 0, j \in O_m : O_m \subset (H \setminus S)\} \\
a_m = j, \forall \{m \in M'_k : i = l_m, j \neq i, r_{i,j} > 0, \sum_{h \in H} w_h \neq 0, q_m = 0, j \in O_m : O_m \subset (H \setminus D)\} \\
a_m = l_m, \forall \{m \in M \setminus M'_k\}\}
\end{aligned} \tag{6}$$

The state S_k transitions deterministically to PDS, $s_k^{a_k}$:

$$s_k^{a_k} = S^{M,a}(s_k, a_k), \tag{7}$$

where the decision is made by the agent ($l^{a_k} = a_k$). This is where the next destination l^{a_k}, arrival time t^{a_k}, capacity of vehicle q^{a_k}, travelled edges status by vehicles e^{a_k}, as well as the demands status w^{a_k} are updated. At this point, the stochastic road capacity is not known; hence r^{a_k} is not updated.

The time of arrival $t_m^{a_k} \in \mathbb{R}, \forall m \in M$ is updated to:

$$t_m^{a_k} = \begin{cases} t_m - Z, & \forall\{m \in M_k' : l_m \in D, \sum_{h \in H} w_h = 0\} \\ t_m - Z, & \forall\{m \in M_k' : i = l_m, r_{i,j} = 0, \quad \forall (i,j) \in E, \\ & |F(m,i)| = ST\} \\ t_{wait}, & \forall\{m \in M_k' : a_m = l_m, l_m \notin D, w_h = 0, \forall h \in H,\} \\ T_k + t_{l_m, a_m}, & \forall\{m \in M_k' : l_m \neq a_m, l_m \notin D, \sum_{h \in H} w_h = 0, \\ & p_{l_m, a_m} = 0\} \\ T_k + t_{l_m, a_m} + (t_{l_m, a_m} \times \frac{p_{l_m, a_m}}{10}), & \forall\{m \in M_k' : l_m \neq a_m, l_m \notin D, \sum_{h \in H} w_h = 0, \\ & p_{l_m, a_m} \neq 0\} \\ t_{wait}, & \forall\{m \in M_k' : a_m = l_m, \sum_{h \in H} w_h \neq 0,\} \\ T_k + t_{l_m, a_m}, & \forall\{m \in M_k' : l_m \neq a_m, \sum_{h \in H} w_h \neq 0, p_{l_m, a_m} = 0\} \\ T_k + t_{l_m, a_m} + (t_{l_m, a_m} \times \frac{p_{l_m, a_m}}{10}), & \forall\{m \in M_k' : l_m \neq a_m, \sum_{h \in H} w_h \neq 0, p_{l_m, a_m} \neq 0\} \\ t_m, & \text{otherwise} \end{cases} \quad (8)$$

where t_{wait} is defined as:

$$t_{wait} = \begin{cases} t_2, & t_k' = (t_1, t_2, \ldots t_n), \quad t_i \in t_k : t_i \geq 0, t_i - t_{i-1} > 0, n \geq 2 \\ \min_{\forall (i,j) \in E} t_{i,j}, & \text{otherwise} \end{cases}, \quad (9)$$

and t_k' is an n-tuple with an increasing order of arrival time.

Meanwhile, the capacity of all vehicles $m \in M$ is updated to:

$$q_m^{a_k} = \begin{cases} Q, & \forall m \in \{M_k' : l_m \in D\} \\ \max(q_m - w_{l_m}, 0), & \forall m \in \{M_k' : l_m \in S\} \\ q_m, & \text{otherwise} \end{cases}. \quad (10)$$

The travelled edges e^{a_k} are updated $\forall (i,j) \in E, \forall m \in M$:

$$e_{i,j,m}^{a_k} = \begin{cases} 1, & \forall m \in \{M_k' : i = l_m, j = a_m, i \neq j\} \\ e_{i,j,m}, & \text{otherwise} \end{cases}. \quad (11)$$

Finally, the demand of emergency shelter is also updated $\forall h \in H$:

$$w_h^{a_k} = \begin{cases} \max(w_{l_m} - q_m, 0), & \forall m \in \{M_k' : l_m \in S\} \\ w_h, & \text{otherwise} \end{cases}. \quad (12)$$

At decision point T_{k+1}, the uncertainty of the road capacity $\hat{r}_{i,j} \forall (i,j) \in E$ is now observed by the agent which leads to the transition from PDS to PRE, s_{k+1}:

$$s_{k+1} = S^{M,W}(s_k^{a_k}, W_{k+1}). \quad (13)$$

The road capacity at this point is no longer uncertain ($r_{i,j} \forall (i,j) \in E$) since it has been sampled/known to vehicles that have arrived at their destinations. This information is thus known to the agent. The next destination $l_m = l_m^{a_k}$ ($\forall m \in M$), the arrival time $t_m = t_m^{a_k}$ ($\forall m \in M$), capacity of the vehicle $q_m = q_m^{a_k}$ ($\forall m \in M$), as well as the shelter demand $w_h = w_h^{a_k}$ ($\forall h \in H$) remain the same.

The travelled edges status, e_k is updated $\forall m \in M$, $\forall (i,j) \in E$:

$$e_{i,j,m} = \begin{cases} 0, & \forall m \in M'_k \\ e^{a_k}_{i,j,m}, & \text{otherwise} \end{cases}. \tag{14}$$

The road capacity r_k is at this point observed and updated:

$$r_{i,j} = \min((\hat{r}_{i,j} - \sum_{m \in M} e_k(i,j,m)), 0) \quad \forall (i,j) \in E, \tag{15}$$

where the random road capacity $\hat{r}_{i,j} \forall (i,j) \in E$ is obtained from a random Poisson distribution as described in [15].

When transitioning to PDS, $s_k^{a_k}$, the agent receives a reward $R_k(s_k, a_k)$ contributed by all vehicles $m \in M$ at decision point k:

$$R_k(s_k, a_k) = \sum_{m \in M} R_{k,m}(s_k, a_k), \tag{16}$$

where $R_{k,m}(s_k, a_k)$, $\forall m \in M$ is given by:

$$R_{k,m}(s_k, a_k) = \begin{cases}
0, & \forall m \in \{M \setminus M'_k\} \\
0, & \forall m \in \{M'_k : i = l_m, l_m = a_m, \sum_{h \in H} w_h \neq 0\} \\
(max(w_{l_m} - q_m, 0) \times G2) - c_{l_m, a_m} - t_{l_m, a_m}, & \\
& \forall m \in \{M'_k : q_m \neq 0, l_m \in S, w_{l_m} > q_m, p_{l_m, a_m} = 0\} \\
(max(q_m - w_{l_m}, 0) \times G2) - c_{l_m, a_m} - t_{l_m, a_m}, & \\
& \forall m \in \{M'_k : q_m \neq 0, l_m \in S, w_{l_m} < q_m, p_{l_m, a_m} = 0\} \\
(max(w_{l_m} - q_m, 0) \times G2) - c_{l_m, a_m} - (t_{l_m, a_m} + t_{l_m, a_m} \times \frac{p_{l_m, a_m}}{10}), & \\
& \forall m \in \{M'_k : q_m \neq 0, l_m \in S, w_{l_m} > q_m, p_{l_m, a_m} \neq 0\} \\
(max(q_m - w_{l_m}, 0) \times G2) - c_{l_m, a_m} - (t_{l_m, a_m} + t_{l_m, a_m} \times \frac{p_{l_m, a_m}}{10}), & \\
& \forall m \in \{M'_k : q_m \neq 0, l_m \in S, w_{l_m} < q_m, p_{l_m, a_m} \neq 0\} \\
G2 - c_{l_m, a_m} - t_{l_m, a_m}, & \\
& \forall m \in \{M'_k : l_m \neq a_m, q_m \neq 0, l_m \in S, w_{l_m} = q_m, p_{l_m, a_m} = 0\} \\
& \text{or } \forall m \in \{M'_k : l_m \neq a_m, q_m = 0, a_m \in D, \sum_{h \in H} w_h \neq 0, \\
& p_{l_m, a_m} = 0\} \\
& \text{or } \forall m \in \{M'_k : l_m \neq a_m, a_m \in D, \sum_{h \in H} w_h = 0, p_{l_m, a_m} = 0\} \\
G2 - c_{l_m, a_m} - (t_{l_m, a_m} + t_{l_m, a_m} \times \frac{p_{l_m, a_m}}{10}), & \\
& \forall m \in \{M'_k : l_m \neq a_m, q_m \neq 0, l_m \in S, w_{l_m} = q_m, p_{l_m, a_m} \neq 0\} \\
& \text{or } \forall m \in \{M'_k : l_m \neq a_m, q_m = 0, a_m \in D, \sum_{h \in H} w_h \neq 0, \\
& p_{l_m, a_m} \neq 0\} \\
& \text{or } \forall m \in \{M'_k : l_m \neq a_m, a_m \in D, \sum_{h \in H} w_h = 0, p_{l_m, a_m} \neq 0\} \\
-c_{l_m, a_m} - t_{l_m, a_m}, & \text{otherwise, } p_{l_m, a_m} = 0, \quad \forall m \in M'_k \\
-c_{l_m, a_m} - (t_{l_m, a_m} + t_{l_m, a_m} \times \frac{p_{l_m, a_m}}{10}), & \text{otherwise, } p_{l_m, a_m} \neq 0, \quad \forall m \in M'_k
\end{cases} \tag{17}$$

Here, a policy of decisions denotes the guiding principle on which the decision is based. For example, a policy $\pi_B \in \Pi$ could be a heuristic if a decision function $A^{\pi_B}(s_k)$ is mapped from that heuristic. In this model formulation, the decision $a_k = A^{\pi}(s_k) \subset A(s_k)$ [67] is selected among other potential decisions in the decision space, $A(s_k)$ following a certain policy $\pi \in \Pi$ such that the decision rule function $A^{\pi}(s_k) : s_k \to a_k$.

The objective (Equation (18)) is to find an optimal policy $\pi^\star$ such that the expected total rewards are maximised (objective function for the Bellman optimality equation [67]):

$$\max_{\pi \in \Pi} \mathbb{E}^{\pi} \left\{ \sum_{k=0}^{K} (R_k(s_k, A^{\pi}(s_k))) \right\}. \quad (18)$$

Hence:

$$\pi^\star = \arg\max_{\pi \in \Pi} \mathbb{E}^{\pi} \left\{ \sum_{k=0}^{K} (R_k(s_k, A^{\pi}(s_k))) \right\}, \quad (19)$$

where for every decision point k, the optimal decision $a_k^\star$ is chosen: $a_k^\star = A^{\pi^\star}(s_k)$ by following the optimal policy $\pi^\star$.

4. MDDVRPSRC Solution Approach

To solve an MDP is to seek an optimal policy $\pi^\star$. Through this optimal policy, every decision made by the agent is optimal: $A^{\pi^\star}(s_k) : s_k \to a_k^\star$ as stated by the principal of optimality [12]. To obtain the optimal policy, the Bellman Equation is solved [12] such that the optimal decision $a_k^\star$ is computed for every decision point k for each given state s_k observed by the agent. This series of optimal computed decisions is said to be guided by the optimal policy $\pi^\star \in \Pi$, and therefore the problem formulated in MDP is solved. To compute the optimal decision, $a_k^\star$, the Bellman Equation could be written as Equation (20) [67]:

$$a_k^\star = \arg\max_{a_k \in A(s_k)} (R_k(s_k, a_k) + \lambda^k \mathbb{E}\{V_{k+1}(s_{k+1})\}). \quad (20)$$

Due to the curse of dimensionality as seen in Equation (20), computing for an optimal decision is often intractable. To alleviate the curse associated with the outcome or transition space, the PDS is introduced [67] (Equation (21)) and the equation was rewritten as in Equation (22):

$$V_k^{a_k}(s_k^{a_k}) = \mathbb{E}\{V_{k+1}(s_{k+1})\}, \quad (21)$$

$$a_k^\star = \arg\max_{a_k \in A(s_k)} (R_k(s_k, a_k) + \lambda^k V_k^{a_k}(s_k^{a_k})). \quad (22)$$

Even with PDS introduced as above, the computation for an optimal decision is usually challenging, especially when computing the value of the PDS, $V_k^{a_k}(s_k^{a_k})$ in Equation (22). The ADP approach approximates the value of PDS instead. This is to deal with the large state space in the MDP. Through the ADP approach, Equation (22) is rewritten as Equation (23), where the value of PDS is approximated and thus the decision is computed to near optimality instead:

$$\widetilde{a_k^\star} = \arg\max_{a_k \in A(s_k)} (R_k(s_k, a_k) + \lambda^k \overline{V_k^{a_k}}(s_k^{a_k})). \quad (23)$$

For MDDVRPSRC, this equation is still challenging to solve since the decision space $A(s_k)$ in Equation (23) is too large for a practical number of vehicles to be involved. Furthermore, the decisions consist of combinations of vehicle assignments that would require a long rollout horizon as well as a large number of Monte Carlo simulations. The concern is that the reward obtained for one vehicle may exaggerate the value of the decision for all vehicles collectively if computed prematurely. This is seen in the initial experiments where, given limited computation capabilities on the machine, inefficient assignments for vehicles resulted.

Alternatively, to cope with this challenge, the near optimal decision could be further approximated as in Equation (24) as proposed in work [15]:

$$\widetilde{a_k^\star} \in H^{|M|} \approx [\widetilde{a_1^\star}, \widetilde{a_2^\star}, \ldots, \widetilde{a_{|M|}^\star}] \quad \forall k, \tag{24}$$

where the decision space, made of combinations of vehicle assignments (which could be astronomical), could be restricted to a decision space of possible assignments for each vehicle O_m instead, as shown in Equation (25):

$$\widetilde{a_m^\star} = \arg\max_{a_m \in O_m}(R_k(s_k, a_k) + \lambda^k \overline{V_k^{a_m}}(s_k^{a_m})) \quad \forall (k, m). \tag{25}$$

Even with such measures, given the machine's capabilities, the computation is only limited to a small number of rollout horizons and Monte Carlo simulations. However, it is shown in this work that the decisions computed are applicable to this type of problem.

To compute Equation (25), the PDS value, $\overline{V_k^{a_m}}(s_k^{a_m})$ is approximated using PDS-RA, as proposed by [40]. However, different base heuristics can be applied to solve for the MDP problems with characteristics such as the one in this work. Finally, this approach is applied to reciprocate the model for the agent's decision in Equation (6).

4.1. PDS-RA Algorithm

PDS-RA is one of the RA families first introduced in [40] as an ADP solution algorithm to the dynamic VRP with stochastic demand. PDS-RA takes advantage of the PDS structures that alleviate the problem associated with the outcome or transition space. This thus reduces the number of rollout executions compared to the conventional RA to approximate the value of PDS in a modified Bellman Equation effectively. The general PDS-RA could be referred to in Algorithm 1. Here, the rollout transitioned PDS (simulation) is denoted as s^a to avoid confusion with the real-time transitioned PDS, $(s_k^{a_k})$ observed by the agent. In this algorithm, the values of PDS, $V_k^{a_k}(s_k^{a_k})$ associated with each respected $a_k \in A(s_k)$ is approximated ($\overline{V_k^{a_k}}(s_k^{a_k})$). For each possible PDS associated with the next decision $a_k \in A(s_k)$, the PDS-RA is executed, and by the end of the execution, the approximated value of PDS, $\overline{V_k^{a_k}}(s_k^{a_k})$ is obtained. In every execution of PDS-RA, the base policy $\pi_{B(s_k^{a_k})} \in \Pi$ is first assigned (policy to apply heuristic B), computing the decision rule function $\varrho^{\pi_{B(s_k^{a_k})}}(s_k)$ for the rollout simulation is based on the heuristic B performed given the PDS, $s_k^{a_k}$. Based on this specific decision rule (which is normally the assignment of vehicles to next destination for VRP), the lookahead into the future as far as horizon K is performed. Transiting from the simulated PRE to PDS is enabled by referring to $\varrho^{\pi_{B(s_k^{a_k})}}(s_k)$ when making a decision during the lookahead. This decision is followed by a stochastic transition, transitioning PDS back to PRE ($s_k = S^{M,W}(s^a, W_{k+1}(\omega(k+1)))$) in the lookahead simulation. Here, the random information of road capacities for all roads, ($W_{k+1}(\omega(k+1))$), is known by sampling $\omega(k+1) \in \Omega$ through a known distribution as part of the Monte Carlo simulation approach. By sampling $\omega(k+1) \in \Omega$, the exhaustive computation for all random transitions of outcomes in the outcome space Ω is prevented as first observed by [37] in her application of RA.

Each time the transition occurs within the lookahead along the horizon, rewards $R_k(s_k, a_k)$ are consecutively amassed. At the end of a one-episode lookahead simulation, the sum of rollout rewards $\widehat{B}^n(\pi_{B(s_k^{a_k})}, k+1, K)$ is obtained. This value is used to update the approximated PDS value of the respective potential decision a_k through an incremental mean approach (Algorithm 1: line 14). The process repeats for N Monte Carlo simulation episodes. After this number of Monte Carlo simulations, the resulting updated approximated PDS value, $\overline{V_k^{a_k}}^N(s_k^{a_k})$ is considered good enough an estimation for the respective decision a_k. This approximated PDS value is mapped to the respective decision by a function: $f: a_k \leftarrow \overline{V_k^{a_k}}^N(s_k^{a_k})$.

Algorithm 1 Compute $\overline{V_k^a}(s_k^{a_k})$ (as shown in [75] based on PDS-RA proposed by [13] and highlighted in [15]).

Require: s_k, λ, a_k
Ensure: $\overline{V_k^a}(s_k^{a_k})$
1: Initialise $n, k, R_k(s_k, a_k), B^n$
2: $s_k^{a_k} = S^{M,a}(s_k, a_k)$
3: $\varrho^{\pi_{\mathcal{B}(s_k^{a_k})}}(s_k) \leftarrow \pi_{\mathcal{B}(s_k^{a_k})} \leftarrow \mathcal{B}(s_k^{a_k})$
4: **while** $n \leq N$ **do**
5: $\quad s^a \leftarrow s_k^{a_k}$
6: $\quad$ **while** $k \neq K$ **do**
7: $\quad\quad R_k(s_k, a_k) = R_k(s_k, a_k) + \lambda^k R_k(s_k, a_k)$
8: $\quad\quad s_k = S^{M,W}(s^a, W_{k+1}(\omega(k+1)))$
9: $\quad\quad a_k \leftarrow \varrho^{\pi_{\mathcal{B}(s_k^{a_k})}}(s_k)$
10: $\quad\quad s^a = S^{M,a}(s_k, a_k)$
11: $\quad\quad k = k + 1$
12: $\quad$ **end while**
13: $\quad \widehat{B}^n(\pi_{\mathcal{B}(s_k^{a_k})}, k+1, K) \leftarrow R_k(s_k, a_k)$
14: $\quad \overline{V_k^a}^n(s_k^{a_k}) = \overline{V_k^a}^{n-1}(s_k^{a_k}) + \frac{1}{n}(\widehat{B}^n(\pi_{\mathcal{B}(s_k^{a_k})}, k+1, K) - \overline{V_k^a}^{n-1}(s_k^{a_k}))$
15: $\quad n = n + 1$
16: **end while**
17: **return** $\overline{V_k^{a_k}}^N(s_k^{a_k})$

The PDS-RA is then executed for the next possible decision $a_k \in A(s_k)$ after which the process repeats. Finally, when the PDS-RA is executed $\forall a_k \in A(s_k)$, Equation (23) can now be computed based on all approximated PDS values associated with each respective potential next decision for agent to make. Based on the computation of Equation (23), a decision is then made.

It should be noted that Algorithm 1 is applied to the rollout and looks into the future of each potential decision where each decision a_k revolves on the assignments of all vehicles $a_m = a_k[m], \forall m \in M$ simultaneously per PDS-RA. The base policy $\pi_{\mathcal{B}(s_k^{a_k})}$ guides the construction of the decision function $\varrho^{\pi_{\mathcal{B}(s_k^{a_k})}}(s_k)$ in one go, per PDS-RA execution $\forall a_k \in A(s_k)$.

In the applied solution, the rollout is executed for every potential next destination for each vehicle $a_m, \forall m \in M$, and the value for each PDS associated with the potential next destination is computed by PDS-RA, such that near optimal assignments a_m^* would be computed in Equation (25). These near optimal individual assignments form the near optimal decision as described in Equation (24). The base policy $\pi_{\mathcal{B}(s_k^{a_k})}$ is based on an iterative policy $\pi_{\mathcal{B}(s_k)}$ applied at each lookahead decision point s_k to construct the decision rule $\varrho^{\pi_{\mathcal{B}(s_k^{a_k})}}$ on-the-go using constructive base heuristics $\mathcal{B}$. The decision rule $\varrho^{\pi_{\mathcal{B}(s_k^{a_k})}}$ is constructed on the go such that $\varrho^{\pi_{\mathcal{B}(s_k^{a_k})}} : s_k \rightarrow \eta^{\pi_{\mathcal{B}(s_k)}}(s_k)$ where $\eta^{\pi_{\mathcal{B}(s_k)}}(s_k)$ is the decision rule computed at every decision epoch k in the lookahead horizon when applying heuristic $\mathcal{B}$ based on the rollout state s_k according to the iterative policy $\pi_{\mathcal{B}(s_k)}$.

In Algorithm 2, for example, CPLEX (denoted as $CPLEX$) is applied instead as the base heuristic. Here, CPLEX is run for a Stochastic Linear Integer Programming (SILP) version of the reduced MDDVRPSRC to construct $\varrho^{\pi_{CP(s_k^{a_k})}}(s_k)$ on the go given the current rollout state s_k and this results in $\eta^{\pi_{CP(s_k)}}(s_k)$. Since here the policy is to apply CPLEX, we denote that the policy that the decision rule follows is of $\pi_{CP(s_k^{a_k})}$.

A detailed explanation on this matheuristic is given in [15] (Algorithm 2). The authors used this exact configuration (with $CPLEX$ as the base heuristic) as a benchmark where tractable. As a solution approach in general, the Algorithm 3 is referred. The authors first introduced the TBIH-1 heuristic (Algorithm 4) based on a pure random insertion for the non-obvious decisions. Furthermore, other constructive heuristics were applied dynamically (TBIH-2 and TBIH-3), extended from TBIH-1, to construct the decision rule on the go ($\varrho^{\pi_{B(s_k^{a_k})}}$) as shown in Algorithm 3, in contrast to Algorithm 2. Additionally from these constructive heuristics, the authors propose another two new variants (TBIH-4 and TBIH-5) for this problem by introducing the exploitation mechanism on both TBIH-2 and TBIH-3.

Algorithm 2 Matheuristic Extended from Algorithm 1 to Compute $\widetilde{a_m^\star}$ [15].

Require: s_k, λ, a_k
Ensure: $a_m^\star$
1: **for** $a_m \in O_m$ at decision point k **do**
2: $\quad$ Initialise $n, k, R_k(s_k, a_k), B^n$
3: $\quad$ **while** $n \leq N$ **do**
4: $\quad\quad$ $s_k^{a_m} = S^{M,a}(s_k, a_m)$
5: $\quad\quad$ $s^a \leftarrow s_k^{a_m}$
6: $\quad\quad$ **while** $k \neq K$ **do**
7: $\quad\quad\quad$ $R_k(s_k, a_k) = R_k(s_k, a_k) + \lambda^k R_k(s_k, a_k)$
8: $\quad\quad\quad$ $s_k = S^{M,W}(s^a, W_{k+1}(n(k+1)))$
9: $\quad\quad\quad$ $\pi_{CP_k(s_k)} \leftarrow CPLEX(s_k)$
10: $\quad\quad\quad$ $\eta^{\pi_{B(s_k)}} \leftarrow \pi_{CP_k(s_k)}$
11: $\quad\quad\quad$ $\varrho^{\pi_{B(s_k^{a_k})}} : s_k \to \eta^{\pi_{B(s_k)}}(s_k)$
12: $\quad\quad\quad$ $a_m \leftarrow \varrho^{\pi_{B(s_k^{a_k})}}(s_k)$
13: $\quad\quad\quad$ $s^a = S^{M,a}(s_k, a_m)$
14: $\quad\quad\quad$ $k = k+1$
15: $\quad\quad$ **end while**
16: $\quad\quad$ $\widehat{B}^n(\pi_{B(s_k^{a_k})}, k+1, K) \leftarrow R_k(s_k, a_k)$
17: $\quad\quad$ $\overline{V_k^{a_m}}^n(s_k^{a_m}) = \overline{V_k^{a_m}}^{n-1}(s_k^{a_m}) + \frac{1}{n}\left(\widehat{B}^n(\pi_{B(s_k^{a_k})}, k+1, K) - \overline{V_k^{a_m}}^{n-1}(s_k^{a_m})\right)$
18: $\quad\quad$ $n = n+1$
19: $\quad$ **end while**
20: $\quad$ $f : a_m \leftarrow \overline{V_k^{a_m}}^N(s_k^{a_m})$
21: **end for**
22: $\widetilde{a_m^\star} = \underset{a_m \in O_m}{\arg\max}(R_k(s_k, a_k) + \lambda^k f(a_m)) \quad \forall (k, m)$
23: **return** $\widetilde{a_m^\star}$

Algorithm 3 Compute $\widetilde{a_m^\star}$ based on [15] using other Base Heuristic, $\mathcal{B}$.

Require: s_k, λ, a_k
Ensure: $a_m^\star$
1: **for** $a_m \in O_m$ at decision point k **do**
2:     Initialise $n, k, R_k(s_k, a_k), \hat{B}^n$
3:     **while** $n \leq N$ **do**
4:         $s_k^{a_m} = S^{M,a}(s_k, a_m)$
5:         $s^a \leftarrow s_k^{a_m}$
6:         **while** $k \neq K$ **do**
7:             $R_k(s_k, a_k) = R_k(s_k, a_k) + \lambda^k R_k(s_k, a_k)$
8:             $s_k = S^{M,W}(s^a, W_{k+1}(n(k+1)))$
9:             $\pi_{\mathcal{B}(s_k)} \leftarrow \mathcal{B}(s_k)$
10:             $\eta^{\pi_{\mathcal{B}(s_k)}} \leftarrow \pi_{\mathcal{B}(s_k)}$
11:             $\varrho^{\pi_{\mathcal{B}(s_k^{a_k})}} : s_k \to \eta^{\pi_{\mathcal{B}(s_k)}}(s_k)$
12:             $a_m \leftarrow \varrho^{\pi_{\mathcal{B}(s_k^{a_k})}}(s_k)$
13:             $s^a = S^{M,a}(s_k, a_m)$
14:             $k = k + 1$
15:         **end while**
16:         $\hat{B}^n(\pi_{\mathcal{B}(s_k^{a_k})}, k+1, K) \leftarrow R_k(s_k, a_k)$
17:         $\overline{V_k^{a_m}}^n(s_k^{a_m}) = \overline{V_k^{a_m}}^{n-1}(s_k^{a_m}) + \frac{1}{n}(\hat{B}^n(\pi_{\mathcal{B}(s_k^{a_k})}, k+1, K) - \overline{V_k^{a_m}}^{n-1}(s_k^{a_m}))$
18:         $n = n + 1$
19:     **end while**
20:     $f : a_m \leftarrow \overline{V_k^{a_m}}^N(s_k^{a_m})$
21: **end for**
22: $\widetilde{a_m^\star} = \underset{a_m \in O_m}{\arg\max}(R_k(s_k, a_k) + \lambda^k f(a_m)) \quad \forall(k, m)$
23: **return** $\widetilde{a_m^\star}$

4.2. Teach Base Insertion Heuristic (TBIH-1)

In this section, the base heuristics applied are described in general (Algorithm 4), and the elaboration of each is described in the subsections that follow. TBIH-1, TBIH-2, TBIH-3, TBIH-4, and TBIH-5 are the heuristics applied in this work to both validate the model and to cross-compare the performance for each of the models.

The algorithm for each heuristic applied here follows the same main structure of: (i) the teaching part (TP) and (ii) the seeking part (SP).

In the TP, the obvious decisions are chosen without running any heuristics to search for the best next destination. These obvious decisions are stated in Equation (6) and applied to each vehicle:

- To serve any shelter $s \in S$ randomly among possible shelters as the next destination;
- To replenish at any depots $d \in D$ randomly among possible depots as the next destination;
- To return to any depots $d \in D$ randomly among possible depots when all demands have been served;
- To remain stationary at the current arrival node i while still having capacity ($q_m \neq 0$) and demands that have not all been served, if the only next possible destination is to a depot;
- To wait at the current arrival node i while still having capacity ($q_m \neq 0$) if the road capacity to the next possible shelter is blocked $r_{i,j} = 0$;
- To remain resting at the depot if the current arrival node is a depot $i \in D$ and all demands have been served;
- To remain stationary at the current arrival node i if all road capacity to a neighbouring node j are blocked $r_{i,j} = 0, \forall(i, j) \in E$.

Algorithm 4 TBIH-1 and General Structure Algorithm. (Note: $|M'_k| \leq 1$ in rollout).

Require: $s_k, M'_k, M \setminus M'_k$
Ensure: *Decision* during lookahead
1: update $q_m, \forall m \in M$ and $w_h, \forall h \in H$ as in Equation (10) and Equation (12)
2: unserved shelters vector, $US = [h]_{\forall h \in H: w_h \neq 0}$
3: **for** $m \in M'_k$ **do**
4:     $i = l_m$
5:     potential next destination vector, $next = [h]_{\forall h \in H: r_{i,h} \in E, r_{i,h} > 0}$
6:     init empty list $nextS, nextD, nextND, Decision$
7:     $nextS = [i : i \in (next \cap US)]$
8:     $nextD = [i : i \in (next \cap D)]$
9:     $nextND = [i : i \in (next \notin D)]$
10:     **if** $q_m \neq 0$ AND len($nextS$!=0) **then**
11:         **if** len($nextS$)!=1 **then**
12:             a_m = random.choice($nextS$)
13:             **while** len($nextS$)!=0 **do**
14:                 **if** $r_{i,a_m} > 0$ **then**
15:                     Decision.append(a_m)
16:                     $r_{i,a_m} = max(r_{i,a_m} - 1, 0)$
17:                     break
18:                 **else**
19:                     $nextS$.remove(a_m)
20:                     **if** len($nextS$)!=0 **then**
21:                         a_m = random.choice($nextS$)
22:                     **else**
23:                         continue
24:                     **end if**
25:                 **end if**
26:             **end while**
27:         **if** *Decision*!= 0 **then**
28:             break
29:         **else**
30:             continue
31:         **end if**
32:         **else**
33:             a_m = random.choice($nextS$)
34:             **if** $r_{i,a_m} > 0$ **then**
35:                 Decision.append(a_m)
36:                 $r_{i,a_m} = max(r_{i,a_m} - 1, 0)$
37:                 break
38:             **else**
39:                 continue
40:             **end if**
41:         **end if**
42:     **else if** $q_m == 0$ AND len($nextD$!=0) **then**
43:         **if** len($nextD$)!=1 **then**
44:             a_m = random.choice($nextD$)
45:             **while** len($nextD$)!=0 **do**
46:                 **if** $r_{i,a_m} > 0$ **then**
47:                     Decision.append(a_m)
48:                     $r_{i,a_m} = max(r_{i,a_m} - 1, 0)$
49:                     break

Algorithm 4 *Cont.*

```
50:              else
51:                  nextD.remove(a_m)
52:                  if len(nextD)!=0 then
53:                      a_m = random.choice(nextD)
54:                  else
55:                      continue
56:                  end if
57:              end if
58:          end while
59:          if Decision!= 0 then
60:              break
61:          else
62:              continue
63:          end if
64:      else
65:          a_m = random.choice(nextD)
66:          if r_{i,a_m} > 0 then
67:              Decision.append(a_m)
68:              r_{i,a_m} = max(r_{i,a_m} - 1, 0)
69:              break
70:          else
71:              continue
72:          end if
73:      end if
74:  else if len(US)==0 AND len(nextD!=0) then
75:      if len(nextD)!=1 then
76:          a_m = random.choice(nextD)
77:          while len(nextD)!=0 do
78:              if r_{i,a_m} > 0 then
79:                  Decision.append(a_m)
80:                  r_{i,a_m} = max(r_{i,a_m} - 1, 0)
81:                  break
82:              else
83:                  nextD.remove(a_m)
84:                  if len(nextD)!=0 then
85:                      a_m = random.choice(nextD)
86:                  else
87:                      continue
88:                  end if
89:              end if
90:          end while
91:          if Decision!= 0 then
92:              break
93:          else
94:              continue
95:          end if
96:      else
97:          a_m = random.choice(nextD)
98:          if r_{i,a_m} > 0 then
99:              Decision.append(a_m)
100:             r_{i,a_m} = max(r_{i,a_m} - 1, 0)
101:             break
```

Algorithm 4 *Cont.*

```
102:            else
103:              continue
104:            end if
105:          end if
106:        else if q_m!=0 AND len(US)!=0 AND len(nextD)!=0 AND len(nextS)== 0 AND
              len(nextND)== 0 then
107:            Decision.append(i)
108:            break
109:        else if q_m!=0 AND ANY(h, ∀h ∈ US ∩ next) AND len(nextS)== 0 AND ANY(w_h ≠
              0, ∀h ∈ next) then
110:            Decision.append(i)
111:            break
112:        else if ALL(w_h == 0, ∀h ∈ H) AND i ∈ D then
113:            Decision.append(i)
114:            break
115:        else if ALL(r_{i,j} == 0, ∀j ∈ next, if (i,j) ∈ E) then
116:            Decision.append(i)
117:            break
118:        else
119:          if len(nextND) > 1 then
120:            a_m = random.choice(nextND)
121:            while len(nextND)!=0 do
122:              if r_{i,a_m} > 0 then
123:                Decision.append(a_m)
124:                r_{i,a_m} = max(r_{i,a_m} − 1, 0)
125:                break
126:              else
127:                nextD.remove(a_m)
128:                if len(nextND)!=0 then
129:                  a_m = random.choice(nextND)
130:                else
131:                  continue
132:                end if
133:              end if
134:            end while
135:            if Decision!= 0 then
136:              break
137:            else
138:              continue
139:            end if
140:          else
141:            Decision.extend(nextND)
142:            break
143:          end if
144:        end if
145:   end for
146:   if M\M'_k then
147:     for m ∈ M\M'_k do
148:       Decision[m] = l_m
149:     end for
150:   end if
151:   if len(Decision) == 0 then
152:     print("error")
153:   end if
          return Decision
```

These decisions are considered obvious decisions where computation efforts should not be focused on. Instead, only when all of the above TP decisions are not applicable (no obvious decisions), will the heuristic be applied. Ideally, none of these obvious decisions should be specified. Instead, the agent should be able to figure out and learn the obvious decision based on the reward obtained. However, such an ideal mechanism would require a humongous amount of rollout episodes with horizons extending to the termination state on each of them. For practical purposes, limited by computation power, the obvious decisions are filtered out to avoid extensive computation efforts. Hence the term "teach" in TBIH-1's "teaching part" (TP).

For the SP, a purely random selection of the next destinations could be applied as in TBIH-1 (Algorithm 4 (line 122)). In the proposed TBIH-1, the obvious decisions are inserted by "teaching". The non-obvious decision is decided by a purely random selection among possible next destinations. The general structure of TBIH-1 is described in Algorithm 4 where the SP part is shown in line (121–147).

The TP consists of updating the capacity of all the vehicles as well as the demand of the shelters (Algorithm 4 (line 1)). This is performed so that the decision selected is based on the current status of the demand and capacity which are otherwise updated/observed by the agent during the transition from PRE to PDS. The next part involves determining the potential next destinations j for vehicle m and sorting these destinations whether they are emergency shelters, depots or non–depot nodes (line 5–9). Afterwards, the obvious decision selection follows as described in Equation (6) (line 10–120). The SP is executed if none of the obvious decisions are suitable (line 121–147). For en route vehicles, the decision is to remain at their current destination (line 149–153). Finally, a decision is selected and returned by the algorithm.

Instead of a purely random selection as in Algorithm 4 (line 121–147), there could be more meaningful guided approaches to select the next destination for the SP. From here, an extend Algorithm 4 (line 121–147) shows the possibilities of inserting a better possible next destination in the route by applying a dynamic SIH-I1 (DSIH) (Algorithm 5) in TBIH-2 and a DCW in TBIH-3 (Algorithm 6), in their respective SP. The authors also experimented with the proposed heuristics TBIH-4 (with an embedded Dynamic Lookahead SIH (DLASIH) in the SP) (Algorithm 7) and TBIH-5 (with an embedded Dynamic Lookahead CW (DLACW) in the SP) (Algorithm 8) to see if both aforementioned heuristics could be enhanced further for better insertion.

4.3. TBIH-2

Among the first to develop SIH is [76], whose work is based on the generalised savings algorithm. Ref. [77] then introduced three types of SIH to solve the VRP and scheduling problem with a time window. The proposed SIH (I1) constructs a route by considering two criteria: the first involves determining the best place for insertion, c_1 based on $c_{1,1}$ and $c_{1,2}$. The second is the consideration for the best un-routed node v to be inserted c_2. For the VRP considering time windows, the SIH (I1) is computed with the following equations [77]:

$$c_{1,1}(i,v,j) = c_{i,v} + c_{v,j} - \xi c_{i,j} \quad \xi \geq 0,$$

$$c_{1,2}(i,v,j) = b_{j_v} - b_j,$$

where $c_{1,1}$ is the generalised savings, and $c_{1,2}$ is the time difference between the new service time for j, b_{j_v} and the time prior to insertion of v. Together, the best insertion place of v is computed as $c(i(v), v, j(v))$ given by:

$$c(i(v), v, j(v)) = \min_{(i,v,j) \in c_1} c_1(i,v,j),$$

where c_1 is given as:

$$c_1 = \theta_1 c_{1,1}(i,v,j) + \theta_2 c_{1,2}, \quad \theta_1 + \theta_2 = 1.$$

Meanwhile, the best v insertion criterion c_2 is given by:

$$c_2(i,v,j) = \zeta c_{0,v} - c_1(i,v,j), \quad \zeta \geq 0,$$

where node 0 in the formulation is the depot; v is then chosen based on:

$$v^\star : (i, v^\star, j) = \underset{(i,v^\star,j) \in c_2}{\arg\max} \; c_2.$$

Since the MDDVRPSRC does not consider time windows, the θ_2 value is given the value of zero and therefore $c_{1,2}$ is not considered. This turns c_1 into a generalisation of [76]. Furthermore, both ζ and θ_1 are given the value of one. Both node 0 and i are considered as the current position of vehicle m at s_k during the lookahead. In the DSIH, the seed j is chosen randomly by looking one step ahead beyond the next destination of m currently at i in a set such that $\{j : (v,j) \in E, r_{v,j} > 0, j \neq i, j \notin$ (set of the immediate neighbor of i), $\forall j \in H, \; \forall v \in$ (set of the immediate neighbor of i)$\}$. This is illustrated in Figure 1a–c. Here, the road capacity is not considered to simplify the description of the DSIH. In Figure 1a, the current position of vehicle m is at node 0 (not a depot) with capacity to serve. Node S5 is an emergency shelter with demand, while the rest are connecting nodes. The purpose of the DSIH is to treat the next possible destination from the current position as v by treating j as the seed when constructing a route from node 0. In Figure 1b, the node j is identified as node S9, node 4, and node 3. In the DSIH, the seed j is then chosen randomly among these three potential seeds. In Figure 1c, node 3 is chosen randomly as the seed j. Here, two possible nodes could be inserted as the v: node 1 and node 5. After applying the SIH(I1) (without time window consideration, θ_1 and ζ is given the value one), node 5 is considered the best inserted node and the route $\eta^{\pi_{B(s_k)}}$ is constructed from node 0–5–3. The next destination of the vehicle from node 0, $a_m = \eta^{\pi_{B(s_k)}}(s_k)$ is then selected as node 5. This also means that at the lookahead decision point k, the lookahead route $\varrho^{\pi_{B(s_k^{a_k})}}$ is constructed on the go/updated such that $\varrho^{\pi_{B(s_k^{a_k})}} : s_k \to \eta^{\pi_{B(s_k)}}(s_k)$ with heuristic $\mathcal{B}$ as per TBIH-2. In addition, when applying TBIH-2, the route-based MDP concept is applied [14]. This means that at the lookahead decision point $k+1$, the vehicle may not necessarily move to node 3 ($\eta^{\pi_{B(s_k)}}(s_{k+1})$) next upon arriving at node 5 as the DSIH will be executed at every decision point. In this example, the road capacity is ignored to simplify the explanation of the DSIH that is used in the SP of TBIH-2. In reality, if the edge $(0,1)$ has no road capacity available ($r_{0,1} = 0$), then SIH(I1) will not be applied as the only possible v is node 5.

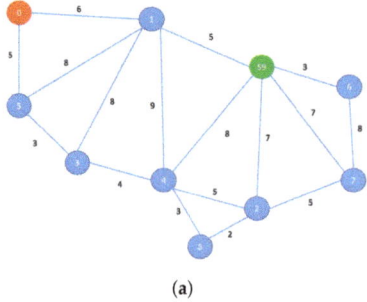
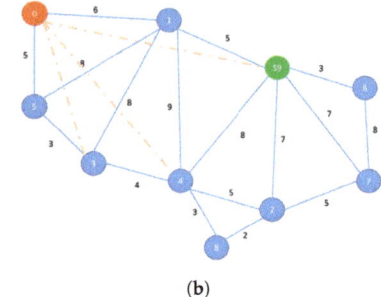

(a) (b)

Figure 1. Cont.

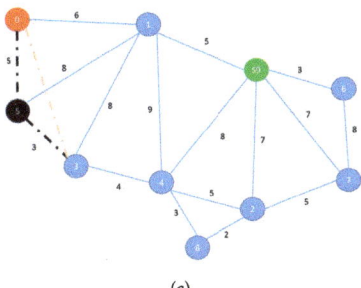

(c)

Figure 1. Performing the DSIH in TBIH-2 in an example network (**a**) with node 0 as current position of vehicle m and node S9 as an emergency shelter. The potential seeds j are considered in (**b**) and chosen randomly in (**c**). As a result, node 5 (v) is inserted and route (0–5–3) is constructed.

The decision selection specific to the DSIH is highlighted in Algorithm 5. Here, the possible seed candidates are selected based on the neighbours of potential destination v for vehicle m (lines 3–5). The seed is then randomly selected (line 7) from which the number of potential destinations v is reduced (line 8). For each of the possible v, the insertion criteria are evaluated according to the SIH(I1) (lines 9–10), and the insertion of v is determined (lines 11–12) from which the decision is made and returned (line 18).

Algorithm 5 TBIH-2 (with Embedded DSIH) Algorithm.

Require: s_k, M'_k, $M \setminus M'_k$, current position of vehicle
Ensure: *Decision*
1: Perform Algorithm 4 (line 1–120)
2: **if** $len(nextND) > 1$ **then**
3: $\quad$ $dict : v \leftarrow \{j : \forall j \in H, (v,j) \in E, r_{v,j} > 0, j \neq i, j \notin nextND\}$ $\qquad \forall v \in nextND$
4: $\quad$ $newnextND = \{j : \forall j \in dict(v), \forall v \in nextND, dict(v) \neq \{\}\}$
5: $\quad$ remove duplicate node: $list(set(newnextND))$
6: $\quad$ **if** $len(newnextND) \neq 0$ **then**
7: $\quad\quad$ $seed = random.choice(newnextND)$
8: $\quad\quad$ list of potential inserted nodes based on the selected *seed*, $InsertList = \{v : \forall v \in nextND, (v, seed) \in E\}$
9: $\quad\quad$ $dictC11 : (i, v, seed) \leftarrow (c_{i,v} + c_{v,seed} - c_{i,seed})$, $\quad \forall j \in InsertList$
10: $\quad\quad$ $dictC2 : (i, v, seed) \leftarrow (\lambda c_{i,seed} - dictC1(i, v, seed))$, $\quad \forall v \in InsertList$
11: $\quad\quad$ choose v from $(i, v, seed) = \underset{(i,v,seed) \in dictC2}{\arg\max}(dictC2)$
12: $\quad\quad$ $a_m = v$
13: $\quad\quad$ $Decision.append(a_m)$
14: $\quad\quad$ $r_{i,a_m} = max(r_{i,a_m} - 1, 0)$
15: $\quad\quad$ **break**
16: $\quad$ **else**
17: $\quad\quad$ $a_m = random.choice(nextND)$
18: $\quad\quad$ $Decision.append(a_m)$
19: $\quad\quad$ $r_{i,a_m} = max(r_{i,a_m} - 1, 0)$
20: $\quad\quad$ **break**
21: $\quad$ **end if**
22: **else**
23: $\quad$ $Decision.extend(nextND)$
24: $\quad$ **break**
25: **end if**
26: continue Algorithm 4 (148–156)
$\qquad$ **return** *Decision*

4.4. TBIH-3

The CW is derived from the work of [78] as an alternative heuristic solution to the method proposed in [79] to solve the general VRP [80]. This algorithm which is also known as the savings algorithm [81] is based on the savings computed for two non-depot nodes (i, j) in a complete graph (where all non-depot nodes have arcs connecting them to the depot). The savings is computed as $\mathbb{S}_{i,j} = 2c_{i,0} + 2c_{j,0} - (c_{i,0} + c_{j,0} + c_{i,j})$ where 0 is the depot [81]. The route is then constructed based on the savings computed for all non-depot nodes in a decreasing order, provided that the capacity constraint is respected and the connection between edges are allowed (normally the theoretical application onto a complete graph). In the event that the capacity constraint is violated, a new route is constructed for the next vehicle in the same manner of the remaining savings pair. The concept of the CW algorithm is illustrated in Figure 2 [82]. One of the few surveys on the CW algorithm for VRP can be referred to in [83]. A good example of the CW application can be referred to in [84].

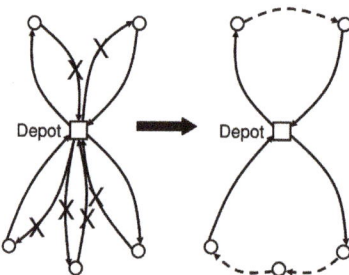

Figure 2. Concept of the Savings Algorithm. Reprinted/adapted with permission from Ref. [82]. 2015, ProQuest Information and Learning Company.

In this work, the application of the Dynamic Clarke and Wright Algorithm (DCW) is proposed and applied. By replacing the random selection of the TBIH-1 in the SP with the DCW, TBIH-1 is then modified to form TBIH-3 and is used as the base heuristic (among other heuristics) in the execution of the PDS–RA. In the DCW, the route-based MDP approach [14] is adopted during the rollout resulting in the on-the-go construction of the decision function $\varrho^{\pi_{B(s_k^{a_k})}}$. The idea is to apply the CW iteratively ($\pi_{B(s_k)}$) when a decision for a single vehicle's next assignment during the lookahead is required, given that the TBIH-3 has been selected as the base heuristic. Iteratively, the CW is applied when no obvious decision can be taken during the lookahead when transitioning. At the point of decision, the current position l_m is regarded as the single depot in the CW while the neighbouring nodes $j \in O_m : O_m \subset H$ are considered customers. The example for applying the DCW is illustrated in Figure 3a,b where node 3 is the current arrival spot of vehicle m. Additionally, a shelter in the network example is denoted as the node S2. Using the CW, route $\eta^{\pi_{B(s_k)}}$ is constructed from the assumed depot (node 3) and back to the depot.

An example of a constructed route $\eta^{\pi_{B(s_k)}}$ could be $(3-5-1-4-3)$ or $(3-4-1-5-3)$, or both if both edges $(5,1)$ and $(4,1)$ happen to have the highest savings. a_m would then be chosen as the first insertion $\varrho^{\pi_{B(s_k^{a_k})}} : s_k \to \eta^{\pi_{B(s_k)}}(s_k)$ of the chosen route to transition within the lookahead horizon.

The algorithm for the TBIH-3 is shown in Algorithm 6 as the extension of Algorithm 4 by replacing lines 121–147. In this algorithm, a decision is computed if no other obvious decision can be chosen. To execute the CW, all possible pairs $(j,k) \in E$ are detected from the possible next destination nodes in the list *nextND* (lines 3–4). If there are no edges that exist, a randomly selected node is chosen as the next destination for the vehicle m (lines 5–9). Otherwise, the savings are computed from these edges and sorted in decreasing order (lines 11–12) prior to constructing the temporary decision function $\eta^{\pi_{B(s_k)}}$ (line 16) which constructs the on-the-go base decision function $\varrho^{\pi_{B(s_k^{a_k})}} : s_k \to \eta^{\pi_{B(s_k)}}(s_k)$ (line 17). Lines 148–156 are similar to Algorithm 4 where the computed decision is returned.

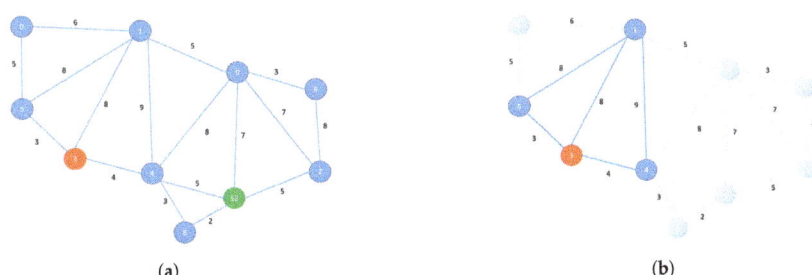

(a)   (b)

Figure 3. Performing DCW in TBIH-3 in an example network (**a**) with node 3 as current position of vehicle m and node S2 as an emergency shelter. The components for performing CW are selected in (**b**).

Algorithm 6 TBIH-3 Algorithm.

Require: s_k, M'_k, $M \setminus M'_k$, current position of vehicle
Ensure: Decision
1: Perform Algorithm 4 (line 1–120)
2: **if** len($nextND$) > 1 **then**
3:     Possible edges from the pair that could be formed in $nextND$, Pairs = $\binom{nextND}{2}$
4:     Remove $(j,k) \in$ Pairs, if $(j,k) \notin E$
5:     **if** len(pairs == 0) **then**
6:        a_m = random.choice($nextND$)
7:        Decision.append(a_m)
8:        $r_{i,a_m} = max(r_{i,a_m} - 1, 0)$
9:        break
10:     **else**
11:        compute savings: $(j,k) \leftarrow c_{i,j} + c_{i,k} - c_{j,k} \quad \forall (j,k) \in$ Pairs
12:        sort $(j,k) \in$ Pairs with decreasing savings
13:        **if** len(Pairs)==1 **then**
14:           $a_m = j : (j,k) \in$ Pairs
15:        **else**
16:           construct route $\varrho^{\pi_{B(s_k^{a_k})}} : s_k \to \eta^{\pi_{B(s_k)}}(s_k)$ from $i = l_m$ by inserting $(j,k) \in$ Pairs as would be done in CW (decreasing savings)
17:           $a_m \leftarrow A^{\pi_{B(s_k^{a_k})}}(s_k)$
18:        **end if**
19:        Decision.append(a_m)
20:        $r_{i,a_m} = max(r_{i,a_m} - 1, 0)$
21:        break
22:     **end if**
23: **else**
24:     Decision.extend($nextND$)
25:     break
26: **end if**
27: continue Algorithm 4 (148–156)
        return Decision

4.5. TBIH-4

The application of the SIH in the MDDVRPSRC for the rollout is quite clear, given the chosen "seed customer" is the main driver of the method. In the MDDVRPSRC, the authors concur with [85] that choosing an appropriate seed is very important for insertion heuristics.

For this particular problem of depending on the capacity status of vehicle m, the seed is either the depot in the route to replenish capacity or the emergency shelter in the route to serve a shelter. This is different from Algorithm 5 where the seed is randomly chosen based on potential destinations v's neighbour. In Figure 1a–c, it is clear that more can be done to guide the vehicles towards fulfilling their task. In these figures, it could be argued that the selection of node 5 (while ignoring the road capacity condition in the network), which might occur through the random selection of seeds that occurs in Algorithm 5, may not be the best choice. Instead, node 1 could be the better choice as it would lead to serving node S9. In the TBIH-4 (Algorithm 7), the potential seeds j are reserved only for those which are either one of the depots, emergency shelters, or neighbours of either. In Figure 1a–c, node 1 will be chosen instead as v since this node would lead to serving shelter S9. Only node 1 could be inserted as only a one-time insertion procedure in DLASIH is performed at every decision point in the lookahead during the construction of the route. For the shelter or depot which is farther than a one-step lookahead, as seen in Figure 4a–c, the neighbour of either that shelter or depot is then chosen as the seed j. In this case where the vehicle is packed with delivery supplies, node 9 shall be chosen as the seed (j) since it is the neighbour of shelter S7. Since only node 1 can connect to node 9 from node 0 in the one-time insertion, node 1 is then regarded as the next destination v. Here, no SIH(I1) computation is necessary as the option is rather obvious. In this illustration case, recognising node 9 as the neighbour of emergency shelter S7 helped in trimming down potential seeds to be considered and thus also reduced the number of potential v.

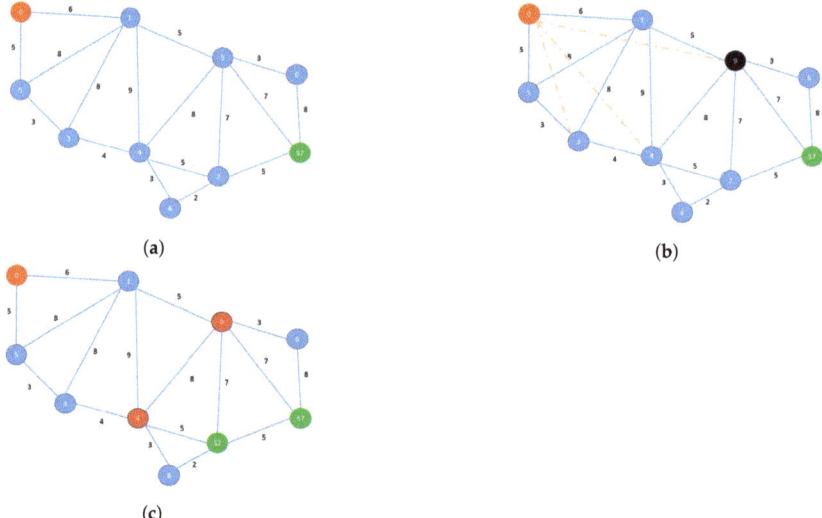

Figure 4. Performing the DLASIH in the TBIH-4 in an example network (**a**) with node 0 as current position of vehicle m ready to serve and node S7 as an emergency shelter. The potential seeds j are considered in (**b**) and Node 9 was selected since it is the neighbour of shelter S7 in (**c**). As a result, node 1 (v) is inserted and route (0–1–9–S7) is constructed. (**c**) shows two potential seeds j (node 4 and node 9) in which case a random selection between node 4 and node 9 as a seed is done.

However, if there are more potential v leading to the neighbours of emergency shelters, then one of these neighbours will be chosen randomly. If more than one possible v is connected to the chosen seed (j), the SIH(I1) will be executed.

In the TBIH-4 algorithm (Algorithm 7), the selection for j is restricted to those that would lead to either a shelter or depot, depending on q_m (lines 5 and 55). However, if such nodes are not available, another lookahead is performed to see if there are potential destinations j that could lead to neighbours of either a depot or shelter (lines 21 and 71). Depending on the case considered, the numbers of possible j from which the seed for the SIH could be chosen from (lines 9, 37, 59, and 94) can be reduced. For either case, the insertion criteria are computed and evaluated such that the on-the-go lookahead route $\varrho^{\pi_{B(s_k^{a_k})}}$ is updated: $\varrho^{\pi_{B(s_k^{a_k})}} : s_k \to \eta^{\pi_{B(s_k)}}(s_k)$, and the decision $a_m = \eta^{\pi_{B(s_k)}}(s_k)$ are returned (line 98 onwards).

Algorithm 7 TBIH-4 (with an embedded DLASIH) Algorithm.

Require: s_k, M'_k, $M \setminus M'_k$, current position of vehicle
Ensure: Decision
1: Perform Algorithm 4 (line 1–120)
2: **if** len($nextND$)> 1 **then**
3: $\quad$ $dict : v \leftarrow \{j : \forall j \in H, (v,j) \in E, r_{v,j} > 0, j \neq i, j \notin nextND\}$ $\quad \forall v \in nextND$
4: $\quad$ **if** $q_m \neq 0$ AND len(US)!= 0 **then**
5: $\quad\quad$ $dictA : v \leftarrow \{j : \forall j \in US, (v,j) \in E, r_{v,j} > 0, j \neq i, j \notin nextND\}$ $\quad \forall v \in nextND$
6: $\quad\quad$ **if** len($dictA$)!= 0 **then**
7: $\quad\quad\quad$ $newnextNDS = \{j : \forall j \in dictA(v), \forall v \in nextND, dictA(v) \neq \{\}$
8: $\quad\quad\quad$ remove duplicate node: list(set($newnextNDS$))
9: $\quad\quad\quad$ $seed$ = random.choice($newnextNDS$)
10: $\quad\quad\quad$ list of potential inserted nodes based on selected $seed$, $InsertList = \{v : \forall v \in nextND, (v, seed) \in E\}$
11: $\quad\quad\quad$ $dictC1 : (i, v, seed) \leftarrow (c_{i,v} + c_{v,seed} - c_{i,seed})$, $\quad \forall v \in InsertList$
12: $\quad\quad\quad$ $dictC2 : (i, v, seed) \leftarrow (\lambda c_{i,seed} - dictC1(i, v, seed))$, $\quad \forall v \in InsertList$
13: $\quad\quad\quad$ choose v from $(i, v, seed) = \arg\max_{(i,v,seed) \in dictC2} (dictC2)$
14: $\quad\quad\quad$ $a_m = v$
15: $\quad\quad\quad$ Decision.append(a_m)
16: $\quad\quad\quad$ $r_{i,a_m} = max(r_{i,a_m} - 1, 0)$
17: $\quad\quad\quad$ break
18: $\quad\quad$ **else**
19: $\quad\quad\quad$ List of shelter's neighbours, $USN = \{n : n \in H, (s, n) \in E, \forall s \in US, n \neq i\}$
20: $\quad\quad\quad$ USN = list(set(USN))
21: $\quad\quad\quad$ $dictB : v \leftarrow \{j : \forall j \in USN, (v,j) \in E, r_{v,j} > 0, j \neq i, j \notin nextND\}$ $\quad \forall v \in nextND$
22: $\quad\quad\quad$ **if** len($dictB$)!=0 **then**
23: $\quad\quad\quad\quad$ $LNS = \{j : \forall j \in dictB(v), \forall v \in nextND, dictB(v) \neq \{\}$
24: $\quad\quad\quad\quad$ LNS = list(set(LNS))
25: $\quad\quad\quad$ **else**
26: $\quad\quad\quad\quad$ continue
27: $\quad\quad\quad$ **end if**
28: $\quad\quad\quad$ init $nextNDS$
29: $\quad\quad\quad$ **if** len(LNS)== 0 **then**
30: $\quad\quad\quad\quad$ $nextNDS = \{j : \forall j \in dict(v), \forall v \in nextND, dict(v) \neq \{\}$
31: $\quad\quad\quad$ **else**
32: $\quad\quad\quad\quad$ $nextNDS$.extend(LNS)
33: $\quad\quad\quad$ **end if**
34: $\quad\quad\quad$ **if** len($nextNDS$)==0 **then**
35: $\quad\quad\quad\quad$ a_m = random.choice($nextND$)
36: $\quad\quad\quad\quad$ Decision.append(a_m)
37: $\quad\quad\quad\quad$ $r_{i,a_m} = max(r_{i,a_m} - 1, 0)$
38: $\quad\quad\quad\quad$ break
39: $\quad\quad\quad$ **else**
40: $\quad\quad\quad\quad$ pass
41: $\quad\quad\quad$ **end if**

Algorithm 7 *Cont.*

42:     seed = random.choice($nextNDS$)
43:     list of potential inserted nodes based on selected $seed$, $InsertList = \{v : \forall v \in nextND, (v, seed) \in E\}$
44:     $dictC1 : (i, v, seed) \leftarrow (c_{i,v} + c_{v,seed} - c_{i,seed}), \quad \forall v \in InsertList$
45:     $dictC2 : (i, v, seed) \leftarrow (\lambda c_{i,seed} - dictC1(i, v, seed)), \quad \forall v \in InsertList$
46:     choose v from $(i, v, seed) = \underset{(i,v,seed) \in dictC2}{\arg\max}(dictC2)$
47:     $a_m = v$
48:     Decision.append(a_m)
49:     $r_{i,a_m} = max(r_{i,a_m} - 1, 0)$
50:     break
51:     **end if**
52:     **else**
53:     $dictC : v \leftarrow \{j : \forall j \in D, (v, j) \in E, r_{v,j} > 0, j \neq i, j \notin nextND\} \quad \forall v \in nextND$
54:     **if** len($dictC$)!= 0 **then**
55:     $newnextNDS = \{j : \forall j \in dictC(v), \forall v \in nextND, dictC(v) \neq \{\}$
56:     remove duplicate node: list(set($newnextNDS$))
57:     seed = random.choice($newnextNDS$)
58:     list of potential inserted nodes based on selected $seed$, $InsertList = \{v : \forall v \in nextND, (v, seed) \in E\}$
59:     $dictC1 : (i, v, seed) \leftarrow (c_{i,v} + c_{v,seed} - c_{i,seed}), \quad \forall v \in InsertList$
60:     $dictC2 : (i, v, seed) \leftarrow (\lambda c_{i,seed} - dictC1(i, v, seed)), \quad \forall v \in InsertList$
61:     choose v from $(i, v, seed) = \underset{(i,v,seed) \in dictC2}{\arg\max}(dictC2)$
62:     $a_m = v$
63:     Decision.append(a_m)
64:     $r_{i,a_m} = max(r_{i,a_m} - 1, 0)$
65:     break
66:     **else**
67:     List of Depot's neighbours, $UDN = \{n : n \in H, (d, n) \in E, \forall d \in D, n \neq i, n \notin D\}$
68:     UDN = list(set(UDN))
69:     $dictD : v \leftarrow \{j : \forall j \in UDN, (v, j) \in E, r_{v,j} > 0, j \neq i, j \notin nextND\} \quad \forall v \in nextND$
70:     **if** len($dictD$)!=0 **then**
71:     $LND = \{j : \forall j \in dictD(v), \forall v \in nextND, dictD(v) \neq \{\}$
72:     LND = list(set(LND))
73:     **else**
74:     continue
75:     **end if**
76:     init $nextNDD$
77:     **if** len(LND)== 0 **then**
78:     $nextNDD = \{j : \forall j \in dict(v), \forall v \in nextND, dict(v) \neq \{\}$
79:     **else**
80:     $nextNDD$.extend(LND)
81:     **end if**

Algorithm 7 *Cont.*

```
82:         if len(nextNDD)==0 then
83:             a_m = random.choice(nextND)
84:             Decision.append(a_m)
85:             r_{i,a_m} = max(r_{i,a_m} - 1, 0)
86:             break
87:         else
88:             pass
89:         end if
90:         seed = random.choice(nextNDD)
91:         list of potential inserted nodes based on selected seed, InsertList = {v : ∀v ∈ nextND, (v, seed) ∈ E}
92:         dictC1 : (i, v, seed) ← (c_{i,v} + c_{v,seed} − c_{i,seed}),  ∀v ∈ InsertList
93:         dictC2 : (i, v, seed) ← (λc_{i,seed} − dictC1(i, v, seed)),  ∀v ∈ InsertList
94:         choose v from (i, v, seed) = arg max_{(i,v,seed)∈dictC2} (dictC2)
95:         a_m = v
96:         Decision.append(a_m)
97:         r_{i,a_m} = max(r_{i,a_m} − 1, 0)
98:         break
99:       end if
100:    end if
101: else
102:    Decision.extend(nextND)
103:    break
104: end if
105: continue Algorithm 4 (148–156)
     return Decision
```

4.6. TBIH-5

In the previous section (Section 4.4), an example network (Figure 3a) is used to demonstrate how the DCW could be applied in constructing a temporary route $\eta^{\pi_{B(s_k)}}$ with $\mathcal{B}$ being the heuristic from TBIH-3. From the temporary route, the first insertion is selected as the decision for the current lookahead state s_k based on the temporary route constructed: $\varrho^{\pi_{B(s_k^{a_k})}} : s_k \to \eta^{\pi_{B(s_k)}}(s_k)$. From the example, it is seen that either node 4 or 5 (Figure 3b) could be selected as the next destination since two routes could be computed from the CW heuristic (if two edges have similar highest savings). However, it is also seen in the example network that node S2 is next to node 4, while node 5 is much further than node S2. If the vehicle is with capacity, inserting node 4 for the on-the-go lookahead route $\varrho^{\pi_{B(s_k^{a_k})}}$ would make more sense.

If TBIH-3 (with an embedded DCW) could perform as a sort of lookahead (for non-obvious decisions, SP) for a nearby emergency shelter when a vehicle m has capacity, then the selection for the next destination would be more accurate. This is illustrated in Figure 5a,b. In Figure 5a, the current position of vehicle m is at node 3, and the nearby emergency shelter is node S9. With the exception of node 5, which is the neighbour of node 3, both nodes 1 and 4 are neighbours of node S9. As a result, only nodes 4 and 1 are considered when constructing $\eta^{\pi_{B(s_k)}}(s_k)$ even though node 5 is also a neighbour of node 3. This leads to a more promising construction of $\varrho^{\pi_{B(s_k^{a_k})}}$ on the go. If node 5 is taken into consideration, there is a possibility of node 5 being selected as the next destination for vehicle m. This is undesirable as that would lead vehicle m, which has capacity, farther from serving S9. With this concept, the DCW is extended into DLACW (turning TBIH-3 into TBIH-5). The principle of the proposed DLACW is, for most parts, similar with the exception of a mechanism to detect a nearby shelter or depot depending on the capacity status of vehicle m.

The algorithm for TBIH-5 is presented in Algorithm 8. Similar to Algorithm 5, Algorithm 6 is extended, resulting in a different base heuristic. When compared to Algorithm 6, some parts of this algorithm consist of detecting the potential next destination j of vehicle m that might lead to either a shelter of depot, depending on the current capacity status q_m (lines 3–9). Through this mechanism, the possible option for j is restricted to only those ideally more guided destinations. Edges are detected (line 10) and removed if they do not exist in the network (line 11), while savings are computed (line 18) and sorted (line 19). Finally the on-the-go base policy $\varrho^{\pi_{B(s_k^{a_k})}}$ is updated for the lookahead state s_k, where $\varrho^{\pi_{B(s_k^{a_k})}} : s_k \to \eta^{\pi_{B(s_k)}}(s_k)$ and the decision $a_m = \eta^{\pi_{B(s_k)}}(s_k)$ is returned.

Algorithm 8 TBIH-5 (with an embedded DLACW) algorithm.

Require: $s_k, M_k', M \backslash M_k'$, current position of vehicle
Ensure: *Decision*
1: Perform Algorithm 4 (line 1–120)
2: **if** len(*nextND*)> 1 **then**
3:    **if** $q_m \neq 0$ AND len(*US*)!= 0 **then**
4:       $dict : j \leftarrow \{k : \forall k \in US, (j,k) \in E, r_{j,k} > 0, k \neq i, k \notin nextND\}$ $\forall j \in nextND$
5:       $newnextND = \{j : \forall j \in nextND, dict(j) \neq \{\}\}$
6:    **else**
7:       $dict : j \leftarrow \{k : \forall k \in D, (j,k) \in E, r_{j,k} > 0, k \neq i, k \notin nextND\}$ $\forall j \in nextND$
8:       $newnextND = \{k : \forall k \in dict(j), \forall j \in nextND, dict(j) \neq \{\}\}$
9:    **end if**
10:   Possible edges from pair that could be formed in *newnextND*, $Pairs = \binom{newnextND}{2}$
11:   Remove $(j,k) \in Pairs$, if $(j,k) \notin E$
12:   **if** len(*pairs* == 0) **then**
13:      a_m = random.choice(*nextND*)
14:      *Decision*.append(a_m)
15:      $r_{i,a_m} = max(r_{i,a_m} - 1, 0)$
16:      **break**
17:   **else**
18:      compute savings, $(j,k) :\leftarrow c_{i,j} + c_{i,k} - c_{j,k}$ $\forall (j,k) \in Pairs$
19:      sort $(j,k) \in Pairs$ with decreasing savings
20:      **if** len(*Pairs*)==1 **then**
21:         $a_m = j : (j,k) \in Pairs$
22:      **else**
23:         construct route $\varrho^{\pi_{B(s_k^{a_k})}} : s_k \to \eta^{\pi_{B(s_k)}}(s_k)$ from $i = l_m$ by inserting $(j,k) \in Pairs$ as would be done in CW (decreasing savings)
24:         $a_m \leftarrow A^{\pi_{B(s_k^{a_k})}}(s_k)$
25:      **end if**
26:      *Decision*.append(a_m)
27:      $r_{i,a_m} = max(r_{i,a_m} - 1, 0)$
28:      **break**
29:   **end if**
30: **else**
31:   *Decision*.extend(*nextND*)
32:   **break**
33: **end if**
34: continue Algorithm 4 (148–156)
      return *Decision*

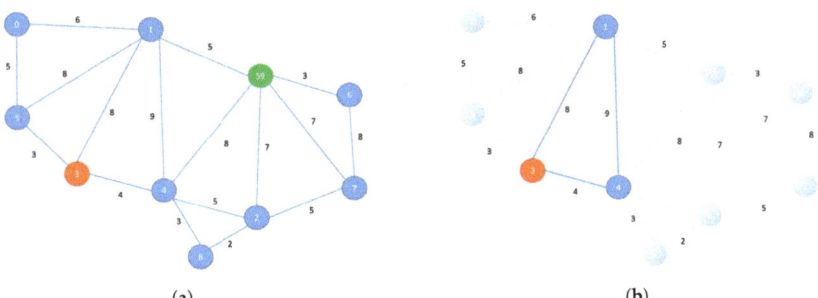

(a) (b)

Figure 5. Performing the DLACW in TBIH-5 in an example network (**a**) with node 3 as the current position of vehicle m and node S9 as an emergency shelter. The components for performing the CW are selected in (**b**).

5. Computational Results

This study presents computational results for the following purposes:

- To validate the model MDDVRPSRC by observing through the simulation tool the ecosystem (emergency medical supplies delivery) simulated.
- To validate the reinforcement learning solution of the agent in conducting the medical delivery operations through decisions computed based on the ADP approach (PDS–RA with 5 proposed base heuristics).
- To study the quality of the learning solution through the resulting simulated data by means of a comparative approach against the matheuristic proposed in the work of [15] in the stochastic setting of road capacity and dynamic road damage.
- To extend the findings in the work of [15] which serves as a preliminary study for this research.

The experiment is conducted using the authors' developed MDDVRPSRC Decision Support System (DSS) program (Figure 6) with codes written in Python 2.7 programming language. Embedded in this program is also a network monitoring layout through which the simulation of medical supplies delivery operations in the setting of the MDDVRPSRC is observed in real time (live simulation). Both the MDDVRPSRC model and the computation of the agent's decision are also implemented at the heart of the DSS. As part of the computation of the agent's decision, this program also executes the matheuristic (upon selection) proposed in work of [15] with CPLEX computation executed through the DOCPLEX API for Python. For the experiment, the MDDVRPSRC DSS is run on a laptop computer running on Intel^R Core^{TM} i7-7500U CPU at 2.70–2.90 GHz with 20 GB RAM.

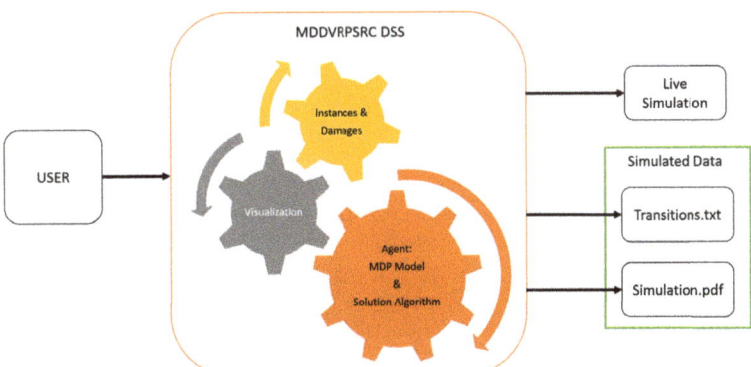

Figure 6. MDDVRPSRC DSS for medical delivery operation.

To test and validate the model and solutions algorithm for such a unique problem as the medical supplies delivery operations with compromising circumstances, the common benchmarks of Perl, Gaskell, and Christofides cannot be applied. So several test instances are designed [86,87], ranging from a small and simple road network, to medium and more challenging networks based on the available experimental apparatus (Figures A1–A10). Along with each test instance are the associated initial damage for each road within the network of the respective test instances [86,87]. These datasets, consisting of test instances and the associated damage files are available in [87] and are shown in Table 3. In Table 3, the test instances are ordered by increasing complexity levels, characterised in terms of total number of nodes as well as the ratio between connecting node to a depot and emergency shelter. The test instances associated with the road network D4N30S10 are placed last as it is hypothesised as the most challenging network among the test instances listed. Each network is comprised of multi-depots, multi emergency shelters with different demands and connecting nodes as described in Section 3.1. The placement of the nodes is based on the lessons learned from the 2015 Nepal earthquake.

In each of the road networks seen in Figures A1–A10, the blue, yellow, and brown nodes each represent the depots, emergency shelters, and connecting nodes, respectively. The violet circle lines represent the outward tremor that originated from an earthquake epicentre (coordinate (460, 180) in all the networks). The degree of the initial road damage is based on the intersection of these circles onto the edges, and the corresponding random road capacity is denoted in red at the center of the edges. The demands of each emergency shelter hovers above in a pink box. The green boxes represent vehicles that have arrived at the nodes where they are currently stationed. The blue boxes represent vehicles en route to each of their next assigned destinations. In Figure A11, the simulation example of an ongoing medical supplies operation is shown. In the road network D8N20S8, five vehicles are assigned to deliver medical supplies to eight emergency shelters with their respective demands. The full road capacity in this network for a city road, normal road, and highway is given in Table 3 as (6, 7, 8), respectively. In all road networks, the highways are placed at the outer part of the network, while the city roads are placed at the innermost sections of the networks. Normal roads can be found connecting highways with city roads in most cases, especially in the larger networks. At decision point 104, which is at the simulated time of 3097 min (translated as 2:3:37:00), the road capacity for each road changes randomly based on the dynamic road capacity mean for the random distribution of each road. These dynamic deteriorating road capacities in turn depend on the initial damage sustained by the road (given in the damage file of each test instance in the repository [87]). Thus the road capacity for the edges with more interceptions with the radial earthquake tremor circles are seen with a tendency to have less road capacity at random when compared with the edges with less or zero intersections. Hence, vehicles travelling at these edges will suffer longer travel times proportional to the initial damage sustained by the edges as accounted for in the MDDVRPSRC model described in Section 3.3. The work [15] is referred to for more explanation on how the random road capacity is sampled at each decision point. The experiment settings for both the simulation and computation of the agent's decision (PDS-RA) is given in Table 4.

For the model and solution validation, simulated data is compiled (Figure 6). For each proposed base heuristics (TBIH-1, TBIH-2, TBIH-3, TBIH-4, and TBIH-5) applied for all test instances in Table 3, 10 complete simulations of a medical supplies delivery operation are performed. Out of the 10 complete simulations, there are 10 readings for 4 key measurements:

1. Total travelled distance (K1);
2. Total travelled time (K2);
3. Total computation time (K3);
4. Average decision computation time (K4).

Table 3. Simulated test instances applied to validate the model and solutions algorithm.

Instance	Depot	Shelter	Nodes	Vehicle	Total Demand	Max Road Capacity
D3N8S3_4	3	3	8	4	550	6, 7, 8
D3N8S3_8	3	3	8	8	550	6, 7, 8
D3N8S3_15	3	3	8	15	550	6, 7, 8
D3N8S3_30	3	3	8	30	550	6, 7, 8
D3N8S3_50	3	3	8	50	550	6, 7, 8
D4N11S4_4	4	4	11	4	550	6, 7, 8
D4N11S4_8	4	4	11	8	550	6, 7, 8
D4N11S4_15	4	4	11	15	550	6, 7, 8
D4N11S4_30	4	4	11	30	550	6, 7, 8
D4N11S4_50	4	4	11	50	550	6, 7, 8
D5N13S5_4	5	5	13	4	650	6, 7, 8
D5N13S5_8	5	5	13	8	650	6, 7, 8
D5N13S5_15	5	5	13	15	650	6, 7, 8
D5N13S5_30	5	5	13	30	650	6, 7, 8
D5N13S5_50	5	5	13	50	650	6, 7, 8
D6N16S6_4	3	3	8	4	950	6, 7, 8
D6N16S6_8	3	3	8	8	950	6, 7, 8
D6N16S6_15	3	3	8	15	950	6, 7, 8
D6N16S6_30	3	3	8	30	950	6, 7, 8
D6N16S6_50	3	3	8	50	950	6, 7, 8
D7N18S7_4	7	7	18	4	1250	6, 7, 8
D7N18S7_8	7	7	18	8	1250	6, 7, 8
D7N18S7_15	7	7	18	15	1250	6, 7, 8
D7N18S7_30	7	7	18	30	1250	6, 7, 8
D7N18S7_50	7	7	18	50	1250	6, 7, 8
D8N20S8_4	8	8	20	4	1350	6, 7, 8
D8N20S8_8	8	8	20	8	1350	6, 7, 8
D8N20S8_15	8	8	20	15	1350	6, 7, 8
D8N20S8_30	8	8	20	30	1350	6, 7, 8
D8N20S8_50	8	8	20	50	1350	6, 7, 8
D8N22S9_4	8	9	22	4	1600	6, 7, 8
D8N22S9_8	8	9	22	8	1600	6, 7, 8
D8N22S9_15	8	9	22	15	1600	6, 7, 8
D8N22S9_30	8	9	22	30	1600	6, 7, 8
D8N22S9_50	8	9	22	50	1600	6, 7, 8
D9N25S10_4	9	10	25	4	1650	6, 7, 8
D9N25S10_8	9	10	25	8	1650	6, 7, 8
D9N25S10_15	9	10	25	15	1650	6, 7, 8
D9N25S10_30	9	10	25	30	1650	6, 7, 8
D9N25S10_50	9	10	25	50	1650	6, 7, 8
D9N30S10_4	9	10	30	4	1650	6, 7, 8
D9N30S10_8	9	10	30	8	1650	6, 7, 8
D9N30S10_15	9	10	30	15	1650	6, 7, 8
D9N30S10_30	9	10	30	30	1650	6, 7, 8
D9N30S10_50	9	10	30	50	1650	6, 7, 8
D4N30S10_4	4	10	30	4	1650	6, 7, 8
D4N30S10_8	4	10	30	8	1650	6, 7, 8
D4N30S10_15	4	10	30	15	1650	6, 7, 8
D4N30S10_30	4	10	30	30	1650	6, 7, 8
D4N30S10_50	4	10	30	50	1650	6, 7, 8

The first three key measurements are self explanatory. The last key measurement is the average time taken for the agent to make one decision at decision point k based on the total computation time divided by the number of decisions made (decision points) to complete the delivery operations simulation. The PDS-RA with the proposed heuristic bases are benchmarked with the matheuristic rollout found in the work of [15] for all vehicle number settings (4, 8, 15, 30, and 50) for the road networks D3N8S8-D7N18S7. For the road network D8N20S8-D4N30S10, however, the benchmarking is completed only up to the vehicle number settings of 4, 8, and 15. This is due to the resultant computational time which is far longer than considered reasonable when compared with the longest computation time obtained among the five proposed heuristics (Figures A14 and A18). With the resulting simulated data, the model is then validated based on the analysis of the output data produced (Figure 6). Furthermore, the performance of the proposed heuristics compared to the matheuristic rollout applied is observed through a descriptive and comparative analysis.

Table 4. Simulation and PDS-RA Configuration.

Parameter	Value
Deterioration Proportional Constant P	0.1
Ω	200
Vehicle Speed	90 km/h
Vehicle Capacity, Q	50
Monte Carlo Simulation	3
Lookahead Horizon K	7

The computational results in the Supplementary file (Tables S1–S81) are collected and recorded for a time span of more than two years; given the hardware available for the experiments. A total of 10 readings were taken for each of the proposed base heuristics applied in the PDS-RA for all test instances. This was for all key measurements (K1–K4) given the stochastic road capacity and dynamic deterioration of the mean road capacity in the problem addressed. From each 10 readings, the descriptive analysis is performed to measure the mean, standard deviation, variance, and covariance of the sample data. The Normality test is performed to determine that a suitable comparative analysis method is applied for benchmarking. A total of 11,600 key readings were recorded as a result of 2900 simulations performed for further analysis involving the key measurements of K1, K2, K3, and K4 mentioned in Section 5. The 2900 simulations consist of 290 sets of 10 readings per set, for each of the 4 key measurements which are then used to compute the average reading. Not all 290 sets tested were found to have a normal distribution based on the Shapiro–Wilk test [88] performed in the Excel [89]. The highest percentage for normal data (around 50%) is only seen in the K3 and K4 measurements. Furthermore, the 10 readings for each key measurement of a test instance is considered small for a parametric test. As such, a non-parametric test (Wilcoxon Signed Rank Test) was applied to test for significance in differences against the matheuristic solution (PDS-RA with CPLEX as base heuristic). Moreover, the Best So Far (BSF) measurement among the solution algorithms applied at each test instance was performed to observe the performance of each PDS-RA of the respective proposed heuristics against the matheuristic rollout.

The full computation results are presented in the supplementary file and the abbreviations applied are listed in Table 5. Furthermore, the general overview of the simulated data collected is shown in Table A1. Thorough investigation and synthesise of the resulting simulation data by means of cross-referencing key values were performed to ensure that no errors are presented.

The results obtained in Tables S1–S81 are further synthesised for numerical analysis focusing on model validation and base heuristics performances. The MDDVRPSRC model is validated based on the trends and patterns observed in Figures A12, A13, A16 and A17. Meanwhile, the performance of the proposed heuristics, as compared to the matheuristic rollout, can be seen in the remaining figures between Figures A12–A27 and in the supplementary file S1 (Figures S1–S62). Figures A12–A15 show the trends for average measurements of each of the 10 sample readings based on all four key measurements, while Figures A16–A19 shows the trends for best measurements among the 10 reading samples for each key measurement. Figures A20–A23 show the total numbers of BSF counts for each algorithm for all 40 instances with the matheuristic rollout benchmark. Figures A24–A27 depict the total numbers of BSF counts in percentage for each algorithm for all 50 instances with and without (omitting 10 test instances for matheuristic rollout due to computation time limitation) the matheuristic rollout benchmark. A more detailed breakdown per test instance of the percentage of BSF associated with each heuristics is shown in Figures S1–S40. Meanwhile, Tables A2–A7 give a more detailed breakdown on numbers of the BSF counts, normal distribution data, and the significant differences for each key measurements. Finally, a detailed performance of each PDS-RA with proposed heuristics for all key measurements is shown in Figures S41–S62.

Table 5. Abbreviation for Tables and Figures.

Base-H	Base Heuristic applied during rollout lookahead
TBIH-1	Teach Based Insertion Heuristic
TBIH-2	TBIH with dynamic SIH
TBIH-3	TBIH with dynamic CW
TBIH-4	TBIH with dynamic lookahead SIH
TBIH-5	TBIH with dynamic lookahead CW
CPLEX	DOCPLEX (Python): solving MDVRPSRC-2S1 and MDVRPSRC-2S2
SW(P)	P value: Shapiro Wilk Test for normality test
Wilcox(P)	P value: Wilcoxon Signed Rank Test for Significance test
BSF	Best So Far Measurement Value
Sig.	Significance
N	Normal
(% V2)	Percentage Performance based on 40 Measurements instead of 50 (CPLEX Application as Base Heuristic for benchmarking)

6. Discussion

In terms of the MDDVRPSRC MDP model validation, the behaviours plotted in Figures A12, A13, A16 and A17 are conforming to the natural expectation on how the humanitarian operational aspects will shape out based on the key measurements. Figures A12 and A16, for example, show a logical increase of total distance travelled with the increase in the number of vehicles. Here, the increase in total distance is also attributed to the policy that all vehicles must be dispatched for delivery to compensate for the potential risk that a vehicle might be stranded while en route due to the road damage incurred. Furthermore, a stochastic road capacity with multiple dispatches of vehicles might ensure a faster delivery time at the cost of an increase in total distance travelled.

For the road network D3N8S3, the increase of total distance is higher than that of networks D4N11S4, D5N13S5, and D6N16S6. This is comparable to that of network D7N18S7 onwards with operations involving 30 and 50 vehicles. This is due to the large amount of vehicles travelling on a road network with limited roads. The random road capacity as well as deteriorating road conditions cause a bottleneck at some connecting nodes. However, a steady increase of roads in more complex networks alleviates this problem, as shown in networks D4N11S4, D5N13S5, and D6N16S6. Given the increasing demands and more complex networks, a different observation could be made.

The road networks of D7N18S7, D8N20S8, D9N25S9, and D9N30S10, for example, indicate roughly the same trend of total distance travelled with an occasional peak at about 10,000 km for networks D8N20S8 and D9N25S10. However, an obvious increase of total distance travelled can be seen for the network D4N30S10, thereby confirming the hypothesis that this network is the most complex in terms of delivery operations. This is explained by the ratio of depots to connecting nodes where the vehicle has only a limited number of depots to replenish supplies in this network as compared to the other networks. Furthermore, the ratio of depots and shelters also contributes to this observation, showing the difficulties of completing the deliveries given the smaller number of depots to replenish.

Additionally, the reduced number of depots in this network also leads to more connecting options between the depots and connecting nodes which may not necessarily be advantageous to the delivery operations. This is especially true for networks that tend to have a shorter route disabled due to random road capacity and a dynamic reduction of the road capacity due to damage to the road. As a result, a longer route is taken leading to the increase of total distance travel by all vehicles.

All of the observations for the total distance travelled shown in Figures A12 and A16 also apply to the observations seen in Figures A13 and A17. In general, the increase of the total vehicle numbers leads to the reduced delivery operations time (total travel time). For the network D3N8S3, a limited number of vehicles in a small network with high demands relative to the number of vehicles led to an increase in total travel time compared to network D4N11S4. This is due to the longer time required by the smaller number of vehicles to satisfy the total demands within the network. Moreover, the deteriorating road capacity for each damaged road may lead to lesser road availability for an already small road network. This leads to vehicles taking the longer route compared to that of network D4N11S4.

Vehicles may also travel back and forth along the same road due to connecting roads becoming increasingly less available. The bottleneck effect is also seen for the larger number of vehicles when comparing the total time travel within the road network of D3N8S3 with the road networks of D4N11S4, D5N13S5, and D6N16S6. It is also shown clearer here that the bottleneck effect could be alleviated through trends observed for networks D7N18S7, D8N20S8, D9N25S9, and D9N30S10. Similarly the reduced ratio between depots to shelters and depots to connecting nodes leads to a more complex network. This is despite not having the highest number of nodes that contributes to a higher total travel time for some of the algorithms. Interestingly, the matheuristic rollout approach does not show the same observations. This shows the potential of the matheuristic rollout in navigating more complex networks compared to the proposed heuristics.

This, however, comes at the cost of computation time as shown in Figures A14, A15, A18, A19, A22, A23, A26 and A27. This was observed when investigating the performance of the proposed base heuristics against the matheuristic rollout as a benchmark. The total computation time increases for the matheuristic rollout applying CPLEX at every lookahead decision point for road network D5N13S5 onwards for all vehicle settings (Figures A14 and A18) when compared with the results obtained with PDS-RA applying the proposed base heuristics. This trend is even more obvious in Figures A15 and A19, showing a clear increase in computation time for the agent in making a decision on average. As a result, no BSF count was ever obtained through the matheuristic rollout for the key measurement of K3 and K4 (Figures A22, A23, A26 and A27).

Apart from showing an exponential increase for both K3 and K4 (see Figures A15 and A19), it is also obvious that this trend depends on the total number of nodes that are involved in the network. This is evident when comparing the two key measurements for networks D9N30S10 and D4N30S10. However, the road networks sharing a similar number of nodes as D4N30S10, such as D9N25S10, do not indicate a similar magnitude of increment. Therefore, it could be concluded that both the number of nodes and complexity associated with each network affect the two key measurements for the matheuristic rollout.

Meanwhile, the performance of the proposed PDS-RA applying base heuristics is further investigated through the BSF count for all instances tested. Figures A22, A23, A26 and A27 confirm the observation made for the matheuristic rollout in terms of computation time (K3 and K4). However, the matheuristic rollout shows clear dominance in terms of the key measurements of K1 and K2 (Figures A20, A21, A24 and A25). This is especially seen in the breakdown of K1 and K2 in Figures S46 and S52 which Figure S46 interestingly also show a good performance of TBIH-1 for K1. This shows the relevance of the matheuristic approach for complex stochastic problems. In most of the individual networks, the matheuristic approach seems to also perform better compared to the other proposed approaches for K1 and K2 (Figures S46 and S52). However, as it can be seen in Figures A12–A17 with the exception of Figures A14 and A15, the application of PDS-RA with proposed heuristics remains competitive with low gaps of difference. This is also supported by the statistical numerical evidence that show lower significance differences recorded throughout all simulated data involving K1 and K2 when compared with data obtained by the matheuristic rollout (Table A1).

Of those, a vast majority of significance difference is seen in Figures A14, A15, A18 and A19 which corroborates findings in terms of computation time for K3 and K4. Judging from the trends, the practicality of the matheuristic rollout as benchmarked, is shown to be poor at least for the given hardware used for the experimentation. This is despite the good performance shown for K1 and K2, albeit with no significance difference.

On the other hand, the TBIH-1 shows clear advantage as shown from Figures A20–A27 in terms of the BSF count. This is perhaps expected considering the stochastic problem which may favour the exploratory approach more than the exploitation part, as is performed in TBIH-1 with random selection for the SP part of the algorithm. The comparable performance of PDS-RA with TBIH-1 compared to the matheuristic rollout is also shown in most of the road networks, respectively. Furthermore, TBIH-1 is seen at times neck to neck with the benchmark when looking into the performance in each individual network, such as in Figures S26, S29, S33, S34, and S36 among others. It is also noteworthy to see that the algorithm also performs rather well for the network D4N30S10, with the exception of key measurement K2. Moreover, the dominance of the TBIH-1 is increasingly more noticeable for larger networks as best seen in Figures S41, S47, S53, and S58. Meanwhile, both the TBIH-2 and TBIH-4 also perform well in the overall BSF count (as seen in Figures A20–A27) when compared to that of TBIH-3 and TBIH-5 which is based on DCW. This highlights the advantages of the DSIH which centred on the concept of inserting and placing promising nodes in ways that optimise the operation.

DCW, on the other hand, tends to ignore the inner part of the nodes and favour the outer nodes in an attempt to reduce parallel connections to the origin node as CW has always been intended for. This is evident by the performance of TBIH-3 which is the lowest followed by TBIH-2 when looking at BSF counts for both the individual network and overall networks (Figures S41–S62). Except for K3 in Figure S55, the TBIH-3 only scores a BSF count of one for all other key measurements (Figures S43, S49 and S60). This translates in a low BSF count obtained in Figures A20–A27 where the TBIH-3 is seen multiple times with BSF counts as low as 0% and 2.5% while topping at most only an 8% as seen in Figure A26. TBIH-5 shows an improved performance when compared to TBIH-3 (for K1, K2, K3, and K4 in Figures S45, S51, and S57) and TBIH-2 (except for K3 and K4) with the addition of a lookahead mechanism for selecting more promising nodes in the route. This demonstrates the strength of exploitation in the heuristics to improve selection. The TBIH-2, however, is better in terms of K3 and K4 (Figures S54 and S59), displaying the trade off for embedding such features.

Similarly the TBIH-2's performance is improved in TBIH-4 by means of an exploitation mechanism that requires a lookahead in selecting more promising nodes and filtering out those that are not. Unlike the TBIH-3 and TBIH-5, however, the gap in the computation speed between the TBIH-2 and TBIH-4 is not obvious. This shows that the TBIH-5 might be more costly to implement compared to TBIH-4 which improves on the TBIH-2 with less trade-off as seen in Figures S54, S56, S59 and S61. As such, the TBIH-4 could be considered an all-rounder with a balanced performance next to TBIH-1.

It should be noted that the PDS–RA is performed per vehicle when making a collective decision for all vehicles. Furthermore, both the number of Monte Carlo simulations and the length of the lookahead horizon shown in Table 4 could be considered low when compared to other similar work. However, the new perspective of the computing decision, as proposed in Equation (24), demands some compromise be made, especially with limited computational power available for this research. Furthermore, the method applied in this research is necessary to break the usual practice of clustering the emergency hot-spots per vehicle and then computing the routing decision afterwards. Additionally, the research for stochastic road capacity problems with additional consideration for damaged roads is very limited among reinforcement-learning-oriented research. Due to the stochastic road capacity, the resulting key measurements are highly varied as shown in the variance and covariance measurement of each of the simulated samples collected (Tables S2–S81). Ideally, a good amount of Monte Carlo simulations of the rollout and a longer horizon for the lookahead would be best to account for such stochastic problems. A trade-off still needs to be made where the limitation of computation is a concern. If anything, this research proves that the proposed methods could be applied to a machine with limited capability to simulate, visualise, and compute decisions as a DSS for an emergency medical supplies delivery humanitarian operation.

However, more study into this research is warranted. With capable machines, the number of lookahead horizons and the number of Monte Carlo simulations should be increased. With such an increase in parameters, perhaps the TP of the algorithm could be discarded; allowing the agent a pure learning opportunity when making decisions. In the experiments here, this could not be achieved; hence the TP is needed. Furthermore, with enough Monte Carlo simulations, the highly stochastic problem concerning routing can be properly addressed. A longer horizon of the lookahead ensures better decisions in a long-term perspective.

The investigation included a one-factor experiment performed by varying the fixed number of vehicles per road networks, which is a limitation. It should be note,d however that various road networks were tested consisting of varying numbers of depots, emergency shelters, and connecting nodes. Furthermore, given the entry level machine that is utilized, this experiment (involving 2900 simulations and 11,600 measurement readings) took more than one year to complete. Given a more capable machine, factorial experiments should be performed to investigate the performance of the proposed heuristics against the matheuristic benchmark. For example, through a factorial experiment, the existing network could be expanded into more challenging networks. In D4N30S10 for instance, it would also be interesting to see how the delivery operation with such a number of depots and an increase of connecting nodes fares with a smaller number of emergency shelters as more options for routing become available. Will the agent with the proposed solution method be able to navigate intelligently among these many options? Hence, more studies should be performed with expanded networks where the combination of ratios between depots, connecting nodes, and emergency shelters are varied. For this experiment, the vehicles are placed randomly at depots initially. This is performed to account for the degree of unpreparedness, where coordination should be planned with random accounts of assets. Hence, even though the key measurements are assessed through 10 average readings for each test instance, the initial situation for each simulation run is varied. There are two ways that this study could be expanded further: (1) to increase the number of simulations per test instance to obtain more than 10 readings for a better average reading, and (2) to apply a fixed assignment of vehicles per depot for all simulations. The latter approach, however would not account for a more realistic scenario of emergency medical supplies delivery operations. Finally, in this study, the placement of depots, connecting nodes, and emergency shelters are made such that the findings obtained from the lessons learned in the 2015 Nepal earthquake are addressed. Instead of utilising a simulated network, a more concrete simulation could be performed by applying real networks and incorporating details of the depots, connecting nodes, emergency shelters, vehicles, road damages, and road capacities during that actual disaster event. It is noted that such data is usually of a sensitive nature. However, developing a simulated network allows for flexibility when completing planning exercise and experiments.

7. Conclusions

As part of the DSS for humanitarian emergency medical supplies delivery operations, the 2015 Nepal earthquake is referred to in developing the MDDVRPSRC MDP model. The presented model focuses on the difficulty in navigating through stochastic road capacity within the compromised road network due to the ongoing tremors from the earthquake. The model also incorporates multi-depots, multi-trips, and split delivery operations. Here the conventional approach of "cluster first, route second" largely applied among related research cannot be applied. Instead, to solve the problem, a lookahead approach of ADP is adopted, where the PDS-RA is applied. As part of the PDS-RA mechanism, five base constructive heuristics are proposed to construct the decision rule on the go dynamically and iteratively. Unlike conventional applications of the PDS-RA in VRP, this research adopted the proposed method in the work of [15] for a consecutive application of the PDS-RA for each vehicle that arrives at every decision point. The resulting individual assignment of vehicles computed collectively forms an MDP decision at every decision point.

The five proposed base heuristics are based on a decision-making strategy that consists of obvious decisions (TP) and non-obvious decisions (SP) to reduce the burden of computation. In the TBIH-1, the SP applied pure random selection for selecting a vehicle's next destination. Alternatively, the principle of constructive heuristics used in SIH(I1) and CW, (coined as DSIH and DCW, respectively) are adopted in the TBIH-2 and the TBIH-3. A lookahead exploitation mechanism is adapted to both the DCW and the DSIH, giving birth to DLASIH and DLACW which is applied in the proposed TBIH-4 and TBIH-5, respectively. These five proposed base heuristics are compared with the matheuristic proposed in the authors' previous work, [15]. Moreover, test instances were developed and made available in the repository [87]. The results presented in the supplementary file validate the model where expected behaviour is observed from the simulated operations based on four key measurements: K1, K2, K3, and K4. Furthermore, the performance of the PDS-RA applied with the proposed five base heuristics shows comparable performance for K1 and K2 with no significant difference recorded. Meanwhile, all the proposed heuristics showed superior performance for K3 and K4 when compared to the matheuristic. The results also highlight the power of exploration associated to pure random selection in the TBIH-1 in addressing a highly stochastic problem such as the MDDVRPSRC. Furthermore, the advantages of exploitation are shown in TBIH-4 and TBIH-5 when compared with the performance of TBIH-2 and TBIH-3, respectively. For problems such as the MDDVRPSRC, it would appear that the DSIH (TBIH-2) and DLASIH (TBIH-4) perform better than their counterparts: DCW (TBIH-3) and DLACW (TBIH-5).

Supplementary Materials: The following are available at https://www.mdpi.com/article/10.3390/math10152699/s1.

Author Contributions: Conceptualisation, W.K.A., L.S.L. and S.P.; methodology, W.K.A., L.S.L. and S.P.; software, W.K.A. and L.S.L.; validation, W.K.A. and L.S.L.; formal analysis, W.K.A., L.S.L. and H.-V.S.; investigation, W.K.A. and L.S.L.; resources, W.K.A.; data curation, W.K.A. and L.S.L.; writing—original draft preparation, W.K.A., L.S.L. and H.-V.S.; writing—review and editing, W.K.A., L.S.L. and H.-V.S.; visualisation, W.K.A.; supervision, L.S.L. and S.P. All authors have read and agreed to the published version of the manuscript.

Funding: This research received no external funding.

Institutional Review Board Statement: Not applicable.

Informed Consent Statement: Not applicable.

Data Availability Statement: The primary simulated data is presented in the supplementary file. The test instances from which the simulated data is generated is found in [87].

Acknowledgments: This research was supported by the Ministry of Higher Education Malaysia through the Fundamental Research Grant Scheme with reference code FRGS/1/2019/STG06/UPM/02/1.

Conflicts of Interest: The authors declare no conflict of interest.

Abbreviations

The following abbreviations are used in this manuscript:

ADP	Approximate Dynamic Programming
MDDVRPSRC	Multi-Depot Dynamic Vehicle Routing Problem with Stochastic Road Capacity
CSM	Supply Chain Management
MDP	Markov Decision Processes
DSS	Decision Support System
LSPs	Logistics Service Providers
ML	Machine Learning
RL	Reinforcement Learning
MIP	Mixed Integer Programming
PRE	Pre Decision State
PDS	Post Decision State
RA	Rollout Algorithm
PDS–RA	Post Decision State Rollout Algorithm
SILP	Stochastic Linear Integer Programming
SIH	Sequential Insertion Heuristic
DSIH	Dynamic Sequential Insertion Heuristic
DLASIH	Dynamic Lookahead Sequential Insertion Heuristic
CW	Clarke and Wright
DCW	Dynamic Clarke and Wright
DLACW	Dynamic Lookahead Clarke and Wright

Appendix A. Simulated Road Networks and Analysis Results

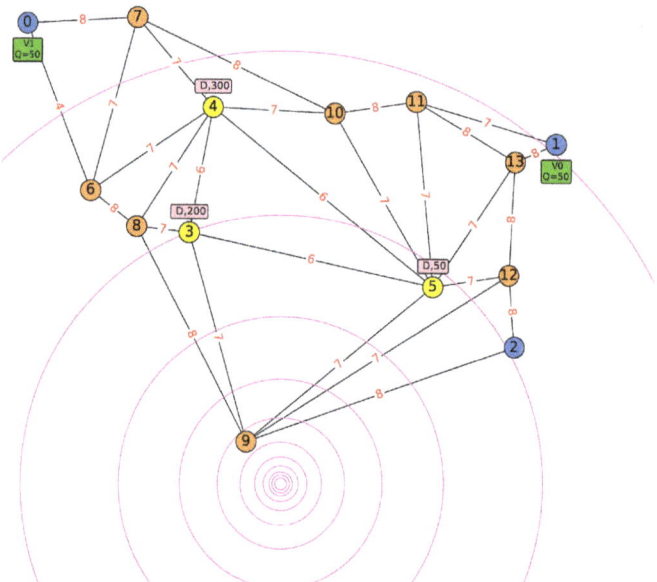

Figure A1. Road network for instance D3N8S3 [15].

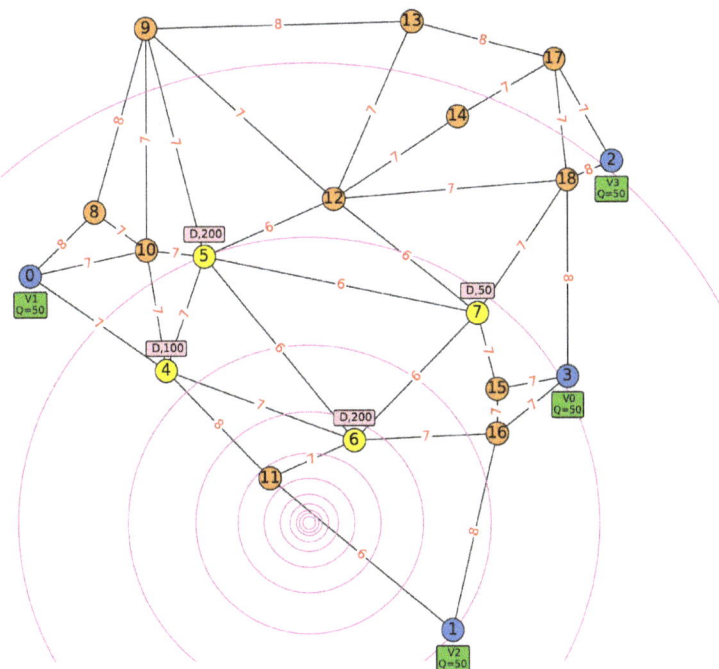

Figure A2. Road network for instance D4N11S4 [15].

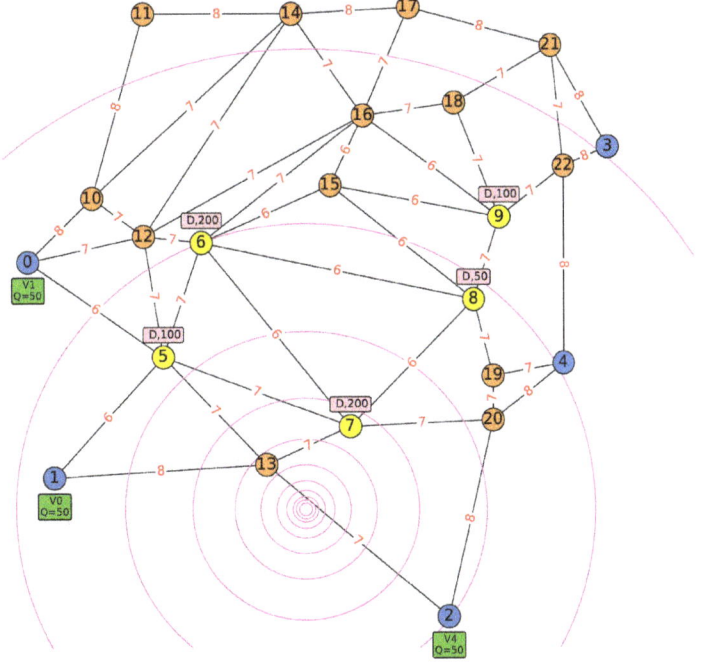

Figure A3. Road network for instance D5N13S5 [15].

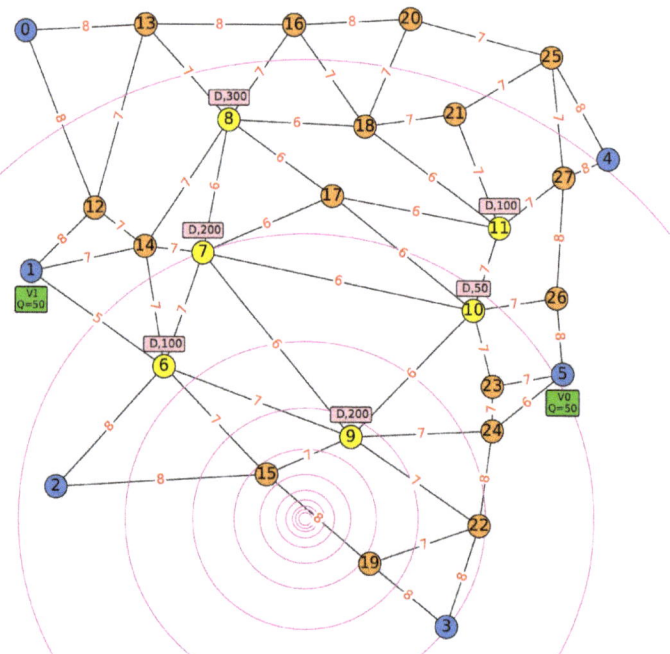

Figure A4. Road network for instance D6N16S6.

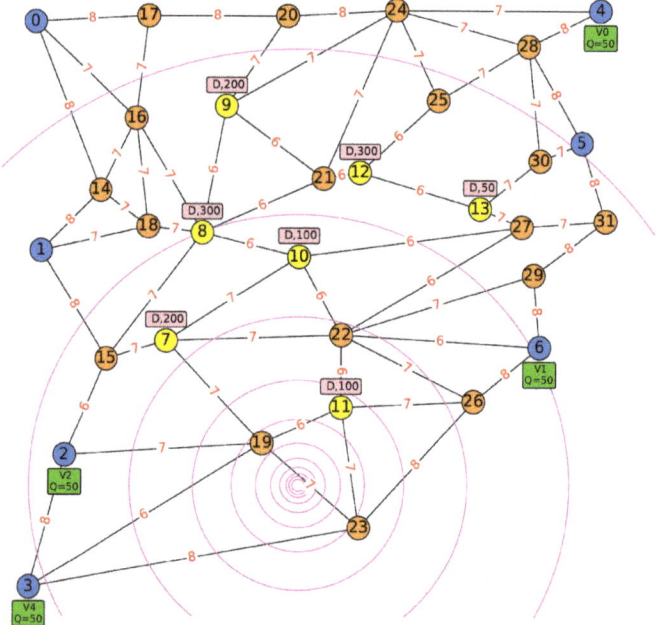

Figure A5. Road network for instance D7N18S7.

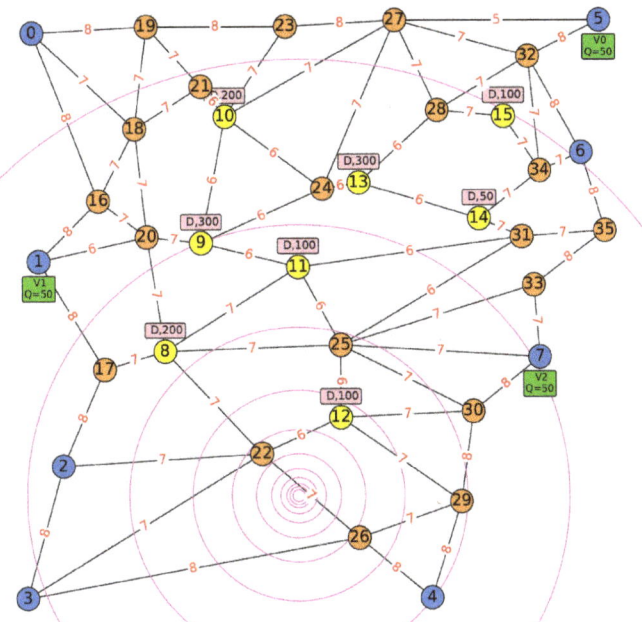

Figure A6. Road network for instance D8N20S8.

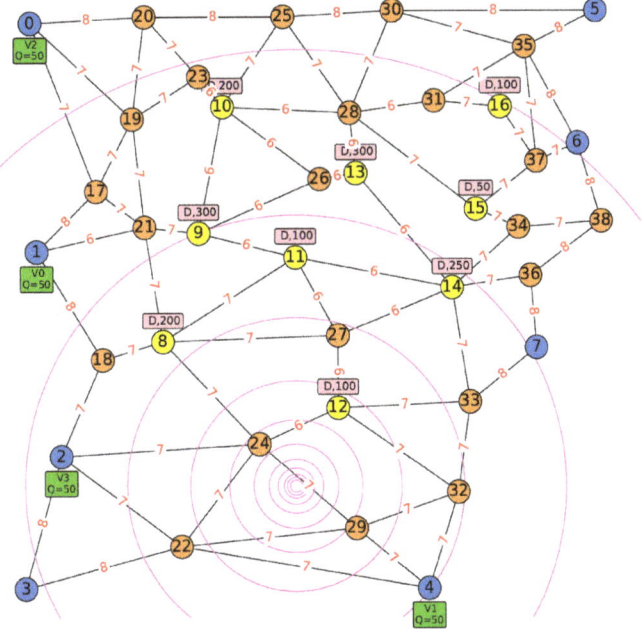

Figure A7. Road network for instance D8N22S9.

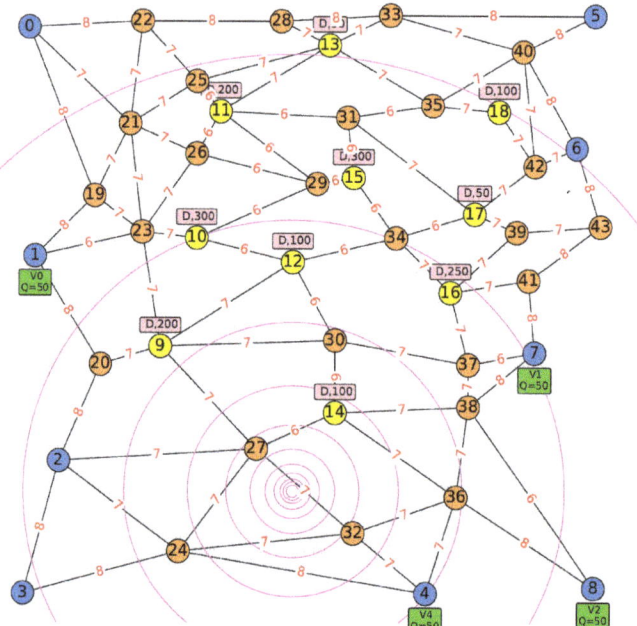

Figure A8. Road network for instance D9N25S10.

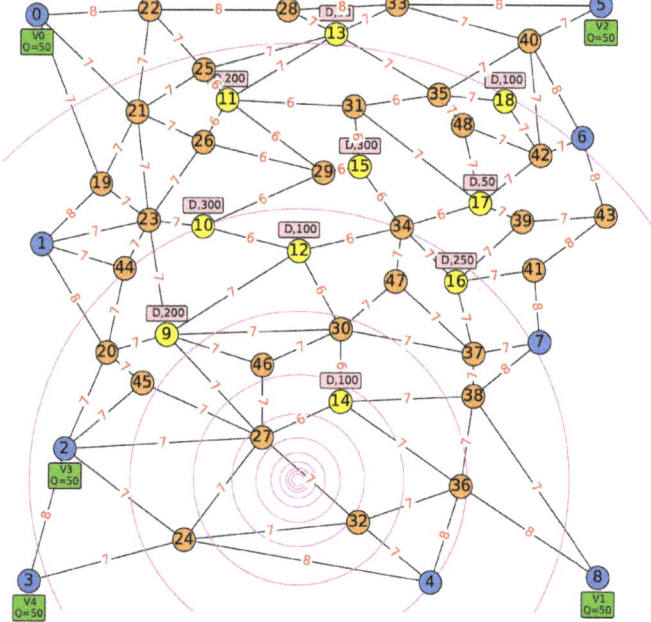

Figure A9. Road network for instance D9N30S10.

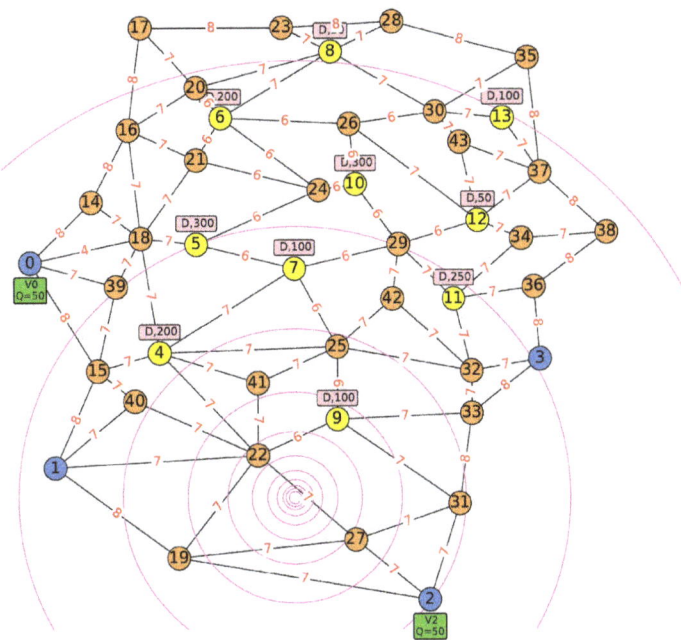

Figure A10. Road network for instance D4N30S10.

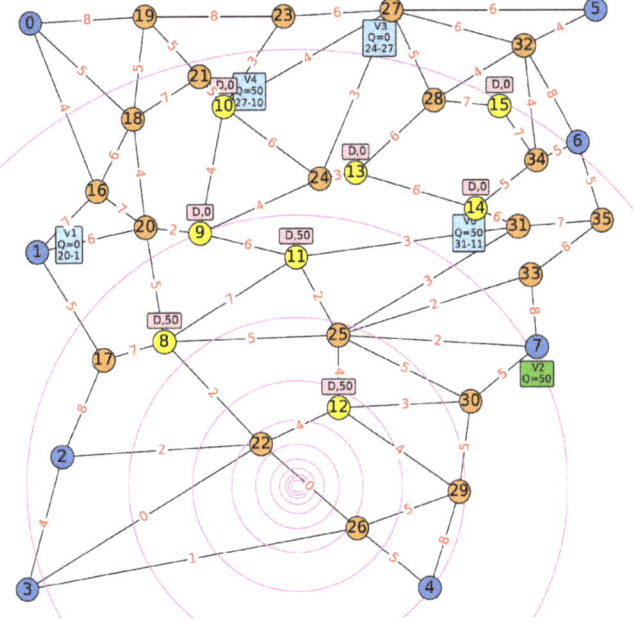

Figure A11. Example of medical supply delivery in progress for the network D8N20S20.

Table A1. Descriptive overall view on simulated data collected.

Total Test Instances: (10 Networks × 5 vehicle settings)	50
Proposed Base Heuristics & Benchmark: (5 + 1)	6
Total Test Instances: Base Heuristic & Benchmark (with 10 Omitted Matheuristic Benchmark: ((50 × 6) − 10))	290
Total Simulation Run	2900
Total Key Measurements	4
Total Set of 10 Samples Readings: 290 × 4 (for Four Key Measurements)	1160
Total Sample Readings	11,600
Total Normality Analysis (Shapiro-Wilk Test) Applied (for Each Key Measurement)	290
Total 10 Normal Sample Reading (Total Travelled Distance)	39 (13.44%)
Total 10 Normal Sample Reading (Total Travelled Time)	42 (14.48%)
Total 10 Normal Sample Reading (Total Computation Time)	148 (51.03%)
Total 10 Normal Sample Reading (Average Decision Computation Time)	166 (57.24%)
Total Comparative Analysis (Wilcoxon Signed-Ranks Test) Applied (for Each Key Measurement: ((50 × 5) − (10 × 5)))	200
Total Significant Difference (Total Travelled Distance)	68 (34%)
Total Significant Difference (Total Travelled Time)	69 (34.5%)
Total Significant Difference (Total Computation Time)	191 (95.5%)
Total Significant Difference (Average Decision Computation Time)	194 (97%)

Table A2. PDS_RA performance with TBIH-1 application as base heuristic.

Test Instance	Total Distance Travelled			Total Travelled Time			Total Computation Time			Average Decision Computation		
	N	Sig.	BSF	N	Sig.	BSF	N	Sig.	BSF	N	Sig.	BSF
D3N8S3_4		✓	✓		✓		✓	✓			✓	
D3N8S3_8		✓						✓			✓	
D3N8S3_15	✓							✓			✓	
D3N8S3_30								✓			✓	
D3N8S3_50		✓	✓				✓			✓		
	1	3	2	0	0	1	3	4	0	1	4	0
D4N11S4_4							✓	✓			✓	
D4N11S4_8					✓			✓		✓	✓	✓
D4N11S4_15	✓	✓		✓	✓			✓		✓	✓	✓
D4N11S4_30		✓			✓		✓	✓		✓	✓	
D4N11S4_50	✓			✓			✓			✓	✓	
	2	2	0	2	2	0	3	4	0	4	5	2

Table A2. *Cont.*

Test Instance	Total Distance Travelled			Total Travelled Time			Total Computation Time			Average Decision Computation		
	N	Sig.	BSF	N	Sig.	BSF	N	Sig.	BSF	N	Sig.	BSF
D5N13S5_4							✓	✓	✓	✓	✓	
D5N13S5_8							✓	✓		✓	✓	
D5N13S5_15		✓					✓	✓	✓		✓	
D5N13S5_30								✓			✓	✓
D5N13S5_50	✓			✓			✓	✓		✓	✓	
	1	0	1	1	0	0	4	5	2	4	5	1
D6N16S6_4							✓	✓	✓	✓	✓	
D6N16S6_8		✓					✓	✓		✓	✓	✓
D6N16S6_15								✓	✓	✓	✓	✓
D6N16S6_30			✓			✓		✓	✓		✓	✓
D6N16S6_50		✓			✓			✓			✓	
	0	2	1	0	1	1	2	5	3	3	5	3
D7N18S7_4	✓	✓		✓			✓	✓		✓	✓	✓
D7N18S7_8			✓				✓	✓	✓	✓	✓	✓
D7N18S7_15							✓	✓		✓	✓	
D7N18S7_30	✓	✓			✓			✓		✓	✓	✓
D7N18S7_50				✓				✓	✓		✓	
	2	2	1	2	1	0	3	5	2	4	5	3
D8N20S8_4			✓		✓		✓	✓	✓	✓	✓	✓
D8N20S8_8	✓		✓				✓	✓	✓	✓	✓	✓
D8N20S8_15							✓	✓		✓	✓	
D8N20S8_30	✓								✓			✓
D8N20S8_50				✓								✓
	2	0	2	1	0	1	3	3	3	3	3	4
D8N22S9_4		✓			✓		✓	✓		✓	✓	
D8N22S9_8								✓	✓		✓	✓
D8N22S9_15			✓				✓	✓	✓	✓	✓	✓
D8N22S9_30			✓	✓		✓			✓	✓		✓
D8N22S9_50			✓			✓			✓			
	0	1	3	1	1	2	2	3	4	3	3	3
D9N25S10_4		✓			✓		✓	✓	✓	✓	✓	✓
D9N25S10_8								✓		✓	✓	✓
D9N25S10_15							✓	✓		✓	✓	
D9N25S10_30			✓				✓			✓		
D9N25S10_50			✓									
	0	1	2	0	1	0	3	3	1	4	3	2
D9N30S10_4		✓			✓		✓	✓	✓	✓	✓	✓
D9N30S10_8	✓						✓	✓		✓	✓	
D9N30S10_15			✓			✓	✓	✓	✓	✓	✓	
D9N30S10_30			✓			✓	✓					
D9N30S10_50				✓								
	1	1	2	1	1	2	4	3	2	4	3	1

Table A2. Cont.

Test Instance	Total Distance Travelled			Total Travelled Time			Total Computation Time			Average Decision Computation		
	N	Sig.	BSF	N	Sig.	BSF	N	Sig.	BSF	N	Sig.	BSF
D4N30S10_4		✓			✓		✓	✓		✓	✓	
D4N30S10_8		✓			✓			✓			✓	
D4N30S10_15		✓			✓			✓			✓	✓
D4N30S10_30			✓				✓		✓			
D4N30S10_50			✓									
	0	3	2	0	3	0	2	3	1	1	3	1
Total	9	15	16	8	10	7	29	38	18	31	39	20
(%)	18.00	30.00	32.00	16.00	20.00	14.00	58.00	76.00	36.00	62.00	78.00	40.00

Table A3. PDS_RA performance with TBIH-2 application as base heuristic.

Test Instance	Total Distance Travelled			Total Travelled Time			Total Computation Time			Average Decision Computation		
	N	Sig.	BSF	N	Sig.	BSF	N	Sig.	BSF	N	Sig.	BSF
D3N8S3_4								✓	✓		✓	✓
D3N8S3_8								✓			✓	✓
D3N8S3_15	✓				✓		✓	✓	✓	✓	✓	✓
D3N8S3_30					✓			✓			✓	
D3N8S3_50							✓					
	1	0	0	0	2	0	2	4	2	1	4	3
D4N11S4_4							✓	✓	✓	✓	✓	✓
D4N11S4_8				✓				✓			✓	
D4N11S4_15			✓				✓	✓			✓	
D4N11S4_30		✓		✓			✓	✓		✓	✓	
D4N11S4_50	✓							✓			✓	
	1	1	1	2	0	0	3	5	1	2	5	1
D5N13S5_4		✓			✓		✓	✓		✓	✓	✓
D5N13S5_8	✓				✓		✓	✓	✓	✓	✓	✓
D5N13S5_15								✓		✓	✓	✓
D5N13S5_30								✓		✓	✓	
D5N13S5_50		✓		✓				✓		✓	✓	✓
	1	2	0	2	1	0	2	5	1	5	5	4
D6N16S6_4							✓	✓		✓	✓	
D6N16S6_8							✓	✓	✓	✓	✓	
D6N16S6_15		✓			✓		✓	✓		✓	✓	
D6N16S6_30								✓			✓	
D6N16S6_50		✓			✓			✓			✓	
	0	2	0	0	2	0	3	5	1	3	5	0
D7N18S7_4							✓	✓		✓	✓	
D7N18S7_8							✓	✓		✓	✓	
D7N18S7_15							✓	✓	✓	✓	✓	✓
D7N18S7_30		✓			✓			✓			✓	
D7N18S7_50		✓			✓			✓			✓	✓
	0	2	0	0	2	0	3	5	1	4	5	2

Table A3. Cont.

Test Instance	Total Distance Travelled			Total Travelled Time			Total Computation Time			Average Decision Computation		
	N	Sig.	BSF	N	Sig.	BSF	N	Sig.	BSF	N	Sig.	BSF
D8N20S8_4					✓		✓	✓		✓	✓	
D8N20S8_8						✓	✓	✓		✓	✓	
D8N20S8_15						✓	✓	✓		✓	✓	
D8N20S8_30										✓		
D8N20S8_50												
	0	0	0	0	1	2	3	3	0	4	3	0
D8N22S9_4							✓	✓		✓	✓	
D8N22S9_8							✓	✓		✓	✓	
D8N22S9_15							✓	✓		✓	✓	
D8N22S9_30												
D8N22S9_50												✓
	0	0	0	0	0	0	3	3	0	3	3	1
D9N25S10_4							✓	✓		✓	✓	
D9N25S10_8								✓			✓	
D9N25S10_15	✓						✓	✓		✓	✓	
D9N25S10_30						✓	✓			✓		
D9N25S10_50												
	1	0	0	0	0	1	3	3	0	3	3	0
D9N30S10_4		✓					✓	✓		✓	✓	
D9N30S10_8		✓			✓		✓	✓		✓	✓	
D9N30S10_15							✓	✓		✓	✓	✓
D9N30S10_30							✓			✓		
D9N30S10_50			✓									
	0	2	1	0	1	0	4	3	0	4	3	1
D4N30S10_4		✓			✓		✓	✓		✓	✓	
D4N30S10_8					✓		✓	✓		✓	✓	
D4N30S10_15					✓			✓	✓	✓	✓	
D4N30S10_30												✓
D4N30S10_50										✓		
	0	1	0	0	3	0	2	3	1	4	3	1
Total	4	10	2	4	12	3	28	39	7	33	39	13
(%)	8.00	20.00	4.00	8.00	24.00	6.00	56.00	78.00	14.00	66.00	78.00	26.00

Table A4. PDS_RA performance with TBIH-3 application as base heuristic.

Test Instance	Total Distance Travelled			Total Travelled Time			Total Computation Time			Average Decision Computation		
	N	Sig.	BSF	N	Sig.	BSF	N	Sig.	BSF	N	Sig.	BSF
D3N8S3_4								✓			✓	
D3N8S3_8	✓							✓			✓	
D3N8S3_15							✓	✓			✓	
D3N8S3_30				✓	✓							
D3N8S3_50					✓		✓			✓		
	1	0	0	1	2	0	2	3	0	1	3	0

Table A4. Cont.

Test Instance	Total Distance Travelled			Total Travelled Time			Total Computation Time			Average Decision Computation		
	N	Sig.	BSF	N	Sig.	BSF	N	Sig.	BSF	N	Sig.	BSF
D4N11S4_4							✓	✓			✓	
D4N11S4_8		✓			✓			✓		✓	✓	
D4N11S4_15		✓			✓			✓			✓	
D4N11S4_30		✓					✓	✓		✓	✓	
D4N11S4_50	✓	✓		✓	✓						✓	
	1	4	0	1	3	0	2	4	0	2	5	0
D5N13S5_4		✓			✓		✓	✓		✓	✓	
D5N13S5_8		✓			✓		✓				✓	
D5N13S5_15					✓			✓		✓	✓	
D5N13S5_30	✓			✓				✓		✓	✓	
D5N13S5_50		✓		✓	✓			✓			✓	
	1	3	0	2	4	0	2	5	0	3	5	0
D6N16S6_4		✓			✓		✓	✓		✓	✓	
D6N16S6_8		✓			✓		✓	✓		✓	✓	
D6N16S6_15		✓			✓		✓	✓		✓	✓	
D6N16S6_30	✓			✓				✓		✓	✓	
D6N16S6_50							✓	✓			✓	
	1	3	0	1	3	0	4	5	0	4	5	0
D7N18S7_4							✓	✓		✓	✓	
D7N18S7_8							✓	✓		✓	✓	
D7N18S7_15							✓	✓		✓	✓	
D7N18S7_30		✓		✓	✓			✓	✓		✓	
D7N18S7_50		✓			✓			✓			✓	
	0	2	0	1	2	0	3	5	1	3	5	0
D8N20S8_4								✓			✓	
D8N20S8_8	✓			✓			✓	✓		✓	✓	
D8N20S8_15							✓	✓		✓	✓	
D8N20S8_30	✓		✓		✓		✓					
D8N20S8_50			✓			✓			✓			
	2	0	2	1	0	2	2	3	1	2	3	0
D8N22S9_4		✓			✓		✓	✓		✓	✓	
D8N22S9_8							✓	✓		✓	✓	
D8N22S9_15							✓	✓		✓	✓	
D8N22S9_30												
D8N22S9_50												
	0	1	0	0	1	0	3	3	0	3	3	0
D9N25S10_4							✓	✓		✓	✓	
D9N25S10_8					✓			✓			✓	
D9N25S10_15							✓	✓		✓	✓	
D9N25S10_30									✓			
D9N25S10_50												
	0	0	0	0	1	0	2	3	1	2	3	0

Table A4. Cont.

	Total Distance Travelled			Total Travelled Time			Total Computation Time			Average Decision Computation		
Test Instance	N	Sig.	BSF	N	Sig.	BSF	N	Sig.	BSF	N	Sig.	BSF
D9N30S10_4		✓			✓		✓	✓		✓	✓	
D9N30S10_8							✓	✓		✓	✓	
D9N30S10_15							✓	✓		✓	✓	
D9N30S10_30										✓		
D9N30S10_50												
	0	1	0	0	1	0	3	3	0	4	3	0
D4N30S10_4		✓			✓			✓			✓	✓
D4N30S10_8		✓			✓			✓		✓	✓	
D4N30S10_15		✓		✓	✓			✓			✓	
D4N30S10_30												
D4N30S10_50									✓			
	0	3	0	1	3	0	0	3	1	1	3	1
Total	6	17	2	8	20	2	23	37	4	25	38	1
(%)	12.00	34.00	4.00	16.00	40.00	4.00	46.00	74.00	8.00	50.00	76.00	2.00

Table A5. PDS_RA performance with TBIH-4 application as base heuristic.

	Total Distance Travelled			Total Travelled Time			Total Computation Time			Average Decision Computation		
Test Instance	N	Sig.	BSF	N	Sig.	BSF	N	Sig.	BSF	N	Sig.	BSF
D3N8S3_4	✓			✓				✓		✓	✓	
D3N8S3_8								✓			✓	
D3N8S3_15	✓							✓		✓	✓	
D3N8S3_30		✓		✓			✓	✓	✓	✓	✓	✓
D3N8S3_50			✓			✓		✓	✓		✓	✓
	2	0	1	2	0	1	1	5	2	3	5	2
D4N11S4_4		✓			✓	✓	✓	✓		✓	✓	
D4N11S4_8								✓	✓	✓	✓	
D4N11S4_15								✓	✓		✓	
D4N11S4_30		✓		✓		✓	✓	✓	✓	✓	✓	✓
D4N11S4_50		✓	✓	✓				✓	✓	✓	✓	✓
	0	2	1	2	1	2	3	5	4	3	5	2
D5N13S5_4	✓						✓	✓		✓	✓	
D5N13S5_8							✓	✓		✓	✓	
D5N13S5_15	✓						✓	✓			✓	
D5N13S5_30							✓	✓	✓		✓	
D5N13S5_50		✓		✓			✓	✓	✓	✓	✓	
	2	1	0	1	0	4	4	5	2	3	5	0
D6N16S6_4								✓		✓	✓	✓
D6N16S6_8		✓					✓	✓		✓	✓	
D6N16S6_15		✓			✓		✓	✓		✓	✓	
D6N16S6_30								✓			✓	
D6N16S6_50		✓			✓			✓	✓		✓	✓
	0	3	0	0	2	0	2	5	1	3	5	2

Table A5. Cont.

Test Instance	Total Distance Travelled			Total Travelled Time			Total Computation Time			Average Decision Computation		
	N	Sig.	BSF	N	Sig.	BSF	N	Sig.	BSF	N	Sig.	BSF
D7N18S7_4		✓			✓		✓	✓		✓	✓	
D7N18S7_8		✓			✓		✓	✓		✓	✓	
D7N18S7_15			✓			✓	✓	✓		✓	✓	
D7N18S7_30		✓			✓			✓			✓	
D7N18S7_50		✓						✓			✓	
	0	4	1	0	3	1	3	5	0	4	5	0
D8N20S8_4							✓	✓		✓	✓	
D8N20S8_8							✓	✓		✓	✓	
D8N20S8_15	✓			✓			✓	✓		✓	✓	
D8N20S8_30												
D8N20S8_50												
	1	0	0	1	0	0	3	3	0	3	3	0
D8N22S9_4		✓			✓		✓	✓		✓	✓	
D8N22S9_8							✓	✓		✓	✓	
D8N22S9_15							✓	✓		✓	✓	
D8N22S9_30												
D8N22S9_50												
	0	1	0	0	1	0	3	3	0	3	3	0
D9N25S10_4							✓	✓		✓	✓	
D9N25S10_8								✓	✓		✓	
D9N25S10_15							✓	✓		✓	✓	
D9N25S10_30							✓			✓		
D9N25S10_50				✓		✓				✓		✓
	0	0	0	1	0	1	3	3	1	4	3	1
D9N30S10_4							✓	✓		✓	✓	
D9N30S10_8							✓	✓	✓	✓	✓	✓
D9N30S10_15				✓			✓	✓		✓	✓	
D9N30S10_30									✓			✓
D9N30S10_50				✓		✓			✓			✓
	0	0	0	2	0	1	3	3	3	3	3	3
D4N30S10_4	✓	✓		✓	✓		✓	✓		✓	✓	
D4N30S10_8					✓		✓	✓		✓	✓	
D4N30S10_15				✓	✓		✓	✓		✓	✓	
D4N30S10_30						✓						
D4N30S10_50						✓	✓			✓		
	1	1	0	2	3	2	4	3	0	4	3	0
Total (%)	6 12.00	12 24.00	3 6.00	11 22.00	10 20.00	12 24.00	29 58.00	40 80.00	13 26.00	33 66.00	40 80.00	10 20.00

Table A6. PDS_RA performance with TBIH-5 application as base heuristic.

Test Instance	Total Distance Travelled			Total Travelled Time			Total Computation Time			Average Decision Computation		
	N	Sig.	BSF	N	Sig.	BSF	N	Sig.	BSF	N	Sig.	BSF
D3N8S3_4								✓		✓	✓	
D3N8S3_8		✓	✓	✓	✓	✓		✓	✓		✓	
D3N8S3_15								✓			✓	
D3N8S3_30		✓			✓		✓			✓		
D3N8S3_50	✓	✓					✓					
	1	3	1	1	2	1	2	3	1	2	3	0
D4N11S4_4							✓	✓			✓	
D4N11S4_8							✓	✓		✓	✓	
D4N11S4_15	✓				✓			✓			✓	
D4N11S4_30		✓					✓	✓		✓	✓	
D4N11S4_50								✓			✓	
	1	1	0	0	1	0	3	5	0	2	5	0
D5N13S5_4		✓			✓		✓	✓		✓	✓	
D5N13S5_8					✓		✓	✓		✓	✓	
D5N13S5_15								✓		✓	✓	
D5N13S5_30							✓	✓		✓	✓	
D5N13S5_50				✓	✓		✓			✓	✓	
	0	1	0	1	3	0	4	4	0	5	5	0
D6N16S6_4		✓			✓		✓	✓		✓	✓	
D6N16S6_8		✓			✓		✓	✓		✓	✓	
D6N16S6_15	✓	✓		✓	✓		✓	✓		✓	✓	
D6N16S6_30	✓							✓			✓	
D6N16S6_50		✓			✓			✓			✓	
	2	4	0	1	4	0	3	5	0	3	5	0
D7N18S7_4						✓	✓	✓	✓	✓	✓	
D7N18S7_8							✓	✓		✓	✓	
D7N18S7_15							✓	✓		✓	✓	
D7N18S7_30		✓			✓		✓	✓		✓	✓	
D7N18S7_50	✓	✓			✓			✓			✓	
	1	2	0	0	2	1	4	5	1	4	5	0
D8N20S8_4							✓	✓		✓	✓	
D8N20S8_8								✓			✓	
D8N20S8_15			✓					✓	✓		✓	✓
D8N20S8_30												
D8N20S8_50												
	0	0	1	0	0	0	1	3	1	2	3	1
D8N22S9_4							✓	✓	✓	✓	✓	✓
D8N22S9_8			✓			✓	✓	✓		✓	✓	
D8N22S9_15							✓	✓		✓	✓	
D8N22S9_30							✓			✓		
D8N22S9_50												
	0	0	1	0	0	1	4	3	1	4	3	1

Table A6. *Cont.*

Test Instance	Total Distance Travelled			Total Travelled Time			Total Computation Time			Average Decision Computation		
	N	Sig.	BSF	N	Sig.	BSF	N	Sig.	BSF	N	Sig.	BSF
D9N25S10_4							✓	✓		✓	✓	
D9N25S10_8								✓			✓	
D9N25S10_15							✓	✓	✓	✓	✓	✓
D9N25S10_30	✓											
D9N25S10_50	✓						✓		✓			✓
	2	0	0	0	0	0	3	3	2	2	3	2
D9N30S10_4		✓			✓		✓	✓		✓	✓	
D9N30S10_8		✓			✓		✓	✓		✓	✓	
D9N30S10_15							✓	✓		✓	✓	
D9N30S10_30	✓						✓			✓		
D9N30S10_50												
	1	2	0	0	2	0	4	3	0	4	3	0
D4N30S10_4		✓			✓		✓	✓		✓	✓	
D4N30S10_8					✓			✓			✓	✓
D4N30S10_15			✓		✓			✓			✓	
D4N30S10_30				✓					✓			
D4N30S10_50									✓			✓
	0	1	1	1	3	0	1	3	2	1	3	2
Total	8	14	4	4	17	3	29	37	8	29	38	6
(%)	16.00	28.00	8.00	8.00	34.00	6.00	58.00	74.00	16.00	58.00	76.00	12.00

Table A7. PDS_RA performance with CPLEX application as base heuristic.

Test Instance	Total Distance Travelled			Total Travelled Time			Total Computation Time			Average Decision Computation		
	N	Sig.	BSF	N	Sig.	BSF	N	Sig.	BSF	N	Sig.	BSF
D3N8S3_4												
D3N8S3_8										✓		
D3N8S3_15			✓	✓		✓						
D3N8S3_30												
D3N8S3_50						✓						
	0	-	1	1	-	2	0	-	0	1	-	0
D4N11S4_4												
D4N11S4_8			✓			✓				✓		
D4N11S4_15	✓			✓		✓						
D4N11S4_30			✓	✓								
D4N11S4_50	✓		✓	✓		✓	✓			✓		
	2	-	3	3	-	3	1	-	0	2	-	0
D5N13S5_4			✓			✓						
D5N13S5_8			✓									
D5N13S5_15												
D5N13S5_30	✓		✓							✓		
D5N13S5_50			✓	✓			✓			✓		
	1	-	4	1	-	1	1	-	0	2	-	0

Table A7. Cont.

Test Instance	Total Distance Travelled			Total Travelled Time			Total Computation Time			Average Decision Computation		
	N	Sig.	BSF	N	Sig.	BSF	N	Sig.	BSF	N	Sig.	BSF
D6N16S6_4			✓			✓	✓			✓		
D6N16S6_8	✓		✓			✓				✓		
D6N16S6_15			✓			✓	✓					
D6N16S6_30										✓		
D6N16S6_50	✓		✓	✓		✓	✓			✓		
	2	-	4	1	-	4	3	-	0	4	-	0
D7N18S7_4			✓									
D7N18S7_8							✓	✓				
D7N18S7_15				✓			✓	✓		✓		
D7N18S7_30			✓				✓					
D7N18S7_50			✓				✓			✓		
	0	-	3	1	-	3	2	-	0	2	-	0
D8N20S8_4							✓			✓		
D8N20S8_8												
D8N20S8_15							✓					
D8N20S8_30												
D8N20S8_50												
	0	-	0	0	-	0	2	-	0	1	-	0
D8N22S9_4			✓			✓	✓			✓		
D8N22S9_8												
D8N22S9_15	✓					✓						
D8N22S9_30												
D8N22S9_50												
	1	-	1	0	-	2	1	-	0	1	-	0
D9N25S10_4			✓			✓						
D9N25S10_8			✓			✓				✓		
D9N25S10_15			✓			✓						
D9N25S10_30												
D9N25S10_50												
	0	-	3	0	-	3	0	-	0	1	-	0
D9N30S10_4			✓			✓						
D9N30S10_8			✓			✓						
D9N30S10_15												
D9N30S10_30												
D9N30S10_50												
	0	-	2	0	-	2	0	-	0	0	-	0
D4N30S10_4			✓			✓				✓		
D4N30S10_8			✓			✓						
D4N30S10_15						✓						
D4N30S10_30												
D4N30S10_50												
	0	-	2	0	-	3	0	-	0	1	-	0
Total	6	-	23	7	-	23	10	-	0	15	-	0
(%)	12.00	-	46.00	14.00	-	46.00	20.00	-	0.00	30.00	-	0.00
(% V2)	15.00	-	57.50	17.50	-	57.50	25.00	-	0.00	37.50	-	0.00

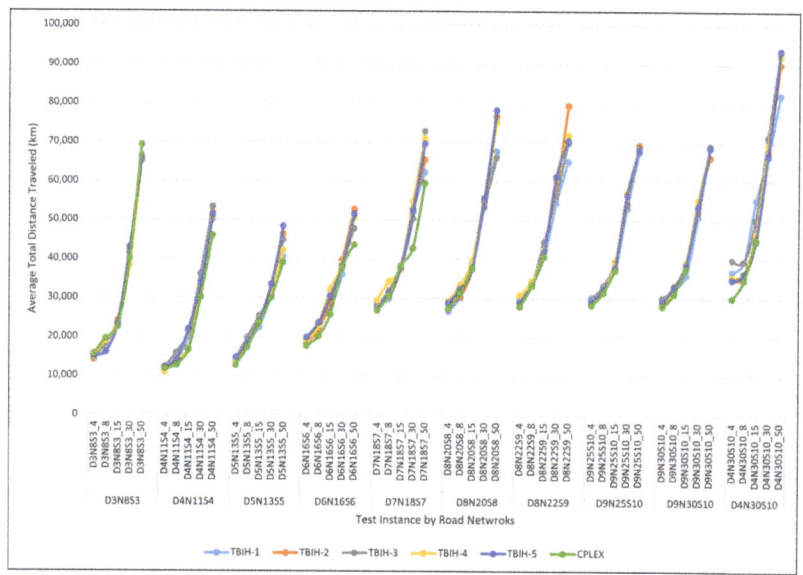

Figure A12. Algorithms performance compared to matheuristic rollout applied in PDS-RA: average total distance travelled (km) based on test instances.

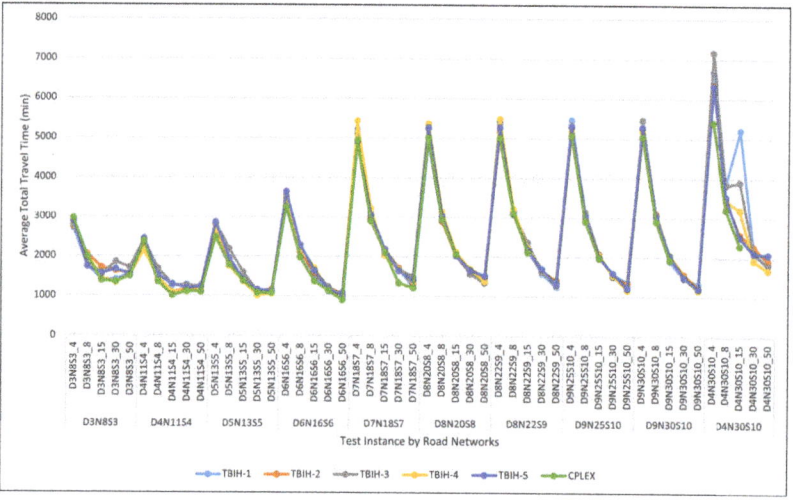

Figure A13. Algorithms performance compared to matheuristic rollout applied in PDS-RA: average total travel time (min) based on test instances.

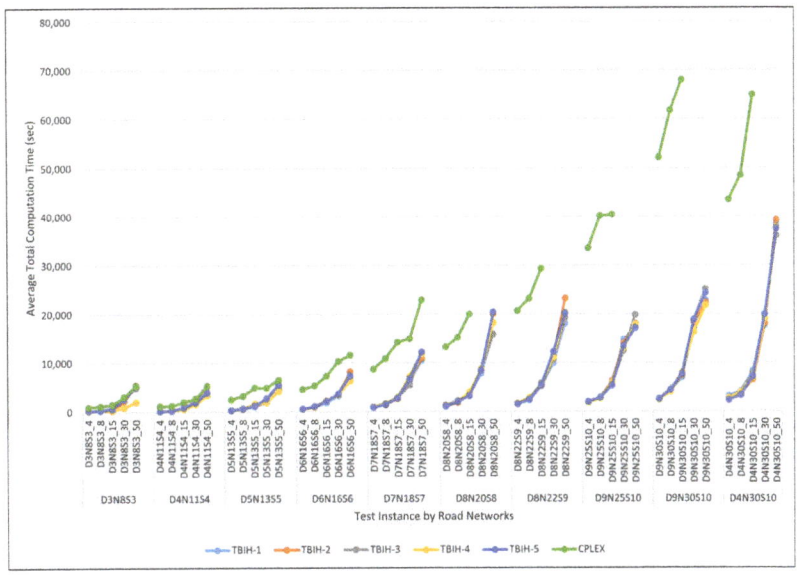

Figure A14. Algorithms performance compared to matheuristic rollout applied in PDS-RA: average total computation time (sec) based on test instances.

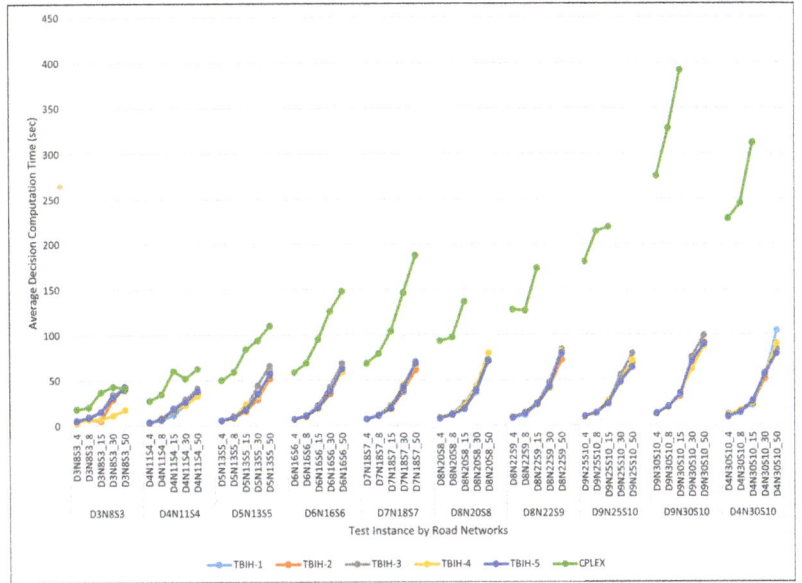

Figure A15. Algorithms performance compared to matheuristic rollout applied in PDS-RA: average decision computation time (sec) based on test instances.

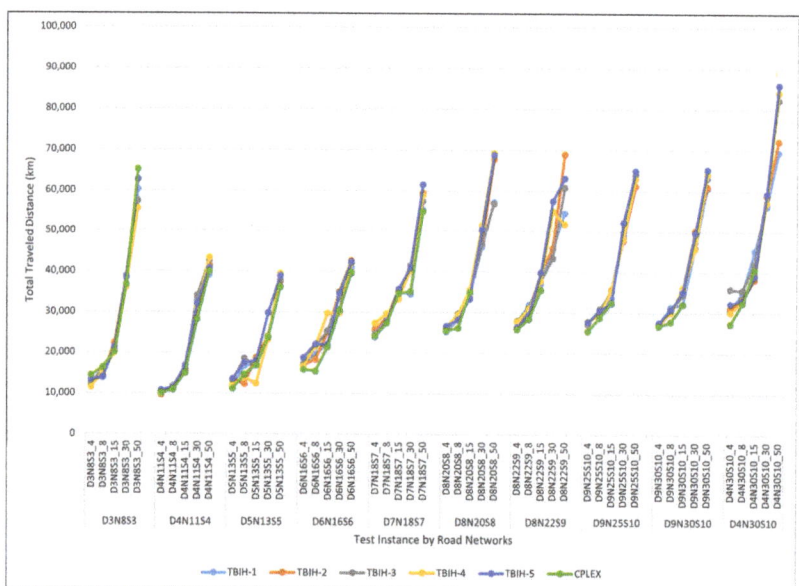

Figure A16. Algorithms performance compared to matheuristic rollout applied in PDS-RA: best total distance travelled (km) measured based on test instances.

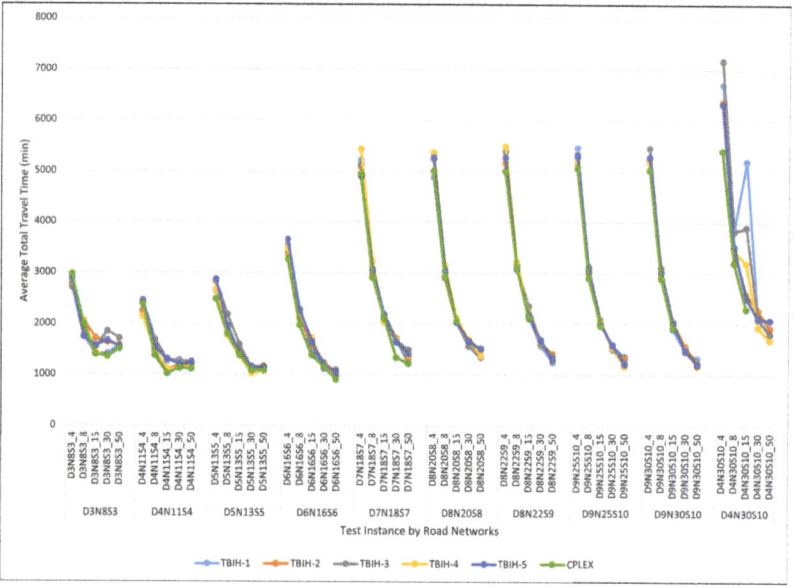

Figure A17. Algorithms performance compared to matheuristic rollout applied in PDS-RA: best total travel time (min) measured based on test instances.

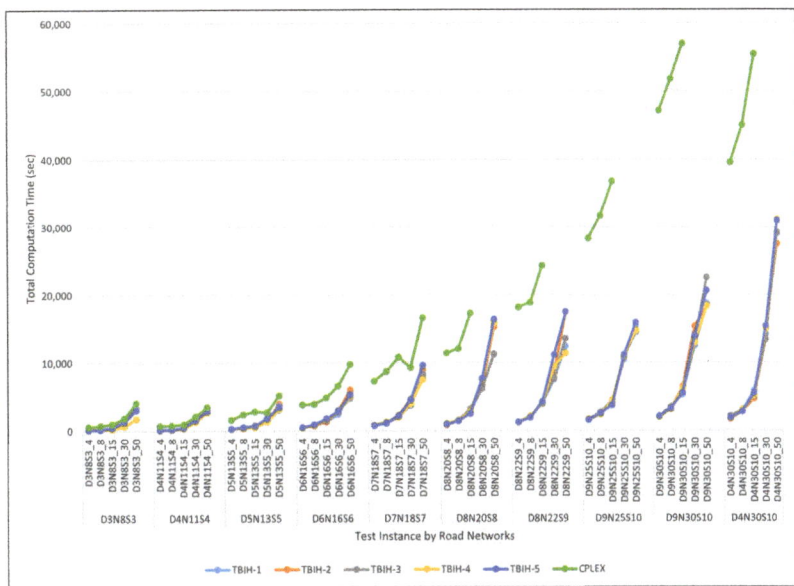

Figure A18. Algorithms performance compared to matheuristic rollout applied in PDS-RA: best total computation time (sec) measured based on test instances.

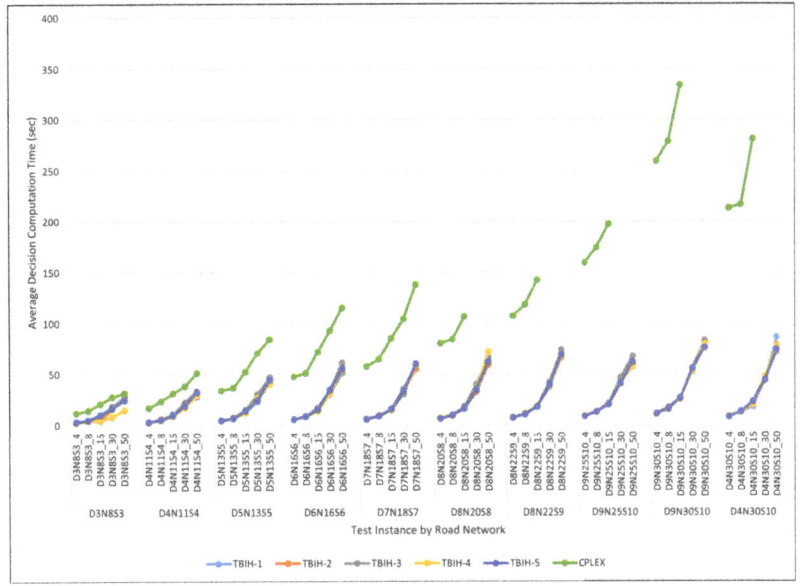

Figure A19. Algorithms performance compared to matheuristic rollout applied in PDS-RA: best average decision computation time (sec) measured based on test instances.

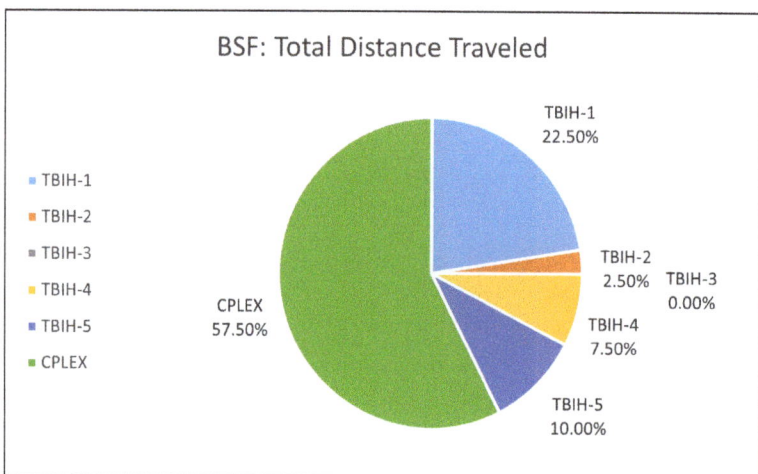

Figure A20. Algorithms performance compared to matheuristic rollout applied in PDS-RA: total BSF measured for total travelled distance over all test instances applied (omitting 10 non-benchmarked measurements).

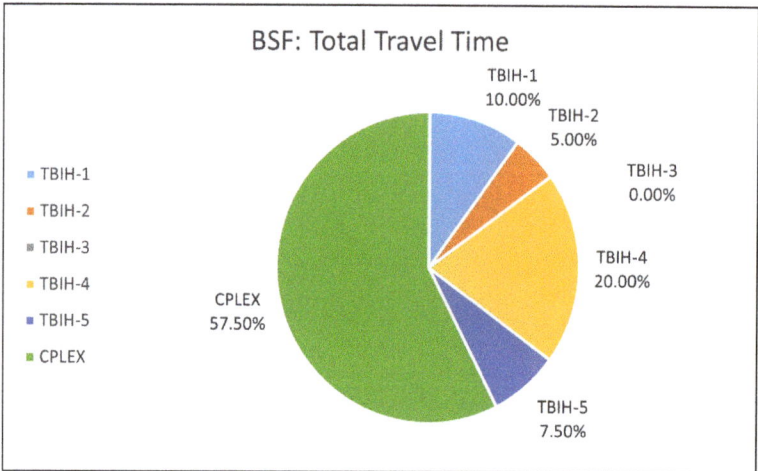

Figure A21. Algorithms performance compared to matheuristic rollout applied in PDS-RA: total BSF measured for total travel time over all test instances applied (omitting 10 non-benchmarked measurements).

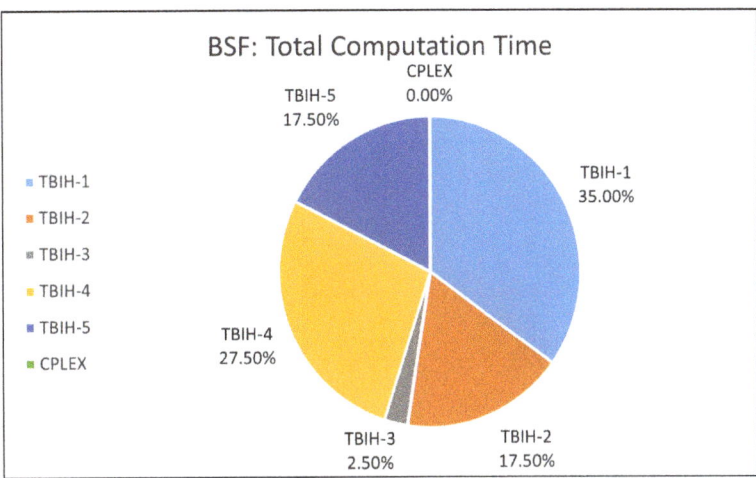

Figure A22. Algorithms performance compared to matheuristic rollout applied in PDS-RA: total BSF measured for total computation time over all test instances applied (omitting 10 non-benchmarked aasurements).

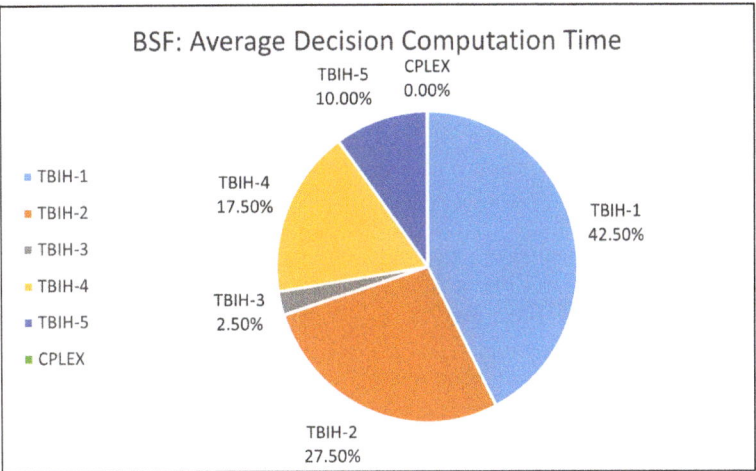

Figure A23. Algorithms performance compared to matheuristic rollout applied in PDS-RA: total BSF measured for average decision computation time over all test instances applied (omitting 10 non-benchmarked measurements).

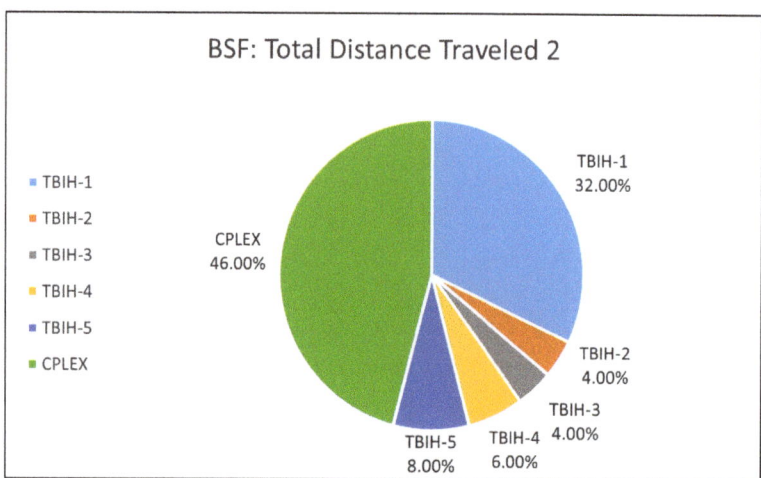

Figure A24. Algorithms performance compared to matheuristic rollout applied in PDS-RA: total BSF measured for total travelled distance over all test instances applied (including 10 non-benchmarked measurements).

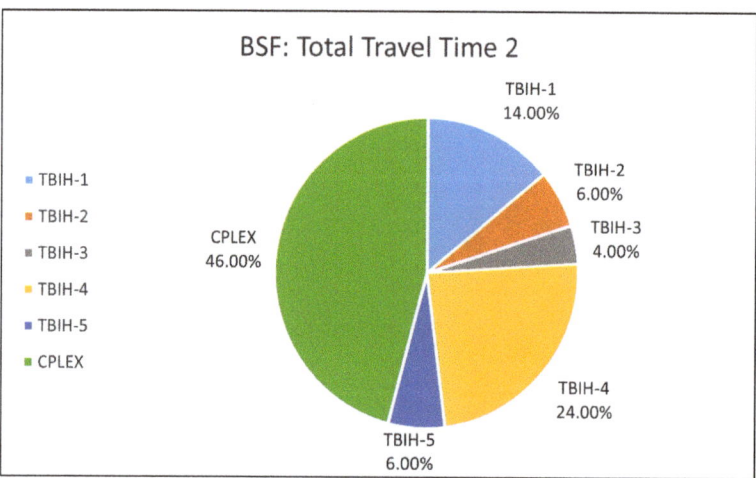

Figure A25. Algorithms performance compared to matheuristic rollout applied in PDS-RA: total BSF measured for total travel time over all test instances applied (including 10 non-benchmarked measurements).

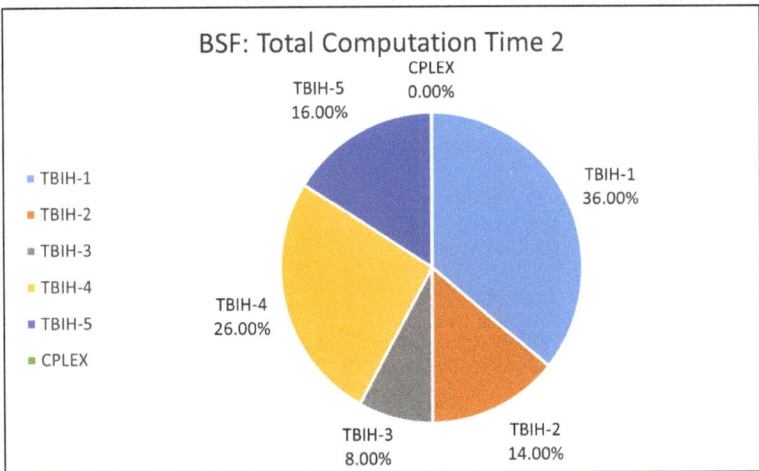

Figure A26. Algorithms performance compared to matheuristic rollout applied in PDS-RA: total BSF measured for total computation time over all test instances applied (including 10 non-benchmarked measurements).

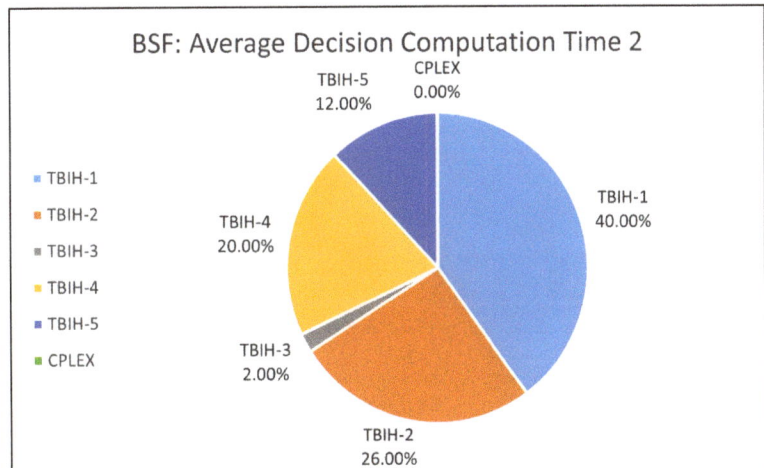

Figure A27. Algorithms performance compared to matheuristic rollout applied in PDS-RA: total BSF measured for average decision computation time over all test instances applied (including 10 non-benchmarked measurements).

References

1. Chauhan, A.; Chopra, B.K. Deployment of medical relief teams of the Indian army in the aftermath of the Nepal earthquake: Lessons learned. *Disaster Med. Public Health Prep.* **2017**, *11*, 394–398. [CrossRef] [PubMed]
2. Sharma, D.C. Nepal earthquake exposes gaps in disaster preparedness. *Lancet* **2015**, *385*, 1819–1820. [CrossRef]
3. Radianti, J.; Hiltz, S.R.; Labaka, L. An overview of public concerns during the recovery period after a major earthquake: Nepal twitter analysis. In Proceedings of the 2016 49th Hawaii International Conference on System Sciences (HICSS), Koloa, HI, USA, 5–8 January 2016; pp. 136–145.
4. Baharmand, H.; Comes, T.; Lauras, M. Managing in-country transportation risks in humanitarian supply chains by logistics service providers: Insights from the 2015 Nepal earthquake. *Int. J. Disaster Risk Reduct.* **2017**, *24*, 549–559. [CrossRef]
5. Tian, Y.; Owen, L.A.; Xu, C.; Ma, S.; Li, K.; Xu, X.; Figueiredo, P.M.; Kang, W.; Guo, P.; Wang, S.; et al. Landslide development within 3 years after the 2015 M w 7.8 Gorkha earthquake, Nepal. *Landslides* **2020**, *17*, 1251–1267. [CrossRef]

6. Xie, Q.; Gaohu, L.; Chen, H.; Xu, C.; Feng, B. Seismic damage to road networks subjected to earthquakes in Nepal, 2015. *Earthq. Eng. Eng. Vib.* **2017**, *16*, 649–670. [CrossRef]
7. Heckmann, I.; Comes, T.; Nickel, S. A critical review on supply chain risk–Definition, measure and modeling. *Omega* **2015**, *52*, 119–132. [CrossRef]
8. Neupane, S.P. Immediate lessons from the Nepal earthquake. *Lancet* **2015**, *385*, 2041–2042. [CrossRef]
9. Archetti, C.; Savelsbergh, M.W.; Speranza, M.G. Worst-case analysis for split delivery vehicle routing problems. *Transp. Sci.* **2006**, *40*, 226–234. [CrossRef]
10. Bellman, R.; Lee, E. History and development of dynamic programming. *IEEE Control Syst. Mag.* **1984**, *4*, 24–28. [CrossRef]
11. Van Roy, B.; Bertsekas, D.P.; Lee, Y.; Tsitsiklis, J.N. A neuro-dynamic programming approach to retailer inventory management. In Proceedings of the 36th IEEE Conference on Decision and Control, San Diego, CA, USA, 12 December 1997; Volume 4, pp. 4052–4057.
12. Bellman, R. The theory of dynamic programming. *Bull. Am. Math. Soc.* **1954**, *60*, 503–515. [CrossRef]
13. Goodson, J.C. Solution Methodologies for Vehicle Routing Problems with Stochastic Demand. Ph.D. Thesis, University of Iowa, Iowa City, IA, USA, 2010.
14. Ulmer, M.W.; Goodson, J.C.; Mattfeld, D.C.; Thomas, B.W. *Route-Based Markov Decision Processes for Dynamic Vehicle Routing Problems*; Technical Report; Braunschweig, Geremany, 2017. Available online: https://web.winforms.phil.tu-bs.de/paper/ulmer/Ulmer_model.pdf (accessed on 7 July 2021).
15. Anuar, W.K.; Lee, L.S.; Seow, H.V.; Pickl, S. A multi-depot vehicle routing problem with stochastic road capacity and reduced two-stage stochastic integer linear programming models for rollout algorithm. *Mathematics* **2021**, *9*, 1572. [CrossRef]
16. Anuar, W.K.; Moll, M.; Lee, L.; Pickl, S.; Seow, H. Vehicle routing optimization for humanitarian logistics in disaster recovery: A survey. In Proceedings of the International Conference on Security and Management (SAM). The Steering Committee of the World Congress in Computer Science, Computer Engineering and Applied Computing (WorldComp), Las Vegas, NV, USA, 28 July–1 August 2019; pp. 161–167. Available online: https://www.proquest.com/openview/24d13cfa7f7ed47c7948a895a66d8a1a/1?pq-origsite=gscholar&cbl=1976342 (accessed on 7 July 2021).
17. Anuar, W.K.; Lee, L.S.; Pickl, S.; Seow, H.V. Vehicle routing optimisation in humanitarian operations: A survey on modelling and optimisation approaches. *Appl. Sci.* **2021**, *11*, 667. [CrossRef]
18. Yan, Y.; Chow, A.H.; Ho, C.P.; Kuo, Y.H.; Wu, Q.; Ying, C. Reinforcement learning for logistics and supply chain management: Methodologies, state of the art, and future opportunities. *Transp. Res. Part E Logist. Transp. Rev.* **2022**, *162*, 102712. [CrossRef]
19. Wang, Q.; Tang, C. Deep reinforcement learning for transportation network combinatorial optimization: A survey. *Knowl.-Based Syst.* **2021**, *233*, 107526. [CrossRef]
20. Rios, B.H.O.; Xavier, E.C.; Miyazawa, F.K.; Amorim, P.; Curcio, E.; Santos, M.J. Recent dynamic vehicle routing problems: A survey. *Comput. Ind. Eng.* **2021**, *160*, 107604.
21. Chang, K.H.; Hsiung, T.Y.; Chang, T.Y. Multi-Commodity distribution under uncertainty in disaster response phase: Model, solution method, and an empirical study. *Eur. J. Oper. Res.* **2022**, *303*, 857-876. [CrossRef]
22. Nodoust, S.; Pishvaee, M.S.; Seyedhosseini, S.M. Vehicle routing problem for humanitarian relief distribution under hybrid uncertainty. *Kybernetes* **2021**. [CrossRef]
23. Balcik, B.; Iravani, S.; Smilowitz, K. Multi-vehicle sequential resource allocation for a nonprofit distribution system. *IIE Trans.* **2014**, *46*, 1279–1297. [CrossRef]
24. Abazari, S.R.; Aghsami, A.; Rabbani, M. Prepositioning and distributing relief items in humanitarian logistics with uncertain parameters. *Socio-Econ. Plan. Sci.* **2021**, *74*, 100933. [CrossRef]
25. Mondal, A.; Roy, S.K. Multi-objective sustainable opened-and closed-loop supply chain under mixed uncertainty during COVID-19 pandemic situation. *Comput. Ind. Eng.* **2021**, *159*, 107453. [CrossRef]
26. Mohammadi, S.; Darestani, S.A.; Vahdani, B.; Alinezhad, A. A robust neutrosophic fuzzy-based approach to integrate reliable facility location and routing decisions for disaster relief under fairness and aftershocks concerns. *Comput. Ind. Eng.* **2020**, *148*, 106734. [CrossRef]
27. Zhong, S.; Cheng, R.; Jiang, Y.; Wang, Z.; Larsen, A.; Nielsen, O.A. Risk-averse optimization of disaster relief facility location and vehicle routing under stochastic demand. *Transp. Res. Part E Logist. Transp. Rev.* **2020**, *141*, 102015. [CrossRef]
28. Bruni, M.; Khodaparasti, S.; Beraldi, P. The selective minimum latency problem under travel time variability: An application to post-disaster assessment operations. *Omega* **2020**, *92*, 102154. [CrossRef]
29. Nadi, A.; Edrisi, A. Adaptive multi-agent relief assessment and emergency response. *Int. J. Disaster Risk Reduct.* **2017**, *24*, 12–23. [CrossRef]
30. Sidrane, C.; Kochenderfer, M.J. Closed-loop planning for disaster evacuation with stochastic arrivals. In Proceedings of the 2018 21st International Conference on Intelligent Transportation Systems (ITSC), Maui, HI, USA, 4–7 November 2018; pp. 2544–2549.
31. Bi, C.; Pan, G.; Yang, L.; Lin, C.C.; Hou, M.; Huang, Y. Evacuation route recommendation using auto-encoder and markov decision process. *Appl. Soft Comput.* **2019**, *84*, 105741. [CrossRef]
32. Çelik, M.; Ergun, Ö.; Keskinocak, P. The post-disaster debris clearance problem under incomplete information. *Oper. Res.* **2015**, *63*, 65–85. [CrossRef]
33. Mills, A.F.; Argon, N.T.; Ziya, S. Dynamic distribution of patients to medical facilities in the aftermath of a disaster. *Oper. Res.* **2018**, *66*, 716–732. [CrossRef]

34. Secomandi, N. *Exact and Heuristic Dynamic Programming Algorithms for the Vehicle Routing Problem with Stochastic Demands*; University of Houston: Houston, TX, USA, 1999.
35. Secomandi, N. A rollout policy for the vehicle routing problem with stochastic demands. *Oper. Res.* **2001**, *49*, 796–802. [CrossRef]
36. Novoa, C.M. *Static and Dynamic Approaches for solving the Vehicle Routing Problem with Stochastic Demands*; Lehigh University: Bethlehem, PA, USA, 2005.
37. Novoa, C.; Storer, R. An approximate dynamic programming approach for the vehicle routing problem with stochastic demands. *Eur. J. Oper. Res.* **2009**, *196*, 509–515. [CrossRef]
38. Thomas, B.W.; White Iii, C.C. Anticipatory route selection. *Transp. Sci.* **2004**, *38*, 473–487. [CrossRef]
39. Fan, J.; Wang, X.; Ning, H. A multiple vehicles routing problem algorithm with stochastic demand. In Proceedings of the 2006 6th World Congress on Intelligent Control and Automation, Dalian, China, 21–23 June 2006; Volume 1, pp. 1688–1692.
40. Goodson, J.C.; Ohlmann, J.W.; Thomas, B.W. Rollout policies for dynamic solutions to the multivehicle routing problem with stochastic demand and duration limits. *Oper. Res.* **2013**, *61*, 138–154. [CrossRef]
41. Goodson, J.C.; Thomas, B.W.; Ohlmann, J.W. Restocking-based rollout policies for the vehicle routing problem with stochastic demand and duration limits. *Transp. Sci.* **2016**, *50*, 591–607. [CrossRef]
42. Ulmer, M.W.; Mattfeld, D.C.; Hennig, M.; Goodson, J.C. A rollout algorithm for vehicle routing with stochastic customer requests. In *Logistics Management*; Springer: Berlin/Heidelberg, Germany, 2016; pp. 217–227.
43. Ulmer, M.W.; Goodson, J.C.; Mattfeld, D.C.; Thomas, B.W. On modeling stochastic dynamic vehicle routing problems. *EURO J. Transp. Logist.* **2020**, *9*, 100008. [CrossRef]
44. Ulmer, M.W.; Soeffker, N.; Mattfeld, D.C. Value function approximation for dynamic multi-period vehicle routing. *Eur. J. Oper. Res.* **2018**, *269*, 883–899. [CrossRef]
45. Ulmer, M.W.; Goodson, J.C.; Mattfeld, D.C.; Hennig, M. Offline–online approximate dynamic programming for dynamic vehicle routing with stochastic requests. *Transp. Sci.* **2019**, *53*, 185–202. [CrossRef]
46. Ulmer, M.W. Horizontal combinations of online and offline approximate dynamic programming for stochastic dynamic vehicle routing. *Cent. Eur. J. Oper. Res.* **2020**, *28*, 279–308. [CrossRef]
47. Yu, X.; Gao, S.; Hu, X.; Park, H. A Markov decision process approach to vacant taxi routing with e-hailing. *Transp. Res. Part B Methodol.* **2019**, *121*, 114–134. [CrossRef]
48. Bertsekas, D.P.; Tsitsiklis, J.N.; Wu, C. Rollout algorithms for combinatorial optimization. *J. Heuristics* **1997**, *3*, 245–262. [CrossRef]
49. Secomandi, N. Comparing neuro-dynamic programming algorithms for the vehicle routing problem with stochastic demands. *Comput. Oper. Res.* **2000**, *27*, 1201–1225. [CrossRef]
50. Dror, M.; Laporte, G.; Trudeau, P. Vehicle routing with stochastic demands: Properties and solution frameworks. *Transp. Sci.* **1989**, *23*, 166–176. [CrossRef]
51. Dror, M. Modeling vehicle routing with uncertain demands as a stochastic program: Properties of the corresponding solution. *Eur. J. Oper. Res.* **1993**, *64*, 432–441. [CrossRef]
52. Bertsekas, D.P. *Dynamic Programming and Optimal Control*, 3rd ed.; Athena Scientific: Belmont, MA, USA, 2011; Volume 2.
53. Bertsekas, D.P.; Tsitsiklis, J.N. *Neuro-Dynamic Programming*; Athena Scientific: Nashua, NH, USA, 1996.
54. Sutton, R.S.; Barto, A.G. *Reinforcement Learning: An Introduction*; MIT Press: Cambridge, MA, USA, 1998; Volume 22447.
55. Shannon, C.E. XXII. Programming a computer for playing chess. *Lond. Edinb. Dublin Philos. Mag. J. Sci.* **1950**, *41*, 256–275. [CrossRef]
56. Samuel, A.L. Some studies in machine learning using the game of checkers. *IBM J. Res. Dev.* **1959**, *3*, 210–229. [CrossRef]
57. Samuel, A.L. Some studies in machine learning using the game of checkers. II—Recent progress. *IBM J. Res. Dev.* **1967**, *11*, 601–617. [CrossRef]
58. Barto, A.G.; Sutton, R.S.; Anderson, C.W. Neuronlike adaptive elements that can solve difficult learning control problems. *IEEE Trans. Syst. Man Cybern.* **1983**, *5*, 834–846. [CrossRef]
59. Sutton, R.S. Learning to predict by the methods of temporal differences. *Mach. Learn.* **1988**, *3*, 9–44. [CrossRef]
60. Watkins, C.J.C.H. *Learning from Delayed Rewards*. 1989. Available online: https://d1wqtxts1xzle7.cloudfront.net/503602 35/Learning_from_delayed_rewards_20161116-28282-v2pwvq-with-cover-page-v2.pdf?Expires=1659006720&Signature= XMv610R4pgdMEva3Jg8e8SqjYPOgg~BcjROgGKK4dak2z5aUwWMbxqGanaYDj9GuKMWKjTsTAGRQilNeQEOOcHtP~52 zthGvsGXmKoa60~jJA3qW6AKYyC1UsDQQX5K~NUZqgaSmRekMdhhrTY8SsZ2gFXj24-Me93ZIBL1GwKXqY~BYVKva1 mfLKWagtRo4xOO4qOD3bItUG5r2jz2CxMwODZLB5NR8xQi3wWdddVRfr2GrThK08nvUwJD4QV~5jaydvc9YLAuLl3 tmUAWlbPj20a0ioTkA3VneMHRMDHItoIfa88KKZC8SPhxtVK7r-iCfiUemnJfFDYzxrS~E~Q__&Key-Pair-Id=APKAJLOHF5 GGSLRBV4ZA (accessed on 7 July 2021).
61. Tesauro, G. Practical issues in temporal difference learning. *Mach. Learn.* **1992**, *8*, 257–277. [CrossRef]
62. Tesauro, G. TD-Gammon, a self-teaching backgammon program, achieves master-level play. *Neural Comput.* **1994**, *6*, 215–219. [CrossRef]
63. Tesauro, G. Temporal difference learning and TD-Gammon. *Commun. ACM* **1995**, *38*, 58–68. [CrossRef]
64. Ghiani, G.; Manni, E.; Quaranta, A.; Triki, C. Anticipatory algorithms for same-day courier dispatching. *Transp. Res. Part E Logist. Transp. Rev.* **2009**, *45*, 96–106. [CrossRef]
65. Voccia, S.A.; Campbell, A.M.; Thomas, B.W. The same-day delivery problem for online purchases. *Transp. Sci.* **2019**, *53*, 167–184. [CrossRef]

66. Secomandi, N. Analysis of a rollout approach to sequencing problems with stochastic routing applications. *J. Heuristics* **2003**, *9*, 321–352. [CrossRef]
67. Powell, W.B. *Approximate Dynamic Programming: Solving the Curses of Dimensionality*; John Wiley & Sons: Hoboken, NJ, USA, 2007; Volume 703.
68. Bertazzi, L.; Secomandi, N. Faster rollout search for the vehicle routing problem with stochastic demands and restocking. *Eur. J. Oper. Res.* **2018**, *270*, 487–497. [CrossRef]
69. Goodson, J.C.; Thomas, B.W.; Ohlmann, J.W. A rollout algorithm framework for heuristic solutions to finite-horizon stochastic dynamic programs. *Eur. J. Oper. Res.* **2017**, *258*, 216–229. [CrossRef]
70. Zhao, Y.; Chen, X.; Jia, Q.S.; Guan, X.; Zhang, S.; Jiang, Y. Long-term scheduling for cascaded hydro energy systems with annual water consumption and release constraints. *IEEE Trans. Autom. Sci. Eng.* **2010**, *7*, 969–976. [CrossRef]
71. Bertazzi, L.; Bosco, A.; Guerriero, F.; Lagana, D. A stochastic inventory routing problem with stock-out. *Transp. Res. Part C Emerg. Technol.* **2013**, *27*, 89–107. [CrossRef]
72. Bertazzi, L.; Bosco, A.; Laganà, D. Managing stochastic demand in an inventory routing problem with transportation procurement. *Omega* **2015**, *56*, 112–121. [CrossRef]
73. Moin, N.H.; Halim, H.Z.A. Solving inventory routing problem with stochastic demand. In *AIP Conference Proceedings*; AIP Publishing LLC: Melville, NY, USA, 2018; Volume 1974, p. 020104. Available online: https://aip.scitation.org/doi/abs/10.1063/1.5041635 (accessed on 22 July 2022).
74. Secomandi, N.; Margot, F. Reoptimization approaches for the vehicle-routing problem with stochastic demands. *Oper. Res.* **2009**, *57*, 214–230. [CrossRef]
75. Ulmer, M.W. *Approximate Dynamic Programming for Dynamic Vehicle Routing*, 1st ed.; Operations Research/Computer Science Interfaces Series; Springer International Publishing: Berlin/Heidelberg, Germany, 2017; Volume 61.
76. Mole, R.; Jameson, S. A sequential route-building algorithm employing a generalised savings criterion. *J. Oper. Res. Soc.* **1976**, *27*, 503–511. [CrossRef]
77. Solomon, M.M. Algorithms for the vehicle routing and scheduling problems with time window constraints. *Oper. Res.* **1987**, *35*, 254–265. [CrossRef]
78. Clarke, G.; Wright, J.W. Scheduling of vehicles from a central depot to a number of delivery points. *Oper. Res.* **1964**, *12*, 568–581. [CrossRef]
79. Dantzig, G.B.; Ramser, J.H. The truck dispatching problem. *Manag. Sci.* **1959**, *6*, 80–91. [CrossRef]
80. Chauhan, C.; Gupta, R.; Pathak, K. Survey of methods of solving tsp along with its implementation using dynamic programming approach. *Int. J. Comput. Appl.* **2012**, *52*, 12–18. [CrossRef]
81. Rand, G. 50 years of the savings method for vehicle routing problems. *Oper. Res. Manag. Sci. Today* **2014**, *41*, 14–15.
82. Nowak, M.A. *The Pickup and Delivery Problem with Split Loads*; Georgia Institute of Technology: Atlanta, GA, USA, 2005.
83. Paessens, H. The savings algorithm for the vehicle routing problem. *Eur. J. Oper. Res.* **1988**, *34*, 336–344. [CrossRef]
84. Larson, R.C.; Odini, A.R. Urban Operations Research. Massachusetts. 1999. Available online: http://web.mit.edu/urban_or_book/www/book/chapter6/6.4.12.html (accessed 7 July 2021).
85. Savelsbergh, M. A parallel insertion heuristic for vehicle routing with side constraints. *Stat. Neerl.* **1990**, *44*, 139–148. [CrossRef]
86. Anuar, W.K.; Lee, L.S.; Pickl, S. Benchmark dataset for multi depot vehicle routing problem with road capacity and damage road consideration for humanitarian operation in critical supply delivery. *Data Brief* **2022**, *41*, 107901. [CrossRef]
87. Anuar, W.K.; Lee, L.S. MDDVRPSRCV1_Test_Instance. Dataset in Mendeley Repository. 2021. Available online: https://www.sciencedirect.com/science/article/pii/S2352340922001135 (accessed on 7 July 2021).
88. Shapiro, S.S.; Wilk, M.B. An analysis of variance test for normality (complete samples). *Biometrika* **1965**, *52*, 591–611. [CrossRef]
89. Zaiontz, C. Real Statistics Using Excel. 2015. Available online: https://www.real-statistics.com (accessed on 11 May 2021).

Article

An Optimized Decision Support Model for COVID-19 Diagnostics Based on Complex Fuzzy Hypersoft Mapping

Muhammad Saeed [1], Muhammad Ahsan [1], Muhammad Haris Saeed [1], Atiqe Ur Rahman [1], Asad Mehmood [1], Mazin Abed Mohammed [2], Mustafa Musa Jaber [3,4] and Robertas Damaševičius [5,*]

1. Department of Mathematics, University of Management and Technology, Lahore 54000, Pakistan; muhammad.saeed@umt.edu.pk (M.S.); ahsan1826@gmail.com (M.A.); abdullahsaeed74@gmail.com (M.H.S.); aurkhb@gmail.com (A.U.R.); a.asadkhan.khi@gmail.com (A.M.)
2. College of Computer Science and Information Technology, University of Anbar, Anbar 31001, Iraq; mazinalshujeary@uoanbar.edu.iq
3. Department of Computer Science, Dijlah University College, Baghdad 00964, Iraq; mustafa.musa@duc.edu.iq
4. Department of Medical Instruments Engineering Techniques, Al-Farahidi University, Baghdad 10021, Iraq
5. Faculty of Applied Mathematics, Silesian University of Technology, 44-100 Gliwice, Poland
* Correspondence: robertas.damasevicius@polsl.pl

Citation: Saeed, M.; Ahsan, M.; Saeed, M.H.; Rahman, A.U.; Mehmood, A.; Mohammed, M.A.; Jaber, M.M.; Damaševičius, R. An Optimized Decision Support Model for COVID-19 Diagnostics Based on Complex Fuzzy Hypersoft Mapping. *Mathematics* **2022**, *10*, 2472. https://doi.org/10.3390/math10142472

Academic Editors: Francois Rivest and Abdellah Chehri

Received: 31 May 2022
Accepted: 12 July 2022
Published: 15 July 2022

Publisher's Note: MDPI stays neutral with regard to jurisdictional claims in published maps and institutional affiliations.

Copyright: © 2022 by the authors. Licensee MDPI, Basel, Switzerland. This article is an open access article distributed under the terms and conditions of the Creative Commons Attribution (CC BY) license (https://creativecommons.org/licenses/by/4.0/).

Abstract: COVID-19 has shaken the entire world economy and affected millions of people in a brief period. COVID-19 has numerous overlapping symptoms with other upper respiratory conditions, making it hard for diagnosticians to diagnose correctly. Several mathematical models have been presented for its diagnosis and treatment. This article delivers a mathematical framework based on a novel agile fuzzy-like arrangement, namely, the complex fuzzy hypersoft ($\mathscr{CFHS}$) set, which is a formation of the complex fuzzy (CF) set and the hypersoft set (an extension of soft set). First, the elementary theory of $\mathscr{CFHS}$ is developed, which considers the amplitude term (A-term) and the phase term (P-term) of the complex numbers simultaneously to tackle uncertainty, ambivalence, and mediocrity of data. In two components, this new fuzzy-like hybrid theory is versatile. First, it provides access to a broad spectrum of membership function values by broadening them to the unit circle on an Argand plane and incorporating an additional term, the P-term, to accommodate the data's periodic nature. Second, it categorizes the distinct attribute into corresponding sub-valued sets for better understanding. The $\mathscr{CFHS}$ set and $\mathscr{CFHS}$-mapping with its inverse mapping (INM) can manage such issues. Our proposed framework is validated by a study establishing a link between COVID-19 symptoms and medicines. For the COVID-19 types, a table is constructed relying on the fuzzy interval of [0, 1]. The computation is based on $\mathscr{CFHS}$-mapping, which identifies the disease and selects the optimum medication correctly. Furthermore, a generalized $\mathscr{CFHS}$-mapping is provided, which can help a specialist extract the patient's health record and predict how long it will take to overcome the infection.

Keywords: COVID-19; disease modelling; complex numbers (C-numbers); complex fuzzy hypersoft set; mapping; inverse mapping

MSC: 03E72, 68U35

1. Introduction

COVID-19 marked itself on the world's map at the end of 2019 in the Hunan Seafood market of Wuhan district (Hubei, China) [1]. After a few days, deep sequencing analysis of the samples taken from the infected patients' lower respiratory tract led to identifying a novel virus that belonged to the Severe Acute Respiratory Syndrome. From there, it was given the name SARS-CoV-2 and was found to be the infection-causing agent of the pneumonia clusters observed in the infected patients [2]. The coronavirus family is thought to be the cause of sickness in both animals and humans, according to [3]. A total of seven family members of the Coronavirus family can produce infection in humans. The most common infection causative agents in humans out of these viruses are namely: 229E, HKU1, NL63, and OC43 [1].

Machine learning and deep learning methods are widely used for COVID-19 diagnostics (see, for example, [4–6]), severity prediction [7], and spread prediction [8,9]. The overview of these methods can be found in review papers [10,11]. Fuzzy-logic-based methods have also been applied extensively for disease diagnostics with various examples ranging from advice on the common cold [12] to Huntington's disease [13].

Conventional methods are insufficient to solve multidimensional challenges in the environment, economics, engineering, and robotics. The four theories discussed here that specialize in solving these types of problems include the fuzzy set theory Zadeh [14], interval mathematics [15], the probability set theory [16], and the rough set theory Pawlak [17]. They are widely used in various fields such as statistics, machine learning, and artificial intelligence. Liu et al. [18] characterized the concept of a correlation coefficient between hesitant fuzzy sets and applied it for medical diagnoses. Molodtsov [19] showed that soft set (SS) theory has significant applications in the fields of data mining, medical imaging, Riemann integration, game theory, and pattern recognition. Soft sets were initially deployed by Maji et al. [20] to handle judgment call dilemmas. S-sets and associated variants are relevant according Yang et al. [21]. The paradigm of imprecise SS and its various forms was established by Maji et al. [22]. Kharal et al. [23,24] established the concepts of mappings on fuzzy soft subclasses and soft classes. They deployed examples and empirical evidence to explore the preservation of the image of fuzzy soft sets and soft sets. In [25], Karaaslan investigated the word smooth class and its relevant functions. Alkhazaleh et al. [26] developed the concepts of a mapping on classes and categorised neutrosophic soft set collections into single-valued neutrosophic classes and also explored and identified a single-valued neutrosophic image and neutrosophic soft images of neutrosophic soft sets. Ropiak [27] combined rough set based granular computing with deep learning methods, which allowed for the improvement of knowledge extraction.

The notion of mappings over collections of multifunctional fuzzy soft sets was pioneered by Sulaiman et al. [28]. They focused on a few factors linked to the image and INI of multi-aspect fuzzy soft sets and demonstrated their findings with numerical examples. The concept of mappings between picture fuzzy soft sets and an intuitionistic fuzzy soft set and INI was defined by Bashir and Salleh [29].

Samarandache [30] offered the fuzzified hypersoft (FHS) and hypersoft sets (HS) as modifications of fuzzy soft and soft settings. Saeed et al. [31–34], Zulqarnain et al. [35], Martin et al. [36], Musa et al. [37], Ajay et al. [38], and Debnath et al. [39] discussed the basics of the HS and their entire mappings in an HS environment, as well as their exposition of the HS in object classification, cell imaging, and multi-eligibility requirements. Ramot et al. [40] proposed an extensive analysis of the mathematical properties of the CF set. Elementary predetermined operations on CF sets were studied, including CF complement, union, and intersection. Thirunavukarasu et al. [41] examined the intuitive understanding of a soft CF set's aggregation operation. They also illustrated uses for consolidation techniques, demonstrating that the approach may be successfully used in a wide range of circumstances including uncertainty and periodicities. In 2020, Rahman et al. [42] combined two major theories complex set and hypersoft set in a fuzzy setting: a sophisticated neutrosophic set, and a complex intuitionistic imprecise information given to build hypersoft mixtures.

The paradigm of a complex multi-fuzzy collection, which is a fusion of CF collections and multi-fuzzy defines, was established by Al-Qudah et al. [43]. Their developed scheme would indeed be equipped to deal with instabilities, ambiguities, and evaluation based of two-dimensional cross inputs by continuously storing the magnitude and P-terms of the C-numbers.

The main objective of this study is to simulate a feasible type of situation of COVID-19-specific diagnosis, as well as to ensure an effective treatment because it is difficult to distinguish other upper-respiratory infections from COVID-19 using existing theoretical and empirical models and techniques [23,24,44,45] because these techniques are restrained from finalizing configurations. The above mentioned strategies are inadequate to thoroughly assess the data to gain a more substantial insight and correct diagnosis. To remedy this defect, these foundations are coupled into a multifaceted system composed of a fuzzy output and a hypersoft (HS) setting.

This approach is far more flexible in two main ways. To continue, it extends the $\mathscr{CFHS}$ to obtain a new term 'P-term' to support the statement's reoccurring aspect, permitting a broad range of weighted parameters. They cannot keep up in two-dimensional quantities to the unit circle in an image plane. Furthermore, the $\mathscr{CFHS}$ traits can be further grouped into sub-values to enhance explanation. A mapping is a correlation between the two or more segments which is handled by guidelines that transfer an embedding feature to its underpinning normative considered appropriate predicated on subsystem and subsurface properties. This tool enables comparable inputs to be treated by a single basic value. The goal of the research is to investigate COVID-19 treatments in the community, as well as the manifestations that correlate with them. It is impossible to discern which characteristic of COVID-19 is causing issues and how substantial it is after gazing at the COVID-19 health consequences. To reduce this issue, the $\mathscr{CFHS}$ set and $\mathscr{CFHS}$-mapping with its INM are often used.

When linked with scientific modelling, these concepts are effective and crucial for appropriately addressing the issues. A table based on the fuzzy region among $[0, 1]$ is constructed for the diverse strains of COVID-19. The approaches rely on $\mathscr{CFHS}$-mapping and would be used to create an index that indicates the ailment and then decides the correct diagnosis. In addition, a detailed $\mathscr{CFHS}$-mapping, which will support a practitioner in estimating the time before the symptoms are alleviated, is established.

The main contributions and the advantages of the proposed method can be summarized as follows:

1. The adopted $\mathscr{CFHS}$ model is more flexible and consistent as compared to existing fuzzy soft set-like models because it is capable of managing the following limitations of the existing literature collectively as a single model:

    (a). Uncertainties involved in the approximation of alternatives.
    (b). Periodic nature of the data.
    (c). Consideration of sub-parametric values as disjointed classes.
    (d). Entitlement of multi-argument approximate function.

    It tackles first issue by assigning a fuzzy membership grade to each alternative corresponding to parameters, the second by considering phase and amplitude terms, and the third and fourth by considering the hypersoft setting. Thus it leads to constructing a reliable decision support system by addressing these issues collectively.

2. An $\mathscr{MADM}$ intelligent algorithm is proposed that aims to support problem-solving for an early assortment of alternatives and identify sufferers with conflicting medical indications.

3. This exploration demonstrates a well-built association between the signs and mathematically records them to ample concern. The scheme is assembled on trimming $\mathscr{CFHS}$ set designs that can predict a patient's state and estimate medical indications over time to analyze a medicine's health effects. It can be carried out to foresee the contagion's reinfection parameters in anticipation that the infection is cured. In the upcoming outlook, such pattern recognition-based algorithms are proposed to diminish medical inaccuracies and receive inspiring results depending on various patient configurations.

The article is presented in the following manner: Section 2 highlights the concept of complex fuzzy hypersoft classes. image The opted approach is validated by practically applying it to a problem with comparative analysis in Section 3, while the conclusion sums up the study in the Section 4.

2. Implementation of 𝒞ℱℋ𝒮 Set for COVID-19

This section's primary focus is to analyze the highlighted problem related to COVID-19. The analysis is based on the cause of the disease, its symptoms, diagnosis, and treatment of patients. 𝒞ℱℋ𝒮 mapping and inverse mapping are applied for precise and accurate analysis and suggest a procedure policy purely based on mathematical strategies presented in this article.

2.1. COVID-19 and Its Variants

With the passage of time, scientists have identified numerous variants of COVID-19 as it has evolved. There are many distinct forms of coronaviruses, but just four are discussed below.

The first is SARS, also known as Severe Acute Respiratory Syndrome, whose causative agent also belongs to the coronavirus family. The SARS-CoV virus has a zoonotic origin, targets the lungs, and causes acute respiratory problems. It was the first virus whose virology or genetic sequence was remotely similar to the COVID-19 virus upon the first examination.

SARS-CoV-2 or COVID-19 is responsible for the pandemic that started back in 2019. As explained in the introduction, it also hinders respiratory functions and is renowned as the successor of the SARS-CoV-1 virus by the US National Institutes of Health.

MERS, or Middle Eastern Respiratory Syndrome, also belongs to the coronavirus family. It first presented itself in the Middle Eastern countries of Asia around 2012, and it is called MERS or the Camel Flu. Its symptoms are quite similar to those of the COVID-19 virus, but the most prominent are mild to high fever, shortness of breath, diarrhea, and cough. MERS is regarded as more severe when compared with other diseases.

The OC43(HCoV-OC43) strain of the human coronavirus is a component of the COVID family and belongs to a group of viruses called the Betacoronavirus 1. This strain is prominent in infecting humans and cattle. As far as the virus's structural integrity goes, it is a simple-stranded RNA, positive-sense, enclosed virus. It is also one of those viruses of the coronavirus family that affects humans out of the seven strains. Its host-entering mechanism involves binding with the N-acetyl-9-O-acetylneuraminic acid receptor of the host cell.

These are the specific symptoms associated with these problems: loss of speech or movement, chest pain or pressure, difficulty breathing or shortness of breath, loss of taste or smell, headache, diarrhea, sore throat, aches and Pain, tiredness, dry cough, and fever.

An algorithm based on 𝒞ℱℋ𝒮-mapping is proposed to diagnose COVID-19, suggest appropriate treatments, and track the treatment steps and improvement measures for the patients.

2.2. Preliminaries

This portion provides a few basic concepts to facilitate the readers for clear understanding proposed approach.

Definition 1 ([14]). *The FS is characterized by a membership mapping $\hat{\omega} : \hat{\Theta} \to \hat{\Omega}$ which is stated as a family of pairs $(\hat{\theta}, \hat{\omega}(\hat{\theta}))$ where $\hat{\omega}(\hat{\theta})$ and $\hat{\Omega}$ are regarded as belonging degree of $\hat{\theta} \in \hat{\Theta}$ and unit closed interval, respectively.*

Definition 2 ([19]). *An SS is stated as the family of pairs $(\hat{o}, \hat{\zeta}(\hat{o}))$ where $\hat{\zeta} : \hat{\Xi} \to \hat{\mathscr{P}}(\hat{\Theta})$ with $\hat{\zeta}(\hat{o}), \hat{\Xi},$ and $\hat{\mathscr{P}}(\hat{\Theta})$ as an $\hat{o}$-approximate member of SS, a set of evaluating indicators and the family of subsets of $\hat{\Theta}$, respectively.*

Definition 3 ([41]). *Let say $\hat{\Theta}$ and $\hat{\Pi}$ are the initial universal set and attributes, respectively. For any $g \in \hat{\Pi}$, let $F \subseteq \hat{\Pi}$ and (φ, F) be a CF soft set over $\hat{\Theta}$. Then, a CF soft set (φ, F) is subjected to $\hat{\Theta}$, which is specified by a function φ_F that represents a mapping $\varphi_F : F \to C(\hat{\Theta})$. Here, φ_F is known as CF approximate function of the CF soft set, and it can be signified as*

$$(\varphi, F) = \{(g, \varphi_F(\mho)) : \mho \in F, \varphi_F(\mho) \in C(\hat{\Theta})\}.$$

Definition 4 ([30]). *An HS is stated as a class of pairs $(\breve{\delta}, \hat{\zeta}_{HS}(\breve{\delta}))$ where $\hat{\zeta}_{HS} : \hat{\Lambda} \to \mathscr{P}(\hat{\Theta})$ with $\hat{\zeta}_{HS}(\breve{\delta})$ as $\breve{\delta}$-multi-argument approximate member of HS for $\breve{\delta} \in \hat{\Lambda}$ and $\hat{\Lambda}$ is equal to $\hat{\Lambda}_1 \times \hat{\Lambda}_2 \times \ldots \times \hat{\Lambda}_n$, whereas all $\hat{\Lambda}_i$ are disjoint sub-classes of parameters having their respective sub-parametric values. For more definition see, [31].*

2.3. Methodology

This section aims to describe the various stages of complete methodology that are adopted for this study. The Figure 1 presents the graphical view of complete methodology adopted in this study.

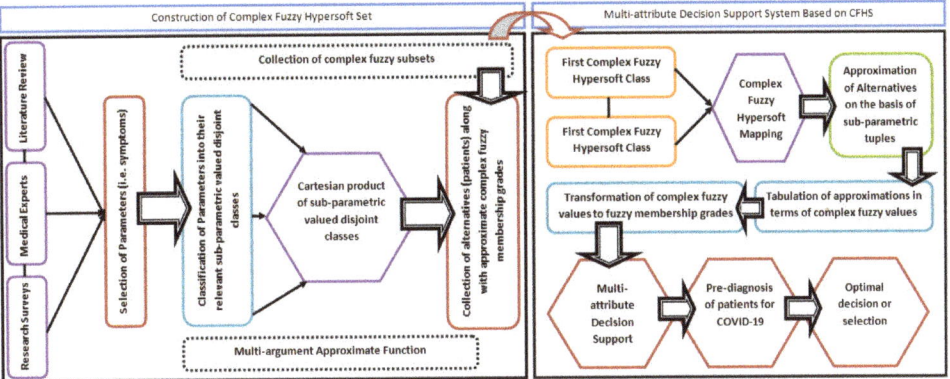

Figure 1. Pictographic view of various stages involved in adopted methodology.

2.3.1. Description of Fuzzy Rules

In accordance with the terminological understanding of "fuzzy rule", the following criteria have been employed to justify fuzzy rule requirements:

1. Consideration of linguistic variables: The linguistic variables are taken as fuzzy input and their corresponding linguistic variable are taken as fuzzy output.
2. Employment of membership function: In this proposed approach, a novel function called multi-argument approximate function is employed which considers the Cartesian product of sub-parametric valued disjointed classes corresponding to parameters as its domain and the collection of complex fuzzy sets as its co-domain. In other words, this function has sub-parametric tuples having multi-argument coordinates. It is the modified version of approximate function used in a soft set. It ensures the entitlement of the hypersoft setting with provision of due status to parameters and their sub-parametric values in the form of disjointed classes. Table 1 presents the comparison of the adopted membership function with other existing membership functions.
3. Designing of fuzzy-valued-based rules: In this step, construction and computation of the relevant fuzzy system are involved.
4. Observation of fuzzy-valued-based output: This step is meant for obtaining the optimum decision.

Table 1. Comparison of employed membership function with other membership functions.

Model	Function	Domain	Co-Domain
Fuzzy Set	Membership function	Universal set	$[0,1]$
Complex fuzzy set	Membership function	Universal set	Complex plane within $[0,1]$
Soft set	Approximate function	Single set of parameters	Power set of universal set
Fuzzy soft set	Approximate function	Single set of parameters	Collection of fuzzy sets
Complex fuzzy soft set	Approximate function	Single set of parameters	Collection of complex fuzzy sets
Hypersoft set	Multi-argument approximate function	Cartesian product of sub-parametric valued disjoint classes	Power set of universal set
Fuzzy hypersoft set	Multi-argument approximate function	Cartesian product of sub-parametric valued disjoint classes	Collection of fuzzy sets
Complex fuzzy hypersoft set	Multi-argument approximate function	Cartesian product of sub-parametric valued disjoint classes	Collection of complex fuzzy sets

2.3.2. Pre-Stage

COVID-19 patients show similar symptoms to the sickness caused by the viruses listed above, making it hard to pinpoint the cause of the ailment and propose an appropriate treatment for the disease. This ambiguity and vagueness are dealt with by using $\mathscr{CFHS}$ in a specialized manner. To translate oral data into numerical language, a fuzzy interval $[0, 1]$ is constructed for various types of COVID. A chart is created to find the actual form of COVID from its different types; see Table 2.

Table 2. COVID diagnosis table with ranges.

Kinds of COVID	Various Ranges
SARS-CoV	$[0.6, 1]$
SARS-CoV-2	$[0.5, 0.6)$
MERS-CoV	$[0.2, 0.5)$
OC43 (beta)	$[0.1, 0.2)$
No COVID	$[0, 0.1)$

Diseases are known to progress over time, so this paper will utilize this fact by collecting the patient's data for 2–3 days, comparing the symptoms and the side effects (if any) presented, leading to a complete workup of the patient's history. Further on, additional graphs regarding the present condition compared to the previous condition of the patients are created for better monitoring and trend identifying purposes. The above statement is expanded in Table 3 and Figure 2. Depending on the conditions of COVID, it is divided into a set of three ranges, namely serious, moderate, and low. Figure 2 defines the ranges along with the constraints allocated to these ranges.

Table 3. COVID is analysed using associated concerns and how they are treated on a daily basis.

Situations	1st Day	2nd and 3rd Days Report	After the 3rd Day
Serious (SARS-CoV)	$0.72 \leq \varrho < 0.8$	$0.8 \leq \varrho < 1$	$=1$
Moderate (SARS-CoV)	$0.75 \leq \varrho < 0.82$	$0.82 \leq \varrho < 0.87$	$0.87 \leq \varrho < 0.92$
Low (SARS-CoV)	$0.6 \leq \varrho < 0.65$	$0.65 \leq \varrho < 0.69$	$0.69 \leq \varrho < 0.74$
Serious (SARS-CoV-2)	$0.55 \leq \varrho < 0.57$	$0.57 \leq \varrho < 0.58$	$0.58 \leq \varrho < 0.59$
Moderate (SARS-CoV-2)	$0.551 \leq \varrho < 0.558$	$0.558 \leq \varrho < 0.559$	$0.559 \leq \varrho < 0.5596$
Low (SARS-CoV-2)	$0.557 \leq \varrho < 0.559$	$0.559 \leq \varrho < 0.5597$	$0.5597 \leq \varrho < 0.5593$
Serious (MERS-CoV)	$0.2 \leq \varrho < 0.3$	$0.3 \leq \varrho < 0.4$	$0.4 \leq \varrho < 0.49$
Moderate (MERS-CoV)	$0.23 \leq \varrho < 0.25$	$0.25 \leq \varrho < 0.27$	$0.27 \leq \varrho < 0.4$
Low (MERS-CoV)	$0.22 \leq \varrho < 0.23$	$0.23 \leq \varrho < 0.235$	$0.235 \leq \varrho < 0.37$
Serious (OC43 (beta))	$0.1 \leq \varrho < 0.15$	$0.15 \leq \varrho < 0.17$	$0.17 \leq \varrho < 0.176$
Moderate (OC43 (beta))	$0.12 \leq \varrho < 0.13$	$0.13 \leq \varrho < 0.15$	$0.15 \leq \varrho < 0.157$
Low (OC43 (beta))	$0.123 \leq \varrho < 0.125$	$0.125 \leq \varrho < 0.129$	$0.129 \leq \varrho < 0.189$
No COVID	$0.00 \leq \varrho < 0.01$	$0.01 \leq \varrho < 0.08$	$0.01 \leq \varrho < 0.08$

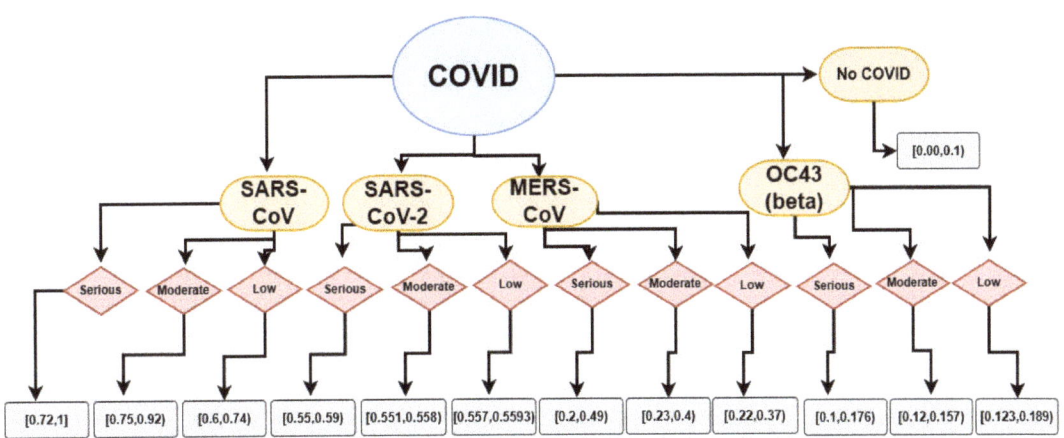

Figure 2. Flowchart of various ranges related to COVID-19's mentioned criteria.

2.4. Proposed Algorithm for Pre-Diagnosis of Patients Based on CFHS Mapping

This section proposes a multi-attribute decision-making-based ($\mathscr{MADM}$) algorithm (Algorithm 1) for pre-diagnosis of COVID-19 in patients who are under observation.

Algorithm 1: Procedural flow of pre-diagnosis of COVID-19 in patients.

▷ **Start**
▷ **Input**

Step 1. To categorise the coronavirus family. Suppose $\mathscr{W} = \{\partial_1, \partial_2, \partial_3, ..., \partial_n\}$ be set of four patients suspected to have COVID and $\mathscr{A} = \{\hat{\omega}_1, \hat{\omega}_2, \hat{\omega}_3, ..., \hat{\omega}_v\}$ be set of symptoms whose sub-values related to sets $\mathscr{F}_i$'s, where $\mathscr{F} = \prod_{i=1}^{v} \mathscr{F}_i$. Following a crucial evaluation at εth times, the consultant's $\mathscr{CFHS}$ set chart is customised as: $z^\varepsilon_{\mathscr{F}} = \{z^\varepsilon_s = \{\partial, \langle \mathcal{T}^\varepsilon_s(\partial) \rangle\}\} : \mathcal{T}^\varepsilon_s(\partial) \in C(F), \partial \in \mathscr{W}, s \in \mathscr{F}\}$, where $\mathcal{T}^\varepsilon_s(\partial)$ are $\mathscr{CFHS}$ membership of SARS-CoV, SARS-CoV-2, MERS-CoV and OC43 (beta) for lth patients and kth symptoms respectively and
($\varepsilon = 1, 2, 3, ..., t; k = 1, 2, 3, ..., |\mathscr{F}|; l = 1, 2, 3, ..., n$). The $\mathscr{CFHS}$ union of all "t" day to clinical charts is used to procure the most relevant data on all patients.

Step 2. It is anticipated that $\mathscr{B} = \{\hat{\omega}'_1, \hat{\omega}'_2, \hat{\omega}'_3, ..., \hat{\omega}'_w\}$ a class having relevant indications and the their respective sub-classes are $\mathscr{F}'_i$'s with $\mathscr{F}' = \prod_{i=1}^{w} \mathscr{F}'_i$.

An $\mathscr{CFHS}$ set is constructed having weights proposed by decision-makers (health experts) after assessing the physical condition of the patient under observation over time ε.

Step 3. Now, mappings are defined as follows: $\lambda : \mathscr{W} \to \mathscr{W}$ and $\omega : \mathscr{F} \to \mathscr{F}'$ characterized as follows; $\lambda(\partial_l) = \partial_l$, $\omega(s_k) = (s'_{k'})$,
($k' = 1, 2, 3, ..., |\mathscr{F}'|; k = 1, 2, 3, ..., |\mathscr{F}|; l = 1, 2, 3, ..., n$) (based on the interrelations with the basic symptoms).

Suppose $\mathscr{CFHS}$-mapping $\sigma = (\lambda, \omega) : \mathscr{CFHS}(\mathscr{W}) \to \mathscr{CFHS}(\mathscr{W})$ defined as;

$$\mathcal{T}_{\sigma(z_\mathscr{F})}(s')(\partial) = |\mathcal{T}_{s'_{k'}}| \begin{cases} \max_{v \in \lambda^{-1}(\partial)} \left(\max_{s \in \omega^{-1}(s') \cap \mathscr{F}} \mathcal{T}_{z_F} \right)(\partial) \text{ if} \\ \lambda^{-1}(\partial) \neq \emptyset, \omega^{-1}(s') \cap \mathscr{F} \neq \emptyset, \\ 0 \text{ if } otherwise \end{cases}$$

where $\mathcal{T}_{s'_{k'}}$ are weights from $z_{\mathscr{F}'}$ that are connected. Get the image of $\sqcup z^\varepsilon_{\mathscr{F}}$ by using the mappings σ and denoted as $z'_{\mathscr{F}'}$.

▷ **Construction**

Step 4. Transform $\mathscr{CFHS}$ set to aggregation values by using,
$\mathcal{T}_{z'(s')}(\partial) = w_1 \mu_{z'(s')}(\partial) + w_2(\frac{1}{2\pi}) \omega_{z'(s')}(\partial)$ [46], where $w_1, w_2 \in [0, 1]$.

Step 5. Then, by making use of the information from Table 3, constitute a set after symptoms and assemble the pre-diagnosis table which leads to the assessment for consistency of the proposed study.

Step 6. Take the mean for each specific patient centred on their clinical manifestations. Now, compare our outcomes to the diagnosis Table 2.

▷ **Computation**

Step 7. Consider a class $\mathscr{B} = \{\hat{\omega}'_1, \hat{\omega}'_2, \hat{\omega}'_3, ..., \hat{\omega}'_w\}$ consists of symptoms which are correlated concurrently, where $k' = \prod_{i=1}^{w} |\mathscr{F}'_i|$ and $C = \{\mho_1, \mho_2, \mho_3, ..., \mho_x\}$ is a list of potential medicines, then it allows for constructing $\chi_{\mathscr{F}'}$, where χ is the $\mathscr{CFHS}$ function from $\mathscr{F}'$ to $\mathscr{W}(C)$ that is the collection with recommendations of physician.

Step 8. Obtain $\mathscr{W}^1_C$ by applying min-max composition over $z'_{\mathscr{F}'}$ and $\chi_{\mathscr{F}'}$.

Step 9. Use medications that offer additional benefits while having fewer side effects. To determine the patient's status, the guidelines are followed.

Algorithm 1: *Cont.*

▷ **Output**

Step 10. Consider two mappings: $\lambda' : J^{q-1} \to J^q$ and
$\lambda' : \mathscr{W}^{q-1} \to \mathscr{W}^q$ and $\varpi' : C^{q-1} \to C^q$ such that $\lambda'(\partial_l) = \partial_l$ and $\varpi'(\mho_x) = \mho_x$.
Then this mapping can be constructed in this mechanism:
$\sigma' = (\lambda', \varpi') : \mathscr{W}_C^{q-1} \to \mathscr{W}_C^q$ and can be regarded as:

$$\mathscr{W}_C^q = \sigma'(\mathscr{W}_C^{q-1})(\mho)(\partial) = \frac{1}{q} \begin{cases} \vee_{\pi \in \lambda'^{-1}(\partial)} (\vee_{\vartheta \in \varpi'^{-1}(\mho) \cap C} \mathscr{W}_C^{q-1}(\pi)) \text{ if} \\ \quad \lambda'^{-1}(\partial) \neq \emptyset, \varpi'^{-1}(\mho) \cap C \neq \emptyset \\ 0 \quad \text{if otherwise} \end{cases}$$

where $g \in \varpi'(C) \subseteq C, v \in \mathscr{W}^q, \pi \in \mathscr{W}^{q-1}, \vartheta \in (C)^{q-1}$ for $q = 2, 3, 4...$ is the number of episodes of treatments.

Step 11. Continue step 10 whenever the outcomes need to be assessed and finally compute the score values by taking arithmetic mean of all final obtained values corresponding to each patient.

Methodological Limitations

Prior to the application of the algorithm above, the following limitations of the technique are checked:

1. As the parameters described have the same base and structure, a mapping will be required to convert the criterion to its parameterized value.
2. The two collections to be compared must belong to the same structural class of the $\mathscr{CFHS}$ set, and their composition must be independent of each other.
3. By using the patient's history and medical records, the doctor should advise the best course of medication based on the symptoms presented by the disease.
4. A database is required that comprises the ranges needed for the disease identification and mapping, which can be constructed with the assistance of a medical professional.
5. If the proposed treatment method is leading to diverse effects on the patient, inverse $\mathscr{CFHS}$-mapping is utilized to remove the adverse effects and restart the medication process all over again.

3. Experimental Study

The usage of the algorithm described above in a clinical situation is the main emphasis of this section. The patient's medical condition is first translated into mathematical syntax with the aid of medical personnel. The next step involves the comparison of the mathematical syntax of the patient with the syntax of the patients recorded in the database beforehand. The patient with distinct symptoms of COVID-19 is monitored with the help of a diagnostic map, and day-by-day reports can be seen in (Tables 2 and 3). These tables can be used for a comparative analysis to deduce the intensity of the disease on a particular patient. The most significant advantage of the algorithm is its use case for determining a particular disease based on its symptoms and severity using mapping functions. The algorithm can propose an optimal treatment method based on the disease based on the patient's condition. The technique's development will be aided by a fully generalized mapping of the physician's rehabilitation and convenient restoration graphs for clinical practice, retrospective cohort analysis, and application users. Four patients present similar symptoms making it complicated for medical professionals to suggest a diagnosis based on their overlapping symptoms. Many dynamics are considered, but some are ruled out for ease of explanation of the algorithm, such as the previous skin color changes, history, and other aspects. Based on the diagnosis presented by the algorithm and the doctor's intuition, a treatment method can be started along with the patient's rehabilitation plan. The following example is performed on hypothetical data, but if real data is used, it can lead to fruitful results and help optimize the workflow in hospitals while minimizing human errors and misdiagnosis problems.

Step 1.
Let $\mathscr{W} = \{\partial_1, \partial_2, \partial_3, \partial_4\}$ be considered a set of four patients. Let $\hat{\omega}_1$ = Fever, $\hat{\omega}_2$ = Cough, $\hat{\omega}_3$ = Pain, be ailments with distinct attributes, the attributes of which are associated to the sets $\mathscr{F}_1, \mathscr{F}_2$ and $\mathscr{F}_3$, respectively. Let $\mathscr{F}_1 = \{\hat{\omega}_{11}$ = Intermittent fever, $\hat{\omega}_{12}$ = Remittent fever$\}$, $\mathscr{F}_2 = \{\hat{\omega}_{21}$ = Dry cough$\}$, $\mathscr{F}_3 = \{\hat{\omega}_{31}$ = Pain in temples of head, $\hat{\omega}_{32}$ = Pain in forehead$\}$. Now, generate the first two ($\varepsilon = 2$) days chart given in Tables 4 and 5 which are in the form of $\mathscr{CFHS}$. After that, take the union between them. The results can be seen in Table 6, where $0 \leq \theta \leq 2\pi$.

Table 4. $z^1_{\mathscr{F}}$: Symptoms from $\mathscr{F}$ on the first day of patient's treatment.

Symptoms/Patients	∂_1	∂_2	∂_3	∂_4
$(\hat{\omega}_{11}, \hat{\omega}_{21}, \hat{\omega}_{31})$	$0.4e^{i0.7\theta}$	$0.1e^{i0.4\theta}$	$0.5e^{i0.2\theta}$	$0.3e^{i0.4\theta}$
$(\hat{\omega}_{11}, \hat{\omega}_{21}, \hat{\omega}_{32})$	$0.1e^{i0.9\theta}$	$0.8e^{i0.1\theta}$	$0.4e^{i0.8\theta}$	$0.1e^{i0.4\theta}$
$(\hat{\omega}_{12}, \hat{\omega}_{21}, \hat{\omega}_{31})$	$0.4e^{i0.2\theta}$	$0.8e^{i0.1\theta}$	$0.7e^{i0.9\theta}$	$0.1e^{i0.4\theta}$
$(\hat{\omega}_{12}, \hat{\omega}_{21}, \hat{\omega}_{32})$	$0.3e^{i0.8\theta}$	$0.1e^{i0.3\theta}$	$0.2e^{i0.4\theta}$	$0.6e^{i0.4\theta}$

Table 5. $z^2_{\mathscr{F}}$: Symptoms from $\mathscr{F}$ on the second day of patient's treatment.

Symptoms/Patients	∂_1	∂_2	∂_3	∂_4
$(\hat{\omega}_{11}, \hat{\omega}_{21}, \hat{\omega}_{31})$	$0.2e^{i0.9\theta}$	$0.2e^{i0.4\theta}$	$0.1e^{i0.5\theta}$	$0.2e^{i0.6\theta}$
$(\hat{\omega}_{11}, \hat{\omega}_{21}, \hat{\omega}_{32})$	$0.2e^{i0.5\theta}$	$0.2e^{i0.3\theta}$	$0.6e^{i0.8\theta}$	$0.2e^{i0.4\theta}$
$(\hat{\omega}_{12}, \hat{\omega}_{21}, \hat{\omega}_{31})$	$0.4e^{i0.2\theta}$	$0.8e^{i0.1\theta}$	$0.7e^{i0.9\theta}$	$0.1e^{i0.4\theta}$
$(\hat{\omega}_{12}, \hat{\omega}_{21}, \hat{\omega}_{32})$	$0.5e^{i0.8\theta}$	$0.3e^{i0.4\theta}$	$0.6e^{i0.1\theta}$	$0.8e^{i0.4\theta}$

Table 6. $\sqcup z^{\varepsilon}_{\mathscr{F}}$: $\mathscr{CFHS}$ union of $z^1_{\mathscr{F}}$ and $z^2_{\mathscr{F}}$.

Symptoms/Patients	∂_1	∂_2	∂_3	∂_4
$(\hat{\omega}_{11}, \hat{\omega}_{21}, \hat{\omega}_{31})$	$0.4e^{i0.9\theta}$	$0.2e^{i0.4\theta}$	$0.5e^{i0.5\theta}$	$0.3e^{i0.6\theta}$
$(\hat{\omega}_{11}, \hat{\omega}_{21}, \hat{\omega}_{32})$	$0.2e^{i0.9\theta}$	$0.8e^{i0.3\theta}$	$0.6e^{i0.8\theta}$	$0.2e^{i0.4\theta}$
$(\hat{\omega}_{12}, \hat{\omega}_{21}, \hat{\omega}_{31})$	$0.4e^{i0.2\theta}$	$0.8e^{i0.1\theta}$	$0.7e^{i0.9\theta}$	$0.1e^{i0.4\theta}$
$(\hat{\omega}_{12}, \hat{\omega}_{21}, \hat{\omega}_{32})$	$0.5e^{i0.8\theta}$	$0.1e^{i0.3\theta}$	$0.6e^{i0.4\theta}$	$0.8e^{i0.4\theta}$

Step 2.
Let $\mathscr{F}'_1 = \{\hat{\omega}'_{11}$ = tightness sensation in the head, $\hat{\omega}'_{12}$ = stroke$\}$, $\mathscr{F}'_2 = \{\hat{\omega}'_{21}$ = Scratchy sensation$\}$, $\mathscr{F}'_3 = \{\hat{\omega}'_{31}$ = Malaise, $\hat{\omega}'_{32}$ = Body aches$\}$ be three sets related to three different attributes $\hat{\omega}'_1$ = Headaches, $\hat{\omega}'_2$ = Sore throat, $\hat{\omega}'_3$ = weakness, respectively, for COVID-related symptoms. Specialists weight clinical conditions depending on clinical knowledge and translate relevant knowledge to quantitative transcription to establish the $\mathscr{CFHS}$ $z_{\mathscr{F}'}$ displayed in Table 7.

Table 7. $z_{\mathscr{F}'}$: Scales assigned to each $\mathscr{CFHS}$ patient's clinical manifestations.

Symptoms/Patients	∂_1	∂_2	∂_3	∂_4
$(\hat{\omega}'_{11}, \hat{\omega}'_{21}, \hat{\omega}'_{31})$	$0.2e^{i0.9\theta}$	$0.8e^{i0.3\theta}$	$0.6e^{i0.8\theta}$	$0.2e^{i0.4\theta}$
$(\hat{\omega}'_{11}, \hat{\omega}'_{21}, \hat{\omega}'_{32})$	$0.4e^{i0.2\theta}$	$0.8e^{i0.1\theta}$	$0.7e^{i0.9\theta}$	$0.1e^{i0.4\theta}$
$(\hat{\omega}'_{12}, \hat{\omega}'_{21}, \hat{\omega}'_{31})$	$0.4e^{i0.9\theta}$	$0.2e^{i0.4\theta}$	$0.5e^{i0.5\theta}$	$0.3e^{i0.6\theta}$
$(\hat{\omega}'_{12}, \hat{\omega}'_{21}, \hat{\omega}'_{32})$	$0.5e^{i0.8\theta}$	$0.1e^{i0.3\theta}$	$0.6e^{i0.4\theta}$	$0.8e^{i0.4\theta}$

Step 3.
Define the mappings listed below; $\lambda : \mathscr{W} \to \mathscr{W}$ and $\omega : F \to \mathscr{F}'$ such that;
$\lambda(\partial_1) = \partial_1, \lambda(\partial_2) = \partial_2, \lambda(\partial_3) = \partial_3, \lambda(\partial_4) = \partial_4$, and
$\omega(\hat{\omega}_{11}, \hat{\omega}_{21}, \hat{\omega}_{31}) = (\hat{\omega}'_{11}, \hat{\omega}'_{21}, \hat{\omega}'_{31})$,
$\omega(\hat{\omega}_{11}, \hat{\omega}_{21}, \hat{\omega}_{32}) = (\hat{\omega}'_{12}, \hat{\omega}'_{21}, \hat{\omega}'_{31})$,
$\omega(\hat{\omega}_{12}, \hat{\omega}_{21}, \hat{\omega}_{31}) = (\hat{\omega}'_{11}, \hat{\omega}'_{21}, \hat{\omega}'_{32})$,
$\omega(\hat{\omega}_{12}, \hat{\omega}_{21}, \hat{\omega}_{32}) = (\hat{\omega}'_{12}, \hat{\omega}'_{21}, \hat{\omega}'_{32})$.
Measure the image of $\sqcup z_F^e$ as well as $z'_{\mathscr{F}'}$ in Table 8.

Table 8. $z'_{\mathscr{F}'}$: The image of $\sqcup z_F^e$ under $\mathscr{CFHS}$ mapping

Symptoms/Patients	∂_1	∂_2	∂_3	∂_4
$(\hat{\omega}'_{11}, \hat{\omega}'_{21}, \hat{\omega}'_{31})$	$0.4e^{i0.7\theta}$	$0.1e^{i0.4\theta}$	$0.5e^{i0.2\theta}$	$0.3e^{i0.4\theta}$
$(\hat{\omega}'_{11}, \hat{\omega}'_{21}, \hat{\omega}'_{32})$	$0.1e^{i0.9\theta}$	$0.8e^{i0.1\theta}$	$0.4e^{i0.8\theta}$	$0.1e^{i0.4\theta}$
$(\hat{\omega}'_{12}, \hat{\omega}'_{21}, \hat{\omega}'_{31})$	$0.4e^{i0.2\theta}$	$0.8e^{i0.1\theta}$	$0.7e^{i0.9\theta}$	$0.1e^{i0.4\theta}$
$(\hat{\omega}'_{12}, \hat{\omega}'_{21}, \hat{\omega}'_{32})$	$0.3e^{i0.8\theta}$	$0.1e^{i0.3\theta}$	$0.2e^{i0.4\theta}$	$0.6e^{i0.4\theta}$

Step 4.
Changed Table 8 to fuzzy values, for this please see Table 9 by applying $\mathscr{T}_{z'(s')}(\partial) = w_1 \mu_{z'(s')}(\partial) + w_2(\frac{1}{2\pi})\omega_{z'(s')}(\partial)$ [46], with weights $w_1 = 0.2$, $w_2 = 0.4$.

Table 9. Scores in the form of FHS set.

Symptoms/Individuals	∂_1	∂_2	∂_3	∂_4
$(\hat{\omega}'_{11}, \hat{\omega}'_{21}, \hat{\omega}'_{31})$	0.22	0.12	0.24	0.2
$(\hat{\omega}'_{11}, \hat{\omega}'_{21}, \hat{\omega}'_{32})$	0.2	0.18	0.24	0.1
$(\hat{\omega}'_{12}, \hat{\omega}'_{21}, \hat{\omega}'_{31})$	0.1	0.18	0.32	0.09
$(\hat{\omega}'_{12}, \hat{\omega}'_{21}, \hat{\omega}'_{32})$	0.22	0.08	0.12	0.2

Step 5.
Compare Table 9 with Table 3 to obtain initial diagnosis and generate a diagnosis Table 10. This table is utilized to check the accuracy of the generated diagnosis.

Step 6.
Determine the average of all the aspects from Table 9 that correspond to each individual's symptoms. This can be seen in Table 11. The COVID chart (Table 2) is currently being compared to the Table 11 findings. Patients ∂_1, ∂_3 are diagnosed with SARS-CoV, while patients ∂_2, ∂_4 are suspected with SARS-CoV-2.

Table 10. Initial treatment chart is developed to assess the validity of the results.

Symptoms/Patients	∂_1	∂_2	∂_3	∂_4
$(\hat{\omega}'_{11}, \hat{\omega}'_{21}, \hat{\omega}'_{31})$	low MERS-CoV	serious OC43 (beta)	moderate MERS-CoV	serious MERS-CoV
$(\hat{\omega}'_{11}, \hat{\omega}'_{21}, \hat{\omega}'_{32})$	serious MERS-CoV	low OC43 (beta)	moderate MERS-CoV	serious OC43 (beta)
$(\hat{\omega}'_{12}, \hat{\omega}'_{21}, \hat{\omega}'_{31})$	serious OC43 (beta)	low OC43 (beta)	serious MERS-CoV	NO COVID
$(\hat{\omega}'_{12}, \hat{\omega}'_{21}, \hat{\omega}'_{32})$	serious MERS-CoV	NO COVID	moderate OC43 (beta)	serious MERS-CoV

Step 7.
The doctor prescribes medicine after accurately assessing the true essence of each clinical condition. The $\mathscr{CFHS}$ set evolves based on critical specific suggestions, along with the adequate care for the different sorts of COVID. Suppose $C = \{\mho_1 = $ Pfizer, $\mho_2 = $ Moderna, $\mho_3 = $ Novavax, $\mho_4 = $ AstraZeneca$\}$ be distinctive sustainable therapies, then $\chi_{\mathscr{F}'}$ is established, which is a set of surgeon's advice for the effective treatments for COVID manifestations, and repurpose $\mathscr{CFHS}$ to fuzzy values using $\mathscr{T}_{z'(s')}(\partial) = w_1\mu_{z'(s')}(\partial) + w_2(\frac{1}{2\pi})\omega_{z'(s')}(\partial)$ [46], with weights $w_1 = 0.2$, $w_2 = 0.4$ to obtain aggregation values. Table 12 contains $\chi_{\mathscr{F}'} \in \mathscr{CFHS}(\mathscr{W})$. The assessment methods in Table 12 are determined depending on each patient's condition.

Step 8.
Measure the $\mathscr{CFHS}$ union among both $\chi_{\mathscr{F}'}, z'_{\mathscr{F}'}$ and collect the linkage among both predicted treatments and doctors as $\mathscr{CFHS}$ set $\chi_{\mathscr{F}'} \sqcup z'_{\mathscr{F}'} = \mathscr{W}_C^1$, see Table 13.

Step 9.
The prescription is pertinent for the patients because it generates more rewards while having low toxicity. Table 14 shows the best medicine dosages for each patient. From Table 14, the treatment $\mho_4$ is most suitable for patient ∂_1, while one of the treatments among $\mho_1, \mho_3$, and $\mho_4$ is to be advised for patient ∂_2; for patient ∂_3 the most suitable treatment is $\mho_1$, and the treatment $\mho_4$ is the most suitable for patient ∂_4. The concluding position relies on the person's actual status, disease features, and disease.

Step 10.
The individual's predicament is classified by the characteristics of ailments and the patient's condition. The incidences will repeat whenever illnesses are cured. By using $\mathscr{CFHS}$-mapping and creating mappings to assess the development of each patient; $\lambda': \mathscr{W}^{q-1} \to \mathscr{W}^q$ and $\omega': C^{q-1} \to C^q$ such that

$$\lambda'(\partial_1) = \partial_1, \lambda'(\partial_2) = \partial_2, \lambda'(\partial_3) = \partial_3, \lambda'(\partial_4) = \partial_4;$$

and

$$\omega'(\mho_1) = \mho_1, \omega'(\mho_2) = \mho_2, \omega'(\mho_3) = \mho_3, \omega'(\mho_4) = \mho_4.$$

This is how the $\mathscr{CFHS}$-mapping can be conveyed;

$$\sigma' = (\lambda', \omega'): \mathscr{W}_C^{q-1} \to \mathscr{W}_C^q$$

The $\mathscr{CFHS}$-mapping is underlying as;

$$\mathscr{W}_C^q = \sigma'(\mathscr{W}_C^{q-1})(\mho)(\partial) = \frac{1}{q}\begin{cases} \vee_{\pi \in \lambda'^{-1}(\partial)}(\vee_{\vartheta \in \omega'^{-1}(\mho) \cap C}\mathscr{W}_C^{q-1}(\pi)) \text{ if} \\ \quad \lambda'^{-1}(\partial) \neq \emptyset, \omega'^{-1}(\mho) \cap C \neq \emptyset \\ 0 \quad \text{if otherwise} \end{cases}$$

where $\mho \in \omega'(C) \subseteq C, \partial \in \mathscr{W}^q, \pi \in \mathscr{W}^{q-1}, \vartheta \in C^{q-1}$ identify the number of remedies and rehabilitation exacerbations in Tables 15–18 for $q = 2, 3, 4, 5$.

Step 11.
Step 10 is reiterated until patients' targets are met. Figures 3–6 depict each patient's status update.

Table 11. Personal information from patient significance levels related to clinical manifestations.

Patients	Total Average Score
∂_1	0.74
∂_2	0.56
∂_3	0.92
∂_4	0.509

Table 12. $\chi_{\mathscr{F}'}$ is represented in a tabular format: Doctor's advice for COVID symptoms and the appropriate treatment.

Treatments/ Symptoms	$(\hat{\omega}'_{11}, \hat{\omega}'_{21}, \hat{\omega}'_{31})$	$(\hat{\omega}'_{11}, \hat{\omega}'_{21}, \hat{\omega}'_{32})$	$(\hat{\omega}'_{12}, \hat{\omega}'_{21}, \hat{\omega}'_{31})$	$(\hat{\omega}'_{12}, \hat{\omega}'_{21}, \hat{\omega}'_{32})$
$\mho_1$	0.2	0.3	0.1	0.5
$\mho_2$	0.6	0.4	0.6	0.6
$\mho_3$	0.6	0.5	0.3	0.2
$\mho_4$	0.5	0.3	0.4	0.7

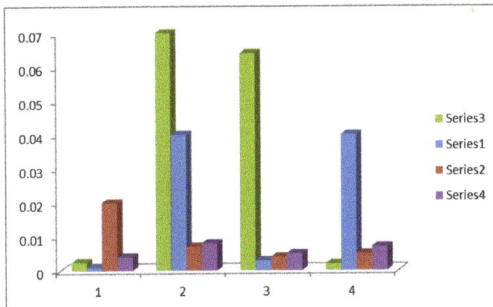

Figure 3. Graph of progress of patient ∂_1.

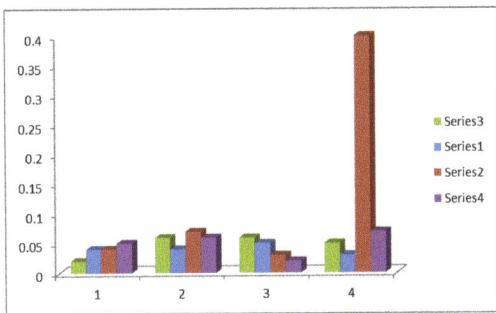

Figure 4. Graph of progress of patient ∂_2.

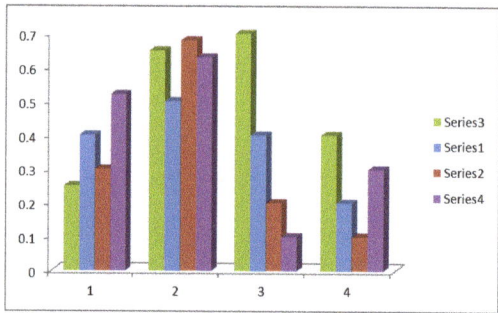

Figure 5. Graph of progress of patient ∂_3.

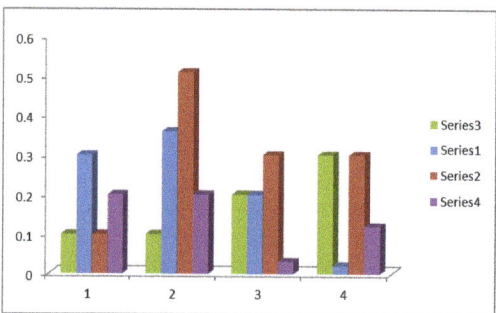

Figure 6. Graph of progress of patient ∂_4.

Table 13. $\mathscr{W}_C^1$ tabular representation: union of $\chi_{\mathscr{F}'}$ and $z'_{\mathscr{F}'}$ to investigate the affiliation for both envisaged treatments and patients.

Patients/Treatments	$\mho_1$	$\mho_2$	$\mho_3$	$\mho_4$
∂_1	0.3	0.4	0.3	0.512
∂_2	0.7	0.5	0.7	0.7
∂_3	0.7	0.6	0.4	0.3
∂_4	0.6	0.4	0.5	0.8

Table 14. Data pertaining to suggested treatment is represented in a tabular format.

Patients/Treatments	$\mho_1$	$\mho_2$	$\mho_3$	$\mho_4$	Maximum Values	Selected Treatment
∂_1	0.22	0.3	0.24	0.5	0.5	$\mho_4$
∂_2	0.6	0.4	0.6	0.6	0.6	$\mho_1$ or $\mho_3$ or $\mho_4$
∂_3	0.6	0.5	0.32	0.2	0.6	$\mho_1$
∂_4	0.5	0.3	0.4	0.7	0.7	$\mho_4$

Table 15. $\mathscr{W}_C^2$ tabular representation: after the second therapy event, the patient's improvement report.

Patients/Treatments	$\mho_1$	$\mho_2$	$\mho_3$	$\mho_4$
∂_1	0.3	0.5	0.4	0.6
∂_2	0.7	0.6	0.7	0.7
∂_3	0.8	0.5	0.3	0.2
∂_4	0.5	0.3	0.2	0.4

Table 16. $\mathscr{W}_C^3$ tabular representation: After the third therapy event, the patient's improvement report.

Patients/Treatments	$\mho_1$	$\mho_2$	$\mho_3$	$\mho_4$
∂_1	0.2	0.4	0.2	0.1
∂_2	0.2	0.2	0.4	0.2
∂_3	0.1	0.1	0.2	0.02
∂_4	0.2	0.01	0.2	0.02

Table 17. $\mathscr{W}_C^4$ tabular representation: After the fourth therapy event, the patient's improvement report.

Patients/Treatments	$\mho_1$	$\mho_2$	$\mho_3$	$\mho_4$
∂_1	0.01	0.03	0.03	0.04
∂_2	0.06	0.03	0.06	0.05
∂_3	0.05	0.04	0.02	0.01
∂_4	0.04	0.02	0.3	0.06

Table 18. $\mathscr{W}_C^5$ tabular representation: After the fifth therapy event, the patient's improvement report.

Patients/Treatments	$\mho_1$	$\mho_2$	$\mho_3$	$\mho_4$
∂_1	0.0014	0.002	0.01	0.003
∂_2	0.06	0.03	0.006	0.007
∂_3	0.05	0.002	0.003	0.004
∂_4	0.001	0.03	0.004	0.006

In Table 19, the symbols ✓ and × are meant for YES and NO, respectively. Similarly, the features such as FMG stand for fuzzy membership grade, COP for "consideration of parameters", COSP for "consideration of sub-parameters", MOPND for "management of periodic nature of data" and REC for "ranking evaluation criteria".

Table 19. The proposed $\mathscr{CFHS}$ is compared to established paradigms.

Literature\Features	FMG	COP	COSP	MOPND	REC
Zadeh [14]	✓	×	×	×	×
Molodtsov [19]	×	✓	×	×	×
Maji et al. [22]	✓	✓	×	×	×
Smarandache [30]	×	✓	✓	×	×
Ahsan et al. [47]	✓	✓	✓	×	×
Ramot et al. [40]	✓	×	×	✓	×
Zadeh [48]	✓	×	×	×	×
Atanassov [49]	✓	×	×	×	×
Smarandache [50]	✓	✓	×	×	×
Zhang & Zhang [51]	✓	×	×	×	×
Chen et al. [52]	✓	×	×	×	×
Deli et al. [53]	✓	✓	×	×	×
Zeb et al. [54]	✓	×	×	×	×
Proposed model	✓	✓	✓	✓	✓

3.1. Target Users of the Proposed Approach

The proposed algorithm aims to be a problem-solving support for early assortment alternatives and identifying sufferers with conflicting medical indications. This exploration demonstrates a well-built association between the signs and mathematically records them. The scheme is assembled on trimming $\mathscr{CFHS}$ set designs that can predict a patient's state and estimate medical indications over time to analyse the health effects of a medicine. It can be carried out to foresee the contagion's reinfection possibilities in anticipation of a cure. In their upcoming implementation, such pattern recognition-based algorithms are committed to diminishing medical inaccuracies and receiving inspiring results depending on various patient configurations.

3.2. Comparative Analysis

The concept of $\mathscr{CFHS}$ mapping is both broad and appropriate for various illnesses. Existing theories cannot be used to cope with and examine the challenges; however, our proposals do have their limits (Table 19). Because of such boundaries, some physicians may be incapable or unwilling to gather all the initial information. The presented method can transform the patient's condition into a quantitative style without gaps or overlaps, permitting us to secure the best diagnosis and treatment. The presented approach is compared to existing theories on structural and computational basis in Tables 19 and 20. When attributes are further split into attribute values and the concerns include complex (2D) data, current techniques fail to execute. The proposed mapping addresses these shortfalls. It reveals that, compared to conventional techniques, our framework is stable and effective in responding to such obstacles satisfactorily.

Now, the recommended plan is discussed along with its comprehensive nature.

- Because the COVID diagnosed individual cannot be comprehensively assessed after the initial assessment, additional days are added to this approximation . All of the patient's facts are contained in the $\mathscr{CFHS}$ set, and its union and severity can be linked to symptoms.
- In each patient trial, a relationship between related and critical indications can be determined, and weights assigned to them, which is crucial. The results will be non-specific if only the initial symptoms are considered.
- A treatment method for the patients is suggested in the second stage of the algorithm based on their COVID type.
- At the third stage, a generalized version of $\mathscr{CFHS}$-mapping tracks the patients' progress. With each scene, all memberships decrease until they reach zero. COVID symptoms, pharmaceutical neutral effects with therapies, and side effects are all falling. As time passes, this model depicts the evolution of the disease.

- If an individual does not progress after that round, inverse $\mathscr{CFHS}$-mapping is used to reinstate him to his initial state, and then the medications must be resumed from the beginning.
- Under the influence of parameterizations, the proposed approach is helpful for many patients with various illnesses and multiform criteria. This research is comprehensive and coherent in dealing with concerns in the medical world and multi-criteria.
- The data recorded by the medical personnel will be evaluated in the form of $\mathscr{CFHS}$. The intensity of the effect and the time the patient has been sick are recorded in the form of a complex number, while the sub-parametric values of the attributes are taken in hypersoft structures. The data recorded is taken between 0 and 1, depending on the degree of % match.
- This framework attempts to identify any illness's prognosis as well as their associated symptoms. By integrating these notions with a scientific prototype, these concepts can ve fully understand. This investigation demonstrates a relationship between symptoms and treatments, which simplifies the issue. The calculation relies on $\mathscr{CFHS}$-mapping to correctly identify the disease and choose the most appropriate treatment for each patient. A generalized mapping is used to predict the physician's progression record and evaluate the spacing of rehabilitation until it is mitigated.

Table 20. Comparison of computational results of proposed algorithm.

Authors	Approach	Approximated Score Values	Ranking of Patients
Zeb et al. [55]	Fermatean fuzzy soft weighted averaging operator (FFSWA)	0.94, 0.91, 0.93, 0.89	$\mho_1 > \mho_3 > \mho_2 > \mho_4$
Zeb et al. [55]	Fermatean fuzzy soft Yager average (FFS_fWA)	0.46, 0.35, 0.39, 0.12	$\mho_1 > \mho_3 > \mho_2 > \mho_4$
Riaz et al. [56]	Grey relational analysis (GRA) based on q-rung orthopair m-polar fuzzy soft set (q-RO-m-PFSS)	0.2854, 0.2825, 0.2820, 0.2921	$\mho_4 > \mho_1 > \mho_2 > \mho_3$
Riaz et al. [56]	TOPSIS based on q-rung orthopair m-polar fuzzy soft set (q-RO-m-PFSS)	0.5545, 0.5342, 0.5324, 0.6084	$\mho_4 > \mho_1 > \mho_2 > \mho_3$
Proposed approach	$\mathscr{CFHS}$ set	0.1124, 0.0640, 0.0230, 0.0020	$\mho_1 > \mho_2 > \mho_3 > \mho_4$

4. Conclusions

COVID-19 and its associated complications have been discussed in this article. A technique is suggested for diagnosing the patient's primary symptoms and analyzing their COVID. As a result, the $\mathscr{CFHS}$-mapping, INM and a few practical works with associated features are described. There are three stages to the calculation that have been established. The model examines the patients' actual COVID in the first stage. In the second step, $\mathscr{CFHS}$-mapping was utilized to locate suitable medications for the patients depending on their COVID-19 severity. Thirdly, generalized mapping is developed for the patient's development. The system predicts which medication will best treat the patient until the patient achieves suitable immune response. By associating this approach with existing knowledge, the findings thus gained are precise, simple to cope with, and have outstanding flexibility to examine MCDM issues. Other zones of the Neutrosophic HS set, Plithogenic HS set, Plithogenic Intuitionistic Fuzzy HS set, Q-Rung Orthopair Fuzzy HS set and their gluing models are to be explored for developing flexible hybrid structures. It may also be adapted for intelligent machines, diagnostic devices, information retrieval, information processing, social bonding, personalized recommendation approaches, algorithms, media platforms, remote sensing, the macroeconomic paradigm, classification techniques, image recognition, virtual architecture, and probabilistic reasoning.

Author Contributions: Conceptualization, M.S., M.A., A.U.R. and M.A.M.; methodology, M.S., M.A., A.U.R. and M.M.J.; software, M.H.S., A.U.R., M.A.M., M.M.J. and R.D.; validation, M.H.S., A.M., M.M.J. and R.D.; formal analysis, M.S., A.U.R., M.A. and R.D.; investigation, M.S., M.A., A.U.R., M.A.M. and M.M.J.; data curation, M.H.S., A.M., M.A.M. and R.D.; writing of the original draft, M.A., A.U.R., M.H.S. and M.A.M.; writing of the review and editing, M.S., M.A., M.A.M. and R.D.; visualization, M.S., M.A., A.U.R., M.H.S. and M.M.J.; supervision, M.S., M.A.M., M.M.J. and R.D.; project administration, M.S., M.A.M. and M.M.J.; funding acquisition, R.D. All authors have read and agreed to the published version of the manuscript.

Funding: This research received no external funding.

Institutional Review Board Statement: Not applicable.

Informed Consent Statement: Not applicable.

Data Availability Statement: Not applicable.

Conflicts of Interest: The authors declare no conflict of interest.

References

1. Hafeez, A.; Ahmad, S.; Siddqui, S.A.; Ahmad, M.; Mishra, S. A review of covid-19 (coronavirus disease-2019) diagnosis, treatments and prevention. *Ejmo* **2020**, *4*, 116–125.
2. Huang, C.; Wang, Y.; Li, X.; Ren, L.; Zhao, J.; Hu, Y.; Zhang, L.; Fan, G.; Xu, J.; Gu, X. Clinical features of patients infected with 2019 novel coronavirus in wuhan, china. *Lancet* **2020**, *395*, 497–506. [CrossRef]
3. Shekhar, S.; Wurth, R.; Kamilaris, C.D.; Eisenhofer, G.; Barrera, F.J.; Hajdenberg, M.; Tonleu, J.; Hall, J.E.; Schiffrin, E.L.; Porter, F.; et al. Endocrine conditions and covid-19. *Horm. Metab. Res.* **2020**, *52*, 471–484. [CrossRef] [PubMed]
4. Abayomi-Alli, O.O.; Damaševičius, R.; Maskeliūnas, R.; Misra, S. An ensemble learning model for COVID-19 detection from blood test samples. *Sensors* **2022**, *22*, 2222. [CrossRef]
5. Allioui, H.; Mohammed, M.A.; Benameur, N.; Al-Khateeb, B.; Abdulkareem, K.H.; Garcia-Zapirain, B.; Maskeliūnas, R. A multi-agent deep reinforcement learning approach for enhancement of COVID-19 CT image segmentation. *J. Pers. Med.* **2022**, *12*, 309. [CrossRef] [PubMed]
6. Rehman, N.U.; Zia, M.S.; Meraj, T.; Rauf, H.T.; Damaševičius, R.; El-Sherbeeny, A.M.; El-Meligy, M.A. A self-activated cnn approach for multi-class chest-related covid-19 detection. *Appl. Sci.* **2021**, *11*, 9023. [CrossRef]
7. Jiang, X.; Coffee, M.; Bari, A.; Wang, J.; Jiang, X.; Huang, J.; Shi, J.; Dai, J.; Cai, J.; Zhang, T.; et al. Towards an artificial intelligence framework for data-driven prediction of coronavirus clinical severity. *Comput. Mater. Contin.* **2020**, *63*, 537–551. [CrossRef]
8. Tuli, S.; Tuli, S.; Tuli, R.; Gill, S.S. Predicting the growth and trend of COVID-19 pandemic using machine learning and cloud computing. *Internet Things* **2020**, *11*, 100222. [CrossRef]
9. Wieczorek, M.; Silka, J.; Polap, D.; Wozniak, M.; Damaševicius, R. Real-time neural network based predictor for cov19 virus spread. *PLoS ONE* **2020**, *15*, e0243189. [CrossRef]
10. Kumar, V.; Singh, D.; Kaur, M.; Damaševičius, R. Overview of current state of research on the application of artificial intelligence techniques for COVID-19. *PeerJ Comput. Sci.* **2021**, *7*, 1–34. [CrossRef]
11. Alyasseri, Z.A.A.; Al-Betar, M.A.; Doush, I.A.; Awadallah, M.A.; Abasi, A.K.; Makhadmeh, S.N.; Alomari, O.A.; Abdulkareem, K.H.; Adam, A.; Damasevicius, R.; et al. Review on COVID-19 diagnosis models based on machine learning and deep learning approaches. *Expert Syst.* **2022**, *39*, e12759. [CrossRef] [PubMed]
12. Omoregbe, N.A.I.; Ndaman, I.O.; Misra, S.; Abayomi-Alli, O.O.; Damaševičius, R. Text messaging-based medical diagnosis using natural language processing and fuzzy logic. *J. Healthc. Eng.* **2020**, *2020*, 8839524. [CrossRef]
13. Lauraitis, A.; Maskeliunas, R.; Damaševičius, R. ANN and fuzzy logic based model to evaluate huntington disease symptoms. *J. Healthc. Eng.* **2018**, *2018*, 4581272. [CrossRef]
14. Zadeh, L.A. Fuzzy sets. In *Fuzzy Sets, Fuzzy Logic, and Fuzzy Systems: Selected Papers by Lotfi A Zadeh*; World Scientific: Singapore, 1996; pp. 394–432.
15. Dawood, H. Interval mathematics as a potential weapon against uncertainty. In *Mathematics of Uncertainty Modeling in the Analysis of Engineering and Science Problems*; IGI Global: Hershey, PA, USA, 2014; pp. 1–38. [CrossRef]
16. Dubois, D.; Prade, H. Interval-valued fuzzy sets, possibility theory and imprecise probability. In Proceedings of the 4th Conference of the European Society for Fuzzy Logic and Technology and 11th French Days on Fuzzy Logic and Applications, EUSFLAT-LFA 2005 Joint Conference, Barcelona, Spain, 7–9 September 2005; pp. 314–319.
17. Pawlak, Z.; Grzymala-Busse, J.; Slowinski, R.; Ziarko, W. Rough set. *Commun. ACM* **1995**, *38*, 88–95. [CrossRef]
18. Liu, X.; Wang, Z.; Zhang, S.; Garg, H. Novel correlation coefficient between hesitant fuzzy sets with application to medical diagnosis. *Expert Syst. Appl.* **2021**, *183*, 115393. [CrossRef]
19. Molodtsov, D. Soft set theory—First results. *Comput. Math. Appl.* **1999**, *37*, 19–31. [CrossRef]
20. Maji, P.; Roy, A.R.; Biswas, R. An application of soft sets in a decision making problem. *Comput. Math. Appl.* **2002**, *44*, 1077–1083. [CrossRef]

21. Yang, X.; Yu, D.; Yang, J.; Wu, C. Generalization of soft set theory: From crisp to fuzzy case. In *Fuzzy Information and Engineering*; Springer: Berlin/Heidelberg, Germany, 2007; pp. 345–354.
22. Maji, P.K.; Biswas, R.; Roy, A. Fuzzy soft sets. *J. Fuzzy Math.* **2001**, *9*, 589–602.
23. Kharal, A.; Ahmad, B. Mappings on soft classes. *New Math. Nat. Comput.* **2011**, *7*, 471–481. [CrossRef]
24. Kharal, A.; Ahmad, B. Mappings on fuzzy soft classes. *Adv. Fuzzy Syst.* **2009**, *2009*, 407890. [CrossRef]
25. Karaaslan, F. Soft classes and soft rough classes with applications in decision making. *Math. Probl. Eng.* **2016**, *2016*, 1584528. [CrossRef]
26. Alkhazaleh, S.; Marei, E. Mappings on neutrosophic soft classes. *Neutrosophic Sets Syst.* **2014**, *2*, 3–8.
27. Ropiak, K.; Artiemjew, P. On a hybridization of deep learning and rough set based granular computing. *Algorithms* **2020**, *13*, 63. [CrossRef]
28. Sulaiman, N.H.; Mohamad, D. Mappings on multiaspect fuzzy soft classes. In *AIP Conference Proceedings*; American Institute of Physics: University Park, PA, USA, 2014; Volume 1602, pp. 716–722.
29. Bashir, M.; Salleh, A.R. Mappings on intuitionistic fuzzy soft classes. In *AIP Conference Proceedings*; American Institute of Physics: University Park, PA, USA, 2013; Volume 1522, pp. 1022–1032.
30. Smarandache, F. Extension of soft set to hypersoft set, and then to plithogenic hypersoft set. *Neutrosophic Sets Syst.* **2018**, *22*, 168–170.
31. Saeed, M.; Ahsan, M.; Siddique, M.K.; Ahmad, M.R. A study of the fundamentals of hypersoft set theory. *Int. J. Sci. Eng. Res.* **2020**, *11*, 320–329.
32. Saeed, M.; Ahsan, M.; Abdeljawad, T. A development of complex multifuzzy hypersoft set with application in mcdm based on entropy and similarity measure. *IEEE Access* **2021**, *9*, 60026–60042. [CrossRef]
33. Saeed, M.; Ahsan, M.; Saeed, M.H.; Mehmood, A.; Khalifa, H.A.E.W.; Mekawy, I. The Prognosis of Allergy Based Diseases using Pythagorean Fuzzy Hypersoft Mapping Structures and Recommending Medication. *IEEE Access* **2022**, *10*, 5681–5696. [CrossRef]
34. Saeed, M.; Ahsan, M.; Saeed, M.H.; Mehmood, A.; Abdeljawad, T. An application of neutrosophic hypersoft mapping to diagnose hepatitis and propose appropriate treatment. *IEEE Access* **2021**, *9*, 70455–70471. [CrossRef]
35. Zulqarnain, M.; Dayan, F.; Saeed, M. Topsis analysis for the prediction of diabetes based on general characteristics of humans. *Int. J. Pharm. Sci. Res.* **2018**, *9*, 2932–2939.
36. Martin, N.; Smarandache, F. Introduction to combined plithogenic hypersoft sets. *Neutrosophic Sets Syst.* **2020**, *35*, 503–510. [CrossRef]
37. Musa, S.Y.; Asaad, B.A. Bipolar hypersoft sets. *Mathematics* **2021**, *9*, 1826. [CrossRef]
38. Ajay, D.; Charisma, J.J.; Boonsatit, N.; Hammachukiattikul, P.; Rajchakit, G. Neutrosophic semiopen hypersoft sets with an application to MAGDM under the COVID-19 scenario. *J. Math.* **2021**, *2021*, 5583218. [CrossRef]
39. Debnath, S. Interval-valued intuitionistic hypersoft sets and their algorithmic approach in multi-criteria decision making. *Neutrosophic Sets Syst.* **2022**, *48*, 226–250.
40. Ramot, D.; Milo, R.; Friedman, M.; Kandel, A. Complex fuzzy sets. *IEEE Trans. Fuzzy Syst.* **2002**, *10*, 171–186. [CrossRef]
41. Thirunavukarasu, P.; Suresh, R.; Ashokkumar, V. Theory of complex fuzzy soft set and its applications. *Int. J. Innov. Res. Sci. Technol.* **2017**, *3*, 13–18.
42. Rahman, A.U.; Saeed, M.; Smarandache, F.; Ahmad, M.R. Development of hybrids of hypersoft set with complex fuzzy set, complex intuitionistic fuzzy set and complex neutrosophic set. *Neutrosophic Sets Syst.* **2020**, *38*, 335–355.
43. Al-Qudah, Y.; Hassan, N. Operations on complex multi-fuzzy sets. *J. Intell. Fuzzy Syst.* **2017**, *33*, 1527–1540. [CrossRef]
44. Riaz, M.; Tehrim, S.T. Bipolar fuzzy soft mappings with application to bipolar disorders. *Int. J. Biomath.* **2019**, *12*, 1950080. [CrossRef]
45. Riaz, M.; Hashmi, M.R. M-polar neutrosophic soft mapping with application to multiple personality disorder and its associated mental disorders. *Artif. Intell. Rev.* **2021**, *54*, 2717–2763. [CrossRef]
46. Al-Qudah, Y.; Hassan, N. Complex multi-fuzzy soft set: Its entropy and similarity measure. *IEEE Access* **2018**, *6*, 65002–65017. [CrossRef]
47. Ahsan, M.; Saeed, M.; Rahman, A.U. A theoretical and analytical approach for fundamental framework of composite mappings on fuzzy hypersoft classes. *Neutrosophic Sets Syst.* **2021**, *45*, 268–285.
48. Zadeh, L.A. The concept of a linguistic variable and its application to approximate reasoning—II. *Inf. Sci.* **1975**, *8*, 301–357. [CrossRef]
49. Atanassov, K. Intuitionistic fuzzy sets. *Fuzzy Sets Syst.* **1986**, *20*, 87–96. [CrossRef]
50. Smarandache, F. *Neutrosophy: Neutrosophic Probability, Set, and Logic: Analytic Synthesis & Synthetic Analysis*; American Research Press: Santa Fe, NM, USA, 1998.
51. Zhang, W.R.; Zhang, L. YinYang bipolar logic and bipolar fuzzy logic. *Inf. Sci.* **2004**, *65*, 265–287. [CrossRef]
52. Chen, J.; Li, S.; Ma, S.; Wang, X. -Polar fuzzy sets: An extension of bipolar fuzzy sets. *Sci. World J.* **2014**, *2014*, 416530. [CrossRef]
53. Deli, I.; Ali, M.; Smarandache, F. Bipolar neutrosophic sets and their application based on multi-criteria decision making problems. In Proceedings of the International Conference on Advanced Mechatronic Systems (ICAMechS), Beijing, China, 22–24 August 2015; pp. 249–254.
54. Heilpern, S. Fuzzy mappings and fixed point theorem. *J. Math. Anal. Appl.* **1981**, *83*, 566–569. [CrossRef]

55. Zeb, A.; Khan, A.; Juniad, M.; Izhar, M. Fermatean fuzzy soft aggregation operators and their application in symptomatic treatment of COVID-19 (case study of patients identification). *J. Ambient Intell. Humaniz. Comput.* **2022**, 1–18. [CrossRef] [PubMed]
56. Riaz, M.; Garg, H.; Hamid, M.T.; Afzal, D. Modelling uncertainties with TOPSIS and GRA based on q-rung orthopair m-polar fuzzy soft information in COVID-19. *Expert Syst.* **2021**, *39*, e12940. [CrossRef]

Article

Application of ANN in Induction-Motor Fault-Detection System Established with MRA and CFFS

Chun-Yao Lee [1,*], Meng-Syun Wen [1], Guang-Lin Zhuo [1] and Truong-An Le [2]

[1] Department of Electrical Engineering, Chung Yuan Christian University, Taoyuan 320314, Taiwan; g10878027@cycu.org.tw (M.-S.W.); s10528245@cycu.org.tw (G.-L.Z.)
[2] Department of Electrical and Electronic Engineering, Thu Dau Mot University, Thu Dau Mot 75000, Binh Duong, Vietnam; anlt@tdmu.edu.vn
* Correspondence: cyl@cycu.edu.tw

Abstract: This paper proposes a fault-detection system for faulty induction motors (bearing faults, interturn shorts, and broken rotor bars) based on multiresolution analysis (MRA), correlation and fitness values-based feature selection (CFFS), and artificial neural network (ANN). First, this study compares two feature-extraction methods: the MRA and the Hilbert Huang transform (HHT) for induction-motor-current signature analysis. Furthermore, feature-selection methods are compared to reduce the number of features and maintain the best accuracy of the detection system to lower operating costs. Finally, the proposed detection system is tested with additive white Gaussian noise, and the signal-processing method and feature-selection method with good performance are selected to establish the best detection system. According to the results, features extracted from MRA can achieve better performance than HHT using CFFS and ANN. In the proposed detection system, CFFS significantly reduces the operation cost (95% of the number of features) and maintains 93% accuracy using ANN.

Keywords: multiresolution analysis (MRA); correlation and fitness values-based feature selection (CFFS); artificial neural network (ANN); feature selection

MSC: 68T07

1. Introduction

With the fourth industrial revolution developing, the way factories operate will no longer be the same. Factory automation can save manpower and avoid equipment failures with online fault-detection systems [1–3]. In factories, motors can cause production equipment failure and a significant impact on the economy [4]. Therefore, establishing a motor-detection system could solve the failure problems before severe damages are caused to factory productions. This study analyzes and builds a fault-detection system for common cases of motor failure [5]: (1) bearing fault, (2) interturn short circuit, and (3) broken rotor bar, based on motor-current signature analysis (MCSA) [6].

In recent years, many signal-processing methods have received high attention in the problem of fault-detection systems. For example, R. Romero-Troncoso improved the fast Fourier transform (FFT) by fractional resampling and proposed a multirate signal-processing technique for induction-motor fault detection [7]. M. Riera-Guasp et al. proposed the Gabor analysis of the current via the chirp z-transform to obtain high-resolution time–frequency images of transient motor currents [8]. V. Climente-Alarcon used a combination of Wigner–Ville distribution (WVD) and particle-filtering feature extraction to study in detail the evolution of principal slot harmonics (PSH) in induction motors under different load profiles [9]. M. Z. Ali et al. proposed a threshold-based fault-diagnosis method for induction motors, first using discrete wavelet transform to process the stator current, and then calculating the threshold value of the motor load through a curve-fitting equation [10].

The above signal-processing methods have their own advantages, but the current signal may obtain nonlinear and nonstationary noise signals in the time and frequency domains due to the faulty motor, which limits the performance of these methods. For example, FFT and GT are sensitive to noise [7]. The cross-term interference of nonstationary signals limits the performance of WVD [11]. The predefined wavelet-based parameters cause the WT may not be able to adaptively process nonstationary signals [12].

In recent years, several studies have demonstrated the advantages of multiresolution analysis (MRA) [13,14] and Hilbert Huang transform (HHT) [15–17] in analyzing nonlinear and nonstationary noise signals of induction motors. Therefore, this study compares two signal-processing approaches: (1) MRA, (2) HHT. The result of the research could help establish the best fault-detection system for induction motors. (1) MRA can analyze undetectable fault information in the time and frequency domain with current signals that are composed of detail coefficients and approximation coefficients. MRA is used to analyze motor-failure-current signals and extract the important features for fault-detection system from noisy signals; (2) HHT is widely used to analyze nonlinear and nonstationary signals. In conclusion, the HHT is used to analyze the noisy current signals that are caused by a faulty motor in order to find the noise frequency through the Hilbert transform to improve the accuracy of the fault-detection system.

The fault-detection system established with the features extracted from signal-processing approaches. Therefore, this study uses feature engineering to improve the system. Feature engineering can be divided into three categories [18]: feature construction [19,20], feature extraction [21–23], and feature selection [24–26]. Feature construction can increase the number of features by creating the new features based on old features. If the new features are important information, the fault-detection system may achieve better performance. Feature extraction can decrease the dimension of features from high-dimensional features with transfer function, and also avoid a situation where the accuracy of the system would be reduced when the Hughes phenomenon occurs. Feature selection has two methods: filter and wrapper. The filter selects the features based on feature correlation. The wrapper selects the features based on the evaluation function. Therefore, this study uses correlation and fitness values-based feature selection (CFFS) [27] to select the features. The CFFS is improved from correlation-based feature selection (CFS) [28]. CFFS uses Relief [29,30] and ReliefF [31] to calculate the correlation. CFFS selects the features based on evaluation function (performance of artificial neural network (ANN)) and features correlation. In conclusion, the CFFS obtains the advantages from the filter method and the wrapper method.

The selected classifier is the last part of fault-detection system. In [32], most classifier types are compiled, the advantages and disadvantages are discussed, and it is shown that ANNs are supervised by machine learning and achieve robust performance for irrelevant input data and noise and nonlinear data. This study also trains the neural network with Levenberg–Marquardt (LM) [33,34]. LM has advantages when training the neural network with small or medium data, so it is widely used for training feedforward networks [35–37]. Therefore, this study uses an artificial neural network with LM to establish a fault-detection system, selects important features via feature-selection method, and adds additive white Gaussian noise with a different signal-to-noise ratio (SNR) to test the efficiency of the fault-detection system.

2. Measure and Analyze the Current Signals

The classes of motor faults and damages are shown in Figure 1. As the equipment layout is shown in Figure 2, this study uses the AC power supply with 3 phases and 220 volts for motors. The control panel could adjust the load of the servo motor, which has a 220 V rated voltage, a 60 Hz power frequency, a 2 Hp output, a 1764 rpm rated speed, and a 0.8 power factor. The data-acquisition equipment (PXI-1033) captures the current from all types of motors. Labview can save each observation for 2 s and save sampling frequency for 1 kHz. Corresponding to four types (one healthy motor and three faulty motors) Labview can collect 400 observations for each case, save each observation for 2 s, and save the sampling frequency at 1 kHz.

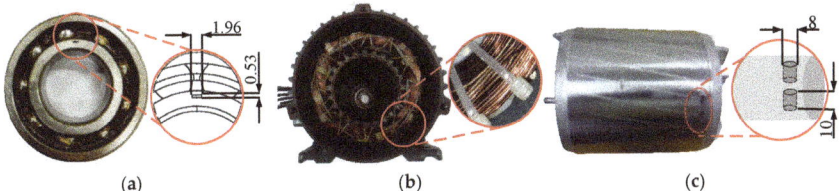

Figure 1. Faulty motor failure sample. (**a**) Bearing fault (0.53 mm width and 1.96 mm length), (**b**) interturn short circuit (5 insulation destructive coils), (**c**) broken rotor bar (2 holes—10 mm depth and 8 mm diameter).

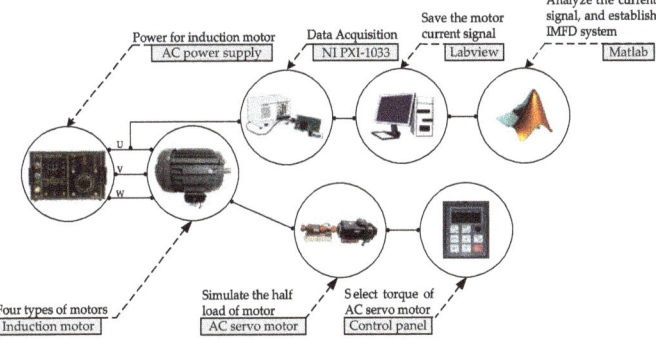

Figure 2. Equipment layout.

After measuring the data, this study establishes the fault-detection system with Matlab as shown in Figure 3. This classification system is divided into five parts: (a) NI PXI-1033 is used to capture 400 observations of current signals for four types of motors. The current signals will be processed by normalization, benefiting system operation. (b) A total of 1600 observations (4 classes) of normalized current signals were analyzed using MRA and HHT, while features were captured by Matlab. In this section, a fault dataset of 4 types of induction motors with 1600 observations and 4 classes is established. The number of extracted features is described in detail in the next subsection. (c) Critical features are selected by feature-selection approaches to lower the number of features. (d) In the dataset, each type is divided into 300 observations for training and 100 observations for testing. The artificial neural network is trained by the LM to build the fault-detection system. (e) Finally, the accuracy of the fault-detection system can be calculated.

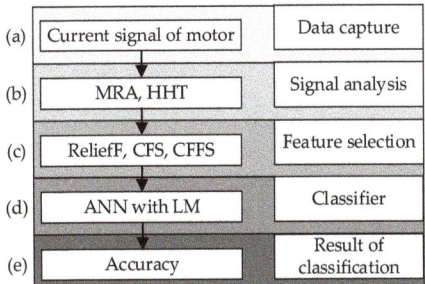

Figure 3. Schematic diagram of classification system. (**a**) capture the observations, (**b**) build fault detection dataset, (**c**) feature selection, (**d**) train the ANN, (**e**) classification result.

2.1. MRA and Feature Distribution of Current Signals

The MRA is used to analyze the current signals of four motors. According to [38], the MRA function in (1) demonstrates that signal $f(t)$ can be decomposed into approximation coefficient a_j and detail coefficient d_j. $\varphi(t)$ is the scaling function. $\psi(t)$ is the wavelet function, where g_0 and h_0 are filter coefficients.

$$f(t) = \sum_k a_{j0,k} \varphi_{j0,k}(t) + \sum_j \sum_k d_{j,k} \psi_{j,k}(t) \tag{1}$$

$$\varphi(t) = \sum_k g_0(k) + \varphi_k(2t - k) \tag{2}$$

$$\psi(t) = \sqrt{2} \sum_k h_0(t) + \varphi_k(2t - k) \tag{3}$$

Firstly, the MRA decomposes the signal and uses detail coefficients and approximation coefficients to compose the signal, as shown in Figure 4, where x-axis is the time and y-axis is the amplitude. Then, 60 features extracted from the signal will be composed with d1–5 and a5, as shown in Table 1, namely (1) Tmax; (2) Tmin; (3) Tmean; (4) Tmse; (5) Tstd; (6) Fmax; (7) Fmin; (8) Fmean; (9) Fmse; (10) Fstd. Features are summarily presented below. The frequency domain is analyzed with FFT. Finally, Figure 5 shows the feature distribution of IM.

(1) Tmax: maximum of each coefficient in time domain;
(2) Tmin: minimum of each coefficient in time domain;
(3) Tmean: average of each coefficient in time domain;
(4) Tmse: root mean square of each coefficient in time domain;
(5) Tstd: standard of each coefficient in time domain;
(6) Fmax: maximum of each coefficient in frequency domain;
(7) Fmin: minimum of each coefficient in frequency domain;
(8) Fmean: average of each coefficient in frequency domain;
(9) Fmse: root mean square of each coefficient in frequency domain;
(10) Fstd: standard of each coefficient in frequency domain.

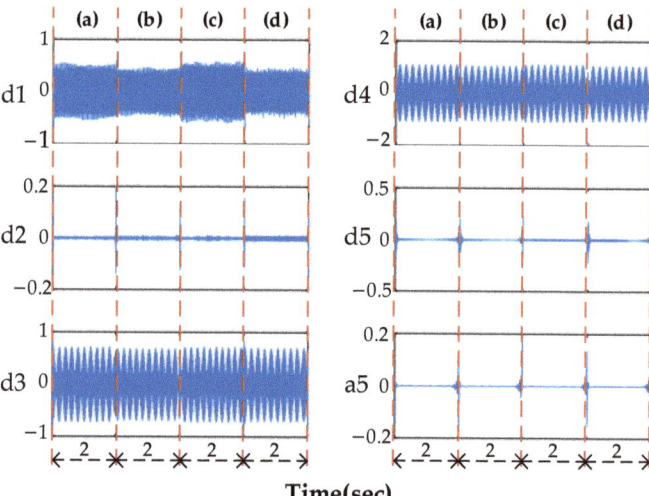

Figure 4. The MRA of current signal. (a) Normal motor, (b) bearing fault, (c) interturn short circuit, (d) broken rotor bar.

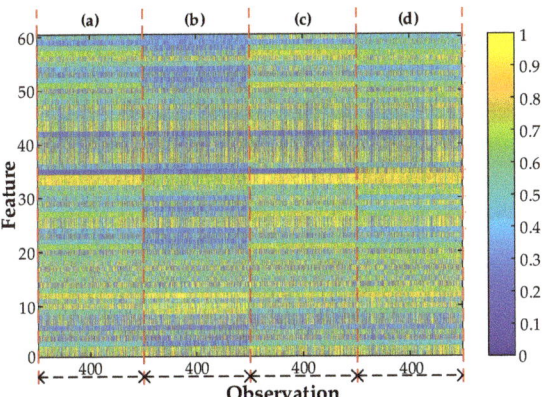

Figure 5. Feature distribution of the MRA. (**a**) Normal motor, (**b**) bearing fault, (**c**) interturn short circuit, (**d**) broken rotor bar.

Table 1. Feature extraction of the MRA.

	a5	d5	d4	d3	d2	d1
Tmax	F1	F2	F3	F4	F5	F6
Tmin	F7	F8	F9	F10	F11	F12
Tmean	F13	F14	F15	F16	F17	F18
Tmse	F19	F20	F21	F22	F23	F24
Tstd	F25	F26	F27	F28	F29	F30
Fmax	F31	F32	F33	F34	F35	F36
Fmin	F37	F38	F39	F40	F41	F42
Fmean	F43	F44	F45	F46	F47	F48
Fmse	F49	F50	F51	F52	F53	F54
Fstd	F55	F56	F57	F58	F59	F60

2.2. Hilbert–Huang Transform and Feature Distribution of Current Signals

This study uses Hilbert–Huang transform (HHT) to analyze the current signals of four classes of motors. According to [39], the HHT decomposes the signal into several intrinsic mode functions (IMF) c_i by empirical mode decomposition (EMD) and calculates $H_i(t)$ from c_i with Hilbert transform (HT) in (4), as shown. (5) and (6) calculate the instantaneous amplitude $a_i(t)$ and instantaneous phase angle $\theta_i(t)$. Finally, (7) differentiates the instantaneous phase angle $\theta_i(t)$ and obtains instantaneous frequency $\omega_i(t)$.

$$H_i(t) = \frac{1}{\pi} \int_{-\infty}^{\infty} \frac{c_i}{t-\tau} d\tau \quad (4)$$

$$a_i(t) = \sqrt{c_i^2(t) + H_i^2(t)} \quad (5)$$

$$\theta_i(t) = \tan^{-1} \frac{H_i(t)}{c_i(t)} \quad (6)$$

$$\omega_i(t) = \frac{d\theta_i(t)}{dt} \quad (7)$$

Firstly, the HHT decomposes the signal into seven (limitation of the signal) intrinsic mode functions, IMF1 (c1) to IMF7 (c7) by EMD, as shown in Figure 6, where x-axis is the amplitude, y-axis is the time. Then, instantaneous frequencies w1 to w7 are calculated with c1 to c7, as shown in Figure 7, where x-axis is the time, y-axis is the frequency. In w1, most of the bandwidths are around 60 Hz (fundamental frequency), and some of the bandwidths are close to 1 kHz, because the value of AC current emerged close to zero has a great slope. Furthermore, 70 features are extracted from c1 to c7 and w1 to w7, as shown in Table 2, namely (1) max; (2) min; (3) mean; (4) mse; (5) std. Features are summarily presented below. Finally, Figure 8. shows the feature distribution of IM.

(1) max: maximum of w1 to w7 and c1 to c7;
(2) min: minimum of w1 to w7 and c1 to c7;
(3) mean: average of w1 to w7 and c1 to c7;
(4) mse: root mean square of w1 to w7 and c1 to c7;
(5) std: standard of w1 to w7 and c1 to c7.

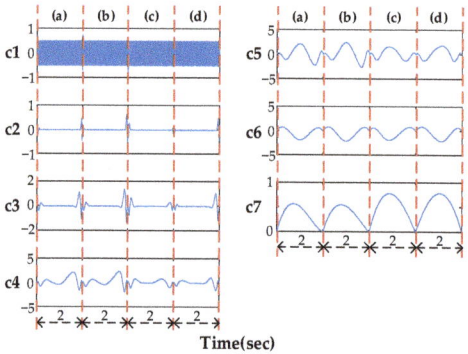

Figure 6. The EMD of current signal. (**a**) Normal motor, (**b**) bearing fault, (**c**) interturn short circuit, (**d**) broken rotor bar.

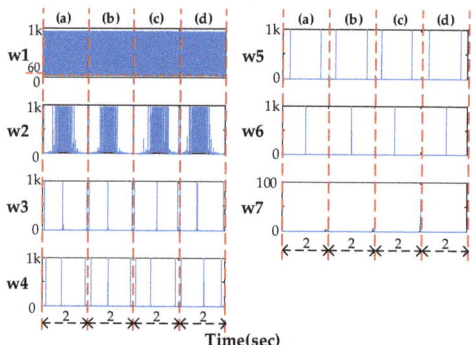

Figure 7. Instantaneous frequency of EMD. (**a**) Normal motor, (**b**) bearing fault, (**c**) interturn short circuit, (**d**) broken rotor bar.

Table 2. Feature extraction of the HHT.

		max	min	mean	mse	std
	c1	F1	F2	F3	F4	F5
	c2	F6	F7	F8	F9	F10
	c3	F11	F12	F13	F14	F15
EMD	c4	F16	F17	F18	F19	F20
	c5	F21	F22	F23	F24	F25
	c6	F26	F27	F28	F29	F30
	c7	F31	F32	F33	F34	F35

Table 2. Cont.

		max	min	mean	mse	std
HT	w1	F36	F37	F38	F39	F40
	w2	F41	F42	F43	F44	F45
	w3	F46	F47	F48	F49	F50
	w4	F51	F52	F53	F54	F55
	w5	F56	F57	F58	F59	F60
	w6	F61	F62	F63	F64	F65
	w7	F66	F67	F68	F69	F70

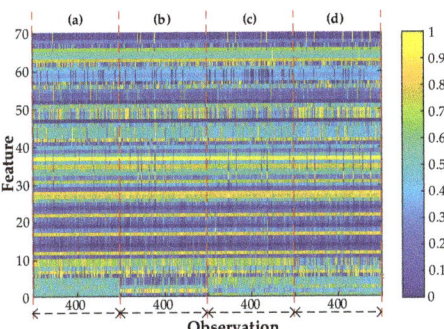

Figure 8. Feature distribution of the HHT. (a) Normal motor, (b) bearing fault, (c) interturn short circuit, (d) broken rotor bar.

3. Feature-Selection Approaches for Features of the MRA and HHT

3.1. ReliefF

The ReliefF algorithm shows as Algorithm 1. ReliefF is improved for multiclass classification situations. This study uses ReliefF to calculate the correlation between feature and classification. The algorithm selects the feature (F_h) from all of the features, and F_h is selected as one value of the set. Then, the feature (F_h) chooses the nearest values of the same classification and other classifications. In addition, function (8) is used to calculate the correlation, and features with greater correlation will be considered more important.

Algorithm 1: ReliefF

1: **repeat**
2:   Choose one of the features F_h;
3:   Choose one value f_h randomly from F_h;
4:   Choose the nearest values f_{nh} and f_{nmb} with f_h;
5:   Calculate the F_h correlation R_{fFh} in (8);
6: **until** obtain all correlations R_{fF} with ReliefF for feature selection
7: Choose the best performance of feature set for establish ANN

$$R_{fF} = W_i - (\frac{1}{km})diff(f_h, f_{nh}) + (\frac{p(m \not\subset n)}{1 - p(n)})(\frac{1}{km}) \times diff(f_h, f_{nmb}) \quad (8)$$

where

$$RfF \begin{pmatrix} R_{fF1} \\ \vdots \\ R_{fFi} \\ \vdots \\ R_{fFm} \end{pmatrix},$$

is the correlation between feature and classification.

3.2. CFS

The CFS algorithm is shown as Algorithm 2. CFS calculates the Merit value for selecting the features under three conditions: (I) feature correlation and (II) correlation between feature and classification. The algorithm calculates the correlation R_f between features with Relief that is shown in (9). Next, ReliefF is used to calculate the correlation R_{fF} between feature and classification in (8). In addition, (III) calculates the Merit value in (10).

Algorithm 2: CFS

1: (I) The feature correlation:
2: **repeat**
3:    Choose two of the features F_h and F_i;
4:    Choose one value f_h randomly from F_h;
5:    Choose the nearest values f_{nh} and f_{nm} with f_h;
6:    Calculate the correlation between F_h and F_i with (9);
7: **until** obtain all correlation R_F with Relief.
8: (II) The correlation between feature and classification:
9: Use ReliefF to calculate R_{fF} in (8);
10: (III) Calculate the Merit value:
11: **repeat**
14:    Calculate the Merit value in (10);
15: **until** obtain the whole Merit value.
16: Choose the best performance of feature set for establish ANN.

$$R_f = W_i - (\frac{1}{k})diff(f_h, f_{nh})^2 + (\frac{1}{k}) \times diff(f_h, f_{nm})^2 \tag{9}$$

where

$$Rf \begin{pmatrix} 1 & R_{f12} & R_{f13} & \cdots & \cdots & R_{f1m} \\ 0 & 1 & R_{f23} & \cdots & \cdots & \vdots \\ \vdots & 0 & \ddots & \cdots & R_{fhm} & \vdots \\ \vdots & 0 & 0 & \ddots & \cdots & \vdots \\ \vdots & \vdots & \vdots & 0 & 1 & \vdots \\ 0 & \cdots & \cdots & \cdots & 0 & 1 \end{pmatrix},$$

is the correlation between features;

$$\text{Merit} = \frac{n_f \times \overline{R}_{fFi}}{\sqrt{n_f + n_f(k-1) \times \overline{R}_{fij}}} \tag{10}$$

3.3. CFFS

The CFFS algorithm is shown as Algorithm 3. CFFS is the feature-selection approach improved by CFS, which is proposed in our previous study [28]. CFFS selects the features under four conditions. The algorithm calculates (I) correlation between features in (9), (II) correlation between features and classification in (8), (III) Merit value in (10). Then, (IV) fitness value W_{fi} is calculated for Merit_new value in (11).

$$\text{Merit\_new} = \text{Merit} \times W_{fi} \tag{11}$$

The fitness value was calculated by PSO. The PSO is used to optimize the weights of features [40,41] and selects the best-known solution in swarms. Therefore, this study could establish the best induction-motor fault-detection system with the features selected by CFFS and the weights of these features after training ANN.

To compare the feature-selection approach's performance, this study chooses the 1st to the 10th feature-selection approach orders through the MRA and the HHT, which are shown in Table 3. The MRA–ReliefF, MRA–CFS, and MRA–CFFS have the same 9 features (F35, F24, F54, F60, F27, F57, F30, F51, and F58). The HHT–ReliefF, HHT–CFS, and HHT–CFFS only have the same 2 features (F5 and F4). The important features mentioned above are marked in Figures 5 and 8 (the red dot •). Inferring to Table 3, the features extracted from the MRA with feature-selection approaches are more similar than the HHT. According to the result, the performance of feature selection is affected by the features extracted from signal processing.

Algorithm 3: CFFS

1: (I) The correlation between features:
2: Use Relief to calculate the correlation;
3: (II) The correlation between feature and classification:
4: Use ReliefF to calculate the correlation;
5: (III) Calculate the Merit value:
6: Use CFS to calculate the Merit value;
7: (IV) Calculate the Merit_new value:
8: **repeat**
9:     Select the feature set to training ANN with PSO;
10:    Calculate the fitness value W_{fi} from PSO;
11:    Calculate the Merit_new value in (11);
12: **until** obtain all the Merit_new value.
13: Choose the best performance of feature set for establish ANN.

Table 3. Features order.

Signal Processing	Feature-Selection Approach	Features Order of 1st to 10th									
		1st	2nd	3rd	4th	5th	6th	7th	8th	9th	10th
MRA	ReliefF	F35	F24	F54	F60	F27	F57	F30	F21	F51	F58
	CFS	F35	F54	F60	F24	F57	F51	F58	F30	F27	F21
	CFFS	F35	F57	F58	F27	F24	F51	F60	F30	F22	F54
HHT	ReliefF	F5	F4	F61	F32	F56	F12	F40	F58	F44	F10
	CFS	F39	F40	F38	F5	F4	F13	F64	F65	F14	F45
	CFFS	F39	F5	F4	F13	F64	F43	F25	F46	F24	F45

4. The Result of Induction-Motor Fault Detection

This section demonstrates the results of the fault-detection system and analyzes the current signals using MRA and HHT. As shown in Figure 9, the feature-selection method is used to reduce the number of features to test the efficiency of IMFD with noise current signals (including SNR: 40 dB, 30 dB, 20 dB, and 10 dB): (a) Use Matlab to add the AWGN into current signals; (b) analyze the data; (c) select the features. The feature order after adding noise is the same as the feature-selection method applied to the original signal. (d) Training the fault-detection system. (e) Finally, obtain the accuracy of this fault-detection system. ReliefF and CFS both select features based on feature correlation, whereby the feature orders of ReliefF and CFS are the same. CFFS selects the features based on feature correlation and the performance of the fault-detection system, whereby feature orders will change every time according to accuracy. Therefore, the accuracies of the MRA–ReliefF, MRA–CFS, HHT–ReliefF, and HHT–CFS are at an average level through 50 rounds of training and testing. The MRA–CFFS and HHT–CFFS only undergo the training and testing process once, whereby the accuracy curves are more unstable than the accuracy curves of the MRA–ReliefF, MRA–CFS, HHT–ReliefF, and HHT–CFS. In conclusion, this study compares the accuracy curve of all results and proposed the best model to establish the fault-detection system.

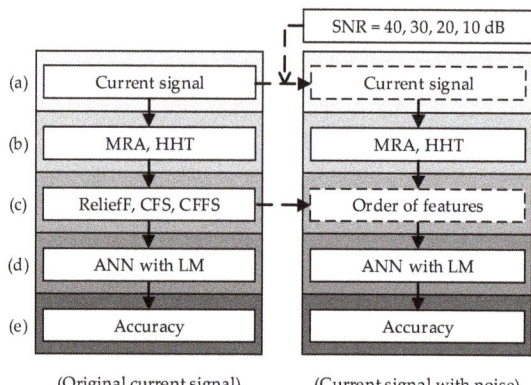

Figure 9. Schematic diagram of current signal added the noise to establish fault-detection system. (**a**) capture the observations, (**b**) build fault detection dataset, (**c**) feature selection, (**d**) train the ANN, (**e**) classification result.

4.1. Parameter Setting of ANN

The ANN is composed of the input layer, hidden layer, output layer, and neurons. In the hidden layer, the input is computed via weights, biases, and activation functions. The classification result is computed by the output layer. In ANN, the weight and bias of each neuron are adjusted by calculating the error between the output and the target. Updating the weights and biases during the iteration will reduce the cross-entropy loss. The parameter settings of the ANN used in this study are shown in Table 4.

Table 4. Parameter setting of ANN.

Parameters	Value
Hidden layer size	10
Output layer size	4
Training ratio	75/100
Testing ratio	25/100
Training function	Levenberg-Marquardt
Learning rate	0.007
Iteration	50
Activation function	Softmax
Performance function	Cross-Entropy
Transfer function	Hyperbolic tangent sigmod

4.2. Compare the Signal-Processing Aproaches: The MRA, and the HHT

The accuracies of the MRA–ReliefF (Figure 10) are displayed at 60 feature numbers and the accuracies of the HHT–ReliefF (Figure 11) are displayed at 70 feature numbers under different noise conditions. The comparison results are summarized below. The accuracies under different noise conditions of the MRA–ReliefF is higher than the accuracies of the HHT–ReliefF.

(1) In ∞ dB, MRA: 94.8%, HHT: 85.8%;
(2) In 40 dB, MRA: 92.2%, HHT: 84.4%;
(3) In 30 dB, MRA: 92%, HHT: 81.9%;
(4) In 20 dB, MRA: 88.2%, HHT: 68.4%;
(5) In 10 dB, MRA: 69.2%, HHT: 43.9%.

The accuracies of the MRA–CFS (Figure 12) are displayed at 60 feature numbers and the accuracies of the HHT–CFS (Figure 13) are displayed at 70 feature numbers under different noise conditions. The comparison results are summarized below. The accuracies under different noise conditions of the MRA–CFS are higher than the accuracy of the HHT–CFS.

(1) In ∞ dB, MRA: 94.8%, HHT: 85.9%;
(2) In 40 dB, MRA: 94.5%, HHT: 83.4%;
(3) In 30 dB, MRA: 93.7%, HHT: 81.9%;
(4) In 20 dB, MRA: 87.7%, HHT: 68%;
(5) In 10 dB, MRA: 70.3%, HHT: 44.1%.

The accuracies of the MRA–CFFS (Figure 14) are displayed at 60 feature numbers and the accuracies of the HHT–CFFS (Figure 15) are displayed at 70 feature numbers under different noise conditions. The comparison results are summarized below. The accuracies under different noise conditions of the MRA–CFFS are higher than the accuracy of the HHT–CFFS.

(1) In ∞ dB, MRA: 92%, HHT: 83.5%;
(2) In 40 dB, MRA: 91.8%, HHT: 82.7%;
(3) In 30 dB, MRA: 91.3%, HHT: 81.5%;
(4) In 20 dB, MRA: 91%, HHT: 73.3%;
(5) In 10 dB, MRA: 89.8%, HHT: 66%.

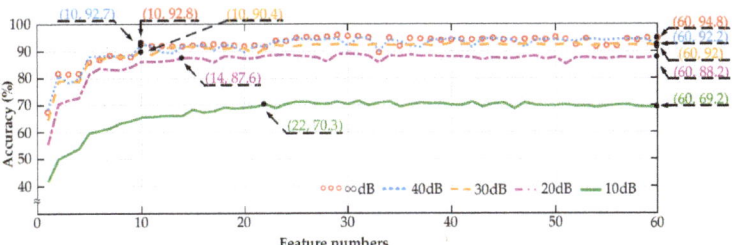

Figure 10. Accuracy curves of the MRA–ReliefF.

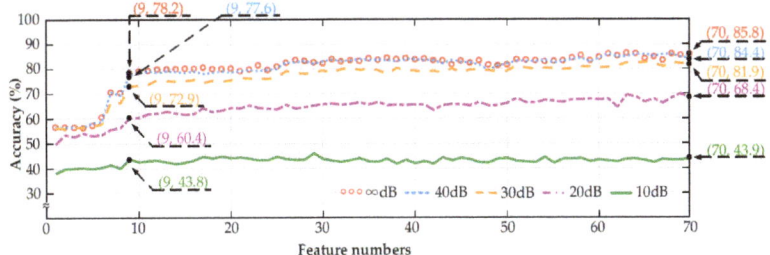

Figure 11. Accuracy curves of the HHT–ReliefF.

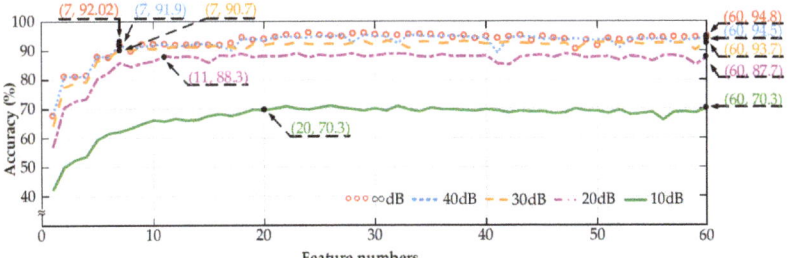

Figure 12. Accuracy curves of the MRA–CFS.

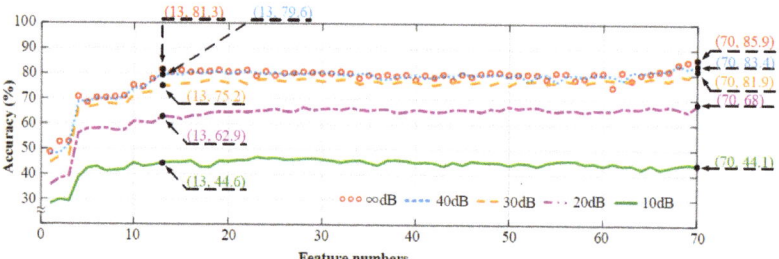

Figure 13. Accuracy curves of the HHT–CFS.

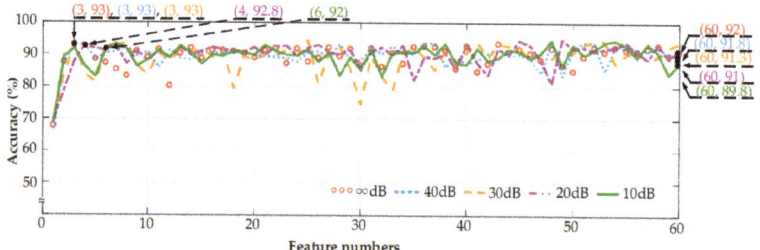

Figure 14. Accuracy curves of the MRA–CFFS.

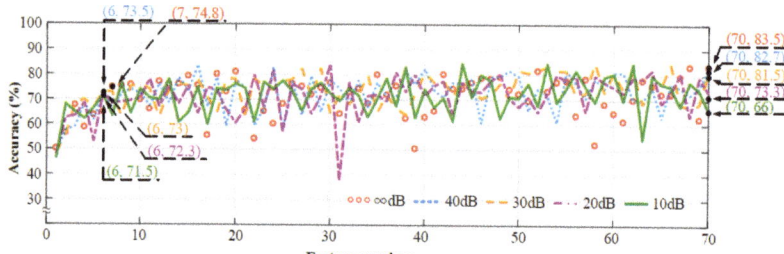

Figure 15. Accuracy curves of the HHT–CFFS.

4.3. Compare the Feature-Selection Approaches: ReliefF, CFS, and CFFS

The highest efficiencies of the MRA with different feature-selection approaches under different noise conditions are shown in Tables 5–7. The comparison is summarized as below. The accuracies of the CFFS are slightly higher than the accuracy of ReliefF and the CFS under ∞ dB, 40 dB, and 30 dB. Under severe noise conditions such as 20 dB and 10 dB, the CFFS achieves a better performance than ReliefF and the CFS.

(1) In ∞ dB, ReliefF: 10 features and 92.8%, CFS: 7 features aFnd 92.02%, CFFS: 3 features and 93%;
(2) In 40 dB, ReliefF: 10 features and 92.7%, CFS: 7 features and 91.9%, CFFS: 3 features and 93%;
(3) In 30 dB, ReliefF: 10 features and 90.4%, CFS: 7 features and 90.7%, CFFS: 3 features and 93%;
(4) In 20 dB, ReliefF: 14 features and 87.6%, CFS: 11 features and 88.3%, CFFS: 4 features and 92.8%;
(5) In 10 dB, ReliefF: 22 features and 70.3%, CFS: 20 features and 70.3%, CFFS: 6 features and 92%.

The highest efficiencies of the HHT with different feature-selection approaches under different noise conditions are shown in Tables 8–10. The comparison is summarized below.

The accuracies of the CFFS are slightly lower than the accuracy of ReliefF and the CFS under ∞ dB, 40 dB, and 30 dB. Under severe noise conditions such as 20 dB and 10 dB, the CFFS achieves a better performance than ReliefF and the CFS.

(1) In ∞ dB, ReliefF: 9 features and 78.2%, CFS: 13 feature and 81.3%, CFFS: 7 features and 74.8%;
(2) In 40 dB, ReliefF: 9 features and 77.6%, CFS: 13 features and 79.6%, CFFS: 6 features and 73.5%;
(3) In 30 dB, ReliefF: 9 features and 72.9%, CFS: 13 features and 75.2%, CFFS: 6 features and 73%;
(4) In 20 dB, ReliefF: 9 features and 60.4%, CFS: 13 features and 62.9%, CFFS: 6 features and 72.3%;
(5) In 10 dB, ReliefF: 9 features and 43.8%, CFS: 13 features and 44.6%, CFFS: 6 features and 71.5%.

According to the comparison of the signal-processing approaches and feature-selection approaches, the performance of the MRA is better than the HHT, and the CFFS can establish an effective fault-detection system than ReliefF and CFS. The result could be inferred by the feature distribution of MRA (Figure 5) and the HHT (Figure 8). The features of MRA (Figure 5) have more significant features than the HHT (Figure 8). For establishing the fault-detection system, the selected signal-processing approach has an impact on the system, and the system established with the feature-selection approach could reduce the considerable feature numbers.

Table 5. Result of the MRA–ReliefF.

SNR	Feature Numbers	Accuracy (%)	The Elements of the Feature Vector
∞	10	92.8	F35, F24, F54, F60, F27, F57, F30, F21, F51, F58
40	10	92.7	F35, F24, F54, F60, F27, F57, F30, F21, F51, F58
30	10	90.4	F35, F24, F54, F60, F27, F57, F30, F21, F51, F58
20	14	87.6	F35, F24, F54, F60, F27, F57, F30, F21, F51, F58, F34, F36, F28, F22
10	22	70.3	F35, F24, F54, F60, F27, F57, F30, F21, F51, F58, F34, F36, F28, F22, F52, F33, F9, F3, F49, F19, F31, F13

Table 6. Result of the MRA–CFS.

SNR	Feature Numbers	Accuracy (%)	The Elements of the Feature Vector
∞	7	92.02	F35, F54, F60, F24, F57, F51, F58
40	7	91.9	F35, F54, F60, F24, F57, F51, F58
30	7	90.7	F35, F54, F60, F24, F57, F51, F58
20	11	88.3	F35, F54, F60, F24, F57, F51, F58, F30, F27, F21, F52
10	20	70.3	F35, F54, F60, F24, F57, F51, F58, F30, F27, F21, F52, F34, F36, F28, F22, F33, F49, F59, F55, F31

Table 7. Result of the MRA–CFFS.

SNR	Feature Numbers	Accuracy (%)	The Elements of the Feature Vector
∞	3	93	F35, F57, F58
40	3	93	F35, F57, F58
30	3	93	F35, F57, F58
20	4	92.8	F35, F57, F58, F27
10	6	92	F35, F57, F58, F27, F24, F51

Table 8. Result of the HHT–ReliefF.

SNR	Feature Numbers	Accuracy (%)	The Elements of the Feature Vector
∞	9	78.2	F5, F4, F61, F32, F56, F12, F40, F58, F44
40	9	77.6	F5, F4, F61, F32, F56, F12, F40, F58, F44
30	9	72.9	F5, F4, F61, F32, F56, F12, F40, F58, F44
20	9	60.4	F5, F4, F61, F32, F56, F12, F40, F58, F44
10	9	43.8	F5, F4, F61, F32, F56, F12, F40, F58, F44

Table 9. Result of the HHT–CFS.

SNR	Feature Numbers	Accuracy (%)	The Elements of the Feature Vector
∞	13	81.3	F39, F40, F38, F5, F4, F13, F64, F65, F14, F45, F63, F15, F46
40	13	79.6	F39, F40, F38, F5, F4, F13, F64, F65, F14, F45, F63, F15, F46
30	13	75.2	F39, F40, F38, F5, F4, F13, F64, F65, F14, F45, F63, F15, F46
20	13	62.9	F39, F40, F38, F5, F4, F13, F64, F65, F14, F45, F63, F15, F46
10	13	44.6	F39, F40, F38, F5, F4, F13, F64, F65, F14, F45, F63, F15, F46

Table 10. Result of the HHT–CFFS.

SNR	Feature Numbers	Accuracy (%)	The Elements of the feature Vector
∞	7	74.8	F39, F5, F4, F13, F64, F43, F25
40	6	73.5	F39, F5, F4, F13, F64, F43
30	6	73	F39, F5, F4, F13, F64, F43
20	6	72.3	F39, F5, F4, F13, F64, F43
10	6	71.5	F39, F5, F4, F13, F64, F43

5. Conclusions

The study proposes the CFFS with the advantage of filter and wrapper; therefore, the CFFS has significant performance in the fault-detection system. According to the results of this research, the choice of signal processing and feature-selection approach is a crucial influence on the accuracy of the fault-detection system. MRA is one useful method to analyze the faulty motor in this paper, which provides good features for the CFFS, which has a significant effect on the system, reducing 57 (95%) of the features from MRA and achieving 93% accuracy. The system established with CFFS also achieves excellent performance under 40 to 10 dB AWGN, reducing about 54 to 57 (90% to 95%) features and maintaining an accuracy of about 92% to 93%. In this research, the low-dimensional feature is suitable to use CFFS. In other words, CFFS uses in other cases with high-dimensional features could have higher operating costs; this factor is the limitation for CFFS. Therefore, this study establishes the fault-detection system with MRA and CFFS for the faulty motors in this study.

Author Contributions: Conceptualization, M.-S.W. and G.-L.Z.; methodology, M.-S.W.; software, G.-L.Z.; validation, C.-Y.L., M.-S.W. and G.-L.Z.; formal analysis, M.-S.W.; resources, C.-Y.L.; data curation, M.-S.W.; writing—original draft preparation, M.-S.W.; writing—review and editing, C.-Y.L., G.-L.Z. and T.-A.L.; visualization, M.-S.W.; supervision, C.-Y.L. and T.-A.L.; project administration, C.-Y.L. All authors have read and agreed to the published version of the manuscript.

Funding: This research received no external funding.

Institutional Review Board Statement: Not applicable.

Informed Consent Statement: Not applicable.

Data Availability Statement: Not applicable.

Conflicts of Interest: The authors declare no conflict of interest.

Nomenclature

a_j	approximation coefficient
$a_i(t)$	instantaneous amplitude
c_i	intrinsic mode function
d_j	detail coefficient
$diff(f_h, f_{nm})$	distance between f_h and f_{nh}
$diff(f_h, f_{nm})$	distance between f_h and f_{nm}
$diff(f_h, f_{nmb})$	sum of the distance between f_h and f_{nmb}
f_h	one value of F_h
f_{nh}	nearest values of F_h with f_h
f_{nm}	nearest values of F_i with f_h
f_{nmb}	nearest values of other classification different with f_h
g_0	filter coefficients 1
h_0	filter coefficients 2
k	maximum times of sampling
n	the class belong f_h
n_f	number of features
m	the all classification
R_{fF}	correlation between feature and classification
R_{fFi}	the average of R_{fFi}
R_{fFi}	the average of R_{fij}
W_i	initial value of correlation
$\psi(t)$	wavelet function
$\varphi(t)$	scaling function
$\theta_i(t)$	instantaneous phase angle
$\omega_i(t)$	instantaneous frequency

References

1. Zhang, P.; Shu, S.; Zhou, M. An online fault detection model and strategies based on SVM-grid in clouds. *IEEE/CAA J. Autom. Sin.* **2018**, *5*, 445–456. [CrossRef]
2. Wang, H.; Lu, S.; Qian, G.; Ding, J.; Liu, Y.; Wang, Q. A two-step strategy for online fault detection of high-resistance connection in BLDC motor. *IEEE Trans. Power Electron.* **2020**, *35*, 3043–3053. [CrossRef]
3. Mao, W.; Chen, J.; Liang, X.; Zhang, X. A new online detection approach for rolling bearing incipient fault via self-adaptive deep feature matching. *IEEE Trans. Instrum. Meas.* **2019**, *69*, 443–456. [CrossRef]
4. Antonino-Daviu, J.; Aviyente, S.; Strangas, E.G.; Riera-Guasp, M. Scale invariant feature extraction algorithm for the automatic diagnosis of rotor asymmetries in induction motors. *IEEE Trans. Ind. Inform.* **2013**, *9*, 100–108. [CrossRef]
5. Bazurto, A.J.; Quispe, E.C.; Mendoza, R.C. Causes and failures classification of industrial electric motor. In Proceedings of the 2016 IEEE Andescon, Arequipa, Peru, 19–21 October 2016; pp. 1–4.
6. Rodriguez-Donate, C.; Romero-Troncoso, R.J.; Garcia-Perez, A.; Razo-Montes, D.A. FPGA based embedded system for induction motor failure monitoring at the start-up transient vibrations with wavelets. *IEEE Trans. Instrum. Meas.* **2010**, *59*, 63–72.
7. Romero-Troncoso, R. Multirate signal processing to improve FFT-based analysis for detecting faults in induction motors. *IEEE Trans. Ind. Electron.* **2016**, *13*, 1291–1300. [CrossRef]
8. Riera-Guasp, M.; Pineda-Sanchez, M.; Pérez-Cruz, J.; Puche-Panadero, R.; Roger-Folch, J.; Antonino-Daviu, J.A. Diagnosis of induction motor faults via Gabor analysis of the current in transient regime. *IEEE Trans. Instrum. Meas.* **2012**, *61*, 1583–1596. [CrossRef]
9. Climente-Alarcon, V.; Antonino-Daviu, J.A.; Haavisto, A.; Arkkio, A. Diagnosis of induction motors under varying speed operation by principal slot harmonic tracking. *IEEE Trans. Ind. Appl.* **2015**, *51*, 3591–3599. [CrossRef]
10. Ali, M.Z.; Liang, X. Threshold-based induction motors single- and multifaults diagnosis using discrete wavelet transform and measured stator current signal. *Can. J. Electr. Comput. Eng.* **2020**, *43*, 136–145. [CrossRef]
11. Fan, H.; Shao, S.; Zhang, X.; Wan, X.; Cao, X.; Ma, H. Intelligent fault diagnosis of rolling bearing using FCM clustering of EMD-PWVD vibration images. *IEEE Access* **2020**, *8*, 45194–145206. [CrossRef]
12. Huo, Z.; Zhang, Y.; Francq, P.; Shu, L.; Huang, J. Incipient fault diagnosis of roller bearing using optimized wavelet transform based multi-speed vibration signatures. *IEEE Access* **2017**, *5*, 19442–19456. [CrossRef]

13. Trujillo-Guajardo, L.A.; Rodriguez-Maldonado, J.; Moonem, M.A.; Platas-Garza, M.A. A multiresolution Taylor–Kalman approach for broken rotor bar detection in cage induction motors. *IEEE Trans. Instrum. Meas.* **2018**, *67*, 1317–1328. [CrossRef]
14. Rabbi, S.F.; Little, M.L.; Saleh, S.A.; Rahman, M.A. A novel technique using multiresolution wavelet packet decomposition for real time diagnosis of hunting in line start IPM motor drives. *IEEE Trans. Ind. Appl.* **2017**, *53*, 3005–3019. [CrossRef]
15. Mishra, M.; Rout, P.K. Detection and classification of micro-grid faults based on HHT and machine learning techniques. *IET Gener. Transm. Distrib.* **2017**, *12*, 388–397. [CrossRef]
16. Alvarez-Gonzalez, F.; Griffo, A.; Wang, B. Permanent magnet synchronous machine stator windings fault detection by Hilbert-Huang transform. In Proceedings of the International Conference on Power Electronics, Machines and Drives, Liverpool, UK, 17–19 April 2018; pp. 3505–3509.
17. Esfahani, E.T.; Wang, S.; Sundararajan, V. Multisensor wireless system for eccentricity and bearing fault detection in induction motors. *IEEE/ASME Trans. Mech.* **2014**, *19*, 818–826. [CrossRef]
18. Espinosa, A.G.; Rosero, J.A.; Cusido, J.; Romeral, L.; Ortega, J.A. Fault detection by means of Hilbert–Huang transform of the stator current in a PMSM with demagnetization. *IEEE Trans. Energy Convers.* **2010**, *25*, 312–318. [CrossRef]
19. Oyamada, M. Extracting feature engineering knowledge from data science notebooks. In Proceedings of the IEEE International Conference on Big Data (Big Data), Los Angeles, CA, USA, 9–12 December 2019.
20. Al-Otaibi, R.; Jin, N.; Wilcox, T.; Flach, P. Feature construction and calibration for clustering daily load curves from smart-meter data. *IEEE Trans. Ind. Inform.* **2016**, *12*, 6452–6654. [CrossRef]
21. Neshatian, K.; Zhang, M.; Andreae, P. A filter approach to multiple feature construction for symbolic learning classifiers using genetic programming. *IEEE Trans. Evol. Comput.* **2012**, *16*, 645–661. [CrossRef]
22. Imani, M.; Ghassemian, H. Band clustering-based feature extraction for classification of hyperspectral images using limited training samples. *IEEE Geosci. Remote Sens. Lett.* **2014**, *11*, 1325–1329. [CrossRef]
23. Godse, R.; Bhat, S. Mathematical morphology-based feature-extraction technique for detection and classification of faults on power transmission line. *IEEE Access* **2020**, *8*, 38459–38471. [CrossRef]
24. Yang, H.; Meng, C.; Wang, C. Data-driven feature extraction for analog circuit fault diagnosis using 1-D convolutional neural network. *IEEE Access* **2020**, *8*, 18305–18315. [CrossRef]
25. Panigrahy, P.S.; Santra, D.; Chattopadhyay, P. Feature engineering in fault diagnosis of induction motor. In Proceedings of the 2017 3rd International Conference on Condition Assessment Techniques in Electrical Systems (CATCON), Rupnagar, India, 16–18 November 2017.
26. Rauber, T.W.; de Assis Boldt, F.; Varejão, F.M. Heterogeneous feature models and feature selection applied to bearing fault diagnosis. *IEEE Trans. Ind. Electron.* **2015**, *62*, 637–646. [CrossRef]
27. Van, M.; Kang, H.J. Bearing-fault diagnosis using non-local means algorithm and empirical mode decomposition-based feature extraction and two-stage feature selection. *Sci. Meas. Technol.* **2015**, *9*, 671–680. [CrossRef]
28. Lee, C.Y.; Wen, M.S. Establish induction motor fault diagnosis system based on feature selection approaches with MRA. *Processes* **2020**, *8*, 1055. [CrossRef]
29. Hu, B.; Li, X.; Sun, S.; Ratcliffe, M. Attention recognition in EEG-based affective learning research using CFS+KNN algorithm. *IEEE/ACM Trans. Comput. Biol. Bioinform.* **2018**, *15*, 38–45. [CrossRef]
30. Fu, R.; Wang, P.; Gao, Y.; Hua, X. A new feature selection method based on Relief and SVM-RFE. In Proceedings of the 2014 12th International Conference on Signal Processing (ICSP), Hangzhou, China, 19–23 October 2014.
31. Fu, R.; Wang, P.; Gao, Y.; Hua, X. A combination of relief feature selection and fuzzy k-nearest neighbor for plant species identification. In Proceedings of the 2016 International Conference on Advanced Computer Science and Information Systems (ICACSIS), Malang, Indonesia, 15–16 October 2016.
32. Huang, Z.; Yang, C.; Zhou, X.; Huang, T. A hybrid feature selection method based on binary state transition algorithm and ReliefF. *IEEE J. Biomed. Health Inform.* **2019**, *23*, 1888–1898. [CrossRef]
33. Singh, A.; Thakur, N.; Sharma, A. A review of supervised machine learning algorithms. In Proceedings of the 2016 3rd International Conference on Computing for Sustainable Global Development (INDIACom), New Delhi, India, 16–18 March 2016; pp. 1310–1315.
34. Wilamowski, B.M.; Yu, H. Improved computation for Levenberg-Marquardt training. *IEEE Trans. Neural Netw.* **2010**, *21*, 930–937. [CrossRef]
35. Fu, X.; Li, S.; Fairbank, M.; Wunsch, D.C.; Alonso, E. Training recurrent neural networks with the Levenberg—Marquardt Algorithm for optimal control of a grid-connected converter. *IEEE Trans. Neural Netw. Learn. Syst.* **2014**, *26*, 1900–1912. [CrossRef]
36. Lv, C.; Xing, Y.; Zhang, J.; Na, X.; Li, Y.; Liu, T.; Cao, D.; Wang, F.-Y. Levenberg–Marquardt backpropagation training of multilayer neural networks for state estimation of a safety-critical cyber-physical system. *IEEE Trans. Ind. Inform.* **2018**, *14*, 3436–3446. [CrossRef]
37. Ngia, L.S.H.; Sjoberg, J. Efficient training of neural nets for nonlinear adaptive filtering using a recursive Levenberg–Marquardt algorithm. *IEEE Trans. Signal Process.* **2000**, *48*, 1915–1927. [CrossRef]
38. Mallat, G. A theory for multi-resolution signal decomposition (The wavelet representation). *IEEE Trans. Pattern Anal. Mach. Intell.* **1989**, *PAMI-11*, 674–693. [CrossRef]
39. Yi, L.; Hao, A.; Shuangshuang, B. Hilbert-Huang transform and the application. In Proceedings of the 2020 IEEE International Conference on Artificial Intelligence and Information Systems (ICAIIS), Dalian, China, 20–22 March 2020; pp. 534–539.

40. Lee, C.Y.; Tuegeh, M. An optimal solution for smooth and non-smooth cost functions-based economic dispatch problem. *Energies* **2020**, *13*, 3721. [CrossRef]
41. Fernández-Martínez, J.L.; García-Gonzalo, E. Stochastic stability analysis of the linear continuous and discrete PSO models. *IEEE Trans. Evol. Comput.* **2011**, *15*, 405–423. [CrossRef]

Article

HIFA-LPR: High-Frequency Augmented License Plate Recognition in Low-Quality Legacy Conditions via Gradual End-to-End Learning

Sung-Jin Lee [1,†], Jun-Seok Yun [1,†], Eung Joo Lee [2] and Seok Bong Yoo [1,*]

1. Department of Artificial Intelligence Convergence, Chonnam National University, Gwangju 61186, Korea; 218824@jnu.ac.kr (S.-J.L.); 218062@jnu.ac.kr (J.-S.Y.)
2. Department of Radiology, MGH and Harvard Medical School, Boston, MA 02115, USA; elee66@mgh.harvard.edu
* Correspondence: sbyoo@jnu.ac.kr; Tel.: +82-62-530-3437
† These authors contributed equally to this work.

Abstract: Scene text detection and recognition, such as automatic license plate recognition, is a technology utilized in various applications. Although numerous studies have been conducted to improve recognition accuracy, accuracy decreases when low-quality legacy license plate images are input into a recognition module due to low image quality and a lack of resolution. To obtain better recognition accuracy, this study proposes a high-frequency augmented license plate recognition model in which the super-resolution module and the license plate recognition module are integrated and trained collaboratively via a proposed gradual end-to-end learning-based optimization. To optimally train our model, we propose a holistic feature extraction method that effectively prevents generating grid patterns from the super-resolved image during the training process. Moreover, to exploit high-frequency information that affects the performance of license plate recognition, we propose a license plate recognition module based on high-frequency augmentation. Furthermore, we propose a gradual end-to-end learning process based on weight freezing with three steps. Our three-step methodological approach can properly optimize each module to provide robust recognition performance. The experimental results show that our model is superior to existing approaches in low-quality legacy conditions on UFPR and Greek vehicle datasets.

Keywords: gradual end-to-end learning; single-image super-resolution; automatic license plate recognition; low-quality legacy conditions; holistic feature extraction; high-frequency augmentation

MSC: 68T45

1. Introduction

1.1. License Plate Recognition in a Real-World Scenario

Scene text detection and recognition is a task that detects text regions and recognizes letters and numbers in image frames. This task can be utilized in various applications in smart parking and driving such as illegal parking detection and traffic sign recognition. When this task is applied to image frames in real-world scenarios, it does not assure satisfactory performance due to the varying resolutions of the input images. Specifically, this is a critical issue for the license plate recognition task. As shown in Figure 1, the plate regions detected in vehicle LP images may have small resolutions depending on the distance between the camera and the vehicle object. Even if the detected region images are input directly to the LP recognition module, it causes severe recognition accuracy degradation, as shown in the result of the low-resolved LP recognition approach in Figure 1. To address this problem, a bicubic-interpolation-based approach can be considered. However, this approach also generates low recognition accuracy with resized low-quality images, as shown in the result of the bicubic-interpolation-based LP recognition approach in Figure 1. To acquire high-quality LP images, super-resolution (SR) techniques can be considered. Nevertheless, conventional SR modules may not be suitable for enhancing recognition accuracy because the SR modules only focus on improving image quality, not recognition. For this reason, such an approach causes insufficient recognition performance, as shown in the result of the super-resolved LP recognition approach in Figure 1. Hence, in the real world, there is a necessity for an integrated model to improve LP recognition accuracy by restoring LP images in terms of LP recognition.

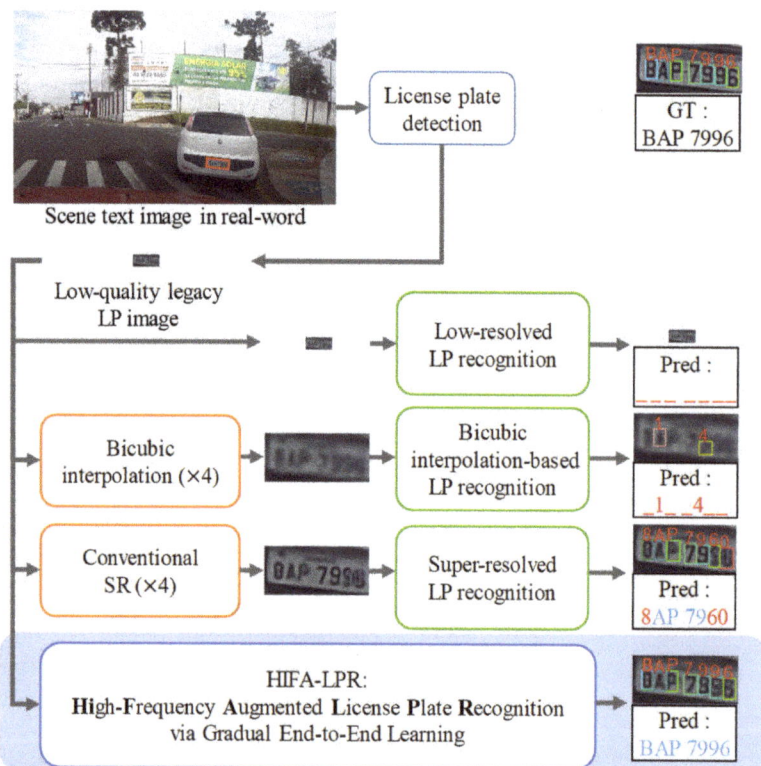

Figure 1. Examples of LP recognition approaches in a real-world scenario. Our proposed HIFA-LPR model outperforms conventional approaches. "_" denotes a missing character recognition. Red character denotes incorrect prediction. Blue character denotes correct prediction. "GT" denotes ground truth. "Pred" denotes the prediction result.

1.2. High-Frequency Augmented License Plate Recognition Model

To tackle this issue in Section 1.1, we propose a high-frequency augmented license plate recognition (HIFA-LPR) model. The HIFA-LPR model can improve the input image resolution optimally from the point of view of LP recognition and robustly classify the LP characters in the optimal super-resolved image, as shown in the last row of Figure 1. To this end, we suggest gradual end-to-end learning so that LP recognition accuracy is robust to input data with various image qualities and resolutions. When performing the gradual end-to-end learning method, most SR modules are trained with a small-sized image patch such as about 8×8 pixels. However, this patch-based SR approach is not suitable for end-to-end learning due to the grid patterns generated by the SR module. Since grid patterns cut off characters, the patch-based SR approaches cannot preserve character information that is closely related to LP recognition accuracy. Hence, we propose a holistic image feature extraction method that is adopted for preventing grid pattern generation while preserving character information in the SR module.

In recognition tasks, high-frequency information, such as edge, contrast, and texture, is closely related to recognition performance. For this reason, we propose an LP recognition module based on high-frequency augmentation to exploit enhanced high-frequency information. Our LP recognition module mainly consists of high-frequency augmentation blocks (HAB). We utilize the discrete cosine transform (DCT) principle that the component corresponds to the higher-frequency component as it goes to the right and bottom directions in the DCT domain. In the HAB, we extract the desired high-frequency components using the DCT principle and augment the high frequency of the feature map.

The training process of HIFA-LPR consists of three steps based on a weight freezing technique. First, the SR and the LP recognition modules are independently trained for stabilizing the training process. Second, to properly restore images in terms of LP recognition, the SR module is trained with SR loss and recognition loss while the LP recognition module weights are frozen. Third, the recognition module is trained with super-resolved LP images for enriching LP recognition accuracy. By using the weight freezing technique, we enhance the collaborative correlations between each module. To verify HIFA-LPR, we perform experiments with SR and recognition performance in low-quality legacy conditions using the UFPR [1] and Greek vehicle datasets [2]. The UFPR dataset is organized with Brazilian LP images and character labels for detecting LP and recognizing LP characters. The Greek vehicle dataset is organized with Greek LP images for LP detection only. To utilize this dataset for low-resolution (LR) recognition, we build the LP recognition dataset by manually annotating each LP character in the LP images. The contributions of this study can be summarized as follows:

- A gradual end-to-end learning-based optimization method that collaboratively learns the SR and LP recognition modules is designed. We suggest this method in three steps based on the weight freezing technique.
- An LP recognition module based on high-frequency augmentation is proposed to improve the recognition performance using HABs. The HAB extracts the desired high-frequency components using the DCT principle and augments the high frequency of the feature map.
- A novel holistic image feature extraction method is proposed to prevent generating grid patterns during the SR module. This enables the utilization of more complete character information than using patch-based SR with the character area cut off.
- To evaluate the performance of the proposed HIFA-LPR model, we build the LP recognition dataset by manually annotating 2415 characters in 345 images from the Greek vehicle dataset. Our model is superior to existing state-of-the-art works in low-quality legacy conditions. Even if the LP image resolution is 19×6, our model provides robust recognition performance relatively.

2. Related Works

2.1. Single-Image Super-Resolution

Single-image SR is a method to predict a high-resolution (HR) image from the corresponding LR image. However, single-image SR is an ill-posed problem because there are various methods of degradation while reducing the image quality from HR to LR. To address this problem, several studies have been conducted with deep-learning-based methods. A super-resolution convolutional neural network (SRCNN) [3] proposed the SR method based on convolutional neural networks for the first time, and it showed innovative restoration performance. A very deep convolutional network (VDSR) [4] proposed a deeper SR neural network with a residual learning strategy. An efficient sub-pixel convolutional neural network (ESPCNN) [5] proposed a pixel-shuffling layer that can learn an up-sampling module. Using this layer, ESPCNN solved the limitation of feature map magnification in the neural network. A deep back-projection network (DBPN) [6] proposed an iterative up-sampling and down-sampling module that repeatedly stacks the image upscaling and downscaling layers. A residual channel attention network (RCAN) [7] proposed a channel attention mechanism that helps to create a deep model. A dual regression network (DRN) [8] proposed a closed circuit and added an LR domain loss function that calculates the difference from the input image. A residual dense network (RDN) [9] proposed a neural network that can learn the hierarchical representation of all feature maps through the residual density structure. A second-order attention network (SAN) [10] showed outstanding performance by strongly improving the representation of image feature maps and learning the interdependencies between feature maps. Meta-transfer learning for zero-shot SR (MZSR) [11] proposed a flexible algorithm for restoring images that are blurred under actual blur conditions by training on various kernels. Shifted windows using image restoration (SwinIR) [12] proposed the SR method for image restoration by using a shifted windows (Swin) transformer which performs reliable performance on high-level vision tasks. By using this method, SwinIR outperforms the state-of-the-art SR method.

However, these SR modules only focus on image reconstruction. Since the SR modules cannot appropriately restore the image in terms of LP recognition, the recognition performance is degraded. To obtain better recognition performance, we propose a stepwise gradual end-to-end learning method using combined loss and weight freezing. Specifically, the above SR modules [3–12] generate grid patterns during the end-to-end training process due to patch-extraction-based approaches. The extracted patches that include insufficient character information hinder the optimization of the LP recognition module. To address this issue, we propose the holistic-feature-extraction-based SR module that takes the whole LP image as input. Since our method uses full character information, our SR module can be trained to improve LP character recognition compared with existing patch-extraction-based SR modules.

2.2. License Plate Recognition

LP recognition is the task to recognize the LP characters in the vehicle image. Various studies have been conducted to boost LP character recognition performance. OpenALPR [13] is the LP recognition API and it is based on OpenCV and TesseractOCR [14]. Lee et al. [15] mentioned that LP recognition performance is improved with the SR mode when the LP image is too small to recognize with the recognition module, which has a fixed input size. This shows that the SR method can improve the LP recognition performance with LR images. A super-resolved recognition method [16] was proposed for LR image character recognition and the data augmentation algorithm for left-right reversal. Wang et al. [17] proposed a method that can exploit a synthetic data generation approach based on a generative adversarial network (GAN) for a data generation procedure to obtain a large representative LP dataset. Hamdi et al. [18] proposed double GAN for image enhancement with LP images. They performed SR training used for constructive LP denoising and SR to increase the LP recognition accuracy when an LR image was used for recognition. Wang et al. [19] proposed a convolutional recursive neural network followed by the connectionist temporal classification for LP character recognition. Combining with multitask cascaded convolutional neural network detection, they proposed a recognition module that can detect the LP region and classify characters of LP.

LPRNet [20] proposed the LP character recognition module with the end-to-end method for automatic LP recognition (ALPR) without preliminary character segmentation. Moreover, this method is lightweight enough to run on a variety of platforms, including embedded devices. Laroca et al. [1] proposed the LP dataset with 4500 fully annotated images focused on usual and different real-world scenarios to help address the inadequacy of an LP database and to address the low-recognition problem. Nguyen et al. [21] proposed the LP detection and LP recognition module which is embedded with the spatial transformer to increase the accuracy of LP character detection and recognition with the CCPD dataset [22]. Xu et al. [23] proposed the location-aware 2D attention-based recognition module that recognizes both single-line and double-line plates with perspective deformation. Vasek et al. [24] proposed the LP recognition neural network with the CNN method in LR frames. Lee et al. [25] proposed the GAN-based SR method that can be adopted in LP-recognition-challenged environments. Zhang et al. [26] proposed the multitask generative adversarial network (MTGAN) which combines the SR and recognition modules in a one-step end-to-end learning method. Li et al. [27] proposed the unified deep neural network for the LP image localizing and recognizing the characters at once in a single forward pass. This method operates the LP detection and recognition jointly by a single network to avoid intermediate error accumulation and accelerate the LP processing speed. However, these methods are not the end-to-end training method for LP recognition that cannot guarantee the training stability for stable performance. Moreover, these methods cannot make the recognition module be optimized so that the loss function of LP recognition approaches the global minimum. Zhang et al. [28] proposed the robust LP recognition module in the wild situation. This method also proposed the GAN-based LP generation engine to reduce the exhausting human annotation work. However, there is significant performance degradation when these methods are applied to the image frames in real-world scenarios because the input images have various image resolutions and qualities.

Even if the SR-based approach [15–17,24,25] is applied to the low-quality legacy image, it produces insufficient performance due to irreverent relationships with the recognition module. Moreover, other approaches [18,26] tried to figure it out using the single-step end-to-end learning method. However, these methods based on single-step end-to-end learning cannot optimally strengthen the collaborative correlations between the SR and LP recognition modules. Meanwhile, these LP recognition modules [13–28] do not have any module that augments the high frequency of characters, which is the main clue of LP recognition. For this reason, the LP recognition performance of the referred LP recognition module is not satisfactory at recognizing low-quality characters.

To tackle this issue, in this study, we propose a gradual end-to-end learning method with three steps: Step 1: the independent training of the SR module and LP recognition module; Step 2: SR module training with LP recognition module weight freezing; Step 3: LP recognition module training with SR module weight freezing.

Furthermore, we propose the LP recognition module based on high-frequency augmentation. Our LP module mainly consists of HAB which reinforces the high frequencies of precise character components such as edge, texture, and contrast. Due to HAB, our LP recognition can provide robust recognition performance even if low-quality legacy LP images are inputted.

3. Proposed Method

In this section, we present our methodological contributions. First, a holistic image feature-extraction SR module is proposed to guarantee a stable end-to-end learning process, unlike DBPN [6]. Second, an LP recognition module based on high-frequency augmentation is proposed to strengthen the high-frequency component for LP recognition accuracy, unlike the state-of-the-art object recognition module, Yolov5 [29]. Our LP recognition module mainly consists of HAB. The proposed HAB extracts only the desired frequency by using our new DCT-based frequency mask. Finally, a gradual end-to-end learning process with three steps based on weight freezing is suggested to strengthen the collaborative correlations with each module.

3.1. Architecture of Each Module in HIFA-LPR Model

In this section, we introduce the HIFA-LPR model architecture. The HIFA-LPR model consists of a holistic-feature-extraction-based SR module and an LP recognition module based on high-frequency augmentation.

Holistic-Feature-Extraction-based SR Module. The existing SR methods [3–12] randomly extract patches with about 8×8 pixels by cropping the LR image, due to a lack of computing power. The extracted patches pass through the SR module and LP recognition module in an end-to-end learning process. However, character information is not fully considered because of the truncated character information. It causes severe training performance degradation of the recognition module in the end-to-end learning process. On the other hand, our holistic-feature-extraction-based SR ensures the training stability of the LP recognition module because our module utilizes the character position and full character information by using the whole image. Due to a lack of computing power, we set the training batch size to 1 during the end-to-end learning process.

In this study, considering end-to-end learning for super-resolved character recognition, we propose the holistic-feature-extraction-based SR that takes the whole LP image as input. The DBPN [6] is benchmarked to improve the quality of LP images. Our holistic feature extraction consists of a 3 × 3 convolution layer and a 1 × 1 convolution layer. Unlike the original DBPN method, our SR method takes the whole LP image and performs SR by extracting holistic features and repeatedly upscaling and downscaling the holistic features through the convolution layers, as shown in Figure 2. The SR module extracts the feature map of the input image. The extracted feature maps pass through the up-blocks and down-blocks to obtain feature maps of 64 channels per block. The SR module connects the feature maps obtained for each block so that feature maps are passed to the final output layer, and then, the super-resolved RGB 3-channel image is acquired. This SR module can magnify the image resolution and improve the image quality. However, training stability cannot be guaranteed since patch-based SR models generate grid patterns in the super-resolved image. Such generated grid patterns cause restoration performance degradation. As shown in Figure 3a, since the patch-based end-to-end training process loses character information, it causes severe training performance degradation. It is a critical issue in terms of LP recognition. In addition, LP recognition model training is impossible with the patch that has a small part of the input image. On the other hand, our holistic image feature extraction consisting of a 3 × 3 convolution layer and a 1 × 1 convolution layer preserves character information in the super-resolved image while alleviating annoying grid patterns, as shown in Figure 3b. By using this method, our LP recognition module can be trained with a stable training process. Algorithm 1 shows the pseudocode of the holistic-feature-extraction-based SR module for scale factor of ×4. Our holistic-feature-extraction-based SR module utilizes character position and character information by using the whole image, unlike DBPN.

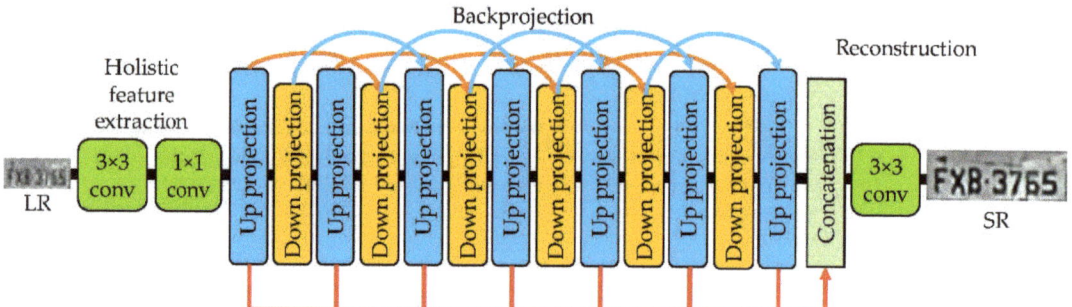

Figure 2. Architecture of holistic-feature-extraction-based SR module.

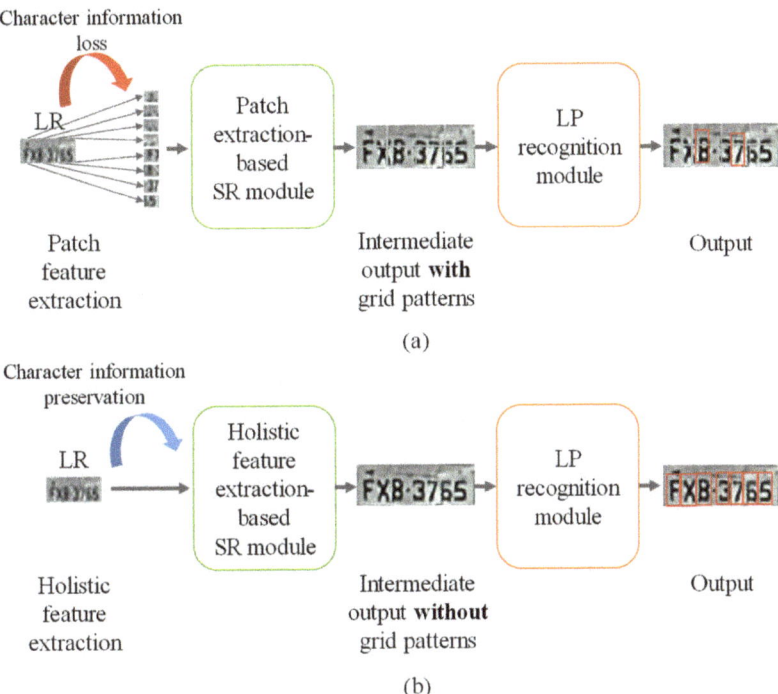

Figure 3. (**a**) Diagram of the patch-based end-to-end training process. (**b**) Diagram of the holistic-feature-based end-to-end training process. In output images, red boxes denote the detected character region.

LP Recognition Module based on High-frequency Augmentation. In the LP recognition task, high-frequency information, such as edge, contrast, and texture, affects LP recognition performance. Hence, to improve LP recognition performance, high-frequency components should be appropriately augmented. To this end, we propose the LP recognition module which is benchmarked and improved from Yolov5 [29]. Since there is no correlation between adjacent numbers or characters in a single LP, our proposed LP recognition module independently detects and recognizes each character in the LP instead of a whole-character-based recognition. To this end, we adopt and improve Yolov5, which is known to provide state-of-the-art accuracy in the object detection field. We note that we utilize high-frequency components to promote LP recognition accuracy, unlike Yolov5.

To augment the high-frequency component, it is necessary to extract only the desired high frequency. Therefore, we utilize the DCT, which has the principle that low-frequency components are concentrated on the upper left and high-frequency components are concentrated on the lower right in the DCT spectrum. A two-dimensional image of size $N \times M$ can be transformed into the frequency domain through DCT, as shown in Equation (1).

Algorithm 1. The pseudocode of the holistic-feature-extraction-based SR module for scale factor ×4.

LR: LR images
W: Width of LR image
H: Height of LR image
$\mathbf{F}^{(W,H)}(k)$: Feature map with $W \times H$ pixels at stage k
G_k: Convolutional layers at stage k
P_k: Deconvolutional layers at stage k
N: Number of training images
I: Number of iterations in the SR module
set * = Convolution operation
set Conv_3 = 3 × 3 convolution layer
set Conv_1 = 1 × 1 convolution layer

do:
1: For i = 1 to N do:
2:    //holistic feature extraction process of the single image
3:    $\mathbf{F}^{(W,H)}(0) = \text{Conv\_1}(\text{Conv\_3}(\mathbf{LR}_i^{(W,H)}))$
4:    For k = 1 to I do:
5:      $\mathbf{F}^{(4W,4H)}(k) = \mathbf{F}^{(W,H)}(k-1) * \mathbf{P}_k$
6:      $\mathbf{F}^{(W,H)}(k) = \mathbf{F}^{(4W,4H)}(k) * \mathbf{G}_k$
7:      $\mathbf{F}^{(4W,4H)}(k) = \mathbf{F}^{(W,H)}(k) * \mathbf{P}_k$
8:      if k > 1:
9:         $\mathbf{F}^{(4W,4H)}(k) = \text{concatenation}(\mathbf{F}^{(4W,4H)}(k-1), \mathbf{F}^{(4W,4H)}(k))$
10:     $\mathbf{F}^{(W,H)}(k) = \mathbf{F}^{(4W,4H)}(k) * \mathbf{G}_k$
11:     $\mathbf{F}^{(4W,4H)}(k) = \mathbf{F}^{(W,H)}(k) * \mathbf{P}_k$
12:     $\mathbf{F}^{(W,H)}(k) = \mathbf{F}^{(4W,4H)}(k) * \mathbf{G}_k$
13:     if k > 1:
14:        $\mathbf{F}^{(W,H)}(k) = \text{concatenation}(\mathbf{F}^{(W,H)}(k-1), \mathbf{F}^{(W,H)}(k))$
15:     $\mathbf{F}^{(W,H)} = \mathbf{F}^{(W,H)}(k)$
16:    end for
17:    $\mathbf{F}^{(4W,4H)} = \mathbf{F}^{(W,H)} * \mathbf{P}$
18:    $\mathbf{F}^{(W,H)} = \mathbf{F}^{(4W,4H)} * \mathbf{G}$
19:    $\mathbf{F}^{(4W,4H)} = \mathbf{F}^{(W,H)} * \mathbf{P}$
20:    //Convert SR feature map to SR image
21:    $\mathbf{S}_i^{(4W,4H)} = \text{Conv\_3}(\mathbf{F}^{(4W,4H)})$
22:    return $\mathbf{S}_i^{(4W,4H)}$
23: end for

$$\mathbf{F}(u,v) = \alpha(u)\beta(v)\sum_{i=0}^{N}\sum_{j=0}^{M}\mathbf{f}(i,j)\gamma(i,j,u,v) \tag{1}$$

$$\gamma(i,j,u,v) = \cos\left(\frac{\pi(2i+1)u}{2N}\right)\cos\left(\frac{\pi(2j+1)v}{2M}\right) \tag{2}$$

$$\alpha(u) = \begin{cases} \sqrt{\frac{1}{N}}, & u = 0 \\ \sqrt{\frac{2}{N}}, & u \neq 0 \end{cases} \tag{3}$$

$$\beta(v) = \begin{cases} \sqrt{\frac{1}{M}}, & v = 0 \\ \sqrt{\frac{2}{M}}, & v \neq 0 \end{cases} \tag{4}$$

$$\mathbf{f}(i,j) = \sum_{u=0}^{N}\sum_{v=0}^{M}\alpha(u)\beta(v)\mathbf{F}(u,v)\gamma(x,y,u,v) \tag{5}$$

In Equation (1), $\mathbf{f}(i,j)$ is the pixel value of the (i,j) position of the image, and $\mathbf{F}(u,v)$ is the DCT coefficient value at the (u,v) position. Equations (2)–(4) show the definitions of the cosine basis function and regularization constant, respectively. As shown in Equation (5), the frequency domain signal can be transformed into the spatial domain using a two-dimensional inverse DCT (IDCT).

By using the DCT principle, we can dynamically extract high-frequency components via a frequency mask $\mathcal{M}$. The frequency mask $\mathcal{M}$ consists of a binary value and is determined depending on the hyper-parameter ε as given below.

$$\mathcal{M}(x,y) = \begin{cases} 0, & y < -x + 2\varepsilon h \\ 1, & \text{otherwise} \end{cases}, \qquad (6)$$

where h denotes the height of the input image and x, y denote the horizontal and vertical coordinates of $\mathcal{M}$, respectively. The hyper-parameter ε ranges from 0 to 1. Since the more directed from the top left to the bottom right in the zigzag direction is, the higher the frequency component in the DCT domain is, we can extract the desired high-frequency components. Figure 4 shows examples of $\mathcal{M}$ according hyper-parameter ε.

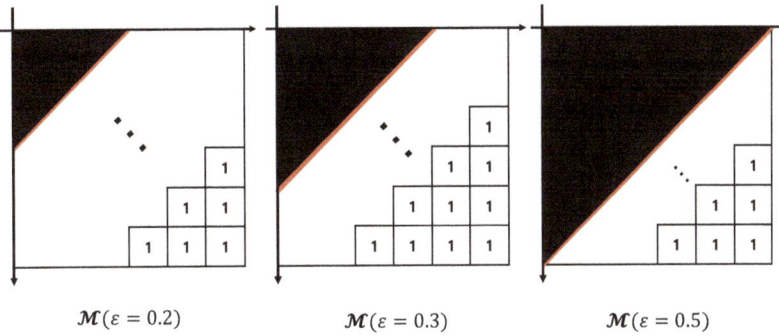

Figure 4. Examples of $\mathcal{M}$ according to ε. Because of the larger hyper-parameter ε, more low-frequency components are masked. We empirically set ε to 0.2.

Our LP recognition module mainly consists of HABs which reinforce the high frequency of the feature map. As shown in Figure 5, the HAB receives the feature map as input. Then, the feature map is transformed into the DCT domain using 2D-DCT. To extract the high frequency in the DCT domain, the element-wise product of the feature map and frequency mask $\mathcal{M}$ determined by hyper-parameter ε is conducted. The extracted high-frequency feature map is transformed into the spatial domain by 2D-IDCT. The obtained high-frequency feature map is added to the original feature map.

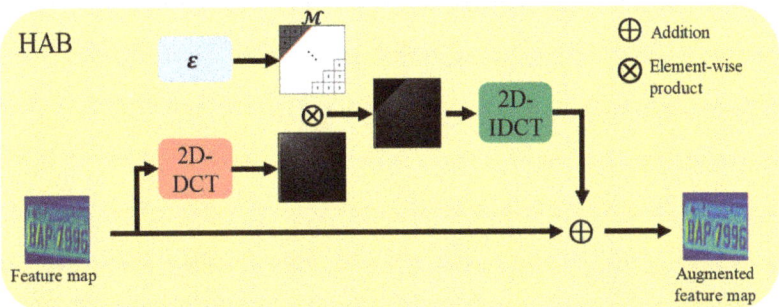

Figure 5. Architecture of HAB.

Our LP recognition module based on high-frequency augmentation is illustrated in Figure 6. The Focus layer downscales the input image with as little information loss as possible for fast recognition by transforming input image space into depth. By transporting to a convolution batch normalization leaky ReLU (CBL) and a cross-stage partial (CSP) layer, feature maps obtain richer gradient combinations while maintaining lower computations. Moreover, by splitting the gradient flow, CSP reduces the computation of the architecture with the residual unit, which maintains the gradient of the neural network. Then, the feature map passes through the spatial pyramid pooling (SPP) layer to generate a fixed one-dimensional array as input to the fully connected layer to predict. The up-sample block performs up-sampling of the feature map to expand the feature map size, and it allows for small-object detection. Before the concatenation of each feature map, the proposed HAB is employed to exploit enhanced high-frequency information. Finally, the LP recognition module can obtain three different-sized feature maps to detect and recognize the characters of the LP image. The character recognition loss (localization, classification, and confidence losses) is obtained by comparing the result of the LP recognition module with the ground truth label. For training for LP recognition, we define 10 numerical classes for 0–9 and 26 character classes for A–Z. Algorithm 2 shows the pseudocode of the LP recognition module based on high-frequency augmentation.

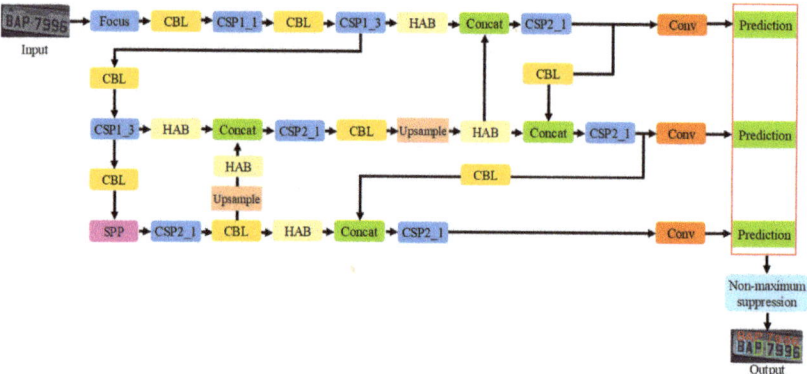

Figure 6. Flowchart of LP recognition module based on high-frequency augmentation.

Algorithm 2. The pseudocode of the LP recognition module based on high-frequency augmentation.

I: Input LP image
M: Frequency mask as in Equation (6)
set Conv = Convolution layer
set CBL = Convolution, batch normalization, leaky ReLU layers
set Up-sample = Bicubic interpolation
set • = Element-wise product
set CSP1 = Combination of CBL and a residual unit layer
set CSP2 = Combination of convolution and a residual unit layer

---

do:
1:   //Convert the input image to four depth maps by focus layer
2:   D_1, D_2, D_3, D_4 = channel slice(**I**)
3:   F = concatenation(D_1, D_2, D_3, D_4)
4:   //Feature extraction.
5:   F = CBL(F)
6:   //CSP layer

7: F_1, F_2 = channel slice(F)
8: F_1 = CBL(F_1)
9: F = concatenation(F_1, F_2)
10: F = CSP1_3(F)
11: //Getting three feature maps with different sizes
12: F_1 = CBL(F)
13: F_2 = CBL(CSP1_1(CBL(F_1)))
14: F_3 = CBL(CSP2_1(CBL(SPP(CBL(CBL(F_2))))))
15: F_3 = Up-sample(F_3)
16: //High-frequency augmentation
17: F_3_dct = DCT(F_3) as in Equation (1)
18: F_3_H = F_3_dct • M
19: F_3_H = IDCT(F_3_H) as in Equation (5)
20: F_3_Aug = F_3 + F_3_H
21: //Concatenate the F_2 and F_3_Aug
22: C_1 = concatenation(CBL(F_2), F_3_Aug))
23: F_1 = CBL(F_1)
24: //High-frequency augmentation
25: F_1_dct = DCT(F_1) as in Equation (1)
26: F_1_H = F_1 • M
27: F_1_H = IDCT(F_1_H) as in Equation (5)
28: F_1_Aug = F_1 + F_1_H
29: C_1_dct = DCT(C_1) as in Equation (1)
30: C_1_H = C_1_dct • M
31: C_1_H = IDCT(C_1_H) as in Equation (5)
32: C_1_Aug = C_1 + C_1_H
33: //Concatenate F_1_Aug and C_1_Aug
34: C_2 = concatenation(CBL(F_1_Aug), Up-sample(CBL(CSP2_1(C_1_Aug))))
35: //Getting first LP recognition feature map
36: P_1 = Conv(CBL(CSP2_1(C_2)))
37: //Concatenate the C_1 and C_2
38: C_3 = concatenation(CBL(CSP2_1(C_1)), Conv(CBL(CSP2_1(C_2))))
39: //Getting second LP recognition feature map
40: P_2 = Conv(CBL(CSP2_1(C_3)))
41: //Concatenate the high-frequency augmented F_3 and the C_3
42: C_4 = concatenation(F_3, CBL(CSP2_1(C_3)))
43: //Getting third LP recognition feature map
44: P_3 = Conv(CBL(CSP2_1(C_4)))
45: //Calculating the confidence of each output feature map P_1, P_2, P_3.
46: **Output** = Non-maximum suppression (P_1, P_2, P_3)

3.2. Gradual End-to-End Learning Process Based on Weight Freezing

A schematic diagram of the gradual end-to-end learning method is shown in Figure 7. We implemented the training process based on weight freezing in Steps 1, 2, and 3 as follows. The gradual end-to-end learning process based on weight freezing is one of our methodological contributions.

Step 1 process. Step 1 requires the pretrained weights of both modules to guarantee optimized performance. As shown in Figure 7a, we independently train the SR and LP recognition modules using SR loss and LP recognition loss, respectively. The SR loss $Loss_{SR}$ reduces the L1 difference in pixel values between SR images and HR images. The $Loss_{SR}$ is defined as

$$Loss_{SR} = \sum_{i=1}^{N} |HR_i - f(LR_i)|, \qquad (7)$$

where N is the number of training images, LR_i is the i-th LR training image, $f(LR_i)$ is the SR result of LR_i, and HR_i is the i-th HR training image corresponding to the SR image $f(LR_i)$.

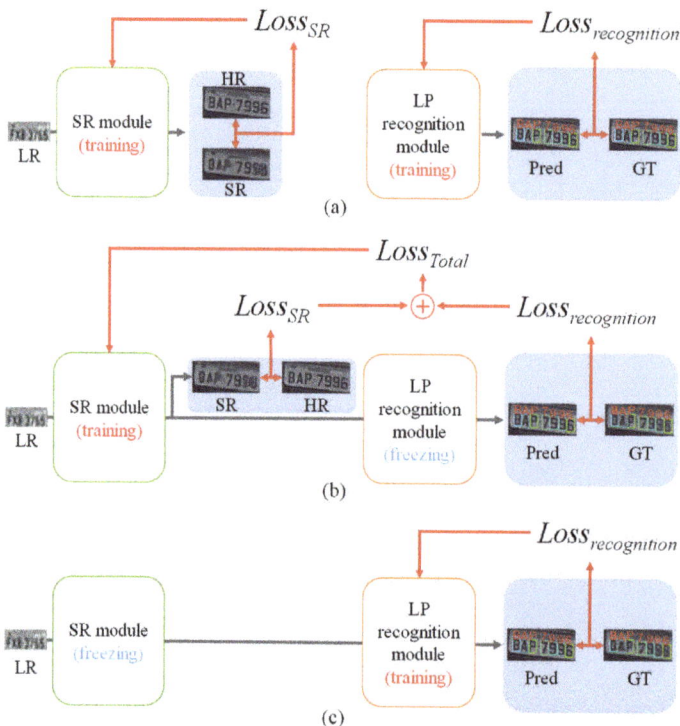

Figure 7. Flowchart of gradual end-to-end learning method. (**a**) Step 1: Independent training of the SR module and LP recognition module. (**b**) Step 2: SR module training while freezing LP recognition module. (**c**) Step 3: LP recognition module training while freezing SR module. "GT" denotes ground truth. "Pred" denotes the prediction result.

The LP recognition loss $Loss_{recognition}$ consists of localization, confidence, and classification losses [29]. The loss function is defined as

$$Loss_{recognition} = \lambda_{coord} \sum_{i=0}^{S^2} \sum_{j=0}^{B} 1_{ij}^{obj} [(x_i - \hat{x}_i)^2 + (y_i - \hat{y}_i)^2]$$

$$+ \lambda_{coord} \sum_{i=0}^{S^2} \sum_{j=0}^{B} 1_{ij}^{obj} [(\sqrt{w_i} - \sqrt{\hat{w}_i})^2 + [(\sqrt{h_i} - \sqrt{\hat{h}_i})^2] \quad (8)$$

$$+ \sum_{i=0}^{S^2} \sum_{j=0}^{B} 1_{ij}^{obj} (C_i - \hat{C}_i)^2 + \lambda_{noobj} \sum_{i=0}^{S^2} \sum_{j=0}^{B} 1_{ij}^{noobj} (C_i - \hat{C}_i)^2 + \sum_{i=0}^{S^2} 1_i^{obj} \sum_{c \in classes} (p_i(c) - \hat{p}_i(c))^2,$$

where S^2 denotes the grid cell for recognition. This grid cell gets a value of one if the LP character is recognized and zero otherwise. λ_{coord} denotes the constants to take into account more aspects of the loss function. The first and second lines denote the localization loss that computes the error of the position of the bounding box for accurate box detection. x_i denotes the horizontal coordinate of the i-th input image, y_i denotes the vertical coordinate of the i-th input image, w_i denotes the width of the i-th image, and h_i denotes the height of the i-th image. The LP recognition module calculates the sum of squared errors for the x_i, y_i, w_i, and h_i between the predicted bounding box of the LP recognition module and the ground truth. C_i denotes the confidence of the class in the i-th image grid box. This C_i is a probability value between zero and one that is determined when a character is detected in the box. When no character is detected, λ_{noobj} is used for the LP recognition loss. $p_i(c)$ denotes the confidence of the detected class of the i-th image.

Step 2 process. Step 2 is constructed to associate the irrelevant SR modules with the LP recognition module based on the weight freezing method. The SR and LP recognition losses are summed to strengthen collaborative correlations with each other. To generate images that are robust to LP recognition, the summed loss is backpropagated to the SR module, as shown in Figure 7b. In this process, if the parameters of the LP recognition module are changed, the end-to-end learning process cannot be performed properly. Therefore, weights for the LP recognition module are frozen during the training process. Using this process, the SR module is trained so that it reduces both the SR and LP recognition losses. Then, we obtain SR weights that can restore the super-resolved image to improve LP recognition accuracy. The summed loss is calculated as

$$Loss_{Total} = \alpha \times Loss_{SR} + Loss_{recognition}, \qquad (9)$$

where α is a hyper-parameter that scales the SR loss. In Step 2, α is set to 0.1 to equalize the scales between $Loss_{SR}$ and $Loss_{recognition}$.

Step 3 process. Step 3 is designed by converting LP recognition module freezing to SR module freezing, as shown in Figure 7c. Although the SR module reconstructs the image to improve LP recognition accuracy, the LP recognition module is not yet adapted to the enhanced super-resolved image. To address this issue, the super-resolved image is used to train the LP recognition module using $Loss_{Total}$ with $\alpha = 0$. Through this, the LP recognition module presents superior recognition accuracy to other existing approaches.

As shown in Algorithm 3, a pseudocode capable of gradual end-to-end learning based on weight freezing is implemented.

Algorithm 3. A pseudocode of the gradual end-to-end learning method based on weight freezing.

L: LR image
H: HR image
N: Number of training images
W_{SR}: SR weights
W_{LP}: LP recognition weights
do:
set SR = SR module of gradual end-to-end learning method
set LP = LP recognition module of gradual end-to-end learning method

---

(Step 1) Independent training of SR for getting initial weights
1: For $p = 1$ to N do:
2:     **S** = SR(**L**)
3:     $Loss_{SR} = |\mathbf{H} - \mathbf{S}|_1$ as in (7)
4:     $grad_{SR}$ = Backpropagate (SR, $Loss_{SR}$)
5:     $W_{SR} \leftarrow W_{SR} - grad_{SR}$
6: end for
7: return W_{SR}
Independent training of LP
8: For $q = 1$ to N do:
9:     **H** = Bicubic_interpolation(**H**, 256)
10:    $label_{pred}$ = LP(**H**)
11:    $Loss_{recognition} = Loss(label_{pred}, label_{GT})$ as in (8)

```
12:     grad_LP = Backpropagate (LP, Loss_recognition)
13:     W_LP ← W_LP − grad_LP
14: end for
15: return W_LP
```

(Step 2) Freeze LP with W_LP and Train SR.
SR loss calculation
```
16:     For p = 1 to N do:
17:         S = SR(L)
18:         Loss_SR = | H − S |_1
19:     end for
```
Recognition loss calculation
```
20: For q = 1 to N do:
21:     S = Bicubic_interpolation(S, 256)
22:     label_pred = LP(S)
23:     Loss_recognition = Loss(label_pred, label_GT) as in (8)
24: end for
```
Total loss calculation
```
25: For p = 1 to N do:
26:     Loss_total = Loss_SR + Loss_recognition × a as in (9)
27: end for
```
SR weight update via total loss backpropagation
```
28: For q = 1 to N do:
29:     grad_SR = Backpropagate (SR, Loss_total)
30:     W_SR ← W_SR − grad_SR
31: return W_SR
32: end for
```

(Step 3) Freeze SR with W_SR and Train LP.
SR loss calculation
```
33: For p = 1 to N do:
34:     S = SR(L)
35:     Loss_SR = | H − S |_1 as in (7)
36: end for
```
LP loss calculation
```
37: For p = 1, N do
38:     S = Bicubic_interpolation(S, 256)
39:     label_pred = LP(S)
40:     Loss_recognition = Loss(label_pred, label_GT) as in (8)
41: end for
```
LP weight update via LP loss backpropagation
```
42: For q = 1, N do
43: grad_LP = Backpropagate (LP, Loss_recognition)
44:     W_LP ← W_LP − grad_LP
45: return W_LP
46: end for
```

Optimizer. Our HIFA-LPR model utilizes the adaptive moment (Adam) optimizer [30] to search a minimum of our loss function $Loss_{Total}$ with the iterative operation as follows:

$$m^{(n+1)} = \beta_1 m^{(n)} + (1 - \beta_1) \nabla Loss_{Total}(W^{(n)}), \quad (10)$$

$$v^{(n+1)} = \beta_2 m^{(n)} + (1 - \beta_2) \nabla Loss_{Total}(W^{(n)}) \bullet \nabla Loss_{Total}(W^{(n)}), \quad (11)$$

$$W^{(n+1)} = W^{(n)} - \frac{h}{\sqrt{v^{(n+1)} + \omega}} m^{(n+1)}, \quad (12)$$

where $\nabla Loss_{Total}$ denotes the gradient of our loss function $Loss_{Total}$, each β_1 and β_2 denote the exponential decay rates for the moment estimates, $m^{(n)}$ denotes the estimate of the first moment of the gradient, $v^{(n)}$ denotes the estimate for the second moment, $W^{(n)}$ denotes the vector before the optimization, $W^{(n+1)}$ denotes the updated vector by the Adam optimizer, h denotes the step size for the optimization process, • denotes the element-wise product, and ω denotes the variable that prevents the dividing by zero error in Equation (12). h is the important parameter for optimization because it gives a balance between the speed and convergence of the proposed model.

4. Experiments and Analysis

4.1. Experimental Setup

Dataset. To verify the effectiveness of our model, we utilize the UFPR [1] and Greek vehicle datasets [2]. The UFPR dataset that consists of Brazilian vehicle LP is organized into 1800 training sets, 900 validation sets, and 1800 test sets. To accurately measure the performance of our framework, we reorganize the UFPR [1] dataset into 3600 training sets and 900 validation sets. We organize the Greek vehicle dataset [2] into 280 training sets and 65 validation sets, and those sets are annotated by ourselves. To simulate low-quality legacy conditions, we resize the HR images to LR images by using the built-in resize function of MATLAB for each scale factor ($\times 3$, $\times 4$).

Metric. To analyze the performance of SR modules, we use the peak signal-to-noise ratio (PSNR), which evaluates the difference between the original image and the super-resolved image. To quantify the recognition accuracy, the mean average precision (mAP) is utilized.

Environments. Our framework is implemented in Pytorch 1.8.0., and we use Python 3.8.3, CUDA 11.2, and cuDNN 8.2.0. Our experiment is performed with AMD Ryzen 5 5600X 6-Core Processor CPU, 32GB memory, and NVIDIA RTX 3080 GPU. The 2D-DCT and 2D-IDCT are implemented using the built-in functions of torch.fft.rfft and torch.fft.irfft, respectively. Our HIFA-LPR model is trained by the Adam optimizer [30] with $\beta_1 = 0.9$ and $\beta_2 = 0.999$, as shown in Equation (12). The training batch size of our study is set to 16, the number of epochs to 200, ω is set to 10^{-8}, and the learning rate to 10^{-4}.

4.2. Experimental Results

We compare our model with other approaches combined with SR modules [8,11,12] and LP recognition modules [14,29]. Among the recent LP recognition modules, we exclude modules that do not provide the source codes [21,23,25–28]. We set the LR image-based LP recognition module trained with LR LP images as the baseline. For a fair comparison, each SR module is trained and validated by the same datasets. In addition, Yolov5 [29] is trained with the corresponding HR LP images. Then, for a fair comparison, each LP recognition module fine-tunes their SR results like Step 3 of our gradual end-to-end learning method. Tables 1 and 2 show the comparison between our HIFA-LPR model and other existing approaches. According to each training step, our HIFA-LPR model is denoted as HIFA-LPR (Steps 1, 2, and 3). Our model outperforms other existing approaches, as shown in Tables 1 and 2. In particular, HIFA-LPR (Step 3) presents that the PSNR is increased by 0.8 dB and the mean average precision (mAP) is increased by 19.7% more than that of HIFA-LPR (Step 1) for a scale factor of $\times 3$. Moreover, HIFA-LPR (Step 3) shows that the PSNR is increased by 0.14 dB and the mAP is increased by 26.5% more than that of HIFA-LPR (Step 1) for the scale factor $\times 4$. These experimental results indicate that our proposed gradual end-to-end learning method is superior to individual learning.

Table 1. Comparison between the HIFA-LPR model and other existing approaches for scale factor (×3) on the UFPR dataset.

PSNR and mAP on UFPR Validation Dataset			
Method		PSNR (dB)	mAP (%)
SR Module	Recognition Module		
LR baseline	Tesseract-OCR [14]	-	17.8
Bicubic		24.10	29.1
MZSR [11]		17.64	22.7
DRN [8]		25.11	33.3
SwinIR [12]		25.66	36.4
LR baseline	Yolov5 [29]	-	49.9
Bicubic		24.10	50.1
MZSR [11]		17.64	43.7
DRN [8]		25.11	58.5
SwinIR [12]		25.66	61.1
HIFA-LPR (Step 1)		26.40	62.7
HIFA-LPR (Step 2)		27.20	67.7
HIFA-LPR (Step 3)		27.20	82.4

Table 2. Comparison between the HIFA-LPR model and other existing approaches for scale factor (×4) on the UFPR dataset.

PSNR and mAP on UFPR Validation Dataset			
Method		PSNR (dB)	mAP (%)
SR Module	Recognition Module		
LR baseline	Tesseract-OCR [14]	-	12.7
Bicubic		22.18	18.8
MZSR [11]		17.99	11.2
DRN [8]		22.74	19.7
SwinIR [12]		23.33	21.8
LR baseline	Yolov5 [29]	-	32.4
Bicubic		22.18	35.8
MZSR [11]		17.99	27.3
DRN [8]		22.74	36.7
SwinIR [12]		23.33	38.1
HIFA-LPR (Step 1)		23.77	34.4
HIFA-LPR (Step 2)		23.91	42.2
HIFA-LPR (Step 3)		23.91	60.9

Figure 8 shows experimental results from SR modules with the scale factor (×4) on the UFPR dataset. As shown in Figure 8b–d, the SR modules cannot properly improve image quality from the LR image in Figure 8a. As shown in Figure 8f, SwinIR presents a better image quality when compared with the other SR modules. As illustrated in Figure 8h, our HIFA-LPR model provides enhanced edges and textures that are closely related to the LP recognition accuracy. As shown in Figure 9, the LP recognition results are used to quantitatively compare our model and existing approaches. As shown in Figure 9b–e, the

LP recognition results obtained from existing approaches include many missing characters as well as several incorrect predictions. Although the result of HIFA-LPR (Step 3) includes one missing character, it outperforms other approaches in terms of recognition accuracy, as shown in Figure 9h. In addition, Figure 10 shows the mAP results for a numeric class (0–9) for the bicubic method and HIFA-LPR (Step 1, Step 2, and Step 3), respectively. We focus on only numeric class for detailed observation. The mAP result for the numerical class of HIFA-LPR (Step 3) is increased by 21.6% more than HIFA-LPR (Step 1). As the gradual end-to-end learning process progresses step by step, the mAP is increased. It demonstrates the effectiveness of the gradual end-to-end learning method.

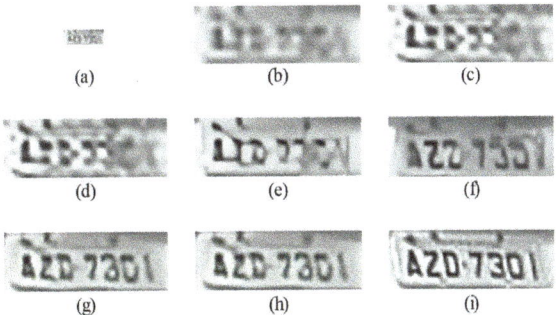

Figure 8. SR results on the LP image of the UFPR dataset for scale factor (×3): (**a**) input low-quality legacy image (24 × 8), (**b**) bicubic (96 × 32), (**c**) MZSR, (**d**) DRN, (**e**) SwinIR, (**f**) HIFA-LPR (Step 1), (**g**) HIFA-LPR (Step 2), (**h**) HIFA-LPR (Step 3), (**i**) HR image.

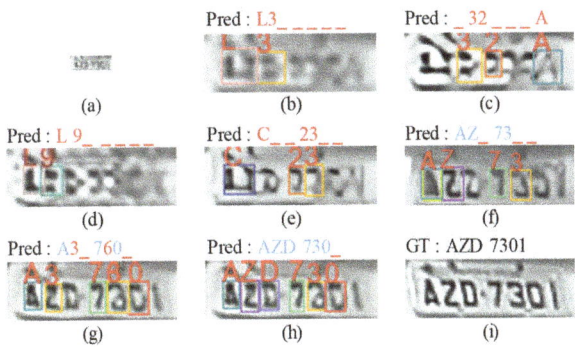

Figure 9. LP recognition results on (**a**) input low-quality legacy image (24 × 8), (**b**) bicubic image (96 × 32), (**c**) MZSR result, (**d**) DRN result, (**e**) SwinIR result, (**f**) HIFA-LPR (Step 1) result, (**g**) HIFA-LPR (Step 2) result, (**h**) HIFA-LPR (Step 3) result, (**i**) HR image. "_" denotes a missing character. Red character denotes an incorrect prediction. Blue character denotes a correct prediction. "GT" denotes ground truth. "Pred" denotes the prediction result.

Tables 3 and 4 show the comparison between our HIFA-LPR model and other approaches to the Greek vehicle datasets. As shown in Table 3, HIFA-LPR (Step 3) presents that the mAP is increased by 1.5%, while the PSNR is decreased by 2.93 dB compared to that of SwinIR for scale factor ×3. As shown in Table 4, although HIFA-LPR (Step 3) shows that the PSNR is decreased by 3.6 dB less than SwinIR, the mAP of our model is increased by 1.4%. As shown in Figure 11b–e, the SR modules also cannot properly enhance the quality of the image from the LR image in Figure 11a. On the other hand, our HIFA-LPR model produces enhanced edge components, as shown in Figure 11h. It helps improve the performance of LP recognition. Figure 12 shows the results of the LP recognition module using SR results for scale factor ×4 on the Greek vehicle dataset. As illustrated in Figure 12, HIFA-LPR (Step 3) accurately predicts all characters, while other approaches include several missing characters and incorrect predictions. These experimental results indicate that the proposed HIFA-LPR model produces high recognition performance because the model performs SR to improve recognition accuracy, despite PSNR degradation. In addition, Figure 13 shows the mAP results for the numeric class (0–9) for the bicubic method and HIFA-LPR (Step 1, 2, and 3), respectively. The mAP result for the numerical class for HIFA-LPR (Step 3) is increased by 18.6% more than that of HIFA-LPR (Step 1).

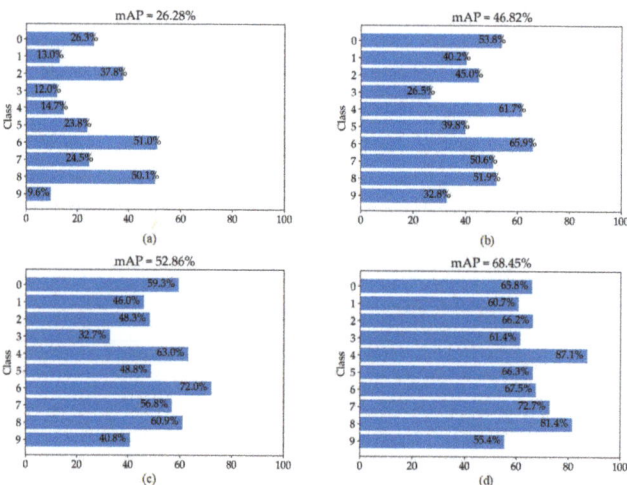

Figure 10. mAP comparison results for only numbers (0–9) on the UFPR dataset for scale factor (×4). (**a**–**d**) represent the mAP results on bicubic results, HIFA-LPR (Step 1) results, HIFA-LPR (Step 2) results, and HIFA-LPR (Step 3) results, respectively.

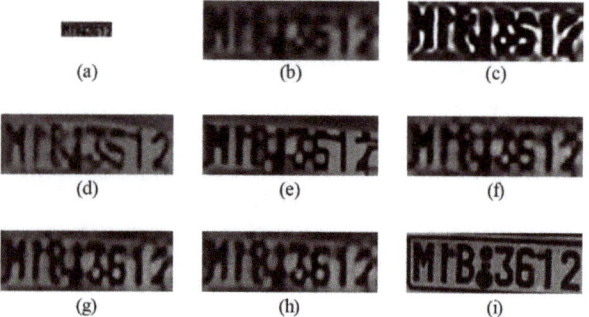

Figure 11. SR results on the LP image of the Greek vehicle dataset for scale factor (×4): (**a**) input low-quality legacy image (24 × 8), (**b**) Bicubic (96 × 32), (**c**) MZSR, (**d**) DRN, (**e**) SwinIR, (**f**) HIFA-LPR (Step 1), (**g**) HIFA-LPR (Step 2), (**h**) HIFA-LPR (Step 3), (**i**) HR image.

Table 3. Comparison between the HIFA-LPR model and other existing approaches for scale factor (×3) on the Greek vehicle dataset.

Method		PSNR (dB)	mAP (%)
SR Module	Recognition Module		
LR baseline	Tesseract-OCR [14]	-	48.2
Bicubic	Tesseract-OCR [14]	21.33	60.3
MZSR [11]	Tesseract-OCR [14]	16.07	47.2
DRN [8]	Tesseract-OCR [14]	25.08	70.4
SwinIR [12]	Tesseract-OCR [14]	25.58	74.7
LR baseline	Yolov5 [29]	-	72.1
Bicubic	Yolov5 [29]	21.33	92.1
MZSR [11]	Yolov5 [29]	16.07	91.8
DRN [8]	Yolov5 [29]	25.08	95.9
SwinIR [12]	Yolov5 [29]	25.58	96.8
HIFA-LPR (Step 1)		21.43	91.9
HIFA-LPR (Step 2)		22.65	94.4
HIFA-LPR (Step 3)		22.65	98.3

Table 4. Comparison between the HIFA-LPR model and other existing approaches for scale factor (×4) on the Greek vehicle dataset.

Method		PSNR (dB)	mAP (%)
SR Module	Recognition Module		
LR baseline	Tesseract-OCR [14]	-	27.4
Bicubic	Tesseract-OCR [14]	21.33	31.1
MZSR [11]	Tesseract-OCR [14]	16.07	22.3
DRN [8]	Tesseract-OCR [14]	25.08	52.1
SwinIR [12]	Tesseract-OCR [14]	25.58	55.1
LR baseline	Yolov5 [29]	-	57.1
Bicubic	Yolov5 [29]	19.63	77.3
MZSR [11]	Yolov5 [29]	15.96	74.1
DRN [8]	Yolov5 [29]	23.83	87.5
SwinIR [12]	Yolov5 [29]	23.61	89.1
HIFA-LPR (Step 1)		20.01	75.2
HIFA-LPR (Step 2)		20.60	80.6
HIFA-LPR (Step 3)		20.60	90.5

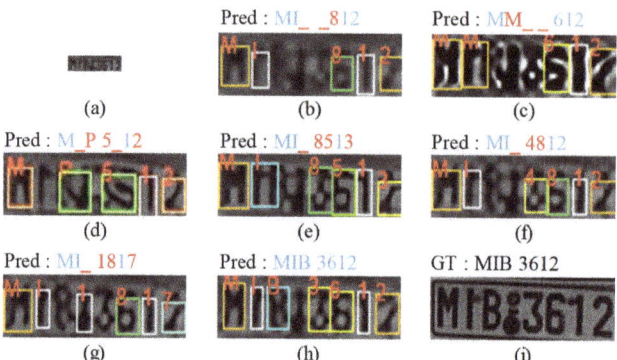

Figure 12. LP recognition results on the Greek vehicle dataset with (**a**) input low-quality legacy image (28 × 8), (**b**) bicubic result (112 × 32), (**c**) MZSR result, (**d**) DRN result, (**e**) SwinIR result, (**f**) HIFA-LPR (Step 1) result, (**g**) HIFA-LPR (Step 2) result, (**h**) HIFA-LPR (Step 3) result. (**i**) HR image. "_" denotes a missing character. Red character denotes an incorrect prediction. Blue character denotes a correct prediction. "GT" denotes ground truth. "Pred" denotes the prediction result.

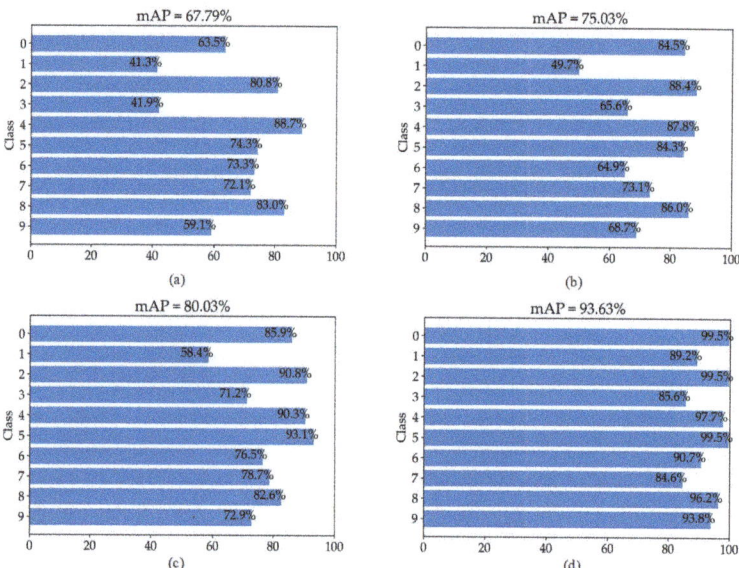

Figure 13. mAP comparison results for only numbers (0–9) on the Greek vehicle dataset for scale factor (×4). (**a**–**d**) represent the mAP results on bicubic results, HIFA-LPR (Step 1) results, HIFA-LPR (Step 2) results, and HIFA-LPR (Step 3), respectively.

4.3. Ablation Study

The effect of holistic feature extraction. In this section, we verify the effectiveness of the holistic image feature-extraction-based SR module by comparison with the patch-extraction-based SR module. For a fair comparison, each module is trained and validated using the same datasets and LP recognition module. As shown in Table 5, the holistic-extraction-based SR presents better mAP results than patch-extraction-based SR due to the elimination of grid patterns during the gradual end-to-end learning process.

Table 5. Comparison between the patch extraction-based SR and the holistic extraction-based SR for scale factor (×4) on the UFPR dataset.

PSNR and mAP on UFPR Validation Dataset			
Method		PSNR (dB)	mAP (%)
SR Module	Recognition Module		
Patch-extraction-based SR	Yolov5 [29]	23.77	34.4
Holistic-extraction-based SR		24.65	44.7

The effect of the LP recognition module based on high-frequency augmentation. In this section, we investigate the effect of our LP recognition module. As we mentioned, the HAB extracts desired high-frequency components according to the hyper-parameter ε and augments the extracted high-frequency components. We compare our LP recognition module with Tesseract-OCR [14] and Yolov5 [29] which is our baseline module. Since OpenALPR [13] only provides cloud demo service for a single image, we provide only visual recognition results of OpenALPR, as shown in Figure 14. For a fair comparison, each LP module is trained by the same SR results. As shown in Table 6, our LP recognition module with high-frequency augmentation outperforms other modules because the HAB effectively exploits high-frequency components which are closely related to LP recognition. As shown in Figure 14, while our LP recognition module recognizes all characters, the other modules provide missing or misrecognized characters.

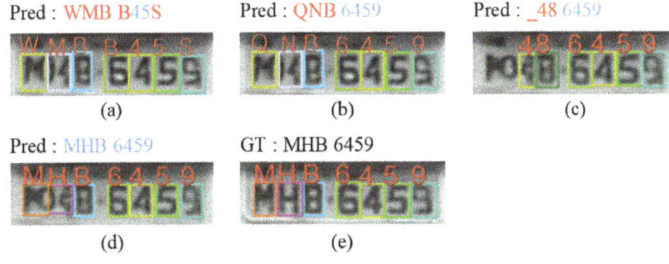

Figure 14. LP recognition results on same SR result (80 × 60). (a) Tesseract-OCR result, (b) OpenALPR result (c) Yolov5 result, (d) HIFA-LPR result, (e) HR image. "_" denotes a missing character. Red character denotes an incorrect prediction. Blue character denotes a correct prediction. "GT" denotes ground truth. "Pred" denotes the prediction result.

Table 6. Comparison between the LP recognition module based on high-frequency augmentation and other modules for scale factor (×4) on the UFPR dataset.

PSNR and mAP on UFPR Validation Dataset	
Method	mAP (%)
Tesseract-OCR [14]	19.1
Yolov5 [29]	34.4
LP recognition module **without** high-frequency augmentation	57.2
LP recognition module **with** high-frequency augmentation	60.9

Extension to other countries' LP images. Our HIFA-LPR model can be extended to other countries' LP images that include different language characters, such as Korean, by building LP datasets and redefining character classes. To verify our framework, we conduct an additional experiment on the Korean LP dataset. Our model presents that the PSNR is increased by about 1.7 dB and the mAP is increased by about 16.4% compared with SwinIR-based LP recognition. Note that our model also surpasses other approaches on the Korean LP dataset.

Limitations. Our HIFA-LPR model may have limitations in practical applications. First, our experiments only assume that the LR image is downscaled with the known bicubic kernel. Hence, there is a possibility that the SR restoration performance will be degraded in the real world where the blur kernel is unknown. Second, our HIFA-LPR model requires more training time due to gradual stepwise learning. However, the inference time of our model is the same as that of other combination methods. The inference time of the proposed HIFA-LPR model is 3.2 ms when the size of the HR LP image is 168×168 pixels as input. The input image is 42×42 pixels in size scaled by a scale factor of $\times 4$, and the LP recognition module's input size is 168×168 pixels. Moreover, the training time of our HIFA-LPR model can be reduced by optimization techniques such as network weight compression or weight sharing.

5. Conclusions

This study focuses on LP recognition in low-quality legacy conditions. For this, we propose the HIFA-LPR model via gradual end-to-end learning. To this end, we suggest the gradual end-to-end learning method based on weight freezing. This method consists of three steps. In Step 1, the SR and LP recognition modules are independently trained for stabilizing the training process. In Step 2, the SR module is trained with a combined loss function by freezing the LP recognition module weights to strengthen collaborative correlations with each module. In Step 3, the LP recognition module is trained with super-resolved images by freezing the SR module weights to obtain higher LP recognition accuracy. Due to this method, we can enhance collaborative correlations between each module. To optimally train our model, we propose the holistic feature extraction method that can prevent grid pattern generation in the training process. To exploit high-frequency information, we propose an LP recognition module based on high-frequency augmentation. Our LP recognition module extracts only the desired high frequency and enhances the high-frequency component of the feature map. The experimental results show that our HIFA-LPR model provides the best performance in terms of mAP among various existing approaches. Although our HIFA-LPR model is intended for LP recognition, it can be extended to other object recognition tasks by building the related datasets and redefining object classes. In addition, our HIFA-LPR model can be considered in real-world scene text recognition applications such as smart parking and autonomous driving. In the smart parking task, our method can be applied to parking in designated areas and crackdown on illegal parking. In addition, our HIFA-LPR model can be applied to character recognition on traffic signs to help in autonomous driving.

Author Contributions: Conceptualization, S.B.Y.; methodology, S.-J.L., J.-S.Y. and S.B.Y.; software, S.-J.L.; validation, J.-S.Y.; formal analysis, S.-J.L. and J.-S.Y.; investigation, E.J.L. and S.B.Y.; resources, S.-J.L. and S.B.Y.; data curation, S.-J.L. and J.-S.Y.; writing—original draft preparation, S.-J.L. and J.-S.Y.; writing—review and editing, E.J.L. and S.B.Y.; visualization, S.B.Y.; supervision, S.B.Y.; project administration, S.B.Y.; funding acquisition, S.B.Y. All authors have read and agreed to the published version of the manuscript.

Funding: This work was supported by the National Research Foundation of Korea (NRF) grant funded by the Korea government (MSIT) (NRF-2020R1G1A1100798). This work was supported by an Institute of Information & Communications Technology Planning & Evaluation (IITP) grant funded by the Korea government (MSIT) (No. 2020-0-00004, Development of Previsional Intelligence based on Long-term Visual Memory Network). This work was partly supported by an Institute of Information & Communications Technology Planning & Evaluation (IITP) grant funded by the Korea government (MSIT) (No. 2021-0-02068, Artificial Intelligence Innovation Hub).

Institutional Review Board Statement: Not applicable.

Informed Consent Statement: Not applicable.

Data Availability Statement: Not applicable.

Conflicts of Interest: The authors declare no conflict of interest.

References

1. Laroca, R.; Severo, E.; Zanlorensi, L.; Oliveira, L.; Gonçalves, G.; Schwartz, W.; Menotti, D. A robust real-time automatic license plate recognition based on the YOLO detector. In Proceedings of the 2018 International Joint Conference on Neural Networks, Rio de Janeiro, Brazil, 8–13 July 2018; pp. 1–10.
2. Anagnostopoulos, C.N.E.; Anagnostopoulos, I.E.; Psoroulas, I.D.; Loumos, V.; Kayafas, E. License plate recognition from still images and video sequences: A survey. *IEEE Trans. Intell. Transp. Syst.* **2008**, *9*, 377–391. [CrossRef]
3. Dong, C.; Loy, C.C.; He, K.; Tang, X. Image super-resolution using deep convolutional networks. *IEEE Trans. Pattern Anal. Mach. Intell.* **2015**, *38*, 295–307. [CrossRef]
4. Kim, J.W.; Lee, J.K.; Lee, K.M. Accurate image super-resolution using very deep convolutional networks. In Proceedings of the IEEE Conference on Computer Vision and Pattern Recognition, Las Vegas, NV, USA, 27–30 June 2016; pp. 1646–1654.
5. Shi, W.; Caballero, J.; Huszár, F.; Totz, J.; Aitken, A.P.; Bishop, R.; Rueckert, D.; Wang, Z. Real-time single image and video super-resolution using an efficient sub-pixel convolutional neural networks. In Proceedings of the IEEE Conference on Computer Vision and Pattern Recognition, Las Vegas, NV, USA, 27–30 June 2016; pp. 1874–1883.
6. Haris, M.; Shakhnarovich, G.; Ukita, N. Deep back-projection networks for super-resolution. In Proceedings of the IEEE Conference on Computer Vision and Pattern Recognition, Salt Lake City, UT, USA, 18–22 June 2018; pp. 1664–1673.
7. Zhang, Y.; Li, K.; Li, K.; Wang, L.; Zhong, B.; Fu, Y. Image super-resolution using very deep residual channel attention networks. In Proceedings of the European Conference on Computer Vision, Munich, Germany, 8–14 September 2018; pp. 286–301.
8. Guo, Y.; Chen, J.; Wang, J.; Chen, Q.; Cao, J.; Deng, Z.; Xu, Y.; Tan, M. Closed-loop matters: Dual regression networks for single image super-resolution. In Proceedings of the IEEE Conference on Computer Vision and Pattern Recognition, Seattle, WA, USA, 14–19 June 2020; pp. 5407–5416.
9. Zhang, Y.; Tian, Y.; Kong, Y.; Zhong, B.; Fu, Y. Residual dense network for image super-resolution. In Proceedings of the IEEE Conference on Computer Vision and Pattern Recognition, Salt Lake City, UT, USA, 18–22 June 2018; pp. 2472–2481.
10. Dai, T.; Cai, J.; Zhang, Y.; Xia, S.T.; Zhang, L. Second-order attention network for single image super-resolution. In Proceedings of the IEEE Conference on Computer Vision and Pattern Recognition, Long Beach, CA, USA, 16–20 June 2019; pp. 11065–11074.
11. Soh, J.W.; Cho, S.; Cho, N.I. Meta-transfer learning for zero-shot super-resolution. In Proceedings of the IEEE/CVF Conference on Computer Vision and Pattern Recognition, Virtual, Seattle, WA, USA, 14–19 June 2020; pp. 3516–3525.
12. Liang, J.; Cao, J.; Sun, G.; Zhang, K.; Van, G.; Timofte, R. SwinIR: Image restoration using swin transformer. In Proceedings of the IEEE International Conference on Computer Vision, Montréal, QC, Canada, 11–17 October 2021; pp. 1833–1844.
13. OpenALPR. Available online: https://www.openalpr.com (accessed on 29 October 2021).
14. Tesseract Open Source OCR Engine. Available online: https://github.com/tesseract-ocr/tesseract (accessed on 25 October 2021).
15. Lee, S.J.; Kim, T.J.; Lee, C.H.; Yoo, S.B. Image super-resolution for improving object recognition accuracy. *JKIICE* **2021**, *25*, 774–784.
16. Lee, S.J.; Yoo, S.B. Super-resolved recognition of license plate characters. *Mathematics* **2021**, *9*, 2494. [CrossRef]
17. Wang, X.; Man, J.; You, M.; Shen, C. Adversarial generation of training examples: Applications to moving vehicle license plate recognition. *arXiv* **2017**, arXiv:1707:03124.
18. Hamdi, A.; Chan, Y.K.; Koo, V.C. A new image enhancement and super resolution technique for license plate recognition. *Heliyon* **2021**, *7*, 8341. [CrossRef] [PubMed]
19. Wang, W.; Yang, J.; Chen, M.; Wang, P. A light CNN for end-to-end car license plates detection and recognition. *IEEE Access* **2019**, *7*, 173875–173883. [CrossRef]
20. Zherzdev, S.; Gruzdev, A. LPRNet: License plate recognition via deep neural networks. *arXiv* **2018**, arXiv:1806:10447.
21. Nguyen, D.L.; Putro, M.D.; Vo, X.T.; Jo, K.H. Triple detector based on feature pyramid network for license plate detection and recognition system in unusual conditions. In Proceedings of the International Symposium on Industrial Electronics (ISIE), Kyoto, Japan, 20–23 June 2021; pp. 1–6.
22. Xu, Z.; Yang, W.; Meng, A.; Lu, N.; Huang, H.; Ying, C.; Huang, L. Towards end-to-end license plate detection and recognition: A large dataset and baseline. In Proceedings of the European Conference on Computer Vision, Munich, Germany, 8–14 September 2018; pp. 255–271.
23. Xu, H.; Guo, Z.H.; Wang, D.H.; Zhou, X.D.; Shi, Y. 2D License plate recognition based on automatic perspective rectification. In Proceedings of the IEEE International Conference on Pattern Recognition, Milan, Italy, 10–15 January 2021; pp. 202–208.
24. Vasek, V.; Franc, V.; Urban, M. License plate recognition and super-resolution from low-resolution videos by convolutional neural networks. In Proceedings of the British Machine Vision Conferences, Newcastle, UK, 3–6 September 2018; p. 132.
25. Lee, Y.; Yun, J.; Hong, Y.; Lee, J.; Jeon, M. Accurate license plate recognition and super-resolution using a generative adversarial networks on traffic surveillance video. In Proceedings of the International Conference on Consumer Electronics Asia, Jeju, Korea, 24–26 June 2017; pp. 1–4.
26. Zhang, M.; Liu, W.; Ma, H. Joint license plate super-resolution and recognition in one multi-task Gan framework. In Proceedings of the International Conference on Acoustics, Speech, and Signal Processing, Calgary, AB, Canada, 15–20 April 2018; pp. 1443–1447.

27. Li, H.; Wang, P.; Shen, C. Toward end-to-end car license plate detection and recognition with deep neural networks. *IEEE Trans. Intell. Transp. Syst.* **2019**, *20*, 1126–1136. [CrossRef]
28. Zhang, L.; Wang, P.; Li, H.; Li, Z.; Shen, C.; Zhang, Y. A robust attentional framework for license plate recognition in the wild. *IEEE Trans. Intell. Transp. Syst.* **2021**, *22*, 6967–6976. [CrossRef]
29. YOLOv5. Available online: https://github.com/ultralytics/yolov5 (accessed on 2 October 2021).
30. Kingma, D.P.; Ba, J. Adam: A Method for Stochastic Optimization. *arXiv* **2014**, arXiv:1412.6980.

Article

An Accelerated Convex Optimization Algorithm with Line Search and Applications in Machine Learning

Dawan Chumpungam [1], Panitarn Sarnmeta [2] and Suthep Suantai [1,3,*]

1. Data Science Research Center, Department of Mathematics, Faculty of Science, Chiang Mai University, Chiang Mai 50200, Thailand; dawan_c@cmu.ac.th
2. KOSEN-KMITL, Bangkok 10520, Thailand; panitarn.sa@kmitl.ac.th
3. Research Group in Mathematics and Applied Mathematics, Department of Mathematics, Faculty of Science, Chiang Mai University, Chiang Mai 50200, Thailand
* Correspondence: suthep.s@cmu.ac.th

Abstract: In this paper, we introduce a new line search technique, then employ it to construct a novel accelerated forward–backward algorithm for solving convex minimization problems of the form of the summation of two convex functions in which one of these functions is smooth in a real Hilbert space. We establish a weak convergence to a solution of the proposed algorithm without the Lipschitz assumption on the gradient of the objective function. Furthermore, we analyze its performance by applying the proposed algorithm to solving classification problems on various data sets and compare with other line search algorithms. Based on the experiments, the proposed algorithm performs better than other line search algorithms.

Keywords: forward–backward algorithm; line search; accelerated algorithm; convex minimization problems; data classification; machine learning

MSC: 65K05; 90C25; 90C30

1. Introduction

The convex minimization problem in the form of the sum of two convex functions plays a very important role in machine learning. This problem has been analyzed and studied by many authors because of its applications in various fields such as data science, computer science, statistics, engineering, physics, and medical science. Some examples of these applications are signal processing, compressed sensing, medical image reconstruction, digital image processing, and data prediction and classification; see [1–8].

As we know in machine learning, especially in data prediction and classification problems, the main objective is to minimize loss functions. Many loss functions can be viewed as convex functions; thus by employing convex minimization, one could find the minimum of such functions, which in turn solve data prediction and classification problems. Many works have implemented this strategy; see [9–11] and the references therein for more information. In this work, we apply *extreme learning machine* together with the *least absolute shrinkage and selection operator* to solve classification problems; more detail will be discussed in a later section. First, we introduce a convex minimization problem, which can be formulated as the following form:

$$\min_{x \in H}\{f(x) + g(x)\}, \qquad (1)$$

where $f : H \to \mathbb{R} \cup \{+\infty\}$ is proper, convex differentiable on an open set containing $dom(g)$ and $g : H \to \mathbb{R} \cup \{+\infty\}$ is a proper, lower semicontinuous convex function defined on a real Hilbert space H.

A solution of (1) is in fact a fixed point of the operator $prox_{\alpha g}(I - \alpha \nabla f)$, i.e.,

$$x^* = prox_{\alpha g}(I - \alpha \nabla f)(x^*), \qquad (2)$$

where $\alpha > 0$, and $prox_{\alpha g}(I - \alpha \nabla f)(x) = \arg\min_{y \in H}\{g(y) + \frac{1}{2\alpha}\|(x - \alpha \nabla f(x)) - y\|^2\}$, which is known as the *forward–backward operator*. In order to solve (1), the *forward–backward algorithm* [12] was introduced as follows:

$$x_{n+1} = \underbrace{prox_{\alpha_n g}}_{\text{backward}} \underbrace{(I - \alpha_n \nabla f)}_{\text{forward}}(x_n), \text{ for all } n \in \mathbb{N}, \qquad (3)$$

where α_n is a positive number. If ∇f is L-Lipschitz continuous and $\alpha_n \in (0, \frac{2}{L})$, then a sequence generated by (3) converges weakly to a solution of (1). There are several techniques that can improve the performance of (3). For instance, we could utilize an inertial step, which was first introduced by Polyak [13], to solve smooth convex minimization problems. Since then, there have been several works that included an inertial step in their algorithms to accelerate the convergence behavior; see [14–19] for examples.

One of the most famous forward–backward-type algorithms that implements an inertial step is the *fast iterative shrinkage–thresholding algorithm* (FISTA) [20]. It is defined as the following Algorithm 1.

Algorithm 1. FISTA.

1: **Input** Given $y_1 = x_0 \in \mathbb{R}^n$, and $t_1 = 1$, for $n \in \mathbb{N}$,

$$x_n = prox_{\frac{1}{L}g}(y_n - \frac{1}{L}\nabla f(y_n)),$$

$$t_{n+1} = \frac{1 + \sqrt{1 + 4t_n^2}}{2}, \quad \theta_n = \frac{t_n - 1}{t_{n+1}},$$

$$y_{n+1} = x_n + \theta_n(x_n - x_{n-1}),$$

where L is a Lipschitz constant of ∇f.

The term $x_n + \theta_n(x_n - x_{n-1})$ is known as an inertial term with an inertial parameter θ_n. It has been shown that FISTA performs better than (3). Later, other forward–backward-type algorithms have been introduced and studied by many authors; see for instance [2,8,18,21,22]. However, most of these works assume the Lipschitz assumption on ∇f, which is difficult for computation in general. Therefore, in this paper, we focus on another approach where ∇f is not necessarily Lipschitz continuous.

In 2016, Cruz and Nghia [23] introduced a line search technique as the following Algorithm 2.

Algorithm 2. Line search 1. $(x, \delta, \sigma, \theta)$.

1: **Input** Given $x \in dom(g)$, $\delta > 0$, $\sigma > 0$ and $\theta \in (0,1)$.

2: Set $\gamma = \sigma$.

3: **while** $\gamma \|\nabla f(prox_{\gamma g}(x - \gamma \nabla f(x))) - \nabla f(x)\| > \delta \|prox_{\gamma g}(x - \gamma \nabla f(x)) - x\|$ **do**

4:     Set $\gamma = \theta \gamma$

5: **end while**

6: **Output** γ.

They asserted that Line Search 1 stops after finitely many steps and proposed the following Algorithm 3.

Algorithm 3. Algorithm with Line Search 1.

1: **Input** Given $x_0 \in dom(g)$, $\delta \in (0, \frac{1}{2})$, $\sigma > 0$, and $\theta \in (0,1)$, for all $n \in \mathbb{N}$,

$$x_{n+1} = prox_{\gamma_n g}(I - \gamma_n \nabla f)(x_n),$$

where $\gamma_n :=$ Line Search $1(x_n, \delta, \sigma, \theta)$.

They also showed that the sequence $\{x_n\}$ defined by Algorithm 3 converges weakly to a solution of (1) under Assumptions A1 and A2 where:

A1. f, g are proper lower semicontinuous convex functions with $dom(g) \subseteq dom(f)$;
A2. f is differentiable on an open set containing $dom(g)$, and ∇f is uniformly continuous on any bounded subset of $dom(g)$ and maps any bounded subset of $dom(g)$ to a bounded set in H.

It is noted that the L-Lipschitz continuity of ∇f is not necessarily assumed. Moreover, if ∇f is L-Lipschitz continuous, then A2 is satisfied.

In 2019, Kankam et al. [3] proposed the new line search as the following Algorithm 4.

Algorithm 4. Line search 2. $(x, \delta, \sigma, \theta)$.

1: **Input** Given $x \in dom(g)$, $\delta > 0$, $\sigma > 0$ and $\theta \in (0,1)$. Set

$$L(x, \gamma) = prox_{\gamma g}(x - \gamma \nabla f(x)), \text{ and}$$

$$S(x, \gamma) = prox_{\gamma g}(L(x, \gamma) - \gamma \nabla f(L(x, \gamma))).$$

2: Set $\gamma = \sigma$.
3: **while**

$$\gamma \max\{\|\nabla f(S(x,\gamma)) - \nabla f(L(x,\gamma))\|, \|\nabla f(L(x,\gamma)) - \nabla f(x)\|\}$$
$$> \delta(\|S(x,\gamma) - L(x,\gamma)\| + \|L(x,\gamma) - x\|)$$

do
4: Set $\gamma = \theta \gamma$, $L(x,\gamma) = L(x, \theta \gamma)$, $S(x, \gamma) = S(x, \theta \gamma)$
5: **end while**
6: **Output** γ.

They also asserted that Line Search 2 stops at finitely many steps and proposed the following Algorithm 5.

Algorithm 5. Algorithm with Line Search 2.

1: **Input** Given $x_0 \in dom(g)$, $\delta \in (0, \frac{1}{8})$, $\sigma > 0$ and $\theta \in (0,1)$, for all $n \in \mathbb{N}$,

$$y_n = prox_{\gamma_n g}(x_n - \gamma_n \nabla f(x_n)),$$
$$x_{n+1} = prox_{\gamma_n g}(y_n - \gamma_n \nabla f(y_n)),$$

where $\gamma_n :=$ Line Search 2 $(x_n, \delta, \sigma, \theta)$.

A weak convergence result of this algorithm was obtained under Assumptions A1 and A2. Although Algorithms 3 and 5 obtained weak convergence results without the Lipschitz assumption on ∇f, the two algorithms did not utilize an inertial step yet. Therefore, some improvements of their convergence behavior using this technique are interesting to investigate.

Motivated by the works mentioned earlier, we aim to introduce a new line search technique and prove that it is well-defined. Then, we employ it to construct a novel forward–backward algorithm that utilizes an inertial step to improve its performance to be better than the other line search algorithms. We prove a weak convergence theorem of the proposed algorithm without the Lipschitz assumption on ∇f and apply it to solve classification problems on various data sets. We also compare its performance with Algorithms 3 and 5 to show that the proposed algorithm performs better.

This work is organized as follows: In Section 2, we recall some important definitions and lemmas used in later sections. In Section 3, we introduce a new line search technique and algorithm for solving (1). Then, we analyze the convergence and complexity of the proposed algorithm under Assumptions A1 and A2. In Section 4, we apply the proposed algorithm to solve data classification problems and compare its performance with other algorithms. Finally, the conclusion of this work is presented in Section 5.

2. Preliminaries

In this section, some important definitions and lemmas, which will be used in later sections, are presented.

Let $\{x_n\}$ be a sequence in H and $x \in H$. We denote $x_n \to x$ and $x_n \rightharpoonup x$ as a strong and weak convergence of $\{x_n\}$ to x, respectively. Let $f : H \to \mathbb{R} \cup \{+\infty\}$ be a proper lower semicontinuous and convex function. We denote $dom(f) = \{x \in H : f(x) < +\infty\}$. A *subdifferential* of f at x is defined by

$$\partial f(x) := \{u \in H : \langle u, y - x \rangle + f(x) \leq f(y),\ y \in H\}.$$

A *proximal operator* $prox_{\alpha f} : H \to dom(f)$ is defined as follows:

$$prox_{\alpha f}(x) = (I + \alpha \partial f)^{-1}(x),$$

where I is an identity mapping and α is a positive number. It is well known that this operator is single-valued, nonexpansive, and

$$\frac{x - prox_{\alpha f}(x)}{\alpha} \in \partial f(prox_{\alpha f}(x)), \text{ for all } x \in H \text{ and } \alpha > 0; \qquad (4)$$

see [23] for more details. Next, we present some important lemmas for this work.

Lemma 1 ([24]). *Let ∂f be a subdifferential of f. Then, the following hold:*

(i) ∂f *is maximal monotone;*
(ii) $Gph(\partial f) := \{(x,y) \in H \times H : y \in \partial f(x)\}$ *is demiclosed, i.e., for any sequence $\{(x_n, y_n)\} \subseteq Gph(\partial f)$ such that $\{x_n\} \rightharpoonup x$ and $\{y_n\} \to y$, then $(x,y) \in Gph(\partial f)$.*

Lemma 2 ([25]). *Let $f, g : H \to \mathbb{R} \cup \{+\infty\}$ be proper lower semicontinuous convex functions with $dom(g) \subseteq dom(f)$ and $J(x, \alpha) = prox_{\alpha g}(x - \alpha \nabla f(x))$. Then, for any $x \in dom(g)$ and $\alpha_2 \geq \alpha_1 > 0$, we have*

$$\frac{\alpha_2}{\alpha_1}\|x - J(x, \alpha_1)\| \geq \|x - J(x, \alpha_2)\| \geq \|x - J(x, \alpha_1)\|.$$

Lemma 3 ([26]). *Let H be a real Hilbert space. Then, for all $a, b, c \in H$ and $\zeta \in [0,1]$, the following hold:*

(i) $\|a \pm b\|^2 = \|a\|^2 \pm 2\langle a, b \rangle + \|b\|^2$;
(ii) $\|\zeta a + (1 - \zeta)b\|^2 = \zeta\|a\|^2 + (1 - \zeta)\|b\|^2 - \zeta(1 - \zeta)\|a - b\|^2$;
(iii) $\|a + b\|^2 \leq \|a\|^2 + 2\langle b, a + b \rangle$;
(iv) $\langle a - b, b - c \rangle = \frac{1}{2}(\|a - c\|^2 - \|a - b\|^2 - \|b - c\|^2)$.

Lemma 4 ([8]). *Let $\{a_n\}$ and $\{b_n\}$ be sequences of non-negative real numbers such that*

$$a_{n+1} \leq (1 + b_n)a_n + b_n a_{n-1}, \text{ for all } n \in \mathbb{N}.$$

Then, the following holds:

$$a_{n+1} \leq K \cdot \prod_{j=1}^{n}(1+2b_j), \text{ where } K = \max\{a_1, a_2\}.$$

Moreover, if $\sum_{n=1}^{+\infty} b_n < +\infty$, then $\{a_n\}$ is bounded.

Lemma 5 ([26]). *Let $\{\alpha_n\}, \{\beta_n\}$ and $\{\gamma_n\}$ be sequences of non-negative real numbers such that*

$$\alpha_{n+1} \leq (1+\gamma_n)\alpha_n + \beta_n, \text{ for all } n \in \mathbb{N}.$$

If $\sum_{n=1}^{+\infty} \gamma_n < +\infty$ and $\sum_{n=1}^{+\infty} \beta_n < +\infty$, then $\lim_{n \to +\infty} \alpha_n$ exists.

Lemma 6 ([27], Opial). *Let $\{x_n\}$ be a sequence in a Hilbert space H. If there exists a nonempty subset Ω of H such that the following hold:*
(i) *For any $x^* \in \Omega$, $\lim_{n \to +\infty} \|x_n - x^*\|$ exists;*
(ii) *Every weak-cluster point of $\{x_n\}$ belongs to Ω.*

Then, $\{x_n\}$ converges weakly to an element in Ω.

3. Main Results

In this section, we define a new line search technique and a new accelerated algorithm with the new line search for solving (1). We denote S_* the set of all solutions of (1) and suppose that $f, g : H \to \mathbb{R} \cup \{+\infty\}$ are two convex functions that satisfy Assumptions A1 and A2, and $dom(g)$ is closed. Furthermore, we also suppose that $S_* \neq \emptyset$.

We first introduce a new line search technique as the following Algorithm 6.

Algorithm 6. Line Search 3 $(x, \delta, \sigma, \theta)$.

1: **Input** Given $x \in dom(g)$, $\delta > 0$, $\sigma > 0$ and $\theta \in (0,1)$. Set

$$L(x, \gamma) = prox_{\gamma g}(x - \gamma \nabla f(x)), \text{ and}$$

$$S(x, \gamma) = prox_{\gamma g}(L(x, \gamma) - \gamma \nabla f(L(x, \gamma))).$$

2: Set $\gamma = \sigma$.
3: **while**

$$\frac{\gamma}{2}(\|\nabla f(S(x,\gamma)) - \nabla f(L(x,\gamma))\| + \|\nabla f(L(x,\gamma)) - \nabla f(x)\|)$$
$$> \delta(\|S(x,\gamma) - L(x,\gamma)\| + \|L(x,\gamma) - x\|),$$
$$\text{or} \quad \gamma\|\nabla f(L(x,\gamma)) - \nabla f(x)\| > 4\delta\|L(x,\gamma) - x\|.$$

   do
4:   Set $\gamma = \theta\gamma$, $L(x,\gamma) = L(x,\theta\gamma)$, $S(x,\gamma) = S(x,\theta\gamma)$
5: **end while**
6: **Output** γ.

We first show that Line Search 3 terminates at finitely many steps.

Lemma 7. *Line Search 3 stops at finitely many steps.*

Proof. If $x \in S_*$, then $x = L(x,\sigma) = S(x,\sigma)$, so Line Search 3 stops with zero steps. If $x \notin S_*$, suppose by contradiction that, for all $n \in \mathbb{N}$, the following hold:

$$\frac{\sigma\theta^n}{2}(\|\nabla f(S(x,\sigma\theta^n)) - \nabla f(L(x,\sigma\theta^n))\| + \|\nabla f(L(x,\sigma\theta^n)) - \nabla f(x)\|)$$
$$> \delta(\|S(x,\sigma\theta^n) - L(x,\sigma\theta^n)\| + \|L(x,\sigma\theta^n) - x\|), \tag{5}$$

or

$$\sigma\theta^n \|\nabla f(L(x,\sigma\theta^n)) - \nabla f(x)\| > 4\delta\|L(x,\sigma\theta^n) - x\|. \tag{6}$$

Then, from these assumptions, we can find a subsequence $\{\sigma\theta^{n_k}\}$ of $\{\sigma\theta^n\}$ such that (5) or (6) holds. First, we show that

$$\{\|\nabla f(L(x,\sigma\theta^n)) - \nabla f(x)\|\} \quad \text{and} \quad \{\|\nabla f(S(x,\sigma\theta^n)) - \nabla f(L(x,\sigma\theta^n))\|\}$$

are bounded. It follows from Lemma 2 that

$$\|L(x,\sigma\theta^n) - x\| \leq \|L(x,\sigma) - x\|,$$

for all $n \in \mathbb{N}$. In combination with A2, we conclude that $\{\|\nabla f(L(x,\sigma\theta^n)) - \nabla f(x)\|\}$ is bounded. Next, we prove that $\{\|\nabla f(S(x,\sigma\theta^n)) - \nabla f(L(x,\sigma\theta^n))\|\}$ is bounded. Since $prox_{\gamma g}$ is nonexpansive, for any $\gamma > 0$, then

$$\|S(x,\sigma\theta^n) - \nabla L(x,\sigma\theta^n)\|$$
$$= \|prox_{\sigma\theta^n g}(L(x,\sigma\theta^n) - \sigma\theta^n \nabla f(L(x,\sigma\theta^n))) - prox_{\sigma\theta^n g}(x - \sigma\theta^n \nabla f(x))\|$$
$$\leq \|(L(x,\sigma\theta^n) - \sigma\theta^n \nabla f(L(x,\sigma\theta^n))) - (x - \sigma\theta^n \nabla f(x))\|$$
$$\leq \|L(x,\sigma\theta^n) - x\| + \sigma\theta^n \|\nabla f(L(x,\sigma\theta^n)) - \nabla f(x)\|$$
$$\leq \|L(x,\sigma\theta^n) - x\| + \sigma\|\nabla f(L(x,\sigma\theta^n)) - \nabla f(x)\|,$$

for all $n \in \mathbb{N}$; hence, $\{\|S(x,\sigma\theta^n) - \nabla L(x,\sigma\theta^n)\|\}$ is bounded. Again, it follows from A2 that $\{\|\nabla f(S(x,\sigma\theta^n)) - \nabla f(L(x,\sigma\theta^n))\|\}$ is bounded. To complete the proof, we consider the only two possible cases to find a contradiction.

Case 1: Suppose that there exists a subsequence $\{\sigma\theta^{n_k}\}$ of $\{\sigma\theta^n\}$ such that (5) holds, for all $k \in \mathbb{N}$. Then, it follows that $\|S(x,\sigma\theta^{n_k}) - L(x,\sigma\theta^{n_k})\| \to 0$ and $\|L(x,\sigma\theta^{n_k}) - x\| \to 0$, as $k \to +\infty$. Since ∇f is uniformly continuous, we obtain:

$$\|\nabla f(S(x,\sigma\theta^{n_k})) - \nabla f(L(x,\sigma\theta^{n_k}))\| \to 0 \quad \text{and} \quad \|\nabla f(L(x,\sigma\theta^{n_k})) - \nabla f(x)\| \to 0,$$

as $k \to +\infty$. Therefore, it follows from (5) that $\frac{\|L(x,\sigma\theta^{n_k}) - x\|}{\sigma\theta^{n_k}} \to 0$, as $k \to +\infty$. By (4), we obtain

$$\frac{x - \sigma\theta^{n_k} \nabla f(x) - L(x,\sigma\theta^{n_k})}{\sigma\theta^{n_k}} \in \partial g(L(x,\sigma\theta^{n_k})).$$

Thus, $\frac{L(x,\sigma\theta^{n_k}) - x}{\sigma\theta^{n_k}} - \nabla f(x) \in \partial g(L(x,\sigma\theta^{n_k}))$. Since $L(x,\sigma\theta^{n_k}) \to x$, as $k \to +\infty$, we obtain from Lemma 1 that $0 \in \nabla f(x) + \partial g(x) \subseteq \partial (f+g)(x)$. Hence, $x \in S_*$, which is a contradiction.

Case 2: Suppose that there is a subsequence $\{\sigma\theta^{n_k}\}$ of $\{\sigma\theta^n\}$ satisfying (6), for all $k \in \mathbb{N}$. Then, $\|L(x,\sigma\theta^{n_k}) - x\| \to 0$, as $k \to +\infty$. Again, from the uniform continuity of ∇f, we have

$$\|\nabla f(L(x,\sigma\theta^{n_k})) - \nabla f(x)\| \to 0,$$

as $k \to +\infty$. From (6), we conclude that

$$\frac{\|L(x,\sigma\theta^{n_k}) - x\|}{\sigma\theta^{n_k}} \to 0,$$

as $k \to +\infty$. By the same argument as in Case 1, we can show that $0 \in \partial(f+g)(x)$, and hence, $x \in S_*$, a contradiction. Therefore, we conclude that Line Search 3 stops with finite steps, and the proof is complete. □

We propose a new inertial algorithm with Line Search 3 as following Algorithm 7.

Algorithm 7. Inertial algorithm with Line Search 3.

1: **Input** Given $x_0, x_1 \in dom(g), \alpha_n \in [0,1], \beta_n \geq 0, \sigma > 0, \theta \in (0,1)$ and $\delta \in (0, \frac{1}{8})$, for $n \in \mathbb{N}$,

$$y_n = x_n + \beta_n(x_n - x_{n-1}),$$
$$z_n = P_{dom(g)}y_n,$$
$$w_n = prox_{\gamma_n g}(z_n - \gamma_n \nabla f(z_n)),$$
$$x_{n+1} = (1 - \alpha_n)w_n + \alpha_n prox_{\gamma_n g}(w_n - \gamma_n \nabla f(w_n)),$$

where $\gamma_n :=$ Line Search $3(z_n, \delta, \sigma, \theta)$, and $P_{dom(g)}$ is a metric projection map onto $dom(g)$.

The diagram of Algorithm 7 can be seen in Figure 1.

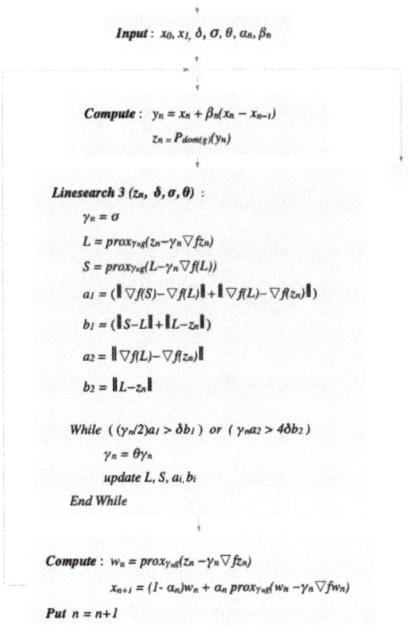

Figure 1. Diagram of Algorithm 7.

Next, we prove the following lemma, which will play a crucial role in our main theorems.

Lemma 8. *Let $\gamma_n :=$ Line Search $3(z_n, \delta, \sigma, \theta)$. Then, for all $n \in \mathbb{N}$ and $x \in dom(g)$, the following hold:*

(I) $\|z_n - x\|^2 - \|w_n - x\|^2 \geq 2\gamma_n[(f+g)(w_n) - (f+g)(x)] + (1 - 8\delta)\|w_n - z_n\|^2;$

(II) $\|z_n - x\|^2 - \|v_n - x\|^2 \geq 2\gamma_n[(f+g)(w_n) + (f+g)(v_n) - 2(f+g)(x)]$
$\qquad + (1 - 8\delta)(\|w_n - z_n\|^2 + \|v_n - w_n\|^2).$

where $v_n = \text{prox}_{\gamma_n g}(w_n - \gamma_n \nabla f(w_n))$.

Proof. First, we show that (I) is true. From (4), we know that

$$\frac{z_n - w_n}{\gamma_n} - \nabla f(z_n) \in \partial g(w_n), \text{ for all } n \in \mathbb{N}.$$

Moreover, it follows from the definitions of $\partial g(w_n)$, $\nabla f(z_n)$ and $\nabla f(w_n)$ that

$$g(x) - g(w_n) \geq \langle \frac{z_n - w_n}{\gamma_n} - \nabla f(z_n), x - w_n \rangle,$$

$$f(x) - f(z_n) \geq \langle \nabla f(z_n), x - z_n \rangle \text{ and } f(z_n) - f(w_n) \geq \langle \nabla f(w_n), z_n - w_n \rangle,$$

for all $n \in \mathbb{N}$. Consequently,

$$\begin{aligned}
f(x) - f(z_n) + g(x) - g(w_n) &\geq \frac{1}{\gamma_n} \langle z_n - w_n, x - w_n \rangle + \langle \nabla f(z_n), w_n - z_n \rangle \\
&= \frac{1}{\gamma_n} \langle z_n - w_n, x - w_n \rangle + \langle \nabla f(z_n) - \nabla f(w_n), w_n - z_n \rangle \\
&\quad + \langle \nabla f(w_n), w_n - z_n \rangle \\
&\geq \frac{1}{\gamma_n} \langle z_n - w_n, x - w_n \rangle - \|\nabla f(z_n) - \nabla f(w_n)\| \|w_n - z_n\| \\
&\quad + \langle \nabla f(w_n), w_n - z_n \rangle \\
&\geq \frac{1}{\gamma_n} \langle z_n - w_n, x - w_n \rangle - \frac{4\delta}{\gamma_n} \|w_n - z_n\|^2 + f(w_n) - f(z_n),
\end{aligned}$$

for all $n \in \mathbb{N}$. It follows that

$$\frac{1}{\gamma_n} \langle z_n - w_n, w_n - x \rangle \geq (f+g)(w_n) - (f+g)(x) - \frac{4\delta}{\gamma_n} \|w_n - z_n\|^2, \text{ for all } n \in \mathbb{N}.$$

From Lemma 3, we have $\langle z_n - w_n, w_n - x \rangle = \frac{1}{2}(\|z_n - x\|^2 - \|z_n - w_n\|^2 - \|w_n - x\|^2)$, and hence,

$$\frac{1}{2\gamma_n}(\|z_n - x\|^2 - \|z_n - w_n\|^2 - \|w_n - x\|^2) \geq (f+g)(w_n) - (f+g)(x) - \frac{4\delta}{\gamma_n} \|w_n - z_n\|^2,$$

for all $n \in \mathbb{N}$. Then, it follows that, for any $x \in \text{dom}(g)$,

$$\|z_n - x\|^2 - \|w_n - x\|^2 \geq 2\gamma_n[(f+g)(w_n) - (f+g)(x)] + (1 - 8\delta)\|w_n - z_n\|^2,$$

and (I) is proven. Next, we show (II). From (4), we have that

$$\frac{z_n - w_n}{\gamma_n} - \nabla f(z_n) \in \partial g(w_n), \text{ and}$$

$$\frac{w_n - v_n}{\gamma_n} - \nabla f(w_n) \in \partial g(v_n).$$

Then,

$$g(x) - g(w_n) \geq \langle \frac{z_n - w_n}{\gamma_n} - \nabla f(z_n), x - w_n \rangle, \text{ and}$$

$$g(x) - g(v_n) \geq \langle \frac{w_n - v_n}{\gamma_n} - \nabla f(w_n), x - v_n \rangle, \text{ for all } n \in \mathbb{N}.$$

Moreover,

$$f(x) - f(z_n) \geq \langle \nabla f(z_n), x - z_n \rangle,$$
$$f(x) - f(w_n) \geq \langle \nabla f(w_n), x - w_n \rangle,$$

$$f(z_n) - f(w_n) \geq \langle \nabla f(w_n), z_n - w_n \rangle, \text{ and}$$
$$f(w_n) - f(v_n) \geq \langle \nabla f(v_n), w_n - v_n \rangle, \text{ for all } n \in \mathbb{N}.$$

The above inequalities imply

$$f(x) - f(z_n) + f(x) - f(w_n) + g(x) - g(w_n) + g(x) - g(v_n)$$
$$\geq \frac{1}{\gamma_n}\langle z_n - w_n, x - w_n\rangle + \langle \nabla f(z_n), w_n - z_n\rangle + \frac{1}{\gamma_n}\langle w_n - v_n, x - v_n\rangle + \langle \nabla f(w_n), v_n - w_n\rangle$$
$$= \frac{1}{\gamma_n}\langle z_n - w_n, x - w_n\rangle + \langle \nabla f(z_n) - \nabla f(w_n), w_n - z_n\rangle + \langle \nabla f(w_n), w_n - z_n\rangle$$
$$+ \frac{1}{\gamma_n}\langle w_n - v_n, x - v_n\rangle + \langle \nabla f(w_n) - \nabla f(v_n), v_n - w_n\rangle + \langle \nabla f(v_n), v_n - w_n\rangle$$
$$\geq \frac{1}{\gamma_n}\langle z_n - w_n, x - w_n\rangle + \frac{1}{\gamma_n}\langle w_n - v_n, x - v_n\rangle - \|\nabla f(w_n) - \nabla f(z_n)\|\|w_n - z_n\|$$
$$+ \langle \nabla f(w_n), w_n - z_n\rangle - \|\nabla f(v_n) - \nabla f(w_n)\|\|v_n - w_n\| + \langle \nabla f(v_n), v_n - w_n\rangle$$
$$\geq \frac{1}{\gamma_n}\langle z_n - w_n, x - w_n\rangle + \frac{1}{\gamma_n}\langle w_n - v_n, x - v_n\rangle$$
$$- \|\nabla f(w_n) - \nabla f(z_n)\|(\|w_n - z_n\| + \|v_n - w_n\|) + \langle \nabla f(w_n), w_n - z_n\rangle$$
$$- \|\nabla f(v_n) - \nabla f(w_n)\|(\|w_n - z_n\| + \|v_n - w_n\|) + \langle \nabla f(v_n), v_n - w_n\rangle$$
$$= \frac{1}{\gamma_n}\langle z_n - w_n, x - w_n\rangle + \frac{1}{\gamma_n}\langle w_n - v_n, x - v_n\rangle + \langle \nabla f(w_n), w_n - z_n\rangle + \langle \nabla f(v_n), v_n - w_n\rangle$$
$$- (\|\nabla f(w_n) - \nabla f(z_n)\| + \|\nabla f(v_n) - \nabla f(w_n)\|)(\|w_n - z_n\| + \|v_n - w_n\|)$$
$$\geq \frac{1}{\gamma_n}\langle z_n - w_n, x - w_n\rangle + \frac{1}{\gamma_n}\langle w_n - v_n, x - v_n\rangle + \langle \nabla f(w_n), w_n - z_n\rangle$$
$$+ \langle \nabla f(v_n), v_n - w_n\rangle - \frac{2\delta}{\gamma_n}(\|w_n - z_n\| + \|v_n - w_n\|)^2$$
$$\geq \frac{1}{\gamma_n}\langle z_n - w_n, x - w_n\rangle + \frac{1}{\gamma_n}\langle w_n - v_n, x - v_n\rangle + f(v_n) - f(z_n)$$
$$- \frac{4\delta}{\gamma_n}(\|w_n - z_n\|^2 + \|v_n - w_n\|^2),$$

for all $x \in dom(g)$ and $n \in \mathbb{N}$. Hence,

$$\frac{1}{\gamma_n}\langle z_n - w_n, w_n - x\rangle + \frac{1}{\gamma_n}\langle w_n - v_n, v_n - x\rangle$$
$$\geq (f+g)(w_n) + (f+g)(v_n) - 2(f+g)(x) - \frac{4\delta}{\gamma_n}\|w_n - z_n\|^2 - \frac{4\delta}{\gamma_n}\|v_n - w_n\|^2.$$

Moreover, from Lemma 3, we have, for all $n \in \mathbb{N}$,

$$\langle z_n - w_n, w_n - x\rangle = \frac{1}{2}(\|z_n - x\|^2 - \|z_n - w_n\|^2 - \|w_n - x\|^2), \text{ and}$$

$$\langle w_n - v_n, v_n - x\rangle = \frac{1}{2}(\|w_n - x\|^2 - \|w_n - v_n\|^2 - \|v_n - x\|^2).$$

As a result, we obtain

$$\frac{1}{2\gamma_n}(\|z_n - x\|^2 - \|z_n - w_n\|^2) - \frac{1}{2\gamma_n}(\|w_n - v_n\|^2 + \|v_n - x\|^2)$$
$$\geq (f+g)(w_n) + (f+g)(v_n) - 2(f+g)(x) - \frac{4\delta}{\gamma_n}\|w_n - z_n\|^2 - \frac{4\delta}{\gamma_n}\|v_n - w_n\|^2,$$

for all $x \in dom(g)$, and $n \in \mathbb{N}$. Therefore,

$$\|z_n - x\|^2 - \|v_n - x\|^2 \geq 2\gamma_n[(f+g)(w_n) + (f+g)(v_n) - 2(f+g)(x)] \\ + (1-8\delta)(\|w_n - z_n\|^2 + \|v_n - w_n\|^2),$$

for all $x \in dom(g)$, and $n \in \mathbb{N}$, and hence, (II) is proven. □

Next, we prove the weak convergence result of Algorithm 7.

Theorem 9. *Let $\{x_n\}$ be a sequence generated by Algorithm 7. Suppose that the following hold:*

B1. $\sum_{n=1}^{+\infty} \beta_n < +\infty;$

B2. *There exists $\gamma > 0$ such that $\gamma_n \geq \gamma$, for all $n \in \mathbb{N}$.*

Then, $\{x_n\}$ converges weakly to some point in S_*.

Proof. Let $x^* \in S_*$; obviously, $x^* \in dom(g)$. The following are direct consequences of Lemma 8:

$$\|z_n - x^*\|^2 - \|w_n - x^*\|^2 \geq 2\gamma_n[(f+g)(w_n) - (f+g)(x^*)] + (1-8\delta)\|w_n - z_n\|^2 \\ \geq (1-8\delta)\|w_n - z_n\|^2, \tag{7}$$

and

$$\|z_n - x^*\|^2 - \|v_n - x^*\|^2 \geq 2\gamma_n[(f+g)(w_n) + (f+g)(v_n) - 2(f+g)(x^*)] \\ + (1-8\delta)(\|w_n - z_n\|^2 + \|v_n - w_n\|^2) \\ \geq (1-8\delta)(\|w_n - z_n\|^2 + \|v_n - w_n\|^2), \tag{8}$$

where $v_n = prox_{\gamma_n g}(w_n - \gamma_n \nabla f(w_n))$. Then, we have

$$\|x_{n+1} - x^*\| \leq (1-\alpha_n)\|w_n - x^*\| + \alpha_n\|v_n - x^*\| \\ \leq (1-\alpha_n)\|w_n - x^*\| + \alpha_n\|z_n - x^*\| \tag{9} \\ \leq \|z_n - x^*\|.$$

Next, we show that $\lim_{n\to\infty} \|x_n - x^*\|$ exists. Since $P_{dom(g)}$ is nonexpansive, we have

$$\|x_{n+1} - x^*\| \leq \|z_n - x^*\| \\ = \|P_{dom(g)}y_n - P_{dom(g)}x^*\| \\ \leq \|y_n - x^*\| \tag{10} \\ \leq \|x_n - x^*\| + \beta_n\|x_n - x_{n-1}\| \\ \leq (1+\beta_n)\|x_n - x^*\| + \beta_n\|x_{n-1} - x^*\|, \quad \text{for all } n \in \mathbb{N}.$$

By using Lemma 4, we have that $\{x_n\}$ is bounded. Consequently, $\sum_{n=1}^{+\infty} \beta_n\|x_n - x_{n-1}\| < +\infty$, and

$$\|y_n - x_n\| = \beta_n\|x_n - x_{n-1}\| \to 0, \text{ as } n \to +\infty.$$

By (10) together with Lemma 5, we conclude that $\lim_{n\to+\infty} \|x_n - x^*\|$ exists. Since $x_n \in dom(g)$, for all $n \in \mathbb{N}$, we obtain

$$\|y_n - z_n\| \leq \|y_n - x_n\|, \quad \text{for all } n \in \mathbb{N},$$

which implies that $\lim_{n\to+\infty}\|y_n - z_n\| = 0$. Consequently, $\lim_{n\to+\infty}\|x_n - z_n\| = 0$, and hence, $\lim_{n\to+\infty}\|x_n - x^*\| = \lim_{n\to+\infty}\|z_n - x^*\|$. Now, we will show that $\lim_{n\to+\infty}\|x_n - w_n\| = 0$. To do this, we consider the following two cases.

Case 1. $\limsup_{n\to+\infty} \alpha_n = c < 1$, then from (9), we obtain

$$\limsup_{n\to+\infty}\|w_n - x^*\| = \limsup_{n\to+\infty}\|x_n - x^*\| = \limsup_{n\to+\infty}\|z_n - x^*\|.$$

Therefore, we obtain from (7) that $\lim_{n\to+\infty}\|w_n - z_n\| = 0$. As a result, we have $\lim_{n\to+\infty}\|x_n - w_n\| = 0$.

Case 2. $\limsup_{n\to+\infty} \alpha_n = 1$, then it follows from (9) that

$$\limsup_{n\to+\infty}\|v_n - x^*\| = \limsup_{n\to+\infty}\|x_n - x^*\| = \limsup_{n\to+\infty}\|z_n - x^*\|.$$

It follows from (8) that $\lim_{n\to+\infty}\|w_n - z_n\| = 0$, and hence, $\lim_{n\to+\infty}\|x_n - w_n\| = 0$.

We claim that every weak-cluster point of $\{x_n\}$ belongs to S_*. To prove this claim, let w be a weak-cluster point of $\{x_n\}$. Then, there exists a subsequence $\{x_{n_k}\}$ of $\{x_n\}$ such that $x_{n_k} \rightharpoonup w$, and hence, $w_{n_k} \rightharpoonup w$. Next, we show that $w \in S_*$. From A2, we know that ∇f is uniformly continuous, so $\lim_{k\to+\infty}\|\nabla f w_{n_k} - \nabla f z_{n_k}\| = 0$. From (4), we also have

$$\frac{z_{n_k} - \gamma_{n_k}\nabla f z_{n_k} - w_{n_k}}{\gamma_{n_k}} \in \partial g(w_{n_k}), \text{ for all } k \in \mathbb{N}.$$

Hence,

$$\frac{z_{n_k} - w_{n_k}}{\gamma_{n_k}} - \nabla f z_{n_k} + \nabla f w_{n_k} \in \partial g(w_{n_k}) + \nabla f w_{n_k} = \partial(f+g)(w_{n_k}), \text{ for all } k \in \mathbb{N}.$$

By letting $k \to +\infty$ in the above inequality, we can conclude from (1) that $0 \in \partial(f+g)(w)$, and hence, $w \in S_*$. It follows directly from Lemma 6 that $\{x_n\}$ converges weakly to a point in S_*, and the proof is now complete. □

If we set $\beta_n = 0$, for all $n \in \mathbb{N}$, in Algorithm 7, we obtain the following Algorithm 8.

Algorithm 8. Algorithm with Line Search 3.

1: **Input** Given $x_0 \in dom(g)$, $\sigma > 0$, $\theta \in (0,1)$, $\delta \in (0, \frac{1}{8})$ and $\alpha_n \in [0,1]$, for $n \in \mathbb{N}$,

$$w_n = prox_{\gamma_n g}(x_n - \gamma_n \nabla f(x_n)),$$
$$x_{n+1} = (1-\alpha_n)w_n + \alpha_n prox_{\gamma_n g}(w_n - \gamma_n \nabla f(w_n)),$$

where $\gamma_n :=$ Line Search $3(x_n, \delta, \sigma, \theta)$.

The diagram of Algorithm 8 can be seen in Figure 2.

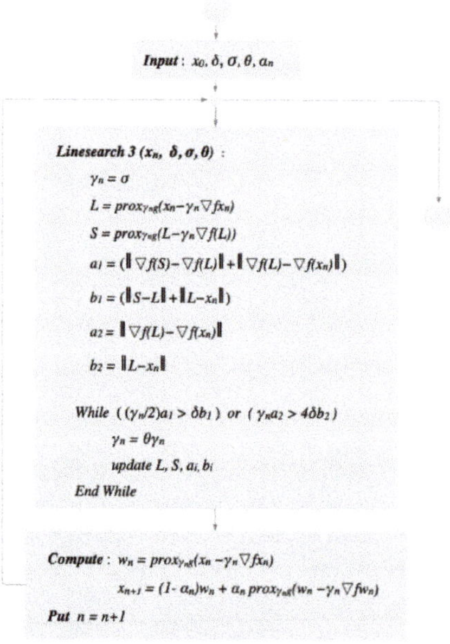

Figure 2. Diagram of Algorithm 8.

We next prove the complexity of Algorithm 8.

Theorem 10. *Let $\{x_n\}$ be a sequence generated by Algorithm 8. Suppose that there exists $\gamma > 0$ such that $\gamma_n \geq \gamma$, for all $n \in \mathbb{N}$, then $\{x_n\}$ converges weakly to a point in S_*. In addition, if $\delta \in (0, \frac{1}{16})$, then the following also holds:*

$$(f+g)(x_n) - \min_{x \in H}(f+g)(x) \leq \frac{1}{2\gamma} \frac{[d(x_0, S_*)]^2}{n}, \tag{11}$$

for all $n \in \mathbb{N}$.

Proof. A weak convergence of $\{x_n\}$ is guaranteed by Theorem 9. It remains to show that (11) is true. Let $v_n = prox_{\gamma_n g}(w_n - \gamma_n \nabla f(w_n))$ and $x^* \in S_*$.

We first show that $f(x_{k+1}) \leq f(x_k)$, for all $k \in \mathbb{N}$. We know that $x_k = z_k$ in Lemma 8, so for any $x \in dom(g)$ and $k \in \mathbb{N}$, we have:

$$\|x_k - x\|^2 - \|w_k - x\|^2 \geq 2\gamma_k[(f+g)(w_k) - (f+g)(x)] + (1-8\delta)\|w_k - x_k\|^2, \tag{12}$$

and

$$\|x_k - x\|^2 - \|v_k - x\|^2 \geq 2\gamma_k[(f+g)(w_k) + (f+g)(v_k) - 2(f+g)(x)] \\ + (1-8\delta)(\|w_k - x_k\|^2 + \|v_k - w_k\|^2). \tag{13}$$

Putting $x = x_k$ in (12) and (13), we obtain

$$-\|w_k - x_k\|^2 \geq 2\gamma_k[(f+g)(w_k) - (f+g)(x_k)] + (1-8\delta)\|w_k - x_k\|^2, \tag{14}$$

and

$$-\|v_k - x_k\|^2 \geq 2\gamma_k[(f+g)(w_k) + (f+g)(v_k) - 2(f+g)(x_k)] \\ + (1-8\delta)(\|w_k - x_k\|^2 + \|v_k - w_k\|^2), \tag{15}$$

respectively. Substituting x with w_k in (13), we obtain

$$\|x_k - w_k\|^2 - \|v_k - w_k\|^2 \geq 2\gamma_k[(f+g)(v_k) - (f+g)(w_k)] \\ + (1 - 8\delta)(\|w_k - x_k\|^2 + \|v_k - w_k\|^2). \quad (16)$$

By summing (15) and (16), we obtain

$$(16\delta - 1)\|x_k - w_k\|^2 + (16\delta - 4)\|v_k - w_k\|^2 \geq 4\gamma_k[(f+g)(v_k) - (f+g)(x_k)]. \quad (17)$$

It follows from (14) and (17) that

$$(f+g)(w_k) \leq (f+g)(x_k) \quad \text{and} \quad (f+g)(v_k) \leq (f+g)(x_k),$$

respectively, for all $k \in \mathbb{N}$. Hence,

$$(f+g)(x_{k+1}) - (f+g)(x_k) \leq (1 - \alpha_k)(f+g)(w_k) + \alpha_k(f+g)(v_k) - (f+g)(x_k) \leq 0, \quad (18)$$

for all $k \in \mathbb{N}$. Hence, $\{(f+g)(x_k)\}$ is a non-increasing sequence. Now, put $x = x^*$ in (12) and (13), then we obtain

$$\|w_k - x^*\|^2 - \|x_k - x^*\|^2 \leq 2\gamma_k[(f+g)(x^*) - (f+g)(w_k)], \quad (19)$$

and

$$\|v_k - x^*\|^2 - \|x_k - x^*\|^2 \leq 2\gamma_k[2(f+g)(x^*) - (f+g)(w_k) - (f+g)(v_k)] \\ \leq 2\gamma_k[(f+g)(x^*) - (f+g)(v_k)]. \quad (20)$$

Inequalities (19) and (20) imply that

$$\|x_{k+1} - x^*\|^2 - \|x_k - x^*\|^2 \leq (1 - \alpha_k)\|w_k - x^*\|^2 + \alpha_k\|v_k - x^*\|^2 - \|x_k - x^*\|^2 \\ \leq 2\gamma_k(1 - \alpha_k)[(f+g)(x^*) - (f+g)(w_k)] \\ + 2\gamma_k\alpha_k[(f+g)(x^*) - (f+g)(v_k)] \\ = 2\gamma_k(f+g)(x^*) - 2\gamma_k[(1-\alpha_k)(f+g)(w_k) + \alpha_k(f+g)(v_k)] \\ \leq 2\gamma_k[(f+g)(x^*) - (f+g)(x_{k+1})],$$

for all $k \in \mathbb{N}$. Since $\gamma_k \geq \gamma$, we obtain

$$0 \geq (f+g)(x^*) - (f+g)(x_{k+1}) \geq \frac{1}{2\gamma_k}(\|x_{k+1} - x^*\|^2 - \|x_k - x^*\|^2) \\ \geq \frac{1}{2\gamma}(\|x_{k+1} - x^*\|^2 - \|x_k - x^*\|^2), \quad (21)$$

for all $k \in \mathbb{N}$. Summing the above inequality over $k = 1, 2, 3, \ldots, n-1$, we obtain

$$n(f+g)(x^*) - \sum_{k=0}^{n-1}(f+g)(x_k) \geq \frac{1}{2\gamma}\|x_n - x^*\|^2 - \|x_0 - x^*\|^2,$$

for all $n \in \mathbb{N}$. Since, $\{(f+g)(x_k)\}$ is a non-increasing, we have

$$n(f+g)(x^*) - n(f+g)(x_n) \geq \frac{1}{2\gamma}\|x_n - x^*\|^2 - \|x_0 - x^*\|^2,$$

for all $n \in \mathbb{N}$. Hence,

$$(f+g)(x_n) - (f+g)(x^*) \leq \frac{1}{2\gamma}\frac{\|x_0 - x^*\|^2}{n} \quad (22)$$

Since x^* is arbitrarily chosen from S_*, we obtain

$$(f+g)(x_n) - \min_{x \in H}(f+g)(x) \leq \frac{1}{2\gamma} \frac{[d(x_0, S_*)]^2}{n},$$

for all $n \in \mathbb{N}$, and the proof is now complete. □

4. Some Applications on Data Classification

In this section, we apply Algorithms 3, 5, 7, and 8 to solve some classification problems based on a learning technique called *extreme learning machine (ELM)* introduced by Huang et al. [28]. It is formulated as follows:

Let $\{(x_k, t_k) : x_k \in \mathbb{R}^n, t_k \in \mathbb{R}^m, k = 1, 2, \ldots, N\}$ be a set of N samples where x_k is an *input* and t_k is a *target*. A simple mathematical model for the output of ELM for SLFNs with M hidden nodes and activation function G is defined by

$$o_j = \sum_{i=1}^{M} \eta_i G(\langle w_i, x_j \rangle + b_i),$$

where w_i is the weight that connects the i-th hidden node and the input node, η_i is the weight connecting the i-th hidden node and the output node, and b_i is the bias. The hidden layer output matrix **H** is defined by

$$\mathbf{H} = \begin{bmatrix} G(\langle w_1, x_1 \rangle + b_1) & \cdots & G(\langle w_M, x_1 \rangle + b_M) \\ \vdots & \ddots & \vdots \\ G(\langle w_1, x_N \rangle + b_1) & \cdots & G(\langle w_M, x_N \rangle + b_M) \end{bmatrix}.$$

The main objective of ELM is to calculate an optimal weight $\eta = [\eta_1^T, \ldots, \eta_M^T]^T$ such that $\mathbf{H}\eta = \mathbf{T}$, where $\mathbf{T} = [t_1^T, \ldots, t_N^T]^T$ is the training target. If the *Moore–Penrose generalized inverse* $\mathbf{H}^\dagger$ of **H** exists, then $\eta = \mathbf{H}^\dagger \mathbf{T}$ is the solution. However, in general cases, $\mathbf{H}^\dagger$ may not exist or be difficult for computation. Thus, in order to avoid such difficulties, we transformed the problem into a convex minimization problem and used our proposed algorithm to find the solution η without $\mathbf{H}^\dagger$.

In machine learning, a model can be overfit in the sense that it is very accurate on a training sets, but inaccurate on a testing set. In other words, it cannot be used to predict unknown data. In order to prevent overfitting, the *least absolute shrinkage and selection operator (LASSO)* [29] is used. It can be formulated as follows:

$$\text{Minimize: } \|\mathbf{H}\eta - \mathbf{T}\|_2^2 + \lambda \|\eta\|_1, \tag{23}$$

where λ is a regularization parameter. If we set $f(x) := \|\mathbf{H}x - \mathbf{T}\|_2^2$ and $g(x) := \lambda \|x\|_1$, then the problem (23) is reduced to the problem (1). Hence, we can use our algorithm as a learning method to find the optimal weight η and solve classification problems.

In the experiments, we aim to classify three data sets from https://archive.ics.uci.edu (accessed on 15 November 2021):

Iris data set [30]. Each sample in this data set has four attributes, and the set contains three classes with 50 samples for each type.

Heart disease data set [31]. This data set contains 303 samples each of which has 13 attributes. In this data set, we classified two classes of data.

Wine data set [32]. In this data set, we classified three classes of 178 samples. Each sample contains 13 attributes.

In all experiments, we used the sigmoid as the activation function. The number of hidden nodes $M = 30$. We calculate the accuracy of the output data by:

$$\text{accuracy} = \frac{\text{correctly predicted data}}{\text{all data}} \times 100.$$

We chose control parameters for each algorithm as seen in Table 1.

Table 1. Chosen parameters of each algorithm.

	Algorithm 3	Algorithm 5	Algorithm 7	Algorithm 8
σ	0.49	0.124	0.124	0.124
δ	0.1	0.1	0.1	0.1
θ	0.1	0.1	0.1	0.1
α_n	-	-	$\frac{1}{2}$	$\frac{1}{3}$

In our experiments, the inertial parameters β_n for Algorithm 7 were chosen as follows:

$$\beta_n = \begin{cases} 0.95, & \text{if } n \leq 1000 \\ \frac{1}{n^2}, & \text{if } n \geq 1001. \end{cases}$$

In the first experiment, we chose the regularization parameter $\lambda = 0.1$ for all algorithms and data sets. Then, we used 10-fold cross-validation and utilized *Average ACC* and $ERR_\%$ for evaluating the performance of each algorithm.

$$\text{Average ACC} = \sum_{i=1}^{N} \frac{x_i}{y_i} \times 100\%/N,$$

where N is the number of folds ($N = 10$), x_i is the number of data correctly predicted at fold i, and y_i is the number of all data at fold i.

Let err_{Lsum} = the sum of errors in all 10 training sets, err_{Tsum} = the sum of errors in all 10 testing sets, $Lsum$ = the sum of all data in all 10 training sets, and $Tsum$ = the sum of all data in all 10 testing sets. Then,

$$ERR_\% = (\text{err}_{L\%} + \text{err}_{T\%})/2,$$

where $\text{err}_{L\%} = \frac{\text{err}_{Lsum}}{Lsum} \times 100\%$ and $\text{err}_{T\%} = \frac{\text{err}_{Tsum}}{Tsum} \times 100\%$.

With these evaluation tools, we obtained the results for each data set as seen in Tables 2–4.

Table 2. The performance of each algorithm in the first experiment at the 200th iteration with 10-fold cv. on the Iris data set.

	Algorithm 3		Algorithm 5		Algorithm 7		Algorithm 8	
	acc.train	acc.test	acc.train	acc.test	acc.train	acc.test	acc.train	acc.test
Fold 1	87.41	86.67	93.33	86.67	97.78	100	97.04	93.33
Fold 2	88.15	93.33	92.59	100	96.30	100	96.30	100
Fold 3	88.15	100	92.59	100	97.78	93.33	96.30	100
Fold 4	88.15	100	92.59	100	97.78	100	96.30	100
Fold 5	86.67	86.67	93.33	86.67	97.78	100	96.30	100
Fold 6	88.15	73.33	92.59	80	99.26	86.67	97.78	86.67
Fold 7	87.41	100	92.59	100	97.78	100	96.30	100
Fold 8	88.15	86.67	93.33	93.33	97.04	93.33	97.78	86.67
Fold 9	88.89	80	93.33	93.33	98.52	93.33	96.30	93.33
Fold 10	88.15	73.33	92.59	93.33	97.78	100	95.56	100
Average acc.	87.93	88	92.89	93.33	97.78	96.67	96.59	96
$ERR_\%$	12.04		6.89		2.78		3.70	
Time	0.0609		0.0901		0.0781		0.0767	

Table 3. The performance of each algorithm in the first experiment at the 200th iteration with 10-fold cv. on the Heart disease data set.

	Algorithm 3		Algorithm 5		Algorithm 7		Algorithm 8	
	acc.train	acc.test	acc.train	acc.test	acc.train	acc.test	acc.train	acc.test
Fold 1	79.85	86.67	81.32	86.67	83.15	93.33	82.05	86.67
Fold 2	80.15	80.65	80.15	80.65	84.19	83.87	81.62	83.87
Fold 3	81.25	77.42	82.35	77.42	84.93	77.42	83.09	80.65
Fold 4	80.51	83.87	82.35	87.10	84.56	80.65	82.72	90.32
Fold 5	79.85	90	81.32	90	84.98	86.67	82.42	86.67
Fold 6	81.68	80	83.15	83.33	84.62	86.67	83.52	83.33
Fold 7	80.22	86.67	81.68	83.33	84.25	83.33	82.05	83.33
Fold 8	82.05	66.67	82.42	66.67	84.98	73.33	82.42	66.67
Fold 9	81.32	70	81.68	70	86.08	73.33	82.05	70
Fold 10	80.95	76.67	82.05	80	84.25	83.33	82.05	80
Average acc.	80.78	79.86	81.85	80.52	84.60	82.19	82.40	81.15
ERR%	19.67		18.81		16.61		18.21	
Time	0.0726		0.1048		0.1004		0.0921	

Table 4. The performance of each algorithm in the first experiment at the 200th iteration with 10-fold cv. on the Wine data set.

	Algorithm 3		Algorithm 5		Algorithm 7		Algorithm 8	
	acc.train	acc.test	acc.train	acc.test	acc.train	acc.test	acc.train	acc.test
Fold 1	96.89	100	96.89	100	99.38	100	98.14	100
Fold 2	96.88	100	97.50	100	99.38	100	98.13	100
Fold 3	97.50	100	98.13	100	99.38	100	98.13	100
Fold 4	97.50	100	96.88	100	99.38	100	98.13	100
Fold 5	96.88	100	97.50	100	99.38	100	98.13	100
Fold 6	97.50	94.44	96.88	100	99.38	100	98.13	100
Fold 7	97.50	94.44	98.13	94.44	100	94.44	98.75	94.44
Fold 8	97.50	100	96.88	100	99.38	100	98.13	100
Fold 9	98.75	88.89	98.13	88.89	99.38	88.89	99.38	88.89
Fold 10	98.76	88.24	98.76	88.24	99.38	100	98.14	100
Average acc.	97.57	96.60	97.57	97.16	99.44	98.33	98.31	98.33
ERR%	2.90		2.62		1.12		1.69	
Time	0.0624		0.0997		0.0870		0.0810	

As seen in Tables 2–4, with the same regularization $\lambda = 0.1$, Algorithms 7 and 8 perform better than Algorithms 3 and 5 in terms of accuracy, while the computation times are relatively close among the four algorithms.

In the second experiment, the regularization parameters λ for each algorithm and data set were chosen using 10-fold cv. We compared the error of each model and data set with various λ, then chose the λ that gives the lowest error ($ERR\%$) for the particular model and data set. Hence, the parameter λ varies depending on the algorithm and data set. The choice of parameters λ can be seen in Table 5.

Table 5. Chosen λ of each algorithm.

	Regularization Parameter λ		
	Iris	Heart Disease	Wine
Algorithm 3	0.001	0.003	0.02
Algorithm 5	0.01	0.03	0.006
Algorithm 7	0.003	0.13	0.0001
Algorithm 8	0.01	0.008	0.003

With the chosen λ, we also evaluated the performance of each algorithm using 10-fold cross-validation and similar evaluation tools as in the first experiment. The results can be seen in the following Tables 6–8.

Table 6. The performance of each algorithm in the second experiment at the 200th iteration with 10-fold cv. on the Iris data set.

	Algorithm 3		Algorithm 5		Algorithm 7		Algorithm 8	
	acc.train	acc.test	acc.train	acc.test	acc.train	acc.test	acc.train	acc.test
Fold 1	88.15	86.67	93.33	86.67	98.52	100	97.04	93.33
Fold 2	88.15	93.33	92.59	100	98.52	100	96.30	100
Fold 3	88.89	100	93.33	100	98.52	100	96.30	100
Fold 4	88.15	100	92.59	100	98.52	100	96.30	100
Fold 5	86.67	86.67	93.33	86.67	98.52	100	96.30	100
Fold 6	88.15	73.33	93.33	80	99.26	86.67	97.78	86.67
Fold 7	87.41	100	92.59	100	98.52	100	96.30	100
Fold 8	88.15	86.67	93.33	93.33	97.78	100	97.78	86.67
Fold 9	88.89	80	93.33	93.33	98.52	100	96.30	93.33
Fold 10	88.15	73.33	92.59	93.33	98.52	100	95.56	100
Average acc.	88.07	88	93.04	93.33	98.52	98.67	96.59	96
ERR$_\%$	11.96		6.81		1.41		3.70	
Time	0.0618		0.0973		0.0793		0.0783	

With the chosen regularization parameters λ as in Table 5, we see that the $ERR_\%$ of each algorithm in Tables 6–8 is lower than that of Tables 2–4. We can also see that Algorithms 7 and 8 perform better than Algorithms 3 and 5 in terms of accuracy in all experiments conducted.

In Figure 3, we show the graph of $ERR_\%$ for each algorithm of the second experiment. As we can see, Algorithms 7 and 8 have lower $ERR_\%$, which means they perform better than Algorithm 3 and 5.

Table 7. The performance of each algorithm in the second experiment at the 200th iteration with 10-fold cv. on the Heart disease data set.

	Algorithm 3		Algorithm 5		Algorithm 7		Algorithm 8	
	acc.train	acc.test	acc.train	acc.test	acc.train	acc.test	acc.train	acc.test
Fold 1	79.49	86.67	82.05	86.67	84.25	80	82.05	86.67
Fold 2	80.15	80.65	80.51	83.87	83.82	87.10	81.62	83.87
Fold 3	81.62	77.42	81.99	80.65	84.56	80.65	83.46	80.65
Fold 4	80.51	83.87	82.72	90.32	83.82	87.10	83.09	87.10
Fold 5	79.85	90	82.42	86.67	86.45	76.67	82.78	86.67
Fold 6	81.68	80	83.52	83.33	85.35	86.67	83.52	83.33
Fold 7	80.22	86.67	81.68	83.33	84.98	73.33	82.05	83.33
Fold 8	82.42	66.67	82.42	66.67	83.15	90	82.78	66.67
Fold 9	80.95	70.00	82.05	70	84.62	83.33	82.42	70
Fold 10	80.95	76.67	82.05	80	84.98	90	82.78	83.33
Average acc.	80.78	79.86	82.14	81.15	84.60	83.48	82.66	81.16
ERR$_\%$	19.67		18.34		15.95		18.08	
Time	0.0794		0.1129		0.1013		0.097	

From Tables 6–8, we can notice that the computational time of Algorithms 7 and 8 is 30% slower than Algorithm 3 at the same number of iterations. However, from Figure 3, we see that at the 120th iteration, both Algorithms 7 and 8 have lower $ERR_\%$ than Algorithm 3 at the 200th iteration. Therefore, the time needed for Algorithms 7 and 8 to achieve the same accuracy as or higher accuracy than Algorithm 3 is actually lower because we can compute the 120-step iteration much faster than the 200-step iteration.

Table 8. The performance of each algorithm in the second experiment at the 200th iteration with 10-fold cv. on the Wine data set.

	Algorithm 3		Algorithm 5		Algorithm 7		Algorithm 8	
	acc.train	acc.test	acc.train	acc.test	acc.train	acc.test	acc.train	acc.test
Fold 1	96.89	100	97.52	100	99.38	100	98.14	100
Fold 2	96.88	100	97.50	100	100	100	98.75	100
Fold 3	97.50	100	97.50	100	100	100	98.13	100
Fold 4	97.50	100	98.13	100	99.38	100	98.13	100
Fold 5	97.50	100	98.13	100	99.38	100	98.13	100
Fold 6	97.50	94.44	98.13	100	99.38	100	98.13	100
Fold 7	97.50	94.44	98.75	94.44	100	94.44	98.75	94.44
Fold 8	97.50	100	97.50	100	99.38	100	98.13	100
Fold 9	98.75	88.89	98.75	88.89	99.38	100	99.38	88.89
Fold 10	98.76	88.24	98.14	88.24	100	100	98.14	100
Average acc.	97.63	96.60	98	97.16	99.63	99.44	98.38	98.33
ERR%	2.87		2.40		0.47		1.65	
Time	0.0644		0.0971		0.0874		0.0819	

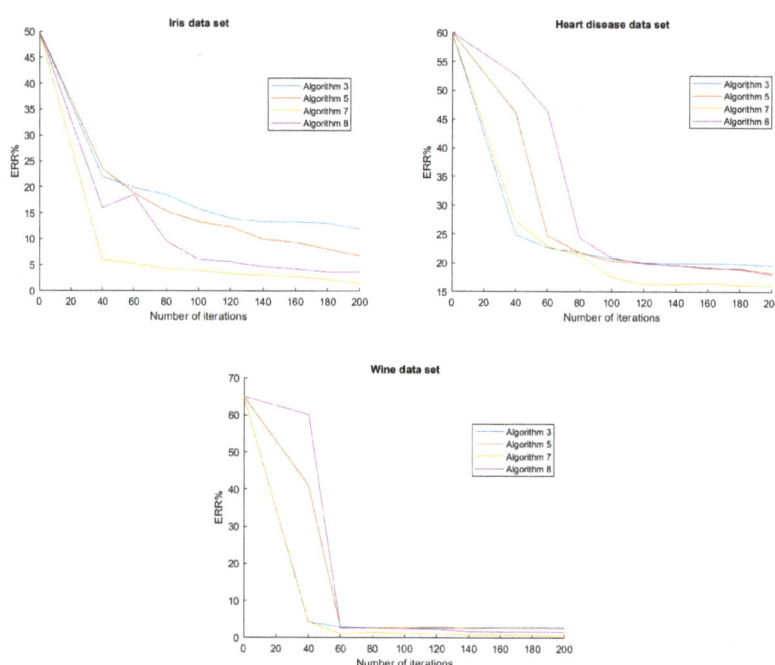

Figure 3. ERR% of each algorithm and data set of the second experiment.

5. Conclusions

We introduced a new line search technique and employed it in order to introduce new algorithms, namely Algorithms 7 and 8. Furthermore, Algorithm 7 also utilizes an inertial step to accelerate its convergence behavior. Both algorithms converge weakly to a solution of (1) without the Lipschitz assumption on ∇f. The complexity of Algorithm 8 was also analyzed and studied. Then, we applied the proposed algorithms to the data classification of the Iris, Heart disease, and Wine data set, then their performances were evaluated and compared with other line search algorithms, namely Algorithms 3 and 5. We observed from our experiments that Algorithm 7 achieved the highest accuracy in all data sets under the same number of iterations. Moreover, Algorithm 8, which is not an inertial algorithm, also performed better than Algorithms 3 and 5. Furthermore, from Figure 3, we see that at a lower number of iterations, the proposed algorithms were more accurate than the other algorithms at a higher iteration number.

Based on the experiments on various data sets, we conclude that the proposed algorithms perform better than the previously established algorithms. Therefore, for our future works, we would like to implement the proposed algorithm to predict and classify the data of patients with non-communicable diseases (NCDs) collected from Sriphat Medical Center, Faculty of Medicine, Chiang Mai University, Thailand. We aim to make an innovation for screening and preventing non-communicable diseases, which will be used in hospitals in Chiang Mai, Thailand.

Author Contributions: Writing—original draft preparation, P.S.; software and editing, D.C.; supervision, review and funding acquisition, S.S. All authors have read and agreed to the published version of the manuscript.

Funding: The NSRF via the Program Management Unit for Human Resources & Institutional Development, Research and Innovation (Grant Number B05F640183).

Data Availability Statement: All data can be obtained from https://archive.ics.uci.edu (accessed on 15 November 2021).

Acknowledgments: This research has received funding support from the NSRF via the Program Management Unit for Human Resources & Institutional Development, Research and Innovation (Grant Number B05F640183). This research was also supported by Chiang Mai University.

Conflicts of Interest: The authors declare no conflict of interest.

References

1. Chen, M.; Zhang, H.; Lin, G.; Han, Q. A new local and nonlocal total variation regularization model for image denoising. *Clust. Comput.* **2019**, *22*, 7611–7627. [CrossRef]
2. Combettes, P.L.; Wajs, V. Signal recovery by proximal forward–backward splitting. *Multiscale Model. Simul.* **2005**, *4*, 1168–1200. [CrossRef]
3. Kankam, K.; Pholasa, N.; Cholamjiak, C. On convergence and complexity of the modified forward–backward method involving new line searches for convex minimization. *Math. Meth. Appl. Sci.* **2019**, 1352–1362. [CrossRef]
4. Luo, Z.Q. Applications of convex optimization in signal processing and digital communication. *Math. Program.* **2003**, *97*, 177–207. [CrossRef]
5. Xiong, K.; Zhao, G.; Shi, G.; Wang, Y. A Convex Optimization Algorithm for Compressed Sensing in a Complex Domain: The Complex-Valued Split Bregman Method. *Sensors* **2019**, *19*, 4540. [CrossRef]
6. Zhang, Y.; Li, X.; Zhao, G.; Cavalcante, C.C. Signal reconstruction of compressed sensing based on alternating direction method of multipliers. *Circuits Syst. Signal Process* **2020**, *39*, 307–323. [CrossRef]
7. Hanjing, A.; Bussaban, L.; Suantai, S. The Modified Viscosity Approximation Method with Inertial Technique and Forward–Backward Algorithm for Convex Optimization Model. *Mathematics* **2022**, *10*, 1036. [CrossRef]
8. Hanjing, A.; Suantai, S. A fast image restoration algorithm based on a fixed point and optimization method. *Mathematics* **2020**, *8*, 378. [CrossRef]
9. Zhong, T. Statistical Behavior and Consistency of Classification Methods Based on Convex Risk Minimization. *Ann. Stat.* **2004**, *32*, 56–134. [CrossRef]
10. Elhamifar, E.; Sapiro, G.; Yang, A.; Sasrty, S.S. A Convex Optimization Framework for Active Learning. In Proceedings of the 2013 IEEE International Conference on Computer Vision, Sydney, Australia, 1–8 December 2013; pp. 209–216. [CrossRef]
11. Yuan, M.; Wegkamp, M. Classification Methods with Reject Option Based on Convex Risk Minimization. *J. Mach. Learn. Res.* **2010**, *11*, 111–130.
12. Lions, P.L.; Mercier, B. Splitting algorithms for the sum of two nonlinear operators. *SIAM J. Numer. Anal.* **1979**, *16*, 964–979. [CrossRef]
13. Polyak, B.T. Some methods of speeding up the convergence of iteration methods. *USSR Comput. Math. Math. Phys.* **1964**, *4*, 1–17. [CrossRef]
14. Attouch, H.; Cabot, A. Convergence rate of a relaxed inertial proximal algorithm for convex minimization. *Optimization* **2019**, *69*, 1281–1312. [CrossRef]
15. Alvarez, F.; Attouch, H. An inertial proximal method for maximal monotone operators via discretization of a nonlinear oscillator with damping. *Set-Valued Anal.* **2001**, *9*, 3–11. [CrossRef]
16. Van Hieu, D. An inertial-like proximal algorithm for equilibrium problems. *Math. Meth. Oper. Res.* **2018**, *88*, 399–415. [CrossRef]
17. Chidume, C.E.; Kumam, P.; Adamu, A. A hybrid inertial algorithm for approximating solution of convex feasibility problems with applications. *Fixed Point Theory Appl.* **2020**, *2020*, 12. [CrossRef]

18. Moudafi, A.; Oliny, M. Convergence of a splitting inertial proximal method for monotone operators. *J. Comput. Appl. Math.* **2003**, *155*, 447–454. [CrossRef]
19. Sarnmeta, P.; Inthakon, W.; Chumpungam, D.; Suantai, S. On convergence and complexity analysis of an accelerated forward–backward algorithm with line search technique for convex minimization problems and applications to data prediction and classification. *J. Inequal. Appl.* **2021**, *2021*, 141. [CrossRef]
20. Beck, A.; Teboulle, M. A fast iterative shrinkage–thresholding algorithm for linear inverse problems. *SIAM J. Imaging Sci.* **2009**, *2*, 183–202. [CrossRef]
21. Boţ, R.I.; Csetnek, E.R. An inertial forward–backward-forward primal-dual splitting algorithm for solving monotone inclusion problems. *Numer. Algor.* **2016**, *71*, 519–540. [CrossRef]
22. Verma, M.; Shukla, K.K. A new accelerated proximal gradient technique for regularized multitask learning framework. *Pattern Recogn. Lett.* **2017**, *95*, 98–103. [CrossRef]
23. Bello Cruz, J.Y.; Nghia, T.T. On the convergence of the forward–backward splitting method with line searches. *Optim. Methods Softw.* **2016**, *31*, 1209–1238. [CrossRef]
24. Burachik R.S.; Iusem, A.N. *Set-Valued Mappings and Enlargements of Monotone Operators*; Springer: Berlin, Germany, 2008.
25. Huang Y.; Dong Y. New properties of forward–backward splitting and a practical proximal-descent algorithm. *Appl. Math. Comput.* **2014**, *237*, 60–68. [CrossRef]
26. Takahashi, W. *Introduction to Nonlinear and Convex Analysis*; Yokohama Publishers: Yokohama, Japan, 2009.
27. Moudafi, A.; Al-Shemas, E. Simultaneous iterative methods for split equality problem. *Trans. Math. Program. Appl.* **2013**, *1*, 1–11.
28. Huang, G.B.; Zhu, Q.Y.; Siew, C.K. Extreme learning machine: Theory and applications. *Neurocomputing* **2006**, *70*, 489–501. [CrossRef]
29. Tibshirani, R. Regression shrinkage and selection via the lasso. *J. R. Stat. Soc. B Methodol.* **1996**, *58*, 267–288. [CrossRef]
30. Fisher, R.A. The use of multiple measurements in taxonomic problems. *Ann. Eugen.* **1936**, *7*, 179–188. [CrossRef]
31. Detrano, R.; Janosi, A.; Steinbrunn, W.; Pfisterer, M.; Schmid, J.J.; Sandhu, S.; Guppy, K.H.; Lee, S.; Froelicher, V. International application of a new probability algorithm for the diagnosis of coronary artery disease. *Am. J. Cardiol.* **1989**, *64*, 304–310. [CrossRef]
32. Forina, M.; Leardi, R.; Armanino, C.; Lanteri, S. *PARVUS: An Extendable Package of Programs for Data Exploration*; Elsevier: Amsterdam, The Netherlands, 1988.

MDPI
St. Alban-Anlage 66
4052 Basel
Switzerland
Tel. +41 61 683 77 34
Fax +41 61 302 89 18
www.mdpi.com

Mathematics Editorial Office
E-mail: mathematics@mdpi.com
www.mdpi.com/journal/mathematics

www.ingramcontent.com/pod-product-compliance
Lightning Source LLC
LaVergne TN
LVHW070138100526
838202LV00015B/1843